International Law and International Relations

This volume is intended to help readers understand the relationship between international law and international relations (IL/IR). As a testament to this dynamic area of inquiry, new research on IL/IR is now being published in a growing list of traditional law reviews and disciplinary journals. The excerpted articles in this volume, all of which were first published in *International Organization*, represent some of the most important research since serious social science scholarship began in this area more than twenty years ago. They are important milestones toward making IL/IR a central concern of scholarly research in international affairs. The contributions have been selected to cover some of the main topics of international affairs and to provide readers with a range of theoretical perspectives, concepts, and heuristics that can be used to analyze the relationship between international law and international relations.

Beth A. Simmons is Professor of Government and Director of the Weatherhead Center for International Affairs at Harvard University, Cambridge, Massachusetts.

Richard H. Steinberg is Professor of Law at the University of California, Los Angeles, and Senior Scholar in the Division of International, Comparative and Area Studies at Stanford University, Stanford, California.

International Law and International Relations

Edited by

BETH A. SIMMONS and RICHARD H. STEINBERG

 CAMBRIDGE
UNIVERSITY PRESS

Stephen D. Krasner, "Structural Causes and Regime Consequences: Regimes as Intervening Variables," IO
36 (2) (spring 1982); Robert O. Keohane, "The Demand for International Regimes," IO 36 (2) (spring
1982); Kurt Taylor Gaubatz, "Democratic States and Commitment in International Relations," IO 50 (1)
(winter 1996); Abram Chayes and Antonia Handler Chayes, "On Compliance," IO 47 (2) (spring 1993);
GeorgeW. Downs, David M. Rocke, and Peter N. Barsoom, "Is the Good News About Compliance Good
News About Cooperation?" IO 50 (3) (summer 1996); Kenneth W. Abbot, Robert O. Keohane, Andrew
Moravcsik, Anne-Marie Slaughter, and Duncan Snidal, "The Concept of Legalization," IO 54 (3) (summer
2000); Robert O. Keohane, Andrew Moravcsik, and Anne-Marie Slaughter, "Legalized Dispute
Resolution: Interstate and Transnational," IO 54 (3) (summer 2000); Judith Goldstein and Lisa L. Martin,
"Legalization, Trade Liberalization, and Domestic Politics: A Cautionary Note," IO 54 (3) (summer 2000);
Martha Finnemore and Stephen J. Toope, "Alternatives to 'Legalization': Richer Views of Law and
Politics," IO 55 (3) (summer 2001); Robert H. Jackson, "Quasi-States, Dual Regimes, and Neoclassical
Theory: International Jurisprudence and the Third World," IO 41 (4) (autumn 1987); Jeffrey W. Legro,
"Which Norms Matter? Revisiting the 'Failure' of Internationalism," IO 51 (1) (winter 1997); Mark W.
Zacher, "The Territorial Integrity Norm: International Boundaries and the Use of Force," IO 55 (2) (spring
2001); Charles Lipson, "Why Are Some International Agreements Informal?" IO 45 (4) (autumn 1991);
James McCall Smith, "The Politics of Dispute Settlement Design: Explaining Legalism in Regional Trade
Pacts," IO 54 (1) (winter 2000); Barbara Koremenos, "Loosening the Ties that Bind: A Learning Model of
Agreement Flexibility," IO 55 (2) (spring 2001); Alexander Wendt, "Driving with the Rearview Mirror: On
the Rational Science of Institutional Design," IO 55 (4) (autumn 2001); Paul F. Diehl, Charlotte Ku,
Daniel Zamora, "The Dynamics of International Law: The Interaction of Normative and Operating
Systems," IO 57 (1) (winter 2003); Anne-Marie Slaughter [Burley] and Walter Mattli, "Europe Before the
Court: A Political Theory of Legal Integration," IO 47 (1) (winter 1993); Geoffrey Garrett, R. Daniel
Kelemen, and Heiner Schulz, "The European Court of Justice, National Governments, and Legal
Integration in the European Union," IO 52 (1) (winter 1998); Virginia Page Fortna, "Scraps of Paper?
Agreements and the Durability of Peace," IO 57 (2) (summer 2003); Richard H. Steinberg, "In the Shadow
of Law or Power? Consensus-Based Bargaining and Outcomes in the GATT/WTO," IO 56 (2) (spring
2002); Beth A. Simmons, "The Legalization of International Monetary Affairs," IO 54 (3) (summer 2000);
Christopher Rudolph, "Constructing an Atrocities Regime: The Politics of War Crimes Tribunals," IO 55
(3) (summer 2001), Andrew Moravcsik, "The Origins of Human Rights Regimes: Democratic Delegation
in Postwar Europe," IO 54 (2) (spring 2000); Ronald B. Mitchell, "Regime Design Matters: Intentional Oil
Pollution and Treaty Compliance," IO 48 (3) (winter 1994); Kal Raustiala and David G. Victor, "The
Regime Complex for Plant Genetic Resources," IO 58 (2) (spring 2004).

Library of Congress Cataloging-in-Publication Data

International law and international relations : an international organization reader / edited by
Beth A. Simmons and Richard H. Steinberg.
p. cm.
Includes bibliographical references and index.
ISBN-13: 978-0-521-86186-1 (hardback)
ISBN-10: 0-521-86186-1 (hardback)
ISBN-13: 978-0-521-67991-6 (pbk.)
ISBN-10: 0-521-67991-5 (pbk.)
1. International law. 2. International relations. I. Simmons, Beth A., 1958–
II. Steinberg, Richard H., 1960– III. Title.

KZ1250.I537   2006
341—dc22
2006032902

Contents

Intellectual Property

Contributors

Volume Editors

Beth A. Simmons is Professor of Government and Director of the Weatherhead Center for International Affairs at Harvard University, Cambridge, Massachusetts.

Richard H. Steinberg is Professor of Law at the University of California, Los Angeles, and Senior Scholar in the Division of International, Comparative and Area Studies at Stanford University, Stanford, California.

Contributors

Kenneth W. Abbot is Professor of Law at Arizona State University, Tempe, Arizona.

Peter N. Barsoom is Director of Credit Card Services at Merrill Lynch, New York, New York.

Abram Chayes (1922–2000) was Professor of Law at Harvard University, Cambridge, Massachusetts.

Antonia Handler Chayes is Adjunct Lecturer in Public Policy at the John F. Kennedy School of Government at Harvard University, Cambridge, Massachusetts.

Paul F. Diehl is Professor of Political Science at the University of Illinois at Urbana-Champaign.

George W. Downs is Professor of Politics at New York University, New York, New York.

Martha Finnemore is Professor of Political Science and International Affairs at George Washington University, Washington, D.C.

Virginia Page Fortna is Assistant Professor of Political Science at Columbia University, New York, New York.

Geoffrey Garrett is Professor of International Relations at University of Southern California, Los Angeles, and President of the Pacific Council on International Policy, Los Angeles, California.

Kurt Taylor Gaubatz is Associate Professor of International Studies at Old Dominion University, Norfolk, Virginia.

Judith Goldstein is Professor of Political Science, Sakurako and William Fisher Family Director of International, Comparative and Area Studies, and The Kaye University Fellow in Undergraduate Education at Stanford University, Stanford, California.

Robert H. Jackson is Professor of International Relations and Political Science at Boston University, Boston, Massachusetts.

R. Daniel Kelemen is University Lecturer and Tutorial Fellow at Lincoln College, University of Oxford.

Robert O. Keohane is Professor of International Affairs at Princeton University, Princeton, New Jersey.

Barbara Koremenos is Assistant Professor of Political Science at the University of Michigan, Ann Arbor.

Stephen D. Krasner is Director of Policy Planning at the United States Department of State, Washington, D.C., and Professor of Political Science at Stanford University, Stanford, California.

Charlotte Ku is Executive Vice President and Executive Director of the American Society of International Law, Washington, D.C.

Jeffrey W. Legro is Associate Professor of International Relations at the University of Virginia, Charlottesville, Virginia.

Charles Lipson is Professor of Political Science at the University of Chicago, Chicago, Illinois.

Lisa L. Martin is Professor of Government and a member of the Executive Committee of The Weatherhead Center for International Affairs at Harvard University, Cambridge, Massachusetts.

Walter Mattli is the Fellow in Politics at St. John's College and Professor of International Political Economy, Oxford University, Oxford, England.

Ronald B. Mitchell is Professor of Political Science at the University of Oregon, Eugene, Oregon.

Andrew Moravcsik is Professor of Politics at Princeton University, Princeton, New Jersey.

Kal Raustiala is Professor of Law and Global Studies at the University of California, Los Angeles.

David M. Rocke is Professor of Biostatistics, Professor of Applied Science, and Co-Director of the Institute for Data Analysis and Visualization at the University of California, Davis.

Christopher Rudolph is Professor of International Politics at American University, Washington, D.C.

Heiner Schulz is Assistant Professor of Political Science at University of Pennsylvania, Philadelphia, Pennsylvania.

Anne-Marie Slaughter [Burley] is Dean of the Woodrow Wilson School of Public and International Affairs at Princeton University, Princeton, New Jersey.

James McCall Smith is Assistant Professor of Political Science and International Affairs at George Washington University, Washington, D.C.

Duncan Snidal is Associate Professor of Political Science and a member of the Committee on International Relations at the University of Chicago, Chicago, Illinois.

Stephen J. Toope is Professor of Law at McGill University, Quebec, Canada.

David G. Victor is Associate Professor of Political Science at Stanford University and director of the Program on Energy and Sustainable Development at the Center for Environmental Science and Policy, Stanford, California.

Alexander Wendt is the Ralph D. Mershon Professor of International Security and the Mershon Center Professor of Political Science at Ohio State University, Columbus, Ohio.

Mark W. Zacher is Professor Emeritus of Political Science, Senior Research Fellow at the Centre of International Relations, and Faculty Fellow, St. John's College, University of British Columbia, Vancouver, Canada.

Daniel Zamora is an associate at the law firm of Tobin & Tobin, San Francisco, California.

Abstracts

Structural Causes and Regime Consequences: Regimes as Intervening Variables (1982)
by Stephen D. Krasner

International regimes are defined as principles, norms, rules, and decision-making procedures around which actor expectations converge in a given issue-area. As a starting point, regimes have been conceptualized as intervening variables, standing between basic causal factors and related outcomes and behavior. There are three views about the importance of regimes: conventional structural orientations dismiss regimes as being at best ineffectual; Grotian orientations view regimes as an intimate component of the international system; and modified structural perspectives see regimes as significant only under certain constrained conditions. For Grotian and modified structuralist arguments, which endorse the view that regimes can influence outcomes and behavior, regime development is seen as a function of five basic causal variables: egoistic self-interest, political power, diffuse norms and principles, custom and usage, and knowledge.

The Demand for International Regimes (1982)
by Robert O. Keohane

International regimes can be understood as results of rational behavior by the actors – principally states – that create them. Regimes are demanded in part because they facilitate the making of agreements, by providing information and reducing transaction costs in world politics. Increased interdependence among issues – greater "issue density" – will lead to increased demand for regimes. Insofar as regimes succeed in providing high-quality information, through such processes as the construction of generally accepted norms or the development of transgovernmental relations, they create demand for their own continuance, even if the structural conditions (such as hegemony) under which they were first supplied change. Analysis of the demand for international regimes thus helps us to understand lags between structural change and regime change, as well as to assess the significance of transgovernmental policy networks. Several assertions of structural theory seem problematic in light of this analysis. Hegemony may not be a necessary condition for stable international regimes; past patterns of institutionalized cooperation may be able to compensate, to some extent, for increasing fragmentation of power.

Democratic States and Commitment in International Relations (1996)
by Kurt Taylor Gaubatz

Making credible commitments is a formidable problem for states in the anarchic international system. A long-standing view holds that this is particularly true for democratic states in which changeable public preferences make it difficult for leaders to sustain commitments over time. However, a number of important elements in the values and institutions that have characterized the liberal democratic states should enhance their ability to sustain international commitments. Indeed, an examination of the durability of international military alliances confirms that those between democratic states have endured longer than either alliances between nondemocracies or alliances between democracies and nondemocracies.

On Compliance (1993)
by Abram Chayes and Antonia Handler Chayes

A new dialogue is beginning between students of international law and international relations scholars concerning compliance with international agreements. This article advances some basic propositions to frame that dialogue. First, it proposes that the level of compliance with international agreements in general is inherently unverifiable by empirical procedures. That nations generally comply with their international agreements, on the one hand, or that they violate them whenever it is in their interest to do so, on the other, are not statements of fact or even hypotheses to be tested. Instead, they are competing heuristic assumptions. Some reasons why the background assumption of a propensity to comply is plausible and useful are given. Second, compliance problems very often do not reflect a deliberate decision to violate an international undertaking on the basis of a calculation of advantage. The article proposes a variety of other reasons why states may deviate from treaty obligations and why in many circumstances those reasons are properly accepted by others as justifying apparent departures from treaty norms. Third, the treaty regime as a whole need not and should not be held to a standard of strict compliance but to a level of overall compliance that is "acceptable" in the light of the interests and concerns the treaty is designed to safeguard. How the acceptable level is determined and adjusted is considered.

Is the Good News About Compliance Good News About Cooperation? (1996)
by George W. Downs, David M. Rocke, and Peter N. Barsoom

Recent research on compliance in international regulatory regimes has argued (1) that compliance is generally quite good; (2) that this high level of compliance has been achieved with little attention to enforcement; (3) that those compliance problems that do exist are best addressed as management rather than enforcement problems; and (4) that the management rather than the enforcement approach holds the key to the evolution of future regulatory cooperation in the international system. While the descriptive findings are largely correct, the policy inferences are dangerously contaminated by endogeneity and selection problems. A high rate of compliance is often the result of states formulating treaties that require them to do little more than they would do in the absence of a treaty. In those cases where noncompliance does occur and where the effects of selection are attenuated, both self-interest and enforcement play significant roles.

The Concept of Legalization (2000)
by Kenneth W. Abbot, Robert O. Keohane, Andrew Moravcsik, Anne-Marie Slaughter, and Duncan Snidal

We develop an empirically based conception of international legalization to show how law and politics are intertwined across a wide range of institutional forms and to frame the analytic and empirical articles that follow in this volume. International legalization is a form of institutionalization characterized by three dimensions: obligation, precision, and delegation. Obligation means that states are legally bound by rules or commitments and are therefore subject to the general rules and procedures of international law. Precision means that the rules are definite, unambiguously defining the conduct they require, authorize, or proscribe. Delegation grants authority to third parties for the implementation of rules, including their interpretation and application, dispute settlement, and (possibly) further rule making. These dimensions are conceptually independent, and each is a matter of degree and gradation. Their various combinations produce a remarkable variety of international legalization. We illustrate a continuum ranging from "hard" legalization (characteristically associated with domestic legal systems) through various forms of "soft" legalization to situations where law is largely absent. Most international legalization lies between the extremes, where actors combine and invoke varying degrees of obligation, precision, and delegation to create subtle blends of politics and law.

Legalized Dispute Resolution: Interstate and Transnational (2000)
by Robert O. Keohane, Andrew Moravcsik, and Anne-Marie Slaughter

We identify two ideal types of international third-party dispute resolution: interstate and transnational. Under interstate dispute resolution, states closely control selection of, access to, and compliance with international courts and tribunals. Under transnational dispute resolution, by contrast, individuals and nongovernmental entities have significant influence over selection, access, and implementation. This distinction helps to explain the politics of international legalization – in particular, the initiation of cases, the tendency of courts to challenge national governments, the extent of compliance with judgments, and the long-term evolution of norms within legalized international regimes. By reducing the transaction costs of setting the process in motion and establishing new constituencies, transnational dispute resolution is more likely than interstate dispute resolution to generate a large number of cases. The types of cases brought under transnational dispute resolution lead more readily to challenges of state actions by international courts. Transnational dispute resolution tends to be associated with greater compliance with international legal judgments, particularly when autonomous domestic institutions such as the judiciary mediate between individuals and the international institutions. Overall, transnational dispute resolution enhances the prospects for long-term deepening and widening of international legalization.

Legalization, Trade Liberalization, and Domestic Politics: A Cautionary Note (2000)
by Judith Goldstein and Lisa L. Martin

If the purpose of legalization is to enhance international cooperation, more may not always be better. Achieving the optimal level of legalization requires finding a balance between reducing the risks of opportunism and reducing the potential negative effects of legalization on domestic political processes. The global trade regime, which aims to liberalize trade, has become increasingly legalized over time. Increased legalization has changed the information environment and the nature of government obligations, which in turn have affected the pattern of mobilization of domestic interest groups on trade. From the perspective of encouraging the future expansion of liberal trade, we suggest some possible negative consequences of legalization, arguing that these consequences must be weighed against the positive effects of legalization on increasing national compliance. Since the weakly legalized GATT institution proved sufficient to sustain widespread liberalization, the case for further legalization must be strong to justify far-reaching change in the global trade regime.

Alternatives to "Legalization": Richer Views of Law and Politics (2001)
by Martha Finnemore and Stephen J. Toope

The authors of "Legalization and World Politics" (*International Organization*, 54, 3, summer 2000) define "legalization" as the degree of obligation, precision, and delegation that international institutions possess. We argue that this definition is unnecessarily narrow. Law is a broad social phenomenon that is deeply embedded in the practices, beliefs, and traditions of societies. Understanding its role in politics requires attention to the legitimacy of law, to custom and law's congruence with social practice, to the role of legal rationality, and to adherence to legal processes, including participation in law's construction. We examine three applications of "legalization" offered in the volume and show how a fuller consideration of law's role in politics can produce concepts that are more robust intellectually and more helpful to empirical research.

Quasi-States, Dual Regimes, and Neoclassical Theory: International Jurisprudence and the Third World (1987)
by Robert H. Jackson

Decolonization in parts of the Third World and particularly Africa has resulted in the emergence of numerous "quasi-states," which are independent largely by international courtesy. They exist by virtue of an external right of self-determination – negative sovereignty – without yet demonstrating much internal capacity for effective and civil government – positive sovereignty. They therefore disclose a new dual international civil regime in which two standards of statehood now coexist: the traditional empirical standard of the North and a new juridical standard of the South. The biases in the constitutive rules of the sovereignty game today and for the first time in modern international history arguably favor the weak. If international theory is to account for this novel situation, it must acknowledge the possibility that morality and legality can, in certain circumstances, be independent of power in international relations. This suggests that contemporary international theory must accommodate not only Machiavellian realism and the sociological discourse of power but also Grotian rationalism and the jurisprudential idiom of law.

Which Norms Matter? Revisiting the "Failure" of Internationalism (1997)
by Jeffrey W. Legro

Scholars tend to believe either that norms are relatively inconsequential or that they are powerful determinants of international politics. Yet the former view overlooks important effects that norms can have, while the latter inadequately specifies which norms matter, the ways in which the norms have an impact, and the magnitude of norm influence relative to other factors. Three different norms on the use of force from the interwar period varied in their influence during World War II. The variation in state adherence to these norms is best explained by the cultures of national military organizations that mediated the influence of the international rules. This analysis highlights the challenge and importance of examining the relative effects of the often cross-cutting prescriptions imbedded in different types of social collectivities.

The Territorial Integrity Norm: International Boundaries and the Use of Force (2001)
by Mark W. Zacher

Scholars and observers of the international system often comment on the decreasing importance of international boundaries as a result of the growth of international economic and social exchanges, economic liberalization, and international regimes. They generally fail to note, however, that coercive territorial revisionism has markedly declined over the past half century – a phenomenon that indicates that in certain ways states attach greater importance to boundaries in our present era. In this article I first trace states' beliefs and practices concerning the use of force to alter boundaries from the birth of the Westphalian order in the seventeenth century through the end of World War II. I then focus on the increasing acceptance of the norm against coercive territorial revisionism since 1945. Finally, I analyze those instrumental and ideational factors that have influenced the strengthening of the norm among both Western and developing countries.

Why Are Some International Agreements Informal? (1991)
by Charles Lipson

Informal agreements are the most common form of international cooperation and the least studied. Ranging from simple oral deals to detailed executive agreements, they permit states to conclude profitable bargains without the formality of treaties. They differ from treaties in more than just a procedural sense. Treaties are designed, by long-standing convention, to raise the credibility of promises by staking national reputation on their adherence. Informal agreements have a more ambiguous status and are useful for precisely that reason. They are chosen to avoid formal and visible national pledges, to avoid the political obstacles of ratification, to reach agreements quickly and quietly, and to provide flexibility for subsequent modification or even renunciation. They differ from formal agreements not because their substance is less important (the Cuban missile crisis was solved by informal agreement) but because the underlying promises are less visible and more equivocal. The prevalence of such informal devices thus reveals not only the possibilities of international cooperation but also the practical obstacles and the institutional limits to endogenous enforcement.

The Politics of Dispute Settlement Design: Explaining Legalism in Regional Trade Pacts (2000)
by James McCall Smith

Dispute settlement mechanisms in international trade vary dramatically from one agreement to another. Some mechanisms are highly legalistic, with standing tribunals that resemble national courts in their powers and procedures. Others are diplomatic, requiring only that the disputing countries make a good-faith effort to resolve their differences through consultations. In this article I seek to account for the tremendous variation in institutional design across a set of more than sixty post-1957 regional trade pacts. In contrast to accounts that emphasize the transaction costs of collective action or the functional requirements of deep integration, I find that the level of legalism in each agreement is strongly related to the level of economic asymmetry, in interaction with the proposed depth of liberalization, among member countries.

Loosening the Ties that Bind: A Learning Model of Agreement Flexibility (2001)
by Barbara Koremenos

How can states credibly make and keep agreements when they are uncertain about the distributional implications of their cooperation? They can do so by incorporating the proper degree of flexibility into their agreements. I develop a formal model in which an agreement characterized by uncertainty may be renegotiated to incorporate new information. The uncertainty is related to the division of gains under the agreement, with the parties resolving this uncertainty over time as they gain experience with the agreement. The greater the agreement uncertainty, the more likely states will want to limit the duration of the agreement and incorporate renegotiation. Working against renegotiation is noise – that is, variation in outcomes not resulting from the agreement. The greater the noise, the more difficult it is to learn how an agreement is actually working; hence, incorporating limited duration and renegotiation provisions becomes less valuable. In a detailed case study, I demonstrate that the form of uncertainty in my model corresponds to that experienced by the parties to the Nuclear Non-proliferation Treaty, who adopted the solution my model predicts.

Driving with the Rearview Mirror: On the Rational Science of Institutional Design (2001)
by Alexander Wendt

The Rational Design project is impressive on its own terms. However, it does not address other approaches relevant to the design of international institutions. To facilitate comparison I survey two "contrast spaces" around it. The first shares the project's central question – What explains institutional design? – but addresses alternative explanations of two types: rival explanations and explanations complementary but deeper in the causal chain. The second contrast begins with a different question: What kind of knowledge is needed to design institutions in the real world? Asking this question reveals epistemological differences between positive social science and institutional design that can be traced to different orientations toward time. Making institutions is about the future and has an intrinsic normative element. Explaining institutions is about the past and does not necessarily have this normative dimension. To avoid "driving with the rearview mirror" we need two additional kinds of knowledge beyond that developed in this volume: knowledge about institutional effectiveness and knowledge about what values to pursue. As such, the problem of institutional design is a fruitful site for developing a broader and more practical conception of social science that integrates normative and positive concerns.

The Dynamics of International Law: The Interaction of Normative and Operating Systems (2003)
by Paul F. Diehl, Charlotte Ku, and Daniel Zamora

This article describes the basic components of the operating and normative systems as a conceptual framework for analyzing and understanding international law. There are many theoretical questions that follow from the framework that embodies a normative and operating system. We briefly outline one of those in this article, namely how the operating system changes. In doing so, we seek to address the puzzle of why operating system changes do not always respond to alterations in the normative sphere. A general theoretical argument focuses on four conditions. We argue that the operating system only responds to normative changes when response is "necessary" (stemming from incompatibility, ineffectiveness, or insufficiency) for giving the norm effect and when the change is roughly coterminous with a dramatic change in the political environment (that is, "political shock"). We also argue, however, that opposition from leading states and domestic political factors might serve to block or limit such operating system change. These arguments are illustrated by reference to three areas of the operating system as they concern the norm against genocide.

Europe Before the Court: A Political Theory of Legal Integration (1993)
by Anne-Marie Slaughter [Burley] and Walter Mattli

The European Court of Justice has been the dark horse of European integration, quietly transforming the Treaty of Rome into a European Community (EC) constitution and steadily increasing the impact and scope of EC law. While legal scholars have tended to take the Court's power for granted, political scientists have overlooked it entirely. This article develops a first-stage theory of community law and politics that marries the insights of legal scholars with a theoretical framework developed by political scientists. Neofunctionalism, the theory that dominated regional integration studies in the 1960s, offers a set of independent variables that convincingly and parsimoniously explain the process of legal integration in the EC. Just as neofunctionalism predicts, the principal forces behind that process are supranational and subnational actors pursuing their own self-interests within a politically insulated sphere. Its distinctive features include a widening of the ambit of successive legal decisions according to a functional logic, a gradual shift in the expectations of both government institutions and private actors participating in the legal system, and the strategic subordination of immediate individual interests of member states to postulated collective interests over the long term. Law functions as a mask for politics, precisely the role neofunctionalists originally forecast for economics. Paradoxically, however, the success of legal institutions in performing that function rests on their self-conscious preservation of the autonomy of law.

The European Court of Justice, National Governments, and Legal Integration in the European Union (1998)
by Geoffrey Garrett, R. Daniel Kelemen, and Heiner Schulz

We develop a game theoretic model of the conditions under which the European Court of Justice can be expected to take "adverse judgments" against European Union member governments and when the governments are likely to abide by these decisions. The model generates three hypotheses. First, the greater the clarity of EU case law precedent, the lesser the likelihood that the Court will tailor its decisions to the anticipated reactions of member governments. Second, the greater the domestic costs of an ECJ ruling to a litigant government, the lesser the likelihood that the litigant government will abide by it (and hence the lesser the likelihood that the Court will make such a ruling). Third, the greater the activism of the ECJ and the larger the number of member governments adversely affected by it, the greater the likelihood that responses by litigant governments will move from individual noncompliance to coordinated retaliation through new legislation or treaty revisions. These hypotheses are tested against three broad lines of case law central to ECJ jurisprudence: bans on agricultural imports, application of principles of equal treatment of the sexes to occupational pensions, and state liability for violation of EU law. The empirical analysis supports our view that though influenced by legal precedent, the ECJ also takes into account the anticipated reactions of member governments.

Scraps of Paper? Agreements and the Durability of Peace (2003)
by Virginia Page Fortna

In the aftermath of war, what determines whether peace lasts or fighting resumes, and what can be done to foster durable peace? Drawing on theories of cooperation, I argue that belligerents can overcome the obstacles to peace by implementing measures that alter incentives, reduce uncertainty about intentions, and manage accidents. A counterargument suggests that agreements are epiphenomenal, merely reflecting the underlying probability of war resumption. I test hypotheses about the durability of peace using hazard analysis. Controlling for factors (including the decisiveness of victory, the cost of war, relative capabilities, and others) that affect the baseline prospects for peace, I find that stronger agreements enhance the durability of peace. In particular, measures such as the creation of demilitarized zones, explicit third-party guarantees, peacekeeping, and joint commissions for dispute resolution affect the duration of peace. Agreements are not merely scraps of paper; rather, their content matters in the construction of peace that lasts.

In the Shadow of Law or Power? Consensus-Based Bargaining and Outcomes in the GATT/WTO (2002)
by Richard H. Steinberg

This article explains how consensus decision making has operated in practice in the General Agreement on Tariffs and Trade/World Trade Organization (GATT/WTO). When GATT/WTO bargaining is law-based, consensus outcomes are Pareto-improving and roughly symmetrical. When bargaining is power-based, states bring to bear instruments of power that are extrinsic to rules, invisibly weighting the process and generating consensus outcomes that are asymmetrical and may not be Pareto-improving. Empirical analysis shows that although trade rounds have been launched through law-based bargaining, hard law is generated when a round is closed, and rounds have been closed through power-based bargaining. Agenda setting has taken place in the shadow of that power and has been dominated by the European Community and the United States. The decision-making rules have been maintained because they help generate information used by powerful states in the agenda-setting process. Consensus decision making at the GATT/WTO is organized hypocrisy, allowing adherence to the instrumental reality of asymmetrical power and the sovereign equality principle upon which consensus decision making is purportedly based.

The Legalization of International Monetary Affairs (2000)
by Beth A. Simmons

For the first time in history, international monetary relations were institutionalized after World War II as a set of legal obligations. The Articles of Agreement that formed the International Monetary Fund contain international legal obligations of the rules of good conduct for IMF members. Members were required to maintain a par value for their currency (until 1977), to use a single unified exchange-rate system, and to keep their current account free from restrictions. In this article I explore why governments committed themselves to these rules and the conditions under which they complied with their commitments. The evidence suggests that governments tended to make and keep commitments if other countries in their region did so as well. Governments also complied with their international legal commitments if the regime placed a high value on the rule of law domestically. One inference is that reputational concerns have a lot to do with international legal commitments and compliance. Countries that have invested in a strong reputation for protecting property rights are more reluctant to see it jeopardized by international law violations. Violation is more likely, however, in the face of widespread noncompliance, suggesting that compliance behavior should be understood in its regional context.

Constructing an Atrocities Regime: The Politics of War Crimes Tribunals (2001)
by Christopher Rudolph

From the notorious "killing fields" of Cambodia to programs of "ethnic cleansing" in the former Yugoslavia and Rwanda, the grizzly nature of ethnic and identity-centered conflict incites horror, outrage, and a human desire for justice. While the drive to humanize warfare can be traced to the writing of Hugo Grotius, current efforts to establish an atrocities regime are unparalleled in modern history. Combining approaches in international relations theory and international law, I examine the role political factors (norms, power and interests, institutions) and legal factors (precedent and procedure) play in the development of an atrocities regime. International tribunals have convicted generally low-level war criminals in both Rwanda and the former Yugoslavia, but they have had much more limited success in achieving their more expansive goals – deterring atrocities and fostering national reconciliation in regions fraught with ethnic violence. This analysis reveals additional institutional modifications needed to construct a more effective regime and highlights the importance of placing this new regime within a comprehensive international strategy of conflict management.

The Origins of Human Rights Regimes: Democratic Delegation in Postwar Europe (2000)
by Andrew Moravcsik

Most formal international human rights regimes establish international committees and courts that hold governments accountable to their own citizens for purely internal activities. Why would governments establish arrangements so invasive of domestic sovereignty? Two views dominate the literature. "Realist" theories assert that the most powerful democracies coerce or entice weaker countries to accept norms; "ideational" theories maintain that transnational processes of diffusion and persuasion socialize less-democratic governments to accept norms. Drawing on theories of rational delegation, I propose and test a third "republican liberal" view: Governments delegate self-interestedly to combat future threats to domestic democratic governance. Thus it is not mature and powerful democracies, but new and less-established democracies that will most strongly favor mandatory and enforceable human rights obligations. I test this proposition in the case of the European Convention on Human Rights – the most successful system of formal international human rights guarantees in the world today. The historical record of its founding – national positions, negotiating tactics, and confidential deliberations – confirms the republican liberal explanation. My claim that governments will sacrifice sovereignty to international regimes in order to dampen domestic political uncertainty and "lock in" more credible policies is then generalized theoretically and applied to other human rights regimes, coordination of conservative reaction, and international trade and monetary policy.

Regime Design Matters: Intentional Oil Pollution and Treaty Compliance (1994)
by Ronald B. Mitchell

Whether a treaty elicits compliance from governments or nonstate actors depends upon identifiable characteristics of the regime's compliance systems. Within the international regime controlling intentional oil pollution, a provision requiring tanker owners to install specified equipment produced dramatically higher levels of compliance than a provision requiring tanker operators to limit their discharges. Since both provisions entailed strong economic incentives for violation and regulated the same countries over the same time period, the variance in compliance clearly can be attributed to different features of the two subregimes. The equipment requirements' success stemmed from establishing an integrated compliance system that increased transparency, provided for potent and credible sanctions, reduced implementation costs to governments by building on existing infrastructures, and prevented violations rather than merely deterring them.

The Regime Complex for Plant Genetic Resources (2004)
by Kal Raustiala and David G. Victor

This article examines the implications of the rising density of international institutions. Despite the rapid proliferation of institutions, scholars continue to embrace the assumption that individual regimes are decomposable from others. We contend that an increasingly common phenomenon is the "regime complex": a collective of partially overlapping and nonhierarchical regimes. The evolution of regime complexes reflects the influence of legalization on world politics. Regime complexes are laden with legal inconsistencies because the rules in one regime are rarely coordinated closely with overlapping rules in related regimes. Negotiators often attempt to avoid glaring inconsistencies by adopting broad rules that allow for multiple interpretations. In turn, solutions refined through implementation of these rules focus later rounds of negotiation and legalization. We explore these processes using the issue of plant genetic resources (PGR). Over the last century, states have created property rights in these resources in a Demsetzian process: As new technologies and ideas have made PGR far more valuable, actors have mobilized and clashed over the creation of property rights that allow the appropriation of that value.

Preface

This volume is intended to help readers understand the relationship between international law and international relations (IL/IR). The excerpted articles, all of which were first published in *International Organization*, represent some of the most important research since serious social science scholarship began in this area more than twenty years ago. The contributions have been selected to provide readers with a range of theoretical perspectives, concepts, and heuristics that can be used to analyze the relationship between international law and international relations. These articles also cover some of the main topics of international affairs. In this brief preface, we note the rise of law in interstate relations and flag some of the most important theoretical approaches to understanding this development. We also introduce the topics chosen and discuss the volume's organization.

THE RISE OF LAW IN INTERNATIONAL RELATIONS

The study of international law has enjoyed something of a renaissance in the last two decades. Of course, international affairs have long been assumed to include international legal issues. Yet, in the first third of the twentieth century, analysts did not sharply distinguish "international law" from "international relations." International relations courses were often about international law and frequently confounded the prescripts of international law with the way states were said to behave in fact. By the time the United States entered the Second World War, that illusory mistake was exposed: it was clear that international legal rules and processes had not operated the way many had hoped. The failure to contain German and Japanese aggression, the weakness of agreements to keep the international economy functioning, and the humanitarian disasters of the Second World War made most observers acutely aware of the limits of law in international affairs. For more than thirty years after the end of the war, American political science turned its back on international law, focusing its study of international relations on the material interests and observed behavior of states.

Yet by the early 1980s, many international relations scholars had rediscovered a role for law in interstate relations. Reflecting on the post-war order, many recognized that it was built not only upon power relationships but also on explicitly negotiated agreements. These agreements in themselves increasingly piqued scholarly interest. One reason may have been the sheer proliferation of such agreements. A century ago, most international law was said to arise from custom – evidenced by continuous, recurrent state practice and *opinion juris* (i.e., the practice was compelled by legal obligation). For a number of reasons – including the growth of independent states, the lack of consent implied by many approaches to customary law, the increasingly detailed nature of international agreements, and the rise of multilateral treaty-making capacity, e.g. by various working groups of the United Nations – today, many (if not most) international legal obligations are expressed in treaty form. Some treaties codify customary law, but in a way that respects the express consent of the states that are parties to them.

Figure 1 shows the number of new multilateral treaties concluded in each quarter of the last century. While the number of new multilateral treaties grew from 1900 to 1975 and then began to decline in the 1976–95 period, Figure 1 strongly suggests that the aggregate number of multilateral treaties in force has grown rapidly in the last hundred years.

Not only has the number of treaties grown, so has the scope of topics and subjects addressed by treaty law. As Figure 1 suggests, treaty growth has been especially marked in economic affairs, as well as in areas of human welfare and the environment. Moreover, in the late nineteenth century, most international law defined the rights and responsibilities of *states* toward each other – purely "public" international law. Over the course of the twentieth century, international law increasingly began to address the responsibilities of states toward individuals and nonstate actors (characteristic of human rights treaties), and set forth rules governing the relationships of private individuals and nonstate actors toward each other – an expansion of private international law. This latter development is reflected in such important treaties as the United Nations

Figure 1. Number of New Multilateral Treaties Concluded

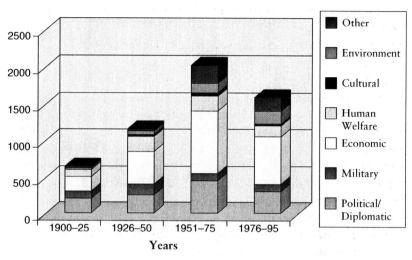

Convention on the International Sale of Goods, which is essentially a global commercial code, and the United Nations Convention on the Recognition and Enforcement of Foreign Arbitral Awards, which has enhanced the effectiveness of private international dispute settlement.

In this context, it is perhaps not surprising that the authority to adjudicate international disputes has been delegated increasingly to international courts. Figure 2 shows that the number of international judicial, quasi-judicial, and dispute settlement bodies has grown from just a handful in 1900 to nearly a hundred today. Moreover, the rate at which dispute settlement bodies are growing has accelerated in the last 25 years. Interstate disputes over territory, trade, human rights, environmental protection, intellectual property, labor protection, and criminal matters may now be resolved in international institutions that more or less resemble well-developed domestic legal systems in the way they apply legal standards, procedures, and norms to dispute resolution. Some of these institutions, such as the European Court of Justice (ECJ) and the World Trade Organization's (WTO) dispute settlement system, have compulsory jurisdiction over member states or territories and enjoy impressive rates of compliance with their decisions.

What explains the explosive growth of treaty law, the broader scope of international law topics and subjects, and expansion of international venues for law-based dispute resolution? Does international law affect the behavior of individuals, states, and nonstate actors? How

Preface

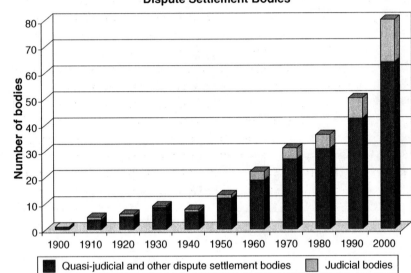

Figure 2. Growth in International Judicial, Quasi-judicial, and Dispute Settlement Bodies

does international law – and how do particular international rules and procedures – affect interstate relations? These are some of the questions addressed by social science and legal scholarship, of which the articles in this volume are examples.

THEORIES OF LAW IN INTERNATIONAL AFFAIRS

One way to understand the proliferation of legal arrangements is to view them as an epiphenomenon of more basic relationships between states. This is the position of scholars informed by structural realist theories: The interests of powerful states determine the content of international law, which in and of itself has little independent impact on behavior or outcomes. In conceptualizing "international regimes," Stephen Krasner's contribution in Part I of this volume sets forth this position in its pure form (Krasner 1982). Another selection in this volume, by Downs, Rocke, and Barsoom (1996), reflects similar skepticism about the extent to which international law has autonomous explanatory power. Other realist work, however, such as Steinberg (2002) and Garrett, Kelemen, and Schulz (1998) in this volume, affords some important functions to international law, while maintaining that law nonetheless reflects underlying power.

If law does simply reflect underlying power relationships, this raises the question of why states bother to create rules to order their inter-actions at all. A rationalist institutionalist theory was offered in early form by Robert Keohane (1982), an excerpt from which appears in Part I of this volume. Using a rationalist logic that was built on the same assumptions employed by structural realism, Keohane showed that international institutions could facilitate cooperative, positive sum outcomes that would not otherwise occur. Keohane's paradigmatic example was the prisoners dilemma, which he (and others following him) argued was a metaphor for much of international life. Rationalist argumentation that infuses legal institutions with autonomous explanatory power has since been a main-stay of much IL/IR literature. Increasingly, rationalist institutionalist scholarship has shifted from questions about how international law matters to questions about why legal forms vary (see, e.g., Lipson 1991, in this volume) and why treaty design varies (see, e.g., Smith 2000 and Koremenos 2001, both in this volume).

Much of the early rationalist work, whether realist or institutionalist, has treated states as unitary actors with interests that are exogenous to the argument. This evades a crucial question: where do interests come from? Liberal theories offer an answer: "State interests" are best under-stood as an aggregation and intermediation of individual and group interests. International law in this view is driven from the bottom up. For example, a selection from Andrew Moravcsik in this volume argues that the European human rights regime expanded rapidly in the wake of the Cold War, as nascent democracies that supported human rights pro-tection emerged in Eastern Europe (Moravcsik 2000).

Liberalism may explain much of the content of international law, but it affords little autonomous role to law; however, when liberal processes are viewed as operating in the context of particular institutional arrange-ments, law may be afforded a crucial explanatory role. For example, Slaughter and Mattli's contribution to this volume shows how the ECJ offered a path for European interests that differed from the European Community's legislative path, reconfiguring European interests in ways that reshaped outcomes (Slaughter and Mattli 1993). Similarly, Keohane, Moravcsik, and Slaughter show how variance in the legal structure of international dispute resolution may explain the extent to which the various processes expand international law (Keohane, Moravcsik, and Slaughter 2000). Other selections in this volume, such as Goldstein and Martin (2000) and Gaubatz (1996), also combine liberal and institutional elements to generate interesting explanations.

Influenced by postmodern social theory, constructivists delved even more deeply into the question: Where do interests come from? Constructivists launched an ontological attack on the rationalist work that preceded it, claiming that neither interests nor power exists independent of the social context in which actors are enmeshed. Interests and identity are constructed socially; they are plastic and may be redefined. International law may be understood as both a reflection of identities and as a social artifact that reinforces identities, interests, and power. Variations on this view are articulated by several selections in this volume, including critiques of nonconstructivist approaches in Wendt (2001) and Finnemore and Toope (2001) and arguments about the importance of norms in shaping and understanding the operation of international law by Jackson (1987), Legro (1997), and Zacher (2001).

CONTEMPORARY RESEARCH AND THE ORGANIZATION OF THIS VOLUME

Increasingly, contemporary IL/IR research organizes less around abstract theoretical debates and more around particular methods and concepts that may be seen as hybrids of the main approaches. Increasingly, there is conscious engagement across meta-theories, with a focus on mid-level analysis of international legal and political developments using hybrid theories and powerful methods to test those theories.

Part II of this volume is largely organized around these developments, and newer heuristics and debates associated with them. This part highlights the distinction between making a commitment to an international rule and compliance with it. Gaubatz (1996) introduces the "credible commitment" concept (which suggests that a costly commitment by one state may induce other states to behave differently from the way they would otherwise behave) to the debate about treaty effects and suggests that at least some treaty commitments by democracies may be more credible than commitments by nondemocracies. Chayes and Chayes (1993) present what has become known as the "managerial" theory of treaty compliance, offering reasons that explain why states generally comply with treaties. Downs, Rocke, and Barsoom (1996) offer a skeptical counterpoint to Chayes and Chayes (1993) and others, arguing that apparent state "compliance" frequently results from treaty provisions that require little more than states would do in the absence of treaties, and that in other cases compliance is usually explained by self-interest or enforcement pressures from powerful states.

Part III explores the "legalization" of international relations, which was the topic of a widely read *IO* special issue in 2000. The first contribution (Abbott et al. 2000) defines the concept of legalization. Keohane, Moravcsik, and Slaughter (2000) argue that transnational adjudication causes more expansive international law-making than interstate dispute resolution. Goldstein and Martin (2000) offer reasons to be cautious about concluding that legalization is normatively desirable. Finnemore and Toope (2001) suggest that most of the work on "legalization" is limited by its narrow definition and the associated ontological orientation, which prevents the concept from adequately accounting for the reciprocal relationship between international law and social practice.

Part IV explores the relationship between international law and international norms. The first piece, by Robert Jackson (1987), argues that competing definitions of sovereignty and statehood suggest that international theory must accommodate morality and legality as autonomous variables. Legro (1997) shows that some norms affect state behavior more than others, and he identifies factors that influenced which norms concerning the use of force mattered most in World War II. Zacher (2001) suggests ideational and instrumental factors that influence the strength of norms, examining the norm against coercive territorial revisionism.

Part V considers the growing literature on treaty design and dynamics. Three of the selections (Lipson 1991, Smith 2000, and Koremenos 2001) offer a rationalist explanation for a particular attribute of international agreement design – why some international agreements are informal; why the extent of legalism in dispute settlement mechanisms varies across agreements; and why some agreements contain escape clauses or provide for a short duration. Wendt (2001) offers a constructivist critique of the rationalist approach to understanding treaty design, suggesting limits of the approach. Diehl, Ku, and Zamora (2003) present a perspective suggesting that international law can only be understood systemically and dynamically, by considering how international law changes (or does not change) as norms or other political factors change.

Part VI presents two competing views of the European Court of Justice (ECJ), which is considered by many to be the world's most legalized and sophisticated international court. Slaughter [Burley] and Mattli (1993) is a classic article, using neofunctionalist theory to argue how the authority and independence of the ECJ have grown and how the court has played an autonomous role in European integration. Garrett, Keleman, and Schulz (1998) challenge this view, arguing that the ECJ is so constrained by European politics that it should not be seen as a truly autonomous actor.

Part VII presents some classic articles that use IL/IR theory to understand particular substantive areas of international law. This includes articles that explore the extent to which international agreements maintain peace after conflict (Fortna 2003), how powerful countries use "invisible weighting" to influence outcomes under "consensus-based" decision-making rules at the World Trade Organization (Steinberg 2002), and why governments commit themselves to particular International Monetary Fund rules and the conditions under which they comply with those rules (Simmons 2000). Other selections consider the politics of war crimes tribunals (Rudolph 2001), explain the surge of commitment to human rights regimes in postwar Europe (Moravcsik 2000), identify treaty features that favor compliance with the international oil pollution control regime (Mitchell 1994), and explore state behavior in the "regime complex" of overlapping treaties governing plant genetic resources (Raustiala and Victor 2004).

CONCLUSION

The scholarship linking international law and international relations has developed significantly over the past three decades. *International Organization* has published some of the most important research in this area, and the articles reprinted here represent major theoretical and empirical contributions. As a testament to this dynamic area of inquiry, new research on IL/IR is now being published in a growing range of traditional law reviews and disciplinary journals. The articles reprinted here were important milestones toward making IL/IR a central concern of scholarly research in international affairs.

Beth A. Simmons   Richard H. Steinberg
Cambridge, Massachusetts   Los Angeles, California

Editors' Note

In order to offer broad coverage of theories, approaches, and topics in this volume, each contribution has been edited down to approximately two-thirds of its originally published length. The authors of each contribution actively supported this endeavor.

While citations within articles have been maintained, complete references have been omitted from the book. However, a complete set of references for each of the chapters in the book may be found at http//: www.cambridge.org/9780521861861.

The deletion of originally published text is signified in this book by the insertion of asterisks. Where three asterisks appear within or at the end of a paragraph, part of the originally published paragraph has been deleted. Where three asterisks appear between paragraphs, one or more paragraphs have been removed. A single asterisk marks where a footnote was deleted. Text appearing within brackets signifies that those words have been changed from the originally published article or added during the editing process. Neither asterisks nor brackets appear in Chapter 4, which was substantially revised from the original by one of its co-authors.

PART I

INTERNATIONAL REGIMES THEORY: DOES LAW MATTER?

Structural Causes and Regime Consequences: Regimes as Intervening Variables

Stephen D. Krasner

DEFINING REGIMES AND REGIME CHANGE

* * *

Regimes can be defined as sets of implicit or explicit principles, norms, rules, and decision-making procedures around which actors' expectations converge in a given area of international relations. Principles are beliefs of fact, causation, and rectitude. Norms are standards of behavior defined in terms of rights and obligations. Rules are specific prescriptions or proscriptions for action. Decision-making procedures are prevailing practices for making and implementing collective choice.

This usage is consistent with other recent formulations. Keohane and Nye, for instance, define regimes as "sets of governing arrangements" that include "networks of rules, norms, and procedures that regularize behavior and control its effects."[1] Haas argues that a regime encompasses a mutually coherent set of procedures, rules, and norms.[2] Hedley Bull, using a somewhat different terminology, refers to the importance of rules and institutions in international society where rules refer to "general imperative principles which require or authorize prescribed classes of persons or groups to behave in prescribed ways."[3] Institutions for Bull

---

[1] Robert O. Keohane and Joseph S. Nye, *Power and Interdependence* (Boston: Little, Brown, 1977), p. 19.
[2] Ernst Haas, "Technological Self-Reliance for Latin America: The OAS Contribution," *International Organization* 34, 4 (Autumn 1980), p. 553.
[3] Hedley Bull, *The Anarchical Society: A Study of Order in World Politics* (New York: Columbia University Press, 1977), p. 54.

help to secure adherence to rules by formulating, communicating, administering, enforcing, interpreting, legitimating, and adapting them.

Regimes must be understood as something more than temporary arrangements that change with every shift in power or interests. Keohane notes that a basic analytic distinction must be made between regimes and agreements. Agreements are *ad hoc*, often "one-shot," arrangements. The purpose of regimes is to facilitate agreements. *** As interest and power change, behavior changes. Waltz's conception of the balance of power, in which states are driven by systemic pressures to repetitive balancing behavior, is not a regime; Kaplan's conception, in which equilibrium requires commitment to rules that constrain immediate, short-term power maximization (especially not destroying an essential actor), is a regime.[4]

Similarly, regime-governed behavior must not be based solely on short-term calculations of interest. Since regimes encompass principles and norms, the utility function that is being maximized must embody some sense of general obligation. One such principle, reciprocity, is emphasized in Jervis's analysis of security regimes. When states accept reciprocity they will sacrifice short-term interests with the expectation that other actors will reciprocate in the future, even if they are not under a specific obligation to do so. This formulation is similar to Fred Hirsch's brilliant discussion of friendship, in which he states: "Friendship contains an element of direct mutual exchange and to this extent is akin to private economic good. But it is often much more than that. Over time, the friendship 'transaction' can be presumed, by its permanence, to be a net benefit on both sides. At any moment of time, though, the exchange is very unlikely to be reciprocally balanced."[5] It is the infusion of behavior with principles and norms that distinguishes regime-governed activity in the international system from more conventional activity, guided exclusively by narrow calculations of interest.

A fundamental distinction must be made between principles and norms on the one hand, and rules and procedures on the other. Principles and norms provide the basic defining characteristics of a regime. There may be many rules and decision-making procedures that are consistent with the same principles and norms. *Changes in rules and decision-making*

---

[4] Kenneth Waltz, *Theory of International Relations* (Reading, Mass.: Addison-Wesley, 1979); Morton Kaplan, *Systems and Process in International Politics* (New York: Wiley, 1957), p. 23; Kaplan, *Towards Professionalism in International Theory* (New York: Free Press, 1979), pp. 66–69, 73.

[5] Fred Hirsch, *The Social Limits to Growth* (Cambridge: Harvard University Press, 1976), p. 78.

procedures are changes within regimes, provided that principles and norms are unaltered. * * * *Changes in principles and norms are changes of the regime itself.* When norms and principles are abandoned, there is either a change to a new regime or a disappearance of regimes from a given issue-area. * * *

Fundamental political arguments are more concerned with norms and principles than with rules and procedures. Changes in the latter may be interpreted in different ways. For instance, in the area of international trade, recent revisions in the Articles of Agreement of the General Agreement on Tariffs and Trade (GATI) provide for special and differential treatment for less developed countries (LDCs). All industrialized countries have instituted generalized systems of preferences for LDCs. Such rules violate one of the basic norms of the liberal postwar order, the most-favored-nation treatment of all parties. However, the industrialized nations have treated these alterations in the rules as temporary departures necessitated by the peculiar circumstances of poorer areas. At American insistence the concept of graduation was formally introduced into the GATT Articles after the Tokyo Round. Graduation holds that as countries become more developed they will accept rules consistent with liberal principles. Hence, Northern representatives have chosen to interpret special and differential treatment of developing countries as a change within the regime.

Speakers for the Third World, on the other hand, have argued that the basic norms of the international economic order should be redistribution and equity, not nondiscrimination and efficiency. They see the changes in rules as changes of the regime because they identify these changes with basic changes in principle. There is a fundamental difference between viewing changes in rules as indications of change within the regime and viewing these changes as indications of change between regimes. The difference hinges on assessments of whether principles and norms have changed as well. Such assessments are never easy because they cannot be based on objective behavioral observations. "We know deviations from regimes," Ruggie avers, "not simply by acts that are undertaken, but by the intentionality and acceptability attributed to those acts in the context of an intersubjective framework of meaning."[6]

Finally, it is necessary to distinguish the weakening of a regime from changes within or between regimes. *If the principles, norms, rules, and*

---

[6] John Ruggie, "International Regimes, Transactions, and Change: Embedded Liberalism in the Postwar Economic Order," *International Organization* 36, 2 (Spring 1982), p. 380.

decision-making procedures of a regime become less coherent, or if actual practice is increasingly inconsistent with principles, norms, rules, and procedures, then a regime has weakened. Special and differential treatment for developing countries is an indication that the liberal regime has weakened, even if it has not been replaced by something else. The use of diplomatic cover by spies, the bugging of embassies, the assassination of diplomats by terrorists, and the failure to provide adequate local police protection are all indications that the classic regime protecting foreign envoys has weakened. However, the furtive nature of these activities indicates that basic principles and norms are not being directly challenged. In contrast, the seizure of American diplomats by groups sanctioned by the Iranian government is a basic challenge to the regime itself. Iran violated principles and norms, not just rules and procedures.[7]

In sum, change within a regime involves alterations of rules and decision-making procedures, but not of norms or principles; change of a regime involves alteration of norms and principles; and weakening of a regime involves incoherence among the components of the regime or inconsistency between the regime and related behavior.

DO REGIMES MATTER?

*** The first attempt to analyze regimes thus assumed the following set of causal relationships (see Figure 1.1).

BASIC CAUSAL VARIABLES $\longrightarrow$ REGIMES $\longrightarrow$ RELATED BEHAVIOR AND OUTCOMES

FIGURE 1.1

Regimes do not arise of their own accord. They are not regarded as ends in themselves. Once in place they do affect related behavior and outcomes. They are not merely epiphenomenal.

The independent impact of regimes is a central analytic issue. The second causal arrow implies that regimes do matter. However, there is no general agreement on this point, and three basic orientations can be distinguished. The conventional structural views the regime concept [as] useless, if not misleading. Modified structural suggests that regimes may matter, but only under fairly restrictive conditions. And Grotian sees

---

[7] Iran's behavior may be rooted in an Islamic view of international relations that rejects the prevailing, European-derived regime. See Richard Rosecrance, "International Theory Revisited," *International Organization* 35, 4 (Autumn 1981) for a similar point.

regimes as much more pervasive, as inherent attributes of any complex, persistent pattern of human behavior.

*** The conventional view argues that regimes, if they can be said to exist at all, have little or no impact. They are merely epiphenomenal. The underlying causal schematic is one that sees a direct connection between changes in basic causal factors (whether economic or political) and changes in behavior and outcomes. Regimes are excluded completely, or their impact on outcomes and related behavior is regarded as trivial.

*** Structural orientations conceptualize a world of rational self-seeking actors. The actors may be individuals, or firms, or groups, or classes, or states. They function in a system or environment that is defined by their own interests, power, and interaction. These orientations are resistant to the contention that principles, norms, rules, and decision-making procedures have a significant impact on outcomes and behavior.

Nowhere is this more evident than in the image of the market, the reigning analytic conceptualization for economics, the most successful of the social sciences. A market is characterized by impersonality between buyers and sellers, specialization in buying and selling, and exchange based upon prices set in terms of a common medium of exchange.[8] Max Weber states that in the market "social actions are not determined by orientation to any sort of norm which is held to be valid, nor do they rest on custom, but entirely on the fact that the corresponding type of social action is in the nature of the case best adapted to the normal interests of the actors as they themselves are aware of them."[9] The market is a world of atomized, self-seeking egoistic individuals.

The market is a powerful metaphor for many arguments in the literature of political science, not least international relations. The recent work of Kenneth Waltz exemplifies this orientation. For Waltz, the defining characteristic of the international system is that its component parts (states) are functionally similar and interact in an anarchic environment. International systems are distinguished only by differing distributions of relative capabilities among actors. States are assumed to act in their own self-interest. At a minimum they "seek their own preservation and, at a maximum, drive for universal domination."[10] They are constrained only by their interaction with other states in the system. Behavior is, therefore,

[8] Cyril Belshaw, *Traditional Exchange and Modern Markets* (Englewood Cliffs, N.J.: Prentice-Hall, 1965), pp.8–9.

[9] Max Weber, *Economy and Society* (Berkeley: University of California Press, 1977), p. 30.

[10] Waltz, *Theory of International Relations*, p. 118.

a function of the distribution of power among states and the position of each particular state. When power distributions change, behavior will also change. Regimes, for Waltz, can only be one small step removed from the underlying power capabilities that sustain them.[11]

The second orientation to regimes is modified structural. *** Authors start from a conventional structural realist perspective, a world of sovereign states seeking to maximize their interest and power. ***

In a world of sovereign states the basic function of regimes is to coordinate state behavior to achieve desired outcomes in particular issue-areas.[12] Such coordination is attractive under several circumstances. *** If, as many have argued, there is a general movement toward a world of complex interdependence, then the number of areas in which regimes can matter is growing. However, regimes cannot be relevant for zero-sum situations in which states act to maximize the difference between their utilities and those of others. *** Pure power motivations preclude regimes. Thus, the second orientation, modified structuralism, sees regimes emerging and having a significant impact, but only under restrictive conditions. It suggests that the first cut should be amended as in Figure 1.2.

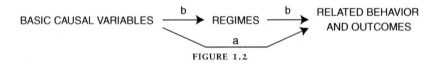

BASIC CAUSAL VARIABLES →(b) REGIMES →(b) RELATED BEHAVIOR AND OUTCOMES / a

FIGURE 1.2

For most situations there is a direct link between basic causal variables and related behavior (path a); but under circumstances that are not purely conflictual, where individual decision making leads to suboptimal outcomes, regimes may be significant (path b).[13]

The third approach to regimes *** reflects a fundamentally different view of international relations than the two structural arguments just described. ***

---

[11] Ibid., especially chapters 5 and 6. This conventional structuralist view for the realist school has its analog in Marxist analysis to studies that focus exclusively on technology and economic structure.

[12] Vinod K. Aggarwal emphasizes this point. See his "Hanging by a Thread: International Regime Change in the Textile/Apparel System, 1950–1979," Ph.D. diss., Stanford University, 1981, chap. 1.

[13] The modified structural arguments are based upon a realist analysis of international relations. In the Marxist tradition this position has its analog in many structural Marxist writings, which emphasize the importance of the state and ideology as institutions that act to rationalize and legitimate fundamental economic structures.

* * *

While the modified structural approach does not view the perfect market as a regime, because action there is based purely upon individual calculation without regard to the behavior of others, the third orientation does regard the market as a regime. Patterns of behavior that persist over extended periods are infused with normative significance. A market cannot be sustained by calculations of self-interest alone. It must be, in Ruggie's terms, *embedded* in a broader social environment that nurtures and sustains the conditions necessary for its functioning. Even the balance of power, regarded by conventional structural realist analysts as a purely conflictual situation, can be treated as a regime.[14] The causal schema suggested by a Grotian orientation either closely parallels the first cut shown in Figure 1.1, or can be depicted as in Figure 1.3.

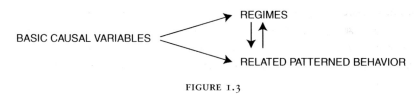

FIGURE 1.3

Patterned behavior reflecting calculations of interest tends to lead to the creation of regimes, and regimes reinforce patterned behavior. * * * States are (rarified) abstractions. Elites have transnational as well as national ties. Sovereignty is a behavioral variable, not an analytic assumption. The ability of states to control movements across their borders and to maintain dominance over all aspects of the international system is limited. Security and state survival are not the only objectives. Force does not occupy a singularly important place in international politics. Elites act within a communications net, embodying rules, norms, and principles, which transcends national boundaries.

This minimalist Grotian orientation has informed a number of theoretical postulates developed during the postwar period. Functionalism saw the possibility of eroding sovereignty through the multiplication of particularistic interests across national boundaries. Karl Deutsch's 1957 study of integration, with its emphasis on societal communication, made a distinction between security communities and anarchy.[15] Some authors associated

---

[14] Bull, *The Anarchical Society*, chap. 5.
[15] See Arend Lijphart, "The Structure of the Theoretical Revolution in International Relations," *International Studies Quarterly* 18, 1 (March 1974), pp. 64–65, for the development of this argument.

with the concept of transnationalism have posited a web of interdependence that makes any emphasis on sovereignty analytically misleading and normatively questionable. Keohane and Nye's discussion of complex interdependence rejects the assumptions of the primacy of force and issue hierarchy assumed by a realist perspective.[16] Ernst Haas points out that what he calls organic theories – eco-environmentalism, eco-reformism, and egalitarianism – deny conventional power-oriented assumptions.

*** The issue is not so much whether one accepts the possibility of principles, norms, rules, and decision-making procedures affecting outcomes and behavior, as what one's basic assumption is about the normal state of international affairs. Adherents of a Grotian perspective accept regimes as a pervasive and significant phenomenon in the international system. Adherents of a structural realist orientation see regimes as a phenomenon whose presence cannot be assumed and whose existence requires careful explanation. The two "standard cases" are fundamentally different, and it is the definition of the standard case that identifies the basic theoretical orientation. *** From a realist perspective, regimes are phenomena that need to be explained; from a Grotian perspective, they are data to be described.

In sum, conventional structural arguments do not take regimes seriously: if basic causal variables change, regimes will also change. Regimes have no independent impact on behavior. Modified structural arguments, represented here by a number of adherents of a realist approach to international relations, see regimes as mattering only when independent decision making leads to undesired outcomes. Finally, Grotian perspectives accept regimes as a fundamental part of all patterned human interaction, including behavior in the international system.

EXPLANATIONS FOR REGIME DEVELOPMENT

* * *

1. Egoistic Self-Interest

The prevailing explanation for the existence of international regimes is egoistic self-interest. By egoistic self-interest I refer to the desire to maximize one's own utility function where that function does not include the utility of another party. The egoist is concerned with the behavior of

---

[16] Keohane and Nye, *Power and Interdependence*, especially chap. 8.

others only insofar as that behavior can affect the egoist's utility. All contractarian political theories from Hobbes to Rawls are based on egoistic self-interest. In contrast, pure power seekers are interested in maximizing the difference between their power capabilities and those of their opponent.

*   *   *

*** It is not so clear that coordination involves regimes. Coordination may only require the construction of rules. If these rules are not informed by any proximate principles or norms, they will not conform to the definition of regimes set forth earlier. ***

[The benefits provided by regimes are likely to outweigh the costs of regime formation and maintenance when there is asymmetric information, moral hazard, potential dishonesty, or high issue density. In addition, the costs of forming regimes will be lower when there is a high level of formal and informal communication among states, a condition more likely to be found in open political systems operating under conditions of complex interdependence. *** Hence calculations of egoistic self-interest emerge as central elements in most of the [chapters] in this [book].

2. Political Power

The second major basic causal variable used to explain regime development is political power. Two different orientations toward power can be distinguished. The first is cosmopolitan and instrumental: power is used to secure optimal outcomes for the system as a whole. In game-theoretic terms power is used to promote joint maximization. It is power in the service of the common good. The second approach is particularistic and potentially consummatory. Power is used to enhance the values of specific actors within the system. These values may include increasing power capabilities as well as promoting economic or other objectives. In game-theoretic terms power is used to maximize individual payoffs. It is power in the service of particular interests.

a. Power in the Service of the Common Good

The first position is represented by a long tradition in classical and neoclassical economics associated with the provision of public goods. The hidden hand was Adam Smith's most compelling construct: the good of all from the selfishness of each; there could be no more powerful defense of egoism. But Smith recognized that it was necessary for the state to provide certain collective goods. These included defense, the maintenance of order, minimum levels of welfare, public works, the protection of infant industries, and standards for commodities.[17] Economists have pointed to the importance of the state for establishing property rights and enforcing contracts; that is, creating conditions that prevent predatory as opposed to market behavior. The state must create institutions that equate public and private rates of return.[18] Keynesian analysis gives the state a prominent role in managing macroeconomic variables. For all of these arguments the purpose of state action is to further general societal interests.

* * *

b. Power in the Service of Particular Interests

* * * A game-theoretic analogy makes it easier to distinguish between two important variants of the viewpoint of power in the service of particular interests. The first assumes that payoffs are fixed and that an actor's choice of strategy is autonomously determined solely by these payoffs. The second assumes that power can be used to alter payoffs and influence actor strategy.

The first approach closely follows the analysis that applies when purely cosmopolitan objectives are at stake, except that political power is used to maximize individual, not joint, payoffs. Under certain configurations of interest, there is an incentive to create regimes and the provision of these regimes is a function of the distribution of power. * * * [Keohane has] argued that hegemons play a critical role in supplying the collective goods that are needed for regimes to function effectively.[19] Hegemons provide

---

[17] There is a lively debate over precisely how much of a role Smith accords to the state. Some (see for instance Albert Hirschman, *The Passions and the Interests* [Princeton: Princeton University Press, 1977], pp. 103–104) maintain that Smith wanted to limit the folly of government by having it do as little as possible. Others (see for instance Colin Holmes, "Laissez-faire in Theory and Practice: Britain 1800–1875," *Journal of European Economic History* 5, 3 [1976], p. 673; and Carlos Diaz-Alejandro, "Delinking North and South: Unshackled or Unhinged," in Albert Fishlow et al., *Rich and Poor Nations in the World Economy* [New York: McGraw-Hill, 1978], pp. 124–25) have taken the intermediate position endorsed here. Others see Smith trying to establish conditions for a moral society that must be based on individual choice, for which a materialistically oriented, egoistically maintained economic system is only instrumental. See, for instance, Leonard Billet, "The Just Economy: The Moral Basis of the Wealth of Nations," *Review of Social Economy* 34 (December 1974).

[18] Jack Hirschleifer, "Economics from a Biological Viewpoint," *Journal of Law and Economics* 20 (April 1977); Weber, *Economy and Society*, pp. 336–37; Douglass C. North and Robert Paul Thomas, *The Rise of the Western World: A New Economic History* (Cambridge: Cambridge University Press, 1973), chap. 1.

[19] Robert O. Keohane, "The Theory of Hegemonic Stability and Changes in International Economic Regimes, 1967–77," in Ole R. Holsti et al., *Changes in the International System* (Boulder, Col.: Westview, 1980).

these goods not because they are interested in the well-being of the system as a whole, but because regimes enhance their own national values. * * *

The theory of hegemonic leadership suggests that under conditions of declining hegemony there will be a weakening of regimes. Without leadership, principles, norms, rules, and decision-making procedures cannot easily be upheld. No one actor will be willing to provide the collective goods needed to make the regime work smoothly and effectively. * * * On the other hand, * * * as hegemony declines there will be greater incentives for collaboration because collective goods are no longer being provided by the hegemon. The international system more closely resembles an oligopoly than a perfect market. Actors are aware of how their behavior affects others. When smaller states perceive that a hegemon is no longer willing to offer a free ride, they are likely to become paying customers. * * *

The second line of argument associated with power in the service of specific interests investigates the possibility that powerful actors may be able to alter the pay-offs that confront other actors or influence the strategies they choose. Here power becomes a much more central concept – the element of compulsion is close at hand. Weaker actors may not be able to make autonomous choices. The values assigned to a particular cell may be changed.

* * *

When a hegemonic state acts to influence the strategy of other actors, the regime is held hostage to the persistence of the existing distribution of power in the international system. If the hegemon's relative capabilities decline, the regime will collapse. * * * For instance, the norms of the colonial regime collapsed because the power of its supporter, the major European states, eroded. This set of arguments about regime change and hegemonic decline differs from the analysis emerging from a focus on the provision of collective goods for either cosmopolitan or particularistic reasons. Here a decline in power leads to a change in regime because the hegemon is no longer able to control the payoff matrix or influence the strategies of the weak, not because there is no actor to provide the collective goods needed for efficient regime functioning.

3. Norms and Principles

To this point in the discussion, norms and principles have been treated as endogenous: they are the critical defining characteristics of any given regime. However, norms and principles that influence the regime in a particular issue-area but are not directly related to that issue-area can also be regarded as explanations for the creation, persistence, and dissipation of regimes. The most famous example of such a formulation is Max Weber's *Protestant Ethic and the Spirit of Capitalism.* Weber argues that the rise of capitalism is intimately associated with the evolution of a Calvinist religious doctrine that fosters hard work while enjoining profligacy and uses worldly success as an indication of predestined fate.[20] Fred Hirsch has argued that without precapitalist values such as hard work, self-sacrifice, loyalty, and honor, capitalist systems would fall apart. Such values are critical constraints on self-interested calculations that would too often lead to untrustworthy and dishonest behavior.[21]

Financing by various pariah groups around the world offers a clear example of the way in which noneconomic norms have facilitated market activity. For instance, bills of exchange were devised by Jewish bankers during the late Middle Ages to avoid violence and extortion from the nobility: safer to carry a piece of paper than to carry specie. However, the piece of paper had to be honored by the recipient. This implied a high level of trust and such trust was enhanced by conventions: established practices were reinforced by the exclusionary nature of the group, which facilitated surveillance and the application of sanctions. The importance of conventions for the use of bills of exchange is reflected in the fact that they were frequently used in the Mediterranean basin in the 16th century but they were not used at the interface with the non-Mediterranean world in Syria where, according to Braudel, "two mutually suspicious worlds met face to face." Here all dealings were in barter, or gold and silver.[22]

* * *

Discussion by other authors suggests that there is a hierarchy of regimes. Diffuse principles and norms, such as hard work as a service to God, condition behavior in specific issue-areas. In international relations, the most important diffuse principle is sovereignty. Hedley Bull refers to

---

[20] See David Laitin, "Religion, Political Culture, and the Weberian Tradition," *World Politics* 30, 4 (July 1978), especially pp. 568–69. For another discussion of noneconomic values in the rise of capitalism see Hirschman, *The Passions and the Interests.*

[21] Hirsch, *The Social Limits to Growth*, chap. 11. See also Michael Walzer, "The Future of Intellectuals and the Rise of the New Class," *New York Review of Books* 27 (20 March 1980).

[22] Fernand Braudel, *The Mediterranean and the Mediterranean World in the Age of Philip II* (New York: Harper, 1975), p. 370. For the tie between bills of exchange and Jewish bankers see Hirschman, *The Passions and the Interests*, p. 72, and Immanuel Wallerstein, *The Modern World-System* (New York: Academic Press, 1974), p. 147.

sovereignty as the constitutive principle of the present international system. The concept of exclusive control within a delimited geographic area and the untrammeled right to self-help internationally, which emerged out of late medieval Europe, have come to pervade the modern international system.[23]

In this usage sovereignty is not an analytic assumption, it is a principle that influences the behavior of actors. With a few exceptions, such as Antarctica, Namibia, and the West Bank, sovereignty prevails. Those areas where sovereignty is not applied are governed by vulnerable regimes or lack regimes altogether. Sovereignty designates states as the only actors with unlimited rights to act in the international system. Assertions by other agencies are subject to challenge. If the constitutive principle of sovereignty were altered, it is difficult to imagine that any other international regime would remain unchanged.

4. Usage and Custom

The last two sets of causal variables affecting regime development are usage and custom, and knowledge. Usage and custom will be discussed in this section, knowledge in the next. Usage and custom, and knowledge, are not treated in this [book] as exogenous variables capable of generating a regime on their own. Rather, they supplement and reinforce pressures associated with egoistic self-interest, political power, and diffuse values.

Usage refers to regular patterns of behavior based on actual practice; custom, to long-standing practice.[24] * * * Patterned behavior accompanied by shared expectations is likely to become infused with normative significance: actions based purely on instrumental calculations can come to be regarded as rule-like or principled behavior. They assume legitimacy. A great deal of western commercial law, in fact, developed out of custom and usage initially generated by self-interest. Practices that began as *ad hoc* private arrangements later became the basis for official commercial law.[25]

* * * Certain patterns of behavior are first adopted because they promote individual utility. Once established, such practices are reinforced by the growth of regimes. Most American drivers (outside New York City) would

---

[23] Bull, *The Anarchical Society*, pp. 8–9, 70.
[24] Weber, *Economy and Society*, p. 29.
[25] Leon E. Trakman, "The Evolution of the Law Merchant: Our Commercial Heritage," Part I, *Journal of Maritime Law and Commerce* 12, 1 (October 1980) and Part II, ibid., 12, 2 (January 1981); Harold Berman and Colin Kaufman, "The Law of International Commercial Transactions (*Lex Mercatoria*)," *Harvard International Law Journal* 19, 1 (Winter 1978).

feel at least a twinge of discomfort at driving illegally through a red light at an empty intersection. Behavior that was originally only a matter of egoistic self-interest is now buttressed by widely shared norms. *** A pattern of behavior initially established by economic coercion or force may come to be regarded as legitimate by those on whom it has been imposed. Usage leads to shared expectations, which become infused with principles and norms.

5. Knowledge

The final variable used to explain the development of regimes is knowledge. Like usage and custom, knowledge is usually treated as an intervening, not an exogenous, variable. In an earlier study Ernst Haas, a prominent exponent of the importance of knowledge, defined knowledge as "the sum of technical information and of theories about that information which commands sufficient consensus at a given time among interested actors to serve as a guide to public policy designed to achieve some social goal."[26] In another essay Haas points to the potentialities inherent in a stance of "cognitive evolutionism," which emphasizes sensitivity to the consequences of the generation of new knowledge.[27] Knowledge creates a basis for cooperation by illuminating complex interconnections that were not previously understood. Knowledge can not only enhance the prospects for convergent state behavior, it can also transcend "prevailing lines of ideological cleavage."[28] It can provide a common ground for both what Haas calls mechanical approaches (most conventional social science theories) and organic approaches (egalitarianism and various environmentally-oriented arguments).

For knowledge to have an independent impact in the international system, it must be widely accepted by policy makers. *** Without consensus, knowledge can have little impact on regime development in a world of sovereign states. If only some parties hold a particular set of beliefs, their significance is completely mediated by the power of their adherents.

*   *   *

[26] Ernst Haas, "Why Collaborate? Issue-Linkage and International Regimes," *World Politics* 32, 3 (April 1980), pp. 367–68.

[27] [Ernst B. Haas, "Words Can Hurt You; Or, Who Said What to Whom about Regimes, *International Organization* 36, 2 (Spring 1982).]

[28] Haas, "Why Collaborate?", p. 368.]

The two most prominent exogenous variables are egoistic self-interest, usually economic, and political power. In addition, diffuse values and norms such as sovereignty and private property may condition behavior within specific issue-areas. Finally, usage and custom and knowledge may contribute to the development of regimes.

CONCLUSION

* * * The Grotian perspective * * * sees regimes as a pervasive facet of social interaction. It is catholic in its description of the underlying causes of regimes. Interests, power, diffuse norms, customs, and knowledge may all play a role in regime formation. These causal factors may be manifest through the behavior of individuals, particular bureaucracies, and international organizations, as well as states.

The structural realist orientation is * * * more circumspect. The exemplar or standard case for the realist perspective does not include international regimes. Regimes arise only under restrictive conditions characterized by the failure of individual decision making to secure desired outcomes. The basic causal variables that lead to the creation of regimes are power and interest. The basic actors are states. * * *

[Modified structural orientations] reject a narrow structural analysis that posits a direct relationship between changes in basic causal variables and related behavior and outcomes, and denies the utility of the regime concept. * * * However, the basic parametric constraints for these analyses are identical with those applied by more conventional structural arguments. The basic analytic assumptions are the same. Arguments that treat regimes as intervening variables, and regard state interests and state power as basic causal variables, fall unambiguously within the structural realist paradigm. A more serious departure from structural reasoning occurs when regimes are seen as autonomous variables independently affecting not only related behavior and outcomes, but also the basic causal variables that led to their creation in the first place. * * *

2

The Demand for International Regimes

Robert O. Keohane

We study international regimes because we are interested in understanding order in world politics. Conflict may be the rule; if so, institutionalized patterns of cooperation are particularly in need of explanation. The theoretical analysis of international regimes begins with what is at least an apparent anomaly from the standpoint of Realist theory: the existence of many "sets of implicit or explicit principles, norms, rules, and decision-making procedures around which actor expectations converge," in a variety of areas of international relations.

This article constitutes an attempt to improve our understanding of international order, and international cooperation, through an interpretation of international regime formation that relies heavily on rational-choice analysis in the utilitarian social contract tradition. I explore why self-interested actors in world politics should seek, under

The original idea for this paper germinated in discussions at a National Science Foundation-sponsored conference on International Politics and International Economics held in Minneapolis, Minnesota, in June 1978.

I am indebted to Robert Holt and Anne Krueger for organizing and to the NSF for funding that meeting. Several knowledgeable friends, particularly Charles Kindleberger, Timothy J. McKeown, James N. Rosse, and Laura Tyson, provided bibliographical suggestions that helped me think about the issues discussed here. For written comments on earlier versions of this article I am especially grateful to Robert Bates, John Chubb, John Conybeare, Colin Day, Alex Field, Albert Fishlow, Alexander George, Ernst B. Haas, Gerald Helleiner, Harold K. Jacobson, Robert Jervis, Stephen D. Krasner, Helen Milner, Timothy J. McKeown, Robert C. North, John Ruggie, Ken Shepsle, Arthur Stein, Susan Strange, Harrison Wagner, and David Yoffie. I also benefited from discussions of earlier drafts at meetings held at Los Angeles in October 1980 and at Palm Springs in February 1981, and from colloquia in Berkeley, California, and Cambridge, Massachusetts.

certain circumstances, to establish international regimes through mutual agreement; and how we can account for fluctuations over time in the number, extent, and strength of international regimes, on the basis of rational calculation under varying circumstances.

Previous work on this subject in the rational-choice tradition has emphasized the "theory of hegemonic stability": that is, the view that concentration of power in one dominant state facilitates the development of strong regimes, and that fragmentation of power is associated with regime collapse.[1] This theory, however, fails to explain lags between changes in power structures and changes in international regimes; does not account well for the differential durability of different institutions within a given issue-area; and avoids addressing the question of why international regimes seem so much more extensive now in world politics than during earlier periods (such as the late 19th century) of supposed hegemonic leadership.[2]

The argument of this article seeks to correct some of these faults of the hegemonic stability theory by incorporating it within a supply-demand approach that borrows extensively from microeconomic theory. The theory of hegemonic stability can be viewed as focusing only on the supply of international regimes: according to the theory, the more concentrated power is in an international system, the greater the supply of international regimes at any level of demand.[3] But fluctuations in demand for international regimes are not taken into account by the theory; thus it is necessarily incomplete. This article focuses principally on the demand for international regimes in order to provide the basis for a more comprehensive and balanced interpretation.

---

[1] See especially Robert O. Keohane, "The Theory of Hegemonic Stability and Changes in International Economic Regimes, 1967–1977," in Ole R. Holsti, Randolph Siverson, and Alexander George, eds., *Changes in the International System* (Boulder: Westview, 1980); and Linda Cahn, "National Power and International Regimes: The United States and International Commodity Markets," Ph.D. diss., Stanford University, 1980.

[2] Current research on the nineteenth century is beginning to question the assumption that Britain was hegemonic in a meaningful sense. See Timothy J. McKeown, "Hegemony Theory and Trade in the Nineteenth Century," paper presented to the International Studies Association convention, Philadelphia, 18–21 March 1981; and Arthur A. Stein, "The Hegemon's Dilemma: Great Britain, the United States, and the International Economic Order," paper presented to the American Political Science Association annual meeting, New York, 3–6 September 1981.

[3] The essential reason for this (discussed below) is that actors that are large relative to the whole set of actors have greater incentives both to provide collective goods themselves and to organize their provision, than do actors that are small relative to the whole set. The classic discussion of this phenomenon appears in Mancur Olson Jr., *The Logic of Collective Action: Political Goods and the Theory of Groups* (Cambridge: Harvard University Press, 1965).

Emphasizing the demand for international regimes focuses our attention on why we should want them in the first place, rather than taking their desirability as a given. I do not assume that "demand" and "supply" can be specified independently and operationalized as in microeconomics. The same actors are likely to be the "demanders" and the "suppliers." Furthermore, factors affecting the demand for international regimes are likely simultaneously to affect their supply as well. Yet supply and demand language allows us to make a distinction that is useful in distinguishing phenomena that, in the first instance, affect the desire for regimes, on the one hand, or the ease of supplying them, on the other. "Supply and demand" should be seen in this analysis as a metaphor, rather than an attempt artificially to separate, or to reify, different aspects of an interrelated process.[4]

* * *

I. SYSTEMIC CONSTRAINT-CHOICE ANALYSIS: VIRTUES AND LIMITATIONS

The argument developed here is deliberately limited to the *systemic* level of analysis. In a systemic theory, the actors' characteristics are given by assumption, rather than treated as variables; changes in outcomes are explained not on the basis of variations in these actor characteristics, but on the basis of changes in the attributes of the system itself. Microeconomic theory, for instance, posits the existence of business firms, with given utility functions, and attempts to explain their behavior on the basis of environmental factors such as the competitiveness of markets. It is therefore a systemic theory, unlike the so-called "behavioral theory of the firm," which examines the actors for internal variations that could account for behavior not predicted by microeconomic theory.

A systemic focus permits a limitation of the number of variables that need to be considered. In the initial steps of theory-building, this is a great advantage: attempting to take into account at the outset factors at the foreign policy as well as the systemic level would lead quickly to descriptive complexity and theoretical anarchy. Beginning the analysis at the systemic level establishes a baseline for future work. By seeing how well a simple model accounts for behavior, we understand better the value of introducing more variables and greater complexity into the analysis. Without the systemic microeconomic theory of the firm, for instance, it would not

---

[4] I am indebted to Albert Fishlow for clarifying this point for me.

have been clear what puzzles needed to be solved by an actor-oriented behavioral theory.

* * *

This analysis follows the tradition of microeconomic theory by focusing on constraints and incentives that affect the choices made by actors.[5] We assume that, in general, actors in world politics tend to respond rationally to constraints and incentives. Changes in the characteristics of the international system will alter the opportunity costs to actors of various courses of action, and will therefore lead to changes in behavior. In particular, decisions about creating or joining international regimes will be affected by system-level changes in this way; in this model the demand for international regimes is a function of system characteristics.

This article therefore employs a form of rational-choice analysis, which I prefer to term "constraint-choice" analysis to indicate that I do not make some of the extreme assumptions often found in the relevant literature. I assume a prior context of power, expectations, values, and conventions; I do not argue that rational-choice analysis can derive international regimes from a "state of nature" through logic alone.[6] This paper also eschews de-terministic claims, or the *hubris* of believing that a complete explanation can be developed through resort to deductive models. To believe this would commit one to a narrowly rationalistic form of analysis in which expectations of gain provide both necessary and sufficient explanations of behavior.[7] Such beliefs in the power of Benthamite calculation have been undermined by the insufficiency of microeconomic theories of the firm – despite their great value as initial approximations – as shown by the work of organization theorists such as Simon, Cyert, and March.[8]

---

[5] Stimulating discussions of microeconomic theory can be found in Martin Shubik, "A Curmudgeon's Guide to Microeconomics," *Journal of Economic Literature* 8 (1970): 405–434; and Spiro J. Latsis, "A Research Progrmme in Economics," in Latsis, ed., *Method and Appraisal in Economics* (Cambridge: Cambridge University Press, 1976).

[6] I am indebted to Alexander J. Field for making the importance of this point clear to me. See his paper, "The Problem with Neoclassical Institutional Economics: A Critique with Special Reference to the North/Thomas Model of Pre–1500 Europe," *Explorations in Economic History* 18 (April 1981).

[7] Lance E. Davis and Douglass C. North adopt this strong form of rationalistic explanation when they argue that "an institutional arrangement will be innovated if the expected net gains exceed the expected costs." See their volume, *Institutional Change and American Economic Growth* (Cambridge: Cambridge University Press, 1971).

[8] Two of the classic works are James March and Herbert Simon, *Organizations* (New York: Wiley, 1958); and Richard Cyert and James March, *The Behavioral Theory of the Firm* (Englewood Cliffs, N.J.: Prentice-Hall, 1963).

Rational-choice theory is not advanced here as a magic key to unlock the secrets of international regime change, much less as a comprehensive way of interpreting reality. Nor do I employ it as a means of explaining particular actions of specific actors. Rather, I use rational-choice theory to develop models that help to explain trends or tendencies toward which patterns of behavior tend to converge. That is, I seek to account for typical, or modal, behavior. This analysis will not accurately predict the decisions of all actors, or what will happen to all regimes; but it should help to account for overall trends in the formation, growth, decay, and dissolution of regimes. The deductive logic of this approach makes it possible to generate hypotheses about international regime change on an *a priori* basis. In this article several such hypotheses will be suggested, although their testing will have to await further specification. We shall therefore be drawing on microeconomic theories and rational-choice approaches heuristically, to help us construct nontrivial hypotheses about international regime change that can guide future research.

The use of rational-choice theory implies that we must view decisions involving international regimes as in some meaningful sense voluntary. Yet we know that world politics is a realm in which power is exercised regularly and in which inequalities are great. How, then, can we analyze international regimes with a voluntaristic mode of analysis?

My answer is to distinguish two aspects of the process by which international regimes come into being: the imposition of constraints, and decision making. Constraints are dictated not only by environmental factors but also by powerful actors. Thus when we speak of an "imposed regime," we are speaking (in my terminology) of a regime agreed upon within constraints that are mandated by powerful actors.[9] Any agreement that results from bargaining will be affected by the opportunity costs of alternatives faced by the various actors: that is, by which party has the greater need for agreement with the other.[10] Relationships of power and dependence in world politics will therefore be important determinants of the characteristics of international regimes. Actor choices will be constrained in such a way that the preferences of more powerful actors will

---

[9] For a discussion of "spontaneous," "negotiated," and "imposed" regimes, see Oran Young's contribution to this volume.

[10] For a lucid and original discussion based on this obvious but important point, see John Harsanyi, "Measurement of Social Power, Opportunity Costs and the Theory of Two-Person Bargaining Games," *Behavioral Science* 7, 1 (1962): 67–80. See also Albert O. Hirschman, *National Power and the Structure of Foreign Trade* (1945; Berkeley: University of California Press, 1980), especially pp. 45–48.

be accorded greater weight. Thus in applying rational-choice theory to the formation and maintenance of international regimes, we have to be continually sensitive to the structural context within which agreements are made. Voluntary choice does not imply equality of situation or outcome.

We do not necessarily sacrifice realism when we analyze international regimes as the products of voluntary agreements among independent actors within the context of prior constraints. Constraint-choice analysis effectively captures the nonhierarchical nature of world politics without ignoring the role played by power and inequality. Within this analytical framework, a systemic analysis that emphasizes constraints on choice and effects of system characteristics on collective outcomes provides an appropriate way to address the question of regime formation.

Constraint-choice analysis emphasizes that international regimes should not be seen as quasi-governments – imperfect attempts to institutionalize centralized authority relationships in world politics. Regimes are more like contracts, when these involve actors with long-term objectives who seek to structure their relationships in stable and mutually beneficial ways.[11] In some respects, regimes resemble the "quasi-agreements" that Fellner discusses when analyzing the behavior of oligopolistic firms.[12] In both contracts and quasi-agreements, there may be specific rules having to do with prices, quantities, delivery dates, and the like; for contracts, some of these rules may be legally enforceable. The most important functions of these arrangements, however, are not to preclude further negotiations, but to establish stable mutual expectations about others' patterns of behavior and to develop working relationships that will allow the parties to adapt their practices to new situations. Rules of international regimes are frequently changed, bent, or broken to meet the exigencies of the moment. They are rarely enforced automatically, and they are not self-executing. Indeed, they are often matters for negotiation and renegotiation; as Puchala has argued, "attempts to enforce EEC regulations open political cleavages up and down the supranational-to-local continuum and spark intense politicking along the cleavage lines."[13]

* * *

[11] S. Todd Lowry, "Bargain and Contract Theory in Law and Economics," in Warren J. Samuels, ed., *The Economy as a System of Power* (New Brunswick, N.J.: Transaction Books, 1979), p. 276.

[12] William Fellner, *Competition among the Few* (New York: Knopf, 1949).

[13] Donald J. Puchala, "Domestic Politics and Regional Harmonization in the European Communities," *World Politics* 27,4 (July 1975), p. 509.

2. THE CONTEXT AND FUNCTIONS OF INTERNATIONAL REGIMES

Analysis of international regime formation within a constraint-choice framework requires that one specify the nature of the context within which actors make choices and the functions of the institutions whose patterns of growth and decay are being explained. Two features of the international context are particularly important: world politics lacks authoritative governmental institutions, and is characterized by pervasive uncertainty. Within this setting, a major function of international regimes is to facilitate the making of mutually beneficial agreements among governments, so that the structural condition of anarchy does not lead to a complete "war of all against all."

The actors in our model operate within what Waltz has called a "self-help system," in which they cannot call on higher authority to resolve difficulties or provide protection.[14] Negative externalities are common: states are forever impinging on one another's interests.[15] In the absence of authoritative global institutions, these conflicts of interest produce uncertainty and risk: possible future evils are often even more terrifying than present ones. All too obvious with respect to matters of war and peace, this is also characteristic of the international economic environment.

Actors in world politics may seek to reduce conflicts of interest and risk by coordinating their behavior. Yet coordination has many of the characteristics of a public good, which leads us to expect that its production will be too low.[16] That is, increased production of these goods, which would yield net benefits, is not undertaken. This insight is the basis of the major "supply-side" argument about international regimes, epitomized by the theory of hegemonic stability. According to this line of argument, hegemonic international systems should be characterized by levels of public goods production higher than in fragmented systems; and,

[14] Kenneth N. Waltz, *Theory of International Politics* (Reading, Mass.: Addison-Wesley, 1979).

[15] Externalities exist whenever an acting unit does not bear all of the costs, or fails to reap all of the benefits, that result from its behavior. See Davis and North, *Institutional Change and American Economic Growth*, p. 16.

[16] Olson, *The Logic of Collection Action;* Bruce M. Russett and John D. Sullivan, "Collective Goods and International Organization," with a comment by Mancur Olson Jr., *International Organization* 25,4 (Autumn 1971); John Gerard Ruggie, "Collective Goods and Future International Collaboration," *American Political Science Review* 66, 3 (September 1972); Duncan Snidal, "Public Goods, Property Rights, and Political Organization," *International Studies Quarterly* 23,4 (December 1979), p. 544.

if international regimes provide public goods, by stronger and more extensive international regimes.[17]

This argument, important though it is, ignores what I have called the "demand" side of the problem of international regimes: why should governments desire to institute international regimes in the first place, and how much will they be willing to contribute to maintain them? Addressing these issues will help to correct some of the deficiencies of the theory of hegemonic stability, which derive from its one-sidedness, and will contribute to a more comprehensive interpretation of international regime change. The familiar context of world politics – its competitiveness, uncertainty, and conflicts of interest – not only sets limits on the supply of international regimes, but provides a basis for understanding why they are demanded.

Before we can understand why regimes are demanded, however, it is necessary to establish what the functions of international regimes, from the perspective of states, might be.[18]

At the most specific level, students of international cooperation are interested in myriads of particular agreements made by governments: to maintain their exchange rates within certain limits, to refrain from trade discrimination, to reduce their imports of petroleum, or progressively to reduce tariffs. These agreements are made despite the fact that, compared to domestic political institutions, the institutions of world politics are extremely weak: an authoritative legal framework is lacking and regularized institutions for conducting transactions (such as markets backed by state authority or binding procedures for making and enforcing contracts) are often poorly developed.

[17] Keohane, "The Theory of Hegemonic Stability"; Charles P. Kindleberger, *The World in Depression, 1929–1939* (Berkeley: University of California Press, 1974); Mancur Olson and Richard Zeckhauser, "An Economic Theory of Alliances," *Review of Economics and Statistics* 48,3 (August 1966), reprinted in Bruce M. Russett, ed., *Economic Theories of International Politics* (Chicago: Markham, 1968). For a critical appraisal of work placing emphasis on public goods as a rationale for forming international organizations, see John A. C. Conybeare, "International Organizations and the Theory of Property Rights," *International Organization* 34,3 (Summer 1980), especially pp. 329–32.

[18] My use of the word "functions" here is meant to designate consequences of a certain pattern of activity, particularly in terms of the utility of the activity; it is not to be interpreted as an explanation of the behavior in question, since there is no teleological premise, or assumption that necessity is involved. Understanding the function of international regimes helps, however, to explain why actors have an incentive to create them, and may therefore help to make behavior intelligible within a rational-choice mode of analysis that emphasizes the role of incentives and constraints. For useful distinctions on functionalism, see Ernest Nagel, *The Structure of Scientific Explanation* (New York: Harcourt, Brace, 1961), especially "Functionalism and Social Science," pp. 520–35. I am grateful to Robert Packenham for this reference and discussions of this point.

Investigation of the sources of specific agreements reveals that they are not, in general, made on an *ad hoc* basis, nor do they follow a random pattern. Instead, they are "nested" within more comprehensive agreements, covering more issues. An agreement among the United States, Japan, and the European Community in the Multilateral Trade Negotiations to reduce a particular tariff is affected by the rules, norms, principles, and procedures of the General Agreement on Tariffs and Trade (GATT) – that is, by the trade regime. The trade regime, in turn, is nested within a set of other arrangements – including those for monetary relations, energy, foreign investment, aid to developing countries, and other issues – that together constitute a complex and interlinked pattern of relations among the advanced market-economy countries. These, in turn, are related to military-security relations among the major states.[19]

Within this multilayered system, a major function of international regimes is to facilitate the making of specific agreements on matters of substantive significance within the issue-area covered by the regime. International regimes help to make governments' expectations consistent with one another. Regimes are developed in part because actors in world politics believe that with such arrangements they will be able to make mutually beneficial agreements that would otherwise be difficult or impossible to attain. In other words, regimes are valuable to governments where, in their absence, certain mutually beneficial agreements would be impossible to consummate. In such situations, *ad hoc* joint action would be inferior to results of negotiation within a regime context.

Yet this characterization of regimes immediately suggests an explanatory puzzle. Why should it be worthwhile to construct regimes (themselves requiring agreement) in order to make specific agreements within the regime frameworks? Why is it not more efficient simply to avoid the regime stage and make the agreements on an *ad hoc* basis? In short, why is there any demand for international regimes apart from a demand for international agreements on particular questions?

An answer to this question is suggested by theories of "market failure" in economics. Market failure refers to situations in which the outcomes of market-mediated interaction are suboptimal (given the utility functions of actors and the resources at their disposal). Agreements that

---

[19] Vinod Aggarwal has developed the concept of "nesting" in his work on international regimes in textiles since World War II. I am indebted to him for this idea, which has been elaborated in his "Hanging by a Thread: International Regime Change in the Textile/Apparel System, 1950–1979," Ph.D. diss., Stanford University, 1981.

would be beneficial to all parties are not made. In situations of market failure, economic activities uncoordinated by hierarchical authority lead to *in*efficient results, rather than to the efficient outcomes expected under conditions of perfect competition. In the theory of market failure, the problems are attributed not to inadequacies of the actors themselves (who are presumed to be rational utility-maximizers) but rather to the structure of the system and the institutions, or lack thereof, that characterize it.[20] Specific attributes of the system impose transactions costs (including information costs) that create barriers to effective cooperation among the actors. Thus institutional defects are responsible for failures of coordination. To correct these defects, conscious institutional innovation may be necessary, although a good economist will always compare the costs of institutional innovation with the costs of market failure before recommending tampering with the market.

Like imperfect markets, world politics is characterized by institutional deficiencies that inhibit mutually advantageous coordination. Some of the deficiencies revolve around problems of transactions costs and uncertainty that have been cogently analyzed by students of market failure. Theories of market failure specify types of institutional imperfections that may inhibit agreement; international regimes may be interpreted as helping to correct similar institutional defects in world politics. Insofar as regimes are established through voluntary agreement among a number of states, we can interpret them, at least in part, as devices to overcome the barriers to more efficient coordination identified by theories of market failure.[21]

---

[20] Of particular value for understanding market failure is Kenneth J. Arrow, *Essays in the Theory of Risk-Bearing* (New York: North Holland/American Elsevier, 1974).

[21] Helen Milner suggested to me that international regimes were in this respect like credit markets, and that the history of the development of credit markets could be informative for students of international regimes. The analogy seems to hold. Richard Ehrenberg reports that the development of credit arrangements in medieval European Bourses reduced transaction costs (since money did not need to be transported in the form of specie) and provided high-quality information in the form of merchants' newsletters and exchanges of information at fairs: "during the Middle Ages the best information as to the course of events in the world was regularly to be obtained in the fairs and the Bourses" (p. 317). The Bourses also provided credit ratings, which provided information but also served as a crude substitute for effective systems of legal liability. Although the descriptions of credit market development in works such as that by Ehrenberg are fascinating, I have not been able to find a historically-grounded theory of these events. See Richard Ehrenberg, *Capital and Finance in the Age of the Renaissance: A Study of the Fuggers and Their Connections*, translated from the German by H. M. Lucas (New York: Harcourt, Brace, no date), especially chap. 3 (pp. 307–333).

The analysis that follows is based on two theoretical assumptions. First, the actors whose behavior we analyze act, in general, as rational utility-maximizers in that they display consistent tendencies to adjust to external changes in ways that are calculated to increase the expected value of outcomes to them. Second, the international regimes with which we are concerned are devices to facilitate the making of agreements among these actors. From these assumptions it follows that the demand for international regimes at any given price will vary directly with the desirability of agreements to states and with the ability of international regimes actually to facilitate the making of such agreements. The condition for the theory's operation (that is, for regimes to be formed) is that sufficient complementary or common interests exist so that agreements benefiting all essential regime members can be made.

The value of theories of market failure for this analysis rests on the fact that they allow us to identify more precisely barriers to agreements. They therefore suggest insights into how international regimes help to reduce those barriers, and they provide richer interpretations of previously observed, but unexplained, phenomena associated with international regimes and international policy coordination. In addition, concepts of market failure help to explain the strength and extent of international regimes by identifying characteristics of international systems, or of international regimes themselves, that affect the demand for such regimes and therefore, given a supply schedule, their quantity. Insights from the market-failure literature therefore take us beyond the trivial cost-benefit or supply-demand propositions with which we began, to hypotheses about relationships that are less familiar.

The emphasis on efficiency in the market-failure literature is consistent with our constraint-choice analysis of the decision-making processes leading to the formation and maintenance of international regimes. Each actor must be as well or better off with the regime than without it – given the prior structure of constraints. This does not imply, of course, that the whole process leading to the formation of a new international regime will yield overall welfare benefits. Outsiders may suffer; indeed, some international regimes (such as alliances or cartel-type regimes) are specifically designed to impose costs on them. These costs to outsiders may well outweigh the benefits to members. In addition, powerful actors may manipulate constraints prior to the formation of a new regime. In that case, although the regime *per se* may achieve overall welfare improvements compared to the immediately preceding situation, the results of the joint process may be inferior to those that existed before the constraints were imposed.

3. ELEMENTS OF A THEORY OF THE DEMAND
FOR INTERNATIONAL REGIMES

We are now in a position to address our central puzzle – why is there any demand for international regimes? – and to outline a theory to explain why this demand exists. First, it is necessary to use our distinction between "agreements" and "regimes" to pose the issue precisely: given a certain level of demand for international agreements, what will affect the demand for international regimes? The Coase theorem, from the market-failure literature, will then be used to develop a list of conditions under which international regimes are of potential value for facilitating agreements in world politics. This typological analysis turns our attention toward two central problems, *transactions cost* and *informational imperfections*. Questions of information, involving uncertainty and risk, will receive particular attention, since their exploration has rich implications for interpretation and future research.

The Demand for Agreements and the Demand for Regimes

It is crucial to distinguish clearly between international regimes, on the one hand, and mere *ad hoc* substantive agreements, on the other. Regimes, as argued above, facilitate the making of substantive agreements by providing a framework of rules, norms, principles, and procedures for negotiation. A theory of international regimes must explain why these intermediate arrangements are necessary.

In our analysis, the demand for agreements will be regarded as exogenous. It may be influenced by many factors, particularly by the perceptions that leaders of governments have about their interests in agreement or nonagreement. These perceptions will, in turn, be influenced by domestic politics, ideology, and other factors not encompassed by a systemic, constraint-choice approach. In the United States, "internationalists" have been attracted to international agreements and international organizations as useful devices for implementing American foreign policy; "isolationists" and "nationalists" have not. Clearly, such differences cannot be accounted for by our theory. We therefore assume a given desire for agreements and ask: under these conditions, what will be the demand for international regimes?

Under certain circumstances defining the demand and supply of agreements, there will be no need for regimes and we should expect none to form. This will be the situation in two extreme cases, where demand for agreements is nil and where the supply of agreements is infinitely elastic and free (so that all conceivable agreements can be made costlessly). But where the demand for agreements is positive at some level of feasible cost, and the supply of agreements is not infinitely elastic and free, there may be a demand for international regimes *if* they actually make possible agreements yielding net benefits that would not be possible on an *ad hoc* basis. In such a situation regimes can be regarded as "efficient." We can now ask: under what specific conditions will international regimes be efficient?

One way to address this question is to pose its converse. To ask about the conditions under which international regimes will be *worthless* enables us to draw on work in social choice, particularly by Ronald Coase. Coase was able to show that the presence of externalities alone does not necessarily prevent Pareto-optimal coordination among independent actors: under certain conditions, bargaining among these actors could lead to Pareto-optimal solutions. The key conditions isolated by Coase were (a) a legal framework establishing liability for actions, presumably supported by governmental authority; (b) perfect information; and (c) zero transactions costs (including organization costs and costs of making side-payments).[22] If all these conditions were met in world politics, *ad hoc* agreements would be costless and regimes unnecessary. *At least one of them must not be fulfilled if international regimes are to be of value, as facilitators of agreement, to independent utility-maximizing actors in world politics.* Inverting the Coase theorem provides us, therefore, with a list of conditions, at least one of which must apply if regimes are to be of value in facilitating agreements among governments:[23]

(a) lack of a clear legal framework establishing liability for actions;

[22] Ronald Coase, "The Problem of Social Cost," *Journal of Law and Economics* 3 (October 1960). For a discussion, see James Buchanan and Gordon Tullock, *The Calculus of Consent: Logical Foundations of Constitutional Democracy* (Ann Arbor: University of Michigan Press, 1962), p. 186.

[23] If we were to drop the assumption that actors are strictly self-interested utility-maximizers, regimes could be important in another way: they would help to develop noms that are internalized by actors as part of their own utility functions. This is important in real-world political-economic systems, as works by Schumpeter, Polanyi, and Hirsch on the moral underpinnings of a market system indicate. It is likely to be important in many international systems as well. But it is outside the scope of the analytical approach taken in this article – which is designed to illuminate some issues, but not to provide a comprehensive account of international regime change. See Joseph Schumpeter, *Capitalism, Socialism, and Democracy* (New York: Harper & Row, 1942), especially Part II, "Can Capitalism Survive?"; Kari Polanyi, *The Great Transformation: The Political and Economic Origins of Our Time* (1944; Boston: Beacon Press, 1957); and Fred Hirsch, *Social Limits to Growth* (Cambridge: Harvard University Press, 1976).

(b) information imperfections (information is costly);

(c) positive transactions costs.[24]

In world politics, of course, *all* of these conditions are met all of the time: world government does not exist; information is extremely costly and often impossible to obtain; transactions costs, including costs of organization and side-payments, are often very high. Yet the Coase theorem is useful not merely as a way of categorizing these familiar problems, but because it suggests how international regimes can improve actors' abilities to make mutually beneficial agreements. Regimes can make agreement easier if they provide frameworks for establishing legal liability (even if these are not perfect); improve the quantity and quality of information available to actors; or reduce other transactions costs, such as costs of organization or of making side-payments. This typology allows us to specify regime functions – as devices to make agreements possible – more precisely, and therefore to understand demand for international regimes. Insofar as international regimes can correct institutional defects in world politics along any of these three dimensions (liability, information, transactions costs), they may become efficient devices for the achievement of state purposes.

Regimes do not establish binding and enforceable legal liabilities in any strict or ultimately reliable sense, although the lack of a hierarchical structure does not prevent the development of bits and pieces of law.[25] Regimes are much more important in providing established negotiating frameworks (reducing transactions costs) and in helping to coordinate actor expectations (improving the quality and quantity of information available to states). An explanation of these two functions of international regimes, with the help of microeconomic analysis, will lead to hypotheses about how the demand for international regimes should be expected to vary with changes in the nature of the international system (in the case of transactions costs) and about effects of characteristics of the international regime itself (in the case of information).

---

[24] Information costs could be considered under the category of transaction costs, but they are so important that I categorize them separately in order to give them special attention.

[25] For a discussion of "the varieties of international law," see Louis Henkin, *How Nations Behave: Law and Foreign Policy*, 2d ed. (New York: Columbia University Press for the Council on Foreign Relations, 1979), pp. 13–22.

International Regimes and Transactions Costs

Neither international agreements nor international regimes are created spontaneously. Political entrepreneurs must exist who see a potential profit in organizing collaboration. For entrepreneurship to develop, not only must there be a potential social gain to be derived from the formation of an international arrangement, but the entrepreneur (usually, in world politics, a government) must expect to be able to gain more itself from the regime than it invests in organizing the activity. Thus organizational costs to the entrepreneur must be lower than the net discounted value of the benefits that the entrepreneur expects to capture for itself.[26] As a result, international cooperation that would have a positive social payoff may not be initiated unless a potential entrepreneur would profit sufficiently. This leads us back into questions of supply and the theory of hegemonic stability, since such a situation is most likely to exist where no potential entrepreneur is large relative to the whole set of potential beneficiaries, and where "free riders" cannot be prevented from benefiting from cooperation without paying proportionately.

Our attention here, however, is on the demand side: we focus on the efficiency of constructing international regimes, as opposed simply to making *ad hoc* agreements. We only expect regimes to develop where the costs of making *ad hoc* agreements on particular substantive matters are higher than the sum of the costs of making such agreements within a regime framework and the costs of establishing that framework.

With respect to transactions costs, where do we expect these conditions to be met? To answer this question, it is useful to introduce the concept of *issue density* to refer to the number and importance of issues arising within a given policy space. The denser the policy space, the more highly interdependent are the different issues, and therefore the agreements made about them. Where issue density is low, *ad hoc* agreements are quite likely to be adequate: different agreements will not impinge on one another significantly, and there will be few economies of scale associated with establishing international regimes (each of which would encompass only one or a few agreements). Where issue density is high, on the other hand, one substantive objective may well impinge on another and regimes will achieve economies of scale, for instance in establishing

---

[26] Davis and North, *Institutional Change and American Economic Growth*, especially pp. 51–57.

negotiating procedures that are applicable to a variety of potential agreements within similar substantive areas of activity.[27]

Furthermore, in dense policy spaces, complex linkages will develop among substantive issues. Reducing industrial tariffs without damaging one's own economy may depend on agricultural tariff reductions from others; obtaining passage through straits for one's own warships may depend on wider decisions taken about territorial waters; the sale of food to one country may be more or less advantageous depending on other food-supply contracts being made at the same time. As linkages such as these develop, the organizational costs involved in reconciling distinct objectives will rise and demands for overall frameworks of rules, norms, principles, and procedures to cover certain clusters of issues – that is, for international regimes – will increase.

International regimes therefore seem often to facilitate side-payments among actors within issue-areas covered by comprehensive regimes, since they bring together negotiators to consider a whole complex of issues. Side-payments in general are difficult in world politics and raise serious issues of transaction costs: in the absence of a price system for the exchange of favors, these institutional imperfections will hinder cooperation.[28] International regimes may provide a partial corrective.[29] The well-known literature on "spillover" in bargaining, relating to the European Community and other integration schemes, can also be interpreted as being concerned with side-payments. In this literature,

[27] The concept of issue density bears some relationship to Herbert Simon's notion of "decomposability," in *The Sciences of the Artificial* (Cambridge: MIT Press, 1969). In both cases, problems that can be conceived of as separate are closely linked to one another functionally, so that it is difficult to affect one without also affecting others. Issue density is difficult to operationalize, since the universe (the "issue-area" or "policy space") whose area forms the denominator of the term cannot easily be specified precisely. But given a certain definition of the issue-area, it is possible to trace the increasing density of issues within it over time. See, for example, Robert O. Keohane and Joseph S. Nye, *Power and Interdependence: World Politics in Transition* (Boston: Little, Brown, 1977), chap. 4.

[28] On questions of linkage, see Arthur A. Stein, "The Politics of Linkage," *World Politics* 33, 1 (October 1980): 62–81; Kenneth Oye, "The Domain of Choice," in Oye et al., *Eagle Entangled: U.S. Foreign Policy in a Complex World* (New York: Longmans, 1979), pp. 3–33; and Robert D. Tollison and Thomas D. Willett, "An Economic Theory of Mutually Advantageous Issue Linkage in International Negotiations," *International Organization* 33, 4 (Autumn 1979).

[29] GATT negotiations and deliberations on the international monetary system have been characterized by extensive bargaining over side-payments and complex politics of issue-linkage. For a discussion see Nicholas Hutton, "The Salience of Linkage in International Economic Negotiations," *Journal of Common Market Studies* 13, 1–2 (1975): 136–60.

expectations that an integration arrangement can be expanded to new issue-areas permit the broadening of potential side-payments, thus facilitating agreement.[30]

It should be noted, however, that regimes may make it more difficult to link issues that are clustered separately. Governments tend to organize themselves consistently with how issues are treated internationally, as well as vice versa; issues considered by different regimes are often dealt with by different bureaucracies at home. Linkages and side-payments become difficult under these conditions, since they always involve losses as well as gains. Organizational subunits that would lose, on issues that matter to them, from a proposed side-payment are unlikely to support it on the basis of another agency's claim that it is in the national interest. Insofar as the dividing lines between international regimes place related issues in different jurisdictions, they may well make side-payments and linkages between these issues less feasible.

The crucial point about regimes to be derived from this discussion of transactions costs can be stated succinctly: the optimal size of a regime will increase if there are increasing rather than diminishing returns to regime-scale (reflecting the high costs of making separate agreements in a dense policy space), or if the marginal costs of organization decline as regime size grows. The point about increasing returns suggests an analogy with the theory of imperfect competition among firms. As Samuelson notes, "increasing returns is the prime case of deviations from perfect competition."[31] In world politics, increasing returns to scale lead to more extensive international regimes.

The research hypothesis to be derived from this analysis is that increased issue density will lead to greater demand for international regimes and to more extensive regimes. Since greater issue density is likely to be a feature of situations of high interdependence, this forges a link between interdependence and international regimes: increases in the former can be expected to lead to increases in demand for the latter.[32]

* * *

---

[30] Ernst B. Haas, *The Uniting of Europe* (Stanford: Stanford University Press, 1958).

[31] Paul A. Samuelson, "The Monopolistic Competition Revolution," in R. E. Kuenne, ed., *Monopolistic Competition Theory* (New York: Wiley, 1967), p. 117.

[32] Increases in issue density could make it more difficult to supply regimes; the costs of providing regimes could grow, for instance, as a result of multiple linkages across issues. The 1970s Law of the Sea negotiations illustrate this problem. As a result, it will not necessarily be the case that increases in interdependence will lead to increases in the number, extensiveness, and strength of international regimes.

The Demand for Specific Information

The problems of organization costs discussed earlier arise even in situations where actors have entirely consistent interests (pure coordination games with stable equilibria). In such situations, however, severe information problems are not embedded in the structure of relationships, since actors have incentives to reveal information and their own preferences fully to one another. In these games the problem is to reach some agreement point; but it may not matter much which of several is chosen.[33] Conventions are important and ingenuity may be required, but serious systemic impediments to the acquisition and exchange of information are lacking.[34]

The norm of generalized commitment can be seen as a device for coping with the conflictual implications of uncertainty by imposing favorable assumptions about others' future behavior. The norm of generalized commitment requires that one accept the veil of ignorance but act *as if* one will benefit from others' behavior in the future if one behaves now in a regime-supporting way. Thus it creates a coordination game by ruling out potentially antagonistic calculations.

Yet in many situations in world politics, specific and calculable conflicts of interest exist among the actors. In such situations, they all have an interest in agreement (the situation is not zero-sum), but they prefer different types of agreement or different patterns of behavior (e.g., one may prefer to cheat without the other being allowed to do so). As Stein points out in this volume, these situations are characterized typically by unstable equilibria. Without enforcement, actors have incentives to deviate from the agreement point:

[Each] actor requires assurances that the other will also eschew its rational choice [and will not cheat, and] such collaboration requires a degree of formalization. The regime must specify what constitutes cooperation and what constitutes cheating.[35]

In such situations of strategic interaction, as in oligopolistic competition and world politics, systemic constraint-choice theory yields no

---

[33] The classic discussion is in Thomas C. Schelling, *The Strategy of Conflict* (1960; Cambridge: Harvard University Press, 1980), chap. 4, "Toward a Theory of Interdependent Decision." See also Schelling, *Micromotives and Macrobehavior* (New York: Norton, 1978).

[34] For an interesting discussion of regimes in these terms, see the paper in this volume by Oran R. Young. On conventions, see David K. Lewis, *Convention: A Philosophical Study* (Cambridge: Cambridge University Press, 1969).

[35] Arthur A. Stein, article in this volume, p. 312.

determinate results or stable equilibria. Indeed, discussions of "black-mailing" or games such as "prisoners' dilemma" indicate that, under certain conditions, suboptimal equilibria are quite likely to appear. Game theory, as Simon has commented, only illustrates the severity of the problem; it does not solve it.[36]

Under these circumstances, power factors are important. They are particularly relevant to the supply of international regimes: regimes involving enforcement can only be supplied if there is authority backed by coercive resources. As we have seen, regimes themselves do not possess such resources. For the means necessary to uphold sanctions, one has to look to the states belonging to the regime.

Yet even under conditions of strategic interaction and unstable equilibria, regimes may be of value to actors by providing information. Since high-quality information reduces uncertainty, we can expect that there will be a demand for international regimes that provide such information.

Firms that consider relying on the behavior of other firms within a context of strategic interaction – for instance, in oligopolistic competition – face similar information problems. They also do not understand reality fully. Students of market failure have pointed out that risk-averse firms will make fewer and less far-reaching agreements than they would under conditions of perfect information. Indeed, they will eschew agreements that would produce mutual benefits. Three specific problems facing firms in such a context are also serious for governments in world politics and give rise to demands for international regimes to ameliorate them.

(1) Asymmetric information. Some actors may have more information about a situation than others. Expecting that the resulting bargains would be unfair, "outsiders" may therefore be reluctant to make agreements with "insiders."[37] One aspect of this in the microeconomic literature is "quality uncertainty," in which a buyer is uncertain about the real value of goods being offered. In such a situation (typified by the market for used cars when sellers are seen as unscrupulous), no exchange may take place despite the fact that with perfect information, there would be extensive trading.[38]

---

[36] Herbert Simon, "From Substantive to Procedural Rationality," in Latsis, ed., *Method and Appraisal in Economics*; Spiro J. Latsis, "A Research Programme in Economics," in ibid.; and on blackmailing, Oye, "The Domain of Choice."

[37] Oliver E. Williamson, *Markets and Hierarchies: Analysis and Anti-Trust Implications* (New York: Free Press, 1975).

[38] George A. Ackerlof, "The Market for 'Lemons': Qualitative Uncertainty and the Market Mechanism," *Quarterly Journal of Economics* 84, 3 (August 1970).

(2) Moral hazard. Agreements may alter incentives in such a way as to encourage less cooperative behavior. Insurance companies face this problem of "moral hazard." Property insurance, for instance, may make people less careful with their property and therefore increase the risk of loss.[39]

(3) Deception and irresponsibility. Some actors may be dishonest, and enter into agreements that they have no intention of fulfilling. Others may be "irresponsible," and make commitments that they are unlikely to be able to carry out. Governments or firms may enter into agreements that they intend to keep, assuming that the environment will continue to be benign; if adversity sets in, they may be unable to keep their commitments. Banks regularly face this problem, leading them to devise standards of "creditworthiness." Large governments trying to gain adherents to international agreements may face similar difficulties: countries that are enthusiastic about cooperation are likely to be those that expect to gain more, proportionately, than they contribute. This is analogous to problems of self-selection in the market-failure literature. For instance, if rates are not properly adjusted, people with high risks of heart attack will seek life insurance more avidly than those with longer life expectancies; people who purchased "lemons" will tend to sell them earlier on the used-car market than people with "creampuffs."[40] In international politics, self-selection means that for certain types of activities – for example, sharing research and development information – weak states (with much to gain but little to give) may have greater incentives to participate than strong ones. But without the strong states, the enterprise as a whole will fail. From the perspective of the outside observer, irresponsibility is an aspect of the problem of public goods and free-riding;[41] but from the standpoint of the actor trying to determine whether to rely on a potentially irresponsible partner, it is a problem of uncertainty and risk. Either way, information costs may prevent mutually beneficial agreement, and the presence of these costs will provide incentives to states to demand international regimes (either new regimes or the maintenance of existing ones) that will ameliorate problems of uncertainty and risk.

* * *

[39] Arrow, *Essays in the Theory of Risk-Bearing.*
[40] Ackerlof, "The Market for 'Lemons' "; Arrow, *Essays in the Theory of Risk-Bearing.*
[41] For an analysis along these lines, see Davis B. Bobrow and Robert T. Kudrle, "Energy R&D: In Tepid Pursuit of Collective Goods," *International Organization* 33, 2 (Spring 1979): 149–76.

4. CONCLUSIONS

The argument of this paper can be summarized under [five] headings. First, international regimes can be interpreted, in part, as devices to facilitate the making of substantive agreements in world politics, particularly among states. Regimes facilitate agreements by providing rules, norms, principles, and procedures that help actors to overcome barriers to agreement identified by economic theories of market failure. That is, regimes make it easier for actors to realize their interests collectively.

Second, public goods problems affect the supply of international regimes, as the "theory of hegemonic stability" suggests. But they also give rise to demand for international regimes, which can ameliorate problems of transactions costs and information imperfections that hinder effective decentralized responses to problems of providing public goods.

Third, two major research hypotheses are suggested by the demand-side analysis of this article.

(a) Increased issue density will lead to increased demand for international regimes.
(b) The demand for international regimes will be in part a function of the effectiveness of the regimes themselves in developing norms of generalized commitment and in providing high-quality information to policymakers.

Fourth, our analysis helps us to interpret certain otherwise puzzling phenomena, since our constraint-choice approach allows us to see how demands for such behavior would be generated. We can better understand transgovernmental relations, as well as the lags observed between structural change and regime change in general, and between the decline of the United States' hegemony and regime disruption in particular.

Fifth, in the light of our analysis, several assertions of structural theories appear problematic. In particular, it is less clear that hegemony is a necessary condition for stable international regimes under all circumstances. Past patterns of institutionalized cooperation may be able to compensate, to some extent, for increasing fragmentation of power.

* * *

None of these observations implies an underlying harmony of interests in world politics. Regimes can be used to pursue particularistic and parochial interests, as well as more widely shared objectives. They do not necessarily increase overall levels of welfare. Even when they do, conflicts among units will continue. States will attempt to force the burdens of adapting to change onto one another. Nevertheless, as long as the situations involved are not constant-sum, actors will have incentives to coordinate their behavior, implicitly or explicitly, in order to achieve greater collective benefits without reducing the utility of any unit. When such incentives exist, and when sufficient interdependence exists that *ad hoc* agreements are insufficient, opportunities will arise for the development of international regimes. If international regimes did not exist, they would surely have to be invented.

PART II

COMMITMENT AND COMPLIANCE

3

Democratic States and Commitment in International Relations

Kurt Taylor Gaubatz

[T]he Four Hundred . . . departed widely from the democratic system of government. . . . They also sent to Agis, the Lacedaemonian king, at Decelea, to say that they desired to make peace, and that he might reasonably be more disposed to treat now that he had them to deal with instead of the inconstant commons.

—Thucydides

Confederations are dissolved for the sake of some advantage, and in this republics abide by their agreements far better than do princes. Instances might be cited of treaties broken by princes for a very small advantage, and of treaties which have not been broken by a republic for a very great advantage.

—Machiavelli

The traditional view of popular government as shifting and unreliable, which Thucydides attributes to the Athenian oligarchs, has a long and distinguished history. Machiavelli, who takes issue with this view,

I have benefited greatly in this project from the comments of the participants in the Social Science Research Council workshop on Liberalization and Foreign Policy and from the comments of three anonymous reviewers. John Ferejohn, Jeffry Frieden, Joanne Gowa, Miles Kahler, Lisa Martin, and Barry Weingast have been particularly helpful. I am indebted to Kenneth Schultz and Marissa Myers for their able research assistance. Funding was generously provided by the Center for International Security and Arms Control and by the Institute for International Studies, both at Stanford University. Doug Rivers was of considerable help in thinking about the statistical dimensions of this article. For much of the data used in this project, I am grateful to the Correlates of War Project and the Inter-university Consortium for Political and Social Research. *** The epigraphs are from Thucydides [400 B.C.] 1951, 2.25.70; and Machiavelli [1530] 1970, 1.59.

attributes it to "all writers" and "all historians."[1] The significant, if still somewhat tenuous worldwide trend toward democratization of the past decade has renewed interest in the implications of democratic governance for the international behavior of states.[2] Most of that interest has focused on the relationship between democracy and conflict. *** I return here to the basic question suggested by Thucydides and Machiavelli, which asks about the ability of democratic states to make commitments in their international relations. I argue that there is both a theoretical and an empirical basis for rejecting the traditional view of "the inconstant commons."

The ability of states to make commitments is a critical dimension of the international system. Between two states, commitments run the gamut from formal defense treaties to casual assurances between diplomats. For liberal institutionalists, the ability to make commitments is central to the process of international institutionalization.[3] But commitments do not have to reflect only cooperative behavior. Even for realists, the ability to make commitments is critical to international interactions. The efficacy of deterrence threats and the functioning of alliance politics clearly hinge on the ability of actors to make credible commitments.[4]

The dominant assumption in the study of international relations has been that the ability, or the lack of ability, to make commitments is a function of the anarchic international system.[5] *** Given the importance of commitment and the traditional concern about the inconstancy of popular rule, the possibility that liberal and democratic domestic political and economic arrangements may have distinct effects on the ability of states to make credible international commitments would seem well worth investigating.

On the face of it, the challenge of signaling and maintaining commitment in political systems that require public deliberation and approval for major international actions would seem formidable. But the relationship between international commitments and domestic politics is more complex than might be assumed from a narrow focus on the idea of the inconstant commons. In this article I set out a working definition of liberal democracy and draw out of that definition several implications for the

---

[1] Machiavelli [1530] 1970, 1.58.
[2] Huntington 1991.
[3] Keohane 1984.
[4] Schelling 1960; 1966.
[5] Grieco 1988.

ability of states to make international commitments. As against the common perspective of democratic inconstancy, I argue that there are both normative and structural characteristics of liberal democratic states that can significantly enhance the strength of their international commitments. I then turn to a consideration of democratic alliance behavior as a preliminary empirical indicator for the distinctive nature of democratic commitments in the international system. In particular, I bring forward strong empirical evidence to show that alliances between liberal democratic states have proved more durable than either alliances between nondemocratic states or alliances between democratic and non-democratic states.

Democracy and commitment both are complex phenomena. Many books have been written on both subjects. For the purpose of this analysis, I offer working definitions that, while inadequate as complete philosophical statements, can serve as the basis for a discussion of these phenomena within the context of international affairs.

A state makes a commitment to a course of action when it creates a subjective belief on the part of others that it will carry through with a certain course of action. Commitments may be trivial and involve doing things that are clearly in one's interest to do. The more interesting commitments are those that bind the state to take some set of actions that do not look to be in its narrow self-interest as an international actor. Thus, the commitment problem for the United States when it used nuclear deterrence to defend Europe against a Soviet attack was how to convince both the Europeans and the Soviets that in the event of a war, American leaders would be prepared to sacrifice New York in order to save Berlin or Paris.[6] In this article I will deal in particular with alliance commitments. Alliances, at their core, are a reaction to the problem of nontrivial commitment.[7] If the narrow self-interest of one alliance partner would be served by defending the other, the two would not need to formalize their commitment on paper, beyond some minimal efforts to coordinate defense policies and practices. The creation of a formal alliance is an attempt to signal to both the alliance partners and other states that a genuine commitment to some level of mutual defense exists.

The definition of democracy is even more problematic. I focus in this article on the notion of "liberal democracy." Scholars, of course, continue to debate the relationship between these two terms, but my argument

---

[6] Schelling 1966, chap. 3.
[7] Kegley and Raymond 1990.

proceeds analytically from both concepts. Liberalism refers to a conception of the state that faces juridical limits on its powers and functions.[8] Democracy refers to a form of government in which power rests with the majority. Democracy requires governments to be able to garner majority approval of their performance in order to stay in power. At the same time, liberalism will require that minority opinions can be expressed and that rivals for power will be able to exercise their rights to try to form alternative majorities. The demands that power be limited and that it rest with the majority can be in tension.[9] In the modern world, however, liberalism and democracy have become strongly, though not perfectly interconnected. Indeed, a number of scholars argue that modern democracy in its juridical or institutional sense is a natural extension of liberalism.[10] For the purposes of this analysis, then, liberal democracies comprise states that are limited in their conduct of international affairs by constitutionally defined institutions of popular will and of juridical constraint.

At the domestic level, the survival of liberal democracy and the ability of governments to make credible commitments are inherently intertwined. The existence of liberal democracy ultimately rests on the ability of the majority to convince minorities that it will not remake institutions when its narrow self-interests might be better served by abandoning the notion of limited government. A central question of liberal democratic theory, then, is how it is that the majority commits to accept limits on its power.[11]

Similarly, scholars have long debated the implications of limited government and majority rule for external commitments. Before moving to the analytic portion of this inquiry, it is worth a brief detour to summarize some of these perspectives about the ability of liberal democratic states to make commitments in their international relations.

THREE PERSPECTIVES ON DEMOCRATIC COMMITMENTS

The traditional views on the ability of democratic states to make international commitments can be grouped into three perspectives. The first perspective emerges from the dictate of structural realism that internal organization will be irrelevant to the external behavior of states.[12] In this view, the ability of states to make commitments will be based on the

---

[8] See Manning 1976, 15; and Bobbio 1990, 1.

[9] Bobbio 1990, 2.

[10] Ibid., 31. See also Rawls 1993.

[11] For some recent treatments of this vexing issue, see Hochschild 1981 and Riker 1982.

[12] On some of the limitations of the realist approach in this area, see Barnett and Levy 1991.

demands of the distribution of power in the anarchic international system. There is little room, then, for different behaviors to arise systematically from variations in domestic regimes. In the words of Kenneth Waltz: "International politics consists of like units duplicating one another's activities."[13] All states will have trouble making commitments because the system is anarchic, and the incentives for keeping or breaking commitments will be no different for democratic or nondemocratic regimes. To date, the vast majority of the literature on the nature of commitments in international relations has treated regime type as irrelevant.

Those who have addressed domestic dynamics and the impact of regime type have tended to take a second perspective that views democratic states as distinctively less capable of making strong commitments. As Machiavelli asserts, there is a long tradition of skepticism regarding the efficacy of internal democracy for external relations in general and in particular about the ability of democratic states to make external commitments. Democratic foreign policy, in this view, is dependent on the vagaries and passions of public opinion. *** Alexis de Tocqueville's oft-quoted observation that "in the control of society's foreign affairs democratic governments do appear decidedly inferior to others" is bolstered with his claim that a democratic government tends "to obey its feelings rather than its calculations and to abandon a long-matured plan to satisfy a momentary passion."[14] Lord Salisbury, the nineteenth-century British Prime Minister, points to the regular changes of leadership demanded by democratic publics as a significant limitation on the ability of any given leader to commit the state to a course of action: "for this reason, if no other," he argues, "Britain could not make military alliances on the continental pattern."[15]

The third perspective sees democracies as well able to enter into long-term commitments. Some holding this view make a positive argument about the characteristics of democracy that will enhance the strength of international commitments, while others attribute the strength of democratic commitments to an inability to change course rapidly. Machiavelli typifies the more negative view that the cumbersome machinery of democratic foreign policymaking will increase democratic reliability even after objective interests have changed. Immanuel Kant exemplifies the positive view, holding that states with "republican" forms of government

---

[13] Waltz 1979, 97.
[14] Tocqueville [1835] 1969, 2.5.13.
[15] Lowe 1967, 10.

will be united by bonds of trade and shared norms. In Kant's regime of "asocial sociability," the democratic norms of nonviolent problem solving will be operative between as well as within democratic states.[16] It is for this third perspective that I will argue here: distinctive institutions and preferences should enhance the ability of democratic states to make credible international commitments.

THE THEORETICAL BASES FOR DEMOCRATIC DISTINCTIVENESS

I make the argument for a distinctive democratic capability to make lasting international commitments in three parts. First, I look at several arguments about the basic stability of democratic foreign policy. I then argue that there are particular and distinctive values and foreign policy preferences in democratic states that can contribute to stable international commitments. Finally, I suggest that some characteristics of the internal institutions of democratic states are critical in enhancing the credibility of external commitments.

The Stability of Foreign Policy in Liberal Democratic States

The central argument of those who question the ability of democratic states to make credible commitments in the international system focuses on the putative instability of democratic policy choices. It is, therefore, with those arguments that I will begin in setting out the case for strong democratic commitments. *** I briefly assess foreign policy stability here in terms of the stability of public preferences, the stability of democratic leadership, and the stability of foreign policy institutions. In each case I begin with a look at the traditional view of democratic instability and then turn to a positive argument for the stability of the international commitments of democratic states.

The Stability of Public Preferences

Gabriel Almond sets the tone for the view of fickle democratic foreign policymaking in his classic analysis of the American public and foreign policy: "An overtly interventionist and 'responsible' United States hides a covertly isolationist longing, . . . an overtly tolerant America is at the same time barely stifling intolerance reactions, . . . an idealistic America is muttering *soto voce* cynicisms, . . . a surface optimism in America

---

[16] Kant [1795] 1991. For a more recent proponent of this position, see Dixon 1994. See also Maoz and Russett 1993.

conceals a dread of the future."[17] This image has been further bolstered by the public opinion work that emphasizes the weakness of political conceptions in the general public.[18] If democratic publics are fickle, and if democratic foreign policies are especially sensitive to public preferences, then we might expect democratic foreign policies to be highly unpredictable.[19]

While the image of changeability is a strong one, it is not one we should accept too hastily. The most significant of recent work in this area has argued that democratic states actually are quite stable in their domestic preference orderings.[20] In assessing the stability of democratic policy, it is well to remember Waltz's warning that when evaluating the abilities of democratic states in the foreign policy arena, it is important to consider those abilities relative to the abilities of nondemocratic states.[21] That democratic states flip and flop between isolationism and interventionism may be true, but this does not mean that other states have stable preferences simply because they are headed by a single despot.[22] Machiavelli makes such a comparative argument in rejecting the view of the masses as fickle – a view that he ascribes to Titus Livy and "all other historians":

I claim, then, that for the failing for which writers blame the masses, any body of men one cares to select may be blamed, and especially princes. . . . The nature of the masses, then, is no more reprehensible than is the nature of princes, for all do wrong and to the same extent when there is nothing to prevent them doing wrong. Of this there are plenty of examples besides those given, both among the Roman emperors and among other tyrants and princes; and in them we find a degree of inconstancy and changeability in behaviour such as is never found in the masses.[23]

In the more contemporary setting, we can consider the frequent criticisms of the response of democratic states to the rise of Nazi Germany. If analysts wish to draw strong lessons from the vacillation of the democracies in the interwar years, then it is only fair to point to the dramatic shifts in German–Soviet relations in that period as well.[24]

---

[17] Almond 1950, 67.

[18] Converse 1964.

[19] On the fickleness of democratic publics and their influence on foreign policies, see Monroe 1979; and Page and Shapiro 1983.

[20] See Shapiro and Page 1988; and Russett 1990, 92–95.

[21] Waltz 1967, 17.

[22] For two different approaches to democracies' tendency to waver between isolationism and interventionism, see Hartz 1955; and Klingberg 1952.

[23] Machiavelli [1530] 1970, 1.58.

[24] On the behavior of democracies in the interwar years, see, for example, Taylor 1961, xi.

The democratic states were uncertain about how to interpret their obligations to Czechoslovakia. They did, however, finally pursue their treaty obligations with Poland in quite certain terms. Meanwhile, the Germans and Soviets were experimenting with dramatic shifts in their positions toward one another. Ultimately, of course, the Nazi–Soviet pact proved worthless. The democratic states, on the other hand, maintained the basic shape of their commitments to one another despite very high international and domestic costs.

Contrary to the pessimism of many analysts, foreign policy issues do seem to have played an important role in American electoral politics.[25] This role has not led to either the extremes of chaos or paralysis that the critics of democratic foreign policy have predicted. The policy views of the public in aggregate have been reasonably stable and well-connected to the exigencies of external events.[26] When we look at the issue of policy stability from an empirical angle, the reality seems to be that democracies can maintain stable equilibrium policies.[27]

* * *

The Stability of Democratic Leadership

A central fact of the constraints on government power in the modern liberal democracies has been limitations on the tenure of government leaders. *** Regular leadership change is an important element in thinking about the relationship between democracy and commitment. Henry Bienen and Nicholas Van de Walle have shown that the leaders of democratic states do tend to have shorter tenures than the leaders of nondemocratic states.[28] Those who would enter into commitments with democracies must face the possibility that a new leader will be less inclined to honor previous commitments. The United States faces the prospect of major leadership change every four years. In parliamentary systems, the government could fall at any time. Some kinds of agreements surely will survive across governments, but it is plausible that the myriad small understandings that condition relations between states might be threatened by a new administration. ***

The simple fact that leadership change is more frequent is not, however, necessarily a negative factor for commitment. Again, a comparative

---

[25] Aldrich, Sullivan, and Borgida 1989.
[26] See Page and Shapiro 1991; Holsti 1992; and Nincic 1992.
[27] See Russett 1990; and Page and Shapiro 1991.
[28] Bienen and Van de Walle 1991.

perspective is important. Democratic leadership changes are *regularized* as well as being regular. The ability of democratic states to make smooth leadership transitions can help improve the stability of commitments. Indeed, Riker argues that rapid elite circulation can itself stabilize policies.[29] Nondemocratic states that do not have effective means for making leadership transitions may have fewer leadership changes, but those changes may be accompanied by greater shifts in preferences and policies. *** The transition from Presidents Carter to Reagan pales in comparison to the change from the Shah of Iran to Ayatollah Khomeini, from Mao Tse-tung to Deng Xiaoping, from Joseph Stalin to Nikita Khrushchev, or from Leonid Brezhnev to Mikhail Gorbachev.

Finally, it is important to remember that the juridical nature of liberal democracy gives current leaders the power to commit future leaders. Political power in liberal democracies rests abstractly with the office and is limited by juridical principles, rather than resting with specific individuals or being unlimited. Thus, future leaders are bound by the domestic legal environment to honor the treaty commitments of their predecessors. ***

The Stability of Democratic Institutions

While the political life of individual leaders may be relatively short and unpredictable in liberal democracies, domestic political institutions themselves are considerably more stable. As I have argued above, liberal democracy requires that majorities be able to commit to stable institutional arrangements that codify minority rights and constraints on majority powers. To the degree that democratic states possess institutional stability despite regular and regularized leadership change, it should be easier for them to enter into commitments. Stable civil service bureaucracies that handle foreign affairs, for example, help ensure some degree of policy continuity. ***

The Distinctive Preferences of Liberal Democracies

*** In responding to the traditional critique of democratic foreign policy-making, we also need to look at the kinds of values democratic states bring to bear in thinking about international commitments in general. It is common for analysts of the liberal democratic states to focus on their political culture. This line of argument sees something distinctive about the ideas and values that are held by democratic publics. ***

[29] Riker 1982.

Tocqueville made a number of assertions about the distinctive preferences that would emerge in democratic political culture. *** He viewed
these preferences as largely inimical to effective foreign policy commitments and sustained international involvement in general.[30] Isolationism
is a characteristic frequently attributed to democratic states. To the degree
that democratic states turn inward, they will pay less attention to their
international obligations and may thus prove less reliable. But this logic
is not definitive. At least two other possible connections between isolationism and international commitments are possible. First, following
Machiavelli's argument, an isolationist turn may make states take less
account of the need to abandon a commitment that begins to conflict
with their interests.[31] Second, the isolationist state may be inclined to
make only those commitments that involve truly vital national interests
and thus are more likely to be honored.[32]

The Role of Law in Liberal Democracy

Tocqueville also suggests that respect for law is a critical component of
democratic political culture.[33] *** The internal practice of liberal
democracy requires a basic respect for legal commitments. More recently, some have argued that these internal norms are also reflected in
preferences over external policies.[34] While the force of law in democratic
foreign policymaking is still being argued, international commitments
and domestic legal commitments do seem to be connected. For example,
international law has long been expressly incorporated into the domestic
legal order in the Anglo-American legal tradition and has spread to most
of the other major liberal democracies as well.[35] In relations between
states, legalism and the reputation of a state for reliability do seem to have
at least significant rhetorical appeal in democratic polities. Whether the
respect for law emerges from practice, from ideology, or from some other
primitive of inclination, if democratic peoples hold legal norms to be of
some overarching legitimacy, then this will increase their sense of the
binding nature of international commitments.[36]

---

[30] Tocqueville [1835] 1969, 1.2.5.13.
[31] Machiavelli [1530] 1970, 1.59.
[32] I am indebted to an anonymous reviewer for this second point.
[33] Tocqueville [1835] 1969, 1.2.6.4.
[34] Doyle 1983, 230. See also Dixon 1994; and Maoz and Russett 1993.
[35] von Glahn [1965] 1992, chap. 3.
[36] For a discussion of the effect of transnational legal arrangements on liberal democracies,
see Burley 1993. On the relation between domestic dispute resolution procedures and
international relations, see Dixon 1993.

Democratic Interdependence

Tocqueville identifies a third source of distinctive preferences in liberal democratic states pointing to the effects of "interdependence." *** Liberal economic orders that lead to increased trade and other associations between their citizens will naturally make them more interdependent. This logic follows closely Kant's argument about the pacific union of democratic states, based on the free flow of people and goods.[37] Tocqueville suggests interdependence as a basis for the lack of war between democratic states: "As the spread of equality, taking place in several countries at once, simultaneously draws the inhabitants into trade and industry, not only do their tastes come to be alike, but their interests become so mixed and entangled that no nation can inflict on others ills which will not fall back on its own head. So that in the end all come to think of war as a calamity almost as severe for the conqueror as for the conquered."[38] *** A third-party attack on an ally might be almost as severe a calamity for the interdependent ally as it is for the attacked state. Thus, interdependence can increase the credibility of commitments between states faced with an outside threat.

* * *

The Institutional Resources for Democratic Commitments

Liberal democracy makes it more likely that interdependent interest groups will be able to push the larger society to take their interests into consideration. The role of interest groups with vested interests in international commitments not only reflects on the distinctive preferences of liberal states but also points to the role of their internal institutions in strengthening commitments.

The Multiple Levels of Democratic Domestic Politics

The notion of liberal democracy as a system of majoritarian and juridical limits on government action is suggestive of Robert Putnam's recent argument that two-level games are a useful analog for many aspects of international politics.[39] In his model, state leaders must negotiate in the international arena and then return home to sell commitments in the domestic arena. *** If foreign policy is dependent on public approval,

---

[37] Kant [1794] 1991, 50. For a recent review of the notion of a cosmopolitan international economic order see Neff 1990.

[38] Toqueville [1835] 1969, 2.3.26.

[39] Putnam 1988.

and if public preferences are either distinct from leader preferences or are constantly and dramatically changing, then the state will have difficulty making the credible commitments it would otherwise choose. In this regard, Putnam makes a particularly interesting distinction between voluntary and involuntary defection from cooperative schemes. As with Woodrow Wilson and the League of Nations or Jimmy Carter and the second strategic arms limitation talks treaty, democratic leaders can enter into international agreements in good faith but then find themselves unable to implement the agreement because of democratic constraints on their power at home.

This, however, is not a sufficient consideration of the role of domestic constraints. Walter Lippmann worried in *The Public Philosophy* that democratic states would be frozen into undesirable policies by the inability to mobilize public support for change.[40] This is also the basis of Machiavelli's assertion that democratic states are less likely to break treaties, even when they have strong incentives to do so.[41] By this logic, the same factors that make it difficult for democratic states to enter into commitments also make it harder to get out of them. * * *

Domestic politics will be particularly effective at increasing the ability of democratic leaders to make commitments that accord with the interests of a strong domestic constituency. * * * The United States can make effective commitments to Israel even without a formal alliance because it has a substantial domestic audience that will monitor and enforce that commitment in the domestic arena. * * * Germany's somewhat reticent acquiescence to the 1994 round of the Basel convention banning all exports of hazardous wastes * * * will be closely monitored not only by the other parties but also by Germany's own environmental activists. Thus, the combination of interdependence and a strong voice for domestic actors has the potential to increase significantly the ability of democratic states to make commitments when the interests of other states are shared by significant domestic groups.

The Transparency of Democratic Domestic Politics

The multiple levels of democratic policymaking take on particular significance because democratic political systems are relatively transparent. Without the ability to observe what the government is doing and the freedom to express and organize alternative political views, the

---

[40] Lippmann 1955, 18–19.
[41] Machiavelli [1530] 1970, 1.59.

liberal notions of limited government and political competition would be meaningless. It is very difficult, however, to discriminate against external actors in providing transparency to internal actors. *** Any embassy can subscribe to the major newspapers that provide day-to-day investigative services on the policymaking activities of the democratic state. *** Outsiders can observe linkages between commitments made to them and commitments made to the domestic audience. When a democratic leader makes a public commitment to a specific course of action, deviation from that course might bring domestic as well as international repercussions. When President Bush vowed to remove Iraqi troops from Kuwait, the Iraqis should have known that that vow would bear on the ensuing election as well as on the international situation.

Recent work at the interstices of economics and political science has shed new light on the relationship between social organization and the ability of states to make commitments to domestic audiences. Two particularly interesting examples of this literature are Douglas North and Barry Weingast's interpretation of the Glorious Revolution as an exercise in recasting a constitution in order to increase the ability of the state to make commitments and François Velde and Thomas Sargent's similar interpretation of the French Revolution.[42] In these pieces, the respective authors argue that democratic institutions can increase the ability of the state to make commitments to large numbers of domestic actors. *** In the international arena, the ability to link external commitments transparently with internal commitments will allow democratic states to draw on domestic audiences to aid their international credibility.

Thomas Schelling points to the importance of political costs for enhancing the credibility of international commitments.[43] He focuses on incurring political costs within the international system itself. But similar benefits can be derived from incurring these costs at home if they can be adequately observed from outside. The linkage between external commitments and internal political costs is represented formally in James Fearon's work on the role of audience costs in international interactions.[44] When democratic leaders send signals in the international arena that bear domestic costs at home, those signals will have more credibility than would similar signals that bear no significant domestic costs. All

---

[42] See North and Weingast 1989; and Velde and Sargent 1990, respectively.

[43] Schelling 1966, 49.

[44] Fearon 1990.

states face some domestic costs for their international actions, but democratic states may be distinctive in the degree of domestic accountability. *** Statements and actions may create domestic expectations that will lead to audience costs or electoral punishment if a leader fails to carry out an international commitment.

Making credible international commitments is difficult at best for all states. I have argued here that, contrary to the traditional image of unreliability, democratic states should be relatively effective at making international commitments. The task now is to turn to some empirical attempts to assess the overall ability of democratic states to make commitments and to abide by them.

EMPIRICAL SOUNDINGS: DEMOCRATIC ALLIANCE BEHAVIOR

Alliances are the most salient form of commitment behavior in the current international system. States join formal alliances in order to indicate both to their alliance partner and to other states that the level of commitment between the two states is greater than the level of commitment that would be expected based simply on observed international interests. *** If democratic states are unreliable because of shifting majority preferences, we would expect to see this reflected in the length of time that they are able to maintain alliances.

*   *   *

The analysis of alliance commitments is also appropriate to the degree that alliance commitments are an indicator of international community. Drawing on Kant's essay *On Perpetual Peace,* Michael Doyle's explanation for the liberal peace turns on a natural community of liberal states:

Since morally autonomous citizens hold rights to liberty, the states that democratically represent them have the right to exercise political independence. Mutual respect for these rights then becomes the touchstone of international liberal theory. When states respect each other's rights, individuals are free to establish private international ties without state interference. Profitable exchanges between merchants and educational exchanges among scholars then create a web of mutual advantages and commitments that bolsters sentiments of public respect. These conventions of mutual respect have formed a cooperative foundation for relations among liberal democracies of a remarkably effective kind.[45]

*   *   *

[45] Doyle 1983, 213.

Some empirical work on the question of democratic alliance behavior has been done. Ole Holsti, Terrence Hopmann, and John Sullivan included a polity variable in their 1973 analysis of alliance politics.[46] Their conclusions about democratic alliance behavior are mixed. In their survey of all alliances between 1815 and 1939, they find that ideological similarity disposes states to ally with each other and leads to some increase in the length of alliances, although they conclude that after alliances are formed, the impact of ideological differences is minimal.[47] They also find some areas of democratic distinctiveness in their case study work. For example, looking at the differences between Chinese and French defection from their respective alliance systems in the 1950s, they argue that in pluralistic polities, intra-alliance disputes tend to be confined to a narrow range of issues, while in nonpluralistic polities, intra-alliance disputes tend to spill over into all issue-areas.[48] In an argument that echoes the Kantian hypothesis, the mechanism they posit for this effect is basically the influence of complex interdependence, which creates a large number of nongovernmental ties between pluralistic states.

Randolph Siverson and Juliann Emmons, in a recent analysis that focuses specifically on democratic states, confirm with more rigorous statistics the observation of Holsti, Hopmann, and Sullivan that ideologically similar states are more likely to form high-commitment defense pacts rather than lower commitment entente or neutrality pacts (as coded by the Correlates of War Project).[49] They show that at the dyadic level there is a strong tendency for democratic states to form alliances with each other at a greater rate than would be expected from the null model assumption that alliance formation should be independent of ideological orientation.

My goal here is to expand on these results with an attempt to assess the relative durability of democratic and nondemocratic alliances. The statistical analysis of Holsti, Hopmann, and Sullivan is largely limited to contingency table analysis. In this article, I focus on the case of democratic states to confirm the rather tentative relationship they describe for the relationship between alliance duration and ideological affinity. By using more sophisticated techniques for analyzing duration data, I am able to provide a more nuanced assessment of the effect of shared democratic norms on alliance duration.

---

[46] Holsti, Hopmann, and Sullivan 1973.
[47] Ibid., 61–68.
[48] Ibid., 160–61.
[49] Siverson and Emmons 1991.

The Data: Measuring Democracy and Measuring Alliances

Two kinds of data are required for this analysis: data about polities and data about alliances. *** I have used Doyle's coding of liberal regimes and the coding of alliances from the Correlates of War Project.[50] ***

For my purposes here, the democracy measure is reasonably straight-forward. It is not necessary to resolve the significant debates about the meaning of these terms in political philosophy and comparative politics in order to advance propositions about the implications of liberal democracy for foreign policy and international relations. Even the problematic distinction between "liberal" and "democratic" retreats in importance in the face of the empirical reality that the two phenomena have been highly coincident in modern history. There is a relatively clear set of states that have been regularly labeled as either "democratic" or "liberal." While one might disagree about some cases on the edges, the results I report here are not sensitive to small definitional changes. ***

The conceptual problems surrounding the measurement of alliances are more immediately serious. *** One particularly vexing conceptual issue is whether alliance behavior should be analyzed with the alliance as the unit of measurement or with the dyad as the unit. *** Conceptual arguments are valid in both directions. A focus on formal treaties would lead us to concentrate on the alliance as the observation: how long treaties are in force would be the most relevant question. If, however, we are interested conceptually in the underlying relations between individual countries, we will need to turn to the analysis of dyads. A focus on the alliance as the unit of observation also runs into problems when multiple treaties reflect the same relationship. For example, while a single treaty unites the North Atlantic Treaty Organization (NATO) countries, the Warsaw Pact countries cemented their relationship with a large number of bilateral treaties. The use of treaties as the unit of observation would bias the data toward this kind of multilateral relationship. The use of dyads as the unit of observation would give extra weight to multilateral treaties. Both biases present serious problems. In both cases, multilateral alliances lead to problems in assessing the relationship between individual states when formal relationships end because of a falling out between other alliance members. *** My approach is to statistically test both kinds of data. The fact that the findings are reasonably robust with both data sets increases our confidence in the results.

---

[50] See Doyle 1983; and Singer and Small 1966, respectively.

* * *

Translating the Singer–Small data to the alliance level from the dyadic level is more complex than it might appear on first blush. The decisions I have made in this regard are not always transparent and thus bear some discussion. Should we count the West European Union as a different treaty than NATO? Is the Rio Pact with Cuba a different alliance than the Rio Pact without Cuba? I have used two different kinds of decision rules, and the results seem reasonably insensitive to these coding variations. First, I tried to identify the individual treaties and gave them their longest life, regardless of new members coming and going (reduced model 1). Second, I identified starting and ending dates in the dyadic data set and collapsed the data around these values (reduced model 2). The first method tends to overcount multilateral alliances that use bilateral treaties, such as the Warsaw Pact. The second method overcounts multilateral alliances that have more changes over time, such as NATO or the Arab League.

Multilateral treaties are also problematic for coding the democracy variable when they include states with different political systems. My focus in this article is on relationships between democratic states, so I have chosen in both of these reduced data sets to decompose treaties that have mixed democratic and nondemocratic members. Thus, for example, I code NATO as three observations: a relationship between democracies, a relationship between democracies and nondemocracies, and a relationship between nondemocracies. Interestingly, this affected only six alliances, including three nineteenth-century alliances involving Britain, France, or Italy in their democratic periods, NATO, the Rio Pact, and the Arab League (which included Lebanon when it was coded as liberal).

International Alliance Behavior and Democratic States

Figure 3.1 tracks the average number of alliance relationships for democratic and nondemocratic states for each decade between 1815 and 1965. *** Before 1870 there were very few democratic states, and those states had decidedly fewer alliance relationships of any kind than the nondemocratic states. After 1870, the curves for the democratic and nondemocratic states follow one another very closely. From 1870 until 1920, alliance relationships were at a fairly low level for both democratic and nondemocratic states. Finally, in 1920 a strong trend began toward an increasing number of alliance relationships. The significant changes over

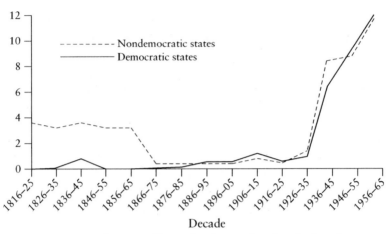

FIGURE 3.1. Average alliance density per decade, 1816–1965.

time support the notion that alliance norms have evolved over the past two centuries.[51]

* * *

Figure 3.1 is, of course, a simple representation of the relationship between alliances and democracy with no controls for confounding factors. On its face, this pattern would give the most support to the expectation that domestic regime type should not make much difference in international behavior in general and in the ability to make commitments in particular. These results do not support the idea that democratic states should be more alliance-prone, but neither do they support the more often expressed concern that democratic states cannot make credible commitments. Democratic states find just as many alliance partners as nondemocratic states. *** Either Salisbury was wrong or something has changed since he suggested that democratic states cannot keep their promises and thus will have trouble entering into alliances. At a minimum, democratic states are finding other states that are at least willing to sign the papers.

*** The question in which we are most interested is not simply how many alliance relationships democratic states enter, but rather what level of commitment those relationships represent. We can move one analytic step closer to this more fundamental issue by considering the length of time that democratic and nondemocratic alliances tend to last.

---

[51] On the evolution of alliance norms, see Kegley and Raymond 1990.

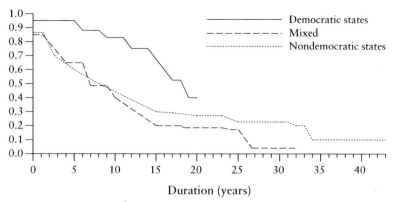

FIGURE 3.2. Alliance survival functions (Kaplan–Meier estimates) for alliances by treaty (reduced model 1).

The Duration of Alliances

Statistical analysis of duration data is made treacherous by several factors. Briefly, the two primary problems are nonlinear relationships and the censoring of data.[52] Duration data are said to be right-censored when the events are still ongoing at the end of the observation period. For example, a seemingly robust alliance that starts just two years before the end of the observation period should not be coded as having ended after just two years. If we did not take censoring into account, we would bias our analysis for all the cases of alliances that were still in effect at the end of the period of observation. This bias is nontrivial because it would tend to be the alliances that were the longest lasting that would be censored. This is of particular importance in the study of alliances, because a large number of alliances are still ongoing.

The most common method for examining survival data, given these problems, is the use of Kaplan–Meier or product-limit estimates of the survival function. *** The Kaplan–Meier estimate of the probability that an alliance will last k years is the product of the estimate of the probability that the alliance will last $k - 1$ years and the observed survival rate in year k. Thus, censored and uncensored observations will provide information as to the number of alliances that last $k - 1$ years, while the uncensored observations will provide the observed survival rate in any given year.[53] Figure 3.2 displays the Kaplan–Meier estimates of survival times for the

[52] For a thorough review of the statistical issues, see Kiefer 1988. For a discussion that is more oriented toward political science, see Bienen and Van de Walle 1991, chap. 3.
[53] Lee 1992, chaps. 4 and 5.

TABLE 3.1. *Predicted Alliance Durations (expected duration in years of a defense pact starting in 1925 between two major powers)*

	Democratic alliances	Mixed alliances	Nondemocratic alliances
All alliances			
Dyads	17.1	9.8	10.7
Model 1	8.8	3.4	4.2
Model 2	12.6	6.7	6.6
Defense pacts			
Dyads	39.0	16.3	10.6
Model 1	30.6	18.5	18.4
Model 2	30.8	18.7	18.5

first reduced data set based on treaties. The three lines show the estimated survival function for democratic alliances, nondemocratic alliances, and mixed alliances. The distinctiveness of democratic alliances is clearly visible in this figure. Reading across the chart at the 50-percent survival mark, we can see that the median survival time for both mixed and nondemocratic alliances is about seven years, while democratic alliances have a median survival time of about seventeen years. A generalized Wilcoxon rank test shows this difference to be significant at the 0.005 level.

The central limitation of the Kaplan–Meier estimates is that they are nonparametric. While they provide an effective visual indicator of survival patterns, it is difficult to control for important covariates or to specify more exactly the independent effect of democracy on alliance duration. A next step, then, is to turn to a parametric survival model. The model I use here to assess the effects of democracy on alliance duration is an accelerated failure time model *** using the LIFEREG procedure in SAS.

* * *

This model does show a significant effect for the duration of alliances between liberal domocracies. These effects are consistent in direction across all of the aggregations of the data and are statistically significant for the dual democracy coefficient in all of the models that use all alliances and for one of the dual democracy coefficients in the defense pact models. *** The impact *** can be seen more concretely in the examples given in Table 3.1. For the purposes of illustration, I have presented the predicted durations of a defense pact between two major powers that starts in 1925.

With all of the other independent variables held constant, the effect of the democracy variables is clearly visible in each row of the table. Most of the models predict fairly similar results.

As in the Siverson and Emmons work and the work on democracies and wars, it is again the dyadic effects of democracy that are the most notable.[54] We can make a distinction between the case of two democracies and either one or no democracies. But there is no statistically significant separation between the cases of one democracy and no democracies. Democracies are no different than nondemocracies when it comes to relationships with nondemocracies. It is only alliances between democracies that appear to be more durable. If alliance duration is an indicator of the ability to make commitments, then democracy by itself does not appear to either increase or decrease the ability of a state to make commitments to nondemocracies.

That democracies would be no worse at making commitments than nondemocracies is itself interesting in light of the frequent concerns about the instability of democratic decision making. The dyadic finding, however, suggests that the important explanations do not lie within the stability of democratic institutions themselves. Rather, the most promising source of explanation for these findings is likely to be either in the distinctive preferences democratic states may hold for maintaining their relationships with each other or in the institutional elements that develop in the relationships between democratic states.

* * *

CONCLUSIONS

The central characteristic of liberal democracies is juridically limited majority rule. For foreign policy decision making, this has meant that decision makers are limited in their ability to commit the state both because of the limits in their power at any given time – for example, the requirement that the President of the United States submit treaties to the Senate for ratification – and because of the possibility that public preferences will change. Drawing on these characteristics, the most traditional argument about the relationship between democratic states and commitment in the international system focuses on the inconstant commons and the expectation that democratic governance will be particularly ill-suited to

[54] Siverson and Emmons 1991. On democracy and war, see, for example, Small and Singer 1976; Maoz and Abdolali 1989; Russett 1990; and 1993.

long lasting commitments. The relationship between polity type and the ability to make commitments is more complex than this traditional argument would allow. As Riker has argued, there is a theoretical basis for policy stability in liberal democratic regimes; and this has been supported in several studies of foreign policy stability. Moreover, at the theoretical level, the creation of links between external commitments and internal commitments and the development of shared preferences through interdependence should also enhance the ability of liberal democracies to forge effective international commitments.

Ultimately, these factors will have to be disentangled and their individual importance assessed empirically to discern the net effect of the factors that push for and against democratic commitments. I have offered here a start on that empirical task with a broad analysis of the duration of democratic alliances. Consistent with the conjectures of Doyle and Kant, there are distinctive elements in the alliance behavior of democratic states. As Siverson and Emmons have shown, democracies tend to ally with other democracies.[55] I have shown here that these alliances tend to last longer than either the relationships between nondemocracies or the relationships that mix democracies and nondemocracies. Democratic alliances do appear distinctively durable when measured against the background of the constantly shifting international environment. More work will be required before we will want to endorse a robust version of the "pacific union" of democratic states. We can be more emphatic in the assertion that contrary to the pessimistic views of the likes of Tocqueville or Salisbury, democratic states have not demonstrated an inability to make lasting commitments.

[55] Siverson and Emmons 1991.

4

On Compliance

Abram Chayes and Antonia Handler Chayes

In an increasingly complex and interdependent world, negotiation, adoption, and implementation of international agreements is a major component of the foreign policy activity of every state.[1] International agreements come in a variety of shapes and sizes formal and informal, bilateral and multiparty, universal and regional. Our concern is with contemporary agreements of relatively high political salience in fields such as security, economics, and environment, where the treaty is a central structural element in a broader international regulatory regime. Some of these agreements are little more than statements of general principle, while others contain detailed prescriptions for a defined field of inter-action. Still others may be umbrella agreements for consensus building

---

[1] Barry E. Carter and Phillip R. Trimble, *International Law* (Boston: Little, Brown, 1991), pp. 133–252, cite a statistical study showing that of 10,189 U.S. treaties and international agreements made between 1789 and 1979, 8,955 were concluded between 1933 and 1979 (see p. 169). In the U.S. lexicon, the term "treaty" is reserved for international agreements ratified with the advice and consent of the Senate in accordance with Article 2, cl. 2 of the Constitution. Other international agreements are concluded by the President, in the great majority of cases with the authorization of Congress. All of these are "treaties" according to international usage, which defines a treaty as "an international agreement, concluded between states in written form and governed by international law." See Vienna Convention on the Law of Treaties (entered into force on 27 January 1980) Article 2(1)(a), in *International Legal Materials*, vol. 8 (Washington, D.C.: The American Society of International Law, July 1969), pp. 679–735, at 701 (hereafter cited as Vienna Convention on the Law of Treaties). The computer bank of the United Nations (UN) Treaty Office shows treaty growth, including multilateral and bilateral treaties and amendments, as follows: 373 treaties were entered into during the ten-year period ending in 1955; 498 in the period ending in 1965; 808 in the period ending in 1975; 461 in the period ending in 1985; and 915 in the period ending in 1991.

in preparation for more specific regulation. Most of the agreements of concern are [now] multilateral.

We believe that when nations enter into an international agreement of this kind, they alter their behavior, their relationships, and their expectations of one another over time in accordance with its terms. That is, they will to some extent comply with the undertakings they have made.[2] How or why this should be so is the subject of a burgeoning literature and debate in which, for the first time in half a century, the possibility of fruitful dialogue between international lawyers and students of international relations has emerged. This article explores some basic propositions we think should frame this discussion.

First, the general level of compliance with international agreements cannot be fully empirically verified. That nations generally comply with their international agreements, on the one hand, and that they violate them whenever it is "in their interests to do so" are not statements of fact or even hypotheses to be tested, but assumptions. We give some reasons why we think the background assumption of a propensity to comply is plausible and useful.

Second, compliance problems often do not reflect a deliberate decision to violate an international undertaking on the basis of a calculation of interests. We propose a variety of other (and in our view more usual) reasons why states may deviate from treaty obligations and why, in particular circumstances, these reasons are accepted by the parties as justifying such departures.

Third, the treaty regime as a whole need not and should not be held to a standard of strict compliance but to a level of overall compliance that is "acceptable" in the light of the interests and concerns the treaty is designed to safeguard. We consider how the "acceptable level" is determined and adjusted.

BACKGROUND ASSUMPTION

According to Louis Henkin, *"almost all nations observe almost all principles of international law and almost all of their obligations almost all*

---

[2] We are mindful of the distinction between treaty compliance and regime effectiveness. See Oran Young, "The Effectiveness of International Institutions: Hard Cases and Critical Variables," in James N. Rosenau and Ernst-Otto Czempiel, eds., *Governance Without Government: Order and Change in World Politics* (Cambridge: Cambridge University Press, 1992), pp. 160–92.

of the time."[3] The observation is frequently repeated [without either empirical support or refutation.] A moment's reflection shows that it would not be easy to devise a statistical protocol that would generate such evidence. For example, how would Iraq's unbroken respect for the borders of Turkey, Jordan, and Saudi Arabia count in the reckoning against the invasions of Iran and Kuwait?

Equally, and for much the same reasons, there is no way to validate empirically the position of mainstream realist international relations theory going back to Machiavelli, that "a prudent ruler cannot keep his word, nor should he, where such fidelity would damage him, and when the reasons that made him promise are no longer relevant."[4] Contemporary realists accept that the interest in reciprocal observation of treaty norms by other parties or a more general interest in the state's reputation as a reliable contractual partner should be counted in the trade-off of costs and benefits on which a decision is based (an extension that detracts considerably from the power and elegance of the realist formula).[5] No calculus, however, will supply a rigorous, non-tautological answer to the question whether a state observed a particular treaty obligation, much less its treaty obligations generally, only when it was in its interest to do so. Anecdotal evidence abounds for both the normative and the realist propositions, but neither of them, in their general form, is subject to statistical or empirical proof. The difference between the two schools is not one of fact but of the background assumption that informs their approach to the subject.

A critical question for any study of compliance, then, is which background assumption to adopt, and that question is to be resolved not on the basis of whether the assumption is "true" or "false" but whether or not it is helpful for the particular inquiry. Thus, for game-theoretic approaches that focus on the abstract structure of the relationship between

---

[3] See Louis Henkin. How *Nations Behave,* 2d ed. (New York: Columbia University Press, 1979), p. 47; and p. 69 of Louis Henkin, "International Law: Politics, Values, and Functions: General Course on Public International Law," *Recueil Des Cours, vol.* 216, 1989, pp. 1–416, emphasis original.

[4] Niccolo Machiavelli, *The Prince,* eds. Quentin Skinner and Russell Price (Cambridge: Cambridge University Press, 1988), pp. 61–62. For a modern instance, see Hans J. Morgenthau, *Politics Among Nations: The Struggle for Power and Peace,* 5th ed. (New York: Alfred A. Knopf, 1978), p. 560: "In my experience [states] will keep their bargains as long as it is in their interest."

[5] See, for example, James A. Caporaso, "International Relations Theory and Multilateralism: The Search for Foundations," *International Organization* 46 (Summer 1992), pp. 599–632.

states, the realist assumption of a unitary rational actor optimizing utilities distributed along smooth preference curves may have value. As Thomas Schelling said at the beginning of his classic work, "The premise of 'rational behavior' is a potent one for the production of theory. Whether the resulting theory provides good or poor insight into actual behavior is ... a matter for subsequent judgment."

Our interest in this work is in improving the prospects for compliance with treaties, both at the drafting stage and later as the parties live and operate under them. From this perspective, the realist analysis, focusing on a narrow set of externally defined "interests" primarily, in the classical version, the maintenance or enhancement of state military and economic power is not very helpful. Improving compliance becomes a matter of the manipulation of burdens and benefits defined in terms of those interests, which translates into the application of military or economic sanctions. Because these are costly, difficult to mobilize, and of doubtful efficacy, they are infrequently used in practice. Meanwhile, analytic attention is diverted from a wide range of institutional and political mechanisms that in practice bear the burden of efforts to enhance treaty compliance.

For a study of the methods by which compliance can be improved, the background assumption of a general propensity of states to comply with international obligations, which is the basis on which most practitioners carry out their work, seems more illuminating.[6]

Efficiency

Decisions are not a free good. Governmental resources for policy analysis and decision making are costly and in short supply. Individuals and organizations seek to conserve those resources for the most urgent and pressing matters.[7] In these circumstances, standard economic analysis argues against the continuous recalculation of costs and benefits in the absence of convincing evidence that circumstances have changed since the original decision. Efficiency dictates considerable policy continuity.

---

[6] See Oran R. Young, *Compliance and Public Authority: A Theory with International Applications* (Baltimore, Md.: Johns Hopkins University Press, 1979), pp. 31–34.

[7] See George Stigler, "The Economics of Information," *Journal of Political Economy* 69 (June 1961), pp. 213–25; G. J. Stigler and G. S. Becker, "De Gustibus non Est Disputandum" (There is no disputing taste), in Karen S. Cook and Margaret Levi, eds., *The Limits of Rationality* (Chicago: University of Chicago Press, 1990), pp. 191–216; Charles E. Lindblom, *The Policy Making Process* (Englewood Cliffs, N.J.: Prentice-Hall, 1968), p. 14.

In areas of activity covered by treaty obligations, the alternative to recalculation is to follow the established rule.

Organization theory would reach the same result as economic analysis, but by a different route. In place of the continuously calculating, maximizing rational actor, it substitutes a "satisficing" model of bounded rationality that reacts to problems as they arise and searches for solutions within a familiar and accustomed repertoire.[8] In this analysis, bureaucratic organizations are viewed as functioning according to routines and standard operating procedures, often specified by authoritative rules and regulations. The adoption of a treaty, like the enactment of any other law, establishes an authoritative rule system. Compliance is the normal organizational presumption.

The bureaucracy is not monolithic, of course, and it will likely contain opponents of the treaty regime as well as supporters. When there is an applicable rule in a treaty or otherwise, opposition ordinarily surfaces in the course of rule implementation and takes the form of argument over interpretation of language and definition of the exact content of the obligation. Such controversies are settled in accordance with normal bureaucratic procedures in which, again, the presumption is in favor of "following" the rule.

Interests

The assertion that states carry out treaty commitments only when it is in their interest to do so seems to imply that commitments are somehow unrelated to interests. In fact, the opposite is true. The most basic principle of international law is that states cannot be legally bound except with their own consent. So, in the first instance, the state need not enter into a treaty that does not conform to its interests.

More important, a treaty does not present the state with a simple binary alternative, to sign or not to sign. Treaties, like other legal arrangements, are artifacts of political choice and social existence. The process by which they are formulated and concluded is designed to ensure that the final result will represent, to some degree, an accommodation of the interests of the negotiating states. Modern treaty making, like legislation in

---

[8] Herbert Simon, *Models of Man: Social and Rational Mathematical Essays on Rational Human Behavior in a Social Setting* (New York: John Wiley & Sons, 1957), pp. 200–204. See also James G. March and Herbert A. Simon, *Organizations* (New York: John Wiley & Sons, 1958), p. 169. For an example of this model of organizational behavior applied to the analysis of international affairs, see Graham T. Allison, *The Essence of Decision: Explaining the Cuban Missile Crisis* (Glenview, Ill.: Scott, Foresman, 1971).

a democratic polity, can be seen as a creative enterprise through which the parties not only weigh the benefits and burdens of commitment but explore, redefine, and sometimes discover their interests. It is at its best a learning process in which not only national positions but also conceptions of national interest evolve.

This process goes on both within each state and at the international level. In a state with a well-developed bureaucracy, the elaboration of national positions in preparation for treaty negotiations requires extensive interagency vetting. Different officials with different responsibilities and objectives engage in what amounts to a sustained internal negotiation. The process can be seen in every major U.S. international negotiation. For example, at the end of what Ambassador Richard Benedick calls "the interagency minuet" in preparation for the Vienna Convention for the Protection of the Ozone Layer, the final U.S. position "was drafted by the State Department and was formally cleared by the Departments of Commerce and Energy, The Council on Environmental Quality, EPA [Environmental Protection Agency], NASA, NOAA [National Oceanographic and Atmospheric Administration], OMB [Office of Management and Budget], USTR [U.S. Trade Representative], and the Domestic Policy Council (representing all other interested agencies)."[9] In addition to this formidable alphabet soup, White House units, like the Office of Science and Technology Policy, the Office of Policy Development, and the Council of Economic Advisers, also got into the act. According to Trimble, "each agency has a distinctive perspective from which it views the process and which influences the position it advocates.... All these interests must be accommodated, compromised or overriden by the President before a position can even be put on the table."[10]

In the United States in recent years, increasing involvement of Congress and with it nongovernmental organizations (NGOs) and the broader public has introduced a new range of interests that must ultimately be reflected in the national position.[11] Similar developments seem to be occurring in other democratic countries.

---

[9] Richard Benedick, *Ozone Diplomacy: New Directions in Safeguarding the Planet* (Cambridge, Mass: Harvard University Press, 1991), pp. 51–53. Other states, at least in advanced industrialized societies, exhibit similar, if perhaps not quite as baroque, internal practices in preparation for negotiations. Developing countries, with small resources to commit to bureaucratic coordination, may rely more on the judgment and inspiration of representatives on the scene.

[10] Trimble, "Arms Control and International Negotiation Theory," p. 550.

[11] See Benedick, *Ozone Diplomacy*, p. 57; Robert O. Keohane and Joseph S. Nye, *Power and Interdependence*, 2d ed. (Glenview, Ill.: Scott, Foresman, 1989). p. 35.

In contrast to day-to-day foreign policy decision making that is oriented toward current political exigencies and imminent deadlines and is focused heavily on short-term costs and benefits, the more deliberate process employed in treaty making may serve to identify and reinforce longer range interests and values. Officials engaged in developing the negotiating position often have an additional reason to take a long-range view, since they may have operational responsibility under any agreement that is reached.[12] What they say and how they conduct themselves at the negotiating table may return to haunt them once the treaty has gone into effect. Moreover, they are likely to attach considerable importance to the development of governing norms that will operate predictably when applied to the behavior of the parties over time. All these convergent elements tend to influence national positions in the direction of broad-based conceptions of the national interest that, if adequately reflected in the treaty, will help to induce compliance.

The internal analysis, negotiation, and calculation of the benefits, burdens, and impacts are repeated, for contemporary regulatory treaties, at the international level.[13] In anticipation of negotiations, the issues are reviewed in international forums long before formal negotiation begins. The negotiating process itself characteristically involves intergovernmental debate often lasting years and involving not only other national governments but also international bureaucracies and NGOs. The most notable case is the UN Conference on the Law of the Sea, in which that process lasted for more than ten years, spawning innumerable committees, subcommittees, and working groups, only to be torpedoed in the end by the United States, which had sponsored the negotiations in the first place.[14] Current environmental negotiations on ozone and on global warming follow very much the Law of the Sea pattern. The first conference on

---

[12] Hudec uses the examples of the General Agreement on Tariffs and Trade (GATT) and the International Trade Organization (ITO): "For the better part of the first decade, GATT meetings resembled a reunion of the GATT/ITO draftsmen themselves. Failure of the code would have meant a personal failure to many of these officials, and violation of rules they had helped to write could not help being personally embarrassing." See p. 1365 of Robert E. Hudec, "GATT or GABB? The Future Design of the General Agreement of Tariffs and Trade," *Yale Law Journal* 80 (June 1971), pp. 1299–386. See also Robert E. Hudec, *The GATT Legal System and World Trade Diplomacy*, 2d ed. (Salem, N. H.: Butterworth Legal Publishers, 1990), p. 54.

[13] Robert D. Putnam, "Diplomacy and Domestic Politics: The Logic of Two-Level Games," *International Organization* 42 (Summer 1988), pp. 427–60.

[14] See James K. Sebenius, *Negotiating the Law of the Sea* (Cambridge, Mass.: Harvard University Press, 1984); and William Wertenbaker, "The Law of the Sea," parts 1 and 2, *The New Yorker*, 1 August 1983, pp. 38–65, and 8 August 1983, pp. 56–83, respectively.

stratospheric ozone was convoked by the UN Environment Program (UNEP) in 1977, eight years before the adoption of the Vienna Convention on the Protection of the Ozone Layer.[15] The formal beginning of the climate change negotiations in February 1991 was preceded by two years of work by the Intergovernmental Panel on Climate Change, convened by the World Meteorological Organization and the UNEP to consider scientific, technological, and policy response questions.[16]

Much of this negotiating activity is open to some form of public scrutiny, triggering repeated rounds of national bureaucratic and political review and revision of tentative accommodations among affected interests. The treaty as finally signed and presented for ratification is therefore likely to be based on considered and well-developed conceptions of national interest that have themselves been shaped to some extent by the preparatory and negotiating process.

Treaty making is not purely consensual, of course. Negotiations are heavily affected by the structure of the international system, in which some states are much more powerful than others. As noted, the Convention of the Law of the Sea, the product of more than a decade of international negotiations, was ultimately derailed when a new U.S. administration found it unacceptable. On the other hand, a multilateral negotiating forum provides opportunities for weaker states to form coalitions and exploit blocking positions. In the same UN Conference on the Law of the Sea, the caucus of what were known as "land-locked and geographically disadvantaged states," which included such unlikely colleagues as Hungary, Switzerland, Austria, Uganda, Nepal, and Bolivia, had a crucial strategic position. The Association of Small Island States, chaired by Vanuatu, played a similar role in the global climate negotiations. Like domestic legislation, the international treaty-making process leaves a good deal of room for accommodating divergent interests. In such a setting, not even the strongest state will be able to achieve all of its objectives, and some participants may have to settle for much less. The treaty is necessarily a compromise, "a bargain that

[15] As early as 1975, the UNEP funded a World Meteorological Organization (WMO) technical conference on implications of U.S. ozone layer research. But the immediate precursor of the negotiating conference in Vienna came in March 1977, when the UNEP sponsored a policy meeting of governments and international agencies in Washington, D.C., that drafted a "World Plan of Action on the Ozone Layer." See Benedick, *Ozone Diplomacy*, p. 40.

[16] The Intergovernmental Panel of Climate Change was set up by the UNEP and WMO after the passage of UN General Assembly Resolution 43/53, A/RES/43/53, 27 January 1989, "Resolution on the Protection of the Global Climate."

[has] been made."[17] From the point of view of the particular interests of any state, the outcome may fall short of the ideal. But if the agreement is well designed, sensible, comprehensible, and with a practical eye to probable patterns of conduct and interaction–compliance problems and enforcement issues are likely to be manageable. If issues of noncompliance and enforcement are endemic, the real problem is likely to be that the original bargain did not adequately reflect the interests of those that would be living under it, rather than mere disobedience.[18]

It is true that a state's incentives at the treaty-negotiating stage may be different from those it faces when the time for compliance rolls around. Parties on the giving end of the compromise, especially, might have reason to seek to escape the obligations they have undertaken. Nevertheless, the very act of making commitments embodied in an international agreement changes the calculus at the compliance stage, if only because it generates expectations of compliance in others that must enter into the equation.

Moreover, although states may know they can violate their treaty commitments in a crunch, they do not negotiate agreements with the idea that they can do so in routine situations. Thus, the shape of the substantive bargain will itself be affected by the parties' estimates of the costs and risks of their own compliance and expectations about the compliance of others. Essential parties may be unwilling to accept or impose stringent regulations if the prospects for compliance are doubtful. The negotiation will not necessarily collapse on that account, however. The result may be a looser, more general engagement. Such an outcome is often deprecated as a lowest-common-denominator outcome, with what is really important left on the cutting room floor. But it may be the beginning of increasingly serious and concerted attention to the problem.

Finally, the treaty that comes into force does not remain static and unchanging. Treaties that last must be able to adapt to inevitable changes in the economic, technological, social, and political setting. Treaties may be formally amended, of course, or modified by the addition of a protocol, but these methods are slow and cumbersome. Since they are subject to the same ratification process as the original treaty, they can be blocked or

---

[17] Susan Strange, "Cave! Hic Dragones: A Critique of Regime Analysis," in Stephen D. Krasner, ed., *International Regimes* (Ithaca, N.Y.: Cornell University Press, 1983), pp. 337–54; at 353.

[18] Systems in which compliance can only be achieved through extensive use of coercion are rightly regarded as authoritarian and unjust. See Michael Barkun, *Law Without Sanctions: Order in Primitive Societies and the World Community* (New Haven, Conn.: Yale University Press, 1968), p. 62.

avoided by a dissatisfied party. As a result, treaty lawyers have devised a number of ways to deal with the problem of adaptation without seeking formal amendment. The simplest is the device of vesting the power to "interpret" the agreement in some organ established by the treaty. The U.S. Constitution, after all, has kept up with the times not primarily by the amending process but by the Supreme Court's interpretation of its broad clauses. The International Monetary Fund (IMF) Agreement gives such power to the Governing Board, and numerous key questions including the crucial issue of "conditionality," whether drawings against the fund's resources may be conditioned on the economic performance of the drawing member have been resolved by this means.[19]

A number of treaties establish authority to make regulations on technical matters by vote of the parties (usually by a special majority), which are then binding on all, though often with the right to opt out. The International Civil Aeronautics Organization has such power with respect to operational and safety matters in international air transport.[20] In many regulatory treaties, "technical" matters may be relegated to an annex that can be altered by vote of the parties.[21] In sum, treaties characteristically contain self-adjusting mechanisms by which, over a significant range, they can be and in practice are commonly adapted to respond to shifting interests of the parties.

NORMS

Treaties are acknowledged to be legally binding on the states that ratify them.[22] In common experience, people, whether as a result of socialization

---

[19] Articles of Agreement of the IMF, 27 December 1945, as amended, Article 8, sec. 5, in *United Nations Treaty Series (UNTS)*, vol. 2, Treaty no. 20 (New York: United Nations, 1947), p. 39. For the conditionality decision, see decision no. 102-(52/11) 13 February 1952, "Selected Decisions of the Executive Directors and Selected Documents," p. 16.

[20] Convention on International Civil Aviation, 7 December 1944, Article 90, in UNTS, vol. 15, Treaty no. 102, 1948, p. 295.

[21] Montreal Protocol on Substances that Deplete the Ozone Layer, in *International Legal Materials*, vol. 26, 1987, p. 1541, Article 2(9) (signed 16 September 1987 and entered into force 1 January 1989; hereafter cited as Montreal Protocol) as amended, London Adjustment and Amendments to the Montreal Protocol on Substances that Deplete the Ozone Layer, in *International Legal Materials*, vol. 30, 1991, p. 537 (signed 29 June 1990 and entered into force 7 March 1991; hereafter cited as London Amendments).

[22] The Vienna Convention on the Law of Treaties, signed 23 May 1969 (entered into force on 27 January 1980), Article 2(1)(a), states that "'treaty' means an international agreement concluded between States in written form and governed by international law, whether embodied in a single instrument or in two or more related instruments and whatever its particular designation." See UN Doc. A/CONF. 39/27.

or otherwise, accept that they are obligated to obey the law. So it is with states. It is often said that the fundamental norm of international law is *pacta sunt servanda* (treaties are to be obeyed).[23] In the United States and many other countries, they become a part of the law of the land. Thus, a provision contained in an agreement to which a state has formally assented entails a legal obligation to obey and is presumptively a guide to action.

This proposition is deeply ingrained in common understanding and often reflected in the speech of national leaders. Yet the realist argument that national actions are governed entirely by calculation of interests (including the interest in stability and predictability served by a system of rules) is essentially a denial of the operation of normative obligation in international affairs. This position has held the field for some time in mainstream international relations theory (as have closely related postulates in other positivist social science disciplines).[24] But it is increasingly being challenged by a growing body of empirical study and academic analysis.

Such scholars as Elinor Ostrom and Robert Ellickson show how relatively small communities in contained circumstances generate and secure compliance with norms, even without the intervention of a supervening sovereign authority.[25] Others, like Frederick Schauer and Friedrich Kratochwil, analyze how norms operate in decision-making processes, whether as "reasons for action" or in defining the methods and terms of discourse.[26] Even Jon Elster says "I have come to believe that social norms provide an important kind of motivation for action that is irreducible to rationality or indeed to any other form of optimizing mechanism."[27]

[23] The Vienna Convention on the Law of Treaties, Article 26, specifies that "every treaty in force is binding upon the parties to it and must be performed in good faith." See also chap. 30 of Arnold Duncan McNair, *The Law of Treaties* (Oxford: Clarendon Press, 1961), pp. 493–505.

[24] William Eskridge, Jr., and G. Peller, "The New Public Law: Moderation as a Postmodern Cultural Form," *Michigan Law Review* 89 (February 1991), pp. 707–91.

[25] See Elinor Ostrom, *Governing the Commons: The Evolution of Institutions for Collective Action* (Cambridge: Cambridge University Press, 1990): and Robert C. Ellickson, *Order Without Law: How Neighbors Settle Disputes* (Cambridge, Mass.: Harvard University Press, 1991).

[26] See Frederick F. Schauer, *Playing by the Rules: A Philosophical Examination of Rule-based Decision-making in Law and Life* (Oxford: Clarendon Press, 1991): Kratochwil, *Rules, Norms and Decisions*; and Sally Falk Moore, *Law as Process* (London: Routledge & Kegan Paul, 1978).

[27] Jon Elster, *The Cement of Society: A Study of Social Order* (Cambridge: Cambridge University Press, 1989), p. 15. See also Margaret Levi, Karen S. Cook, Jodi A. O'Brien, and Howard Fay, "Introduction: The Limits of Rationality," in Cook and Levi, *The Limits of Rationality*, pp. 1–16.

The strongest circumstantial evidence for the sense of an obligation to comply with treaties is the care that states take in negotiating and entering into them. It is not conceivable that foreign ministries and government leaders could devote time and energy on the scale they do to preparing, drafting, negotiating, and monitoring treaty obligations unless there is an assumption that entering into a treaty commitment ought to and does constrain the state's own freedom of action and an expectation that the other parties to the agreement will feel similarly constrained. The care devoted to fashioning a treaty provision no doubt reflects the desire to limit the state's own commitment as much as to make evasion by others more difficult. In either case, the enterprise makes sense only on the assumption that, as a general rule, states acknowledge an obligation to comply with agreements they have signed. In the United States and other Western countries, the principle that the exercise of governmental power in general is subject to law lends additional force to an ethos of national compliance with international undertakings.[28] And, of course, appeals to legal obligations are a staple of foreign policy debate and of the continuous critique and defense of foreign policy actions that account for so much of diplomatic interchange and international political commentary.

All this argues that states, like other subjects of legal rules, operate under a sense of obligation to conform their conduct to governing norms.

VARIETIES OF NONCOMPLYING BEHAVIOR

If the state's decision whether or not to comply with a treaty is the result of a calculation of costs and benefits, as the realists assert, the implication is that noncompliance is the premeditated and deliberate violation of a treaty obligation. Our background assumption does not exclude that such decisions may occur from time to time, especially when the circumstances underlying the original bargain have changed significantly.[29] Or, as in the

---

[28] It is not clear, however, that democracies are more law-abiding. See Diggs v. Shultz, 470 F. 2d 461 (D.C. Cir. 1972): "Under our constitutional scheme, Congress can denounce treaties if it sees fit to do so, and there is nothing the other branches of the government can do about it. We consider that is precisely what Congress has done in this case" (pp. 466–67).

[29] International law recognizes a limited scope for abrogation of an agreement in such a case. See the Vienna Convention on the Law of Treaties, Article 62. Generally, however, the possibility of change is accommodated by provisions for amendment, authoritative interpretation, or even withdrawal from the agreement. See, for example, the withdrawal provision of the ABM Treaty, Article 25(2), or the Limited Test Ban Treaty, Article 4. None of these actions poses an issue of violation of legal obligations, though they may weaken the regime of which the treaty is a part.

area of international human rights, it may happen that a state will enter into an international agreement to appease a domestic or international constituency but have little intention of carrying it out. A passing familiarity with foreign affairs, however, suggests that only infrequently does a treaty violation fall into the category of a willful flouting of legal obligation.[30]

At the same time, general observation as well as detailed studies often reveal what appear or are alleged to be significant departures from established treaty norms. If these are not deliberate violations, what explains this behavior? We discuss three circumstances, infrequently recognized in discussions of compliance, that in our view often lie at the root of behavior that may seem prima facie to violate treaty requirements: (1) ambiguity and indeterminacy of treaty language, (2) limitations on the capacity of parties to carry out their undertakings, and (3) the temporal dimension of the social and economic changes contemplated by regulatory treaties.

These factors might be considered "causes" of noncompliance. But from a lawyer's perspective, it is illuminating to think of them as "defenses" – matters put forth to excuse or justify or extenuate a prima facie case of breach. A defense, like all other issues of compliance, is subject to the overriding obligation of good faith in the performance of treaty obligations.[31]

AMBIGUITY

Treaties, like other canonical statements of legal rules, frequently do not provide determinate answers to specific disputed questions. Language often is unable to capture meaning with precision. Treaty drafters do not foresee many of the possible applications, let alone their contextual settings. Issues that are foreseen often cannot be resolved at the time of treaty negotiation and are swept under the rug.

Economic, technological, scientific, and even political circumstances change. All these inescapable incidents of the effort to formulate rules to

---

[30] Keohane surveyed two hundred years of U.S. foreign relations history and identified only forty "theoretically interesting" cases of "inconvenient" commitments in which there was a serious issue of whether or not to comply. See the chapter entitled "Commitments and Compromise," in Robert O. Keohane, "The Impact of Commitments on American Foreign Policy," manuscript, 1993, pp. 1–49.

[31] See Vienna Convention on the Law of Treaties, Article 26; Lassa Oppenheim, *International Law: A Treatise*, 8th ed., ed. H. Lauterpacht (London: Longmans, 1955), p. 956; and McNair, *The Law of Treaties*, p. 465.

govern future conduct frequently produce a zone of ambiguity within which it is difficult to say with precision what is permitted and what is forbidden.

Of course, treaty language, like other legal language, comes in varying degrees of specificity. The broader and more general the language, the wider the ambit of permissible interpretations to which it gives rise. Yet there are frequently reasons for choosing a more general formulation of the obligation: the political consensus may not support more precision, or, as with certain provisions of the U.S. Constitution, it may be wiser to define a general direction, to try to inform a process, rather than seek to foresee in detail the circumstances in which the words will be brought to bear. If there is some confidence in those who are to apply the rules, a broader standard defining the general policy behind the law may be more effective in realizing it than a series of detailed regulations. The North Atlantic Treaty has proved remarkably durable, though its language is remarkably general: "In order more effectively to achieve the objectives of this Treaty, the Parties, separately and jointly, by means of continuous and effective self-help and mutual aid, will maintain and develop their individual and collective capacity to resist armed attack."[32]

Detail also has its difficulties. As in the U.S. Internal Revenue Code, precision generates loopholes, necessitating some procedure for continuous revision and authoritative interpretation. The complexities of the rule system may give rise to shortcuts that reduce inefficiencies when things are going well but may lead to friction when the political atmosphere darkens.

In short, there will often be a considerable range within which parties may reasonably adopt differing positions as to the meaning of the obligation. In domestic legal systems, courts or other authoritative institutions are empowered to resolve such disputes about meaning. The international legal system can provide tribunals to settle such questions if the parties consent. But compulsory means of authoritative dispute resolution by adjudication or otherwise are not generally available at the international level.[33] Moreover, the issue of interpretation may not arise in the context of an adversarial two-party dispute. In such cases, it

---

[32] North Atlantic Treaty, Article 3, 63 stat. 2241, in UNTS, vol. 34, no. 541, 1949, p. 243.

[33] Abram Chayes and Antonia Handler Chayes, "Compliance Without Enforcement: State Behavior Under Regulatory Treaties," *Negotiation Journal* 7 (July 1991), pp. 311–31. See also Louis B. Sohn, "Peaceful Settlement of Disputes in Ocean Conflicts: Does UN Clause 3 Point the Way?" *Law and Contemporary Problems* 46 (Spring 1983), pp. 195–200.

remains open to a state, in the absence of bad faith, to maintain its position and try to convince the others.

In many such disputes, a consensus may exist or emerge among knowledgeable professionals about the legal rights and wrongs.[34] In many others, however, the issue will remain contestable. Although one party may charge another with violation and deploy legions of international lawyers in its support, a detached observer often cannot readily conclude that there is indeed a case of noncompliance. In fact, it can be argued that if there is no authoritative arbiter (and even sometimes when there is), discourse among the parties, often in the hearing of a wider public audience, is an important way of clarifying the meaning of the rules.

In the face of treaty norms that are indeterminate over a considerable range, even conscientious legal advice may not avoid issues of compliance. At the extreme, a state may consciously seek to discover the limits of its obligation by testing its treaty partners' responses.

Justice Oliver Wendell Holmes said, "The very meaning of a line in the law is that you intentionally may come as close to it as you can if you do not pass it."[35] Perhaps a more usual way of operating in the zone of ambiguity is to design the activity to comply with the letter of the obligation, leaving others to argue about the spirit. The General Agreement on Tariffs and Trade (GATT) prohibits a party from imposing quotas on imports. When Japanese exports of steel to the United States generated pressures from U.S. domestic producers that the Nixon administration could no longer contain, U.S. trade lawyers invented the "voluntary restraint agreement," under which private Japanese producers agreed to limit their U.S. sales.[36] The United States imposed no official quota, although the Japanese producers might well have anticipated some such action had they not "volunteered." Did the arrangement violate GATT obligations?

Questions of compliance with treaty obligations ordinarily arise as [incidental obstacles] to objectives that decisionmakers regard as important.[37] Lawyers may be consulted or may intervene. Decisions about how the desired program is to be carried out emerge from a complex interaction of legal and policy analysis that generates its own subrules and

---

[34] Oscar Schachter, "The Invisible College of International Lawyers," *Northwestern University Law Review*, vol. 72, no. 2, 1977, pp. 217–26.

[35] Superior Oil Co. v. Mississippi, 280 U.S. 390 (1920), p. 395.

[36] Consumers Union v. Kissinger, 506 F. 2d 136 (D.C. Cir. 1974).

[37] Chayes and Chayes, "Living Under a Treaty Regime," pp. 197 and 200.

precedents. The process parallels that in a classic U.S. bureaucracy or corporation.

Even in the stark, high politics of the Cuban Missile Crisis, State Department lawyers argued that the United States could not lawfully react unilaterally, since the Soviet emplacement of missiles in Cuba did not amount to an "armed attack" sufficient to trigger the right of self-defense in Article 51 of the UN Charter. Use of force in response to the missiles would only be lawful if approved by the Organization of American States (OAS). Though it would be foolish to contend that the legal position determined President John Kennedy's decision, there is little doubt that the asserted need for advance OAS authorization for any use of force contributed to the mosaic of argumentation that led to the decision to respond initially by means of the quarantine rather than an air strike. Robert Kennedy said later, "It was the vote of the Organization of American States that gave a legal basis for the quarantine ... and changed our position from that of an outlaw acting in violation of international law into a country acting in accordance with twenty allies legally protecting their position."[38] This was the advice he had heard from his lawyers, and it was a thoroughly defensible position. Nevertheless, many international lawyers in the United States and elsewhere disagreed because they thought the action was inconsistent with the UN Charter.[39]

CAPABILITY

According to classical international law, legal rights and obligations run among states and is an undertaking by them as to their future conduct. The object of the agreement is to affect state behavior. This simple relationship between agreement and relevant behavior continues to exist for many treaties. The LTBT is such a treaty. It prohibits nuclear testing in the atmosphere, in outer space, or underwater. Only states conduct nuclear weapons tests, so only state behavior is implicated in the undertaking. The state, by governing its own actions, without more, determines whether it will comply with the undertaking or not. Moreover, there is no doubt about the state's capacity to do what it has undertaken.

---

[38] Robert Kennedy, *Thirteen Days* (New York: W. M. Norton, 1971), p. 99. See also Abram Chayes "The Role of Law in the Cuban Missile Crisis."

[39] See, for example, Quincy Wright, "The Cuban Quarantine," *American Journal of International Law* 57 (July 1963), pp. 546–65; James S. Campbell, "The Cuban Crisis and the UN Charter: An Analysis of the United States Position" *Stanford Law Review* 16 (December 1963), pp. 160–76; and William L. Standard, "The United States Quarantine of Cuba and the Rule of Law," *American Bar Association Journal* 49 (August 1963), pp. 744–48.

Every state, no matter how primitive its structure or limited its resources, can refrain from conducting atmospheric nuclear tests.

Even when only state behavior is at stake, the issue of capacity may arise when the treaty involves an affirmative obligation. In the 1980s it was a fair assumption that the Soviet Union had the capability to carry out its undertaking to destroy certain nuclear weapons as required by the START agreement. In the 1990s, that assumption was threatened by the emergence of a congeries of successor states in place of the Soviet Union, many of which did not have the necessary technical knowledge or material resources to do the job.[40]

The problem is pervasive in contemporary regulatory treaties. Much of the work of the International Labor Organization (ILO) from the beginning has been devoted to improving its members' domestic labor legislation and enforcement. The current spate of environmental agreements poses the difficulty in acute form. Such treaties formally are among states, and the obligations are cast as state obligations for example, to reduce sulfur dioxide (SO_2) emissions by 30 percent against a certain baseline. However, the real object of such treaties is usually not to affect state behavior but to regulate the behavior of nonstate actors carrying out activities that produce SO_2, using electricity, or gasoline. The ultimate impact on the relevant private behavior depends on a complex series of intermediate steps. It will normally require an implementing decree or legislation followed by detailed administrative regulations. In essence, the state will have to establish and enforce a full-blown domestic regime designed to secure the necessary reduction in emissions.

The state may be "in compliance" when it has taken the formal legislative and administrative steps, and, despite the vagaries of legislative and domestic politics, it is perhaps appropriate to hold it accountable for failure to do so. However, the construction of an effective domestic regulatory apparatus is not a simple mechanical task. It entails choices and requires scientific and technical judgment, bureaucratic capability, and fiscal resources. Even developed Western states have not been able to construct such systems with confidence that they will achieve the desired objective.[41]

[40] Kurt M. Campbell, Ashton B. Carter, Steven E. Miller, and Charles A. Zraket, *Soviet Nuclear Fission: Control of the Nuclear Arsenal in a Disintegrating Soviet Union*, CSIA Studies in International Security, no. 1. Harvard University, Cambridge, Mass., November 1991, pp. 24, 25, and 108.

[41] Kenneth Hanf, "Domesticating International Commitments: Linking National and International Decision-making," prepared for a meeting entitled Managing Foreign Policy Issues Under Conditions of Change, Helsinki, July 1992.

Although there are surely differences among developing countries, the characteristic situation is a severe dearth of the requisite scientific, technical, bureaucratic, and financial wherewithal to build effective domestic enforcement systems. Four years after the Montreal Protocol was signed, only about half the member states had complied fully with the requirement of the treaty that they report annual chlorofluorocarbon (CFC) consumption.[42] The Conference of the Parties promptly established an Ad Hoc Group of Experts on Reporting, which recognized that the great majority of the nonreporting states were developing countries that for the most part were simply unable to comply without technical assistance from the treaty organization.[43]

The Montreal Protocol is the first treaty under which the parties undertake to provide significant financial assistance to defray the incremental costs of compliance for developing countries. The same issue figured on a much larger scale in the negotiations for a global climate change convention and in the UN Conference on Environment and Development, held in Brazil in June 1992. The last word has surely not been spoken in these forums, nor is the problem confined to environmental agreements.

The Temporal Dimension

Significant changes in social or economic systems mandated by regulatory treaty regimes[44] take time to accomplish. Thus, a cross section at any particular moment in time may give a misleading picture of the state of compliance. Wise treaty drafters recognize at the negotiating stage that

---

[42] See Report of the Secretariat on the Reporting of Data by the Parties in Accordance with Article 7 of the Montreal Protocol, UNEP/OzL.Pro.3/5, 23 May 1991, pp. 6–12 and 22–24; and Addendum, UNEP/OzL.Pro3/5/Add.l, 19 June 1991.

[43] For the establishment of the Ad Hoc Group of Experts, see Report of the Second Meeting of the Parties to the Montreal Protocol on Substances that Deplete the Ozone Layer, UNEP/ OzL.Pro.2/3, Decision 2/9, 29 June 1990, p. 15. At its first meeting in December 1990, the Ad Hoc Group of Experts concluded that countries "lack knowledge and technical expertise necessary to provide or collect" the relevant data and made a detailed series of recommendations for addressing the problem. See Report of the First Meeting of the Ad Hoc Group of Experts on the Reporting of Data, UNEP/OzL.Pro/WG.2/1/4, 7 December 1990.

[44] The now-classical definition of an international regime appears in Krasner, "Structural Causes and Regime Consequences," p. 2: "Regimes are sets of implicit or explicit principles, norms, rules, and decision-making procedures around which actors' expectations converge in a given area of international relations."

there will be a considerable time lag after the treaty is concluded before some or all of the parties can bring themselves into compliance. Thus modern treaties, from the IMF Agreement in 1945 to the Montreal Protocol in 1987, have provided for transitional arrangements and made allowances for special circumstances.[45] Nevertheless, whether or not the treaty provides for it, a period of transition will be necessary.

Similarly, if the regime is to persist over time, adaptation to changing conditions and underlying circumstances will require a shifting mix of regulatory instruments to which state and individual behavior cannot instantaneously respond. Often the original treaty is only the first in a series of agreements addressed to the issue-area.

Activists in all fields lament that the treaty process tends to settle on a least-common-denominator basis. But the drive for universality (or universal membership in the particular region of concern) may necessitate accommodation to the response capability of states with large deficits in financial, technical, or bureaucratic resources. A common solution is to start with a low obligational ante and increase the level of regulation as experience with the regime grows. The convention-protocol strategy adopted in a number of contemporary environmental regimes exemplifies this conception. The Vienna Convention on the Protection of the Ozone Layer, signed in 1985, contained no substantive obligations but required only that the parties "in accordance with the means at their disposal and their capabilities" cooperate in research and information exchange and in harmonizing domestic policies on activities likely to have an adverse effect on the ozone layer.[46] Two years later, as scientific consensus jelled on the destructive effect of CFCs on the ozone layer, the Montreal Protocol was negotiated, providing for a 50 percent reduction from 1986 levels of CFC consumption by the year 2000.[47] By June 1990, the parties agreed to a complete phaseout.[48]

The pattern has a long pedigree, extending back to the ILO, the first of the modern international regulatory agencies, whose members agreed in 1921 only to "bring the recommendation[s] or draft convention[s] [prepared by the organization] before the authority or authorities within

---

[45] See Articles of Agreement of the International Monetary Fund, Article 14, in UNTS, vol. 2, 1945, p. 1501; and Montreal Protocol, Article 5.

[46] Vienna Convention for the Protection of the Ozone Layer (signed 22 March 1985 and entered into force 22 September 1988; hereafter cited as Vienna Ozone Convention), Article 2(2), in *International Legal Materials*, vol. 26, 1986, p. 1529.

[47] Montreal Protocol, Article 2(4).

[48] London Amendments, Annex 1, Articles 2A(5) and 2B(3).

whose competence the matter lies, for the enactment of legislation or other action.[49] The ILO then became the forum for drafting and propagating a series of specific conventions and recommendations on the rights of labor and conditions of employment for adoption by the parties.

The effort to protect human rights by international agreement may be seen as an extreme case of time lag between undertaking and performance. Although the major human rights conventions have been widely ratified, compliance leaves much to be desired. It is apparent that some states adhered without any serious intention of abiding by them. But it is also true that even parties committed to the treaties had different expectations about compliance than with most other regulatory treaties. Indeed, the Helsinki Final Act, containing important human rights provisions applicable to Eastern Europe, is by its terms not legally binding.[50]

Even so, it is a mistake to call these treaties merely "aspirational" or "hortatory." To be sure, they embody "ideals" of the international system, but like other regulatory treaties, they were designed to initiate a process that over time, perhaps a long time, would bring behavior into greater congruence with those ideals. These expectations have not been wholly disappointed. The vast amount of public and private effort devoted to enforcing these agreements evinces their obligational content.

ACCEPTABLE LEVELS OF COMPLIANCE

The foregoing section identified a range of matters that might be put forward by the individual actor in defense or excuse of a particular instance of deviant conduct. From the perspective of the system as a whole, however, the central issue is different. For a simple prohibitory norm like a highway speed limit, it is in principle a simple matter to determine whether any particular driver is in compliance. Yet most communities and law enforcement organizations in the United States seem to be perfectly comfortable with a situation in which the average speed on interstate highways is perhaps ten miles above the limit. Even in individual cases, the enforcing officer is not likely to pursue a driver operating within that zone. The fundamental problem for the system is not how to induce all drivers to obey the speed limit but how to contain

---

[49] Constitution of the International Labor Organization, 11 April 1919, Article 405, 49 stat. 2722.

[50] Conference on Security and Cooperation in Europe, Final Act (1 August 1975), Article 10, in *International Legal Materials*, vol. 14, 1975, p. 1292.

deviance within acceptable levels. So, too, it is for international treaty obligations.

"An acceptable level of compliance" is not an invariant standard. The matter is further complicated because many legal norms are not like the speed limit that permits an on-off judgment as to whether an actor is in compliance. As noted above, questions of compliance are often contestable and call for complex, subtle, and frequently subjective evaluation. What is an acceptable level of compliance will shift according to the type of treaty, the context, the exact behavior involved, and over time.

It would seem, for example, that the acceptable level of compliance would vary with the significance and cost of the reliance that parties place on the others' performance.[51] On this basis, treaties implicating national security would demand strict compliance because the stakes are so high, and to some extent that prediction is borne out by experience. Yet even in this area, some departures seem to be tolerable.

In the case of the NPT, indications of deviant behavior by parties have been dealt with severely. In the 1970s, U.S. pressures resulted in the termination of programs to construct reprocessing facilities in South Korea and Taiwan.[52] Recently, a menu of even more stringent pressures was mounted against North Korea, which signed an IAEA safeguard agreement and submitted to inspection [for a time].[53] The inspection and destruction requirements placed on Iraq under UN Security Council resolution 687 [and the sanctions imposed for violation represent], an extreme case of this severity toward deviation by NPT parties.

Although over 130 states are parties to the NPT, the treaty is not universal, and some nonparties have acquired or are seeking nuclear weapons capability.[54] Despite these important holdouts, compliance

---

[51] Charles Lipson, "Why Are Some International Agreements Informal," *International Organization* 45 (Autumn 1991), pp. 495–538.

[52] See Joseph A. Yager, "The Republic of Korea," and "Taiwan," in Joseph A. Yager, ed., *Nonproliferation and U.S. Foreign Policy* (Washington, D.C.: Brookings Institution, 1980), pp. 44–65 and 66–81, respectively.

[53] See David Sanger "North Korea Assembly Backs Atom Pact," *The New York Times*, 10 April 1992, p. A3; and David Sanger, "North Korea Reveals Nuclear Sites to Atomic Agency, *The New York Times*, 7 May 1992, p. A4. The initial U.S. response included behind-the-scenes diplomatic pressure and encouraging supportive statements by concerned states at IAEA meetings. See L. Spector, *Nuclear Ambitions: The Spread of Nuclear Weapons, 1989–1990* (Boulder, Colo.: Westview Press, 1990), pp. 127–30. Japan apparently has refused to consider economic assistance or investment in North Korea until the nuclear issue is cleared up.

[54] Countries that have not ratified the NPT include Argentina, Brazil, China, France, India, Israel, and Pakistan. See Spector, *Nuclear Ambitions*, p. 430.

with the NPT by the parties remains high. In fact, prominent nonparties including Argentina, Brazil, and South Africa have either adhered to the treaty or announced that they will comply with its norms.[55] Although there have been some significant departure from its norms and less than universal acquiescence, the nonproliferation regime is surviving.

If national security regimes have not collapsed in the face of significant perceived violation, it should be no surprise that economic and environmental treaties can tolerate a good deal of noncompliance. Such regimes are in fact relatively forgiving of violations plausibly justified by extenuating circumstances in the foreign or domestic life of the offending state, provided the action does not threaten the survival of the regime. As noted above, a considerable amount of deviance from strict treaty norms may be anticipated from the beginning and accepted, whether in the form of transitional periods, special exemptions, limited substantive obligations, or informal expectations of the parties.

The generally disappointing performance of states in fulfilling reporting requirements is consistent with this analysis.[56] It is widely accepted that failure to file reports reflects a low domestic priority or deficient bureaucratic capacity in the reporting state. Since the reporting is not central to the treaty bargain, the lapse can be viewed as "technical." When, as in the Montreal Protocol, accurate reporting was essential to the functioning of the regime, the parties and the secretariat made strenuous efforts to overcome the deficiency, and with some success.[57]

The Convention on International Trade in Endangered Species (CITES) ordinarily displays some tolerance for noncompliance, but the alarming and widely publicized decline in the elephant population in East African habitats in the 1980s galvanized the treaty regime. The parties took a decision to list the elephant in Appendix A of the treaty (shifting it from Appendix B, where it had previously been listed), with the effect of banning all commercial trade in ivory. The treaty permits any party to enter

[55] Reuters News Service, "Argentina and Brazil Sign Nuclear Accord," *The New York Times*, 14 December 1991, p. 7; "Brazil and Argentina: IAEA Safeguard Accord," U.S. Department of State Dispatch, 23 December 1991, p. 907; Reuters News Service, "South Africa Signs a Treaty Allowing Nuclear Inspection," *The New York Times*, 9 July 1991, p. A11; and "Fact Sheet: Nuclear Non-proliferation Treaty," U.S. Department of State Dispatch, 8 July 1991, p. 491.

[56] U.S. General Accounting Office, *International Environment: International Agreements Are Not Well-Monitored*, GAO, RCED-92-43, January 1992.

[57] See Report of the Secretariat on the Reporting of Data by the Parties in Accordance with Article 7 of the Montreal Protocol, UNEP/OzL.Pro.3/5, 23 May 1991, pp. 6–12 and 22–24; and Addendum, UNEP/OzL.Pro.3/5/Add.1, 19 June 1991.

a reservation to such an action, in which case the reserving party is not bound by it. Nevertheless, through a variety of pressures, the United States together with a group of European countries insisted on universal adherence to the ban, bringing such major traders as Japan and Hong Kong to heel.[58] The head of the Japanese Environment Agency supported the Japanese move in order "to avoid isolation in the international community."[59] It was freely suggested that Japan's offer to host the next meeting of the conference of parties, which was accepted on the last day of the conference after Japan announced its changed position, would have been rejected had it reserved on the ivory ban.

The meaning of the background assumption of general compliance is that most states will continue to comply, even in the face of considerable deviant behavior by other parties. In other words, the free-rider problem has been overestimated. The treaty will not necessarily unravel in the face of defections. As Mancur Olson recognized, if the benefits of the collective good to one or a group of parties outweigh the costs to them of providing the good, they will continue to bear the costs regardless of the defections of others.[60]

It seems plausible that treaty regimes are subject to a kind of critical-mass phenomenon, so that once defection reaches a certain level, or in the face of massive violation by a major player, the regime might collapse.[61] Thus, either the particular character of a violation or the identity of the violator may pose a threat to the regime and evoke a higher demand for compliance. [Thus, in many of the situations in which the United States

---

[58] For a report of Japan's announcement of its intention not to enter a reservation on the last day of the conference, see United Press International, "Tokyo Agrees to Join Ivory Import Ban," *Boston Globe*, 21 October 1989, p. 6. Japan stated that it was "respecting the overwhelming sentiment of the international community." As to Hong Kong, see Jane Perlez, "Ivory Ban Said to Force Factories Shut," *The New York Times*, 22 May 1990, p. A14. The Hong Kong reservation was not renewed after the initial six-month period. Five African producer states with effective management programs did enter reservations but agreed not to engage in trade until at least the next conference of the parties. See Michael J. Glennon, "Has International Law Failed the Elephant," *American Journal of International Law* 84 (January 1990), pp. 1–43, especially p. 17. At the 1992 meeting they ended their opposition. See "Five African Nations Abandon Effort to Resume Elephant Trade in CITES Talks," *Bureau of National Affairs Environment Daily*, electronic news service, 12 March 1992.

[59] United Press International, "Tokyo Agrees to Join Ivory Import Ban," *Boston Globe*, 21 October 1989.

[60] Mancur Olson, *The Logic of Collective Action* (Cambridge, Mass.: Harvard University Press, 1971), pp. 33–36.

[61] For a discussion of critical-mass behavior models, see Thomas Schelling, *Micromotives and Macrobehavior* (New York: Norton, 1978), pp. 91–110.

accused the Soviet Union of egregious violations of the ABM Treaty, and although nuclear security was involved,] the violations did not threaten the basic treaty bargain. The United States responded with a significant enforcement effort but did not itself destroy the basic bargain by abrogating the treaty. In the CITES elephant case, involving relatively peripheral national interests from the realist perspective, a reservation by Japan would have threatened the collapse of the regime. A concerted and energetic defense resulted.

DETERMINING THE ACCEPTABLE COMPLIANCE LEVEL

If, as we argue above, the "acceptable level of compliance" is subject to broad variance across regimes, times, and occasions, how is what is "acceptable" to be determined in any particular instance? The economists have a straightforward answer: invest additional resources in enforcement (or other measures to induce compliance) up to the point at which the value of the incremental benefit from an additional unit of compliance exactly equals the cost of the last unit of additional enforcement resources.[62] Unfortunately, the usefulness of this approach is limited by the impossibility of quantifying or even approximating, let alone monetizing, any of the relevant factors in the equation and markets are not normally available to help.

In such circumstances, as Charles Lindblom has told us, the process by which preferences are aggregated is necessarily a political one.[63] It follows that the choice whether to intensify (or slacken) the international enforcement effort is necessarily a political decision. It implicates all the same interests pro and con that were involved in the initial formulation of the treaty norm, as modified by intervening changes of circumstances. Although the balance will to some degree reflect the expectations of compliance that the parties entertained at that time, it is by no means rare, in international as in domestic politics, to find that what the lawmaker has given in the form of substantive regulation is taken away in the implementation. What is "acceptable" in terms of compliance will reflect

[62] See Gary Becker, "Crime and Punishment: An Economic Approach," *Journal of Political Economy* 76 (March/April 1968), pp. 169–217; and Stigler," *The Optimum Enforcement of Laws*," p. 526.

[63] Charles E. Lindblom, *Politics and Markets* (New York: Basic Books, 1977), pp. 254–55. At the domestic level, the decision whether to intensify enforcement of the treaty implicates a similar political process, as the continuous debates in the United States over GATT enforcement testify. Our work-in-progress includes a consideration of second-level enforcement.

the perspectives and interests of participants in the ongoing political process rather than some external scientific or market-validated standard.

If the treaty establishes a formal organization, that body may serve as a focus for mobilizing the political impetus for a higher level of compliance. A strong secretariat can sometimes exert compliance pressure, as in the IMF or ILO. The organization may serve as a forum for continuing negotiation among the parties about the level of compliance. An example of these possibilities is the effort of the International Maritime Consultative Organization (IMCO) – and after 1982 its successor, the International Maritime Organization (IMO) – to control pollution of the sea by tanker discharges of oil mixed with ballast water.[64] IMCO's regulatory approach was to impose performance standards limiting the amount of oil that could be discharged on any voyage. From 1954, when the first oil pollution treaty was signed, until the 1978 revisions, there was continuous dissatisfaction with the level of compliance. IMCO responded by imposing increasingly strict limits, but these produced only modest results because of the difficulty of monitoring and verifying the amount of oil discharged. Finally, in 1978 IMO adopted a new regulatory strategy and imposed an equipment standard requiring all new tankers to have separate ballast tanks that physically prevent the intermixture of oil with the discharged ballast water. The new requirement was costly to tanker operators but easily monitored by shipping authorities. Compliance with the equipment standard has been close to 100 percent, and discharge of oil from the new ships is substantially nil. The sequence reflects the changing configuration of political strength between domestic environmental and shipping constituencies in the members of IMO (and IMCO) which was originally referred to as a "shipping industry club."

Again, after a considerable period of fruitless exhortation in the International Whaling Commission, Japan finally agreed to participate in a temporary moratorium on whaling that had been proclaimed by the organization when the United States threatened trade sanctions under the Marine Mammal Protection Act.[65] The Japanese ban on ivory imports shows a mixture of economic and reputational threats. The United States

[64] Ronald Mitchell, "Intentional Oil Pollution of the Oceans: Crises, Public Pressure, and Equipment Standards," in Peter M. Haas, Robert O. Keohane, and Mark A. Levy, eds., *Institutions for the Earth: Sources of Effective International Environmental Protection* (Cambridge, Mass.: MIT Press, forthcoming).

[65] See Steinar Andresen, "Science and Politics in the International Management of Whales," *Marine Policy*, vol. 13, no. 2, 1989, p. 99; and Patricia Birnie, *International Regulation of Whaling* (New York: Oceana, 1985).

hinted at trade sanctions, and the conference of the parties of CITES threatened not to schedule its next meeting in Kyoto if Japan remained out of compliance.

If there are no objective standards by which to recognize an "acceptable level of compliance," it may be possible at least to identify some general types of situations that might actuate the deployment of political power in the interest of greater compliance. First, states committed to the treaty regime may sense that a tipping point is close, so that enhanced compliance would be necessary for regime preservation. As noted above, the actions against Japan on the ivory import ban may have been of this character. After the high visibility given to the CITES moves to ban the ivory trade, there would not have been much left of the regime if Japan had been permitted to import with impunity.

Second, states committed to a level of compliance higher than that acceptable to the generality of the parties may seek to ratchet up the standard. The Netherlands often seems to play the role of "leader" in European environmental affairs both in the North Sea and Baltic Sea regimes and in LRTAP.[66] Similarly, the United States may be a "leader" for improving compliance with the NPT, where its position is far stronger than that of its allies.

Finally, campaigning to improve a compliance level that states concerned would just as soon leave alone is a characteristic activity for NGOs, especially in the fields of the environment and of human rights. NGOs increasingly have direct access to the political process both within the treaty organizations and in the societies of which they are a part. Their technical, organizational, and lobbying skills are an independent resource for enhanced compliance at both levels of the two-level game.

CONCLUSION

The foregoing discussion reflects a view of noncompliance as a deviant rather than an expected behavior, and as endemic rather than deliberate. This in turn leads to de-emphasis of formal enforcement measures and even, to a degree, of coercive informal sanctions, except in egregious cases. It shifts attention to sources of noncompliance that can be managed by routine international political and managerial processes. Thus, the improvement of dispute resolution procedures goes to the problem

---

[66] See Peter M. Haas, "Protecting the Baltic and North Seas," in Haas, Keohane, and Levy, *Institutions for the Earth.*

of ambiguity; technical and financial assistance may help cure the capacity deficit; and transparency will make it likelier that, over time, national policy decisions are brought increasingly into line with agreed international standards.

These approaches merge in the process of "jawboning" an effort to persuade the miscreant to change its ways that is the characteristic form of international enforcement activity. This process exploits the practical necessity for the putative offender to give reasons and justifications for suspect conduct. These reasons and justifications are reviewed and critiqued in a variety of venues, public and private, formal and informal. The tendency is to winnow out reasonably justifiable or unintended failures to fulfill commitments that comport with a good-faith compliance standard and to identify and isolate the few cases of egregious and willful violation. By systematically addressing and eliminating all mitigating circumstances that might possibly be advanced, this process can ultimately demonstrate that what may at first have seemed like ambiguous conduct is a black-and-white case of deliberate violation. The offending state is left with a stark choice between conforming to the rule as defined and applied in the particular circumstances or openly flouting its obligation. This turns out to be a very uncomfortable position for even a powerful state. One example is the now demonstrated Iraqi retreat in showdowns with the UN-IAEA inspection teams.[67]

Enforcement through these interacting measures of assistance and persuasion is less costly and intrusive and is certainly less dramatic than coercive sanctions, the easy and usual policy elixir for noncompliance. It has the further virtue that it is adapted to the needs and capacities of the contemporary international system.

---

[67] For an account of the Iraqi response, see Sean Cote, *A Narrative of the Implementation of Section C of UN Security Council Resolution 687.*

5

Is the Good News About Compliance Good News About Cooperation?

George W. Downs, David M. Rocke, and Peter N. Barsoom

In the past few years many social scientists interested in cooperation have turned their attention to the problem of compliance in international regulatory regimes. Much of the empirical research in this area has been conducted by a group composed mainly of qualitative political scientists and scholars interested in international law.[1] Its message is that (1) compliance is generally quite good; (2) this high level of compliance has been achieved with little attention to enforcement; (3) those compliance problems that do exist are best addressed as management rather than enforcement problems; and (4) the management rather than the enforcement approach holds the key to the evolution of future regulatory cooperation in the international system. As Oran Young notes, "A new understanding of the bases of compliance – one that treats compliance as a management problem rather than an enforcement problem and that has profound practical as well as theoretical implications – is making itself felt among students of international relations."[2] In short, not only are the dreary expectations born of factors such as relative gains concerns, collective action problems, anarchy, and fears of self-interested

---

[1] For example, see Arora and Cason 1995; Chayes and Chayes 1990; 1991; 1993a; 1993b; Duffy 1988; Haas, Keohane, and Levy 1993; Hawkins 1984; Mitchell 1993; 1994a; 1994b; 1995; Scholz 1984; Sparrow 1994; Young 1989; and 1994.

[2] Young's quotation is taken from the dust jacket of Mitchell 1994a.

An earlier version of this article was presented at the annual meeting of the International Studies Association, Chicago, February 1994. The authors thank Abram Chayes, Robert Keohane, Marc Levy, Ron Mitchell, Ken Oye, Michael Ross, the editor of *International Organization*, and the anonymous referees for their helpful comments. The authors also acknowledge the support of the John D. and Catherine T. MacArthur Foundation to the Center of International Studies, Princeton University.

exploitation incorrect but also the enforcement limitations that always have appeared to sharply bound the contributions of international law and many international institutions now appear to have been exaggerated.

In this essay we will argue that the empirical findings of this group, which we refer to as the "managerial" school, are interesting and important but that its policy inferences are dangerously contaminated by selection problems. If we restrict our attention to those regulatory treaties that prescribe reductions in a collectively dysfunctional behavior (e.g., tariffs, arms increases), evidence suggests that the high level of compliance and the marginality of enforcement result from the fact that most treaties require states to make only modest departures from what they would have done in the absence of an agreement. This creates a situation where states often are presented with negligible benefits for even unpunished defections; hence the amount of enforcement needed to maintain cooperation is modest. Nothing is wrong with this situation in itself, but it is unlikely to provide the model for the future that the managerialists claim. Even if we assume that the absolute value of the benefits generated by this small amount of regulation is relatively large, further progress in international regulatory cooperation will almost certainly require the creation of agreements that present far greater incentives to defect than those currently in place (e.g., more demanding environmental standards, fewer non-tariff barriers, steeper arms reductions). We have precious little evidence that such progress can be obtained in the absence of better enforcement.

After discussing the problems posed by endogeneity and selection, we present the theoretical argument for linking enforcement level to what we call "depth of cooperation" and examine the extent to which deep cooperation has been achieved without enforcement. We then present a number of prominent exceptions to the managerial school's unqualified generalizations about the causes and cures of noncompliance. Finally, we discuss the strategic implications of the evolution of increasingly cooperative regimes.

THE MANAGERIAL THESIS

The bedrock of the managerial school is the finding that state compliance with international agreements is generally quite good and that enforcement has played little or no role in achieving and maintaining that record. In Abram Chayes and Antonia Chayes's words, what ensures compliance is not the threat of punishment but "a plastic process of interaction among the parties concerned in which the effort is to reestablish, in the microcontext of the particular dispute, the balance of advantage that brought the agreement into existence."[3] For the members of the managerial school, "noncompliance is not necessarily, perhaps not even usually, the result of deliberate defiance of the legal standard."[4] On those rare occasions when compliance problems do occur they should not be viewed as violations or self-interested attempts at exploitation, but as isolated administrative breakdowns. The causes of noncompliance are to be found in (1) the ambiguity and indeterminacy of treaties, (2) the capacity limitations of states, and (3) uncontrollable social or economic changes.[5]

Not surprisingly, the managerial school takes a dim view of formal and even informal enforcement measures. Punishment not only is inappropriate given the absence of any exploitative intent but it is too costly, too political, and too coercive. As Ronald Mitchell notes, "Retaliatory non-compliance often proves unlikely because the costs of any individual violation may not warrant a response and it cannot be specifically targeted, imposing costs on those that have consistently complied without hurting the targeted violator enough to change its behavior."[6] As a result, according to Young, "arrangements featuring enforcement as a means of eliciting compliance are not of much use in international society."[7] Since sanctions usually are more successful against economically vulnerable and politically weak countries and "unilateral sanctions can be imposed only by the major powers, their legitimacy as a device for treaty enforcement is deeply suspect," as Chayes and Chayes point out.[8] ***

Instances of apparent noncompliance are problems to be solved, rather than violations that have to be punished. According to Chayes and Chayes, "As in other managerial situations, the dominant atmosphere is that of actors engaged in a cooperative venture, in which performance that seems for some reason unsatisfactory represents a problem to be solved by mutual consultation and analysis, rather than an offense to be punished. Persuasion and argument are the principal motors of this process."[9] The strategies necessary to induce compliance and maintain cooperation involve: (1) improving dispute resolution procedures, (2) technical and financial assistance, and (3) increasing transparency. The last is especially important: "For a party deliberately contemplating violation, the high

---

[3] Chayes and Chayes 1991, 303.
[4] Ibid., 301.
[5] Chayes and Chayes 1993b, 188.
[6] Mitchell 1993, 330.
[7] Young 1994, 74 and 134.
[8] Chayes and Chayes 1993a, 29.
[9] Chayes and Chayes 1991, 303.

probability of discovery reduces the expected benefits rather than increasing the costs and would thus deter violation regardless of the prospect of sanctions."[10]

THE ENDOGENEITY AND SELECTION PROBLEMS

It is not difficult to appreciate why the findings of the managerial school suggest that both international institutions and even international law have a far brighter future than most international relations specialists have believed for the past fifty years. Apart from sharply contradicting the pessimistic expectations of many realists and neorealists about the inability of cooperation and self-regulation to flourish in an anarchic world, they also run counter to the claims of cooperation researchers in the rational-choice tradition. Such researchers emphasize the centrality of enforcement concerns in regulatory environments and characterize them as mixed-motive games, where the danger of self-interested exploitation is significant, as opposed to coordination games, where it is not.[11] Such findings certainly add credibility to the frequent speculation that the rational-choice tradition's affection for the repeated prisoners' dilemma has led it to overemphasize enforcement and underemphasize the potential for voluntary compliance and noncoercive dispute resolution.

* * *

To even begin to overcome the problems that endogeneity poses for understanding the role of enforcement in regulatory compliance, we need to control for the basis of state selection; that is, those characteristics of international agreements that play the same role for states as musical difficulty does for the school orchestras. One likely candidate is what we have termed the depth of cooperation. International political economists define the depth of an agreement by the extent to which it requires behind-the-border integration with regard to social and environmental standards as well as with regard to the reduction of barriers to trade. Here, however, the depth of an agreement refers to the extent to which it captures the collective benefits that are available through perfect cooperation in one particular policy area. Given the difficulties involved in identifying the cooperative potential of an ideal treaty, it is most useful to think of

[10] Chayes and Chayes 1993a, 18.
[11] See, for example, Abreu 1988; Abreu, Pearce, and Stacchetti 1986; 1989; Bayard and Elliott 1994; Downs and Rocke 1995; Hungerford 1991; Martin 1992; Staiger 1995; and Sykes 1990.

a treaty's depth of cooperation as the extent to which it requires states to depart from what they would have done in its absence. If we are examining the critical subset of regulatory treaties that require states to reduce some collectively dysfunctional behavior like tariffs or pollution, a treaty's theoretical depth of cooperation would refer to the reduction it required relative to a counterfactual estimate of the tariff or pollution level that would exist in the absence of a treaty. Of course, the depth of cooperation that a treaty actually achieved might be quite different than this figure. Here we measure depth of cooperation by the treaty level because that is the figure which serves as the basis for judging the level of compliance. In the absence of a trustworthy theoretical estimate of this counterfactual, it could be based on the status quo at the time an agreement was signed or on a prediction derived from the year-to-year change rate prior to that time.

Either estimate of depth of cooperation is obviously quite crude. There are doubtless policy areas in which, for any number of reasons, the potential for cooperation is much smaller than others. In such cases our depth measure will make cooperation in these areas appear shallower than it really is. Yet if one is willing to concede, as both managerialists and more conventional institutionalists argue, that there are substantial cooperative benefits that are as yet unrealized in the areas of arms control, trade, and environmental regulation, this depth of cooperation measure provides a rough idea of what states have accomplished. We can in turn use it to interpret compliance data and help assess the role of enforcement. While this measure of depth is hardly perfect, there is no reason to expect that it is biased in such a way as to distort the relationship between the depth of cooperation represented by a given treaty, the nature of the game that underlies it, and the amount of enforcement needed to maintain it.

Depth of cooperation is important to track because just as the role of enforcement differs in mixed-motive and coordination games, it also varies within mixed-motive games according to depth. To appreciate the connection, consider the following model. States A and B are playing a repeated bilateral trade game in which each state in each period chooses a level of protection $P \in [0, \infty)$ that influences the level of trade. The utility of state A is denoted as $U_A(P^A, P^B)$, and the utility of state B is denoted as $U_B(P^A, P^B)$. We do not specify the functional form of these utilities but instead adopt a series of plausible assumptions detailed in Appendix A.[12]

---

[12] These assumptions also contain conditions on the response functions $R_A(P_B)$ and $R_B(P_A)$, which denote the optimal single-period response of one state to a particular level of protection (e.g., tariff) chosen by the other state.

We will adopt the convention of representing the trade game as a prisoners' dilemma. While some have argued that this pattern of incentives emerges from a variety of plausible circumstances, we assume it has emerged from electoral and financial incentives provided by interest groups working to protect domestic products from foreign competition.[13] If we consider only two particular levels of tariffs $P^A < P_o^A$ and $P^B < P_o^B$, then the four outcomes represented by each side choosing P or P_o form a payoff matrix of the prisoners' dilemma type. In this case, each side prefers higher tariffs regardless of the choice of the other side, but both sides prefer mutual cooperation to mutual defection. Unlike the repeated prisoners' dilemma, the choices defined by the present model are continuous rather than discrete. Treaties can be set at any level below the noncooperative tariff rates. Cheating can be limited or flagrant. And punishments can range from a barely perceptible increase in tariffs that lasts for one period to a multiple of current tariffs that lasts indefinitely.

Under the assumptions of our model, if tariff levels are high, both states have an opportunity to benefit by devising an agreement to lower them. Nevertheless, there is an incentive to exploit the other party's trust; that is, A's optimal one-period response to side B's cooperative tariff level will always be to raise tariffs. Self-interest will prevent such cheating only if the consequences of cheating are greater than the benefits. To achieve a situation where this disincentive exists, states must resort to a punishment for defection. In this case, one punishment strategy prescribes that state A begin by observing the treaty, but if B violates it, even modestly, state A should respond by abrogating the agreement (or otherwise reducing its level of compliance) for some specified period of time. During cooperative periods each side's tariff is supposed to be limited to $\bar{P}^A < P_o^A$ and $\bar{P}^B < P_o^B$, while in the punishment periods both sides raise tariffs to some noncooperative level. The most extreme punishment strategy, often called the "grim strategy," occurs when the response to any violation is permanent reversion to the noncooperative Nash equilibrium. A punishment strategy is sufficient to enforce a treaty when each side knows that if it cheats it will suffer enough from the punishment that the net benefit will not be positive.

To make this more concrete, consider an example where the noncooperative tariff is at a level of 100 percent for each side, and plausible

[13] For the former argument, see Staiger 1995, 27. For the latter, see Grossman and Helpman 1994.

treaties would provide for symmetric reductions in tariffs for each side.[14] Figure 5.1 compares the one-period utility of both sides observing the treaty with the temptation to defect. The temptation to cheat in this model rises rapidly with the cooperativeness of the treaty, while the treaty benefits rise less rapidly. This is what imposes a limit on which treaties can be supported. Figure 5.2 shows the punishment periods necessary to support treaties of various sizes. A shorter period would make the treaty vulnerable to cheating because it would be insufficient to remove all of the gains from violating the treaty. For example, a treaty that specifies a 5 percent reduction in tariffs only requires a punishment of two periods; the best treaty that can be supported with the maximal punishment of infinite duration is 37.19 percent. The increase in the ratio of the benefit of cheating to the benefit of cooperating means that increasingly severe punishments are necessary to deter defection – here severity means length of punishment – as the benefits of the treaty and corresponding restrictiveness of its requirements increase. Although the rate of increase in utility with the increase in punishment length decreases, the utility obtainable by very long punishments is still many times that of the utility obtainable with punishment lengths of one or two periods. The essential point the graph demonstrates is the deeper the agreement is, the greater the punishments required to support it.

The only relevant criterion is that punishment must hurt the transgressor state at least as much as that state could gain by the violation. This does not imply that, say, a certain amount of trade restriction should be punished by an equal trade restriction (tit-for-tat); nor does it mean that the transgressor be punished at least as much as the transgressor's violation hurt the other party. Although both of these standards possess aspects of fairness, neither is relevant to supporting the treaty equilibrium. Fairness and justice must take a back seat to the correct disincentive.

The specific mechanism by which states punish violations is less relevant to the relationship between depth of cooperation and enforcement than is the magnitude of enforcement. Although we motivate the model by using a case of centralized enforcement for convenience, nothing in the analysis precludes effective decentralized enforcement schemes. Enforcement can occur through linkages, as in the case of the Soviet Union and United States during the Kissinger years; through formal institutions such as the

---

[14] Of course, in the multiperiod model, the feasibility of maintaining this treaty depends on the discount factor, δ, as well as on the previous parameters. In this case, we use a discount factor of $\delta = .95$, corresponding to an interest rate of 5 percent.

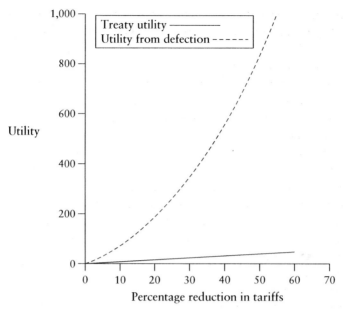

FIGURE 5.1. One-period utility of treaty compliance versus defection.

General Agreement on Tariffs and Trade (GATT) Dispute Settlement Procedure; through unilateral actions, as in the U.S. enforcement of fishery and wildlife agreements under the Pelly and Packwood–Magnuson amendments; or by domestic law as in the European Union and environmental treaties. Given the weakness of current international institutions and the relative difficulty in mobilizing formal sanctions, we suspect – like the majority of managerialists – that the most effective enforcement schemes may well be decentralized and not involve perfectly coordinated action by every signatory of a multilateral agreement.[15] This, however, does not negate the connection between depth of cooperation and the magnitude of the punishment necessary to maintain compliance in mixed-motive games.

DISCUSSION

This logical connection between the depth of cooperation represented by a given treaty and the amount of enforcement that is needed in mixed-motive games suggests that evaluating the importance of enforcement by examining how high compliance is when it is low or absent might

[15] On the role of decentralized enforcement schemes, see Ostrom 1990; and Kandori 1992.

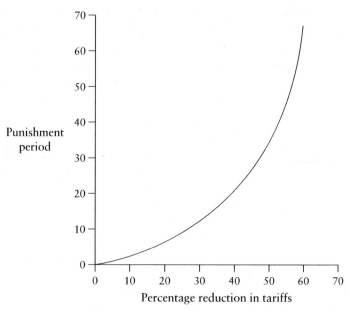

FIGURE 5.2. Punishment required to support treaties of various sizes

be misleading. We need to worry about the possibility that both the high rate of compliance and relative absence of enforcement threats are due not so much to the irrelevance of enforcement as to the fact that states are avoiding deep cooperation – and the benefits it holds whenever a prisoners' dilemma situation exists – because they are unwilling or unable to pay the costs of enforcement. If this were true, prescribing that states ignore enforcement in favor of other compliance strategies would be equivalent to telling the school orchestras to avoid wasting their time rehearsing. Just as the latter would condemn the orchestras to a repertoire of simple compositions, the prescriptions of the managerial school would condemn states to making agreements that represent solutions to co-ordination games and shallow prisoners' dilemmas.

* * *

Given the circumstances, it seems advisable to sidestep any attempt to inventory the nature of the underlying game and to evaluate some of the implications of the rival theories. We examine two. First, we will assess the depth of cooperation and the level of enforcement connected with prominent regulatory agreements that involve the reduction of behaviors that states have concluded are collectively counterproductive but that contain few enforcement provisions. Ideally, one would like to examine the correlation between enforcement and depth of cooperation, but as we noted above, we agree with the managerial school's observation that such strongly enforced regulatory agreements are relatively rare. If the managerial school is correct, the absence of strong enforcement provisions or the informal threat of enforcement should have no bearing on the depth of cooperation. There should be numerous examples of states agreeing to alter dramatically the trajectory that they were following at the time a treaty was signed while paying little attention to enforcement. If the game theorists are correct that most important regulatory agreements are mixed-motive games of some variety, any tendency of states to avoid committing themselves to punishing noncompliance is likely to be associated with either a world in which there are relatively few deeply cooperative agreements or in which violations run rampant. Since we agree that while regulatory violations exist they are not frequent, we expect the former to be true.

Second, we will examine the managerial school's claim that self-interest rarely plays a conspicuous role in the treaty violations that do take place and that violations are driven instead solely by a combination of the ambiguity of treaties, the capacity limitations of states, and uncontrollable social and economic changes. We are skeptical of this assertion because the set of violations should be less distorted by selection than the set of treaties. This is true because we expect that, ceteris paribus, the rate of violation connected with mixed-motive game treaties should in the absence of perfect information and appropriate enforcement be much higher than the rate of violation connected with coordination game treaties. Hence, even if there are fewer such treaties they would be overrepresented relative to coordination game-based treaties in any sample of violations.

The Rarity of Deep Cooperation

Are we correct in our suspicion that inferences about the importance of enforcement are likely to be contaminated by selection? That is, does evidence show that there is little need for enforcement because there is little deep cooperation? Let us begin by considering the set of arms agreements that the United States has made since 1945 (see appendix B). We note at the outset that, however valuable, a number of the treaties such as the "Hot Line" agreement and the United States–Union of Soviet Socialist Republics Ballistic Missile Launch Notification Agreements do not directly regulate an arms output such as the number and/or location of a weapons system. Of those that do, a significant subset such as the Outer Space Treaty, the Seabed Arms Control Treaty, and the Antarctic Treaty involve agreements to maintain the status quo trajectory rather than to alter it significantly. At the time the treaties were signed, neither the Soviet Union nor the United States had cost-effective plans for major weapons systems in these areas or possessed a strategic mission for which such a system was believed necessary. The fact that this situation has basically continued is the reason Chayes and Chayes can report that "there has been no reported deviation from the requirements of these treaties over a period of four decades."[16] That there was more enforcement in this case than officially is embodied in these agreements might also play a role. Both the Soviet Union and the United States likely knew that if one broke an agreement in a dramatic fashion, the other probably would retaliate in kind. Even though these expectations were established tacitly, they are no less real than expectations described formally in the treaty.[17] While we are not denying that obtaining tangible reassurance of a rival's intentions through a treaty is valuable, it is difficult to argue that these treaties exhibit the deep cooperation that would have taken place if the superpowers had each agreed to terminate major modernization programs or dramatically reduce their defense budgets. Much the same argument can be made in connection with the Anti-Ballistic Missiles (ABM) Treaty. While the treaty may have provided a significant benchmark that helped prevent both states from exploiting the technological gains that were made during the period since the treaty was signed, neither side had the technology or the budget to deploy a major system when the treaty was signed in 1972. In 1967 when President Johnson and Premier Kosygin first began to move toward discussion, Soviet ABM efforts were limited to a spare system around Moscow and the United States announced that it would begin deployment of a "thin" system to guard against Chinese attack and possible accidental launches.[18] As the technology of these antiballistic systems gradually has advanced and attention has shifted away from defense against a terrorist state, the depth of the original agreement in terms of today's "counterfactual" (i.e., the ABM system that the United States would construct today in the absence of an agreement) probably has increased. Given a constant or decreasing level of enforcement because of the weakness of the former

---

[16] Chayes and Chayes 1993a, chap. 7, p. 9.
[17] Downs and Rocke 1990.
[18] Arms Control and Disarmament Agency 1990, 150.

Soviet Union and increasing depth, the game theorist would expect the agreement to come under increasing pressure in the form of violations on the part of the most powerful state. This appears to have occurred.

Neither the initial Strategic Arms Limitation Talks (SALT) Interim Agreement nor SALT II was characterized by much depth. The interim agreement froze the number of intercontinental ballistic missile (ICBM) launchers at the status quo level (the United States had none under construction at the time and the Soviet Union was permitted to complete those it was building), but it allowed increases in the number of submarine-launched ballistic missiles (SLBMs) on both sides and failed significantly to restrict qualitative improvements in launchers, missiles, or a host of systems that allowed both sides to increase their nuclear capabilities.[19] SALT II required significant reductions in each side's number of operational launchers or bombers but permitted the number of ICBMs equipped with multiple independently targeted reentry vehicles (MIRVed ICBMs) to increase by 40 percent between the time of signing and 1985. When this figure is added to the number of cruise missiles permitted each bomber, the total number of nuclear weapons was allowed to increase 50–70 percent. As Jozef Goldblat notes, "There is a remarkable compatibility between the Treaty limitations and the projected strategic nuclear weapons programs of both sides."[20]

Intermediate-range nuclear forces (INF), conventional forces in Europe (CFE), and the strategic arms reduction talks (START) agreements are deeper, of course. The first prescribes the elimination of intermediate- and shorter-range missiles in Europe; the second dramatically reduced conventional forces; and the third cuts the arsenals of strategic nuclear delivery vehicles that come under the agreement by about 30 percent and cuts warheads by 40 percent.[21] While one can argue in connection with START that the number of accountable weapons is smaller than the actual number of weapons, the cuts are significant in terms of either the status quo at the time of signing and each state's trajectory. Do these suggest that deep agreements that make no provisions for enforcement play an important role in arms control?

There is no easy answer. On the one hand, we are inclined to simply include these agreements in the set of deep regulatory agreements that seem to require little enforcement. We do not claim that such agreements

---

[19] Ibid., 168.
[20] Goldblat 1993, 35.
[21] Arms Control and Disarmament Agency 1991.

do not exist – they clearly do – simply that many important prospective agreements require enforcement. Yet, it is not clear that these agreements are as deep as they appear to be. After all, the counterfactual – whether estimated on the basis of the status quo or the trajectory of year-to-year differences in arms production – represents the behavior of a political system that no longer exists. No one would gauge the depth of co-operation represented by the North Atlantic Treaty Organization (NATO) by comparing German behavior during wartime with German behavior after the war.

Managerialists might respond to this analysis by arguing that there are good reasons for believing that the connection between enforcement and depth of cooperation in the areas of international trade and the environment is different from that connection in security. Not only are many of the actors obviously different but security historically has been dominated by the realist logic that managerialists find so inadequate. We are not unsympathetic to this argument. The dynamics of cooperation may indeed differ across policy areas, just as they may vary within the same policy area over time. Nonetheless, at least with respect to the relationship between enforcement and depth of cooperation, the areas are not as different as one might imagine or as some might hope.

* * *

Perhaps the best test of the relationship between the depth of co-operation and enforcement can be found when we examine the history of a specific policy area in which regulations have become increasingly strict over time. The game theorist would predict that as regulatory rules tighten, the magnitude of the punishment needed to deter defection would also have to increase. Even if the system achieves some dynamic equilibrium, there should be some tangible sign of this under imperfect information.

If we discount the events that occurred in arms control after the downfall of the Soviet empire, the best examples of steadily increasing depth of cooperation are to be found in the areas of trade and European integration. In each case the role of enforcement has increased accordingly. Thomas Bayard and Kimberly Elliott, for example, conclude that the Uruguay Round has "substantially reduced many of the most egregious trade barriers around the world," but they also emphasize the enhanced ability of the World Trade Organization (WTO) to respond to and punish trade violations.[22] The WTO's procedures for dealing with

---

[22] The quotation is from Bayard and Elliott 1994, 336.

violations are now more automatic and less manipulable by individual parties. Time limits on the establishment of panels have now been set to nine months with the conclusion of panels within eighteen months, eliminating the inexorable delays under GATT. The principle of consensus voting in the adoption of panel reports has been reversed; previously, both parties to a dispute had an automatic veto on panel recommendations and retaliation. The new system provides for automatic adoption of panel reports, including approval for retaliation, unless a unanimous consensus rejects it. Previously, sanctions were utilized only once in GATT's history. Now, retaliation will be authorized automatically in the absence of a withdrawal of the offending practice or compensation to the defendant. We believe that the negotiating history of the WTO demonstrates that the more demanding levels of cooperation achieved by the Uruguay Round would not have been possible without its having reduced the likelihood of self-interested exploitation by member states.

* * *

The Causes and Cures of Noncompliance

The principal goal of the managerial school's investigation of compliance is to design more effective strategies for overcoming compliance problems in regulatory regimes. It is thus useful to shift our attention away from the likelihood of selection and the relationship between depth of cooperation and enforcement to why those compliance problems that do exist have occurred and how they might be remedied.

* * *

As the centerpiece of a sometimes problematic postwar trade regime, the GATT provides researchers with a wealth of material about the sources of noncompliance and the ability of its signatories to deal with them. Typical examples of GATT violations include EC payments and subsidies to oilseed producers, U.S. quantitative restrictions on sugar, Japanese import restrictions on beef and citrus, and Canadian export restrictions on unprocessed salmon and herring.[23] This is just a sample of the long list of commonly employed discriminatory techniques states have used to satisfy protectionist political elements in contravention of the GATT's rules and norms.

---

[23] See, respectively, Hudec 1993, 559 and 568; Bayard and Elliott 1994, 233; and Hudec 1993, 217–19.

Ambiguity about what constitutes noncompliance is a source of some of these problems, but no one denies a considerable number of violations indeed has occurred. The framers of the GATT were careful not to limit its policing or dispute settlement procedures to actions that were prohibited explicitly. Instead, they based enforcement provisions on the nullification or impairment of benefits that countries might expect. Indeed, Article 23 permits that settlement procedures be initiated:

If any contracting patty should consider that any benefit accruing to it directly or indirectly under this agreement is being nullified or impaired or that the attainment of any objective of the agreement is being impeded as the result of (a) the failure of another contracting party to carry out its obligations under this Agreement, or (b) the application by another contracting party of any measure, whether or not it conflicts with the provisions of this Agreement, or (c) the existence of any other situation.[24]

Although variation in expectations doubtless exists, few parties – including the states responsible – have argued that the EC subsidies of wheat flour or pasta or the Multifiber Agreement, which clearly violated the most-favored nation (MFN) principle, were based on confusion about the expectations of other trading partners.

Capacity limitations and uncontrollable social and economic changes rarely are cited as major determinants of violations. This is not so much because they are never present but because their effect is dwarfed by the most conspicuous cause of GATT noncompliance: the demands of domestic interest groups and the significant political benefits often associated with protection. Though GATT supporters would argue that any ill effects have been overshadowed by the GATT's positive achievement of reducing tariffs, the demand for protection is not being entirely ignored.

If the managerialists are wrong about the source of the GATT's problems, are they correct about the steps that appear to have reduced the rate of violations? The GATT provides a better laboratory for evaluating the managerialist claims about how compliance can best be improved than the Washington Treaty because unlike the latter, the GATT has evolved. Dispute resolution in the form of GATT panels undoubtedly has played some role, but certainly not an overwhelming one. Until recently, the panels moved at a ponderous pace and could easily be frustrated, especially by large states.[25] Far more successful have been

---

[24] The article is quoted in Bhagwati 1990, 105–6.
[25] Bayard and Elliott 1994, chaps. 3 and 4.

the rounds of multilateral negotiations that have operated over time to ensure that certain categories of disputes would reappear less often and that have extended the boundaries of the regime.

Nevertheless, enforcement also has played an important, if controversial, role in the operation and evolution of the GATT. Between 1974 and 1994, the United States imposed or publicly threatened retaliation in 50 percent of the cases that it took to the GATT. It did so independent of any GATT action and indeed even in five cases that Bayard and Elliott believe would have fallen under GATT jurisdiction.[26] Observers such as Robert Hudec credit increased enforcement and such "justified disobedience" of the GATT's dispute resolution process with being an important element in the process of GATT legal reform.[27] Others, like Alan Sykes, credit Section 301 and Super 301 unilateralism with having inspired – ironically given the claims of the managerial school – the enhanced dispute settlement procedures of the WTO.[28] As Bayard and Elliott conclude in their recent study, the "USTR [U.S. Trade Representative] generally wielded the Section 301 crowbar deftly and constructively, employing an aggressive unilateral strategy to induce support abroad for strengthening of the multilateral trade system."[29]

Even in the case of environmental regimes, the source of many of the managerialist examples, enforcement plays a greater role in successes than one is led to believe and its absence is conspicuous in some notable failures. For example, until very recently compliance with the weakly enforced agreements issued under eleven international fisheries commissions was highly problematic. Agreement ambiguity and social and economic changes were not a major source of these compliance problems. State capacity was more relevant since monitoring catches is costly, but scholars agree that the developed states that were often the principal violators could have coped with the monitoring issue if they believed it was in their interest to do so. The crux of the problem was the paradox of collective action: states saw little reason to pressure their fishermen to obey rules that other states were likely to flout.[30] The creation of the 200-mile exclusive economic zones was a dramatic improvement because it made enforcement much easier. Consequently, the role of enforcement is growing. For instance, in April 1995 a long-simmering

---

[26] Ibid., 70.
[27] Hudec 1990, 116.
[28] Sykes 1992.
[29] Bayard and Elliott 1994, 350.
[30] Peterson 1993, 280.

dispute over fishing rights in the North Atlantic among Canada, the EC, and the United States was resolved by an agreement that the *New York Times* reported, "could serve as a model for preserving endangered fish stocks throughout the world." The key to the accord, says the article, is "enforcement." The deal provides for elaborate verification measures and "imposes stiff fines and other penalties for violations."[31] The elaborate verification measures testify to the importance of transparency, but to believe that they would be effective in the absence of sanctions is naive. The benefits of cheating are too great to be offset by transparency alone.

The cost of ignoring the connection between enforcement and compliance when there is a substantial incentive to defect is well-illustrated by the Mediterranean Plan, considered by many to be an example of how epistemic communities have been able to play a significant role in effecting international cooperation. The Mediterranean Plan achieved consensus by eliminating any meaningful restrictions on dumping and providing no enforcement mechanism for those minimal targets and restrictions that were agreed to. As a result, it has been an embarrassing failure. Pollution has increased, dolphin hunting continues, and despite a European Union ban on drift nets longer than 2.5 kilometers, the rules are widely flouted.[32] The result has been a collapsing ecosystem in the Mediterranean.

The complementary relationship between transparency and enforcement is exemplified by a case that the managerialists believe to be an archetype of their approach. The case, described by Mitchell, involves the attempt by the International Maritime Consultative Organization (IMCO) and its successor, the International Maritime Organization (IMO), to regulate intentional oil pollution by oil tankers. From 1954 until 1978, the regime had little success and oil discharges were over three to thirty times the legal limit.[33] In 1978 the IMO switched strategies and with the negotiation of the International Convention for the Prevention of Pollution from Ships (MARPOL) began to regulate oil pollution by requiring tankers to be equipped with segregated ballast tanks (SBT). Despite the reduced cargo capacity and increased costs of equipping new and old oil tankers with the new equipment, and "despite strong incentives not to install SBT, tanker owners have done so as required. . . . Compliance is almost perfect."[34]

---

[31] *New York Times*, 17 April 1995, A2.
[32] "Dead in the Water," *New Scientist*, 4 February 1995.
[33] Mitchell 1994b, 439 in particular.
[34] Mitchell 1994a, 291.

Why was the equipment regime so much more effective at inducing compliance? It is not difficult to argue that increased enforcement was anything but irrelevant. We learn for example, that "the [equipment violations regime] provided the foundation for a noncompliance response system involving far more potent sanctions than those available for discharge violations."[35] Statements such as these suggest that while increased transparency was critical to the success of MARPOL, it was also critical that tankers lacking the International Oil Pollution Prevention (IOPP) certificate could be barred from doing business or detained in port.

The huge opportunity costs of having a ship barred from port or detained would force a tanker owner to think twice. . . . A single day of detention cost a tanker operator some $20,000 in opportunity costs, far higher than typical fines being imposed. . . . Detention provisions have altered behavior because they have had the virtue of imposing . . . high costs on the violator, making their use more credible and more potent . . . detention is a large enough penalty to deter a ship from committing future violations.[36]

ENFORCEMENT AND THE FUTURE OF COOPERATION

The significance of the cases discussed above lies not in their representing typical cases of noncompliance but in their salience and role as counterexamples to the unqualified prescriptions of the managerial theory. They should also make us skeptical of any contention that mixed-motive game-based cooperation (with its incentive for one or both sides to defect if they can get away with it) plays only an insignificant role in regulatory regimes. If some persistently have underestimated the value of interstate coordination vis-à-vis the solution of mixed-motive games, others should not commit the opposite error of pretending that the latter – and enforcement – is irrelevant. This is especially true in light of the likely evolution of regulatory cooperation.

Cooperation in arms, trade, and environmental regulation may begin with agreements that require little enforcement, but continued progress seems likely to depend on coping with an environment where defection presents significant benefits. It is not appropriate to counter skepticism about the success of treaties that require steep cuts in nontariff barriers, arms, or air pollution but that contain no enforcement provision with

[35] Ibid., 289.
[36] Ibid., 266 and 182–85.

statistics about the average rate of compliance with international agreements that require states to depart only slightly from what they would have done in the absence of an agreement. Techniques used to ensure compliance with an agreement covering interstate bank transfers cannot be counted on to ensure the success of the WTO's new rules governing intellectual property.

* * *

We do not mean to imply that the managerial model and the failure to embrace the idea that enforcement is often necessary are the only things preventing deeper cooperation. Obviously, states have reasons to refrain from vigorous enforcement. The question is whether it is better to cope with such reluctance by declaring that its importance has been vastly exaggerated or by trying to remedy matters.

We obviously prefer the second course of action, and we believe that the managerialists' vision of cooperation and compliance distracts political scientists from a host of problems that lie squarely within their area of expertise. For example, the vast majority of political economists would argue that the reason the GATT has encountered compliance problems and the reason why states have not obtained the cooperative benefits that would be possible through the use of more aggressive enforcement strategies involves an agency problem. Political leaders, if not the consumers who make up their constituencies, are left better off if they acquiesce to protectionist demands during those periods (e.g., recessions, following a technological breakthrough by foreign competition) when interest groups are likely to pay a premium that is greater than the electoral punishment they are likely to receive. Because the timing of such events is uncertain and most leaders are similarly vulnerable to such events, they deal with this situation by creating penalties for violations that are high enough to prevent constant defection but low enough to allow self-interested defection when circumstances demand it. Even leaders of states that are, for whatever reason, more committed to free trade are reluctant to increase the penalty for violations to a very high level because they suspect (probably correctly) that the "protectionist premium" is at times far greater than the cost of any credible punishment for violations. Thus, their hand is stayed not by any appreciation for the accidental nature of defection but by an appreciation for just how unaccidental it is.[37]

---

[37] Downs and Rocke 1995.

This is a dimension of political capacity that the managerial school rarely discusses and that is unlikely to be exorcized by technical assistance. It is, however, intimately connected to the design of both domestic political institutions and international regimes. One possible strategy is to restrict regime membership to states that will not have to defect very often. The idea is that whatever benefit is lost by excluding such states from the regime will be more than made up by permitting those that are included to set and also enforce a deeper level of cooperation – in this case a higher standard of free trade. This may be a reason, quite different from the large-n coordination concerns of collective action theory, why many deeply cooperative regimes have a limited number of members and why regimes with a large number of members tend to engage in only shallow cooperation. Is this trade-off real? Must states sometimes choose between aggressively addressing an environmental or trade problem and trying to create a community of states? We do not know. What we do know is that to ignore the issue on the basis of high compliance rates and the relative absence of enforcement is dangerously premature.

* * *

PART III

LEGALIZATION AND ITS LIMITS

Obligation: You have to

Precision - You know what you need to do

Delegation - Someone else gets to
make rules

6

The Concept of Legalization

Kenneth W. Abbott, Robert O. Keohane, Andrew Moravcsik, Anne-Marie Slaughter, and Duncan Snidal

* * *

"Legalization" refers to a particular set of characteristics that institutions may (or may not) possess. These characteristics are defined along three dimensions: obligation, precision, and delegation. *Obligation* means that states or other actors are bound by a rule or commitment or by a set of rules or commitments. Specifically, it means that they are *legally* bound by a rule or commitment in the sense that their behavior thereunder is subject to scrutiny under the general rules, procedures, and discourse of international law, and often of domestic law as well. *Precision* means that rules unambiguously define the conduct they require, authorize, or proscribe. *Delegation* means that third parties have been granted authority to implement, interpret, and apply the rules; to resolve disputes; and (possibly) to make further rules.

Each of these dimensions is a matter of degree and gradation, not a rigid dichotomy, and each can vary independently. Consequently, the concept of legalization encompasses a multidimensional continuum, ranging from the "ideal type" of legalization, where all three properties are maximized; to "hard" legalization, where all three (or at least obligation and delegation) are high; through multiple forms of partial or "soft" legalization involving different combinations of attributes; and finally to the complete absence of legalization, another ideal type. None of these dimensions – far less the full spectrum of legalization – can be fully operationalized. We do, however, consider in the section entitled "The Dimensions of Legalization" a number of techniques by which actors manipulate the elements of legalization; we also suggest several corresponding indicators of the strength or weakness of legal arrangements.

* * *

Our conception of legalization creates common ground for political scientists and lawyers by moving away from a narrow view of law as requiring enforcement by a coercive sovereign. This criterion has underlain much international relations thinking on the topic. Since virtually no international institution passes this standard, it has led to a widespread disregard of the importance of international law. But theoretical work in international relations has increasingly shifted attention away from the need for centralized enforcement toward other institutionalized ways of promoting cooperation.[1] In addition, the forms of legalization we observe at the turn of the millennium are flourishing in the absence of centralized coercion.

* * *

THE VARIABILITY OF LEGALIZATION

A central feature of our conception of legalization is the variability of each of its three dimensions, and therefore of the overall legalization of international norms, agreements, and regimes. This feature is illustrated in Figure 6.1. In Figure 6.1 each element of the definition appears as a continuum, ranging from the weakest form (the absence of legal obligation, precision, or delegation, except as provided by the background operation of the international legal system) at the left to the strongest or "hardest" form at the right.[2] Figure 6.1 also highlights the independence of these dimensions from each other: conceptually, at least the authors of a legal instrument can combine any level of obligation, precision, and delegation to produce an institution exactly suited to their specific needs. (In practice, as we shall explain, certain combinations are employed more frequently than others.)

---

[1] See the debate between the "managerial" perspective that emphasizes centralization but not enforcement, Chayes and Chayes 1995, and the "compliance" perspective that emphasizes enforcement but sees it as decentralized, Downs, Rocke, and Barsoom 1996.

[2] On the "obligation" dimension, *jus cogens* refers to an international legal rule – generally one of customary law, though perhaps one codified in treaty form – that creates an especially strong legal obligation, such that it cannot be overridden even by explicit agreement among states.

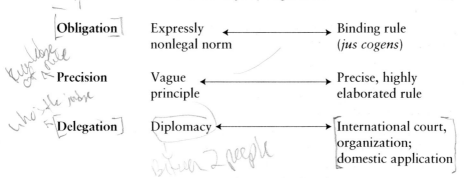

FIGURE 6.1. The dimensions of legalization.

It would be inappropriate to equate the right-hand end points of these dimensions with "law" and the left-hand end points with "politics," for politics continues (albeit in different forms) even where there is law. Nor should one equate the left-hand end points with the absence of norms or institutions; as the designations in Figure 6.1 suggest, both norms (such as ethical principles and rules of practice) and institutions (such as diplomacy and balance of power) can exist beyond these dimensions. Figure 6.1 simply represents the components of legal institutions.

Using the format of Figure 6.1, one can plot where a particular arrangement falls on the three dimensions of legalization. For example, the Agreement on Trade-Related Aspects of Intellectual Property (TRIPs), administered by the World Trade Organization (WTO), is strong on all three elements. The 1963 Treaty Banning Nuclear Weapons Tests in the Atmosphere, in Outer Space, and Under Water is legally binding and quite precise, but it delegates almost no legal authority. And the 1975 Final Act of the Helsinki Conference on Security and Cooperation in Europe was explicitly not legally binding and delegated little authority, though it was moderately precise.

The format of Figure 6.1 can also be used to depict variations in the degree of legalization between portions of an international instrument (John King Gamble, Jr. has made a similar internal analysis of the UN Convention on the Law of the Sea[3]) and within a given instrument or regime over time. The Universal Declaration of Human Rights, for example, was only minimally legalized (it was explicitly aspirational, not overly precise, and weakly institutionalized), but the human rights regime has evolved into harder forms over time. The International Covenant on Civil and Political Rights imposes binding legal obligations,

[3] Gamble 1985.

spells out concepts only adumbrated in the declaration, and creates (modest) implementing institutions.[4]

Table 6.1 further illustrates the remarkable variety of international legalization. Here, for concise presentation, we characterize obligation, precision, and delegation as either high or low. The eight possible combinations of these values are shown in Table 1; rows are arranged roughly in order of decreasing legalization, with legal obligation, a peculiarly important facet of legalization, weighted most heavily, delegation next, and precision given the least weight. A binary characterization sacrifices the continuous nature of the dimensions of legalization as shown in Figure 6.1 and makes it difficult to depict intermediate forms. Yet the table usefully demonstrates the range of institutional possibilities encompassed by the concept of legalization, provides a valuable shorthand for frequently used clusters of elements, and highlights the tradeoffs involved in weakening (or strengthening) particular elements.

Row I on this table corresponds to situations near the ideal type of full legalization, as in highly developed domestic legal systems. Much of European Community (EC) law belongs here. In addition, the WTO administers a remarkably detailed set of legally binding international agreements; it also operates a dispute-settlement mechanism, including an appellate tribunal with significant – if still not fully proven – authority to interpret and apply those agreements in the course of resolving particular disputes.

Rows II–III represent situations in which the character of law remains quite hard, with high legal obligation and one of the other two elements coded as "high." Because the combination of relatively imprecise rules and strong delegation is a common and effective institutional response to uncertainty, even in domestic legal systems (the Sherman Antitrust Act in the United States is a prime example), many regimes in row II should be considered virtually equal in terms of legalization to those in row I. Like the Sherman Act, for example, the original European Economic Community (EEC) rules of competition law (Articles 85 and 86 of the Treaty of Rome) were for the most part quite imprecise. Over time, however, the exercise of interpretive authority by the European courts and the promulgation of regulations by the Commission and Council produced a rich body of law. The 1987 Montreal Protocol on Substances that Deplete the Ozone Layer (row III), in contrast, created a quite precise and elaborate set of

---

[4] The declaration has also contributed to the evolution of customary international law, which can be applied by national courts as well as international organs, and has been incorporated into a number of national constitutions.

TABLE 6.1. *Forms of International Legalization*

Type	Obligation	Precision	Delegation	Examples
Ideal type:				
Hard law				
I	High	High	High	EC; WTO – TRIPs; European human rights convention; International Criminal Court
II	High	Low	High	EEC Antitrust, Art. 85–6; WTO – national treatment
III	High	High	Low	U.S.–Soviet arms control treaties; Montreal Protocol
IV	Low	High	High (moderate)	UN Committee on Sustainable Development (Agenda 21)
V	High	Low	Low	Vienna Ozone Convention; European Framework Convention on National Minorities
VI	Low	Low	High (moderate)	UN specialized agencies; World Bank; OSCE High Commissioner on National Minorities
VII	Low	High	Low	Helsinki Final Act; Nonbinding Forest Principles; technical standards
VIII	Low	Low	Low	Group of 7; spheres of influence; balance of power
Ideal type:				
Anarchy				

legally binding rules but did not delegate any significant degree of authority for implementing them. Because third-party interpretation and application of rules is so central to legal institutions, we consider this arrangement less highly legalized than those previously discussed.

As we move further down the table, the difficulties of dichotomizing and ordering our three dimensions become more apparent. For example, it is not instructive to say that arrangements in row IV are necessarily more legalized than those in row V; this judgment requires a more detailed specification of the forms of obligation, precision, and delegation used in each case. In some settings a strong legal obligation (such as the original Vienna Ozone Convention, row V) might be more legalized than a weaker obligation (such as Agenda 21, row IV), even if the latter were more precise and entailed stronger delegation. Furthermore, the relative significance of delegation vis-à-vis other dimensions becomes less clear at lower levels, since truly "high" delegation, including judicial or quasi-judicial authority, almost never exists together with low levels of legal obligation. The kinds of delegation typically seen in rows IV and VI are administrative or operational in nature (we describe this as "moderate" delegation in Table 6.1). Thus one might reasonably regard a precise but nonobligatory agreement (such as the Helsinki Final Act, row VII) as more highly legalized than an imprecise and nonobligatory agreement accompanied by modest administrative delegation (such as the High Commissioner on National Minorities of the Organization for Security and Cooperation in Europe, row VI).[5] The general point is that Table 6.1 should be read indicatively, not as a strict ordering.

The middle rows of Table 6.1 suggest a wide range of "soft" or intermediate forms of legalization. Here norms may exist, but they are difficult to apply as law in a strict sense. The 1985 Vienna Convention for the Protection of the Ozone Layer (row V), for example, imposed binding treaty obligations, but most of its substantive commitments were expressed in general, even hortatory language and were not connected to an institutional framework with independent authority. Agenda 21, adopted at the 1992 Rio Conference on Environment and Development (row IV), spells out highly elaborated norms on numerous issues but was clearly intended not to be legally binding and is implemented by relatively weak UN agencies. Arrangements like these are often used in settings where norms are contested and concerns for sovereign autonomy are strong, making higher levels of obligation, precision, or delegation unacceptable.

Rows VI and VII include situations where rules are not legally obligatory, but where states either accept precise normative formulations or delegate authority for implementing broad principles. States often delegate discretionary authority where judgments that combine concern for

---

[5] Interestingly, however, while the formal mandate of the OSCE High Commissioner on National Minorities related solely to conflict prevention and did not entail authority to implement legal (or nonlegal) norms, in practice the High Commissioner has actively promoted respect for both hard and soft legal norms. Ratner 2000.

professional standards with implicit political criteria are required, as with the International Monetary Fund (IMF), the World Bank, and the other international organizations in row VI. Arrangements such as those in row VII are sometimes used to administer coordination standards, which actors have incentives to follow provided they expect others to do so, as well as in areas where legally obligatory actions would be politically infeasible.

Examples of rule systems entailing the very low levels of legalization in row VIII include "balances of power" and "spheres of influence." These are not legal institutions in any real sense. The balance of power was characterized by rules of practice[6] and by arrangements for diplomacy, as in the Concert of Europe. Spheres of influence during the Cold War were imprecise, obligations were partly expressed in treaties but largely tacit, and little institutional framework existed to oversee them.

Finally, at the bottom of the table, we approach the ideal type of anarchy prominent in international relations theory. "Anarchy" is an easily misunderstood term of art, since even situations taken as extreme forms of international anarchy are in fact structured by rules – most notably rules defining national sovereignty – with legal or pre-legal characteristics. Hedley Bull writes of "the anarchical society" as characterized by institutions like sovereignty and international law as well as diplomacy and the balance of power.[7] Even conceptually, moreover, there is a wide gap between the weakest forms of legalization and the complete absence of norms and institutions.

Given the range of possibilities, we do not take the position that greater legalization, or any particular form of legalization, is inherently superior.[8] As Kenneth Abbott and Duncan Snidal argue in "Hard and Soft Law in International Governance" (this volume), institutional arrangements in the middle or lower reaches of Table 1 may best accommodate the diverse interests of concerned actors. ***

* * *

In the remainder of this article we turn to a more detailed explication of the three dimensions of legalization. We summarize the discussion in each section with a table listing several indicators of stronger or weaker legalization along the relevant dimension, with delegation subdivided into judicial and legislative/administrative components.

[6] Kaplan 1957.
[7] Bull 1977.
[8] Compare Goldstein, Kahler, Keohane, and Slaughter.

THE DIMENSIONS OF LEGALIZATION

Obligation

Legal rules and commitments impose a particular type of binding obligation on states and other subjects (such as international organizations). Legal obligations are different in kind from obligations resulting from coercion, comity, or morality alone. As discussed earlier, legal obligations bring into play the established norms, procedures, and forms of discourse of the international legal system.

The fundamental international legal principle of *pacta sunt servanda* means that the rules and commitments contained in legalized international agreements are regarded as obligatory, subject to various defenses or exceptions, and not to be disregarded as preferences change. They must be performed in good faith regardless of inconsistent provisions of domestic law. International law also provides principles for the interpretation of agreements and a variety of technical rules on such matters as formation, reservation, and amendments. Breach of a legal obligation is understood to create "legal responsibility," which does not require a showing of intent on the part of specific state organs.

* * *

Establishing a commitment as a legal rule invokes a particular form of discourse. Although actors may disagree about the interpretation or applicability of a set of rules, discussion of issues purely in terms of interests or power is no longer legitimate. * * *

Commitments can vary widely along the continuum of obligation, as summarized in Table 6.2. An example of a hard legal rule is Article 24 of the Vienna Convention on Diplomatic Relations, which reads in its entirety: "The archives and documents of the mission shall be inviolable at any time and wherever they may be." As a whole, this treaty reflects the intent of the parties to create legally binding obligations governed by international law. It uses the language of obligation; calls for the traditional legal formalities of signature, ratification, and entry into force; requires that the agreement and national ratification documents be registered with the UN; is styled a "Convention;" and states its relationship to preexisting rules of customary international law. Article 24 itself imposes an unconditional obligation in formal, even "legalistic" terms.

At the other end of the spectrum are instruments that explicitly negate any intent to create legal obligations. The best-known example is the 1975

TABLE 6.2. *Indicators of Obligation*

High
Unconditional obligation; language and other indicia of intent to be legally bound
Political treaty: implicit conditions on obligation
National reservations on specific obligations; contingent obligations and escape clauses
Hortatory obligations
Norms adopted without law-making authority; recommendations and guidelines
Explicit negation of intent to be legally bound
Low

Helsinki Final Act. By specifying that this accord could not be registered with the UN, the parties signified that it was not an "agreement... governed by international law." Other instruments are even more explicit: witness the 1992 "Non-Legally Binding Authoritative Statement of Principles for a Global Consensus" on sustainable management of forests. Many working agreements among national government agencies are explicitly non-binding.[9] Instruments framed as "recommendations" or "guidelines" – like the OECD Guidelines on Multinational Enterprises – are normally intended not to create legally binding obligations.[10]

* * *

Actors utilize many techniques to vary legal obligation between these two extremes, often creating surprising contrasts between form and substance. On the one hand, *** provisions of legally binding agreements frequently are worded to circumscribe their obligatory force. ***

* * *

On the other hand, a large number of instruments state seemingly unconditional obligations even though the institutions or procedures through which they were created have no direct law-creating authority! Many UN General Assembly declarations, for example, enunciate legal norms, though the assembly has no formal legislative power.[11]

---

[9] Zaring 1998.
[10] Although precise obligations are generally an attribute of hard legalization, these instruments use precise language to avoid legally binding character.
[11] See Chinkin 1989; and Gruchalla-Wesierski 1984.

*** Over time, even nonbinding declarations can shape the practices of states and other actors and their expectations of appropriate conduct, leading to the emergence of customary law or the adoption of harder agreements. Soft commitments may also implicate the legal principle of good faith compliance, weakening objections to subsequent developments. In many issue areas the legal implications of soft instruments are hotly contested. Supporters argue for immediate and universal legal effect under traditional doctrines (for example, that an instrument codifies existing customary law or interprets an organizational charter) and innovative ones (for example, that an instrument reflects an international "consensus" or "instant custom"). As acts of international governance, then, soft normative instruments have a finely wrought ambiguity.[12]

Precision

A precise rule specifies clearly and unambiguously what is expected of a state or other actor (in terms of both the intended objective and the means of achieving it) in a particular set of circumstances. In other words, precision narrows the scope for reasonable interpretation.[13] In Thomas Franck's terms, such rules are "determinate."[14] For a set of rules, precision implies not just that each rule in the set is unambiguous, but that the rules are related to one another in a noncontradictory way, creating a framework within which case-by-case interpretation can be coherently carried out.[15] Precise sets of rules are often, though by no means always, highly elaborated or dense, detailing conditions of

---

[12] Palmer 1992.

[13] A precise rule is not necessarily more constraining than a more general one. Its actual impact on behavior depends on many factors, including subjective interpretation by the subjects of the rule. Thus, a rule saying "drive slowly" might yield slower driving than a rule prescribing a speed limit of 55 miles per hour if the drivers in question would normally drive 50 miles per hour and understand "slowly" to mean 10 miles per hour slower than normal. (We are indebted to Fred Schauer for both the general point and the example.) In addition, precision can be used to define limits, exceptions, and loopholes that reduce the impact of a rule. Nevertheless, for most rules requiring or prohibiting particular conduct – and in the absence of precise delegation – generality is likely to provide an opportunity for deliberate self-interested interpretation, reducing the impact, or at least the potential for enforceable impact, on behavior.

[14] Franck 1990.

[15] Franck labels this collective property "coherence." We use the singular notion of precision to capture both the precision of a rule in isolation and its precision within a rule system.

application, spelling out required or proscribed behavior in numerous situations, and so on.

* * *

In highly developed legal systems, normative directives are often formulated as relatively precise "rules" ("do not drive faster than 50 miles per hour"), but many important directives are also formulated as relatively general "standards" ("do not drive recklessly").[16] The more "rule-like" a normative prescription, the more a community decides *ex ante* which categories of behavior are unacceptable; such decisions are typically made by legislative bodies. The more "standard-like" a prescription, the more a community makes this determination *ex post*, in relation to specific sets of facts; such decisions are usually entrusted to courts. Standards allow courts to take into account equitable factors relating to particular actors or situations, albeit at the sacrifice of some *ex ante* clarity.[17] Domestic legal systems are able to use standards like "due care" or the Sherman Act's prohibition on "conspiracies in restraint of trade" because they include well-established courts and agencies able to interpret and apply them (high delegation), developing increasingly precise bodies of precedent.

* * *

In most areas of international relations, judicial, quasi-judicial, and administrative authorities are less highly developed and infrequently used. In this thin institutional context, imprecise norms are, in practice, most often interpreted and applied by the very actors whose conduct they are intended to govern. In addition, since most international norms are created through the direct consent or practice of states, there is no centralized legislature to overturn inappropriate, self-serving interpretations. Thus, precision and elaboration are especially significant hallmarks of legalization at the international level.

Much of international law is in fact quite precise, and precision and elaboration appear to be increasing dramatically, as exemplified by the WTO trade agreements, environmental agreements like the Montreal (ozone) and Kyoto (climate change) Protocols, and the arms control treaties produced during the Strategic Arms Limitation Talks (SALT) and

---

[16] The standard regime definition encompasses three levels of precision: "principles," "norms," and "rules." Krasner 1983. This formulation reflects the fact that societies typically translate broad normative values into increasingly concrete formulations that decision-makers can apply in specific situations.

[17] Kennedy 1976.

TABLE 6.3. *Indicators of Precision*

High
Determinate rules: only narrow issues of interpretation
Substantial but limited issues of interpretation
Broad areas of discretion
"Standards": only meaningful with reference to specific situations
Impossible to determine whether conduct complies
Low

subsequent negotiations. Indeed, many modern treaties are explicitly designed to increase determinacy and narrow issues of interpretation through the "codification" and "progressive development" of customary law. Leading examples include the Vienna Conventions on the Law of Treaties and on Diplomatic Relations, and important aspects of the UN Convention on the Law of the Sea. * * *

Still, many treaty commitments are vague and general, in the ways suggested by Table 6.3.[18] The North American Free Trade Agreement side agreement on labor, for example, requires the parties to "provide for high labor standards." * * * Commercial treaties typically require states to create "favorable conditions" for investment and avoid "unreasonable" regulations. Numerous agreements call on states to "negotiate" or "consult," without specifying particular procedures. All these provisions create broad areas of discretion for the affected actors; indeed, many provisions are so general that one cannot meaningfully assess compliance, casting doubt on their legal force.[19] As Abbott and Snidal emphasize in their article,[20] such imprecision is not generally the result of a failure of legal draftsmanship, but a deliberate choice given the circumstances of domestic and international politics.

Imprecision is not synonymous with state discretion, however, when it occurs within a delegation of authority and therefore grants to an international body wider authority to determine its meaning. * * * A recent example makes the point clearly. At the 1998 Rome conference that

---

[18] Operationalizing the relative precision of different formulations is difficult, except in a gross sense. Gamble, for example, purports to apply a four-point scale of "concreteness" but does not characterize these points. Gamble 1985.

[19] The State Department's *Foreign Relations Manual* states that undertakings couched in vague or very general terms with no criteria for performance frequently reflect an intent not to be legally bound.

[20] Abbott and Snidal 2000.

approved a charter for an international criminal court, the United States sought to avoid any broad delegation of authority. Its proposal accordingly emphasized the need for "clear, precise, and specific definitions of each offense" within the jurisdiction of the court.[21]

Delegation

The third dimension of legalization is the extent to which states and other actors delegate authority to designated third parties – including courts, arbitrators, and administrative organizations – to implement agreements. The characteristic forms of legal delegation are third-party dispute settlement mechanisms authorized to interpret rules and apply them to particular facts (and therefore in effect to make new rules, at least interstitially) under established doctrines of international law. Dispute-settlement mechanisms are most highly legalized when the parties agree to binding third-party decisions on the basis of clear and generally applicable rules; they are least legalized when the process involves political bargaining between parties who can accept or reject proposals without legal justification.[22]

In practice, as reflected in Table 6.4a, dispute-settlement mechanisms cover an extremely broad range: from no delegation (as in traditional political decision making); through institutionalized forms of bargaining, including mechanisms to facilitate agreement, such as mediation (available within the WTO) and conciliation (an option under the Law of the Sea Convention); nonbinding arbitration (essentially the mechanism of the old GATT); binding arbitration (as in the U.S.-Iran Claims Tribunal); and finally to actual adjudication (exemplified by the European Court of Justice and Court of Human Rights, and the international criminal tribunals for Rwanda and the former Yugoslavia).

* * *

As one moves up the delegation continuum, the actions of decision-makers are increasingly governed, and legitimated, by rules. (Willingness to

---

[21] U.S. Releases Proposal on Elements of Crimes at the Rome Conference on the Establishment of an International Criminal Court, statement by James P. Rubin, U.S. State Department spokesperson, 22 June 1998, <secretary.state.gov/www/briefings/statements/1998/ps980622b.html>, accessed 16 February 1999.

[22] Law remains relevant even here. The UN Charter makes peaceful resolution of disputes a legal obligation, and general international law requires good faith in the conduct of negotiations. In addition, resolution of disputes by agreement can contribute to the growth of customary international law.

TABLE 6.4. *Indicators of Delegation*

---

a. Dispute resolution

High

    Courts: binding third-party decisions; general jurisdiction;
       direct private access; can interpret and supplement rules;
       domestic courts have jurisdiction

    Courts: jurisdiction, access or normative authority limited or consensual

    Binding arbitration

    Nonbinding arbitration

    Conciliation, mediation

    Institutionalized bargaining

    Pure political bargaining

Low

b. Rule making and implementation

High

    Binding regulations; centralized enforcement

    Binding regulations with consent or opt-out

    Binding internal policies; legitimation of decentralized enforcement

    Coordination standards

    Draft conventions; monitoring and publicity

    Recommendations; confidential monitoring

    Normative statements

    Forum for negotiations

Low

---

delegate often depends on the extent to which these rules are thought capable of constraining the delegated authority.) *** Delegation to third-party adjudicators is virtually certain to be accompanied by the adoption of rules of adjudication. The adjudicative body may then find it necessary to identify or develop rules of recognition and change, as it sorts out conflicts between rules or reviews the validity of rules that are the subject of dispute.

Delegation of legal authority is not confined to dispute resolution. As Table 6.4b indicates, a range of institutions – from simple consultative arrangements to fullfledged international bureaucracies – helps to elaborate imprecise legal norms, implement agreed rules, and facilitate enforcement.

                    * * *

Legalized delegation, especially in its harder forms, introduces new actors and new forms of politics into interstate relations. Actors with delegated legal authority have their own interests, the pursuit of which may be more or less successfully constrained by conditions on the grant of authority and concomitant surveillance by member states. Transnational coalitions of nonstate actors also pursue their interests through influence or direct participation at the supranational level, often producing greater divergence from member state concerns. Deciding disputes, adapting or developing new rules, implementing agreed norms, and responding to rule violations all engender their own type of politics, which helps to restructure traditional interstate politics.

CONCLUSION

Highly legalized institutions are those in which rules are obligatory on parties through links to the established rules and principles of international law, in which rules are precise (or can be made precise through the exercise of delegated authority), and in which authority to interpret and apply the rules has been delegated to third parties acting under the constraint of rules. There is, however, no bright line dividing legalized from nonlegalized institutions. Instead, there is an identifiable continuum from hard law through varied forms of soft law, each with its individual mix of characteristics, to situations of negligible legalization.

This continuum presupposes that legalized institutions are to some degree differentiated from other types of international institutions, a differentiation that may have methodological, procedural, cultural, and informational dimensions.[23] Although mediators may, for example, be free to broker a bargain based on the "naked preferences" of the parties,[24] legal processes involve a discourse framed in terms of reason, interpretation, technical knowledge, and argument, often followed by deliberation and judgment by impartial parties. Different actors have access to the process, and they are constrained to make arguments different from those they would make in a nonlegal context. Legal decisions, too, must be based on reasons applicable to all similarly situated litigants, not merely the parties to the immediate dispute.

*** Our conception of legalization reflects a general theme: *** the rejection of a rigid dichotomy between "legalization" and "world politics." Law and politics are intertwined at all levels of legalization. One result of this interrelationship, reflected in many of the articles in this volume, is

[23] Schauer and Wise 1997.
[24] Sunstein 1986.

considerable difficulty in identifying the causal effects of legalization. Compliance with rules occurs for many reasons other than their legal status. Concern about reciprocity, reputation, and damage to valuable state institutions, as well as other normative and material considerations, all play a role. Yet it is reasonable to assume that most of the time, legal and political considerations combine to influence behavior.

At one extreme, even "pure" political bargaining is shaped by rules of sovereignty and other background legal norms. At the other extreme, even international adjudication takes place in the "shadow of politics": interested parties help shape the agenda and initiate the proceedings; judges are typically alert to the political implications of possible decisions, seeking to anticipate the reactions of political authorities. Between these extremes, where most international legalization lies, actors combine and invoke varying degrees of obligation, precision, and delegation to create subtle blends of politics and law. In all these settings, to paraphrase Clausewitz, "law is a continuation of political intercourse, with the addition of other means."

7

Legalized Dispute Resolution: Interstate and Transnational

Robert O. Keohane, Andrew Moravcsik, and Anne-Marie Slaughter

International courts and tribunals are flourishing. Depending on how these bodies are defined, they now number between seventeen and forty.[1] In recent years we have witnessed the proliferation of new bodies and a strengthening of those that already exist. "When future international legal scholars look back at . . . the end of the twentieth century," one analyst has written, "they probably will refer to the enormous expansion of the international judiciary as the single most important development of the post–Cold War age."[2]

These courts and tribunals represent a key dimension of legalization. Instead of resolving disputes through institutionalized bargaining, states choose to delegate the task to third-party tribunals charged with applying general legal principles. Not all of these tribunals are created alike, however. In particular, we distinguish between two ideal types of international dispute resolution: interstate and transnational. Our central argument is that the formal legal differences between interstate and transnational dispute resolution have significant implications for the politics of dispute settlement and therefore for the effects of legalization in world politics.

Interstate dispute resolution is consistent with the view that public international law comprises a set of rules and practices governing

---

[1] Romano 1999, 723–28. By the strictest definition, there are currently seventeen permanent, independent international courts. If we include some bodies that are not courts, but instead quasi-judicial tribunals, panels, and commissions charged with similar functions, the total rises to over forty. If we include historical examples and bodies negotiated but not yet in operation, the total rises again to nearly one hundred.

[2] Ibid., 709.

interstate relationships. Legal resolution of disputes, in this model, takes place between states conceived of as unitary actors. States are the subjects of international law, which means that they control access to dispute resolution tribunals or courts. They typically designate the adjudicators of such tribunals. States also implement, or fail to implement, the decisions of international tribunals or courts. Thus in interstate dispute resolution, states act as gatekeepers both to the international legal process and from that process back to the domestic level.

In transnational dispute resolution, by contrast, access to courts and tribunals and the subsequent enforcement of their decisions are legally insulated from the will of individual national governments. These tribunals are therefore more open to individuals and groups in civil society. In the pure ideal type, states lose their gatekeeping capacities; in practice, these capacities are attenuated. This loss of state control, whether voluntarily or unwittingly surrendered, creates a range of opportunities for courts and their constituencies to set the agenda.

*** It is helpful to locate our analysis in a broader context. *** Legalization is a form of institutionalization distinguished by obligation, precision, and delegation. Our analysis applies primarily when obligation is high.[3] Precision, on the other hand, is not a defining characteristic of the situations we examine. We examine the decisions of bodies that interpret and apply rules, regardless of their precision. Indeed, such bodies may have greater latitude when precision is low than when it is high.[4] Our focus is a third dimension of legalization: delegation of authority to courts and tribunals designed to resolve international disputes through the application of general legal principles.[5]

Three dimensions of delegation are crucial to our argument: independence, access, and embeddedness. As we explain in the first section, independence specifies the extent to which formal legal arrangements ensure that adjudication can be rendered impartially with respect to concrete state interests. Access refers to the ease with which parties other than states can influence the tribunal's agenda. Embeddedness denotes the extent to which dispute resolution decisions can be implemented without governments having to take actions to do so. We define low independence, access, and embeddedness as the ideal type of interstate dispute resolution and high independence, access, and embeddedness as the ideal type

---

[3] Abbott et al., 119 (this book) tab 1, types I–III and V.
[4] Hence we do not exclude types II and V (Abbott et al., tab. 1, 119) from our purview.
[5] See Abbott et al., 119 (this book).

of transnational dispute resolution. Although admittedly a simplification, this conceptualization helps us to understand why the behavior and impact of different tribunals, such as the International Court of Justice (ICJ) and the European Court of Justice (ECJ), have been so different.

In the second section we seek to connect international politics, international law, and domestic politics. Clearly the power and preferences of states influence the behavior both of governments and of dispute resolution tribunals: international law operates in the shadow of power. Yet within that political context, we contend that institutions for selecting judges, controlling access to dispute resolution, and legally enforcing the judgments of international courts and tribunals have a major impact on state behavior. The formal qualities of legal institutions empower or disempower domestic political actors other than national governments. Compared to interstate dispute resolution, transnational dispute resolution tends to generate more litigation, jurisprudence more autonomous of national interests, and an additional source of pressure for compliance. In the third section we argue that interstate and transnational dispute resolution generate divergent longer-term dynamics. Transnational dispute resolution seems to have an inherently more expansionary character; it provides more opportunities to assert and establish new legal norms, often in unintended ways.

This article should be viewed as exploratory rather than an attempt to be definitive. Throughout, we use ideal types to illuminate a complex subject, review suggestive though not conclusive evidence, and highlight opportunities for future research. We offer our own conjectures at various points as to useful starting points for that research but do not purport to test definitive conclusions.

A TYPOLOGY OF DISPUTE RESOLUTION

Much dispute resolution in world politics is highly institutionalized. Established, enduring rules apply to entire classes of circumstances and cannot easily be ignored or modified when they become inconvenient to one participant or another in a specific case. In this article we focus on institutions in which dispute resolution has been delegated to a third-party tribunal charged with applying designated legal rules and principles. This act of delegation means that disputes must be framed as "cases" between two or more parties, at least one of which, the defendant, will be a state or an individual acting on behalf of a state. (Usually, states are the defendants, so we refer to defendants as "states." However, individuals may also be prosecuted by international tribunals, as in the proposed International Criminal Court and various war crimes tribunals.[6]) The identity of the plaintiff depends on the design of the dispute resolution mechanism. Plaintiffs can be other states or private parties – individuals or non-governmental organizations (NGOs) – specifically designated to monitor and enforce the obligatory rules of the regime.

We turn now to our three explanatory variables: independence, access, and embeddedness. We do not deny that the patterns of delegation we observe may ultimately have their origins in the power and interests of major states, as certain strands of liberal and realist theory claim. Nevertheless, our analysis here takes these sources of delegation as given and emphasizes how formal legal institutions empower groups and individuals other than national governments.[7]

Independence: Who Controls Adjudication?

The variable *independence* measures the extent to which adjudicators for an international authority charged with dispute resolution are able to deliberate and reach legal judgments independently of national governments. In other words, it assesses the extent to which adjudication is rendered impartially with respect to concrete state interests in a specific case. The traditional international model of dispute resolution in law and politics places pure control by states at one end of a continuum. Disputes are resolved by the agents of the interested parties themselves. Each side offers its own interpretation of the rules and their applicability to the case at issue; disagreements are resolved through institutionalized interstate bargaining. There are no permanent rules of procedure or legal precedent, although in legalized dispute resolution, decisions must be consistent with international law. Institutional rules may also influence the outcome by determining the conditions – interpretive standards, voting requirements, selection – under which authoritative decisions are made.[8] Even where

---

[6] We do not discuss the interesting case of international criminal law here. See Bass 1998.

[7] This central focus on variation in the political representation of social groups, rather than interstate strategic interaction, is the central tenet of theories of international law that rest on liberal international relations theory. Slaughter 1995a. Our approach is thus closely linked in this way to republican liberal studies of the democratic peace, the role of independent executives and central banks in structuring international economic policy coordination, and the credibility of commitments by democratic states more generally. See Keohane and Nye 1977; Moravcsik 1997; Doyle 1983a,b; and Goldstein 1996.

[8] Helfer and Slaughter 1997.

legal procedures are established, individual governments may have the right to veto judgments, as in the UN Security Council and the old General Agreement on Tariffs and Trade (GATT).

Movement along the continuum away from this traditional interstate mode of dispute resolution measures the nature and tightness of the political constraints imposed on adjudicators. The extent to which members of an international tribunal are independent reflects the extent to which they can free themselves from at least three categories of institutional constraint: selection and tenure, legal discretion, and control over material and human resources.

* * *

Selection and tenure rules vary widely. Many international institutions maintain tight national control on dispute resolution through selection and tenure rules.[9] Some institutions – including the UN, International Monetary Fund, NATO, and the bilateral Soviet–U.S. arrangements established by the Strategic Arms Limitation Treaty (SALT) – establish no authoritative third-party adjudicators whatsoever. The regime creates instead a set of decision-making rules and procedures, a forum for interstate bargaining, within which subsequent disputes are resolved by national representatives serving at the will of their governments. In other institutions, however, such as the EU, governments can name representatives, but those representatives are assured long tenure and may enjoy subsequent prestige in the legal world independent of their service to individual states. In first-round dispute resolution in GATT and the World Trade Organization (WTO), groups of states select a stable of experts who are then selected on a case-by-case basis by the parties and the secretariat, whereas in ad hoc international arbitration, the selection is generally controlled by the disputants and the tribunal is constituted for a single case.

In still other situations – particularly in authoritarian countries – judges may be vulnerable to retaliation when they return home after completing their tenure; even in liberal democracies, future professional advancement may be manipulated by the government.[10] The legal basis of some international dispute resolution mechanisms, such as the European

---

[9] Even less independent are ad hoc and arbitral tribunals designed by specific countries for specific purposes. The Organization for Security and Cooperation in Europe, for example, provides experts, arbiters, and conciliators for ad hoc dispute resolution. Here we consider only permanent judicial courts. See Romano 1999, 711–13.

[10] For a domestic case of judicial manipulation, see Ramseyer and Rosenbluth 1997.

TABLE 7.1. *The Independence Continuum: Selection and Tenure*

Level of independence	Selection method and tenure	International court or tribunal
Low	Direct representatives, perhaps with single-country veto	UN Security Council
Moderate	Disputants control ad hoc selection of third-party judges	PCA
	Groups of states control selection of third-party judges	ICJ, GATT, WTO
High	Individual governments appoint judges with long tenure	ECJ
	Groups of states select judges with long tenure	ECHR, IACHR

Court of Human Rights (ECHR), requires oversight by semi-independent supranational bodies. The spectrum of legal independence as measured by selection and tenure rules is shown in Table 7.1.

Legal discretion, the second criterion for judicial independence, refers to the breadth of the mandate granted to the dispute resolution body. Some legalized dispute resolution bodies must adhere closely to treaty texts; but the ECJ, as Karen Alter describes,[11] has asserted the supremacy of European Community (EC) law without explicit grounding in the treaty text or the intent of national governments. More generally, institutions for adjudication arise, as Abbott and Snidal argue,[12] under conditions of complexity and uncertainty, which render interstate contracts necessarily incomplete. Adjudication is thus more than the act of applying precise standards and norms to a series of concrete cases within a precise mandate; it involves interpreting norms and resolving conflicts between competing norms in the context of particular cases. When seeking to overturn all but the most flagrantly illegal state actions, litigants and courts must inevitably appeal to particular interpretations of such ambiguities. Other things being equal, the wider the range of considerations the body can legitimately consider and the greater the uncertainty concerning the proper interpretation or norm in a given case, the more potential legal independence it possesses. * * *

---

[11] Karen J. Alter, "The European Union's Legal System and Domestic Policy Spillover or Backlash?" *International Organization* 54, 3 (Summer 2000) p. 489.

[12] Kenneth W. Abbott and Duncan Snidal, "Hard and Soft Law in International Governance", International Organization 54, 3 (Summer 2000), p. 421.

The third criterion for judicial independence, *financial and human resources,* refers to the ability of judges to process their caseloads promptly and effectively.[13] Such resources are necessary for processing large numbers of complaints and rendering consistent, high-quality decisions. They can also permit a court or tribunal to develop a factual record independent of the state litigants before them and to publicize their decisions. This is of particular importance for human rights courts, which seek to disseminate information and mobilize political support on behalf of those who would otherwise lack direct domestic access to effective political representation.[14] Many human rights tribunals are attached to commissions capable of conducting independent inquiries. The commissions of the Inter-American and UN systems, for example, have been active in pursuing this strategy, often conducting independent, on-site investigations.[15] Indeed, inquiries by the Inter-American Commission need not be restricted to the details of a specific case, though a prior petition is required. In general, the greater the financial and human resources available to courts and the stronger the commissions attached to them, the greater their legal independence.

In sum, the greater the freedom of a dispute resolution body from the control of individual member states over selection and tenure, legal discretion, information, and financial and human resources, the greater its legal independence.

Access: Who Has Standing?

Access, like independence, is a variable. From a legal perspective, access measures the range of social and political actors who have legal standing to submit a dispute to be resolved; from a political perspective, access measures the range of those who can set the agenda. Access is particularly important with respect to courts and other dispute resolution bodies because, in contrast to executives and legislatures, they are "passive" organs of government unable to initiate action by unilaterally seizing a dispute. Access is measured along a continuum between two extremes. At one extreme, if no social or political actors can submit disputes, dispute resolution institutions are unable to act; at the other, anyone with a legitimate grievance directed at government policy can easily and

---

[13] Helfer and Slaughter 1997.
[14] Keck and Sikkink 1998.
[15] Farer 1998.

inexpensively submit a complaint. In-between are situations in which individuals can bring their complaints only by acting through governments, convincing governments to "espouse" their claim as a state claim against another government, or by engaging in a costly procedure. This continuum of access can be viewed as measuring the "political transaction costs" to individuals and groups in society of submitting their complaint to an international dispute resolution body. The more restrictive the conditions for bringing a claim to the attention of a dispute resolution body, the more costly it is for actors to do so.

Near the higher-cost, restrictive end, summarized in Table 7.2, fall purely interstate tribunals, such as the GATT and WTO panels, the Permanent Court of Arbitration, and the ICJ, in which only member states may file suit against one another. Although this limitation constrains access to any dispute resolution body by granting one or more governments a formal veto, it does not permit governments to act without constraint. Individuals and groups may still wield influence, but they must do so by domestic means. Procedures that are formally similar in this sense may nonetheless generate quite different implications for access, depending on principal-agent relationships in domestic politics. Whereas individuals and groups may have the domestic political power to ensure an ongoing if indirect role in both the decision to initiate proceedings and the resulting argumentation, state-controlled systems are likely to be more restrictive than direct litigation by individuals and groups.

* * *

Within these constraints, GATT/WTO panels and the ICJ differ in their roles toward domestic individuals and groups. In the GATT and now the WTO, governments nominally control access to the legal process, yet in practice injured industries are closely involved in both the initiation and the conduct of the litigation by their governments, at least in the United States. * * * In the ICJ, by contrast, individual access is more costly. The ICJ hears cases in which individuals may have a direct interest (such as the families of soldiers sent to fight in another country in what is allegedly an illegal act of interstate aggression). However, these individuals usually have little influence over a national government decision to initiate interstate litigation or over the resulting conduct of the proceedings. As in the WTO individuals are unable to file suit against their own government before the ICJ. * * *

Near the permissive end of the spectrum is the ECJ. Individuals may ultimately be directly represented before the international tribunal, though

TABLE 7.2. *The Access Continuum: Who Has Standing?*

Level of access	Who has standing	International court or tribunal
Low	Both states must agree	PCA
Moderate	Only a single state can file suit	ICJ
	Single state files suit, influenced by social actors	WTO, GATT
High	Access through national courts	ECJ
	Direct individual (and sometimes group) access if domestic remedies have been exhausted	ECHR, IACHR

the decision to bring the case before it remains in the hands of a domestic judicial body. Under Article 177 of the Treaty of Rome, national courts may independently refer a case before them to the ECJ if the case raises questions of European law that the national court does not feel competent to resolve on its own. The ECJ answers the specific question(s) presented and sends the case back to the national court for disposition of the merits of the dispute. Litigants themselves can suggest such a referral to the national court, but the decision to refer lies ultimately within the national court's discretion. Whether the interests involved are narrow and specific – as in the landmark *Cassis de Dijon* case over the importation of French specialty liquors into Germany – or broad, the cost of securing such a referral is the same. As Karen Alter shows in her article,[16] different national courts have sharply different records of referral, but over time national courts as a body have become increasingly willing to refer cases to the ECJ. These referrals may involve litigation among private parties rather than simply against a public authority.[17]

Also near the low-cost end of the access spectrum lie formal human rights enforcement systems, including the ECHR, the IACHR, the African Convention on Human and People's Rights, and the UN's International Covenant on Civil and Political Rights. Since the end of World War II we have witnessed a proliferation of international tribunals

---

[16] Karen J. Alter, "The European Union's Legal System and Domestic Policy: Spillover or Backlash?", *International Organization* 54, 3 (Summer 2000), p. 489.

[17] It therefore remains unclear, on balance, whether the EC or the ECHR provides more ready access. Whereas the EC system under Article 177 allows only domestic courts, not individuals, to refer cases, the EC does not require, as does the ECHR and all other human rights courts, that domestic remedies be exhausted.

TABLE 7.3. *The Embeddedness Continuum: Who Enforces the Law?*

Level of embeddedness	Who enforces	International court or tribunal
Low	Individual governments can veto implementation of legal judgment	GATT
Moderate	No veto, but no domestic legal enforcement; most human rights systems	WTO, ICJ
High	International norms enforced by domestic courts	EC, incorporated human rights norms under ECHR, national systems in which treaties are self-executing or given direct effect

to which individuals have direct access, though subject to varying restrictions. * * *

* * *

Legal Embeddedness: Who Controls Formal Implementation?

* * * Implementation and compliance in international disputes are problematic to a far greater degree than they are in well-functioning, domestic rule-of-law systems. The political significance of delegating authority over dispute resolution therefore depends in part on the degree of control exercised by individual governments over the legal promulgation and implementation of judgments. State control is affected by formal legal arrangements along a continuum that we refer to as embeddedness.

The spectrum of domestic embeddedness, summarized in Table 7.3, runs from strong control over promulgation and implementation of judgments by individual national governments to very weak control. At one extreme, that of strong control, lie systems in which individual litigants can veto the promulgation of a judgment *ex post*. In the old GATT system, the decisions of dispute resolution panels had to be affirmed by consensus, affording individual litigants an *ex post* veto. Under the less tightly controlled WTO, by contrast, disputes among member governments are resolved through quasi-judicial panels whose judgments are binding unless *reversed* by unanimous vote of the Dispute

Settlement Body, which consists of one representative from each WTO member state.

Most international legal systems fall into the same category as the WTO system; namely, states are bound by international law to comply with judgments of international courts or tribunals, but no domestic legal mechanism assures legal implementation. If national executives and legislatures fail to take action because of domestic political opposition or simply inertia, states simply incur a further international legal obligation to repair the damage. In other words, if an international tribunal rules that state *A* has illegally intervened in state *B*'s internal affairs and orders state *A* to pay damages, but the legislature of state *A* refuses to appropriate the funds, state *B* has no recourse at international law except to seek additional damages. Alternatively, if state *A* signs a treaty obligating it to change its domestic law to reduce the level of certain pollutants it is emitting, and the executive branch is unsuccessful in passing legislation to do so, state *A* is liable to its treaty partners at international law but cannot be compelled to take the action it agreed to take in the treaty.

* * *

At the other end of the spectrum, where the control of individual governments is most constrained by the embeddedness of international norms, lie systems in which autonomous national courts can enforce international judgments against their own governments. The most striking example of this mode of enforcement is the EC legal system. Domestic courts in every member state recognize that EC law is superior to national law (supremacy) and that it grants individuals rights on the basis of which they can litigate (direct effect). When the ECJ issues advisory opinions to national courts under the Article 177 procedure described in detail in Karen Alter's article,[18] national courts tend to respect them, even when they clash with the precedent set by higher national courts. These provisions are nowhere stated explicitly in the Treaty of Rome but have been successfully "constitutionalized" by the ECJ over the past four decades.[19] The European Free Trade Association (EFTA) court system established in 1994 permits such referrals as well, though, unlike the Treaty of Rome, it neither legally obliges domestic courts to refer nor

---

[18] Karen J. Alter, "The European Union's Legal System and Domestic Policy: Spillover or Backlash?", *International Organization* 54, 3 (Summer 2000), p. 489.
[19] Weiler 1991.

TABLE 7.4. *Legal Characteristics of International Courts and Tribunals*

International court or tribunals	Legal characteristics		
	Independence	Access	Embeddedness
ECJ	High	High	High[f]
ECHR, since 1999	High	High	Low to high[c]
ECHR, before 1999	Moderate to high[a]	Low to high[b]	Low to high[c]
IACHR	Moderate to high[a]	High	Moderate
WTO panels	Moderate	Low to moderate[d]	Moderate
ICJ	Moderate	Low to moderate[d]	Moderate
GATT panels	Moderate	Low to moderate[d]	Low
PCA	Low to moderate	Low[e]	Moderate
UN Security Council	Low	Low to moderate[g]	Low

[a] Depends on whether government recognizes optional clauses for compulsory jurisdiction of the court.
[b] Depends on whether government accepts optional clause for individual petition.
[c] Depends on whether domestic law incorporates or otherwise recognized the treaty.
[d] Depends on mobilization and domestic access rules for interest groups concerned.
[e] Both parties must consent. Recent rule changes have begun to recognize nonstate actors.
[f] Embeddedness is not a formal attribute of the regime but the result of the successful assertion of legal sovereignty.
[g] Permanent members of the Security Council can veto; nonmembers cannot.
Source: Sands et al. 1999.

legally binds the domestic court to apply the result. Domestic courts do nonetheless appear to enforce EFTA court decisions.[20]

* * *

Two Ideal Types: Interstate and Transnational Dispute Resolution

The three characteristics of international dispute resolution – independence, access, and embeddedness – are closely linked.*** The characteristics of the major courts in the world today are summarized in Table 7.4, which reveals a loose correlation across categories. Systems with higher values on one dimension have a greater probability of having higher values in the other dimensions. This finding suggests that very high values on one dimension cannot fully compensate for low values on another.

[20] Sands, Mackenzie, and Shany 1999, 148.

Strong support for independence, access, or embeddedness without strong support for the others undermines the effectiveness of a system.

Combining these three dimensions creates two ideal types. In one ideal type – interstate dispute resolution – adjudicators, agenda, and enforcement are all subject to veto by individual national governments. Individual states decide who judges, what they judge, and how the judgment is enforced. At the other end of the spectrum, adjudicators, agenda, and enforcement are all substantially independent of individual and collective pressure from national governments. We refer to this ideal type as transnational dispute resolution.[21] In this institutional arrangement, of which the EU and ECHR are the most striking examples, judges are insulated from national governments, societal individuals and groups control the agenda, and the results are implemented by an independent national judiciary. In the remainder of this article we discuss the implications of variation along the continuum from interstate to transnational dispute resolution for the nature of, compliance with, and evolution of international jurisprudence.

In discussing this continuum, however, let us not lose sight of the fact that *values on the three dimensions move from high to low at different rates*. Table 7.4 reveals that high levels of independence and access appear to be more common than high levels of embeddedness, and, though the relationship is weaker, a high level of independence appears to be slightly more common than a high level of access. In other words, between those tribunals that score high or low on all three dimensions, there is a significant intermediate range comprising tribunals with high scores on independence and/or access but not on the others.[22] Among those international legal institutions that score high on independence and access but are not deeply embedded in domestic legal systems are some international human rights institutions. Among those institutions that score high on independence but not on access or embeddedness are GATT/WTO multilateral trade institutions and the ICJ.

---

[21] We use the term "transnational" to capture the individual to individual or individual to state nature of many of the cases in this type of dispute resolution. However, many of the tribunals in this category, such as the ECJ and the ECHR, can equally be described as "supranational" in the sense that they sit "above" the nation-state and have direct power over individuals and groups within the state. One of the authors has previously used the label "supranational" to describe these tribunals (Helfer and Slaughter 1997); no significance should be attached to the shift in terminology here.

[22] Not surprisingly, domestic legal embeddedness is less common than widespread domestic access, since the former is a prerequisite for the latter.

THE POLITICS OF LITIGATION AND COMPLIANCE: FROM
INTERSTATE TO JUDICIAL POLITICS

Declaring a process "legalized" does not abolish politics. Decisions about the degree of authority of a particular tribunal, and access to it, are themselves sites of political struggle. The sharpest struggles are likely to arise *ex ante* in the bargaining over a tribunal's establishment; but other opportunities for political intervention may emerge during the life of a tribunal, perhaps as a result of its own constitutional provisions. Form matters, however. The characteristic politics of litigation and compliance are very different under transnational dispute resolution than under interstate dispute resolution. In this section we explicate these differences and propose some tentative conjectures linking our three explanatory variables to the politics of dispute resolution.

The Interstate and Transnational Politics of Judicial Independence

* * * As legal systems move from interstate dispute resolution toward the more independent judicial selection processes of transnational dispute resolution, we expect to observe greater judicial autonomy – defined as the willingness and ability to decide disputes against national governments. Other things being equal, the fewer opportunities national governments have to influence the selection of judges, the available information, the support or financing of the court, and the precise legal terms on which the court can decide, the weaker is their likely influence over the decisions of an international tribunal.

* * *

The Interstate and Transnational Politics of Access

What are the political implications of movement from low access (interstate dispute resolution) to high access (transnational dispute resolution)? Our central contention is that we are likely to observe, broadly speaking, a different politics of access as we move toward transnational dispute resolution – where individuals, groups, and courts can appeal or refer cases to international tribunals. As the actors involved become more diverse, the likelihood that cases will be referred increases, as does the likelihood that such cases will challenge national governments – in particular, the national government of the plaintiff. The link between formal access and real political power is not obvious. States might still manipulate access to judicial process regarding both interstate and transnational litigation by establishing stringent procedural rules, bringing political pressure to bear on potential or actual litigants, or simply carving out self-serving exceptions to the agreed jurisdictional scheme. ***

Access to classic arbitral tribunals, such as those constituted under the Permanent Court of Arbitration, requires the consent of both states. *** Slightly more constraining arrangements are found in classic interstate litigation before the Permanent Court of International Justice in the 1920s and 1930s, the ICJ since 1945, and the short-lived Central American Court of Justice. In these systems, a single state decides when and how to sue, even if it is suing on behalf of an injured citizen or group of citizens. The state formally "espouses" the claim of its national(s), at which point the individual's rights terminate (unless entitled to compensation as a domestic legal or constitutional matter), as does any control over or even say in the litigation strategy. The government is thus free to prosecute the claim vigorously or not at all, or to engage in settlement negotiations for a sum far less than the individual litigant(s) might have found acceptable. Such negotiations can resemble institutionalized interstate bargaining more than a classic legal process in which the plaintiff decides whether to continue the legal struggle or to settle the case.

*   *   *

Although in interstate dispute resolution states decide when and whether to sue other states, they cannot necessarily control whether they are sued. If they are sued, whether any resulting judgments can be enforced depends both on their acceptance of compulsory jurisdiction and, where the costs of complying with a judgment are high, on their willingness to obey an adverse ruling. ***

*   *   *

The de facto system is one in which most states, like the United States, reserve the right to bring specific cases to the ICJ or to be sued in specific cases as the result of an ad hoc agreement with other parties to a dispute of specific provisions in a bilateral or multilateral treaty. This system ensures direct control over access to the ICJ by either requiring all the parties to a dispute to agree both to third-party intervention and to choose the ICJ as the third party, or by allowing two or more states to craft a specific submission to the court's jurisdiction in a limited category of disputes arising from the specific subject matter of a treaty.[23] ***

---

[23] Rosenne 1995.

TABLE 7.5. *Access Rules and Dockets of International Courts and Tribunals*

Level of access	International court or tribunal	Average annual number of cases since founding
Low	PCA	0.3
Medium	ICJ	1.7
	GATT	4.4
	WTO	30.5
High	Old ECHR	23.9
	EC	100.1

Source: Sands et al. 1999, 4, 24, 72, 125, 200.

More informally, potential defendants may exert political pressure on plaintiff states not to sue or to drop a suit once it has begun. When confronted by an unfavorable GATT panel judgment (in favor of Mexico) concerning U.S. legislation to protect dolphins from tuna fishing, [for example,] the United States exercised its extra-institutional power to induce Mexico to drop the case before the judgment could be enforced. * * *

The preceding discussion of access suggests two conjectures:

1. The broader and less costly the access to an international court or tribunal, the greater the number of cases it will receive.
2. The broader and less expensive the access to an international court or tribunal, the more likely that complaints challenge the domestic practices of national governments – particularly the home government of the complainant.

* * *

The comparative data summarized in Table 7.5 further support [the first] conjecture. The average caseload of six prominent international courts varies as predicted, with legal systems granting low access generating the fewest number of average cases, those granting high access generating the highest number of cases, and those granting moderate access in between. The difference between categories is roughly an order of magnitude or more. While we should be cautious about imputing causality before more extensive controlled studies are performed, the data suggest the existence of a strong relationship.

Case study evidence supports the conjecture that transnational dispute resolution systems with high levels of access tend to result in cases being brought in national courts against the *home* government. This is the standard method by which cases reach the ECJ. For example, the *Cassis de Dijon* case – a classic ECJ decision in 1979 establishing the principle of mutual recognition of national regulations – concerned the right to export a French liquor to Germany, yet a German importer, not the French producer, sued the German government, charging that domestic regulations on liquor purity were creating unjustified barriers to interstate trade.[24]

The Interstate and Transnational Politics of Embeddedness

Even if cases are brought before tribunals and these tribunals render judgments against states, the extent to which judgments are legally enforceable may differ. We have seen that most international legal systems create a legal obligation for governments to comply but leave enforcement to interstate bargaining. Only a few legal systems empower individuals and groups to seek enforcement of their provisions in domestic courts. However, in our ideal type of transnational dispute resolution, international commitments are embedded in domestic legal systems, meaning that governments, particularly national executives, no longer need to take positive action to ensure enforcement of international judgments. Instead, enforcement occurs directly through domestic courts and executive agents who are responsive to judicial decisions. The politics of embedded systems of dispute resolution are very different from the politics of systems that are not embedded in domestic politics.

* * *

Despite the real successes, in some circumstances, of interstate dispute resolution, it clearly has political limitations, especially where compliance constituencies are weak. Under interstate dispute resolution, pressures for compliance have to operate through governments. The limitations of such practices are clear under arbitration, and notably with respect to the ICJ. In the case involving mining of Nicaragua's harbors, the United States did not obey the ICJ's judgment. Admittedly, the Reagan administration did not simply ignore the ICJ judgment with respect to the mining of Nicaragua's harbors, but felt obliged to withdraw its recognition of the ICJ's jurisdiction – a controversial act with significant domestic political costs for a Republican president facing a Democratic Congress. Nevertheless, in the end the United States pursued a policy contrary to the ICJ's

---

[24] Case 120/78, *Rewe-Zentrale AG v. Bundesmonopolverwaltungfur Branntwein* (Cassis de Dijon), 1978.

decision. Even in trade regimes, political pressure sometimes leads to politically bargained settlements, as in the case of the U.S. Helms-Burton legislation. And a number of countries have imposed unilateral limits on the ICJ's jurisdiction.

*   *   *

The politics of transnational dispute resolution are quite different. By linking direct access for domestic actors to domestic legal enforcement, transnational dispute resolution opens up an additional source of political pressure for compliance, namely favorable judgments in domestic courts. This creates a new set of political imperatives. It gives international tribunals additional means to pressure or influence domestic government institutions in ways that enhance the likelihood of compliance with their judgments. It pits a recalcitrant government not simply against other governments but also against legally legitimate domestic opposition; an executive determined to violate international law must override his or her own legal system. Moreover, it thereby permits international tribunals to develop a constituency of litigants who can later pressure government institutions to comply with the international tribunal's decision.[25] *   *   *

*   *   *

Transnational dispute resolution does not sweep aside traditional interstate politics, but the power of national governments has to be filtered through norms of judicial professionalism, public opinion supporting particular conceptions of the rule of law, and an enduring tension between calculations of short- and long-term interests. Individuals and groups can zero in on international court decisions as focal points around which to mobilize, creating a further intersection between transnational litigation and democratic politics.

This discussion of the politics of interstate and transnational dispute resolution suggests that the following two conjectures deserve more intensive study.

1. Other things being equal, the more firmly embedded an international commitment is in domestic law, the more likely is compliance with judgments to enforce it.
2. Liberal democracies are particularly respectful of the rule of law and most open to individual access to judicial systems; hence attempts to

[25] Helfer and Slaughter 1997.

embed international law in domestic legal systems should be most effective among such regimes. In relations involving nondemocracies, we should observe near total reliance on interstate dispute resolution. Even among liberal democracies, the trust placed in transnational dispute resolution may vary with the political independence of the domestic judiciary.

Although embedding international commitments does not guarantee increased compliance, we find good reason to conclude that embeddedness probably tends to make compliance more likely in the absence of a strong political counteraction. * * *

THE INTERSTATE AND TRANSNATIONAL DYNAMICS OF LEGALIZATION

We have considered the static politics of legalization. Yet institutions also change over time and develop distinctive dynamics. Rules are elaborated. The costs of veto, withdrawal, or exclusion from the "inner club" of an institution may increase if the benefits provided by institutionalized cooperation increase. Sunk costs create incentives to maintain existing practices rather than to begin new ones. Politicians' short time horizons can induce them to agree to institutional practices that they might not prefer in the long term, in order to gain advantages at the moment.[26]

What distinguishes legalized regimes is their potential for setting in motion a distinctive dynamic built on precedent, in which decisions on a small number of specific disputes create law that may govern by analogy a vast array of future practices. This may be true even when the first litigants in a given area do not gain satisfaction. Judges may adopt modes of reasoning that assure individual litigants that their arguments have been heard and responded to, even if they have not won the day in a particular case. Some legal scholars argue that this "casuistic" style helps urge litigants, whether states or individuals, to fight another day.[27]

Although both interstate and transnational dispute resolution have the potential to generate such a legal evolution, we maintain that transnational dispute resolution increases the potential for such dynamics of precedent. The greater independence of judges, wider access of litigants, and greater potential for legal compliance insulates judges, thereby allowing them to

[26] See Keohane and Hoffmann 1991; Alter 1998a; and Pollack 1997.
[27] See White 1990; Glendon 1991; and Sunstein 1996.

develop legal precedent over time without triggering noncompliance, withdrawal, or reform by national governments. We next consider in more detail the specific reasons why.

The Dynamics of Interstate Third-party Dispute Resolution

In interstate legal systems, the potential for self-generating spillover depends on how states perform their gatekeeping roles. As we will show, where states open the gates, the results of interstate dispute resolution may to some degree resemble the results of transnational dispute resolution. However, in the two major international judicial or quasi-judicial tribunals – the Permanent Court of Arbitration and the ICJ – states have been relatively reluctant to bring cases. The great majority of arbitration cases brought before the Permanent Court of Arbitration were heard in the court's early years, shortly after the first case in 1902. The court has seen little use recently – the Iran Claims Tribunal being an isolated if notable exception.

States have been reluctant to submit to the ICJ's jurisdiction when the stakes are large.[28] Hence the ICJ has been constrained in developing a large and binding jurisprudence. *** Still, it is fair to note that use of the ICJ did increase substantially between the 1960s and 1990s, reaching an all-time high of nineteen cases on the docket in 1999.[29] Although this increase does not equal the exponential growth of economic and human rights jurisprudence in this period, it marks a significant shift. In part this reflects pockets of success that have resulted in expansion of both the law in a particular area and the resort to it. The ICJ has consistently had a fairly steady stream of cases concerning international boundary disputes. In these cases the litigants have typically already resorted to military conflict that has resulted in stalemate or determined that such conflict would be too costly. They thus agree to go to court. The ICJ, in turn, has profited from this willingness by developing an extensive body of case law that countries and their lawyers can use to assess the strength of the case on both sides and be assured of a resolution based on generally accepted legal principles.[30]

* * *

---

[28] Chayes 1965.
[29] Ibid.
[30] See, for example, Charney 1994.

The Dynamics of Transnational Dispute Resolution

The key to the dynamics of transnational dispute resolution is access. Transnational dispute resolution removes the ability of states to perform gatekeeping functions, both in limiting access to tribunals and in blocking implementation of their decisions. Its incentives for domestic actors to mobilize, and to increase the legitimacy of their claims, gives it a capacity for endogenous expansion. As we will see with respect to GATT and the WTO, even a formally interstate process may display similar expansionary tendencies, but continued expansion under interstate dispute resolution depends on continuing decisions by states to keep access to the dispute settlement process open. Switching to a set of formal rules nearer the ideal type of transnational dispute resolution makes it much harder for states to constrain tribunals and can give such tribunals both incentives and instruments to expand their authority by expanding their caseload. Indeed, tribunals can sometimes continue to strengthen their authority even when opposed by powerful states – particularly when the institutional status quo is favorable to tribunals and no coalition of dissatisfied states is capable of overturning the status quo.[31]

The pool of potential individual litigants is several orders of magnitude larger than that of state litigants. Independent courts have every incentive to recruit from that pool. Cases breed cases. A steady flow of cases, in turn, allows a court to become an actor on the legal and political stage, raising its profile in the elementary sense that other potential litigants become aware of its existence and in the deeper sense that its interpretation and application of a particular legal rule must be reckoned with as a part of what the law means in practice. Litigants who are likely to benefit from that interpretation will have an incentive to bring additional cases to clarify and enforce it. Further, the interpretation or application is itself likely to raise additional questions that can only be answered through subsequent cases. Finally, a court gains political capital from a growing caseload by demonstrably performing a needed function.

Transnational tribunals have the means at their disposal to target individual litigants in various ways. The most important advantage they have is the nature of the body of law they administer. Transnational litigation, whether deliberately established by states (as in the case of the ECHR) or adapted and expanded by a supranational tribunal itself (as in the case of the ECJ), only makes sense when interstate rules have

---

[31] See Alter 1998a; and Alter 2000.

dimensions that make them directly applicable to individual activity. Thus, in announcing the direct effect doctrine in *Van Gend and Loos,* the ECJ was careful to specify that only those portions of the Treaty of Rome that were formulated as clear and specific prohibitions on or mandates of member states' conduct could be regarded as directly applicable.[32] Human rights law is by definition applicable to individuals in relations with state authorities, although actual applicability will also depend on the clarity and specificity of individual human rights prohibitions and guarantees.

In this way, a transnational tribunal can present itself in its decisions as a protector of individual rights and benefits against the state, where the state itself has consented to these rights and benefits and the tribunal is simply holding it to its word. This is the clear thrust of the passage from *Van Gend and Loos* quoted earlier, in which the ECJ announced that "Community law . . . imposes obligations on individuals but is also intended to confer on them rights that become part of their legal heritage." The ECHR, for its part, has developed the "doctrine of effectiveness," which requires that the provisions of the European Human Rights Convention be interpreted and applied so as to make its safeguards "practical and effective" rather than "theoretical or illusory."[33] Indeed, one of its judges has described the ECHR in a dissenting opinion as the "last resort protector of oppressed individuals."[34] Such rhetoric is backed up by a willingness to find for the individual against the state.[35]

Ready access to a tribunal can create a virtuous circle: a steady stream of cases results in a stream of decisions that serve to raise the profile of the court and hence to attract more cases. When the ECJ rules, the decision is implemented not by national governments – the recalcitrant defendants – but by national courts. Any subsequent domestic opposition is rendered far more difficult. In sum, transnational third-party dispute resolution has led to a de facto alliance between certain national courts, certain types of individual litigants, and the ECJ. This alliance has been the mechanism by which the supremacy and direct effect of EC law, as well as thousands of specific substantive questions, have been established as cornerstones of the European legal order.[36]

---

[32] Case 26/62, *N. V. Algemene Transp. and Expeditie Onderneming Van Gend and Loos v. Nederslandse administratie der belastingen.* 1963 E.C.R. 1, 12.

[33] Bernhardt 1994.

[34] *Cossey v. United Kingdom,* 184 E.C.H.R., ser. A (1990).

[35] Helfer and Slaughter 1997.

[36] See Burley and Mattli 1993; and Weiler 1991 and 1999.

* * *

The motives of these national courts are multiple. They include a desire for "empowerment,"[37] competition with other courts for relative prestige and power,[38] a particular view of the law that could be achieved by following EC precedents over national precedents,[39] recognition of the greater expertise of the ECJ in European law,[40] and the desire to advantage or at least not to disadvantage a particular constituency of litigants.[41] Similar dynamics of intracourt competition may be observed in relations between national courts and the ECHR.[42] National courts appear to have been more willing to challenge the perceived interests of other domestic authorities once the first steps had been taken by other national courts. Weiler has documented the cross-citation of foreign supreme court decisions by national supreme courts accepting the supremacy of EC law for the first time. He notes that though they may have been reluctant to restrict national autonomy in a way that would disadvantage their states relative to other states, they are more willing to impose such restrictions when they are "satisfied that they are part of a trend." An alternative explanation of this trend might be ideational; courts feel such a step is more legitimate.[43]

* * *

Beyond Formalism: The Dynamics of GATT and the WTO

The contrast between the two ideal types of dispute resolution we have constructed – interstate and transnational – illuminates the impact of judicial independence, differential rules of access, and variations in the domestic embeddedness of an international dispute resolution process. The ICJ fits the interstate dispute resolution pattern quite well; the ECJ approximates the ideal type of transnational dispute resolution. The form that legalization takes seems to matter.

Form, however, is not everything. Politics is affected by form but not determined by it. This is most evident when we seek to explain more

---

[37] See Weiler 1991; and Burley and Mattli 1993.
[38] Alter 1996b, and 1998a,b.
[39] Mattli and Slaughter 1998b.
[40] Craig 1998.
[41] Plötner 1998.
[42] Jarmul 1996.
[43] See Weiler 1994; and Finnemore and Sikkink 1998.

fine-grained variations in the middle of the spectrum between the two ideal types. The evolution of the GATT, and recently the WTO, illustrates how politics can alter the effects of form. Formally, as we pointed out earlier, GATT is closer to the ideal type of interstate dispute resolution than to transnational dispute resolution. The independence of tribunals is coded as moderate for both GATT and WTO. On the embeddedness criterion, GATT was low and WTO, with its mandatory procedures, is moderate (see Table 7.4). Most important, however, are access rules: in both the old GATT and the ITO (since 1 January 1995), states have the exclusive right to bring cases before tribunals. In formal terms, therefore, states are the gatekeepers to the GATT/WTO process.

We noted in the first section, however, that the relationships between actors in civil society and representatives of the state are very different in GATT/WTO than in the ICJ. In the GATT/WTO proceedings the principal actors from civil society are firms or industry groups, which are typically wealthy enough to afford extensive litigation and often have substantial political constituencies. Industry groups and firms have been quick to complain about allegedly unfair and discriminatory actions by their competitors abroad, and governments have often been willing to take up their complaints. Indeed, it has often been convenient for governments to do so, since the best defense against others' complaints in a system governed by reciprocity is often the threat or reality of bringing one's own case against their discriminatory measures. In a "tit-for-tat" game, it is useful to have an army of well-documented complaints "up one's sleeve" to deter others from filing complaints or as retaliatory responses to such complaints. Consequently, although states retain formal gatekeeping authority in the GATT/WTO system, they often have incentives to open the gates, letting actors in civil society set much of the agenda.

The result of this political situation is that the evolution of the GATT dispute settlement procedure looks quite different from that of the ICJ: indeed, it seems intermediate between the ideal types of interstate and transnational dispute resolution. Dispute resolution activity levels have increased substantially over time, as the process has become more legalized. Adjudication in the GATT of the 1950s produced vague decisions, which were nevertheless relatively effective, arguably because GATT was a "club" of like-minded trade officials.[44] Membership changes and the emergence of the EC in the 1960s led to decay in the dispute resolution mechanism, which only began to reverse in the 1970s.

---

[44] This paragraph and the subsequent one rely on Hudec 1999, especially 6–17.

Diplomatic, nonlegalized attempts to resolve disputes, however, were severely criticized, leading to the appointment of a professional legal staff and the gradual legalization of the process. With legalization came better-argued decisions and the creation of a body of precedent.

Throughout this period, the formal procedures remained entirely voluntary: defendants could veto any step in the process. This "procedural flimsiness," as Robert E. Hudec refers to it, is often taken as a major weakness of GATT; but Hudec has shown that it did not prevent GATT from being quite effective. By the late 1980s, 80 percent of GATT cases were disposed of effectively – not as a result of legal embeddedness but of political decisions by states. This is a reasonably high level of compliance, though not as high as attained by the EC and ECHR. The WTO was built on the success of GATT, particularly in recent years, rather than being a response to failure.[45]

We infer from the GATT/WTO experience that although the formal arrangements we have emphasized are important, their dynamic effects depend on the broader political context. Our ideal-type argument should not be reified into a legalistic, single-factor explanation of the dynamics of dispute resolution. Even if states control gates, they can under some conditions be induced to open them, or even to encourage actors from civil society to enter the dispute resolution arena. The real dynamics of dispute resolution typically lie in some interaction between law and politics, rather than in the operation of either law or politics alone.

* * *

Conclusion

We have constructed two ideal types of legalized dispute resolution, interstate and transnational, which vary along the dimensions of independence, access, and embeddedness. When we examine international courts, we find that the distinction between the two ideal types appears to be associated with variation in the size of dockets and levels of compliance with decisions. The differences between the ICJ and the ECJ are dramatic along both dimensions. The causal connections between outcomes and

---

[45] The annual number of cases before the WTO has risen to almost twice the number during the last years of GATT; but Hudec argues that this change is accounted for by the new or intensified obligations of the Uruguay Round, rather than being attributable to changes in the embeddedness of the dispute resolution mechanism. Hudec 1999, 21. Hudec acknowledges, however, that he is arguing against the conventional wisdom.

correspondence with one ideal type or the other will require more research and analysis to sort out; but the differences between the ICJ and ECJ patterns cannot be denied. Their dynamics also vary greatly: the ECJ has expanded its caseload and its authority in a way that is unparalleled in the ICJ.

The GATT/WTO mechanisms do not reflect our ideal types so faithfully. States remain formal legal gatekeepers in these systems but have often refrained from tightly limiting access to dispute resolution procedures. As a result, the caseload of the GATT processes, and the effectiveness of their decisions, increased even without high formal levels of access or embeddedness. Hence, GATT and the WTO remind us that legal form does not necessarily determine political process. It is the interaction of law and politics, not the action of either alone, that generates decisions and determines their effectiveness.

What transnational dispute resolution does is to insulate dispute resolution to some extent from the day-to-day political demands of states. The more we move toward transnational dispute resolution, the harder it is to trace individual judicial decisions and states' responses to them back to any simple, short-term matrix of state or social preferences, power capabilities, and cross-issues. Political constraints, of course, continue to exist, but they are less closely binding than under interstate dispute resolution. Legalization imposes real constraints on state behavior; the closer we are to transnational third-party dispute resolution, the greater those constraints are likely to be. Transnational dispute resolution systems help to mobilize and represent particular groups that benefit from regime norms. This increases the costs of reversal to national governments and domestic constituents, which can in turn make an important contribution to the enforcement and extension of international norms. For this reason, transnational dispute resolution systems have become an important source of increased legalization and a factor in both interstate and intrastate politics.

8

Legalization, Trade Liberalization, and Domestic Politics: A Cautionary Note

Judith Goldstein and Lisa L. Martin

*** In this article we consider how increases in the legalization of the international trade regime interact with the trade-related interests of domestic actors. Although legalization may reduce incentives for cheating by individual nations, we identify ways in which the unintended effects of legalization on the activities of domestic economic actors could interfere with the pursuit of progressive liberalization of international trade. Domestic politics cannot be treated as extraneous or as an irrational source of error that obstructs the purposes of legalization. Instead, politics operates in systematic ways and is the mechanism through which legalization exerts its effects. These effects range far beyond reducing opportunism by unitary states.

Through incremental change in the postwar years, the international trade regime has evolved away from its origins as a decentralized and relatively powerless institution and become a legal entity. The number of countries and the amount of trade covered by the rules agreed to in 1947 have expanded greatly. After 1995 and the creation of the World Trade Organization (WTO), the regime further increased its demands on members by elaborating and expanding commercial rules and procedures, including those that relate to the system of settling disputes. In practice the expansion of the regime in the post–World War II period has made trade rules more precise and binding. The result is that the implications or

We thank Bob Keohane, Marc Busch, Eric Anderson, James Fearon, Erica Gould, Barry Weingast, Simon Jackman, Brian Hanson, Richard Steinberg, an anonymous reviewer, and the editors of *IO* for comments on a previous version of this article.

behavioral demands of rules have become increasingly transparent to all participants.[1]

We argue that this increased legalization does not necessarily augur higher levels of trade liberalization, as suggested by supporters. The weakly legalized General Agreement on Tariffs and Trade (GATT) regime was remarkably successful at liberalizing trade; it is not apparent that the benefits of further legalization will outweigh its costs. This finding derives from an analysis of domestic politics and, in particular, from the incentives facing leaders to join and then adhere to the dictates of a liberal international trade regime. We support our position through an analysis of two aspects of trade politics.

First, we examine the effect of legalization on the incentives of domestic groups to mobilize and pressure their governments to adopt policies that favor them.[2] *** We believe that better information will empower protectionists relative to free traders on issues relating to the conclusion of new agreements and free traders relative to protectionists on issues of compliance to existing agreements. Second, we examine the implications of a more "binding" GATT/WTO on member governments. Although GATT rules were always obligatory in a legal sense, the provisions for using escape clauses and other loopholes interacted with domestic political realities in a way that made their use increasingly rare. This fact, combined with a strengthened dispute-resolution mechanism under the WTO, has increased the extent to which governments are "obliged," in a political sense, to maintain their liberal commitments. Reducing the ability of governments to opt out of commitments has the positive effect of reducing the chances that governments will behave opportunistically by invoking phony criteria for protecting their industries. On the other hand, tightly binding, unforgiving rules can have negative effects in the uncertain environment of international trade. When considering the realities of incomplete information about future economic

---

[1] Legalization refers to three aspects of international law: obligation, precision, and level of delegation to a centralized authority. Abbott et al., this issue.

[2] The number and variety of groups participating in the politics of trade has grown in the last decades. Where the classic models assumed three groups with trade-related interests – consumers, import-competing groups, and exporters – other groups, whose interests span from human rights to a clean environment, have come to believe that their interests are influenced by trade negotiations. The logic of this article, explaining the interaction among international regimes, social mobilization, and domestic politics, applies to any interest that groups perceive to be influenced by international trade agreements.

shocks, we suggest that legalization may not result in the "correct" balance between these two effects of binding.

In this article we develop both the theoretical reasoning and the empirical support for our cautionary note on the domestic effects of legalization. We begin by examining information and group mobilization and suggest that the predictability that comes with legalization has both positive and negative effects on the trade liberalization goal of the regime. We then investigate the "bindingness" of trade rules. Through examination of the use of safeguards and the new dispute-resolution procedure, we argue that trade rules have become more binding, even if *pacta sunt servanda* has always applied to such rules, and that enforcement of rules is now more certain.

* * *

LEGALIZATION, INFORMATION, AND THE MOBILIZATION OF DOMESTIC GROUPS

The logic of precision, delegation, obligation, and increased transparency played a large role in negotiations over transforming the GATT into the WTO. The intended effect of these modifications in the WTO was to expand the breadth of the trade regime and enhance compliance so as to increase the benefits of membership. The problem with this logic is that it neglected domestic politics. Maintenance of free trade is politically difficult and is a function of the differential mobilization of those who favor liberalization and those who oppose a further opening of the economy to foreign products. Mobilization itself is a function of a number of factors, including the cost of mobilizing and the potential gains from collective action. One consequence of legalizing the trade regime has been greater transparency and predictability about the effects of trade agreements. Increased information of this sort has mixed effects on the mobilization of domestic interests and therefore on the ability of governments to maintain support for liberal trade policies.

The Logic of Mobilization

Consider first the impact of increased precision of trade rules during the process of trade negotiations. The ability of leaders to sign an accord will depend on the groups mobilized for or against the accord. The pattern of mobilization is not always predictable; mobilizing interest groups requires overcoming collective-action problems that can be quite intense. Actors within these groups must realize first that they have a common interest in government policies. They must then come to believe that it is worthwhile to bear the costs of collective action. A number of factors can undermine mobilization. The factors most relevant to international trade include the large and diffuse nature of some economic interests, lack of information that the interests of actors are at stake in particular international negotiations, and possible calculations that the costs of influencing government policy outweigh anticipated benefits.[3]

From the perspective of encouraging the liberalization of international trade, the fact that groups who prefer economic closure might suffer from collective-action problems is a blessing. If all antitrade forces were well organized and able to exert substantial pressure on their political representatives, the prospects for liberalization would be dim. The interaction with legalization enters the analysis at this point. In that legalization entails a process of increased precision of rules and transparency of agreements, it affects the behavior of domestic groups by increasing the information available to actors about the distributional implications of trade agreements. To the extent that such knowledge enhances the mobilization of antitrade forces relative to already well-organized protrade groups, legalization could undermine liberalization. Information matters for both protectionist and proliberalization interests. However, if these groups are differentially mobilized prior to the process of legalization, information will have the larger marginal effect on the groups that are not as well organized. The structure of the multilateral trade regime, based on the principle of reciprocity, has provided strong incentives for exporters to organize throughout the post-1950 period.[4] Growing dependence on exports and the multinational character of economic interests has also led to strong and effective lobbying efforts by free-trade advocates.[5] We therefore concentrate on the likely impact of greater information on the incentives facing protectionist groups.

* * *

---

[3] Collective-action problems have been central to the literature on endogenous tariff formation. See, for example, Magee, Brock, and Young 1989; and Mayer 1984.

[4] Gilligan 1997.

[5] Milner 1988.

A simple model clarifies the posited relationship between information and mobilization. Define p to be the probability with which a group believes that its interests will be at stake in negotiations. This subjective probability, p, is a random variable that takes on different values as information conditions change. We begin by assuming a poor information environment, where groups know only the total number of groups affected, not which of them will be affected.

Assume that there are N groups with an interest in trade. These groups are not mobilized initially. Assume they know that n groups will be affected by negotiations but have no information about which n groups this will be. This is an extreme assumption of poor information but a useful starting point. Each group therefore estimates that it will have a stake in negotiations with probability n/N, the ratio of affected groups to all groups. Given a lack of information, this is their best guess of the probability of being affected by negotiations. Thus, in the prelegalization environment, the variable p takes on the value n/N; $p = n/N$. The value of p will change as information improves.

Given this value of p prior to legalization, does it make sense for a group to mobilize? The calculation depends on the relationship between the expected benefits and costs of mobilization. The benefits of mobilization, B, are realized only if the group is in n. If the group is not in n, it gains no benefits, but will have to bear the costs of mobilization if it chooses to mobilize. Given the prelegalization value of p, the expected benefits from negotiations are $p*B$, or nB/N. Groups will mobilize if the expected benefits outweigh mobilization costs C; $p*B > C$. Thus each group will mobilize if $nB/N > C$ in the poor information environment. N is a large number, and the ratio n/N is typically small. Thus, unless B is extremely large or the costs of mobilization negligible, groups will not have an incentive to mobilize. Our expectation is that few groups will meet this stringent prelegalization mobilization condition. As information improves, p increases above the n/N minimum. However, with uncertainty about the distributional implications of negotiations, p remains small and the ratio of B to C must be large to allow mobilization.

After legalization, we assume that groups know with certainty whether they will be included in negotiations; that is, their estimate of the probability p now becomes either zero or 1, as groups know whether their interests are at stake or not. The value of the random variable p changes as information conditions change. Groups that do not have their interests at stake will not mobilize. However, the condition for groups that are affected by negotiations to mobilize is now $p*B > C$

with $p = 1$, which is simply $B > C$. This is a much easier condition to meet, as long as collective-action costs are not prohibitive (as they may be for large, diffuse groups such as consumers). Therefore, we expect that many more groups will find it worthwhile to mobilize in the richer information environment postlegalization. Even if p does not improve to the extreme values of zero or 1, it approaches these limits, with the expected effects.

As suggested earlier, information has effects on groups that may be harmed as well as helped by negotiations. Our intention here is not to make precise predictions about the policy outcomes of relative mobilization of exporters and protectionists, but simply to draw attention to the political problems created by enhanced mobilization of antitrade groups. Clearly, information will lead both groups to mobilize, given increased certainty on how interests will fare in an agreement. However, a number of factors suggest that increased information is likely to favor proprotectionist mobilization. This position goes beyond the classic explanation, for example, Schattschneider's, that protectionist interests are concentrated and free-trade interests diffuse, which still has some force.[6]

The first factor is that the status quo favors protected groups, not potential new exporters. Since changes from the status quo require explicit affirmation – for example, ratification of a treaty – those who benefit from the status quo gain veto power. Thus typical institutional procedures that privilege the status quo will tend to favor protectionist over liberalizing interests. Another factor pointing in the same direction is the uncertain nature of gains for exporters. Exporters only know that some market will open up, not whether they will be able to capitalize on this opportunity in the face of international competition. In contrast, protectionists know precisely what protection they will be losing as a result of liberalization, enhancing their incentives to mobilize relative to exporters. Moving beyond a strictly rationalist model, we could also mention experimental evidence that actors tend to react more strongly to losses than to gains, again favoring protectionist groups in this mobilization dynamic. Finally, if we assume, as does Gilligan, that exporters are either fully or almost fully mobilized and are already participating in the political process, the increase in information should lead to a relatively greater mobilization of the less involved, that is, the antitrade groups.

The logic of precision and mobilization does not necessarily lead one to expect economic closure. When we consider the effects of more

---

[6] Schattschneider 1935.

information when maintaining as opposed to creating a trade commit-ment, we get the opposite effect. Although information may mobilize import-competers before the conclusion of an agreement, the effect of a more legalized regime may be to mobilize exporters in cases of certain market losses, *ex post*. In this case, precision about which exporters will bear the costs of retaliation in a trade dispute works to mobilize exporting interests who would otherwise have no involvement in the trade dispute. Given the potential of a market loss, they will press governments to uphold trade rules. The higher the probability that the retaliatory action will hurt them, the greater their interests in expending resources to maintain liberal trade at home.

Therefore, logic suggests that increasing rule precision will have two different, and competing, effects on trade liberalization. Increased de-terminacy can undermine trade deals by activating import-competing groups with veto power. Conversely, precise rules regarding responses to rule breaches will result in more trade liberalization by activating export groups in the offending country. Over time, we should see not only more antitrade groups organizing but also more political activity by export groups if strategies of retaliation are appropriately designed.

Mobilizing Antitrade Groups

Empirical evidence suggests that groups affected by trade policy are often well organized and articulate. Whether the group is farmers in France, auto producers in the United States, or computer companies in Japan, those whose interests will be hurt by either continued or expanded access to foreign goods, services, and markets are articulate spokesper-sons for specific policies. These groups often act as veto players, and leaders who would like to negotiate the opening of world markets find that fear of competition at home undermines support for their free-trade coalition. The ability of leaders to ignore protectionist pressures rests on the willingness of proliberalization groups, those who benefit from liberalized trade, to organize and be equally active in their support. In the absence of exporters or other interested parties who articulate their free-trade positions, governments find it difficult to maintain a free-trade policy.[7]

---

[7] Numerous empirical studies document the importance of groups in setting trade policy. For a cross-national, cross-sectional examination of groups' involvement, see, for ex-ample, Verdier 1994.

Evidence of the effects of this problem of mobilizing and maintaining a free-trade coalition is found in all democracies and partially results from the concentrated benefits of trade barriers and their diffuse costs.[8] Rarely are those who are hurt by higher prices (consumers) present in political debate; more often, trade politics is determined by the balance between groups with specific interests in either openness or closure. In some countries, structural factors affect this balance. For example, groups may be overrepresented because of the electoral process, such as with agricultural producers in Japan, or because they have bureaucratic or corporatist support in government.

Since World War II, protectionist pressures from such groups have been mitigated through changes in the trade policymaking process, both domestic and international.[9] Reciprocal trade agreements, delegation to executive agencies, electoral reform, and changing legislative voting rules help explain why countries support liberal trade policies that were difficult to defend in the pre–World War II period. The fact of liberalization and the specifics of the process are in equilibrium. The process may change either because underlying interests change or for exogenous reasons. Regardless of the particular reason for change, changes in the process have far-reaching consequences for policy. Process changes have made it more difficult for import-competing groups to find a majority to support their position while encouraging the organization of exporter interests.

The success of groups who support liberalization, however, should not be construed as evidence that policymakers no longer need to worry about veto groups undercutting trade policy. Liberalization may have changed the face of the proprotection lobby, but it has not eliminated its potential power. Even in the United States, long a proponent of the liberal trade regime, elected officials repeatedly face pressures from antitrade groups. *** These social pressures have led strategic trade negotiators to bundle the gains to exporters from access to new markets with the losses to import-competing producers from new competition from abroad.

---

[8] On trade and interest groups, see Destler 1995; and Lohmann and O'Halloran 1994.

[9] Whether it was a change in the balance of group interests or a shift in trade policymaking that explains the ability of governments to lower barriers to trade is difficult to determine in the early years of the GATT regime. Certainly, in the United States interest-group activity was muted because the costs of organizing increased when the president obtained increased control of trade policymaking. Still, the shift toward openness would not have occurred without underlying social support. For an analysis of the relationship between institutional and underlying social variables, see Bailey, Goldstein, and Weingast 1997.

Whatever the specifics of this trade-off at the negotiating table, the result must be an agreement that can garner majority support at home. If information about the distributional implication of agreements affects the propensity of groups to organize during negotiations, it may be easier to get to that "optimal bundle" in situations where some uncertainty exists about who is and who is not affected by the trade deal. Providing this information about the effects of either a potential commercial agreement, the behavior of a trading partner, or the dissolution of a trading pact is a central function of the contemporary trade regime. The WTO collects and disseminates trade data in preparation for rounds of trade talks; it monitors compliance and inventories national practices that undermine the free flow of goods and services.

Over time, the GATT/WTO regime has dramatically increased its ability to deliver this information to member countries.[10] In initial rounds of negotiations, tariff information was not systematically collected. Nations relied on data supplied by their negotiating partners, and thus the computation of offers and counteroffers for "balance" was done using often-incomplete statistics. *** In 1989, the Trade Policy Review Mechanism was authorized at the Montreal midterm review of progress in the Uruguay Round. This began a process of regular country studies, providing sector and product information on practices of GATT members. The four largest trading powers – Canada, the European Union (EU), Japan, and the United States – are reviewed every two years; the sixteen member countries that are next in the value of their trade are reviewed every four years; most other members are reviewed every six years.[11] The result has been a more symmetric information environment.[12]

This increased monitoring activity in itself is not a result of "legalization" according to the definition adopted. Still, it has been tightly bound up with increased formalization and precision of commitments both at the time of and during the life of an agreement. The result is a far richer information environment than at any previous time. One aspect of WTO operations, for example, that is more public than in the past is the ministerial meeting. *** Along with changes in WTO policy, a key demand of antitrade groups has been less secrecy in WTO proceedings. Although

---

[10] Keesing 1998.
[11] Ibid.
[12] The GATT's move to the Trade Policy Review Mechanism was motivated by the perception that information was key in negotiations but that it was available only to the larger countries. Ibid.

some Western governments, including the United States, have defended the principle of transparency, most representatives in the WTO strenuously resist this demand.[13] Still, transparency has increased over time. Early rounds were akin to clubs. Deals were struck among a small group of like-minded representatives, behind closed doors. Later rounds eschewed this general negotiating form. Although private negotiations occurred, and were often the most productive, more time was spent in formal settings, with delegates giving prepared speeches that offered few, if any, real trade concessions. Thus the demand for more transparency has been met by more open meetings and more press coverage, but the effect of these particular changes has been muted; delegates continue to worry about domestic constituencies and remain wary of saying anything that would get them into trouble at home.

Increased provision of information to delegates is not, we acknowledge, evidence of complete transparency in the trade regime. Although legalization has resulted in a movement toward transparency, we cannot claim to have reached a situation of complete and perfect information. The WTO retains many of the elements of the GATT, including its preservation of member countries' rights to secrecy. The empirical evidence does not adequately allow us to make precise estimates of the level of transparency. We can, however, identify a trend toward greater openness. When the GATT was established in the late 1940s, the confidentiality rule adopted by member countries was the strictest of any adopted by postwar international institutions.[14] The correspondence of any delegate could be claimed as privileged. If a delegate did not formally rescind a confidentiality request within three years, the information became confidential in perpetuity. Why this rule? Simply, delegates did not want information to leak back home. Offers made during negotiations could be highly sensitive, and although the final package would be made public, it came home as a "closed" deal – groups could not easily pick it apart.

The early delegates to the GATT understood that too much information would incur import-competing group pressures and undermine their ability to make trade-offs among groups. Policymakers need to be able to bundle agreements in order to procure majorities in their home countries. For politicians, the logic of membership in a multilateral trade institution is to facilitate the creation of larger bundles than are possible through bilateral bargaining.

---

[13] *New York Times*, 4 December 1999, A6.
[14] Richard Blackhurst interviews.

TABLE 8.1. *Trade Bills in the U.S. House of Representatives, 1975–98*

	Number of bills	Percentage providing side payments rather than direct protection
1975–78	79	14
1979–82	43	28
1983–86	61	26
1987–90	61	21
1991–94	47	13
1995–98	48	38

Source: Congressional Index, various years.

Efforts to devise free-trade coalitions in an environment of market liberalization help explain the changing structure of trade rounds. ***

* * *

*** Politics was never removed from the liberalization process, although the regime's structure did affect which domestic groups were able to translate their preferences into policy. Thus, adopted formulas were never intended to be binding on parties, and national offers were rife with exceptions. Preparation for rounds involved difficult negotiations with potentially powerful veto groups, often leading to an assortment of side payments issued in the early phase of negotiations.[15] Drawing on U.S. congressional indexes, we illustrate in Table 8.1 one way that this phenomenon manifested. The table summarizes the rise in the number of bills that provided side payments, usually in place of a more direct policy to curb imports. During the 1975–94 period, the number of side-payment bills that made their way to the House floor is high, though fairly stable. The data for 1995–98 suggest that under the WTO even more side-payment bills were used, as our analysis predicts.

Our attention to antitrade groups derives from two related observations. First, although liberalization has been extremely successful in the postwar period, it has always occurred in the shadow of organized opposition. Second, groups respond to information about impending trade talks, which motivates them to pursue particularistic policies. The existence of continued openness should not be interpreted as an absence of

---

[15] Goldstein 1993.

proprotection group pressures. Although proprotection groups may have been more constrained, had less "voice," and been balanced by well-organized exporter groups, once organized, they have powerful effects on policy.

Has there been a rise in interest-group activity since the creation of the WTO, as suggested by our analysis? Given the WTO's brief existence, assessing the data is difficult. However, as evidenced by the significant rise in the number of groups attending the WTO's November 1999 ministerial meeting, the WTO itself has engendered more attention from a wider range of domestic groups than ever before. For a whole host of reasons, some associated with legalization, the WTO has become a focus of attention not only for labor and producer groups, the traditionally interested parties, but also for environmental, health, and safety groups. Such attention is a result of the expansion of knowledge about what the WTO is doing as well as structural changes in the scope of the regime.

The regime's effect on the mobilization of groups may also explain problems faced in initiating a new round of trade talks. The stated focus for a new WTO Millennium Round of talks is far more targeted than ever before; knowledge of who has been targeted has led to more and earlier activity than in previous rounds. The best exemplar is the agricultural sector, where good information about the locus of talks led to a cross-national campaign of producers to undercut negotiations.[16] These types of increasing pressures, generated by more information about the liberalization process, will make it more difficult to find nations willing to launch trade rounds and, for those who do make it to Geneva, more difficult to make the necessary trade-offs among producers, even if export groups stay mobilized. After the November 1999 ministerial meeting the fate of the Millennium Round remains an open question, with most observers offering pessimistic assessments.

Mobilizing Export Groups

Although the mobilization of groups circumscribes the type of new deals that are possible, it also explains the stability of signed agreements. Leaders rarely renege on a GATT trade deal, even when faced with pressure from powerful rent-seeking industries. This stability was not due to GATT sanctions against such changes. Rather, changing specific tariffs, according to the rules, was relatively easy under a number of safeguard

---

[16] Josling 1999.

TABLE 8.2. *Post-Negotiation Tariff Changes by Invoked Article for all GATT Members, 1961–90*

	Open season[a]	Out of season[b]	Article 28:5[c]
1961–66[d]	9	14	3
1967–72	8	7	15
1973–78	5	3	31[e]
1979–84	1	1	66[f]
1985–90	1	1	19
1991–93/94	4	1	5

[a] *Open season* refers to the usage and invocation of GATT Art. XXVIII: 1.

[b] *Out of season* refers to the usage and invocation of GATT Art. XXVIII: 4.

[c] Before the end of a period of "firm validity," a country may reserve to modify their schedule. The numbers in this column refer not to the election of this right, but to its usage (the actual modification).

[d] The time periods correspond to two periods of "firm validity," except the last time period (1991–93/94) for which we have only three years of data. Art. XIX data are as of 1 December 1993. Art. XXVIII data are as of 30 March 1994.

[e] Of these cases, 22 are either New Zealand's or South Africa's.

[f] Of these cases, 32 are South Africa's.

Source: GATT Analytical Index 1994.

provisions of the GATT regime. Under GATT rules, nations could change tariffs every three years during the "open season," in between these times "out of season," and/or under Article 28:5, as long as the general tariff level remained the same. Keeping the overall level of tariffs stable, however, was not easy for politicians at home. The problem with giving compensation was the trade-off it created between the group pressing for aid and some other producer. This type of a trade-off is difficult for politicians.

Table 8.2 shows the use of these provisions for changing particular tariffs post-negotiation. What is striking is that, although the regime legally provided a substantial amount of flexibility, these provisions have only rarely been invoked. Given the thousands of products affected by cuts, only a few countries rescinded an agreement to bind their tariffs. For GATT members, these provisions were akin to a Pandora's Box. Having to change a schedule, item by item, in the absence of reciprocal benefits meant trading off one domestic sector for another. The political problems this engendered assured that few GATT countries chose to deal with import problems through these means.

Another perspective on mobilization is evident in attempts to mobilize export groups in support of free trade by strategically using threats
of retaliation. States making a threat of retaliation that is intended to
mobilize exporters in other countries, such as the United States in
implementing Section 301, must consider how to maximize the pressure
applied by exporters to the other government. Announcing threats of
definite retaliation against just a few groups would not have the desired
effect. These groups would certainly mobilize, but those left off the short
list would not. At the other extreme, announcing a very large or vague
list of possible targets of retaliation would also fail to mobilize many
exporters. This tactic would create massive collective-action problems,
since each exporter would be only part of a potentially universal coalition
and therefore face incentives to free ride. In addition, lack of precision
in the possible targets of retaliation might encourage exporters to wait
and take their chances on being hit, rather than bearing the definite, immediate costs of mobilization.

With these considerations in mind, if our story about mobilization is
correct, the strategic use of retaliatory threats should be quite precise.
In addition, it should target a group of exporters large enough to put
pressure on the government, but not so large as to exacerbate collective-
action problems. Section 301 cases provide a good source of evidence on
the use of retaliatory threats, since they list the potential targets of
retaliation when the other government does not reach a settlement with
the United States.

* * *

The threat of retaliation, if issued with an appropriate degree of
precision, activates export groups. This suggests that the GATT/WTO
should allow or even encourage retaliation in the face of deviation from
regime rules. The GATT structure, incorporating reciprocal retaliation
and/or alternative market access in response to reneging on a concession,
even under safeguard clauses, may have been better than the alternative
adopted by the WTO. WTO rules waive the right to both compensation
and/or retaliation for the first three years of a safeguard action. Those
who supported the change argued that this would encourage nations to
follow the rules – when nations could defend their reasons for invoking
safeguard actions as "just," they should be protected from retaliation.[17]
The logic offered here suggests the opposite. Circumstantial evidence in

---

[17] Krueger 1998.

the United States supports the argument that domestic groups organize in response to government threats that affect their market position. For example, in what was supposed to be a simple incidence of using market restrictions in a Section 301 case, the United States found it politically impossible to raise tariffs on a Japanese car, the Lexus, in large part because of resistance from Lexus dealers in the United States. Lexus dealers are not the type of group that generates great sympathy from the American people. However, during a trade dispute with Japan that came to a head in 1995, they found their interests directly at stake. In an attempt to force more opening of the Japanese market, the United States announced a list of 100 percent retaliatory tariffs on Japanese luxury goods that would go into effect on 28 June.[18] Since this list included cars with a retail value over $30,000, Lexus dealers (along with Infiniti and Acura dealers) found themselves directly threatened. In response they generated a large lobbying and public relations effort. In the end a midnight deal with Japan averted sanctions.

To summarize, we argue that one of the primary political effects of legalizing the trade regime will be an interaction between increased precision about the distributional implications of trade agreements and the mobilization of domestic groups, both protectionist and free trade in orientation. In this section we have surveyed evidence on trade negotiations and the use of retaliatory tariffs during trade disputes to see if mobilization does indeed respond as we expect. From a number of perspectives, we find evidence to support our claims. During negotiations, lobbying activities are conditioned on the information available to particularistic interests. Strategic politicians, who are attempting to design the negotiating process so as to increase their ability to create mutually beneficial bundles of agreements, may find it helpful to have less than complete transparency about the details of negotiations. Antitrade group pressures make negotiations more difficult, and to the extent that transparency encourages mobilization of antitrade groups it will hinder liberalization negotiations.[19] During trade disputes, politicians similarly strategize about how to reveal information so as to mobilize groups appropriately – in this instance to maximize the mobilization of exporters in the target country.

Our findings should not be interpreted as a prediction of trade closure. Rather, we make the more modest claim that attention should be paid to

[18] *New York Times*, 9 June 1995, D3.
[19] See, for example, the history of agricultural trade in Josling 1999.

an underexplored effect of international legalization, that is, the mobilization of domestic groups. The analysis of the interaction of legalization, information, and domestic groups is a requisite to understanding the conditions under which legalization of the trade regime will be successful.

TIGHTLY BINDING TRADE RULES

In the preceding section we argued that legalization enriches the information environment. In this section we examine a second effect of legalization linked to an increase in the obligatory nature of international rules. Legalization at its core refers to *pacta sunt servanda,* or the presumption that, once signed, nations will adhere to treaty obligations. Interpretations of this responsibility are typically rendered by lawyers using a discourse focusing on rules – their exceptions and applicability – and not on interests. Given the expanding breadth of the trade regime, we suggest that the use of legal rule interpretation has made it increasingly difficult for governments to get around obligations by invoking escape clauses and safeguards or by turning to alternative measures, such as nontariff barriers. Partly, this is a result of the increased precision of rules and the inclusion of what were extralegal trade remedies, such as voluntary export restraints, in the regime itself. But the legalization of the trade regime has also moved the nexus of both rule making and adjudicating rule violations into the center of the regime and away from member states.

The Logic of "Bindingness"

The benefits of increased precision and "bindingness" are identified in the functionalist literature on international institutions.[20] The benefit of international institutions lies primarily in the creation of disincentives for states to behave opportunistically by reneging on trade agreements and acting unilaterally. The problem of incentives to renege on cooperative arrangements, and the role of international institutions in helping states

---

[20] We use the term *bindingness* where the term *obligation* would seem appropriate to a political scientist. The reason is that obligation has taken on a particular legal meaning, and that meaning has been adopted in this issue. By *bindingness* we mean the political obligation created by international rules. It is a positive rather than a normative term, meaning the degree to which rules are binding, practically speaking, on governments. Rules with higher probability of enforcement, for example, are more binding (or obligatory) in this political sense.

to overcome these incentives and so reach Pareto-superior outcomes, has been central to the institutional approach to international relations.[21] The key institutional argument is that attaining cooperative outcomes is hindered by the lack of information about the intentions and behavior of others and ambiguity about international obligations that states can manipulate to their advantage. States are often caught in a "prisoners' dilemma" and find it difficult to sustain the necessary enforcement strategies to assure cooperation in the uncertain environment of international politics. The primary function of international institutions, therefore, is to provide politically relevant information and so allow states to escape from the prisoners' dilemma trap.

This argument about international institutions took shape during an era when researchers were anxious to extend their analysis beyond formal international organizations to informal institutions and regimes.[22] By focusing on legalization, the current project returns to the study of formal institutions, but the underlying logic remains the same. Making international commitments precise and explicit makes it more difficult for states to evade them without paying a cost. More precise rules allow for more effective enforcement, and legalization involves a process of increasing precision. Greater precision and transparency about the obligations and behavior of states are also created by other dimensions of legalization. Delegation of monitoring and dispute-resolution functions to centralized organizational agents, away from member states, is intended to increase the quantity and quality of information about state behavior. It therefore leads to more effective enforcement and disincentives to renege on commitments.

As we have argued, legalization has unintended effects on the mobilization of support for and against trade liberalization. Similarly, legal binding has unexpected effects on domestic politics. If agreements are impossible to breach, either because of their level of obligation or because the transparency of rules increases the likelihood of enforcement, elected officials may find that the costs of signing such agreements outweigh the benefits. The downside of increased legalization in this instance lies in the inevitable uncertainties of economic interactions between states and in the need for flexibility to deal with such uncertainty without undermining the trade regime as a whole. Legalization as increased bindingness could therefore constrain leaders and undermine free-trade majorities at home.

[21] Keohane 1984.
[22] Krasner 1983.

* * *

The existence of uncertainty about the costs of trade agreements on the domestic level suggests that fully legalized procedures that apply high, deterministic penalties for noncompliance could backfire, leading to an unraveling of the process of liberalization.[23] Under some conditions it will be inefficient for actors to live up to the letter of the law in their commitments to one another, such as when alternative arrangements exist that increase mutual gains.[24] These alternative arrangements generally involve temporary deviations from the rules with compensation offered to the other party. The problem is to write agreements that recognize the possibility of breach but limit it to the appropriate context, such as when economic shocks occur and all will be better off by temporarily allowing deviation from rules.

At the same time, of course, writing agreements that provide the necessary flexibility creates a moral-hazard problem. If the circumstances that demand temporary deviation are not perfectly observable to other actors, parties will be tempted to cheat. Cheating in this instance would consist of a demand to stretch the rules for a while, which all would benefit from, because of an unanticipated shock, when in fact the actor is simply attempting to get out of inconvenient commitments. Such opportunistic behavior is a constant concern in strategic settings with asymmetric information. In the context of the GATT/WTO, the primary reasons that flexibility is necessary lie in the uncertainties of domestic politics. Flexibility or "imperfection" can lead to stability and success of trade agreements, but incentives also exist for states to evade commitments even when economic conditions do not justify evasion.

The enforcement structures of the GATT/WTO thus face a difficult dilemma: to allow states to deviate from commitments when doing so would be efficient but to deter abuse of this flexibility. If enforcement is too harsh, states will comply with trade rules even in the face of high economic and political costs, and general support for liberalization is likely to decline. On the other hand, if enforcement is too lax, states will cheat, leading to a different dynamic that could similarly undermine the system. Downs and Rocke, drawing on game-theoretic models, suggest that imperfection in the enforcement mechanism is the appropriate

---

[23] Contract law recognizes the same dynamic of uncertainty requiring flexibility in contracts, under the heading of efficient breach. See Roessler, Schwartz, and Sykes 1997, 7.

[24] The idea is similar to that behind the Coase theorem: efficient agreements are reached through the mechanism of one party compensating another.

response. Punishment for infractions of GATT commitments should be probabilistic rather than deterministic.

Changes in WTO procedures have made penalties for rule violation more certain and less probabilistic. At this point, it is difficult to say whether negotiators went too far in limiting the availability of safeguards.[25] However, we can point out one unanticipated effect of the tightening of safeguards that both ties this analysis to our earlier discussion of trade negotiations and generates predictions about future attempts to further liberalize trade. There is a direct connection between states' access to safeguard provisions and their stance during trade negotiations. Domestic interests can anticipate the effects of eliminating safeguards and so will bring more pressure to bear on governments during negotiations.[26] Those who fear the possibility of adverse economic shocks without the protection of an escape clause will be highly resistant to inclusion in liberalization. In response they will demand exclusion or, at a minimum, side payments if their sector is included in liberalizing efforts. Thus extensive tightening of safeguard provisions will lead to tougher, more disaggregated negotiations as some groups lobby strenuously for exclusion. The rise in the use of voluntary export restraints and antidumping and countervailing duty cases is almost certainly a result of this difficulty in using safeguards. It is also likely that more bindingness has led to increases in the side payments governments are forced to make to groups in order to buy their support for trade agreements. Not surprisingly, perhaps, the North American Free Trade Agreement, a highly legalized trade agreement, could only gain approval in the United States after extensive use of side payments by the government.[27]

* * *

Few analysts dispute that the old trade regime was tremendously effective in reducing impediments to trade. Nevertheless, analysts and legal scholars involved in the GATT expressed dissatisfaction about many of its procedures and capacities. One concern was that the dispute-resolution procedures seemed to have a fatal flaw, in that member states could undermine the creation of dispute-resolution panels as well as any decision that went against them. Another concern was that powerful

[25] As we argue later, the safeguard reforms are counterintuitive for two reasons. First, they may be too difficult to invoke, undercutting their purpose. Second, since retaliation is limited, the stability evoked by activating export groups may have been undermined.

[26] See also Sykes 1991, 259.

[27] Hufbauer and Schott 1993.

states, particularly the United States, evaded GATT regulations when convenient. As the United States increasingly turned to unilateral remedies for perceived trade infractions, such as Section 301, other members grew increasingly concerned that the GATT was powerless in preventing unilateralism and not strong enough to provide effective enforcement.

The remedy to these problems, both in theory and in practice, was greater legalization of the GATT. As the GATT evolved into the more formal WTO, the dispute-resolution procedures were made more legal in nature and the organization gained enhanced oversight and monitoring authority. Multilateral rules of trade extended into new and difficult areas, such as intellectual property, and substituted for unilateral practices. The procedures for retaliation and compensation were made more precise and limiting. The process of negotiating the content of rules – including provisions for addressing rule breaches – led to greater precision.[28] In the next sections we evaluate these changes, asking whether or not the changes portend greater trade liberalization. Our inquiry centers on two questions. First, we ask whether the legal framework allows states to abrogate a contract when doing so would be mutually beneficial. Second, we examine the functioning of the dispute-resolution mechanism.

* * *

Exceptions and Escape Clauses

Trade legalization has constrained states by curtailing their ability to utilize safeguards and exceptions. The issue of exceptions, their status and use, has loomed large in many of the rounds of GATT negotiations. Pressure from import-competing groups is strong everywhere, although domestic institutional arrangements vary in how well they can "buy off" or ignore this resistance. The United States, for example, has been notorious for both retaining protection on the upper part of its schedule and for making particular industry side payments before even arriving in Geneva. The United States is also responsible for the inclusion of an escape clause into the GATT's original design, reflecting a desire by Congress to maintain its prerogative to renege on a trade deal if necessary.[29]

Legalization of the regime has resulted in a tightening in the use of safeguard provisions, including the escape clause. Under Article XIX,

---

[28] On the extent of changes in the WTO, see Krueger 1998.
[29] Goldstein 1993.

a country is allowed to increase protection for a home industry if a past tariff concession does damage to it.[30] If a country backs out of an agreement or imposes some additional trade restriction, it must be applied in a nondiscriminatory way; that is, countries whose exports are not hurting your industry cannot retain a preferential position.[31] When the provision is used, other countries are allowed to retaliate by reducing an equivalent amount of concession; otherwise the country imposing Article XIX must reduce tariffs on other products, equivalent to the amount of the original concession.

Two important domestic groups are potentially affected by these limitations on the use of safeguards. If nations retaliate, exporters suffer; if the government compensates, some import-competing industry will feel increased competition. Unless offered some side payment, industries have a strong incentive to have their political representative veto their inclusion into the compensatory package. Thus both the threat of retaliation and the difficulty of reassigning tariff reductions should constrain countries from raising trade barriers as allowed under Article XIX. The logic here is consistent with that offered in the preceding section.

The data on Article XIX provide support for the argument that using this provision is difficult in practice. Table 8.3 shows the aggregate use of the escape clause for all GATT members. Since the 1960s, Article XIX has been invoked at a relatively consistent rate. Given increasing levels of trade, stable numbers of Article XIX invocations imply *declining* use of this mechanism. As with the safeguard measures listed in Table 8.2, the small number of cases, compared with the significant number of industries affected by changing tariffs, should be attributed to the difficult time countries have both with the potential for retaliation and with compensating nations through alternative tariff reductions. This difficulty explains the trend toward alternative methods of protection, such as "administered protection" in the form of subsidies and antidumping and countervailing duty provisions.[32] Nontariff barriers, though not often

---

[30] "Tariff concessions and unforeseen developments must have caused an absolute or relative increase in imports which in turn causes or threatens serious injury to domestic producers . . . of like or directly competitive goods." Although the invoking party is not saddled with the burden of proving that it has met these requirements, the requirements nonetheless have deterred countries from invoking the escape clause.

[31] This often leads to a situation where the producers causing the problems in the first place could remain in a competitive position with the higher-cost home producer. The producers who get penalized are the middle-price traders who were not the problem. Shonfield 1976, 224.

[32] Baldwin 1998.

TABLE 8.3. *Use of Escape Clause by all GATT Members,*
1950–94

	Average number of cases per year	Nontariff barrier remedies as percentage of total uses
1950s	1.9	26
1960s	3.5	56
1970s	4.7	70
1980s	3.7	51
1990s[a]	1.2	75

[a] Data for the 1990s ran only from 1990 to 1 December 1993.
Source: GATT Analytical Index 1994.

used in the 1950s, were, by the 1970s, used by most countries to circumvent problems with GATT rules. Licenses, quotas, and voluntary export restraints were all means to finesse the potential problems *at home* with the GATT compensatory system.

Overall, the figures in Tables 8.2 and 8.3 suggest that use of the legally available mechanisms of flexibility in the trade regime is heavily circumscribed by the interaction of the legal provisions for their use and political realities. The increasing extent to which governments are bound by the lack of realistic escape clauses is apparent when we examine the use of compensation. Although the use of safeguards has been relatively constant, compensation or retaliation in response to the invocation of a safeguard provision was more common in the earlier years – ten cases from 1950 to 1959, ten cases from 1960 to 1969, six cases in the 1970s, and three cases in the 1980s.[33]

Use of compensation and retaliation was concentrated. The United States accounted for twelve of the twenty cases between 1950 and 1970 but only one case thereafter. Australia accounted for seven of the sixteen cases between 1960 and 1980. Although American use of Article XIX did not decline until the 1980s, the kind of remedy administrators chose to use did shift over time. Compensation could occur through reducing tariff barriers elsewhere. However, this would hurt other import-competing groups, so the compensation mechanism of Article XIX is unwieldy if these groups are organized. At the same time, rescinding tariff

[33] GATT *Analytical Index*, various issues.

concessions without compensation opens exporters to the threat of retaliation. For these reasons, the United States had moved toward a non-tariff barrier remedy by the late 1960s. The change was rather dramatic. In the early years of the regime, between 1950 and 1969, the United States compensated for a tariff hike over 93 percent of the time.[34] Thereafter, both the use of compensation and the number of invocations declined precipitously.

Overall, the evidence on the use of safeguards and compensation suggests that strict legal provisions were not necessary to maintain openness. The pattern of use of safeguard provisions in the GATT suggests that the regime gained in politically relevant bindingness, even when in legal terms the obligatory nature of rules did not change. Still, the WTO reforms attempted to clarify and make more stringent the requirements for using safeguards. Drawing on the discussion of economic uncertainty and the need for flexibility in light of the data, we suggest that increased stringency in safeguard use may be misplaced. In fact, even the GATT provisions could be interpreted to have become too tightly binding, not allowing the necessary temporary deviations from rules that contribute to long-term stability. Escape clauses, safeguards, and the like are the legal mechanisms for dealing with a world of economic uncertainty. The provisions for their use must be heavily constrained, so as to reduce the chance that states will invoke them opportunistically. However, it appears that these constraints, interacting with domestic politics, may bind states more tightly than intended.

Our cautionary note may explain why the WTO chose to forestall retaliation for three years in cases where a safeguard provision was sanctioned. Yet the choice of this tool to deal with overbinding may be a problem. Given the logic offered in the preceding section, we suggest that nations abide by their trade agreements because the threat of retaliation mobilizes export groups to counter rent-seeking producer groups. Similarly, our analysis suggests that the mobilization of groups favored those who support openness, which, in turn, deterred states from using even legal exceptions. Given the logic of domestic politics, it is hard to know whether the benefits of this new rule in terms of flexibility will outweigh its effects on the balance between pro- and antitrade groups in WTO members.

---

[34] The United States invoked Article XIX fourteen times between 1950 and 1969. Of these they used nontariff barriers alone in only one case.

Dispute Settlement

One of the major innovations of the WTO was to strengthen the dispute-resolution mechanism. States have lost the ability to wield a veto, which they used under the GATT to protect themselves against GATT-approved retaliation. In effect, residual rights of control have been shifted from states to the WTO, convened as the Dispute Settlement Body. According to proponents of the new system, the existence of veto power encouraged opportunism, whereas not having veto power deters such behavior. If this is the case, we should see predictable effects in the pattern of disputes brought to the WTO.

We suggest that the GATT dispute-settlement structure, by being more attentive to the realities of power and an uncertain economic environment, but also by providing publicity and possible sanctions when states blatantly disregarded regime rules, may have optimized the trade-off between constraint and flexibility that liberalization requires. As a way to examine this hypothesis, we ask whether the pattern of disputes has changed under the WTO in the manner predicted by the logic of reducing opportunism. The strong theoretical argument in favor of legalization claims that legalization is necessary to prevent opportunistic behavior. If we find that the incidence of opportunism has not changed in the face of increasing legalization, the argument in favor of legalization loses much of its force.[35]

If the primary effect of further legalization in dispute settlement is reducing opportunism, it should appear in the data as reduced political manipulation of the regime. Eliminating the power to veto should have observable effects on the activities of states and the outcome of disputes. Political scientists are producing a burgeoning literature on GATT/WTO dispute settlement, using sophisticated statistical techniques. However, this literature, regardless of the techniques involved, cannot escape problems of selection bias, since states chose whether to bring disputes and at what stage to resolve them. Here we suggest a few simple hypotheses about how the pattern of disputes should change with legalization if its major effect is a reduction in opportunism. If the data do not support these simple hypotheses, the case for legalization is substantially weakened.

---

[35] We assume a goal of reducing opportunism on theoretical grounds, without claiming that all negotiators had precisely this goal in mind. Certainly the agendas of negotiators were diverse, and reducing opportunism was only one goal among many.

Adopting the unitary state/opportunism model, we derive propositions about how legalization should influence patterns of disputes. Assuming the problem of opportunism suggests that the loss of veto power should have two primary effects: a *deterrent* effect and a *distributive* effect. States will behave strategically both in deciding when to bring disputes and whether to comply preemptively so that others have no cause to bring a dispute. This two-sided strategic behavior could render many predictions indeterminate. To identify refutable hypotheses, we focus on expected changes in the relative behavior of developed and developing states. Since both are subject to the same incentives in deciding whether to comply with changes in GATT/WTO rules, changes in the proportions of disputes brought are likely caused by changed calculations about the chances of success in a dispute and not by changed patterns of compliance. Although developing countries have more trade restrictions than developed countries, the marginal impact of new dispute-resolution procedures on compliance decisions should be the same for both. In addition, we concentrate on just the first few years of experience under the WTO rules. Since states can change their behavior in bringing disputes more quickly than they can change their basic trade regulations, the patterns we observe should be due primarily to calculations about whether bringing disputes is worthwhile, not fundamental changes in compliance.

A deterrent effect refers to the likelihood that the existence of veto power would deter states from bringing disputes. Bringing a formal dispute is costly and time consuming, and states could calculate that doing so is not worth the trouble if the powerful will simply veto any decision that goes against them. Thus we generate a deterrence hypothesis: *the existence of veto power deters some states from bringing disputes, and with the loss of veto power these states are no longer deterred.*

In order to collect data relevant to this general hypothesis, we need to derive some observable implications from it. We do so on the assumption that the intent of legalizing dispute-resolution procedures is to reduce opportunistic behavior by powerful states such as the United States.[36] One implication is that, since powerful states can no longer veto decisions that go against them, *we should expect the proportion of complaints against developed countries to rise under the WTO* (hypothesis 1). If states were deterred from bringing complaints against the powerful because of the existence of the veto, then such complaints should have a higher probability of success as a result of the loss of the veto. Therefore, we

---

[36] Jackson 1998.

should see more disputes brought against the powerful. This should be true even if states are, for strategic reasons, complying more fully under the WTO. Better compliance should hold for both developed and developing states; there is no reason to expect the proportion of disputes against the powerful to change as a result of changes in compliance patterns.

Second, since less powerful countries may now have a greater chance of having decisions in their favor implemented, *we should see developing countries increasingly bringing complaints* (hypothesis 2). Simply put, the deterrence hypothesis suggests that under the WTO, weak states should no longer be deterred. Like hypothesis 1, hypothesis 2 should hold even if patterns of compliance have improved, since improved compliance should hold for both developed and developing states. There is no reason to expect strategic compliance behavior to lead to a change in the proportion of disputes brought by developing countries.

Finally, a process marred by opportunism should be most evident in relations between powerful and weak states. Thus a third implication of the deterrence hypothesis is that *we should see an increase in the proportion of cases brought by developing countries against developed countries* (hypothesis 3). As the WTO depoliticizes trade and so encourages the less powerful to demand their legal rights, we should see more of these "asymmetric" disputes.

The evidence on these three hypotheses about deterrent effects is mixed.[37] Regarding hypothesis 1, of the complaints raised under the GATT through 1989, 87 percent were brought against developed states.[38] Under the WTO, this percentage has dropped, contrary to the expectation from the opportunism perspective, to 64 percent. This is likely a result of the expansion of regime rules to cover more developing-country trade. The high percentage of complaints brought under the GATT against developed states is not surprising, considering the value of their market for other states. Yet it indicates that the power to veto did not allow powerful states to deter others from bringing complaints against them. This finding suggests that the GATT, in spite of the decentralized nature of its dispute-resolution process, was able to constrain the behavior of developed countries, as Hudec also concludes.[39] Preventing opportunism does not require high levels of legalization.

---

[37] For a more thorough examination of patterns of disputes in the GATT and the WTO, see Hudec 1999; and Sevilla 1998.

[38] Hudec 1993, 297.

[39] Hudec 1999.

Hypothesis 2 posits that developing countries will be more likely to use the WTO procedures than they were to use the GATT mechanism. If this is true, we should see the percentage of complaints brought by developing countries rising under the WTO. This prediction holds up better than the first. Under the GATT (through 1989), only 19 percent of complaints were brought by developing countries.[40] This number has risen to 33 percent in the first few years that the WTO mechanisms have been in effect. However, considering the evidence just discussed on the identity of defendants, it seems likely that this increased reliance on the dispute-resolution mechanism reflects some dynamic other than a decreased ability of the powerful to deter complaints against themselves. In particular, it seems likely that increased legalization has reduced the costs of bringing suits, thus making it more frequently worth the cost of bringing a complaint for poor states, regardless of the identity of the defendant.[41] In other words, legalization has encouraged weaker states to bring more complaints, generally because doing so is easier, not because the powerful will no longer veto them.

Hypothesis 3 predicts an increase in the number of complaints brought by developing countries against developed countries under the WTO. This hypothesis fares badly, because the data show that under the GATT developing countries targeted almost solely the rich world in their disputes. Hudec's data show almost no cases of developing countries bringing complaints against one another. The exceptions are disputes between India and Pakistan. In contrast, the twenty complaints brought by developing countries so far under the WTO have been just about evenly divided between targeting the developed and developing world. Two factors might explain this finding. First, the costs of bringing disputes are now lower, so it is more often worthwhile to bring them against developing countries. Second, the Uruguay Round extended many trade rules to developing countries, so the dispute-resolution procedures can be used against them for the first time. Regardless of the particular mechanism at work, the pattern of complaints shows that the major change under the WTO procedures has been an increased willingness of developing countries to bring complaints against one another. This effect is not consistent with reduced opportunism.

If legalization reduces opportunism as intended, a second effect that should result from eliminating the veto power is enhanced equity in the

---

[40] Hudec 1993, 296.
[41] Sevilla 1998.

outcomes of disputes. We can formalize this as a fourth hypothesis: *legalization of dispute resolution has reduced the bias toward the powerful in the settlement of disputes* (hypothesis 4). A distributive effect could be estimated by comparing the outcomes of disputes brought under the GATT versus under the WTO. Unfortunately, since few cases have yet been resolved under the WTO, we can say nothing definitive on this issue. However, we can look at dispute outcomes under the GATT to see if they tended to favor developed countries as expected. If the weakly legalized GATT mechanisms encouraged opportunism, this trend should appear as a bias toward the powerful in the outcomes of disputes under the GATT. Eric Reinhardt has provided a careful statistical study of the factors determining the distributive outcomes of GATT disputes.[42] He tests the hypothesis that powerful states tend to get a larger share of the benefits of resolved disputes. Employing a number of alternative operationalizations, Reinhardt found no evidence that asymmetries of power work in favor of the powerful. Instead, he found a bias in favor of defendants, regardless of power asymmetries.

As with the data on the choice to bring complaints, in looking at the outcomes of disputes we find little evidence that the GATT operated in an overtly politicized manner, with powerful states using the GATT dispute-resolution procedures to deter weaker states from bringing complaints or to force outcomes of disputes to favor the powerful. The GATT, in spite of its weak level of legalization, provided many of the benefits we expect to see from international institutions. It discouraged opportunism without a resort to highly legalized mechanisms. This finding raises further questions about the benefits that states will be able to derive from further legalization.

Improving the compliance of powerful states with their explicit obligations under the rules of international trade was one of the primary motivations behind the enhanced dispute-resolution mechanisms of the WTO. Thus moving from a politicized process to a more legalized one should have an observable impact on the behavior of powerful states. However, the evidence is weak that the WTO has made the difference intended by proponents of more legalized dispute-resolution procedures. While developing countries appear more willing to lodge formal complaints than they were previously, the complaints do not target the behavior of powerful states any more than they did before. One plausible interpretation of the evidence on the number of complaints being brought

[42] Reinhardt 1995.

is that the GATT was in fact quite influential in constraining powerful states, leading us to ask how much value will be added by increased legalization. Considering the drawbacks of increased legalization discussed earlier, the benefits must be clear in order to justify further moves in this direction. Dispute outcomes do not show evidence of coercion by powerful states, consistent with the idea that the political sensitivity of the GATT was not as much of an impediment to liberalization as legalization proponents presumed.

CONCLUSION

This article was motivated by questions about the relationship between international legalization and trade. The benefits of legalization lie in the fact that the more efficiently a regime provides information, reduces transaction costs, and monitors member behavior, the harder it is for a unitary state to behave opportunistically and renege on trade agreements. However, an analysis of the domestic requisites of free trade suggests potential negative effects of legalization that must be weighed against its benefits. When we consider cooperation with the trade regime to be a function of the interests of domestic political actors, the assumption that increased legalization leads to more trade openness becomes questionable. Although we cannot demonstrate that legalization has gone so far that it threatens liberalization, we do wish to sound a cautionary note based in the impact of legalization on the mobilization of protectionist groups.

We examined three theoretical issues implicated by the legalization of the trade regime. First, we asked how greater precision at the time of negotiating treaties changes the incentives of antitrade groups to mobilize. In that legalization leads to more and better information about the distributional effects of proposed agreements, we suggested that it could actually deter the conclusion of cooperative deals. Faced with certainty of loss, the expected utility of a group's organizing increases, suggesting that negotiators could find themselves confronted by powerful veto groups, undermining their ability to construct a majority in favor of a treaty. This dynamic of information provided by a legalized regime leading to massive mobilization may help explain the level of social activism at the 1999 WTO meetings in Seattle.

Second, we applied the same logic of information and mobilization to expectations about the maintenance of agreements already in force. The logic of information here predicted a different outcome from that during negotiations. By focusing on the incentives of exporters, we argued that when exporters know that they are likely targets of retaliation, they are more motivated to organize in support of the trade regime than those subject to an imprecise threat of retaliation. Thus the prediction about the effect of changes in the information environment varies, depending upon whether we are considering the expansion of trade liberalization or compliance with enacted treaties.

Finally, we looked at the effects of a system of highly deterministic penalties on domestic actors. Here we suggested that trade regimes need to incorporate some flexibility in their enforcement procedures; too little enforcement may encourage opportunism, but too much may backfire, undermining the ability of domestic actors to find support for an open trade policy. By decreasing the ability to breach agreements, WTO nego-tiators may have underestimated the inherently uncertain character of the international economy and so the need to allow practical flexibility in enforcement of regime rules.

* * *

Given the short history of the WTO, the empirical support for our theoretical arguments is inconclusive. Still, evidence suggests that the effects of legalization may not be as glowing as proponents argue. First, legalization may be one reason for the increased attention and activity of antitrade groups. We cannot say whether this will deter nations from further liberalization, since policy will ultimately depend on the balance of national forces between pro- and antitrade groups. Still, it is clear that those groups who are targeted for liberalization in the new round of discussions have become active proponents of particularistic policies. Second, some evidence suggests that changes in WTO rules undermine the incentive for export groups to mobilize in defense of free trade. In that the WTO makes retaliation more difficult, both because of changes in the rules on safeguard provisions and because of the process of dispute resolution, we expect exporters to mobilize less often to balance the action of rent-seeking import-competing groups.

Consideration of the effect of the more precise and binding safeguard and dispute-settlement provisions also raises questions about the turn to-ward legalization. Given the difficulty of their use, few countries turned to GATT safeguards, choosing instead alternative methods to deal with difficulties in compliance. Making these safeguards more difficult to use may have been both unnecessary and counterproductive – if countries found it necessary to turn to alternative mechanisms to deal with the political effects of market dislocation before, the change in rules on safeguards does little to solve the underlying problem. Similarly, our investigation of the WTO dispute-settlement mechanism gives us little reason to think that legalization in the realm of settling disputes will have significant effects on trade compliance. The GATT system was relatively effective at deterring opportunism, in spite of its political nature.

The source of stability of trade agreements is found in domestic political mechanisms. The rules of the regime influence countries by making it easier or harder to find majority support for trade openness; if the regime supports rules that are unhelpful to politicians at home, it may well undercut its own purpose. Thus the legalization of international trade could turn on itself if analysis of the benefits of legalization neglects associated political costs. Thomas Franck has argued that the greater the "determinacy" of a rule, the more legitimate it becomes.[43] Determinacy, however, may be of greater value to lawyers than to politicians, whose interests in trade liberalization will be constrained by elections. Elected officials face a dilemma. If there is too little formalism in international trade rules, politicians will be unable to commit for fear of opportunism by others; too much formalism and they lose their ability to opt out of the regime temporarily during especially intense political opposition or tough economic times. Analyses of legalization that focus on maximizing state compliance neglect complex domestic political dynamics. It is well possible that attempts to maximize compliance through legalization will have the unintended effect of mobilizing domestic groups opposed to free trade, thus undermining hard-won patterns of cooperation and the expansion of trade.

[43] Franck 1995.

9

Alternatives to "Legalization": Richer Views of Law and Politics

Martha Finnemore and Stephen J. Toope

The authors of "Legalization and World Politics" (special issue of *IO*, summer 2000) have done an excellent job connecting one branch of thinking about international law (rooted in the legal theory of H. L. A. Hart) to one branch of thinking about international politics (neoliberal institutionalism).[1] However, the connections between the two disciplines are broader and deeper than the volume indicates. International legal scholars have long understood that international law is more than the formal, treaty-based law on which the volume's authors focus their work. Law is a broad social phenomenon deeply embedded in the practices, beliefs, and traditions of societies, and shaped by interaction among societies.[2] Customary international law displays this richer understanding of law's operation as does the increasingly large body of what has been termed "interstitial law," that is, the implicit rules operating in and around explicit normative frameworks.[3] Similarly, legal pluralist analysis of domestic and international legal systems focuses on the interaction of overlapping state and nonstate normative systems.[4]

We show how a fuller appreciation of what international law is and how it influences behavior allows room for a wealth of intellectual connections between international legal scholarship and research in international

[1] *International Organization* 54, 3, Summer 2000.
[2] Glenn 2000.
[3] Lowe 2000.
[4] See Walzer 1983; and Macdonald 1998.

We thank Jutta Brunnée, H. P. Glenn, Rod Macdonald, René Provost, Bob Wolfe, participants in the University of Chicago Law School International Law Workshop, two anonymous reviewers, and the editors of *IO* for helpful comments on an earlier draft.

relations – connections that are not evident from the framing of the "legalization" phenomenon in the *IO* volume. *** Narrow and stylized frameworks like this one may be useful if they provide conceptual clarity and facilitate operationalization of concepts. However, the empirical applications of legalization in the volume suggest the opposite: the articles reveal that the concept of legalization as defined in the volume is peripheral, in need of revision, or generates hypotheses that are wrong. ***

A RICHER VIEW OF INTERNATIONAL LAW

The framers of the volume are careful in defining their terms. *Legalization* refers to a specific set of characteristics that institutions may (or may not) possess: obligation, precision, and delegation.[5] Each of these characterizations may be present in varying degrees along a continuum, and each can vary independently of the others. This attention to definitions is helpful and lends coherence to the volume, but appropriating the general term *legalization* for only a few features of the law is misleading. It suggests that law *is* and can only be this limited collection of formalized and institutionalized features. The phenomenon the authors investigate might more accurately be termed *legal bureaucratization,* since it seems to involve the structural manifestations of law in public bureaucracies. *** Without a broader view of law that causes us to pay attention to legal procedures, methodologies, institutions, and processes generating legitimacy, the authors' three components of legalization lack theoretical coherence and raise more questions than they answer, as we show.

* * *

The view of law presented in the volume, though important, is limited. In it, law is constructed primarily through cases and courts, or through formal treaty negotiation. The processes of law are viewed overwhelmingly as processes of dispute resolution, mostly within formal institutionalized contexts. The "international legal actions" chosen in the volume's introduction to epitomize the phenomenon of legalization are mainly examples of tribunal decisions. The secondary evidence of legalization is drawn exclusively from explicit obligations imposed by treaties.[6] Law

---

[5] Abbott et al. 2000, 401.
[6] Goldstein et al. 2000, 385–86.

in this view is constraint only; it has no creative or generative powers in social life. Yet law working in the world constitutes relationships as much as it delimits acceptable behavior. The very idea of state sovereignty, both a legal and a political construction, creates the context that allows for the formal articulation of treaty rules.[7] Similarly, property rights, over which political actors battle in many of the volume's articles, are themselves dynamic constructions generated by law. Oddly, given this group of authors, even the role of formal law in creating and shaping the life of institutions like the IMF, GATT, and WTO, explicitly addressed in the volume, is neglected. Theirs is an overwhelmingly liberal and positivist view of law. It is also limited to the bureaucratic formalism described by Weber and so is very "Western" in a narrow sense.[8] We are not implying that Western law, positivism, and liberalism are uninteresting theoretical frameworks, but an analysis of the role of law in world politics that is entirely constrained by these three optics, attending primarily to formal institutions, is at best partial.[9]

Despite the efforts of the framers of the volume to define terms and to expressly bracket issues, at the end of the day it is difficult to decide exactly what the authors have set out to demonstrate and what analytic work their concept of legalization is supposed to accomplish. Is legalization a dependent variable or an independent one? *** If legalization is a phenomenon to be explained, what other factors might explain it, and how important are they? If legalization explains aspects of state behavior, what other independent variables should be considered in assessing legalization's role, and how might these interact with legalization?[10] Equally important for the authors, do the three defining features of legalization all have the same causes, or cause the same effects, and how would we know if they did (or did not)? ***

---

[7] Biersteker and Weber 1996.

[8] Glenn 2000.

[9] For a helpful categorization of various legal theories as they relate to the question of compliance, see Kingsbury 1998. Among the competing theories of international law (and particularly of international obligation) that are not included within the volume's concept of legalization are the "world constitutive process" model of the Yale School (Lasswell and McDougal 1971; Reisman 1992), natural law approaches (Verdross and Koeck 1983), the "transnational legal process" model of Harold Koh (Koh 1997), the "interactional" framework of Brunnée and Toope (Brunnée and Toope 2000), and the rigorously rationalistic law and economics approach of Goldsmith and Posner (Goldsmith and Posner 1999).

[10] See Abbott and Snidal 2000; see also Abbott et al. 2000.

Three Lacunae

Political scientists have understood for decades that formal institutions do not capture many of the most important features of politics. Indeed, the authors of this volume have a fairly broad, and by now standard, political science definition of institutions, one that focuses attention beyond their formal attributes. Institutions are "rules, norms, and decision-making procedures" that shape expectations, interests, and behavior.[11] Marrying such a broad understanding of institutions to a narrow and formal understanding of law seems both unfortunate and unnecessary. A fuller understanding of law would complement our more nuanced understanding of institutions and produce a richer joint research agenda. To illustrate, we discuss three interrelated features of international law neglected in the volume; these features are central to understanding its effects on world politics and, further, are crucial to a theoretically defensible understanding of the very specific legalization phenomenon the volume's authors employ.

Custom

The most obvious casualty of the volume's narrow framing of legalization is customary international law, with which it almost completely fails to engage. Any assessment of law's persuasive influence that neglects to treat seriously the customary law elements of such topics as state responsibility, legal personality, territory, human rights, and the use of force is bound to produce a skewed perspective. For example, customary law on the use of force stands alongside, complements, and even modifies treaty-based norms.[12] Although the UN Charter and humanitarian law treaties establish an explicit framework of norms circumscribing the use of force in international relations, no one analyzing this issue-area can afford to ignore the customary law of self-defense or the impact of the concept of *jus cogens* (peremptory norms) on the attitudes of states toward the legitimate use of force.[13] It is not surprising that the volume contains but the briefest discussion of security issues, for they simply cannot fit within a narrow judicial and treaty-based perspective on law's influence in world affairs.[14] Similarly, in the area of human rights, the broadening

---

[11] Goldstein et al. 2000, 387.
[12] *Nicaragua v. United States (Merits)* [1986] ICJ Rep. 14.
[13] See Bowett 1958; and Ragazzi 1997.
[14] The exception is a brief foray into ASEAN's security relationships in Kahler 2000a. The *Nicaragua Case* (1986) is discussed in Keohane, Moravcsik, and Slaughter 2000, though for purposes unrelated to an analysis of the customary law on the use of force.

of customary law obligations has altered the content of interstate diplomatic rhetoric and affected bilateral political relationships. Canada and
Norway now engage in a trilateral "human rights dialogue" with China,
for example, an engagement that could not take place in the absence of
customary norms, for China has yet to ratify key human rights treaties.[15]
Again, it is not surprising that the one article on human rights concludes that the legalization framework does not explain behavior particularly well.

Defining Characteristics of Law

A second, related issue concerns the selection of obligation, precision,
and delegation as the defining characteristics of legalization. While the
volume's framers offer careful discussion of these terms, their meanings,
and characteristics, they say little about why, among the universe of legal
features, these three are more important than others. These three features
certainly do not define law or distinguish it from other types of normativity, nor are they the source of law's power (or, if they are, that case is not
made in the volume).

Precision and delegation are particularly problematic. In a number of
well-established areas of international law with strong records of influence and compliance, norms are relatively imprecise. Examples include
the delimitation of maritime boundaries (often accomplished on the basis
of "equity"), the bases of state criminal jurisdiction (where overlapping
rules are the norm), and state responsibility (including a very broad duty
not to knowingly allow one's territory to be used in a manner harmful to
another state). Similarly, there are wide swaths of functioning international law that do not depend in any way on extensive "delegation" of
decision-making authority. Outside of the European context, the entire
law of human rights operates and affects world politics without any
mechanisms of compulsory adjudication. *** A comparable pattern of
influence in the absence of delegation is found in international environmental law. Many international environmental commitments continue to
function on the basis of information-sharing and voluntary compliance.
Where modern treaties create mechanisms to promote implementation,
they are often premised on the need for positive reinforcement of

---

[15] For example, although China recently ratified the International Covenant on Economic,
Social, and Cultural Rights, it has yet to ratify the International Covenant on Civil and
Political Rights.

obligations rather than on adjudication and sanctions for noncompliance. There is no extensive delegation of decision-making authority. Why delegation and precision should be defining features of legalization and what they add to the analytic power of this concept is simply not clear.

Further, the relationship among these three characteristics is unexplored, a significant lacuna since these features could contribute to contradictory developments in many circumstances. Increased precision could lead to less obligation, when prospective members of legal regimes are driven away by fears of detailed rules that are inflexible (a point actually supported by the description of the WTO offered by Judith Goldstein and Lisa Martin).[16] Delegation of decision making can also lead to less precision in rules rather than to greater clarity, as presumed by the proponents of legalization. If one considers the decisions of the International Court of Justice in boundary delimitation cases, for example, the results are clearly legal, influential, and effective in promoting compliance, but they are highly imprecise.[17] What we gain by combining, rather than disaggregating, concepts with such complex and tense interrelationships is not well explained.

Most problematic, however, is the volume's conceptualization of obligation, arguably the central preoccupation both of lawyers and of political scientists interested in how norms affect state behavior. Obligation is central to the volume's framework of legalization, yet the authors articulate no theory of obligation and seem remarkably uncurious about how a sense of obligation might be generated. In the volume's lead article, legal obligation is defined in an entirely circular fashion, with reference to its products: "Legal obligations bring into play the established norms, procedures, and forms of discourse of the international legal system."[18] We know obligation by what it achieves, but this approach does not explain how obligation creates these products. To the extent that the bases of obligation are treated at all in the framing article, the conceptualization is very thin, formal, and contractual. Obligation is created when parties enter into treaties or other express agreements. The mechanism for generating obligation is thus choice – presumably choice by

---

[16] Goldstein and Martin 2000.

[17] In the *North Sea Continental Shelf Cases* [1969] ICJ Rep. 3, the court articulated a "rule" of law that the continental shelf should be divided on the basis of "equitable delimitation taking into consideration all of the circumstances." This rule has shaped all subsequent continental shelf negotiations as well as judicial and arbitral decisions.

[18] Abbott et al. 2000, 409.

utility-maximizing actors.[19] Yet both legal scholars and international relations (IR) scholars understand very well that contractual obligations alone are often insufficient to determine behavior.

More careful theorizing of these defining characteristics might have led the framers to explore some alternative features of law and develop more robust concepts. For example, one concept that is notably absent from the various analyses of obligation is legitimacy, yet legal scholars have long focused on legitimacy as an essential source of obligation and "compliance pull" in law.[20] Legitimacy in law has been argued to have a number of interrelated sources. Legitimacy is generated in part through attention to internal legal values that we seem to take for granted in the liberal democratic West but that students of repression will recognize as essential. Law is legitimate only to the extent that it produces rules that are generally applicable, exhibit clarity or determinacy, are coherent with other rules, are publicized (so that people know what they are), seek to avoid retroactivity, are relatively constant over time, are possible to perform, and are congruent with official action.[21] Law that adheres to these values is more likely to generate a sense of obligation, and corresponding behavior change, than law that ignores these values. Legal legitimacy also depends on agents in the system understanding why rules are necessary.[22] Participating in constructing law enhances agents' understanding of its necessity. Finally, adherence to specific legal rationality that all participants understand and accept helps to

[19] In Abbott and Snidal's discussion of "soft law," that quintessentially fluid concept is treated as a preexisting form of institution to be chosen by states for strategic reasons. Abbott and Snidal 2000. This approach misses much of what we know from many legal analyses about how soft law works; see Chinkin 1989; Hillgenberg 1999; and Finnemore 2000. First, soft law is not simply "out there" waiting to be chosen. Part of what is "soft" about this form of law is precisely that it is in flux, in the process of becoming. How states treat it is not exogenous to soft law; it determines and shapes soft law; it is constitutive of it. Equally important, the notion that states "choose" soft law formulations is misleading. Soft law, like customary law, is not always "chosen" in a meaningful strategic sense. For example, the evolution of the "precautionary principle" or "intergenerational equity" in international environmental law is a study in normative entrepreneurship and subtle instantiation as much as in strategic choice. See Brunnée 1993; and Brunnée and Toope 1997.

[20] See Lauterpacht 1947; Lasswell and McDougal 1971 (where legitimacy is not discussed directly but is implicit in the posited relationship between "authority" and "control"); Franck 1990; and Byers 1999.

[21] See Fuller 1969; Franck 1990; and Postema 1994. These legitimating characteristics are much broader than the volume authors' concept of "precision," as indicated by Fuller's term for these values – "internal morality of law." Fuller 1969.

[22] See Fuller 1969; and Postema 1994.

legitimate the collective construction of the law. Legal claims are legitimate and persuasive only if they are rooted in reasoned argument that creates analogies to past practice, demonstrate congruence with the overall systemic logic of existing law, and attend to contemporary social aspirations and the larger moral fabric of society.[23] Law that exhibits this kind of rationality – that is viewed as necessary, involves in its construction those it binds, and adheres to internal legal values – is more likely to be viewed as legitimate than law that does not have these features.

Legitimate law generates obligation, not just in a formal sense but also in a felt sense. Legitimacy thus connects obligation to behavior in important ways.[24] This is a major strain of argument in international law scholarship, one that IR scholars do read, yet the authors of the *IO* volume do not address legitimacy as part of the legalization phenomenon. They never investigate legitimacy's relationship to obligation, precision, and delegation, nor do they explore alternative hypotheses concerning legitimacy.[25] We suspect that legitimacy is a prior variable, generating a felt sense of obligation and empowering those who delegate to do so. Variations in legitimacy almost certainly relate to variations in legalization. The spread of formal legal institutions investigated in the volume is likely to depend on the legitimacy of these formal legal processes generally and on the legitimacy of the particular configurations of these processes (the kind of delegation, the nature and content of the obligation) that these institutions embody.

Law as Process

A third fundamental issue to consider is the nature of legalization itself. The authors of this volume treat law as an artifact – something created by state choice – and equate legalization with three features of the *form* of this artifact (obligation, delegation, precision). Politics thus becomes "legalized," in their view, as it displays these three features. When one thinks about what legitimates law, however, another possibility emerges. Law, and by implication legalization, may be much more about process

---

[23] See Fuller 1969; Franck 1990; and Brunnée and Toope 2000.

[24] Franck 1990.

[25] Abbott and Snidal recognize that legitimacy exists, but they do not theorize or investigate its independent causal effects on strategic choice. Abbott and Snidal 2000, 428–29. Lutz and Sikkink do explore legitimacy issues and find, as we suggest, that these are causally prior to legalization. Lutz and Sikkink 2000, 654–59.

than about form or product. Much of what legitimates law and distinguishes it from other forms of normativity are the processes by which it is created and applied – adherence to legal process values, the ability of actors to participate and feel their influence, and the use of legal forms of reasoning. A view of legalization that focused on legal relationships and processes rather than forms would be more dynamic and better suited to explaining change – which many of us, the volume's authors included, are interested in. Unlike Thomas M. Franck, we would not argue that process is the only thing that legitimates law.[26] Values suffuse legal argument and they underlie legal processes generally, so it is not sufficient to seek the power of law solely in the details of its processes of elaboration and application.[27] But it is equally suspect to craft a framework for the empirical study of legalization that ignores process in favor of an essentially structural, and product-focused, analysis.

As framed in the volume, the world's "move to law" is a move to a very particular kind of law, and not one that resonates with international lawyers who are unaccustomed to the narrow view of obligation espoused by the authors and who would doubt that precision or delegation are the hallmarks of growing normativity in international relations. A broader understanding of law would open up research connections among scholars who would not find the authors' formulation of legalization particularly engaging. Most obviously, a more culturally and sociologically attuned formulation of the role of law speaks to constructivist concerns and builds bridges between that group of IR scholars and like-minded thinkers in law. Situating law in its broader social context allows room for cultural explanations of behavior and identity formation in ways that these scholars will find helpful. It also promises to reveal connections between IR theory and approaches to comparative law that address issues of identity and normative change within legal traditions.[28] Focusing on law as a set of relationships, processes, and institutions embedded in social context has the further advantage of reformulating the lively legal debate over how "soft" law "hardens" and connecting it with the rich and growing body of work on transnational norm dynamics that has occupied constructivists in recent years. ***

[26] Franck 1990.
[27] See Hurrell 2000; and Toope 2000.
[28] See Postema 1991; Kennedy 1997; and Glenn 2000.

WHAT DIFFERENCE DOES LAW MAKE?

A fuller understanding of law is not simply a pleasing accessory to the framework proposed in this volume, however. It is a necessity. The purpose of the legalization concept is presumably to facilitate empirical research. If a narrowly drawn and simplified concept generates new insights for researchers and helps them explain empirical puzzles, it may still be valuable. To assess whether legalization does this, we examine the three articles in the volume that apply the concept of legalization to different issue-areas. Our examination suggests that the concept provides little help to these researchers, not only because it contains such a narrow notion of law but also because it is inadequately theorized.

Beth Simmons, applying the concept of legalization to monetary affairs, asks why states voluntarily declare themselves bound by Article VIII rules concerning current account restrictions and unified exchange rates. She frames this as a credible commitments problem. The policy dilemma for states is to make their commitments to Article VIII rules credible to markets, thus producing desired investment flows. Law's role is to provide a "hook" or signal that makes commitments credible.[29]

The legalization concept does little work here. Simmons certainly does not need it to carry out her analysis. The only aspect of the concept Simmons treats is obligation, recasting it as "credible commitment"; precision and delegation are apparently not relevant. Conceptual equipment for credible commitment and signaling analyses have been around for a long time. Simmons could have completed essentially the same analysis without "legalization." * * *

Adopting a richer view of law, as we suggest, might open this analysis to some important questions and make law more than peripheral in our understanding of these events. A focus on law's role, for example, might prompt us to ask whether or why legal commitments are credible signals to markets for all states. After all, some of the developing countries most successful at attracting investment, such as China and Indonesia, have extremely weak conceptions and applications of the rule of law. If accepting legal obligations is such an important signal to investors, as assumed here, why do investors pour so much money into countries where law is so weak?[30] If Simmons believes that domestic and international rule of law are unconnected, so that investors assume that even countries without

[29] Simmons 2000, 601.
[30] Wang's analysis of exactly this question in the case of China points squarely to the need for a broader view of how law works. Wang 2000.

effective rule of law domestically will be bound unproblematically in the international realm, this would certainly require some elaboration, since it cuts against prominent past work by other authors in the volume.[31]

More generally, equating law with obligation and obligation with credible commitments ignores much of what law does in monetary affairs that might be relevant to Simmons' analysis. The notion that law is merely promise-keeping ignores both the authoritative and the transformative character of law. States are not making the Article VIII decisions in a legal vacuum. The Articles of Agreement (of which Article VIII is a part) created an entire structure of law on monetary affairs, including a Weberian rational-legal bureaucracy (the International Monetary Fund) to make policy on monetary matters. Law thus created a new source of authority in monetary matters, the IMF, which generated new rules for states but also new knowledge about technical matters in economic policy that changed expectations for behavior. Throughout the period examined by Simmons, states are making their decisions about Article VIII commitments in a dynamic environment of law, rules, and economic knowledge about monetary policy, and much of this changing environment is actively promoted by the IMF. * * *

Goldstein and Martin's analysis of trade politics addresses the volume's legalization concept much more directly. They examine the effects of increasing obligation, precision, and delegation in formal trade agreements on international cooperation and compliance. They find that "more is not necessarily better" because more precision and "bindingness" in rules can mobilize protectionist groups who can now better calculate the costs of freer trade.

What work does the legalization concept do here? As in Simmons' article, Goldstein and Martin create a link between legalization and another well-known concept in political analysis, in this case, information. "Increased transparency" (better information) is added to the definition of legalization without comment in this article.[32] Information then becomes the centerpiece of the analysis. "Legalization entails a process of increasing rule precision, [ergo] a more legalized trade regime will provide more and better information about the distributional implications of commercial agreements."[33] Once we understand what legalization

---

[31] For example, Slaughter 1995.
[32] Goldstein and Martin 2000, 604.
[33] Ibid., 604.

does to information, information does most of the heavy analytic lifting in this article, not law.

*** Goldstein and Martin make a strong case that an inverse relationship exists between precision and any sense of felt obligation, since more precision tends to promote greater use of escape clauses and mobilizes interest groups for noncompliance. ***

Unfortunately, however, Goldstein and Martin's findings seem not to have prompted much rethinking of the content of legalization by the volume's framers or by Miles Kahler in the conclusion.[34] Such an overall examination might have revealed additional problematic relationships among their three elements of legalization, even in the Goldstein and Martin article. For example, it is not clear that increased precision in law always increases certainty about distributional effects, as Goldstein and Martin assume. If increased precision involves delegation, uncertainty may remain high or even increase because delegation, by its nature, creates uncertainty in principal-agent relationships. Thus, members of the WTO may have more precise rules about resolving disputes than they did under the GATT, but the workings of the dispute settlement body may be sufficiently opaque or unpredictable that distributional consequences remain uncertain in many areas. Conversely, increased delegation does not guarantee more precise rules for the same principal-agent reasons, so there is no reason to think those co-vary. The overall effect of Goldstein and Martin's interesting finding about the effects of information is thus to suggest a wide array of possible relationships among legalization's core features. This, in turn, suggests that the legalization concept is itself less analytically useful than its component parts, which, as we noted earlier, are not necessarily or uniquely legal.

More attention to law might lead these authors to ask some substantive questions that would bear on their findings. These authors are commendably enthusiastic about including domestic politics in their analysis yet remarkably inattentive to variations in those politics created by widely varying structures of domestic law. Law governing ratification of trade agreements, central to this analysis, differs hugely across even the democratic, industrialized countries on which these authors focus. These differences profoundly change the "logic of [domestic interest group] mobilization" in different countries, around which the analysis revolves. For example, the authors assert that it is the need for treaty ratification, with attendant public processes of debate, that gives rise to the

[34] Kahler 2000b.

possibility of effective protectionist backlash. Yet in Canada, the United States' largest trading partner, the treaty-making power is held by the functional equivalent of the executive branch (in practice the prime minister and cabinet), and there is no constitutional requirement for ratification by Parliament. The entire NAFTA treaty could have been concluded by the executive branch, benefiting from the legitimacy granted by an overwhelming parliamentary majority, without any opportunity for formal political debate. * * *

These differences in legal structure are more than simply differences in the constraints or political opportunity structure surrounding strategic actors. Domestic structures of law are, themselves, mobilizing factors for a wide variety of groups involved in trade politics. Domestic law is what constitutes, empowers, and mobilizes a host of interest groups, from trade unions, to professional organizations, to business groups, to environmentalists and human rights activists. Unions have different forms and powers in different national legal contexts, as do business groups and nongovernmental organizations. Law's role in mobilizing different groups is much more profound than mere provision of information.

* * *

Goldstein and Martin are certainly correct that domestic politics are important in trade politics, but significant variation in domestic legal systems should provoke some caution in claiming generalized effects of domestic ratification on interest group politics. If generalizing their analysis to Canada is problematic, we suspect that generalizing to Europe and Asia, and certainly the developing world, would be even more so. * * *

Ellen Lutz and Kathryn Sikkink apply the legalization concept to human rights to test their hypothesis that increased legalization increases compliance with human rights law.[35] They examine three areas of human rights law – torture, disappearance, and democratic governance – and find the least compliance in the most "legalized" area, torture, and the most compliance in the least "legalized" area, democratic governance. They find stronger explanatory power for compliance in broader social variables and in the "norm cascade" that swept through Latin America in the 1970s and 1980s.

Oddly, the legalization concept seems to be most useful to these researchers who find its effects so limited. Unlike Simmons, or Goldstein and Martin, Lutz and Sikkink take us through an examination of the

---

[35] Lutz and Sikkink 2000.

concept, as defined in the framing chapter, and discuss its application to their issue-area. Lutz and Sikkink do not turn legalization into some other analytic concept (like information or credible commitment) to carry out the analysis. In particular, they engage explicitly with the concept of obligation, suggesting briefly that human rights norms are often rooted in customary law. They also stress that any existing "right" to democratization can only be a social norm or a customary norm. Their findings support the understanding of obligation that we traced out earlier, an approach rooted in social processes of interaction. To be effective, obligation needs to be felt, and not simply imposed through a hierarchy of sources of law. Precision and delegation play absolutely no role in the promotion of compliance, at least with these human rights norms. Once Lutz and Sikkink find the legalization hypothesis wanting, they move into familiar conceptual turf (for Sikkink), employing the "norm cascade" concept elaborated elsewhere to explain the pattern of compliance they see.[36]

That Lutz and Sikkink focus so strongly on legalization's contribution to compliance brings us back to an important problem. As noted earlier, the framing article is not clear about analytic objectives. If the volume's purpose is primarily to describe legalization, then Lutz and Sikkink's article is beside the point. After all, the framing article does not claim that legalization will lead to greater compliance with law. Consequently, the fact that a more highly legalized area engenders less compliance than a less legalized area is neither here nor there for the framers of the volume. Yet the idea that this finding is somehow beside the point and gives no pause to the framers, as revealed by Kahler's dismissive treatment of Lutz and Sikkink's article in the conclusion, is surprising, since elsewhere the volume's authors claim to investigate the consequences of legalization that, presumably, would involve compliance.[37] More generally, if the purpose of the legalization concept is to generate hypotheses that guide research, one would expect disconfirming evidence of the type Lutz and Sikkink present to result in a rethinking of the basic concept. * * *

CONCLUSION

No analysis can do everything, but analysts must justify their choice of focus in the light of other obvious possibilities. The framers of the legalization concept are not explicit, however, about their limited view of

---

[36] Finnemore and Sikkink 1998.
[37] Goldstein et al. 2000, 386.

law or about alternative views of law (or IR theory) that might yield different understandings of their cases. Further, they have not adequately theorized their definition of legalization so as to provide clear help to the empirical researchers seeking to apply the concept. We have called attention to some alternative views of law and suggested ways they can help us to address gaps in the authors' own framework that might lead researchers to examine important questions neglected in this volume. Our hope is the same as the authors' – that international law and IR scholars will begin to read each other's work more carefully and use each other's insights in analysis. Our suspicion, however, is that this process will not yield a long trail of scholarship on the concept of legalization as defined in the volume discussed here. Rather, as IR scholars read more broadly in international law, they will find rich connections between the two fields and will be able to create joint research agendas that are diverse and fruitful.

PART IV

INTERNATIONAL LAW AND INTERNATIONAL NORMS

10

Quasi-States, Dual Regimes, and Neoclassical Theory: International Jurisprudence and the Third World

Robert H. Jackson

PRACTICE AND THEORY

Since the end of World War II we have been witnessing what in retrospect looks more and more like a revolutionary period of international history when sovereign statehood – the constitutive principle of international society – is subjected to major change. It is perhaps most evident in the remarkable role of the United Nations in fostering new sovereignties around the world. In this paper I argue that African states are juridical artifacts of a highly accommodating regime of international law and politics which is an expression of a twentieth-century anticolonial ideology of self-determination. This civil regime has important implications for international theory and particularly the renewed interest in sovereignty.[1]

The discourse characteristic of sovereignty is jurisprudential rather than sociological: the language of rules rather than roles, prescribed norms instead of observed regularities. The study of sovereignty therefore

---

[1] See, for example, Stephen D. Krasner, ed., *International Regimes* (Ithaca and London: Cornell University Press, 1983), particularly the editor's introductory and concluding chapters, and John Gerard Ruggie, "Continuity and Transformation in the World Polity," in Robert O. Keohane, ed., *Neorealism and Its Critics* (New York: Columbia University Press, 1986), pp. 130–57. A major new study which has been very influential in my own thinking is Alan James, *Sovereign Statehood: The Basis of International Society* (London: Allen & Unwin, 1986).

An earlier version of this paper was presented at a panel convened by James Mayall on "The Crisis of the State and International Relations Theory" at the British International Studies Association Annual Conference, University of Reading, 15–17 December 1986. am grateful to Mark Zacher, Stephen Krasner, and two anonymous reviewers for helpful suggestions and the Donner Canadian Foundation for financial support.

involves us in legal theory, international law, and international institutions in the broadest meaning of these terms: what elsewhere I call the "civil science" approach to the study of politics.[2] By "neoclassical international theory" I refer to what Hedley Bull describes as "theorizing that derives from philosophy, history, and law" or what Martin Wight calls "a tradition of speculation about relations between states": the companion of "political theory."[3]

The constitutional tradition generally tends to assume, with Grotius, Burke, and Oakeshott as against Machiavelli, Kant, and Marx, that theory by and large is the child and not the parent of practice in political life. In Hegel's famous phrase: "The owl of Minerva spreads its wings only with the falling of the dusk."[4] The same point is made by the English philosopher Gilbert Ryle: "Intelligent practice is not a stepchild of theory. On the contrary, theorizing is one practice amongst others and is itself intelligently or stupidly conducted."[5] He goes on to argue that "knowing that" (history) and "knowing why" (philosophy) are categorically different from "knowing how" (practice) in much the same way as being a connoisseur of baseball does not depend at all on the ability to pitch strikes or hit home runs. The reverse can be true also. Players are often inarticulate when it comes to explaining their play to observers. "Knowing how to operate is not knowing how to tell how to operate."[6] It is the unusual diplomat, such as Machiavelli or Kissinger, who is also an international theorist of note. According to this epistemology, the project of the practitioner is to shape the world, whereas that of the scholar is to understand it and explain it in coherent terms.

The revolutionaries and nationalists, statesmen and diplomatists who gave effect to the twentieth-century revolt against the West succeeded completely in transferring sovereign statehood to Africa and other parts

---

[2] See Robert H. Jackson, "Civil Science: A Rule-Based Paradigm for Comparative Government" (Delivered at the Annual Conference of the American Political Science Association, Chicago, 3–6 September 1987).

[3] Hedley Bull, "International Theory: The Case for a Classical Approach," in K. Knorr and J. N. Rosenau, eds., *Contending Approaches to International Politics* (Princeton: Princeton University Press, 1969), p. 20 and Martin Wight, "Why Is There No International Theory?" in H. Butterfield and M. Wight, eds., *Diplomatic Investigations* (London: Allen & Unwin, 1966), p. 17.

[4] T. M. Knox, ed., *Hegel's Philosophy of Right* (London: Oxford University Press, 1979), p. 13.

[5] G. Ryle, *The Concept of Mind* (Harmondsworth: Penguin Books, 1968), chap. 2.

[6] G. Ryle, "Ordinary Language," in V. C. Chappell, ed., *Ordinary Language* (Englewood Cliffs, N. J.: Prentice-Hall, 1964), p. 32.

of the non-Western world after a century, more or less, of European colonialism. In the course of doing it they fashioned if not a new, then at least a substantially revised, set of international arrangements which differ dramatically from those imperial ones that previously obstructed the globalization of equal sovereignty. * * *

CIVIL REGIMES

International regimes may be defined as "implicit or explicit principles, norms, rules, and decision-making procedures around which actors' expectations converge in a given area of international relations."[7] Although much of the emphasis in regime analysis has been in areas of political economy, this definition is highly consistent with civil domains in international relations directly related to sovereign statehood, such as recognition, jurisdiction, intervention, human rights, and so forth. It is similar to Hedley Bull's constitutional conception of rules in a society of states: "general imperative principles which require or authorise" behavior and which "may have the status of law, of morality, of custom or etiquette, or simply of operating procedures or 'rules of the game.'"[8] * * *

* * *

Sovereignty, the basic constituent principle of the international civil regime, is not only a normative but essentially a legal relationship. Alan James defines sovereign statehood as "constitutional independence" of other states. "All that constitutional independence means is that a state's constitution is not part of a larger constitutional arrangement."[9] Sovereignty, like any other human convention, is something that can be acquired and lost, claimed or denied, respected or violated, celebrated or condemned, changed or abandoned, and so forth. It is a historical phenomenon.

Because sovereignty is essentially a legal order and basically entails rules, it can very appropriately be understood in terms of a game: an activity constituted and regulated by rules. It is useful to distinguish two logically different but frequently confused kinds of rules: constitutive (civil) and instrumental (organizational). Constitutive rules define

---

[7] Krasner, *International Regimes*, p. 2. Among contemporary British international theorists the term "international society" is used to denote the same phenomenon. See, for example, Hedley Bull, *The Anarchical Society* (London: Macmillan, 1967), chaps. 1 and 3. The term "international regimes" is preferable because it denotes principles and rules and not merely regularities or norms: in other words, it is a better jurisprudential term.

[8] Bull, "International Theory," p. 54.

[9] James, *Sovereign Statehood*, p. 25.

the game, whereas instrumental rules are maxims derived from experience which contribute to winning play. The constitutive rules of the sovereignty game include legal equality of states, mutual recognition, nonintervention, making and honoring treaties, diplomacy conducted in accordance with accepted practices, and other civil international relations. On the other hand, foreign policy (whether public or secret) and similar stratagems, as well as the state organizations which correspond to them, are among the major instruments employed by statesmen in pursuing their interests. Classical reason of state and therefore realism as an international theory belong logically to the instrumental part of the sovereignty game.[10] Classical rationalism belongs to the constitutive part, with which this article is mainly concerned.

Sovereignty began in Europe as an independence de facto between states but became an independence de jure – which is "sovereignty" properly socalled – as natural barriers were overcome by technology, international relations increased, and statesmen subjected their external actions to customary practices which in the course of time acquired the status of law.[11] As the system expanded globally into new continents and oceans, states encountered along the way eventually had to be classified.[12] Ashanti, a traditional West African kingdom, was independent de facto prior to its conquest by Britain in the late 19th century. The Gold Coast, a British colony in which the kingdom was subordinated, was not sovereign because it was not legally independent of Great Britain. To the contrary, it was constitutionally part of the British Empire.[13] Ghana, the sovereign successor to the Gold Coast since 1957 in which Ashanti continues to be subordinated, is legally independent not only of Britain but all other sovereign states. Such changes of status are typical of the movement of international civil regimes over time.

Sovereignty is an extremely important political value in itself, as the 20th-century revolt against the West by Third World anticolonialists

---

[10] Classical realism goes one step farther by suggesting that international relations are totally instrumental and not at all an institutionalized game. Hans Morgenthau discloses this conception in his defining statement: "International politics, like all politics, is a struggle for power." *Politics among Nations* (New York: Knopf, 1966), p. 25.

[11] See C. H. McIlwain, *The Growth of Political Thought in the West* (New York: Macmillan, 1932), p. 268.

[12] See the remarkable collection of essays analyzing this process in Hedley Bull and Adam Watson, ed., *The Expansion of International Society* (Oxford: Clarendon Press, 1984), especially Parts I and II.

[13] See Martin Wight, *British Colonial Constitutions 1947* (Oxford: Clarendon Press, 1952), pp. 80–81.

strikingly indicates. It is significant for this reason alone. In addition, however, it is consequential for other political goods, domestic and international, such as order, justice, economic welfare, and so forth.[14] Sovereignty, like all constitutive rules, has important consequences, intended and unintended. The rules are intrinsically interesting for international lawyers who, as practitioners, treat the law of sovereignty as a text to master. For international theorists, however, sovereignty is a language to understand.[15] Where the rules lead are usually more important than the rules themselves. The unintended consequences are often most interesting theoretically because they are also unexpected and therefore disclose something similar to the refutation of a hypothesis in science.[16] An example relevant to this discussion is the surprising civil and socioeconomic adversities which befell many African jurisdictions following their acquisition of sovereignty.

As with other constitutive rules, there are important conditions which make sovereignty attainable or unattainable in any particular case. In 1885, for example, the constitutional independence of African states was not only unattainable but also inconceivable. *** A hundred years later the rules and the conditions had changed fundamentally. Among the most important conditions affecting changes in the sovereignty game are the differential power and wealth of states, of course, but also prevailing international moralities and ideologies. In some cases the latter may be the most significant, as I suggest below in discussing the spread of sovereignty to tropical Africa.

It should by now be evident that colonialism, in addition to being a socioeconomic phenomenon, is in important and indeed fundamental respects an international civil regime grounded in the law of sovereignty. Colonization and decolonization therefore denote changes in the principles and rules by which people are governed: their movement from one regime to another. More significant than this, however, is a fundamental change of regime which has happened in connection with colonialism: international regime change. *** Decolonization is the sort of basic historical change which we have perhaps come to take for granted but

[14] See J. Roland Pennock, "Political Development, Political Systems, and Political Goods," *World Politics* 18 (1966), pp. 415–34.

[15] The distinction between politics as a literature and as a language is explored by Michael Oakeshott in "The Study of 'Politics' in a University," *Rationalism in Politics and Other Essays* (London: Methuen, 1962), p. 313.

[16] According to Popper this is how science advances. See his *Conjectures and Refutations* (New York: Harper & Row Torchbooks, 1968).

which signals a fundamental alteration in the constitutive principles of sovereignty, particularly as regards the Third World periphery.

DECOLONIZATION

President John F. Kennedy once characterized decolonization as "a worldwide declaration of independence."[17] This is certainly true of sub-Saharan Africa, where in 1955 there were only three independent countries: Ethiopia, Liberia, and South Africa. By the end of 1965, there were thirty-one, and decolonization was looming even in the so-called white redoubt of southern Africa. By 1980, the entire continent was sovereign apart from Namibia.

African decolonization, like the partition of the continent three-quarters of a century earlier, is the instance of a straight line in international history: a political artifact largely and in some cases almost entirely divorced from substantive conditions; a supreme example of "rationalism" in Michael Oakeshott's meaning of politics "as the crow flies."[18] It is not only possible but has become conventional to regard a single year – 1960, the year of Prime Minister Harold Macmillan's famous "wind of change" speech and of the decolonization of the entire French African empire – as a historical dividing line separating the era of European colonialism from that of African independence. That year is matched only by 1884–85, when the continent was subjected to international partition according to rules established by a conference of mainly European states meeting in Berlin.

The political map of Africa is devoid by and large of indigenous determinations in its origins. All but a very few traditional political systems were subordinated or submerged by the colonialists. Decolonization rarely resulted in their elevation. "Most of the boundary lines in Africa are diplomatic in origin and, in very many instances, they are that abomination of the scientific geographers, the straight line."[19] In colonial Africa, according to an important study, "the ultimate decisions in the allocation of territories and the delimitation of borders were always made by Europeans."[20] Despite the fact that it was European in origin, the

[17] Quoted by E. Plischke, *Microstates in World Affairs* (Washington, DC.: American Enterprise Institute, 1977), p. i.
[18] Oakeshott, *Rationalism in Politics*, p. 69.
[19] G. L. Beer, *African Questions at the Paris Peace Conference* (New York: Scribners, 1923), p. 65.
[20] S. Touval, *The Boundary Politics of Independent Africa* (Cambridge, Mass.: Harvard University Press, 1972), p. 4.

political map of Africa was accepted in its entirety by post-colonial African governments. A 1964 resolution of the Organization of African states considered "that the borders of African States, on the day of their independence, constitute a tangible reality" and declared "that all Member States pledge themselves to respect the borders existing on their achievement of national independence."[21] Political Africa is an intrinsically imperial cum international construct.

Colonial governments were never particularly large or imposing, and it is something of a misnomer to speak of them as colonial "states." They were comparable not to states but, rather, to small provincial, county, or municipal governments in European countries. We come close to committing the historical fallacy of retrospective determinism if we conceive of them as emergent or prospective national states. A. H. M. Kirk-Greene refers to the British colonial service in Africa as "the thin white line."[22] When we speak of a colonial government in Africa we are usually referring only to several hundred and occasionally – in the larger dependencies such as Nigeria and the Belgian Congo – several thousand European officials. Their numbers could be small because colonies were not sovereign: rather, they were parts – often small parts – of a far larger transoceanic imperial state which backed up the colony. Their presence was absolutely crucial, however, and enabled the modest governing apparatus to be a going concern. Unlike the Indian civil service, these administrations were never substantially indigenized at decision-making levels before independence. For all intents and purposes they were the colonial state.

In substance, decolonization typically involved the resignation or retirement of European administrators, which therefore meant the elimination of the crucial operative component of empirical statehood. It also involved the loss of the imperial backstop, of course. The new rulers usually could not replace the operative component because there was no group of Africans with comparable experience in running a modern government. After the Europeans left, the new states consequently acquired the unintentional characteristics of "quasi-states" which are summarized below. The Congo, for example, collapsed with the abrupt departure of the Belgians in 1960 and could only be restored to a marginal

---

[21] As quoted in A. McEwen, *International Boundaries of East Africa* (Oxford: Clarendon Press, 1971), p. 22.

[22] A. Kirk-Greene, "The Thin White Line: The Size of the British Colonial Service in Africa," *African Affairs* 79 (1980), pp. 25–44.

semblance of organized statehood by a large-scale UN rescue operation. Most other ex-colonies deteriorated more gradually into pseudo-statehood. They are all preserved more or less in this condition by new accommodating norms of international society.

Independence, therefore, was not a result of the development of individual colonies to the point of meeting classical empirical qualifications for statehood. On the contrary, it stemmed from a rather sudden and widespread change of mind and mood about the international legitimacy of colonialism which aimed at and resulted in its abolition as an international institution. During and after World War II, colonialism became controversial and finally unacceptable in principle. Self-determination for ex-colonies was transformed into a global human right during the same period. Whatever else it may also have been, decolonization was an international regime change of the first importance: a "revolutionary" change, as Puchala and Hopkins put it.

Independence could occur widely and rapidly across Africa because it basically required little more than agreement or acquiescence concerning a new international legal principle that acknowledged as incipiently sovereign all colonies which desired independence. It was essentially a legal transaction: African elites acquired title to self-government from colonial rulers, with the transfer generally recognized – indeed promoted and celebrated – by the international community and particularly the UN General Assembly. * * *

QUASI-STATES

When we look at the contemporary African states, we immediately notice the extent to which most of them depart from current conceptions and expectations of statehood. It is not that they, along with all other states, to some extent fail to live up to their ideals. Rather, it is that they do not disclose the empirical constituents by which real states are ordinarily recognized. African states frequently lack the characteristics of a common or public realm: state offices possess uncertain authority, government organizations are ineffective and plagued by corruption, and the political community is highly segmented ethnically into several "publics" rather than one. The effect is to confuse political obligation almost fatally:

Most educated Africans are citizens of two publics in the same society. On the other hand, they belong to a civic public from which they gain materially but to which they give only grudgingly. On the other hand, they belong to a primordial public from which they derive little or no material benefits but to which they are expected to give generously and do give materially. To make matters more complicated, their relationship to the primordial public is moral, while that to the civic public is amoral. . . . The unwritten law . . . is that it is legitimate to rob the civic public in order to strengthen the primordial public.[23]

This statement discloses what undoubtedly is the fundamental predicament of statehood in Africa: its existence almost exclusively as an exploitable treasure trove devoid of moral value. Unlike solidly established authoritarian states, moreover, the typical African state's apparatus of power is not effectively organized. Corruption and incompetence infiltrate virtually every agency of government, not merely hampering but in most cases undermining state autonomy and capacity. Corruption is integral rather than incidental to African politics.[24] Self-enrichment and personal or factional aggrandizement constitute politics. Many "public" organizations are thoroughly "privatized" in the unusual sense that they are riddled with nepotism, patronage, bribery, extortion, and other personal or black market relationships. In what has become a modern classic Stanislav Andreski coins the apt term "kleptocracy" to characterize African systems of government.[25]

The state in Africa is consequently more a personal- or primordial-favoring political arrangement than a public-regarding realm. Government is less an agency to provide political goods such as law, order, security, justice, or welfare and more a fountain of privilege, wealth, and power for a small elite who control it. If there is a consensus among political scientists it is probably that the state in Africa is neo-patrimonial in character.[26] Those who occupy state offices, civilian and military, high and low, are inclined to treat them as possessions rather than positions: to live off their rents – very luxuriously in some cases – and use them to reward persons and cliques who help maintain their power. According to

---

[23] P. Ekeh, "Colonialism and the Two Publics in Africa," *Comparative Studies in Society and History* 17 (1975), p. 108.

[24] Robert Williams, *Political Corruption in Africa* (Aldershot, England: Gower Publishing, 1987), chap. 1.

[25] Stanislav Andreski, *The African Predicament: A Study in the Pathology of Modernization* (New York: Atherton Press, 1968), chap. 7.

[26] See, among others, Thomas S. Callaghy, *The State-Society Struggle: Zaire in Comparative Perspective* (New York: Columbia University Press, 1984); Christopher Clapham, *Third World Politics* (Madison: The University of Wisconsin Press, 1985); Robert H. Jackson and Carl G. Rosberg, *Personal Rule in Black Africa* (Berkeley: University of California Press, 1982); and Victor T. LeVine, "African Patrimonial Regimes in Comparative Perspective," *The Journal of Modern African Studies* 18 (1980), pp. 657–73.

a candid analysis, "west African governments represent in themselves the single greatest threat to their citizens, treat the rule of law with contempt, and multiply hasty public shemes designed principally for their own private and collective enrichment." "Development" in such circumstances is empty rhetoric: "a world of words and numbers detached from material and social realities."[27]

Large segments of national populations – probably a big majority in most cases – cannot or will not draw the necessary distinction between office and incumbent, between the authority and responsibility of officials and their personal influence and discretion, upon which the realization of modern statehood depends. Many governments are incapable of enforcing their writ throughout their territory. *** Most African countries, even the smallest ones, are fairly loose patchworks of plural allegiances and identities somewhat reminiscent of medieval Europe, with the crucial difference that they are defined and supported externally by the institutional framework of sovereignty regardless of their domestic conditions. ***

Can we speak intelligibly of African "states" in such circumstances? Arguably we cannot, because they obviously are not yet substantial realities in the conduct of public officials and citizens. They are nominal by and large: abstractions represented by written constitutions, laws, regulations, and the like which yet have too little purchase on behavior to realize the conditions of empirical statehood. The reality is the non-statal and anti-public conduct briefly described. ***

Some international theorists therefore speak of these countries as "nascent," "quasi," or "pseudo" states to draw attention to the fact that they are states mainly by international "courtesy."[28] They enjoy equal sovereignty, as Bull and Watson point out, but they lack established legal and administrative institutions capable of constraining and outlasting the individuals who occupy their offices; "still less do they reflect respect for constitutions or acceptance of the rule of law."[29]

African states are indeed states by courtesy, but the real question is why such courtesy has been so extensively and uniformly granted almost entirely in disregard of empirical criteria for statehood. It is surely because a new practice has entered into the determination and preservation of statehood on the margins of international society. The new states ***

---

[27] Keith Hart, *The Political Economy of West African Agriculture* (Cambridge: Cambridge University Press, 1982), pp. 104–5.

[28] Bull and Watson, *International Society,* p. 430.

[29] Ibid.

possess "juridical statehood" derived from a right of self-determination – negative sovereignty – without yet possessing much in the way of empirical statehood, disclosed by a capacity for effective and civil government – positive sovereignty.[30] Juridical statehood can be understood as, among other things, the international institution by which Africa and some other extremely underdeveloped parts of the world were brought into the international community on a basis of equal sovereignty rather than some kind of associate statehood. It was invented because it was, arguably, the only way these places could acquire constitutional independence in a short period of time in conformity with the new international equality.

JURIDICAL STATEHOOD IN INTERNATIONAL LAW

We can begin to clarify the juridical framework of African states by glancing at the relevant international law on the subject. Although "juridical statehood" is not a legal term of art, there are of course established legal practices concerning the criteria of statehood. * * *

The usual point of departure for analysis of these criteria is Article 1 of the Montevideo Convention on Rights and Duties of States (1933), which declares: "The State as a person of international law should possess the following qualifications: (a) a permanent population; (b) a defined territory; (c) government; and (d) capacity to enter into relations with other States."[31] Ian Brownlie notes that the core legal idea of a "state" is a stable political community in a territory with an established legal order. "The existence of effective government, with centralized administrative and legislative organs, is the best evidence of a stable political community."[32]

These empirical criteria are the successors of classical positive international law which emphasized qualifications for admission to the community of states. The main difference from former (late 19th and early 20th century) doctrine is the absence of the standard of "civilization" criterion, which emerged in support of European expansion into the non-Western world to deal not only with the philosophical problem of knowing which governments to recognize as "authentic" sovereigns but

---

[30] See Robert H. Jackson, "Negative Sovereignty in Sub-Saharan Africa," *Review of International Studies* 12 (October 1986), pp. 247–64.

[31] Quoted by Ian Brownlie, *Principles of Public International Law*, third ed. (Oxford: Clarendon Press, 1979), p. 74.

[32] Ibid., p. 75.

also with the practical problem of protecting the persons, property, and liberties of Europeans in non-Western countries.[33] By the 1930s, however, that qualification was controversial and emphasis had shifted to "effective government." It was the latter criterion which defenders of colonialism ordinarily used to ward off demands by African nationalists for immediate self-government.

This criterion is problematical, however. Part of the difficulty is conceptual. *** Governments are "institutional" rather than "brute" facts in which or concepts of government are bound to enter.[34] Legal and political practice is what ultimately determines effective government, and not the reverse. And these practices have changed fundamentally. The problem is disclosed in legal practice.[35] *** Writing of Zaire (the Congo) in the early 1960s, following the abrupt departure of the Belgians, when the government literally collapsed, James Crawford comments:

> Anything less like effective government it would be hard to imagine. Yet despite this there can be little doubt that the Congo was in 1960 a State in the full sense of the term. It was widely recognized. Its application for United Nations membership was approved without dissent.[36]

Other considerations were evidently more important than this one. The criterion is also problematical in reverse cases. For example, Rhodesia was an effective government at least from 1965 to 1975 when, with the independence of neighboring Mozambique, the civil war began to undermine it. Crawford remarks: "There can be no doubt that, if the traditional tests for independence . . . applied, Rhodesia would . . . [have become] . . . an independent state."[37] However, these tests do not apply any longer and have been replaced by something else. *** Crawford concludes: "The proposition that statehood must always be equated with effectiveness is not supported by modern practice."[38]

---

[33] See G. W. Gong, *The Standard of "Civilization" in International Society* (Oxford: Clarendon Press, 1984), chap. 2.

[34] "A State is not a fact in the sense that a chair is a fact; it is a fact in the sense in which it may be said that a treaty is a fact: that is, a legal status attaching to a certain state of affairs by virtue of certain rules." J. Crawford, "The Criteria for Statehood in International Law," *British Yearbook of International Law 1976–1977* (Oxford: Oxford University Press, 1978), p. 95.

[35] See the discussion of "effective control" in Malcolm N. Shaw, *Title to Territory in Africa: International Legal Issues* (Oxford: Clarendon Press, 1986), pp. 16–24.

[36] Crawford, "Criteria for Statehood in International Law," pp. 116–17.

[37] Ibid., p. 162. Also see the penetrating analysis of the Rhodesian case in James, *Sovereign Statehood*, pp. 153–60.

[38] Crawford, "Criteria for Statehood in International Law," p. 144.

Insofar as the criterion has any content today, it is not that of actual effectiveness but of title to exercise authority within a certain territory. In theory this is a "category mistake," but in international legal and political practice, it is merely an expediency. All ex-colonial governments in Africa today have the title, but far from all are actually effective throughout their territorial jurisdictions. The effectiveness of some is extremely dubious.

An international society in which substantial political systems *** are denied legal personality, while quasi-states *** enjoy it, is indicative of new international practice. And according to this practice, once sovereignty is acquired by virtue of independence from colonial rule, then extensive civil strife or breakdown of order or governmental immobility or any other failures are not considered to detract from it. We see international law adapting to the new, inclusive, pluralistic, egalitarian, and far-flung community of states, by a definite and indeed pronounced loosening of empirical qualifications on sovereign statehood. It could not be otherwise if there must be a world exclusively of sovereign states and entirely devoid of colonies, protected states, associate states, or any other nonsovereign jurisdictions.

This change arguably reflects the ascendancy of a highly accommodating international morality which, at its center, contains the principle of self-determination as an unqualified, universal human right of all ex-colonial peoples. It is revealed perhaps most clearly in the 1960 UN Declaration on the Granting of Independence to Colonial Countries and Peoples, which affirmed that "all peoples have the right to self-determination" and that "inadequacy of political, economic, social, or educational preparedness should never serve as a pretext for delaying independence."[39] Subsequently it has been disclosed by various UN Resolutions condemning colonialism as not only illegitimate but also illegal and justifying anticolonial revolutions.[40] In short, one cannot at the same time have empirical qualifications on statehood and such a right institutionalized within the same international regime. Decolonization was necessary to go from old facts to new rights.

Nowadays, at least in Africa *** the key if not the sole criterion of statehood is legal independence, based on the ground of self-determination, which is of course a juridical and not an empirical condition. This is almost exactly the reverse of historical practice. Sovereign statehood, as

[39] *Everyman's United Nations* (New York: United Nations, 1968), pp. 370–71.
[40] See especially UN General Assembly Resolutions 2621, 2627, and 2708 of Session XXV, 1970, and 3103 of Session XXVII, 1973.

previously indicated, originated both logically and historically as a de facto independence between states.[41] States had it "primordially": "the nature of the sovereign state as constitutionally insular is analogous to that of the individual as a developed personality, dependent indeed upon society, yet at the same time inner-directed and self-contained."[42] Traditional sovereignty was like the predemocratic franchise: it was determined by capacities and competencies and therefore acknowledged inequality.

When sovereignty was linked to recognition in nineteenth-century positive international law, it was still based on the postulate that the recognized political entity was primordially capable of modern and civilized government. Recognition was "a sort of juristic baptism."[43] The analogy rings true because of the reasonable assumption that the one being baptized had the marks and merits of a state. This was reflected in the small number of independent as compared to dependent political systems. In short, statehood was still prior to recognition. Even the practice of "constitutive recognition" was the acknowledgment of relevant political facts which warranted the baptism of some but not all political entities. In other words, sovereignty by its original nature was a privilege of the few rather than a right of the many.

Today in * * * Africa this relationship is reversed. Independence is based primarily on an external universal right rather than an internal particular reality. * * * Juridical statehood divorced from the empirical conditions of states now evidently has a place in international law.[44]

* * *

A NEW DUAL CIVIL REGIME

These changes disclose the emergence of a new dual civil regime. According to Martin Wight, "the dual aspect of the states-system" was

---

[41] The historical practice involved was expressed in early modern times by the new and radical claim: *Rex est imperator in regno suo* – the king is emperor within his own realm. See McIlwain, *Political Thought*, p. 268. Also see the brief but penetrating discussion in Martin Wight, *Power Politics*, 2d ed. (Baltimore: Penguin Books and Royal Institute of International Affairs, 1986), pp. 25–26.

[42] Wight, *Power Politics*, p. 307. Also see Crawford, "Criteria for Statehood in International Law," p. 96.

[43] Crawford, "Criteria for Statehood in International Law," p. 98.

[44] Self-determination is part of the jus cogens according to Brownlie, *Principle*, p. 515. He also notes (p. 75) that "self-determination will today be set against the concept of effective government, more particularly when the latter is used in arguments for continuation of colonial rule."

conceived originally, if tentatively, by Grotius. "There is an outer circle that embraces all mankind, under natural law, and an inner circle, the corpus Christianorum, bound by the law of Christ."[45] Dualism in different forms has persisted in international relations ever since. It is a very big subject, of course, and as yet there exists no comprehensive account of which I am aware.[46] However, it is possible to review briefly the changing images of dualism in international relations to gain some background perspective on the dual civil regime which exists today and the place of juridical statehood in it.

Three approximate "stages" are discernible in the development of international dualism. The first is that apprehended by Grotius: an outer or universal circle governing the relations of mankind and reflected in the *jus gentium;* and an inner circle of international law among Christian-European nations. Relations between the two spheres, between Europe and the rest of the world, were nevertheless pragmatic politically, uncertain morally, and untidy legally.[47] They were conducted on a basis of rough equality notwithstanding the accelerating inequality of power in favor of Europe, and they expressed a fair measure of international toleration. There was not yet anything resembling a global regime under common rules.

Insofar as European relations with Africa were concerned,

African heads of state had not yet been downgraded from Kings to Chiefs .... African states were clearly not considered members of the family of nations. They sent no accredited ambassadors to Europe and received none in return .... Nevertheless, their legal rights were recognized in a series of treaties on which the Europeans based their own rights to their footholds along the coast.[48]

It was a tentative and initially accommodating encounter between two utterly different worlds, but Africa was a political world and not merely *terra nullias.* Traditional continental Africa is far better characterized by anthropology or sociology, however, than by political theory, jurisprudence, diplomatic history, or international law. It was a world of societies more than states: "the nation-State in the European sense did not really develop in Africa."[49] Even "states" in the anthropological

[45] M. Wight, "The Origins of Our States-system: Geographical Limits," in *Systems of States* (Leicester: University of Leicester Press, 1977), p. 128.

[46] The closest to it is Bull and Watson, *International Society.*

[47] Ian Brownlie, "The Expansion of International Society: The Consequences for the Law of Nations," in Bull and Watson, *International Society,* p. 359.

[48] P. D. Curtin, *The Image of Africa,* vol. 1 (Madison: University of Wisconsin Press, 1964), pp. 279–80.

[49] Shaw, *Title to Territory,* p. 30.

definition – centralized political systems – of which there were not a large number, exercised uncertain control, and "the authority and power of the central government faded away more and more the further one went from the centre toward the boundary. Thus boundaries between the states were vague, sometimes overlapping."[50] Although there were of course complex and particular customs which regulated intercourse among contiguous local societies, "(t)here was no African international system or international society extending over the continent as a whole, and it is doubtful whether such terms can be applied even to particular areas."[51] Africa scarcely existed even as a politically recognizable, not to mention a diplomatically recognized, international jurisdiction.

* * *

After the middle of the 19th century a new form of international dualism appeared which was connected with European colonial expansion in Asia and Africa: rough equality and diversity was replaced by precise hierarchy and uniformity in the relations between European and non-European countries, with the former in a position of superiority. The determination of sovereignty throughout the world now derived from a Western and specifically liberal concept of a civil state which postulated certain criteria before international personality could be recognized. As previously indicated, these included the standard of "civilization" as well as effective government. Europe had the power and the will to impose this conception on the rest of the world. Even highly credible non-Western states which were never colonized, such as Japan, had to assert their statehood in these terms.[52] The consequence – and arguably the design – was the establishment of numerous colonial dependencies in those parts of the world, such as Africa, which were not considered to have any positive claim to sovereignty on these grounds and could therefore legitimately and legally be ruled by Europeans. The rules were clearly biased in favor of the "civilized," who also happened to be the strong.[53]

---

[50] J. Vansina, *Kingdoms of the Savanna* (Madison: University of Wisconsin Press, 1966), pp. 155–56. Also see Lucy Mair, *African Kingdoms* (Oxford: Clarendon Press, 1967), chap. 1.

[51] H. Bull, "European States and African Political Communities," in Bull and Watson, *International Society*, p. 106.

[52] See Hidemi Suganami, "Japan's Entry into International Society," in Bull and Watson, *International Society*, chap. 12.

[53] "[S]trong states accepted the legitimacy of colonialism and weak states would not challenge the status quo." Puchala and Hopkins, "International Regimes," p. 75.

For the first time the entire globe was organized in terms of European international law: there was a single regime of world politics of which colonialism was an integral institution. Dualism now consisted of a superior inner circle of sovereign states which were recognized members of the family of nations, and an inferior outer circle of their dependencies in Asia, Africa, and Oceania. Apart from a few notable exceptions, such as Turkey at first and later Japan, the inner circle was composed entirely of European countries and their offspring in the Americas. This dualism confined natural law, when it was not completely disregarded in a post-Austinian era of positive law, exclusively to human relations. There was no longer any generally acknowledged *jus gentium*. The very substantial inequalities along with the obvious cultural differences between the predominantly Western family of nations and the rest of the world – differences also marked by the racial boundary between whites and non-whites – were construed as distinctions of moral and political significance and were reflected by international law.

The latest stage of international dualism was first intimated by Wilsonian liberalism and specifically the League of Nations belief in "the virtue of small states" and "the juridical equality of all states."[54] The League did not abandon empirical statehood, however, as indicated by, among other things, the mandates system which was the internationalization of colonialism. That was the result of decolonization and the extension of membership in the community of states and specifically the UN, according to the principle of self-determination, to all dependencies which desired it regardless of any other considerations. This international change was essentially normative and basically entailed abolishing the international legal disabilities imposed on non-Western peoples.

This new dualism is, of course, the current North-South division, which can be defined in jurisprudential as well as political economy terms. It contains two fundamentally different bases of sovereign statehood. The first is the traditional empirical foundation of the competitive states-system which still exists in the developed parts of the world and can be extended only by development and not by constitutional legerdemain. International standing in this familiar sphere is determined primarily by military power and alliances, socioeconomic capabilities and resources, internal unity and legitimacy, science and technology, education and

---

[54] See the perennially apposite discussion in Alfred Cobban, *The Nation State and National Self-Determination* (New York: Crowell, 1969), chap. 4.

welfare, and various other familiar constituents of empirical state-hood.[55] ***

The second is the contemporary moral-legal framework of the accommodative juridical regime which has been fashioned for the most marginal parts of the ex-colonial world and particularly Africa, where extreme underdevelopment still prevails and empirical statehood has yet to be solidly established in most cases. States in this sphere survive primarily by negative sovereignty: the right not to be interfered with that is institutionalized in international law.[56] Reinforcing this negative liberty is the contemporary belief in the inherent equality of all peoples regardless of their empirical capabilities and credibilities as organized political systems. ***

What is fundamentally changed internationally, therefore, is not the distribution of empirical statehood in the world: that is still located in the developed West, *** although shifting perceptibly and in some cases rapidly in the direction of East Asia and a few other substantially developing parts of the Third World. Rather, it is the moral and legal basis of the states-system which has changed in the direction of equality – particularly racial equality.[57] The revolution of the new states is a revolution primarily of international legitimacy and law. ***

The biases in the constitutive rules of the sovereignty game today favor the weak. "For the first time in human history, international law is not on the side of force and power. The novelty of our time resides in the signal divorce between law and force."[58] To this observation of Mohammed Bedjaoui, an Algerian anti-imperialist lawyer and diplomat, one should add that the divorce is also between international legitimacy and national capability, between juridical statehood and empirical statehood. Sovereignty is today the political currency of the weak. *** "It is by insisting upon their privileges of sovereignty that they are able to defend their newly won independence."[59] Why was the international enfranchisement of the weak undertaken? Equality is infectious, as Lynn Miller points out, and once empirical requirements on sovereignty are relaxed to admit

---

[55] See the brilliant analysis in E. L. Jones, *The European Miracle* (Cambridge: Cambridge University Press, 1981), chaps. 6 and 7.

[56] See Jackson, "Negative Sovereignty in Sub-Saharan Africa."

[57] See R. J. Vincent, "Racial Equality," in Bull and Watson, *International Society*, chap. 16.

[58] M. Bedjaoui, "A Third World View of International Organization," in G. Abi-Saab, ed., *The Concept of International Organization* (Paris: UNESCO, 1981), p. 207.

[59] H. Bull, "The State's Positive Role in World Affairs," *Daedalus, The State* 108 (1979), p. 121.

some new members "the tendency is irresistible to qualify still other members of the society as well" until virtually everyone is a member.[60] Decolonization was driven by this international moral pressure.

And why in so many cases was juridical statehood necessary as a vehicle of equal sovereignty? It is, of course, impossible to give anything more than a brief answer in passing. Africa, as already indicated, developed very few organized indigenous governments which were recognizable as modern states and even fewer which were demonstrably as capable. Arguably because there is so little useful and relevant political tradition at the level of international society, it was necessary to invent juridical statehood based on colonial boundaries to incorporate the region into the community of states. * * *

JURIDICAL STATEHOOD AND INTERNATIONAL THEORY

What are the implications of this dual regime for international theory? If this is indeed a new practice, as I have argued, then its corresponding theory must also be novel to some degree. The question can be addressed in terms of Martin Wight's theoretical categories of "rationalism," "realism," and "revolutionism."[61] They are tokens for international constitutionalist theory (Grotius), national interest theory (Machiavelli), and universalist community-of-mankind theory (Kant) * * * usage as far as possible.[62] Kant in particular is in important respects a forerunner of the contemporary constructivist variety of rationalism.[63]

Classical Theory

The classical theory of the states-system is a rationalist-realist theory of collision prevention which has a direct analog in the traditional liberal

---

[60] Lynn H. Miller, *Global Order: Values and Power in International Politics* (Boulder and London: Westview Press, 1985), p. 49.

[61] H. Bull, "Martin Wight and the Theory of International Relations," *British Journal of International Studies* 2 (1976), pp. 104–5.

[62] See, for example, the conceptual controversies surrounding the notion of "neorealism" in Robert O. Keohane, ed., *Neorealism and Its Critics* (New York: Columbia University Press, 1986), especially the contributions by Richard Ashley, Robert Keohane, and Robert Gilpin.

[63] See, for example, Charles R. Beitz, *Political Theory and International Relations* (Princeton: Princeton University Press, 1979), which draws upon the neo-Kantian philosophy of John Rawls.

theory of politics between individuals and groups within states. Classical liberals are realists as well as rationalists. Political good is that which protects the freedom and property of agents: peace, order, and justice. Realists place the emphasis upon power and deterrence, whereas rationalists underline international law. *** Although Hobbes is in some respects a proponent of absolute government, his civil theory has many earmarks of classical liberalism.[64] As we know, however, he saw no evidence of an international civil society. Hobbes is a realist. *** He assumes, nevertheless, that not only humans but also states as a result of the social contract have intrinsic value, and he notes how sovereigns in providing for the security of their subjects have "their weapons pointed, and their eyes fixed on one another."[65] Positive sovereignty for Hobbes is the source of the good life.

Grotius, the rationalist, is more explicit about the value of a state, which is "a complete association of free men, joined together for the enjoyment of rights and for their common interest."[66] States are valuable, according to Hersch Lauterpacht in his definitive essay on Grotius, not because they are "like individuals" but because they are "composed of individual human beings. This is the true meaning of the Grotian analogy of states and individuals."[67] *** For the classical rationalists, state presuppose international civil society and they become subjects of the international law they contract with one another. The sovereign is a constitutionalist not only domestically but also internationally.

* * *

For Kant, traditional customary international law, which might produce order and periodical peace, is not enough to achieve perpetual peace, which is "the highest political good."[68] It is necessary, therefore, to form a peace union of constitutional or "republican" states. Only such states, owing to their domestic civil character, would subscribe to a universal morality – the categorical imperative based on an international social contract – and refrain from war, which is the greatest

---

[64] This is a major feature of Michael Oakeshott's interpretation of Hobbes. See his *Hobbes on Civil Association* (Oxford: Blackwell, 1975), chap. 1.

[65] Hobbes, *Leviathan.*

[66] Hugo Grotius, *De Jure Belli et Pacis Libri*, trans. F. Kelsey (Oxford: Oxford University Press, 1925), vol. 1, chap. 1, section xiv.

[67] Hersch Lauterpacht, "The Grotian Tradition in International Law," in Falk, Kratochwil and Mendlovitz, *International Law*, p. 19.

[68] Immanuel Kant, *Perpetual Peace* (Indianapolis: Bobbs-Merrill/Library of Liberal Arts, 1957), Addendum, p. 59.

political evil. Sovereignty and its built-in hubris would be transcended by a universal community of mankind, and the ultimate political good would finally be realized.[69] Juridical statehood and the new dualism can profitably be interrogated from each of these theoretical perspectives.

Rationalism

Charles Alexandrowicz and others argue that juridical statehood in some cases is a reversion to natural law practice in international relations.[70] Nineteenth-century and early twentieth-century positive law was an interregnum in an older Grotian tradition which postulated the universality of the law of nations, self-determination, and non-discrimination in disregard of civilization, religion, race, or color. These principles arguably are "revived in different shape" within the UN legal framework. Alexandrowicz sees this argument as applying to some traditional Asian states but not to most African countries, which are new state entities.

N. L. Wallace-Bruce argues, to the contrary, that colonialism interrupted the sovereignty of traditional African states and placed it "into an eclipse" but did not terminate it. Thus, African independence was also a reversion to sovereignty and not an attempt to create it for the first time.[71] The difficulty with this argument is the fact that in the vast majority of cases sovereignty in Africa has never reverted to anything remotely resembling traditional states. It has been acquired by ex-colonies which were, as indicated, novel and arbitrary European creations. Most African governments consequently have no authority by virtue of succession to traditional states. One cannot therefore argue that juridical statehood has restored and is protecting the traditional political identities and values of the non-Western world which were the historical subjects of natural law prior to Western imperialism. The new sovereignty, as indicated to the contrary, is far more often undermining and even destroying non-Western political tradition than protecting it.[72]

---

[69] Ibid., Second Article, pp. 16–20.
[70] C. H. Alexandrowicz, "New and Original States: The Issue of Reversion to Sovereignty," *International Affairs* 45 (1969), pp. 465–80, and, by the same author, "The New States and International Law," *Millenium* 3 (1977), pp. 226–33.
[71] N. L. Wallace-Bruce, "Africa and International Law: The Emergence to Statehood," *Journal of Modern African Studies* 23 (1985), pp. 575–602.
[72] See Walker Connor, "Nation-Building or Nation-Destroying," *World Politics* 24, no. 3 (1972), pp. 319–355.

Instead of postulating the existence of states which already afford the good life to inhabitants, the new Third World sovereignty presupposes that international society can promote state-building. Juridical statehood is more appropriately understood, therefore, as a constructive rather than a restorative rationalism. This is an idealist practice and theory which has little in common with the realist and empiricist tendency of classical rationalism.[73] It is a novel twentieth-century and indeed mainly post–World War II international doctrine. It is now part of the conventional wisdom of the international community and is evident, for example, not only in negative sovereignty but also in the positive law of the sea, the principles of UN-CTAD, the Group of 77, international aid, and the North-South dialogue generally.[74] In short, an unprecedented regime of cooperative international law and action has been created, arguably out of necessity, to generate and accommodate a greatly expanded international society containing numerous quasi-states.

Constructivist rationalism is what Burke would call an "innovation": a revolutionary break with the settled international practices of the past.[75] In the contemporary international community, unlike that before World War II, membership is gained more by abstract right than by historical and sociological reason. Protection is afforded and assistance provided for what might valuably exist someday but not for what is necessarily of real value today. It is not a small but otherwise complete state which is being protected, in character with Vattel's famous remark that a dwarf is a man, but rather a quasi-state which someday might be developed into a real state. This is Grotius turned on his head: inverted rationalism.[76]

Realism

Juridical statehood, at first glance, presents difficulties of strict realism because it discloses toleration of powerless quasi-states, *** on the grounds of their absolute claim to sovereignty. Is realism not lurking

---

[73] See F. A. Hayek, "Kinds of Rationalism," *Studies in Philosophy, Politics and Economics* (Chicago: University of Chicago Press, 1967), chap. 5.

[74] See the excellent analysis of these tendencies by Robert A. Mortimer, *The Third World Coalition in International Politics*, 2d ed. (Boulder and London: Westview Press, 1984).

[75] Edmund Burke, "Letter to a Noble Lord," in F. W. Rafferty, ed., *The Works of Edmund Burke*, vol. VI (Oxford: Oxford University Press, 1928), pp. 46–7.

[76] It is perhaps a parallel to what Wight identified as "inverted revolutionism," which is the "pacifist stream" of international thought. See Bull, "Martin Wight and the Theory of International Relations," p. 106.

somewhere in the background, however? For example, is juridical statehood not a consequence perhaps of Africa's lack of global significance in
the balance of power between East and West? Can realism account for the
existence of quasi-states and the contemporary dual international regime? *** The balance of power and other aspects of the competition
among real states, which is a game of hardball, are virtually independent of
quasi-stateland. Thus, *** United States national security policy could be
effective with little real knowledge of Black Africa. This may or may not
please Black governments, but their attitude can cause little concern. Such
knowledge is incidental more than instrumental to the East-West game of
hardball. They are spectators rather than players in that game.

Realists might therefore argue that juridical statehood is an instance
of uninterested toleration on the part of the real states of the world. The
indifference of the major powers enabled African states to become
independent, so the argument goes, and it enables them to continue to
exist despite their obvious debilities. "Indifference" belongs to the language of power and interest rather than legitimacy and law. Juridical
statehood, by this reasoning, *** is only a facade on power: the quasi-
states are states by courtesy only because nothing vital is at stake for those
extending the courtesy. Realism is therefore not refuted or even undermined by juridical statehood and the new international dualism.

The argument is persuasive as far as it goes. Once juridical statehood
is acquired, however, diplomatic courtesies and niceties are set in motion which support it, exaggerate it, and conceal its lack of real substance
and value. A new international community is inaugurated. Quasi-states
are dressed in the robes of sovereignty. An international law of self-
determination and cooperation is created as well as programs of international aid and other actions for the benefit of the underdeveloped
world. A language of global justice and injustice is applied to North–
South relations. A new moral-legal regime comes into existence. The Third
World states acquire and exercise a political voice in world affairs.[77] ***

This is the proprietary "reality" which supports juridical statehood.
"Propriety," of course, belongs to the language of morality rather than
power. It is not about power – certainly not in the classical sense of
Machiavelli and Morgenthau. It is about status, equality, respect, dignity,
decorum, courtesy, and so forth, which is civil conduct characteristic of
the life of clubs: international relations in a community of states. Many
Third World states may amount to little of real substance internationally

---

[77] See Mortimer, *Third World Coalition*, especially chap. 1.

as yet. They do not have to be substantial, however, because they enjoy a universally recognized categorical right of international existence. Numbers and voices of international democracy can be mobilized and organized to count for something today. * * * This is what Bedjaouis is referring to in claiming that international law is no longer on the side of force.

* * * The era of gunboat diplomacy, of speaking softly and carrying a big stick, seems decidedly outdated and increasingly inconceivable in the practical relations of the developed and the underdeveloped worlds.[78] The famous theoretical remark of Thucydides – that "the strong do what they can and the weak suffer what they must" – after many centuries of unquestionable applicability, likewise no longer seems as solidly based.[79] Arguably this international legitimism at least qualifies realism as a theory of pseudo-states.

This argument is consistent with others that identify normative limits of realism – or neorealism – in international theory.[80] However, this is certainly not to imply that realism is outmoded. On the contrary, it remains crucial to an understanding of the international system * * * where the balance of power and other instrumental facets of the game of hardball are still strongly in evidence. It is only to say that in some quarters today and particularly the area of North-South relations a different game more like softball is now being played. This may, of course, be an instance of suspended realism only. * * * Juridical statehood could be among the first casualties if Third World peripheries again became objects of intense rivalry by the major powers as was the case in the late nineteenth century. At this time, however, it does appear more like a regime change than a temporary historical aberration.

Revolutionism

None of this yet addresses arguments characteristic of revolutionism in the Kantian sense of universal morality or what today is understood

---

[78] The skeptic might point to the recent U.S. interventions in Grenada and Libya or the Soviet intervention in Afghanistan. In the former case, however, the Association of East Caribbean states solicited it and the U.S. justified it partly on these grounds. Moreover, most of the world, including many members of NATO, condemned it. In the latter case, Libya is clearly viewed widely not only in the West but also in the nonaligned world as a rogue elephant: an unpredictable international outcast that will not reciprocate. The Soviet Union also claimed that its intervention in Afghanistan was solicited – although it had evidently enthroned the communist regime which made the request.

[79] *The Peloponnesian War* (New York: Modern Library, 1950), p. 331.

[80] See the various selections in Keohane, *Neorealism*.

as international human rights.[81] At first glance much positive international law and organization, especially that which addresses development rights, appears consistent with Kantian theory. It expresses a universal morality reminiscent of the New Testament teachings on what the rich owe to the poor. It is couched in a moral language concerning positive rights of subsistence and positive duties to materially assist beyond borders which is widely and fluently spoken by international practitioners and theoretical commentators alike.[82] It therefore denies that human obligations end at international frontiers. It seeks to ameliorate if not eliminate underdevelopment. It has given rise to an elaborate superstructure of international aid targeted at Third World poverty which is historically unprecedented and can be read as the ascendancy of a cosmopolitan moral community higher than the community of states. In short, it expresses the heightened awareness of people living in the developed quarter of the world of what people in other quarters are suffering which is precisely consistent with Kant's concern to make "a violation of law and right in one place felt in all others."[83]

In practice, however, contemporary positive international law does not and cannot transcend juridical statehood. On the contrary, it postulates it. The duties and obligations acknowledged by it are those not of individuals but of states. If sovereigns object to international policies intended to mitigate human suffering within their borders, perhaps traceable to their own actions or omissions, there is no legitimate or legal basis for overruling them. * * * Indeed, as R. J. Vincent puts it, in the community of states "righteous intervention will be received as imperialism."[84] International borders still intervene strongly

---

[81] The structuralist image of international relations, Marxist or non-Marxist, in which horizontal socioeconomic divisions take precedence over vertical state divisions is a non-Kantian variant of revolutionism which I do not have the space to consider. For recent analyses see Ralph Pettman, "Competing Paradigms in International Politics," *Review of International Studies* 7 (1981), pp. 39–49, and, by the same author, *State and Class: A Sociology of International Affairs* (London: Croom Helm, 1979). For a characteristically brilliant essay pertinent to this discussion, see Ali Mazrui, "Africa Entrapped: Between the Protestant Ethic and the Legacy of Westphalia," in Bull and Watson, *International Society*, chap. 19.

[82] See, for example, Henry Shue, *Basic Rights: Subsistence, Affluence and U.S. Foreign Policy* (Princeton: Princeton University Press, 1980).

[83] As quoted and discussed in R. J. Vincent, *Human Rights and International Relations* (New York: The Royal Institute of International Affairs and Cambridge University Press, 1986), p. 118.

[84] Vincent, *Human Rights*, p. 118.

with individual right and duties.[85] Moreover, when *** international aid transfers are made they are made either between states or with the permission of the recipient state. Individual or private transfers can only be undertaken in stealth if they do not have the sanction of targeted sovereign states.

We live in a world entirely enclosed by equal sovereignty. International aid is profoundly affected by this juridical consideration. On closer inspection development rights look more like sovereign's rights than human rights. The fact of the matter is that southern sovereignty can direct development aid and even redirect it into the pockets of ruling elites. If northern countries could intervene when this happened, then the new sovereignty would be undermined and we would be witnessing a return to the old game of imperialism in which the developed states could legitimately dictate to the underdeveloped in matters affecting their domestic jurisdiction. Juridical statehood only embraces distributive justice insofar as it conforms to the rights of Third World sovereigns. The morality and the elaborate superstructure of international aid which is targeted specifically at countries rather than individuals is inconsistent with Kantian morality.

Kantianism, however, is primarily concerned with individual morality – classical natural rights – in international relations. It is revolutionary because it postulates the priority of human rights over sovereign's rights, which are secondary claims. The ultimate moral agents are individuals. The only authentic moral community is mankind. When statesmen claim rights above individuals or justify their exercise of power in violation of natural rights, injustice is committed. Kantianism, by subordinating sovereign rights to human rights, is therefore revolutionary in regard to the community of states.

Kant's vision of a community of mankind is incipiently evident today only among select developed states, particularly those of the European community, which have freely suspended although not permanently revoked their sovereignty in regard to some important civil rights. They have set up a wholly independent *** European Court of Human Rights which can sit in judgment of them in questions of human rights violations. Moreover, these bodies can hear cases brought by individuals against states and deliver binding judgments. "All this amounts to a

---

[85] See the characteristically subtle and discerning analysis by Stanley Hoffman, *Duties Beyond Borders: On the Limits and Possibilities of Ethical International Politics* (Syracuse: Syracuse University Press, 1981).

substantial retreat from the previously sacred principle of national sovereignty."[86] *** Arguably this achievement has been possible only in a region where domestic democracy and the rule of law is now widely entrenched. It is a historical confirmation of Kant's belief that international humanitarianism is most likely in a league of constitutional states.

This can be contrasted with the UN human rights regime and the situation in Africa. Most UN human rights covenants, which are procedurally slack and deferential to member states, have been ratified and implemented to date only by a minority of those states. The 1981 African Charter on Human and Peoples' Rights, *** explicitly acknowledges the supremacy of sovereign states by differentiating "peoples'" rights from human rights. It is evident that "peoples' rights" is a code word for ex-colonial self-determination and therefore sovereign's rights (Articles 19 and 20). *** The weakness and equivocation of both the UN and the African human rights regimes confirms an inference from Kant's belief: namely that international humanitarianism is not likely to be advanced by a league of authoritarian states.

This interrogation of juridical statehood by Kantian revolutionism suggests that negative sovereignty is well entrenched in Africa and probably other parts of the Third World. At most, a kind of encapsulated revolutionism is evident in which positive laws and organizations of international humanitarianism exist but are subject to the sovereignty of southern governments. In North-South relations the Kantian revolution has yet to occur, and at present there is little prospect that it will soon happen. Revolutionism is therefore a weak theory in the terms of this article: it is recommendatory more than explanatory. In this regard, however, it is very Kantian.[87]

CONCLUSION

Perhaps the threads of these remarks can now be drawn together. Although realism and revolutionism are certainly relevant, as I have

---

[86] Paul Sieghart, *The Lawful Rights of Mankind* (New York: Oxford University Press, 1986), p. 68.

[87] "For my part, I put my trust in the theory of what the relationships between men and states ought to be according to the principle of right. On the cosmopolitan level too, whatever reason shows to be valid in theory, is also valid in practice." Immanuel Kant, "On the Relationship of Theory to Practice in International Right," reprinted in Hans Reiss, ed., *Kant's Political Writings* (New York: Cambridge University Press, 1977), p. 92.

indicated, the classical international theory most apposite to African quasi-states and the external order which sustains them at this time is one which places sovereignty at the forefront of analysis: rationalism. Neither Machiavellianism nor Kantianism adequately captures the practice of juridical statehood. This is only part of the story, however. As indicated, modern rationalist theories of Third World states are inclined to be inverted and idealist in character, unlike traditional European rationalism, which was far more empiricist and realist. If this observation has validity, rationalist theory today at least as regards sovereignty in the Third World is primarily disclosed not as a Grotian theory concerned with protecting the intrinsic value of existing states but as a constructivist theory aimed at creating political value and developing new states.

Rationalism, realism, and revolutionism have a designated place of long standing in the theory of international relations. The point is locating their appropriate and relative position at any historical period. To reduce international theory to any one mode would be to limit the subject unduly. It would be like trying to operate effectively in practical political life only with the language of power or the language of law or the language of morality. Many political goods and certainly the good life would be unobtainable. One could not achieve in practice the modern constitutional democratic state which requires all of these languages. Likewise in theory. Methodological pluralism, although it obviously sacrifices parsimony and elegance, more than makes up for it by affording balance and comprehensiveness. This is, of course, the point of Martin Wight and others who write about international relations in a pluralist manner, as Hedley Bull observes: "the essence of his teaching was that the truth about international politics had to be sought not in any one of these patterns of thought but in the debate among them."[88] Methodological pluralism seeks to be faithful to the observed pluralism of international political life.

* * *

[88] Bull, "Martin Wight and the Theory of International Relations," p. 110.

Which Norms Matter? Revisiting the "Failure" of Internationalism

Jeffrey W. Legro

International relations theorists have in recent years shown an interest in international norms and rules not equaled since the interwar period.[1] This contemporary literature is, of course, quite different – ie., better – than that of the 1920s and 1930s: it has greater intellectual depth, empirical backing, and explanatory power. The promise of this research, bolstered by the opportunities of the post–cold war era, is that norms encouraging free trade, protecting the environment, enhancing human rights, and controlling the spread and use of heinous weapons may have a substantial impact on the conduct and structure of international relations. But pessimists also exist. Some have taken up the stick E. H. Carr skillfully shook at idealists in an earlier period, arguing that the anarchic power-shaped international arena is not so malleable and that international norms and institutions have relatively little influence.[2] On the one hand, we are pointed to the centrality of international norms; on the other, we are cautioned that norms are inconsequential. How do we make sense of these divergent claims? Which is right?

---

[1] For examples, see Axelrod 1986; Kratochwil 1989; Ray 1989; Nadelmann 1990; Goertz and Diehl 1992; Finnemore 1993; Reed and Kaysen 1993; Thomson 1993, 1994; Mayall 1990; Goldstein and Keohane 1993; Jackson 1993; Sikkink 1993; Paul, 1995; Price 1995; Klotz 1995; Gelpi 1995; Katzenstein 1996; Finnemore 1996a; and Cortell and Davis in press.

[2] Carr 1946. For an example, see Mearsheimer 1994–95, 7.

For their help on the ideas presented below, I am grateful to James Davis, Colin Elman, Hein Goemans, Paul Kowert, John Odell, Ido Oren, Richard Price, Brian Taylor, Mark Zacher, participants at seminars at Harvard University's Olin Institute and Brown University's Watson Institute, and several anonymous reviewers for *International Organization*.

I argue that neither of the polarized positions is sustainable. Contrary to what the skeptics assert, norms do indeed matter. But norms do not necessarily matter in the ways or often to the extent that their proponents have argued. The literature on norms has generally misspecified their impact because of several conceptual and methodological biases. In short, by concentrating on showing that norms "matter," analysts have given short shrift to the critical issues of which norms matter, the ways they matter, and how much they matter relative to other factors. The result has been a misguided sense of the range and depth of the impact of international norms. The social focus of norm analysis is indeed central, but recent analyses have overemphasized international prescriptions while neglecting norms that are rooted in other types of social entities – e.g., regional, national, and subnational groups. This oversight has led scholars to ignore significant subsystemic social understandings that can contradict and overwhelm international prescriptions.

To assess the promise and limits of focusing on norms, I draw on a set of cases involving the use of force where the conventional wisdom expects little impact from international prescriptions – that is, "least likely" cases.[3] Furthermore, the study focuses on a time period (the interwar and World War II years) that the standard historiography of international relations theory sees as decisively refuting ideational internationalism.[4] In the 1920s and 1930s, the international community stigmatized three types of warfare as heinous and immoral: submarine attacks against merchant ships, the bombing of nonmilitary targets, and the use of chemical weapons. These prohibitory norms are interesting (and similar to current efforts) because they were not simply part of the "deep structure" of the international system or "invisible" to the participants but instead were explicit objects of construction by states that later had to weigh the desirability of adherence versus violation. Yet, during World War II, these prohibitions had varying effects. Participants ignored the submarine warfare restrictions almost immediately. They respected strategic bombing rules for months and then violated them. But they upheld limitations on chemical weapons, despite expectations and preparations, throughout the war. Why were some norms apparently influential and not others?

---

[3] See Eckstein 1975; and King, Keohane, and Verba 1994, 209–10.
[4] For example, see Bull 1972.

Contrary to the conventional historiography, I argue that international norms were consequential for the use of force during World War II. The prohibitions shaped states' calculations and tactics, inspired leaders' justifications and rationalizations, and, most fundamentally, appear to be a key reason why certain means of warfare were even considered for restraint. Yet while international norms certainly mattered, a norm explanation cannot account for the variation that occurred in the use of force. The explanation is not that strategic security concerns overwhelmed social prescriptions, since neither the military effectiveness of the weapons nor opportunities for relative strategic advantage can explain the differential adherence of states to the three norms. Instead, it lies in an understanding of organizational culture. This approach does emphasize collective prescriptions, but the focus is on national society rather than on international norms. The dominant beliefs in military organizations about the appropriate ways to fight wars shaped how soldiers thought about and prepared for war, which in turn shaped the varying impact of norms on state aims.

This analysis has several implications for international relations theory. First, it demonstrates the value of providing clear concepts, of examining both effective and ineffective norms, and of considering alternative explanations – methodological additions that can advance both positivist and intrepretivist norm research. Second, its results show the benefits of analyzing competing norm, belief, and cultural patterns in international politics. Although many recent accounts have usefully focused on global norms, few have examined such international injunctions in the context of national norms. Yet these intrastate prescriptions (i.e., those of organizational culture) can wield great influence. This, of course, is not to suggest that bureaucratic culture always supersedes international norms or relative power constraints, but it does highlight the need for conceptual tools to weigh the cross-cutting or synthetic effects of different types of cultural and material structures.

The article takes shape in four parts. First, it outlines the limitations of the extant norm literature and develops an approach that seeks to address those shortcomings. Second, it discusses the logic of a competing view based on organizational culture. It then assesses how persuasively these two perspectives explain state preferences on adherence to norms limiting the use of force in World War II. Finally, it addresses the implications of the argument for international relations theory, especially future work on norms.

ON NORMS

Across a range of theoretical and methodological orientations, scholars have shown a renewed interest in the ways that norms – collective understandings of the proper behavior of actors – operate in international politics. Norms are seen as continuous, rather than dichotomous, entities: they do not just exist or not exist but instead come in varying strengths. Analysts typically portray norms as consequential in terms of either constituting, regulating, or enabling actors or their environments.[5] In any of these roles, the central proposition is that norms that are more robust will be more influential regardless of whether the dependent variable is identity, interests, individual behavior, or collective practices and outcomes. Yet in exploring these relationships, the extant norm literature has been prone to three types of biases.[6]

The first is a failure to conceptualize norm robustness independent of the very effects attributed to norms, thus leading to tautology. This failure is compounded because analysts must confront not a dearth but an apparent profusion of norms in the international arena. Given this availability, one can almost always identify a norm to "explain" or "allow" a particular effect. Since different norms can have competing or even contradictory imperatives, it is important to understand why some norms are more influential than others in particular situations. Thus, whether one emphasizes the behavioral or the linguistic/discursive facet of norms, avoiding circular reasoning requires a notion of norm robustness that is independent of the effects to be explained. This is not an easy task. For example, Alexander Wendt suggests that social structures (of shared knowledge) vary in the degree to which they can be transformed, but he does not specify what defines this trait.[7] In different ways, both Robert Keohane and Friedrich Kratochwil link a norm's potency to its institutionalization.[8] But this pushes the problem back to one of theorizing the robustness of institutions, an exercise that has been prone to ambiguity or definition by effect.

A second problem is that efforts to explore norms suffer from a bias toward the norm that "worked." Most studies of norms focus on a single, specific norm – or, at most, on a small set of norms. Typically, the norms

---

[5] See Kratochwil and Ruggie 1986; Kratochwil 1989, 26; and Dessler 1989, 454–58.
[6] Thanks to Paul Kowert for his contribution to this section. For a developed discussion on the strengths and weaknesses of norm research, see Kowert and Legro 1996.
[7] Wendt 1995, 80.
[8] Keohane 1989, 4–5; Kratochwil 1989, 62.

under consideration are "effective" norms that seem to have obvious consequences.[9] Yet, in order to understand how norms operate, studies must allow for more variation: the success or failure, existence or obsolescence of norms. Research on norms has tended to overlook the emerging rules, principles, prohibitions, and understandings that might have had influence but did not. These cases, analyzed in conjunction with comparable cases of norm effectiveness, are critical to the development of this line of thinking.[10] Why norms did not emerge or were not consequential is as important as why they did or were.

The final (but less pervasive) problem of many studies is a neglect of alternative explanations, particularly ideational ones, for the effects attributed to norms. The dangers of not doing so are apparent. One risks spuriously crediting international norms with consequences (e.g., the shaping or enabling of particular identities, interests, beliefs, or actions) that are better explained by other types of factors.

I attempt to avoid these biases by developing an explicit scheme for assessing norm strength; by comparing norms that seem to have been very effectual, such as those proscribing chemical warfare (CW), with those that were less so, such as those concerning submarine warfare and strategic bombing; and by explicitly contrasting a norm approach with an alternative organizational culture explanation and, to a lesser degree, a conventional realist account.

To gauge the robustness of the norms, I propose a conceptualization based on three criteria: *specificity, durability,* and *concordance.*[11] These three traits are, in principle, as applicable to informal institutions as they are to formal ones. Specificity refers to how well the guidelines for restraint and use are defined and understood. Is there a laborious code that is overly complex or ill-defined or is it relatively simple and precise? Do countries argue about what the restraints entail or how to implement them? Specificity is thus assessed by examining actors' understandings of the simplicity and clarity of the prohibition.

Durability denotes how long the rules have been in effect and how they weather challenges to their prohibitions. Have the norms had

---

[9] See, for example, Ray 1989; Finnemore 1993; Jackson 1993; Thomson 1994; Price 1995; Klotz 1995; and Price and Tannenwald 1996.

[10] Examples include Nadelmann 1990; and McElroy 1992.

[11] Though this is my own schema, it is influenced by traits often implicit in discussions of norms and in the institutionalist literature, for example, Keohane 1989, 4–5; Smith 1989, 234–36; and Young 1989, 23.

long-standing legitimacy? Are violators or violations penalized, thus reinforcing and reproducing the norm? Violations of a norm do not necessarily invalidate it, as is seen, for example, in cases of incest. The issue is whether actors are socially or self-sanctioned for doing so. These questions can be assessed by examining the history of a prohibition and agents' related understanding of and reaction to violations.

Concordance means how widely accepted the rules are in diplomatic discussions and treaties (that is, the degree of intersubjective agreement). The concordance dimension may be a sword that cuts both ways. Public efforts to reaffirm a norm may be a sign, not that it is viable, but instead that it is weakening. Which is the case may depend on its context. In the cases examined here, affirmation is more reinforcing because the focus is largely on "nascent" or evolving norms where affirmation seems to contribute to robustness. Do states seem to concur on the acceptability of the rules? Do they affirm their approval by committing reputations to public ratification? Do states put special conditions on their acceptance of prohibitions, thus diminishing concordance? Or do they take the rules for granted, never even considering violating their prescriptions? These questions can be assessed by reviewing the records of national and international discussions that involve the norms.

Overall, the expectation of the norm approach developed above is that the clearer, more durable, and more widely endorsed a prescription is, the greater will be its impact. With respect to the variation in World War II, this suggests, ceteris paribus, that states' adherence to norms is most likely in areas where norms are most robust in terms of specificity, durability, and concordance. Conversely, where norms are less robust, states will be more inclined toward violations. If a norm account is right, we should see restraint in those areas where prohibitions are most developed. States' expectations of future use should shift as the accord becomes more ingrained as part of international society. Leaders should make reference to the norm in making decisions and recognize the penalties of nonadherence. Alternatively, the norm may be so robust, violation of it is not even considered. Countries should react to constrain transgressions of principles, especially ones that are clear, long-standing, and widely endorsed. In those areas where agreements have not been concluded or are thinly developed, restraint is more likely to break down. The costs of violation will be seen as nonprohibitive. Leaders will attempt to cut corners on restrictions. The related norms will not be identified with self-interest or identity. In short, the effect of prohibitions on actors, decision making, and practices will be minimal.

ORGANIZATIONAL CULTURE

An alternative approach to understanding the varying use of force in World War II comes from a conjunction of cultural and organization theory. An organizational culture approach focuses on the way that the pattern of assumptions, ideas, and beliefs that prescribes how a group should adapt to its external environment and manage its internal affairs influences calculations and actions.[12] In a sense, this approach focuses on "norms" that dominate specific organizations: culture is, in effect, a set of collectively held prescriptions about the right way to think and act.[13] Applied to military bureaucracies, an organizational culture perspective highlights how government agencies tasked with vague formal purposes ("provide security") concentrate on modes of warfare that subsequently condition organizational thinking and behavior. Their dominant way of war tends to become such a locus of activity that, in effect, means become ends.[14] Culture shapes how organizations understand their environment: it acts as a heuristic filter for perception and calculation much the same way a theoretical paradigm shapes intellectual thought or a schema structures individual cognition.[15] Culture also has material consequences. Collective beliefs dictate which capabilities are perceived as better and are worthy of support. Organizations will channel resources to weapons suited to culture. Those weapons will appear more feasible than those that are incompatible with culture and that are subsequently deprived of funding and attention.[16]

* * *

*** Governments, however, consist of multiple agencies, so the question is which bureaucracies will matter and when? The brief answer offered here is that a bureaucracy's impact varies with what I call its organizational salience, consisting of at least three dimensions: the extent to which the bureaucracy has monopoly power on expertise, the complexity of the issue, and the time period available for action. When one organization has a monopoly on expertise and no competitors, it faces less pressure to change and no checks on organizational biases. In terms of complexity, the intricacy of an issue affects the degree to which specialist

[12] This definition is loosely based on Schein 1985, 9.
[13] For a thoughtful review of the work on culture in security affairs, see Johnston 1995. Kier 1996 provides an excellent analysis of organizational culture and military doctrine.
[14] See Wilson 1989, especially 32.
[15] See Kuhn 1970; and Khong 1992.
[16] Levitt and March 1988, 322.

knowledge is required for decisions. The more complex the issue, the less effective senior authorities will be in objecting to or intervening in operations and the more organizational preferences will be felt. The time frame for decision making can also affect bureaucratic effect. When decision-making cycles are short, so is time for adjusting prearranged plans.

These traits all suggest that military organizations will have a high salience in choices on the use of force in war. Militaries are key players in such situations because they generally have monopoly control over expertise in the use of force, military operations are complex and not easily understood by nonspecialists, and the time periods for altering prearranged plans are limited. Civilians may have authority to make final choices, but often contrary to their wishes and efforts, military propensity can prevail in the midst of war due to the organizational salience of the armed forces.

In sum, organizational culture is important because it shapes organizational identity, priorities, perception, and capabilities in ways unexpected by noncultural approaches. Those means compatible with the dominant war-fighting culture will be developed and advocated by the military; those that are not will suffer benign neglect. Even as the cultural tendencies of militaries can remain fairly consistent, their heightened organizational salience in war may lead to change in national policy on the use of force. With regard to World War II, this view predicts that, ceteris paribus, a state will favor adherence to norms proscribing a particular form of combat if that form is antithetical to the war-fighting culture of its military bureaucracy. States will prefer violations regarding means that are compatible with organizational cultures. * * *

NORMS AND ORGANIZATIONAL CULTURE IN WORLD WAR II

To assess the relative explanatory power of the two approaches, I rely on two methods. The first is a macrocorrelation of each approach's ability to predict outcomes across a number of cases. The second is an in-depth analysis of some of the history to illustrate the validity of the causal mechanisms.

The cases I examine relate to submarines, strategic bombing, and CW in World War II. These are a good focus because they were the three main types of combat that states had considered for limitation in the interwar period. These three also make sense for assessing the propositions because they allow for variation in both the "independent" (norms and culture) and the "dependent" (state preferences on the use of force) variables, and they "control" other factors, such as the personalities, the causes of conflict, the stakes at risk, and the general international setting. Within the three categories, I investigate a total of eight cases. In submarine warfare, I examine Britain, Germany, and the United States. In strategic bombing, I focus on Britain and Germany. And in CW, the analysis considers Britain, Germany, and the Soviet Union. I selected countries because they were either the central possessors or potential users of a particular means of warfare or because their behavior was anomalous. For example, why did the Soviet Union not use CW in June 1941 when it was facing a devastating German invasion and imminent defeat, had the weapons in its inventory, and had adopted a "scorched earth" strategy? I excluded cases that might at first glance seem relevant because they did not allow a comparable assessment of the norms and culture propositions or because I could not verify that norms or culture were not epiphenomenal to strategic realist concerns (discussed below). For example, I excluded both U.S. strategic bombing (including the dropping of the atom bomb) and CW use against Japan because Japan could not retaliate against the United States with comparable means, thus removing a key balance-of-forces condition that is present in the other cases. While the list of cases examined does not comprise the entire universe of possible cases, it is a representative one.

Macrocorrelation

A first way to assess the two alternative propositions is through a small-n comparison of their predictions versus the outcomes across the cases. This requires specification of the content of their predictions.

Measuring Norms

A norm account requires a sense of the relative robustness, based on the specificity, durability, and concordance, of the prohibitions in the three types of warfare. I offer no precise formula on how to aggregate the three into an overall measure of robustness. Like all coding, this exercise is partly interpretive, but it improves on many studies that offer no way to evaluate norm strength at all or do so tautologically. Any evaluation of robustness must measure it independently from the norm's effects. Here, the evidence for robustness comes from the period prior to 1939 and describes primarily international-level phenomena. In contrast, the dependent variable (discussed below) is national preferences on adherence to norms limiting the use of force after 1939. The prohibitions on submarine warfare, strategic bombing, and CW each deserve brief description.

In submarine warfare, it was not so much the weapon itself that was stigmatized but its employment against civilian ships and personnel. What was considered illegitimate was the destruction of merchant and passenger ships without attention to the safety of those on board – a practice that came to be known as unrestricted submarine warfare.[17]

The norm against such unrestricted warfare is notable as relatively robust in its durability, specificity, and concordance. The rules regulating submarine warfare stood out as relatively durable. Modern international limitations on attacks at sea date back at least to the Hague Peace Conference of 1899. When Germany used unrestricted submarine warfare extensively in World War I, it provoked a significant adverse reaction culminating in the U.S. entrance into the conflict. Over the course of the interwar years, prohibitions on submarines were repeatedly discussed in the context of international conferences and generally approved. Most important, even as other international agreements crumbled in the wake of rising international tension in the late 1930s, countries took pains to reaffirm the illegality of underwater boat attacks on merchant ships. They gathered in 1936 to approve the London Protocol on Submarine Warfare, while the broader London Naval Conference dissolved in disagreement. Significantly, when the London Protocol was anonymously violated (by Italy) in 1937 during the Spanish civil war, countries took action to punish any further violations, and the unrestricted attacks stopped.[18]

Despite the fact that prominent historians have called the rules explicit and legally binding, the protocol did present some problems in specificity.[19] For example, the definition of what constituted a "merchant ship" was not entirely clear. Whether the arming of a vessel, even if for defensive purposes, made it an actual combatant was hotly disputed, Britain was intent on retaining the right to arm its merchants and denied that such armaments altered their civilian status.[20] Nonetheless, even defensive armaments comprised a threat to submarines that were highly vulnerable on the surface while conducting the required search and seizure procedures. The rules about providing for the safety of passengers and

[17] For solid, concise, secondary accounts of the development of the submarine rules, see Burns 1971; and Manson 1993.

[18] See Toynbee 1938, 339–49; and Frank 1990.

[19] See Samuel F. Bemis, "Submarine Warfare in the Strategy of American Defense and Diplomacy, 1915–1945," Study prepared for the U.S. Navy, 15 December 1961, Yale University Library, Box 1603A, 15–16; and Morison 1951, 8.

[20] Burns 1971, 58.

crews when sinking merchant vessels were likewise vague. Because underwater boats had small crews, they could often not afford to leave men to sail the ship into port. Furthermore, they could not generally take the noncombatant's crew and passengers aboard because of the lack of space. These people could be put in their emergency boats, but countries differed on whether this was safe.

Finally, in terms of concordance, the regime received widespread support. Prior to the war, the submarine rules had been accepted and reaffirmed by a total of forty-eight states. Among them were Britain, Germany, Japan, the Soviet Union, and the United States, all central combatants during World War II. Overall, in terms of durability, specificity, and concordance, the submarine rules represented the most robust institution of the three examined in this study.

The second norm constrained strategic bombing. Statesmen made considerable efforts during the interwar years to reduce the quantity of military aircraft and/or to find ways to regulate conflict by agreeing on rules and restrictions. The main distinction they hoped to enforce was between bombing civilians and combatants. Persons participating directly in the war effort were generally seen as legitimate targets of air power. All others were to be considered illegitimate victims, on whom only the inhumane and criminal would drop bombs.[21]

Concordance was low, however. There was little consensus among nations on the rules. No firm agreement on aerial bombing was apparent in the discourse of international negotiations or accepted in treaty language during the interwar years. At the start of World War II, Britain and Germany did agree verbally to an appeal for restraint by U.S. President Roosevelt, but this last-minute accord raised, at a minimum, questions of commitment.[22]

Because concordance was low, resulting in the absence of a finalized agreement, specificity is difficult to evaluate. Generally, however, the participants seemed to use the 1923 Hague Commission of Jurists' product as a benchmark. Even though they were the most detailed of the interwar years, these rules, too, were troubled by disagreement. The main point of contention was what exactly constituted a military objective. Were civilian factories producing parts for airplanes a legitimate target? Was it acceptable to bomb troop barracks surrounded by hospitals and schools? Each state seemed to have a different way of

[21] Spaight 1947, 43.
[22] On this agreement, see ibid. 259–60.

differentiating civilian from combatant, safe zone from battle area, legitimate from illegitimate bombing.[23] In the absence of clear rules, we can only conclude that specificity was indeed low.

Norms on strategic bombing were also as fragile as any studied here.[24] Linked to the prohibition against attacking undefended cities was an agreement at the 1899 Hague conference that dropping weapons from balloons or "other new weapons of a similar nature" was not allowable. Additionally, while the representatives did not elect to include specific language related to the airplane at the 1907 Hague conference, they did reaffirm the prohibition against attacking undefended cities and dwellings.[25] Nonetheless, in World War I some states did bomb cities. By the beginning of World War II, Franklin Roosevelt's last-minute appeal was the only vestige of states' explicit external commitment to restrict bombing. To the extent that the 1923 Hague rules comprised a de facto prohibition, they were not respected very well in the conflicts in China and Spain during the 1930s. Overall, the norms of air warfare were less developed than those relating to either submarine warfare or CW.

The third major target of diplomatic efforts to limit the use of force in this period was CW. While prohibitions against the use of poison agents had existed for centuries, the interwar norm on gas use showed mixed durability. On the one hand, constraints on chemical use had been a part of international law from the turn of the century. On the other, states had violated the constraints egregiously during World War I. Limitations on the use or manufacture of gas were discussed in a number of conferences during the 1920s and 1930s. The issue of limits on CW was first broached at the Paris Peace Conference in 1919 that prohibited Germany from using, manufacturing, or importing poisonous gases or the raw materials and equipment to produce them. CW received considerable attention at the 1921–22 Washington Conference on the Limitation of Armaments, but a provision that prohibited the use of poison gases in war was proposed but never ratified. The 1925 Geneva Conference for the Supervision of the International Trade in Arms and Ammunition and in Implements of War provided another forum in which CW was discussed. After proposals to prohibit the export of poisonous gases and related materials were rejected, diplomats decided to act again on the CW

---

[23] See Moore 1924, 194–202; and Spaight 1947, 43–47.
[24] Parks 1992 argues that the rules were largely illegitimate.
[25] On the development of bombing prohibitions, see Parks 1992; Royse 1928; and De Saussure 1971.

provisions of the Washington treaty.[26] This agreement became known as the Geneva Protocol. It was the only agreement on CW concluded during the interwar period and had a somewhat stormy record of adherence in those years. For example, Italy violated the agreement in 1935 in its war with Ethiopia. The League of Nations responded weakly with limited economic sanctions that were not enforced and were largely ineffectual.[27] In 1938, when Japan used chemical weapons in China, the League of Nations and most other polities simply ignored the event.[28]

Concordance with the norm was moderate. The problem was that neither Japan nor the United States publicly ratified the 1925 protocol before the start of war in 1939. Furthermore, Britain and France agreed to respect the norm only in conflicts with other parties that had ratified the agreement and whose allies also adhered to the agreement. This provision might have had significant ramifications in World War II. For example, since Japan engaged in CW in China and was an ally of Germany, Britain's pledge of restraint would no longer have been guaranteed.

The Geneva Protocol was simple and fairly precise, however. Signatory nations would not use CW first if the other side was a signatory and also showed restraint. It allowed only a few minor gray areas. For example, high explosives released small amounts of chemicals; was this a violation? The use of nonlethal gas (such as tear gas) was another unresolved area. Some countries, such as the United States, wanted the freedom to employ nonlethal gases to control their own populaces.[29] Overall, the anti-CW norm was more robust than that attached to strategic bombing but less than that limiting submarine warfare. Table 11.1 summarizes these relationships along with their predicted effects.

Measuring Organizational Cultures

Organizational culture is gauged according to the ideas and beliefs about how to wage war that characterized a particular military bureaucracy. Specifically, the issue of interest is whether the favored way of war incorporated the specific means prohibited (violation oriented) or designated it either as nonorganic or as peripheral (adherence oriented). A measure of each culture is developed by reviewing available internal correspondence, planning documents, regulations, exercises, and memoirs

---

[26] For studies of the development of the prohibition, see Moon 1993; and Price forthcoming.
[27] See Fair 1985, 45; SIPRI 1971b, 180.
[28] SIPRI 1971b, 189–90.
[29] Ibid., 102–4.

TABLE 11.1. *Assessing Norm Robustness*

	Submarine warfare	Chemical warfare	Strategic bombing
Specificity	Medium	Very high	Low
Durability	High	Low	Low
Concordance	Very high	Medium	Low
Overall relative assessment	High	Medium	Low
Prediction	Most likely adherence	Mixed adherence/ violation	Most likely violation

of individual members. These multiple sources provide a composite picture of the hierarchy of legitimate beliefs within an organization. This is a holistic exercise that depends on the qualitative interpretation of the specific content of each culture. While this makes a priori generalizations difficult, it does allow for the coding of a culture as violation or adherence oriented. Cultural explanations are often accused of being post hoc and tautological: a certain cultural belief can always be found after the fact that "explains" a given action. In this case, however, the sources I have used to measure culture describe bureaucratic thinking and date from the earlier interwar years, while the outcomes to be explained involve national preferences during the later war. Thus the organizational culture hypothesis can be falsified. For example, U.S. Navy culture was oriented toward adhering to prohibitions on unrestricted submarine warfare throughout the interwar period. Yet on the first day of war the United States switched to favoring such warfare. This case tends to disconfirm the organizational culture hypothesis.

Although it is not possible here to document the entire logic of each military's organizational culture and its relationship to the use of stigmatized force, the brief summaries below can give a snapshot of each culture and which prediction – violation of or adherence to the respective norm – follows from it.[30]

In submarine warfare, the German navy, unlike many, viewed the submarine as a valued combat tool, and because the ethos of its underwater force was based on its World War I unrestricted trade offensive, its plans, operations, and advice were biased in favor of violation. In contrast, the British navy, long dominated by a belief in the supremacy of the

---

[30] For a more detailed analysis of these cultures, see Legro 1995.

battleship, considered submarines a strictly ancillary means of combat. Even when Britain had strategic incentives to turn to submarine raiding, it did not. During the interwar period, the Royal Navy's main expected adversary was Japan, a nation vulnerable to a submarine campaign, yet the navy never considered an anticommerce submarine strategy. British naval culture favored adherence to the rules. Finally, the U.S. Navy, like the Royal Navy, was "battleship-bound" in its thinking during the interwar period. It gave little consideration to an unrestricted commerce campaign against Japan, its main expected opponent, despite Japan's vulnerability to such a strategy. This cultural orientation predicts U.S. adherence to the rules.

In contrast to the navy's orientation in submarine warfare, the German army's culture led it to favor adherence to the CW norm. Army thought highlighted the efficacy of the mobile offensive, and CW – perceived as a static defensive weapon – was seen as ill-suited to the dominant mindset. The British military was also inclined toward adherence but for different reasons. The Royal Army was a tradition-governed antitechnology force that was generally hostile to CW, particularly given its institutional experience in World War I. CW was more compatible with the Royal Air Force's strategic bombing thinking, but the army was in charge of CW development. The air force developed its own biases toward fire-bombing and high explosives (even though gas was considered a complement, not a competitor, to those munitions). Finally, the Soviet Union's Red Army was dominated by a faith in the offensive, an orientation that was encouraged by its civil war experience and ensuing debates about the proper political-military orientation for the country. It subsequently paid less attention to means such as CW, which was perceived as primarily useful in defense. This orientation favored adherence to the CW rules.

In strategic bombing, Britain's Royal Air Force developed around a "faith" in the effectiveness of strategic bombing, particularly against civilians and their morale. Personnel, plans, weapons acquisition, and intelligence all were affected by this ideology. This culture favored a violation of the rules, even as geopolitical factors and popular concern cautioned against such action. Although it toyed with strategic bombing, the German air force moved away from such concepts as the war years approached. The Luftwaffe, influenced by Germany's continental tradition of warfare and a variety of circumstantial factors, was more focused on contributing to the ground and sea campaigns than achieving victory by targeting enemy morale in an unrestricted bombing offensive. This culture was more inclined toward adherence to the rules on strategic bombing.

Predictions Versus Outcomes

A macrocomparison of expected effects versus actual outcomes during World War II yields a first look at the influence of norms and organizational culture. For this analysis, "outcome" refers to the preferences of states, not their actions. We can thus distinguish between conscious violation of a norm with those situations where states may have responded to the other side's violation (an allowable action) of where they crossed boundaries by accident. In practice, preferences and action correspond closely. I measured preferences by reviewing the internal discussions of the wartime leadership regarding its desired outcomes. Such decision-making bodies were often small groups that debated and reached a consensus on desired ends.

Table 11.2 summarizes the relative predictive fit of the norm and organizational culture approaches. Predictions from an organizational culture perspective matched the outcome significantly more consistently than predictions from a norm perspective (7 versus 3.5 of 8). In those cases where normative prohibitions are most robust, for instance, we should expect adherence or at least the slowest shift toward the opposite preference. Where norms are thinly developed, a preference for violation should be more likely. As Table 11.2 indicates, however, the relationship between norm robustness and preferences on the use of force seems weak. For example, in submarine warfare, where the institution of restraint was most robust, nations first favored escalation. Yet in CW, where the institution was less developed, nations preferred restraint throughout the conflict.

Table 11.2 displays a relatively consistent link between military culture and state preferences regarding the use of force. When culture favored violation, prohibitions against use generally were disregarded. And when culture was inclined toward adherence, states tended to prefer adherence to international norms. In both absolute and relative terms, organizational culture correlates strongly with the variation in adherence to the limitations on the use of force.

Microassessment of Causal Mechanisms

A closer look at the details of World War II is a necessary complement to the macrocomparison in three ways. First, it provides a better sense of the content and use of analytical constructs such as norms and organizational culture. Second, as sophisticated methodologists are quick to point out, correlation by itself does not tell us what caused the

TABLE 11.2. *A Macrocorrelation: Two Approaches and the Pattern of Norm Adherence*

	Predictions[a]		
Case	Norm	Organizational culture	Outcome (N = 8)
Britain			
Chemical warfare	Mixed (1/2)[b]	Adherence (1)	Adherence
Strategic bombing	Violation (1)	Violation (1)	Violation
Submarine warfare	Adherence (1)	Adherence (1)	Adherence[c]
Germany			
Chemical warfare	Mixed 1/2	Adherence (1)	Adherence
Strategic bombing	Violation (0)	Adherence (1)	Adherence[c]
Submarine warfare	Adherence (0)	Violation (1)	Violation
Soviet Union			
Chemical warfare	Mixed (1/2)	Adherence (1)	Adherence
United States			
Submarine warfare	Adherence (0)	Adherence (0)	Violation
Correlational fit	3.5/8	7/8	

[a] The match between prediction and outcome is in parentheses. It was scored as follows: 0 = no match; 1 = match; 1/2 = half a match (see below).

[b] The mixed pattern represents a middle position on the norm robustness continuum. It predicts that chemical warfare would have shown a varying pattern of preferences for mutual adherence and violation. Since this view also predicts a partial or varying preference for restraint and is indeterminate as to the dominant preference, I have scored it in favor of the norm proposition as half a match.

[c] Though the state eventually violated the norm, it did so only after the other side's first use, as allowed by norms in all three categories, and thus was coded as adherence.

apparent association. Microanalysis allows for better checking of the causal mechanisms posited by each approach.[31] Finally, such analysis is useful for checking to make sure that the presumed relationships are not spurious owing to some other influence. One clear possibility is political-military advantage. A "strategic realist" view would argue that especially in war, states choose means according to their expected contribution to strategic goals; states will prefer violating norms when they expect to reap relative military or political benefits from doing so.

[31] George and McKeown 1985.

In those situations where violations further a state's position, escalation is probable. Likewise, when a relative loss or disadvantage will result from escalation, adherence is more likely.[32]

My microassessment focuses on the *** British submarine warfare case. [For space reasons a section of German submarine warfare is omitted.] Given space limitations, this case offers maximum analytical leverage. *** The norm was most robust in submarine warfare, so that norm effects should be most significant in that area. Moreover, the British case at least seems to offer a priori support for the influence of norms: British preferences matched the predictions of the norm hypothesis. A careful study of the decision-making process reveals, however, that this relationship is problematic and that organizational culture was the more influential cause.

* * *

British Submarine Warfare

Britain preferred restraint in this case, an outcome that the norms, organizational culture, and strategic advantage propositions predict. Examining the decision-making process in this case helps to sort out the relative influence of the three because it increases the number of observations that are theoretically relevant and permits differentiation of causal mechanisms.[33] British calculations on the submarine rules occurred in two key stages: before and after German escalation.

British preferences and actions before the German escalation can be attributed to several causes. The robustness of the submarine norm and Britain's particularly energetic role in promoting it during the interwar period indicate a strong preference for restraint. Strategic realism also predicts restraint because Britain was dependent on trade and defended by a large surface fleet; hence submarine use could only be harmful. From an organizational culture vantage point, the expected effects were the same: the navy orthodoxy saw very limited possibilities for employing the submarine, thus favoring norm adherence.

A second stage, one that allows us to sort out the three propositions, came after Germany had violated the submarine rules in October 1939, when Britain continued to adhere to restraint. A strategic view would expect escalation at this point. Britain no longer had any reason to prefer adherence to the norm because it no longer had to fear that its own

---

[32] For a more developed discussion and assessment of this proposition, see Legro 1995.
[33] George and McKeown 1985, 36.

use would induce the more costly German retaliation: Germany already had transgressed the rules. More important, submarines could play an immediate strategic role. Germany was using merchant ships to import iron ore – a critical material for Nazi war industries – from both Sweden and, in the winter, Norway.[34] In October, some proposed that British submarines should be used to intercept this trade. Because of icebound Baltic ports in the winter, the iron ore was sent to Narvik and shipped through Norwegian coastal waters and across the Skagerrak and Kattegat, areas where unrestricted submarine warfare would be effective but where British surface ships were either vulnerable or would violate Norwegian waters.

A norm perspective predicts expectations, thinking, desires, and actions that reflect the prescriptions of the submarine rules or concerns about the effects of transgressing them. According to this perspective, after Germany had escalated, Britain should have done the same, since the norm was one of quid pro quo restraint. If only to reinforce the norm, Britain should have turned toward escalation, yet it did not.

Some evidence suggests norms were influential in Britain's decision-making process, although again, they were not decisive. Specifically, a view that recognizes both the impact of normative prohibitions and strategic concerns captures at least one part of the process. In the early fall of 1939, it became increasingly clear that Germany was violating the rules of submarine warfare. The British Foreign Office noted that, as of 5 October, nine of thirty-one reported incidents related to the submarine rules were violations, amounting to a "formidable list of illegalities." By the end of October, the navy had concluded Germany was making illegal attacks.[35] As Britain considered how to respond, several ideas were forwarded, ranging from a looser interpretation of the London protocol to permitting unrestricted warfare in the Baltic.[36] These proposals, however, were rejected. Not only was the idea of unrestricted warfare turned down but the Lords of the Admiralty would not approve

---

[34] See U.K. PRO, ADM 199/892, Memorandum from First Lord, 19 September 1939; and Roskill 1968, 156.

[35] See U.K. PRO, ADM 1/10584, Memorandum from William Malkin, Foreign Office, 24 October 1939 and ADM 199/892, Minute by the Head of the Military Branch, October 1939.

[36] See the following U.K. PRO documents: ADM 199/878, 008070/39, Minute by Deputy Chief of the Naval Staff, 25 October 1939; ADM 199/892, Minute by Head of Military Branch, October 1939; and ADM 199/892, Minute by Director of Plans, 3 November 1939.

even loosening Britain's strict interpretation of the protocol's search and seizure rules. Britain was concerned that the goodwill it was attempting to build among neutral countries would be dissipated should submarines be employed. The Lords sensibly feared that some accident would result that would alienate important countries such as Norway and Sweden.[37] Britain wanted to avoid antagonizing neutral countries especially with regard to one issue, the control of German exports. Britain had already instituted a "contraband" system to limit Third Reich imports and now wanted to do the same to Germany's outgoing trade. To accomplish this, however, Britain would need the support of the neutral countries and therefore had to keep their interests in mind. The British plan was to forgo tit-for-tat replies to Germany's breaches of the London Protocol and instead allow the illegalities to accumulate; it would then respond by controlling German exports.[38]

While these incidents indicate the influence of both the prohibitions and the strategic concerns, events that followed cast doubt on whether they were at the heart of British restraint. In December 1939, Britain did implement export controls but in response to Germany's "illegal" mining activity, not its submarine violations. Furthermore, while Britain put plans (Operation Wilfred) into motion in early April 1940 that violated Norwegian waters with underwater mines, it maintained its restraints on submarines.[39] Thus even though Germany conducted unrestricted warfare and neutral country reaction became less of a concern, Britain did not turn to escalation. Although the rules allowed Britain to escalate under the circumstances, restraint obtained for five months beyond German escalation while iron ore shipments continued and even during the first days of the Nazi invasion of Norway in April 1940. Why?

Organizational culture offers an answer to this curious restraint. The British navy was dominated by a battleship creed that considered the big surface ship as the pivotal element in the large clashes of fleets that were expected to decide the war at sea. Navy leadership saw the submarine as a strictly ancillary tool. It gave little attention to and sometimes even disparaged commerce warfare, especially the unrestricted type. Despite the devastating success of German submarines in World War I, the Royal

---

[37] See U.K. PRO, ADM 199/892, Minute by Head of Military Branch, and ADM 199/892, Minute by Director of Plans, the latter of which was approved by the First Lord, First Sea Lord, Deputy Chief of the Naval Staff.

[38] See U.K. PRO, ADM 199/878, Minute by Deputy Chief of the Naval Staff, and ADM 199/892, Minute by Head of Military Branch.

[39] Roskill 1954, 102 and 156–58.

Navy's postwar assessment committee reaffirmed that the "battleship retains her old predominant position."[40] As one captain noted in his diary, the committee "had merely made statements, assertions: had not examined the war to find out what the influence of the big ship was, or whether she was still in the position she used to be {in}. The thing i.e. the future of the battleship must be approached in a far more scientific manner."[41] The navy's exercises in the interwar years, which were meant to be objective measures of competence, gave submarines little chance to prove their worth. Since the dominant creed assumed that submarines were relatively ineffective, the navy structured its exercises accordingly and rejected results that suggested otherwise. At the end of a 1939 exercise, a submarine officer accurately reported to a hall of one thousand sailors that torpedoes had hit 22 percent of their targets. Instead of the normal questions, Admiral Forbes, the commander of the Home Fleet, stood up, declared that the officer was clearly wrong and that 3 percent was the correct figure, and the session ended.[42] The navy's battleship cult also affected its evaluation of the threat of enemy submarines. Ignoring readily available evidence, many believed that the danger from German U-boats had been mastered: Britain did not conduct a single exercise in protection of a slow convoy against the submarine between 1919 and 1939.[43]

In short, it was the battleship orthodoxy that drove decisions on whether to violate the norm on submarine warfare. The deputy chief of the naval staff commented in October 1939 that "if it could be shown that it was essential for us to take full advantage of the latitude allowed by the Submarine Protocol in order to achieve some war aim, then I would say that we should have to do so but, at the present moment, I do not think this is the case."[44] In fact, had the submarine regulations been loosened, the underwater boats could have been used effectively for considerable strategic advantage both off the coast of Norway and in the sea channel between Germany and Sweden and Norway.[45] Even when the gray uniforms

[40] See U.K. PRO, ADM 1/8586, "Final Report of the Post-War Questions Committee," 27 March 1920, as cited in Roskill 1968, 115, Also see Terraine 1989, 117–18.

[41] Diary entry of Captain (later Sir Admiral) Herbert Richmond for 10 November 1919, as cited in Roskill 1968, 115–16.

[42] See Simpson 1972, 48–49, 57–58, and 74–76; Hezlet 1967, 119; Mars 1971, 33; and Roskill 1976, 230 and 430–31.

[43] See Henry 1976, 381–82; Roskill 1976, 336–37 and 477; and Roskill 1954, 45,355, and 536.

[44] U.K. PRO, ADM 199/878, Minute 08070/39 by Deputy Chief of the Naval Staff, 25 October 1939.

[45] See Roskill 1954, 334–35; King 1958, 55–56; and Hezlet 1967, 125 and 138–40.

of the Wehrmacht were spotted on merchant ships, Britain allowed German shipping to continue in the Kattegat during the early stages of the Reich's invasion of Norway in April 1940. As it had twenty submarines in the waters through which the invasion fleet sailed, Britain's restraint in this instance has been called a significant "missed opportunity."[46]

How Norms Matter

To argue that norms do not account as well as organizational culture for the differential use of prohibited warfare in World War II is not to say such prohibitions were meaningless. The record clearly suggests that the norms did indeed "matter" in at least one fundamental sense and a number of less consequential ways related to the way that states thought, communicated, and acted with regard to the use of force.

Constituting Heinous Warfare

The most fundamental effect of norms was to define which means of warfare would even be considered for restraint.[47] Rather than inventory their armories and war plans in search of finding heinous forms of fighting, countries considered for restraint those forms that already were stigmatized by extant norms. This stigmatization was not a simple product of the technological inhumanity of a particular form of combat. States hardly blinked over the use of equally inhumane forms of warfare such as high-explosive artillery shells or flamethrowers. And was it really less moral to bomb London than to besiege Leningrad? Yet bombing was stigmatized while besieging a defended city was not. No objective measure of inhumanity set submarines, strategic bombing, and chemical weapons apart. Only recognized norms dictated the boundaries of acceptable use. At times, these took the form of a moral consideration: whether it was "right" to use such a weapon. For example, when Britain considered the use of CW, one assistant chief of the army general staff argued that "such a departure from our principles and traditions would have the most deplorable effects not only on our own people but even on the fighting services. Some of us would begin to wonder whether it really mattered which side won."[48] More often, the special attention given to these three prohibitions had to do with the material consequences of

---

[46] Simpson 1972, 89.
[47] This thesis is developed in greater depth in Price forthcoming.
[48] U.K. PRO, WO 193/732, Minute from Assistant Chief of the Imperial General Staff (C) to Chief of the Imperial General Staff, 16 June 1940.

violations as seen above. In either case, the effect of the international norms suggests they may be a critical facilitating force in the limitation of otherwise taken-for-granted behavior. To find whether this is in fact the case would entail a broader investigation that would include cases where mutual restraint in using militarily significant weapons obtained but where no legacy of international norms existed. That such cases do not readily come to mind suggests the relevance of norms.

Restricting Preparations

In some cases, norms also affected the way states prepared for war. For example, popular anti-CW sentiment in Britain during the 1920s and 1930s combined with Britain's acceptance of the Geneva Protocol seemed to add slightly to constraints on developing gas warfare. Terms were changed to avoid any reference to offensive CW; training materials were not written or distributed and exercises not conducted to avoid a perception that Britain was preparing for a chemical war. Even the open development of civil defense measures against gas was deferred in 1929 as being ill-timed in light of Britain's ratification that year of the Geneva Protocol.[49] The Foreign Office adamantly opposed proposals to use gas on India's northwest frontier against Afghan tribesmen in the mid-1920s. It found the turnaround in policy to be too quick. Austen Chamberlain, the Foreign Secretary, argued that since Britain had vilified Germany for gas use in World War I, it had to wait until its "charges against Germany were less present in the minds of the public" before advocating gas use.[50] Yet one must be careful not to overstate the influence of the antigas norm. Although Britain's offensive gas program was pushed underground, it was not stopped. After the Geneva Protocol was signed, the work previously done in the Offensive Munitions Department was simply conducted under the heading of "chemical weapons against which defense is required." A variety of research and weapons development for offensive warfare evolved under the guise of this semantic cover.[51] By the late 1930s, any constraining impact that public opinion had exerted

[49] See U.K. PRO, WO 188/390, "Lecture to Staff College, Camberly," 10 April 1931, and WO 188/446, "Preparation of Training Manuals on Chemical Warfare," 30 September 1930; Harris and Paxman 1982, 46–47; SIPRI 1971a, 269 and 300; Haber 1986, 300; and Spiers 1986, 47–49.

[50] The quotation is from U.K. PRO, CAB 2/4, Minute of 215 and 217 Meetings of the Committee on Imperial Defense, 22 July and 11 November 1926, as cited in Spiers 1986, 48.

[51] Harris and Paxman 1982, 42 and 47.

on CW preparations dissipated, as the threat of war with Germany rose.[52]

Rules also inhibited wartime preparations in the United States. Although U.S. Navy culture had ignored commerce warfare in the interwar years, once war with Japan seemed imminent some navy officials began to acknowledge the possible benefits of using submarines against shipping. When the naval leadership considered the matter, however, it advised against changing the rules because doing so would be "contrary to international law and U.S. policy" and instead recommended maintaining a traditional posture until circumstances rendered modification advisable.[53] The Japanese Pearl Harbor attack soon provided such circumstances.

Influencing Third-Party Reactions

Most apparent, international principles affected the expectations of states regarding the reactions of other parties. The rules of warfare set guidelines for what was considered acceptable behavior. States believed that violating such guidelines could cost them the support of other countries or even their own populace. Germany, as mentioned above, fretted that its unrestricted submarine warfare would antagonize Britain or the United States at a time when it wanted accommodation with the former and nonintervention from the latter. Likewise, Britain pondered how its unrestricted bombing or use of chemical weapons would affect the support it desperately needed from the United States.

However, as seen in the case of German submarine warfare, these expected costs led states to alter the manner of policy implementation but not necessarily the direction of decisions. So Britain, when worried that its unrestricted campaign would alienate neutral countries, devised schemes to blame escalation on the enemy in order to mitigate political damage while going ahead with the bombing.[54]

Gaining Advantage

Norms also figured in state calculations of gaining advantage over the enemy. Britain concluded that its own restraint, in the face of German transgressions, would bring it favor with third parties. It planned to

---

[52] Harris 1980, 60–61.
[53] See U.S. National Archives, RG80, General Board Study No. 425, Amendment of Rules for Maritime Commerce, Box 133, Department of the Navy, 15 May 1941; and Samuel F. Bemis study, Yale University Library, Box 1603 A.
[54] Terraine 1985, 143.

accumulate this "normative capital" and then cash it in at a later point. For example, in the summer of 1939 the commander of the submarine force, Rear Admiral B. C. Watson, wanted to announce danger zones around British overseas possessions where submarines could defend against invasion by attacking convoys without restrictions. The admiralty denied the proposal. It feared that if Britain initiated action, it could not then blame the Germans for violating restrictions on submarine attacks or respond with "other measures besides a strict tit-for-tat" that would be even more advantageous.[55] As discussed above, Britain's plan to control German exports was also typical of this thinking.

Signaling Intentions

Norms proved influential in terms of signaling intentions. In this sense they help to define a critical dimension of the concept "threat" that has played so large a role in the international relations literature.[56] Violating prohibitions was an indicator of the nature of one's ambitions. Germany, for example, sought accommodation with Britain after its invasion of Poland in the fall of 1939. Even though it believed that its use of unrestricted submarine warfare was to its military advantage, Germany favored restraint because it acknowledged that violating the submarine rules would indicate to Britain that it aimed for total war; accommodation would then be impossible. Had these norms not developed during the interwar period, the stigma of violation would not have been so great. Norms worked in the same manner in the summer of 1940, Then, Germany refrained from bombing British cities immediately after defeating France. One reason for this restraint was Hitler's interest in striking a deal with Britain; unrestricted bombing would have scuttled such a possibility. Here again the norm was important as a recognized threshold of violence with social significance not applicable to conventional forms of combat.

[Original article includes section addressing possible objections to how I measure norms, the role of strategic pressures, and the impact of national culture and regime type.]

* * *

[55] See U.K. PRO, ADM 1/10360, Rear Admiral (Submarines) to Secretary of the Admiralty, "Remarks on the Use of Submarines in Defence of Territory," 3 August 1939, and ADM 1/10360, Minute 07295/39 by Head of the Military Branch, 21 August 1939.
[56] For example, see Walt 1987, 25–26.

CONCLUSION

The contemporary surge in research on international norms inevitably draws our attention to the past – particularly the interwar years. Traditionally the two decades leading to World War II have comprised a paradigmatic case showing that international norms are ineffective in critical situations and that practical efforts based on norm effectiveness are utopian. To be sure, neither the Kellogg-Briand Pact nor the League of Nations effectively prohibited war. But even in this difficult period for international institutions, not all prohibitions were ineffectual. Oddly enough, in a total war, states struggling for survival altered or transcended the expected use of particular forms of military power, in part because of intentionally constructed international prohibitions on those types of warfare.

Yet by considering the question, which norms matter? the drawbacks of focusing exclusively on international norms are also apparent. In World War II, the robustness of such norms did not directly relate to their impact on the thinking and actions of actors or to systemic outcomes. But contrary to the realist answer, neither relative capabilities nor the situations of states was the primary catalyst. Instead, it was the organizational cultures of militaries that more significantly structured how states understood their situations, what types of capabilities they saw as important, and, ultimately, how desirable it was to violate the norm or maintain mutual restraint. Furthermore, these cultures had a marked autonomous effect relative to both norms and to the balance of power – that is, the way militaries and nations thought about fighting was not reducible either to international norms or to strategic opportunities.

Of course, the response to the prohibitions during World War II was not a monocausal organizational culture story. As seen in the cases above, concerns about international prescriptions and strategic advantage both had roles to play. Although I have assessed these variables as competing hypotheses here, a synthetic model might, for example, develop an explanation of norm influence that takes into account both the robustness of international prescriptions and the impact of national-level social understandings such as political or organizational culture.

* * *

12

The Territorial Integrity Norm: International Boundaries and the Use of Force

Mark W. Zacher

* * *

In the late twentieth century many international relations scholars and observers have commented on the declining importance of interstate territorial boundaries for a variety of national and transnational activities.[1] Concurrently, something very significant has been happening in international relations that raises questions concerning judgments of the decreasing importance of boundaries: the growing respect for the proscription that force should not be used to alter interstate boundaries – what is referred to here as the territorial integrity norm.[2] The development of a norm concerning respect for states' territoriality is particularly important because scholars have established that territorial disputes have been the major cause of enduring interstate rivalries, the frequency of war, and the intensity of war.[3] After reviewing studies on interstate wars, John Vasquez wrote that "Of all the issues over which wars could logically be fought, territorial issues seem to be the ones most often associated with wars. Few interstate wars are fought without any territorial issue being involved in one way or another."[4]

---

[1] See Ohmae 1990 and 1995; Rosecrance 1986 and 1996; Ruggie 1993; Rosenau 1990; Elkins 1994; and Hirst and Thompson 1996.

[2] A norm is generally defined as "a standard of appropriate behavior for actors of a given identity" (Finnemore and Sikkink 1999, 251) and an international regulatory norm is strong when it is respected and viewed as legally binding by the great majority of states.

[3] See Holsti 1991; Goertz and Diehl 1992; Vasquez 1993, 123–52; Huth 1996; Hensel 1999; and Vasquez and Henehan 2001.

[4] Vasquez 1993, 151.

In this article I trace the dramatic change in attitudes and practices of states in the Westphalian international order concerning the use of force to alter interstate boundaries. *** In the first section I briefly outline the attitudes and practices of states regarding territorial boundaries from the seventeenth century until World War II. In the second section I focus on the remarkable changes in beliefs and practices from World War II until the present. In the third section I explore the roots of the territorial integrity norm. States' motivations for accepting the territorial integrity norm have been both instrumental and ideational, and the importance of different motivations has varied among groups of states. ***

INTERNATIONAL BOUNDARIES FROM THE SEVENTEENTH TO THE EARLY TWENTIETH CENTURY

Political life has not always disclosed a clearly defined system of international boundaries. The medieval world did not have international boundaries as we understand them today;[5] authority over territorial spaces was overlapping and shifting. The political change from the medieval to the modern world involved the construction of the delimited territorial state with exclusive authority over its domain. Even at that, precisely surveyed national borders only came into clear view in the eighteenth century.[6] In the words of Hedley Bull, the practice of establishing international boundaries emerged in the eighteenth century as "a basic rule of co-existence."[7]

The birth of the modern interstate system is often dated at the 1648 Peace of Westphalia, although key features of the system emerged gradually and fluctuated in strength before and after 1648. Initially, the legitimacy of interstate borders was defined in dynastic terms: state territory was the exclusive property of ruling families, and they had an absolute right to rule their territories. But this international order did not reflect any absolute right to *particular* territory that could *legitimately* change hands by inheritance, marriage, war, compensation, and purchase.[8] In these early centuries of the Westphalian order territory was the main factor that determined the security and wealth of states, and thus the protection and acquisition of territory were prime motivations of foreign policy. Most wars, in fact, concerned the acquisition of territory,

[5] Clark 1961, chap. 10.
[6] Clark 1972, 144.
[7] Bull 1977, 34–37.
[8] Holsti 1991.

and most of these wars led to exchanges of territory; this practice continued until the middle of the twentieth century (see Table 12.1). These practices were reflected in the legal norm concerning the legitimacy of conquest. To quote the eminent international legal scholar Lassa Oppenheim writing in 1905, "As long as a Law of Nations has been in existence, the states as well as the vast majority of writers have recognized subjugation as a mode of acquiring territory."[9]

In the early centuries of the Westphalian system the populations of the early modern states were often culturally diverse and politically disorganized. Many people were not collectively identified by state borders that moved back and forth without much regard for them.[10] The practice of drawing boundaries in disregard of the people living in the territories was extended from Europe to the rest of the world during the age of Western colonialism from the sixteenth through the nineteenth centuries. This was often carried out with little attention to the cultural and ethnic character of the indigenous peoples of the non-European world. Yet it was the borders that were initially drawn and imposed by Western imperialists that later became the acceptable reference for articulating anticolonial demands for self-determination and independent statehood.[11]

The nineteenth century was, of course, the age of nationalism, which was spurred by the French Revolution and Napoleon's support for popular sovereignty and national self-determination. These intellectual currents began to alter peoples' views concerning the legitimacy of territorial conquests. "From the middle of the nineteenth century the current of opinion, influenced by the growing belief in national self-determination, was moving against the legitimacy of annexation outside the colonial sphere, when effected without the consent of the inhabitants."[12] Sharon Korman referred to this change in attitudes as the beginning of an "important change in the *moral climate* of international relations."[13] This moral climate, with its clear democratic thrust, however, had conflicting implications for the stability of boundaries. On the one hand, nationalism supported the precept that a territory belonged to a national grouping and it was wrong to take the land from a nation. On the other hand, nationalism

---

[9] Quoted in Korman 1996, 7. Juxtapose this with the statement of Professor Lauterpacht in the 1955 edition of Oppenheim's *International Law* in Korman 1996, 179.

[10] Clark 1972, 143.

[11] See Jackson and Rosberg 1982; and Korman 1996, 41–66.

[12] Korman 1996, 93.

[13] Ibid., 39 (italics added). Malcolm Anderson has spoken of "the sacralization of homelands" as a result of the growth of nationalism. Anderson 1996, 3.

TABLE 12.1. *Interstate Territorial Wars, 1648–2000*

a. Wars by historical era

Period	Territorial conflicts	Conflicts resulting in redistribution of territory	Conflicts in which territory was redistributed	Territorial redistributions per year
1648–1712	19	15	79%	0.23
1713–1814	30	24	80%	0.24
1815–1917	25	20	80%	0.19
1918–1945	18	16	88%	0.59
1946–2000	40	12	30%	0.22

b. Wars by half century

Period	Territorial conflicts	Conflicts resulting in redistribution of territory	Conflicts in which territory was redistributed	Territorial redistributions per year
1651–1700	14	11	79%	0.22
1701–1750	16	14	88%	0.28
1751–1800	12	8	67%	0.16
1801–1850	13	11	85%	0.22
1851–1900	14	10	71%	0.20
1901–1950	26	23	89%	0.46
1951–2000	37	10	27%	0.20

Sources: Data used to identify territorial wars between 1648 and 1945 is from Holsti 1991. Holsti classifies wars according to twenty-two issues. Six of these are clearly concerned with control over territory: territory, strategic territory, colonial competition, empire creation, maintaining integrity of empire, and national unification. Additional information on these conflicts was derived from a number of secondary sources, including Goertz and Diehl 1992; Goldstein 1992; McKay and Scott 1983; and Taylor 1954. Wars are classified by their beginning date.

Information on territorial wars between 1946 and 2000 was also obtained from a large number of secondary sources, including Bercovitch and Jackson 1997; Goertz and Diehl 1992; Kacowicz 1994; Huth 1996; and Wallensteen and Sollenberg 1998. Goertz and Diehl focus on territorial conflicts where there were exchanges of territory; Kacowicz examines cases of peaceful territorial change; and Huth includes territorial disputes that involved and did not involve international violence. The Correlates of War list of conflicts was also consulted. It includes territorial wars with over one thousand deaths. Singer and Small 1982. There were five conflicts between 1946 and 2000 that led to minor border alterations and are not included under "Conflicts resulting in redistribution of territory." For descriptions of the territorial aggressions between 1946 and 2000, see Table 12.2.

provided grounds for a national grouping in one state trying to secede to form an independent state or to unite with its ethnic compatriots living in other states. In fact, nationalism had a more disruptive than pacifying effect on international relations in the late nineteenth and early twentieth centuries, as was witnessed in the wars surrounding the unification of the German and Italian peoples and in the division of the Hapsburg, Hohenzollern, and Ottoman empires into numerous national states.[14]

Three interrelated territorial issues during and at the end of World War I were whether the victorious states should be able to take territory from the defeated, whether states should commit themselves to respect the territorial integrity of other states, and whether national self-determination should take precedence over respect for existing state boundaries in shaping the territorial order. On the first issue, in the early years of World War I the major states still supported the right of victorious states to realize territorial gains, and this was reflected in their secret treaties concerning territorial exchanges at the end of the war. This perspective was altered significantly following the United States' entry into the war, the Russian revolution in 1917, and popular pressure against territorial annexation in some countries.[15] In the 1919 Versailles settlement the victorious states only obtained small territorial concessions in Europe, although they realized some significant gains by dividing up the colonies of the defeated powers. Still, these colonies were declared League Mandates, and the new colonial powers were implicitly obligated to prepare the colonial peoples for self-governance – especially in the case of the former Turkish territories.[16] ***

On the second issue, the obligation to uphold the territorial integrity of all states, President Woodrow Wilson was the strongest protagonist. His famous "Fourteenth Point" spoke of "specific covenants for the purpose of affording mutual guarantees of political independence and territorial integrity to great and small states alike."[17] Such a revolutionary proposal took the form of Article 10 of the League of Nations Covenant, whose approval really constituted the beginning of states' formal support for the territorial integrity norm. It read: "The members of the League undertake to respect and preserve as against external aggression the territorial integrity and existing political independence of all Members of the League."

[14] See Cobban 1969; and Mayall 1990.
[15] Korman 1996, 132–36.
[16] See Article 22 of the League Covenant; Claude 1964, 322–28; and Korman 1996, 141–42.
[17] See Zimmern 1939, 199; Egerton 1978; and Knock 1992.

On the third question of the weight that should be given to the right of national self-determination in redrawing international boundaries, there was clearly tension within democratic governments between protagonists of national self-determination and respect for existing boundaries; and the former generally lost. Even President Wilson, who was viewed as the leader of the national self-determination cause, came out fundamentally on the side of respect for territorial integrity. National self-determination for ethnic nations was not mentioned in the covenant, and at the Versailles conference self-determination for ethnic nations was only applied to some of the territories of the defeated states in World War I.[18] Overall, recognition of the territorial boundaries of juridical states gained significant support in post–World War I settlements.

Following the World War I peace settlements, the territorial integrity norm was supported in several multilateral declarations and treaties. The 1928 General Treaty for the Renunciation of War (better known as the Kellogg-Briand Pact) certainly included support for the prohibition against territorial aggressions, although it did not explicitly focus on territorial aggrandizement.[19] The norm was then directly supported by the League's backing for the Stimson Doctrine in 1931, which denied the legitimacy of territorial changes obtained by force.[20]

* * *

At the end of World War II the Western Allied Powers exhibited very strong support for the integrity of interstate boundaries. With one exception they did not request or obtain sovereignty over any territories that belonged to the defeated powers, although they did obtain some UN Trust Territories that were formerly colonies of Japan and Italy and that they were obliged to bring to independence. The exception was the right of the United States to maintain control over some of the Pacific islands that formerly belonged to Japan.[21] The same approach toward territorial gains, however, was not true for the Soviet Union, which continued to operate with a classical view of boundaries, namely, that the victors in wars could claim territorial spoils. The Baltic states were integrated into the Soviet Union by Stalin against the wishes of their populations and without the recognition of major Western powers. The

---

[18] Franck 1990, 154–62.
[19] Korman 1996, 192–99.
[20] Stimson and Bundy 1948, 227–60.
[21] See Korman 1996, 176; and Claude 1964, 339–40.

Soviet Union also absorbed parts of Poland, Germany, Finland, Rumania, the southern half of Japan's Sakhalin Island, and Japan's Kurile Islands. In addition, the territory of postwar Germany was realigned and reduced. These changes were clearly reminiscent of the outcomes of wars in earlier centuries, but they were the last major diplomatic developments in Europe that blatantly defied the consent principle in the determination of international boundaries.[22] Finally, despite most countries' accession to the territorial gains of the Soviet Union, all countries at the 1945 San Francisco conference acceded to the obligation to respect existing boundaries in the UN Charter: "All Members shall refrain in their international relations from the threat or use of force against the territorial integrity or political independence of any state."[23]

THE EVOLUTION OF THE TERRITORIAL INTEGRITY NORM SINCE 1945

General Legal and Declaratory Developments

The UN Charter of 1945, as noted, affirmed states' obligation not to use force to alter states' boundaries. This same respect for the borders of juridical entities influenced the UN's approach to de-colonization. The colonial territory, which was often artificial in terms of delimiting ethnic nations, became the frame of reference for *** responding to claims for self-determination and political independence.[24] The 1960 UN Declaration on Granting Independence to Colonial Countries and Peoples made clear that it was existing colonies, and not ethnic groups, that were eligible for independence. Concerning "dependent peoples," it stated that "the integrity of their national territory shall be respected." It then proclaimed that "any attempt aimed at the partial or total disruption of the national unity or territorial integrity of a country is incompatible with the purposes and principles of the Charter of the United Nations."[25] In 1970 the UN General Assembly approved a comparable normative

---

[22] Korman 1996, 161–78. The new German-Polish border subsequently acquired legitimacy. The need to recognize this border was made abundantly clear to Chancellor Helmut Kohl by Germany's Western allies in 1990 when he voiced a desire to relocate the border; Fritsch-Bournazel 1992, 102–11.

[23] Article 2 (4). On debates over whether the UN prohibition allows any exceptions, see Korman 1996, 199–229.

[24] Jackson 1993.

[25] Declaration on Granting of Independence to Colonial Countries and Peoples, UNGA res. 1514, 1960.

statement in the Declaration of Principles of International Law Concerning Friendly Relations and Cooperation Among States.[26] There is clearly no ambiguity as to whether these major UN declarations supported respect for the territorial integrity of juridical states and existing colonies. To quote Michael Barnett and Martha Finnemore, "The UN encouraged the acceptance of *the norm of sovereignty-as-territorial-integrity* through resolutions, monitoring devices, commissions, and one famous peacekeeping episode in the Congo in the 1960s."[27]

Apart from reviewing UN normative statements, it is important to look at developments relating to respect for international boundaries in several regional organizations. The charters of the Arab League and Organization of American States, which were approved in 1945 and 1948, respectively, contained provisions supportive of the territorial integrity of member states, but the issue was not highlighted by the founding member states.[28] Several decades afterwards, however, the Organization of African Unity (OAU) and the Conference on Security and Cooperation in Europe (CSCE) adopted strong and well-publicized stands in favor of the sanctity of existing state boundaries. The 1963 OAU Charter contains a strong article in support of territorial integrity (Article 3). *** In 1975 the CSCE reiterated the same principle in the Helsinki Final Act: "Frontiers can [only] be changed, in accordance with international law, by peaceful means and by agreement." Separate bilateral treaties between West Germany and its major Communist neighbors (East Germany, Poland, and the Soviet Union) that preceded and anticipated the Helsinki agreements committed the parties to "respect without restriction the territorial integrity" of each state and "reaffirm[ed] the inviolability of existing boundaries."[29] At the end of the Cold War the 1990 Charter of Paris for a New Europe reiterated exactly the same principle, as have all subsequent conferences concerning international boundaries, including the 1995 Dayton peace treaty that settled the wars in Croatia and Bosnia-Herzegovina.[30]***

One other development should be noted with regard to attitudes and practices within Europe and the Western community more generally. In

---

[26] Declaration of Principles of International Law Concerning Friendly Relations and Cooperation Among States, UNGA res. 2625, 1970.

[27] Barnett and Finnemore 1999, 713 (italics in original).

[28] Zacher 1979, 189, 165.

[29] Maresca 1985, 86–87.

[30] See Ullman 1996; and Holbrooke 1998. The Dayton Agreement can be found at (http://www1.umn.edu/humanrts/icty/dayton). See particularly Articles 1 and 10.

the 1990s both the European Union (EU) and NATO proclaimed that all new members must have accords with contiguous states as to their borders. This has necessitated that the East European countries aspiring to membership sign boundary treaties with their neighboring states – sometimes at the cost of sacrificing long-held dreams of absorbing parts of these neighboring countries.[31] ***

The fifteen successor states of the Soviet Union have also followed the Western countries in supporting their existing boundaries. The Commonwealth of Independent States (CIS) has supported the principle of territorial integrity in their main constitutional documents. In part their support for the territorial integrity norm is attributable to pressure from the Western countries, especially through the Organization for Security and Cooperation in Europe (OSCE), but the great majority of these countries have recognized that respect for inherited boundaries (the principle of *uti possidetis*) is in their mutual interest.[32]

Territorial Aggressions Since 1946: International Responses and Outcomes

Prior to discussing the patterns of territorial wars in the post-1945 period I review some data on territorial wars since the seventeenth century because they highlight the marked changes in international practices in the late twentieth century. Table 12.1 contains data on international territorial wars for five historical eras in international relations over the past three and a half centuries and seven half-century periods. The five historical eras are frequently used in historical analyses of the interstate system. They are also employed by Kalevi Holsti from whose book this chapter has drawn the list of wars for the period 1648–1945. The wars listed by Holsti are major military conflicts in "the European and global states system."[33] He includes some civil wars, but they are excluded from the conflicts examined here. Of the 119 interstate wars between 1648 and 1945, 93 were judged to be territorial wars in that Holsti classified them as being concerned with six issues that clearly involve state control over territory.[34] The list is not exhaustive of all territorial aggressions or wars, but it is extensive enough to reveal important patterns.

---

[31] Donald M. Blinken and Alfred H. Moses, Hungary-Romania Pact: Historic but Ignored, *The Daily Yomuri* (Tokyo), 21 September 1996, 11.

[32] See MacFarlane 1999, 4; and Webber 1997.

[33] Holsti 1991, 20.

[34] See note to Table 12.1.

The list of forty "territorial aggressions" for the period 1946–2000 is drawn from extensive research in secondary materials. *** Territorial aggressions or wars include interstate armed conflicts where: a clear purpose of the military attack was the change of boundaries of a state or its colonies; the invading state sought to capture some territory from the attached state; *** the attacking states were widely recognized as sovereign states; and the invasion or occupation lasted at least a week. Using this definition clearly reduces the value of comparisons with the pre-1946 territorial wars, but the value of using a larger group of territorial aggressions for the recent period greatly assists our understanding of recent changes.[35]

Several key patterns emerge from the data in Table 12.1. First, and most importantly, while approximately 80 percent of territorial wars led to redistributions of territory for all periods prior to 1945, this figure dropped to 30 percent after 1945. Second, the number of territorial redistributions per year (given our list of wars) has varied by time period. It was about 0.24 from 1648 to 1814; it dropped to 0.19 between 1815 and 1917; it rose dramatically to 0.59 between 1918 and 1945; and then it dropped back to 0.22 in the post-1945 period.

In looking at the average territorial redistributions per year, it is valuable to take into consideration that a larger population of territorial conflicts is included in the 1946–2000 period than in other periods and, more importantly, that the number of states has increased dramatically over recent centuries – especially since 1945. A recent study provides data on the number of states (with certain characteristics) between 1816 and 1998, and it allows us to control for the number of states in the international system by calculating the number of territorial redistributions per country-year for particular periods of time. The figure for 1816–50 is 0.0032; for 1851–1900, 0.0035; for 1901–50, 0.0073; and 1951–98, 0.0015.[36] These

---

[35] The term "aggression" is more accurate than "war" for some of the conflicts since in a few cases the attacked state did not resist militarily and in some cases the number of deaths was small. However, such territorial occupations are often referred to as "wars" and therefore the terms "war" and "aggression" are used interchangeably.

[36] Gleditsch and Ward 1999. The authors include states that meet the following criteria: (1) they possessed autonomous administration over some territory; (2) they were regarded as distinct entities by local actors; and (3) they had a population over 250,000. The average number of states per year between 1816 and 1850 was 53.05; between 1851 and 1900, 56.70; between 1901 and 1950, 63.42; and between 1951 and 1998, 134.58. The total number of territorial redistributions for these four periods was 6, 10, 23, and 10, respectively. To determine the number of territorial redistributions per country-year for a particular period it is necessary to multiply the total number of years by the average number of countries per year and to divide this sum into the total number of redistributions for the period.

figures indicate, of course, that the number of territorial redistributions per country-year was more than twice as high in the nineteenth century than it was in the last half of the twentieth century. Also, it was almost five times higher in the first half of the twentieth century than in the second half. These figures have to be interpreted in light of the fact that the criteria for the inclusion of wars differs for the pre- and post-1945 years, and there is no claim of statistical significance.

The preceding figures do point to important changes in some patterns of territorial armed conflict. However, it is also crucial to look at post-1945 territorial wars (summarized in Table 12.2) in some detail since the development and management of these conflicts reveal a great deal about the strengthening of the norm. * * *

* * *

It is clear that there have been very few cases of coercive boundary change in the last half century during which UN membership has grown from 50 to 190. No longer is territorial aggrandizement the dominant motif of interstate politics; whereas in the three centuries leading up to 1946, about 80 percent of all interstate territorial wars led to territorial redistributions, for the period 1946–2000, the figure is 30 percent (twelve out of forty) (Table 12.1a). Given the huge increase in the number of states in the international system in the past half century and our definition of territorial wars for the period, the absolute numbers of forty territorial wars and twelve cases of major boundary change are not very large by historical standards. Two of the successful uses of force involved turbulent decolonization processes in 1947 and 1948 in the Indian subcontinent and former British Palestine, and the other ten occurred between 1961 and 1975. Of these ten wars, the UN passed resolutions calling for withdrawal in four of them (Israel-Arab states in 1967, India-Pakistan in 1971, Turkey-Cyprus in 1974, and Morocco-Spanish Sahara in 1975). Another three of the ten (India-Portugal in 1961, Indonesia-Netherlands in 1961–62, and North Vietnam-South Vietnam from 1962 to 1975) were viewed by many countries as stages of the decolonization process. The remaining two involved China's occupation of remote areas – parts of northern India in 1962 and South Vietnam's Paracel Islands in 1974.

An interesting characteristic of territorial wars concerns the role of international organizations in bringing them to an end, since multilateral responses often reflect broad international backing for the norm. In the four territorial wars in Europe (except for the quick war

TABLE 12.2. *Interstate Territorial Aggressions, 1946–2000*

States involved	Issue	Outcome	Change
Europe			
Turkey–Cyprus, 1974–present	Turkey invaded Cyprus to protect the Turkish Cypriot community. It gathered all Turkish Cypriots into the northern 40 percent of the island. In 1983 Turkey supported the creation of the Turkish Republic of Northern Cyprus (TRNC). Turkish troops remain in the TRNC.	The UN and NATO opposed the invasion and recognition of the TRNC. Western and UN attempts to negotiate a settlement based on a federation of the two sections of the island have failed. Only Turkey recognizes the TRNC.	Major change
Yugoslavia–Slovenia, 1991	Yugoslavia's armed forces attacked to try to reverse Slovenia's departure from the federation after Slovenia declared independence on 25 June 1991.	Yugoslavia ceased its attack after eight days of fighting and withdrew from Slovenia.	No change
Yugoslavia–Croatia, 1991–95	Croatia declared independence in 1991. Yugoslavia (Serbia-Montenegro) sent troops to assist Serbs in Croatia (12 percent of pop.) who wanted to attach their areas to Yugoslavia. Most Serb troops defending Serb enclaves came from Croatia, but some came from Yugoslavia.	UN called for withdrawal of foreign troops and a cease-fire. Fighting killed 15,000. Main Serb force was defeated in 1995. Dayton accord in 1995 recognized former boundary. Yugoslavia and Croatia recognized boundary in bilateral treaty in August 1996.	No change
Yugoslavia–Bosnia, 1992–95	Bosnia declared independence in 1992. Serb population of Bosnia (assisted by Yugoslav military) fought against an alliance of Bosnian Muslims and Bosnian Croats. The Serb forces wanted to unite parts of Bosnia with Yugoslavia. The Croatian army intervened at times, and in a few instances it fought Muslim forces.	UN called for withdrawal of non-Bosnian troops and cease-fire. The fighting killed 200,000. The 1995 Dayton accord created a multiethnic government and recognized the original boundaries of Bosnia-Herzegovina. Yugoslavia and Bosnia recognized boundary in bilateral treaty in October 1996.	No change

(continued)

States involved	Issue	Outcome	Change
The Americas			
Nicaragua–Honduras, 1957	Nicaragua occupied a part of Honduras.	Nicaragua withdrew and accepted ICJ arbitration because of OAS pressure. ICJ awarded territory to Houduras in 1959.	No change
Argentina–Britain, 1982	Argentina occupied Malvinas/Falkland islands.	UN called for Argentina's withdrawal. Britain reoccupied islands.	No change
Ecuador–Peru, 1995	Ecuador sent troops into an area it lost in peace treaty at end of 1942 war.	Four guarantor powers of 1942 treaty promoted withdrawal. The two states signed a border treaty in 1998.	No change
Africa			
Egypt–Sudan, 1958	Egypt occupied a small area of Sudanese territory.	Arab League pressured Egypt to withdraw.	No change
Ghana–Upper Volta, 1963–65	Ghana occupied a small border area of Upper Volta in 1963.	In 1965 OAU supported original boundary. Ghana withdrew.	No change
Algeria–Morocco, 1963	Morocco occupied a part of Algeria.	Arab League and OAU called for withdrawal. OAU established mediators. Morocco withdrew.	No change
Somalia–Ethiopia and Kenya, 1964	Somalia provided troops to Somali rebels in eastern Ethiopia and northern Kenya seeking union with Somalia.	OAU supported original boundaries and established mediator. Somalia withdrew.	No change
Libya–Chad, 1973–87	In 1973 Libya secretly occupied a border area of Chad called the Aouzou Strip.	OAU tried to secure Libyan withdrawal in 1980s. Libya was driven out by Chad in 1987. ICJ arbitration was accepted in 1990. ICJ ruled in Chad's favor in 1994.	No change

(continued)

TABLE 12.2 *(continued)*

States involved	Issue	Outcome	Change
Africa (cont.)			
Mali–Burkina Faso, 1975	Mali claimed a small area of Burkina Faso in 1960. Mali occupied the area in 1975.	OAU mediated a cease-fire and withdrawal by Mali.	No change
Somalia–Ethiopia, 1976–80	Somalia occupied most of the Ogaden region of Ethiopia. Ethiopia received military forces from Cuba.	An OAU committee called for respect for former boundary. Somalia withdrew all forces by 1980.	No change
Uganda–Tanzania, 1978	Uganda occupied a small part of Tanzania.	Within several weeks of Tanzanian military action, Uganda withdrew.	No change
Morocco–Spanish Sahara, 1975–2000	Morocco claimed Spanish Sahara prior to independence and sent in military contingents in 1975. Under pressure Spain agreed to cede the colony. Since 1976 Morocco and the independence movement Polisario have conducted a continuous war.	The OAU and the UN have called for Moroccan withdrawal and a referendum. The UN tried to organize a referendum during the 1990s. (Mauritania occupied part of Spanish Sahara from 1976 to 1978.)	Major change
Libya–Chad, 1981–82	Libya pressured Chad to accept a political union in exchange for military assistance in its civil war.	OAU opposed union and provided some troops. Chad ended political union and Libya withdrew troops.	No change
Mali–Burkina Faso, 1985	Dispute over a small strip existed from time of independence and led to violence again.	In 1985 they accepted ICJ arbitration as a result of OAU mediation. In 1986 ICJ divided the area equally between the two states.	Minor change
Eritrea–Ethiopia, 1998–2000	Eritrea and Ethiopia dispute sovereignty over several small border regions. Eritrea occupied some areas in 1998. In 1999 and 2000 Ethiopia regained control of all areas.	The OAU and the Western powers promoted a cease-fire, a withdrawal to the pre-1998 boundary, and arbitration based on colonial treaties. These were accepted in June 2000.	No change

(continued)

States involved	Issue	Outcome	Change
Middle East			
Arab states–Israel, 1948	Britain accepted a UN recommendation to divide Palestine into Israeli and Arab states. Neighboring Arab states attacked Israel at time of independence in May 1948 to support Palestinian Arabs' claim to entire area.	Israel gained territory in each stage of the war. At end of 1948 both sides accepted armistice lines. Arab Palestinians retained control of the West Bank and Gaza Strip (administered by Jordan and Egypt).	Major change
Israel–Arab states, 1967	Israel occupied the West Bank, Gaza Strip, Sinai, and Golan Heights. It later annexed East Jerusalem and applied Israeli law to Golan Heights.	UN Security Council in November 1967 called for withdrawal of Israel to 1948 armistice lines in exchange for recognition by Arab states of Israel. In 1978 Israel agreed to return the Sinai; in 1993 Israel accepted staged implementation of self-rule for West Bank and Gaza.	Major change
Egypt and Syria–Israel, 1973	Egypt and Syria sought to recapture the Sinai and Golan Heights.	UN Security Council called for cease-fire. Fighting ended after two weeks. Egypt was allowed to keep a small enclave in the Sinai.	Minor change
Iraq–Kuwait, 1990–91	Iraq invaded Kuwait and annexed it.	Most UN members called for Iraq's withdrawal. Iraq was expelled by a UN-sanctioned force.	No change
Asia			
Pakistan–India, 1947–48	British India was partitioned and India and Pakistan became independent in 1947. Pakistan army joined Muslim rebels in Kashmir who were seeking union of Kashmir with Pakistan.	Pakistan secured control over a sparsely populated third of Kashmir by end of war. UN Security Council supported plebiscite during war, but India did not accept it. Post-1948 border is the Line of Control.	Major change
North Korea–South Korea, 1950–53	North Korea attempted to absorb South Korea.	Armistice line reflects very minor changes in former boundary.	Minor change

(continued)

TABLE 12.2 (continued)

States involved	Issue	Outcome	Change
Asia (continued)			
China–Burma, 1956	China moved into a small border area of Burma.	The two states negotiated a new border that gave China a part of the area it occupied.	Minor change
Afghanistan–Pakistan, 1961	Afghanistan sent irregular Afghan forces into the Pathanistan region of Pakistan to support local forces favoring union with Afghanistan.	Afghan incursions were defeated by Pakistan.	No change
India–Portugal, 1961	India invaded and absorbed the Portuguese-controlled colony of Goa.	Most states accepted the legitimacy of India's action.	Major change
Indonesia–Netherlands, 1961–62	Indonesia claimed West New Guinea (West Irian) over which the Netherlands had colonial control. Indonesia invaded in 1961.	In 1962 Indonesia and the Netherlands agreed to a plebiscite after one year of UN administration. The plebiscite favored integration with Indonesia.	Major change
China–India, 1962	China occupied Aksai Chin and part of Northeast Frontier Agency that it claimed.	China still occupies the areas.	Major change
North Vietnam–South Vietnam, 1962–75	France administered the northern and southern parts of Vietnam separately prior to 1954. After independence in 1954 South Vietnam did not allow a referendum on unification as provided in the Paris peace accord. By 1962 North Vietnamese forces were fighting with the Viet Cong to promote unification.	In 1975 North Vietnamese and Viet Cong forces defeated the South Vietnamese army, and the two areas were reunified.	Major change
Indonesia–Malaysia, 1963–65	Indonesia claimed the Malaysian territory of North Borneo, and it introduced military contingents to expel Malaysian authorities.	Britain and Australia sent troops to help Malaysia. Indonesia was unsuccessful.	No change
Pakistan–India, April 1965	Pakistan sent a force into the Rann of Kutch.	Britain negotiated a cease-fire and the parties agreed to an arbitration that awarded 10 percent of the area to Pakistan in 1968.	Minor change

(continued)

States involved	Issue	Outcome	Change
Asia (continued)			
Pakistan–India, August 1965	Pakistan attacked India to secure control of the Indian-controlled part of Kashmir.	Pakistan was defeated. USSR and Western powers backed the 1948 Line of Control.	No change
India–Pakistan (creation of Bangladesh), 1971	The Bengali population in East Pakistan sought to secede from Pakistan. Indian troops intervened in the civil war to secure the creation of Bangladesh.	The UN General Assembly called for Indian withdrawal; India did not withdraw, and it facilitated the creation of Bangladesh.	Major change
Iran–United Arab Emirates, 1971	Upon Britain's granting of independence to the UAE Iran occupied some of the islands in the Straits of Hormuz that belonged to the UAE.	Iran maintains control of the islands.	Major change
China–South Vietnam, 1974	China expelled South Vietnam from the western Paracel Islands that it claimed.	China maintains control of the islands.	Major change
Indonesia–Portugal (East Timor), 1975–99	Indonesia invaded East Timor several months before it was to achieve independence from Portugal. It made it a province of Indonesia.	UN demanded Indonesian withdrawal and self-determination through 1982. In 1999 Indonesia relented to international pressure and allowed a referendum that led to independence.	No change
Cambodia–Vietnam, 1977–78	Cambodia attacked Vietnam to establish control over a small border region.	Cambodian forces were defeated. War was the result mainly of political conflicts.	No change
Iraq–Iran, 1980–88	Iraq invaded Iran to seize control of the Shatt al-Arab waterway and some other areas.	UN Security Council backed acceptance of former boundary in 1987. The two states accepted a cease-fire in 1988 and the former boundary in 1990.	No change

Note: Of the forty interstate territorial conflicts listed here, twelve involved major redistributions of territory, and five involved minor alterations of borders. A "minor change" refers to small border adjustments. Any change apart from a minor border alteration is regarded as a "major change." The conflict over the Spratly Islands, which involves China, Taiwan, Vietnam, Philippines, Malaysia, and Brunei, is not included because there has never been any local or international consensus on jurisdictions. See Haller-Trost 1990; and Lo 1989.

between Yugoslavia and Slovenia in 1991) the NATO states and the UN were active in promoting respect for boundaries. In the Western Hemisphere the OAS or an important group of OAS members was active in promoting a withdrawal of forces in two conflicts, and the UN backed withdrawal in the other. In Africa the OAU was very active in ten of the twelve territorial wars (one being prior to the OAU's creation), and the UN played a role in several conflicts as well. In the Middle East the UN played a significant role in promoting a return to the status quo ante in three territorial wars (not the Arab-Israeli war of 1948). In Asia international organizations have not been active in most of the seventeen territorial wars. However, the UN had a major long-term role in promoting Indonesia's recent withdrawal from East Timor.

The Boundaries of Successor States

In discussing the post-1945 stabilization of boundaries another pattern of international behavior should be noted, since it is closely related to support for the prohibition of the use of force to alter boundaries. During the postwar period, all of the successor states that emerged from the nine breakups of existing states have kept their former internal administrative boundaries as their new international boundaries.[37] In fact, in cases where some doubt existed as to whether the successor states would accept these boundaries, outside countries pressured the successor states to adopt their former administrative boundaries as their new interstate borders. This indicates that states generally desire predictability regarding the international territorial order. They do not like secessions, but if they are going to occur, they do not want the successor states fighting over what their boundaries should be.

Some of the best examples of international policy on this issue concern the breakups of the former Yugoslavia and the former Soviet Union.

---

[37] Syria's secession from the UAR in 1961, Singapore's secession from Malaysia in 1965, Bangladesh's secession from Pakistan in 1971, Gambia's secession from Senegambia in 1989, Namibia's secession from South Africa in 1990, Eritrea's secession from Ethiopia in 1993, the breakup of the former Soviet Union into fifteen states in 1991, Yugoslavia's breakup into five states in 1991–92, and Slovakia's secession from Czechoslovakia in 1992. In the case of Eritrea-Ethiopia, they maintained the former internal administrative boundary from 1993 to 1998. In 1998 Eritrea occupied several small border areas, and in 1999 and 2000 Ethiopia regained the lost territories. In 2000 the OAU backed withdrawal of all forces behind the pre-1998 boundary and the establishment of an arbitral body to settle the dispute.

The United States and the European powers went to tremendous lengths to preserve the former internal administrative boundaries of Croatia and Bosnia as their new international boundaries. These boundaries were legitimated in the Western countries' recognition of these states in 1992, the 1995 Dayton accord, and the 1996 accords between Yugoslavia (Serbia), on the one hand, and Croatia and Bosnia, on the other.[38] The Western countries have also been active in promoting respect among the Soviet successor states for the boundaries they originally possessed as Soviet republics. Concerning why the former internal boundaries have been maintained as interstate borders, Neil MacFarlane has remarked:

> Most significant . . . are the norms of sovereignty and non-intervention and the principle of territorial integrity. The 15 republics of the former Soviet space exist in the territorial boundaries defined under Soviet rule, whether or not they make sense in ethno-geographical terms, or correspond to the aspirations of the people living within them. They do so in part because Western states and international organizations . . . have self-consciously promoted these norms. . . . For better or worse, the West is committed to the attempt to address problems relating to minority rights within the context of acceptance of the sovereignty and territorial integrity of the new states.[39]

Western efforts at promoting the territorial integrity of the successor states (often through the OSCE) have focused on keeping Nagorno-Karabakh (an Armenian enclave) within Azerbaijan and keeping Abkahzia and Ossetia within Georgia, but Western policy has had a broader impact as well in strengthening the international territorial order among the Soviet successor states.[40]

It is impossible to declare that the acceptance of internal administrative boundaries as interstate boundaries for secessionist states is now an authoritative rule of international practice. Quite possibly, however, this norm will become entrenched as a part of the new territorial order that flows from states' concern for reducing the incidence of destructive wars and wars' impact on commercial relations. States and international commercial interests increasingly abhor violence and uncertainty over what political entities have jurisdiction over particular geographical spaces.

---

[38] See Weller 1992, 587, 602; and Ullman 1996.

[39] MacFarlane 1999, 4, 16.

[40] See Baranovsky 1966, 267–78; Webber 1997; MacFarlane and Minnear 1997; and Menon 1998. Armenia's support for the Armenian population in Azerbaijan is not regarded as an interstate territorial war because Armenia (some of whose army fought for Nagorno-Karabakh) has not explicitly backed secession by Nagorno-Karabakh.

Overview of Stages in the Development of the Norm

In concluding the discussion of the evolution of normative declarations and state practices concerning coercive territorial revisionism, it is valuable to look at past developments as falling into a number of stages. Two scholars have identified three stages of norm development as emergence, acceptance, and institutionalization.[41] The emergence stage is marked by a growing advocacy of the new norm by important countries and non-governmental groups and some multilateral declarations. The acceptance stage is characterized by growing support for the norm and its integration into treaties to that point where it is viewed as legally binding by most countries. The institutionalization stage includes the integration of the norm in additional international accords and more effective multilateral efforts to promote state compliance.

Before moving to an analysis of the three stages of norm development during the twentieth century, I offer some observations about the nineteenth century. The magnitude of international violence declined from 1815 to 1913 as a result of regular consultations within the framework of the Concert of Europe, but the great powers were involved periodically in territorial aggrandizement within the Western state system as well as in colonial expansion in the Southern Hemisphere. In fact, territorial adjustments in Europe and in the colonial world were central to maintaining a balance of power.

The *emergence stage* of norm development started with the end of World War I and more particularly Article 10 of the League Covenant, and it lasted through the end of World War II. The major proponents of the norm were the Western democratic states. During this period major multilateral treaties and declarations for the first time upheld the territorial integrity norm – particularly the 1919 League Covenant, the 1928 Kellogg-Briand Pact, and the League's approval of the Stimson Doctrine in 1931. At the same time the great powers tolerated a number of territorial aggressions, and Germany, Italy, and Japan became increasingly committed to territorial expansion in the 1930s. The emergence stage was very bloody, but it was states' experience with this era of destructive territorial aggrandizement that increased support for the norm after World War II.

The *acceptance stage* of norm development began with the adoption of Article 2(4) in the UN Charter in June 1945, and it lasted until the

---

[41] Finnemore and Sikkink 1999, 254–61.

mid-1970s. It was not until the 1960s and early 1970s that broad and strong backing for the norm became palpable. The key post-1945 multilateral accords were the 1960 UN declaration that upheld the territorial integrity of states and pronounced that existing colonies (not ethnic groups) were eligible for self-determination; the OAU's 1963 charter provision *** supporting respect for inherited boundaries; and the 1975 CSCE's Helsinki Final Act with its proscription that boundaries could only be altered by consent. In 1975 the last case of significant territorial revisionism occurred – Morocco's absorption of the Spanish Sahara.

The *institutionalization* (strengthening) *stage* of norm development encompassed the period from 1976 to the present; no major cases of successful territorial aggrandizement have occurred during this period. The key events that strengthened the norm were states' responses to individual conflicts. Particularly noteworthy cases were Somalia's war against Ethiopia, 1976–80; Iraq's occupation of Kuwait, 1990–91; and Yugoslavia's attempts to absorb parts of Croatia and Bosnia, 1992–95. Also important was the decision by Indonesia in 1999 to allow a referendum in East Timor. Another noteworthy development during this period was the International Court of Justice's adjudication of several territorial conflicts. The court based its decisions on the principle of *uti possidetis,* which means that states have rights to those territories that were legally ceded to them by prior governing states and that other states do not have the right to take these territories by force.[42]

ROOTS OF THE NEW TERRITORIAL ORDER

International practices regarding the use of force to alter boundaries have changed markedly in recent years, and in this section I analyze the reason for this transformation in the international order. At the heart of this analysis are several general assertions. First, states have backed the norm for both instrumental and ideational reasons, though the former have dominated. Instrumental reasons are rooted in perceptions of how a norm and congruent practices benefit the self-interests of countries. Ideational reasons are rooted in changing views of ethical behavior toward other peoples and states. A number of scholars have recognized that both instrumental and ideational factors influence the evolution of

[42] Prescott 1998, 241–52.

norms and that applying an "either/or" approach concerning their influence is wrong.[43]

Second, the reasons for such a change in beliefs and practices have varied among countries, and no single factor explains the support for the norm among a particular grouping of states.[44] These factors include the perceived relationship between territorial aggrandizement and major international wars, the power relations between possible territorial aggressors and the major powers supporting the norm, the costs and benefits of territorial aggrandizement, and moral predispositions concerning territorial aggression. Although we can speculate about the relative importance of specific factors, providing definitive conclusions about the weight of each is difficult when the factors have generally pressured states in the same direction. It appears that the coincidence of several factors has been crucial for both the Western and the developing states' backing of the norm.

Among the *Western industrialized states, the association of territorial revisionism with major wars* was the central driving force that led these states after World Wars I and II to advocate a prohibition of coercive territorial revisionism. The key international affirmations of the norm were after the world wars in 1919 and 1945 and at the 1975 Helsinki conference whose central purpose was the prevention of a major war between the Western and Soviet alliances. Territorial aggrandizement was not the central motivation of the key antagonists in World War I, but it played a part in states' participation and the postwar settlements. Also, attempts to promote national self-determination and hence border changes exacerbated feelings of international hostility after World War I, and this made many states wary of this justification for territorial revisionism. To quote Michael Howard, "The Mazzinian doctrine, that peace could result only from national self-determination, had left its followers in disarray. It had caused chaos at the Paris peace conference, and it was increasingly clear that this mode of thought lent itself far more readily to right-wing authoritarianism . . . than it did to any form of parliamentary democracy."[45]

---

[43] See Nadelmann 1990; Finnemore 1996; Finnemore and Sikkink 1999; Jackson 1993; and Ruggie 1999.

[44] The Soviet bloc is not specifically discussed in this section. It was generally supportive of existing boundaries because it wanted to legitimize the Eastern European boundaries that were established in 1945. Like the Western powers it occasionally supported territorial revisionism for Cold War reasons, for example, Afghanistan-Pakistan, 1961; and Indonesia-Malaysia, 1963–65.

[45] Howard 1978, 95.

The fear of territorial aggrandizement as a cause of major war was exacerbated by World War II because the origins of the war lay significantly in German and Japanese territorial ambitions. The Western states came to fear the right of national self-determination, and particularly the right to unite national compatriots in different states, since it encouraged territorial irredentism and xenophobic nationalism.[46] * * *

Because Western countries' support for democratic political institutions grew during the development of the norm,[47] it is important to ask whether their *liberal democratic ethos* influenced their acceptance of the territorial integrity norm. This question involves considering the reasons why democratic states might eschew wars of territorial aggrandizement, the views of democratic leaders, and democratic and nondemocratic states' patterns of territorial aggrandizement. The key factor that has probably influenced democratic states' opposition to territorial aggrandizement is touched on in John Owen's study concerning the democratic peace in which he notes that "liberalism as a system of thought" is particularly attached to "self-legislation or self-government" and "self-determination."[48] It is these values that have shaped the policies of democratic leaders toward coercive territorial revisionism.

In the late stages of World War I President Wilson commented that "no right exists anywhere to hand peoples about from sovereignty to sovereignty without their consent,"[49] and Prime Minister David Lloyd remarked that any territorial changes had to be based on "the consent of the governed."[50] If the citizens of liberal states adhered to this principle of not imposing a new government on people by force, they would definitely be opposed to using force to change interstate boundaries – unless possibly a liberal state sought to assist the secession of a national minority in a foreign country. However, the dangers of supporting

---

[46] See Cobban 1969; Mayall 1990; and Franck 1990, 155–74. The destructiveness of past territorial wars also encouraged Latin American states to oppose territorial revisionism. Holsti 1996, 150–84.

[47] Michael Doyle has noted that the number of liberal states grew from three in 1800; to eight in 1850; thirteen in 1900; twenty-nine in 1945; and forty-nine in 1980. Doyle 1996, 56. With recent changes in Eastern Europe, Latin America, and Asia the number is now considerably higher.

[48] Owen 1997, 32. Malcolm Anderson has identified another influence on liberal democrats' support for the sanctity of boundaries – namely, that established boundaries are "essential for ordered constitutional politics." Anderson 1996, 8. For a discussion of institutional and cultural factors that have influenced the democratic zone of peace, see Russett et al. 1993.

[49] Korman 1996, 136.

[50] Lloyd George 1936, 1524–26.

national secessionist groups have been clearly recognized by liberal democratic states. While self-determination for ethnic groups is at times viewed sympathetically by liberals, it is "trumped" by their recognition that the logical outcome of allowing self-determination for every national group would be continual warfare. Self-determination has had to be compromised in the pursuit of physical security, which is itself necessary for individuals' realization of liberty. ***

The proclivity of democratic states to eschew territorial aggrandizement is reflected in their evolving practices regarding territorial annexations at the end of the world wars and in their colonial policies. At the end of World War I, the Triple Entente states and their democratic allies gained little territory. Britain and the United States, whose President Wilson led the fight for "no annexations," did not establish sovereignty over any new territories, and France only *reestablished* sovereignty over Alsace-Lorraine. Among the smaller allies, Belgium obtained a small border area from Germany; Denmark secured two-thirds of Scheswig-Holstein from Germany as a result of a referendum; and Italy and Greece obtained small, but strategic, territories from Austria and Bulgaria. The Italian and Greek gains might be explained by the relatively new and unstable character of their democratic regimes, which collapsed in the interwar period.[51] France, Britain, Australia, and New Zealand (as well as Japan and South Africa) secured League mandates that previously belonged to the defeated powers, and while there was no obligation to bring them to independence, there was an implicit responsibility to move in this direction for the A mandates and to a lesser extent the B mandates as well.[52] Some signs of a new normative orientation on territorial issues were present in the policies of the victorious democratic states at the end of World War I, but the old order that sanctioned annexations and colonialism still had a significant influence. As happened with the expansion of the voting franchise in the Western states, progress in promoting liberal democratic values about territorial revisionism occurred in stages.

In the case of the settlements at the end of World War II, no Western power achieved territorial control over new areas (except UN trusteeships that they were to prepare for independence),[53] whereas the authoritarian Soviet Union obtained sovereign control over significant areas

---

[51] Gleditsch and Ward 2000.
[52] See Howard 1978, 83–84; and Lyons 2000, 302–12. One clearly authoritarian ally of the Triple Entente was Romania, and it gained considerable territory.
[53] Claude 1964, 285–302.

in eastern Europe as well as some of Japan's northern islands. The democratic Western European states still clung to the legitimacy of colonial empires through the immediate post–World War II years, but by the 1950s they had all committed themselves to decolonization. However, the authoritarian regimes in Portugal and Spain resisted granting independence to their colonies until their democratic transformations in 1974. Granting the right of self-determination to colonies flowed from the very same ideational source as did opposition to violent territorial revisionism – namely, a liberal democratic belief that it is wrong to impose rule on the people of another juridical state or a part thereof. * * *

The reluctance of democratic states to engage in territorial aggrandizement is also seen in their infrequent territorial aggressions since World War I. Between 1919 and 1945 there were twenty territorial wars; the only democratic state to achieve territorial gains was Poland in 1922, and its democratic government did not have deep social roots, as the 1926 *coup d'etat* indicated.[54] Since 1945 the only territorial wars that have been initiated by democratic states have been India's absorption of the Portuguese colony of Goa in 1961, Israel's invasion of three Arab neighbors in 1967 following Arab sabre rattling, and Ecuador's invasion of Peru in 1995.[55] The other thirty-seven territorial aggressions have been by nondemocratic states.

In dwelling on whether the association of territorial revisionism and major war or a liberal respect for other states is the crucial factor that shaped Western states' support for the territorial integrity norm, it is interesting to ask what might have happened if the other factor had not been present. First, if democracy had not grown steadily in the Western world during the twentieth century, would the Western states have opted for the sanctity of states' borders because of the linking of territorial revisionism and major war? They might have adopted this strategy after the carnage of the two world wars, but it is problematic whether the policy would have endured without a moral belief that other juridical states deserved their respect. After all, the Western states did not support the territorial integrity norm following major wars prior to the twentieth

---

[54] See Table 12.1a; and Holsti 1991, 213–42. On the war proneness of new and unstable democratic states, see Gleditsch and Ward 2000.

[55] Huth found that of forty-one territorial disputes occurring between 1950 and 1990, the only one where a state with fifteen years of democratic rule was the challenger was the Indian invasion of Goa. Huth 1996, 136–37. Mitchell and Prins found that of the ninety-seven territorial "militarized disputes" occurring between 1815 and 1992, only two were between well-established democracies; and these two occurred between 1945 and 1992. Mitchell and Prins 1999.

century (for example, the Thirty Years' War and the Napoleonic Wars). Second, if territorial revisionism had not been a very important cause of major wars, would the democratic states have come down strongly for a prohibition against coercive territorial revisionism? Again, it is doubtful (probably more doubtful) because without a fear that territorial revisionism could lead to regional or world wars, they probably would have opted for the right of self-determination for all ethnic or national groups. Liberal states were clearly influenced to support the right of self-determination *for juridical states,* and hence the territorial integrity norm, because warfare was so horrific in the twentieth century. Indicative of this perspective is a provision in President Wilson's first draft of the League Covenant: "The parties accept without reservation the principle that the peace of the world is superior in importance to every question of political jurisdiction or boundary."[56] A fear of a major war and a liberal democratic respect for other juridical states clearly have a symbiotic relationship that has motivated these countries to support the territorial integrity norm, and it is highly problematic whether the norm would have achieved the strength it has if both factors had not been present.

In considering the support for the territorial integrity norm by *non-Western or developing states,* we must first recognize that most of them have not experienced very destructive territorial wars in recent centuries and have not had liberal democratic governments in the postwar era. Their backing of the norm generally stems from the existence of *ethnic groups that overlap borders and can provoke territorial irredentism, the military weakness of many developing states vis-à-vis their neighbors, and their weakness vis-à-vis Western supporters of the norm.* However, changing economic costs and benefits of territorial aggrandizement have undoubtedly had an influence in recent decades.

Among developing states, many (especially in Africa) have feared territorial aggressions because of the likelihood of irredentist claims resulting from ethnic groups' overlapping borders and their own military weakness.[57] These developing states made sure that the 1960 UN Declaration on Granting Independence to Colonial Territories and Countries established that the peoples of existing colonial territories, not ethnic groups, are eligible for self-determination and that the territorial integrity of all states should be respected.[58] Through regional organizations

---

[56] Miller 1928, 23 (Art. 3).
[57] See Jackson 1990; and Touval 1972.
[58] Declaration on the Granting of Independence to Colonial Countries and Peoples, UNGA res. 1514, 1960.

and the UN, the African, Middle Eastern, and Latin American states have also been very active in opposing territorial aggrandizement and secessionist movements (for example, Biafra) and in securing great power backing through concerted diplomatic advocacy.

Another concern that has been (and still is) very important in promoting support of the territorial integrity norm among developing states is their recognition that they will probably meet strong Western opposition if they embark on territorial aggression. In the Cold War the Western states provided assistance to their many allies in the developing world if they were subject to territorial revisionist threats or attacks. Good examples are South Korea in 1950, Kuwait in 1961 (a threat of invasion from Iraq), and Malaysia in 1963. In addition, the Western states generally opposed their allies when they pursued territorial expansionism.[59] *** In a few cases, such as South Korea in 1950 and Kuwait in 1990, the Western powers actually sent significant military forces to repel invasions. And in Eastern Europe the NATO countries bombed Serb forces as part of their attempt to promote respect for the boundaries of Bosnia and Croatia. If it had not been for the Western democratic powers' (and especially the United States') willingness to employ their military and economic leverage in many territorial wars over the entire post-1945 era, the norm against coercive territorial revisionism would not have been sustained. However, the Western powers could not have enforced the norm in the developing world without the backing of the great majority of non-Western states. A crucial factor in the strength of the territorial integrity norm in the developing world is the coincidence of most developing states' opposition to coercive territorial revisionism and the willingness of the Western states to use their power to reverse territorial aggressions.

In addition to the aforementioned international conditions and beliefs sustaining the prohibition against coercive territorial change, scholars have observed that a number of *economic trends reduce the benefits and increase the costs of coercive territorial revisionism.* These trends have undoubtedly had an important impact on strengthening support for the norm in recent decades, but it is doubtful whether they could be regarded as important factors in securing its diplomatic acceptance between World War I and the 1960s. These economic trends influence why states are less

---

[59] In a few cases the Western powers backed territorial revisionism for strategic reasons related to the Cold War. They favored the absorption of the Spanish Sahara by Morocco and Mauritania and East Timor by Indonesia in 1975 prior to their independence because of the political orientation of their independence movements during the Cold War.

motivated to pursue territorial aggrandizement themselves, not why they would oppose such actions by other states.

First, the declining value of land as a factor of production in modern economies means that the conquest of foreign territory no longer brings the same benefits that it did in the pre-industrial era. Robert Gilpin has observed that a state can now gain more "through specialization and international trade" than it can "through territorial expansion and conquests."[60] This is clearly true, but land has been viewed by some countries in the twentieth century as quite valuable. It was certainly viewed as valuable by Germany and Japan in the 1930s and 1940s – a time when the territorial integrity norm was beginning to attract strong support. Today the accomplishments of countries such as South Korea and Singapore are leading to a recognition that economic development depends first and foremost on human skills and not on control of territory; but this recognition has not been strong enough, and it did not come soon enough in this century, to be seen as a crucial factor in driving broad acceptance of the territorial integrity norm.

Second, some scholars argue that the occupation of foreign territory is more difficult and costly in an era of national consciousness, and therefore states are less prone toward territorial expansionism.[61] This view is true in many circumstances, but as Peter Lieberman's study has pointed out, the occupation of foreign territories can be beneficial as long as the occupying states do not meet large-scale military resistance and are willing to use considerable force to suppress local populations.[62] In World War II foreign occupiers were certainly willing to adopt such policies of suppression. We should also recognize that quite a few cases of potential territorial revisionism today concern a desire to unite ethnic brethren in different countries, and in this case the problem of needing to suppress local populations would not exist.

Finally, some political observers adopt a traditional liberal stance that war generally, and territorial wars in particular, are increasingly being rejected in this century because they disrupt valuable economic interdependencies.[63] This hypothesis is true to a degree. However, such interdependencies were not adequate to deter major wars throughout most of this century. In fact, such interdependencies were quite strong

[60] See Gilpin 1981, 125, 132; and Kaysen 1990, 54.
[61] See Deutsch 1953; Kaysen 1990, 53; and Lieberman 1996.
[62] Lieberman 1996.
[63] See Rosecrance 1986 and 1996; and Zacher and Matthew 1995, 124–26.

in 1914.[64] Their impacts are certainly stronger at the end of the twentieth century as a result of the recent growth of international economic transactions, but they are unlikely to assure a rejection of coercive territorial revisionism by the majority of countries. For one thing, many states are highly interdependent with a relatively small number of other states (often not including contiguous states), and wars with most countries would not have major impacts on their commercial interactions.

Another way to reflect on the roots of the territorial integrity norm is to look at what has happened to the major incentives for territorial aggrandizement: the search for economic gains, the search for strategic gains, and the protection of national brethren. In the case of a striving for *economic gain*, the benefits of territorial aggression are much lower now since land alone does not provide the resources it once provided when agricultural production was a central source of wealth. Also, the economic costs of occupying land inhabited by a different ethnic group can be very high.

The use of territorial aggrandizement to achieve *strategic gain*, or an improvement in a state's relative power, has concerned the occupation of territories well situated for launching military operations, the exploitation of captured land as a source of national wealth, and the unification of ethnic brethren in other countries so as to increase the state's population base. Having strategically located territory is less important now than it once was because of the mobility of planes, missiles, and ships – in our technologically advanced era, land provides less power potential than it once did. Finally, increasing the population base of loyal nationals still gives a state more power, but in this case an expansionist state would have to meet the costs of international opposition.

The final motivation for territorial aggrandizement, *protecting fellow nationals*, has concerned the protection of ethnic compatriots who are being mistreated in other states and the unification of nationals in a single state. This motivation cannot be squelched, but it is much more difficult now for states to embark on attempts to protect and absorb fellow nationals in foreign states when their civil rights are respected. A central reason why the Western states have been so active in promoting minority rights (particularly through the OSCE) is that they want to remove any justification for foreign intervention and territorial aggrandizement.

---

[64] Thompson and Krasner 1989. Ethan Nadelmann has made an interesting comment about the demise of piracy and privateering in the seventeenth century that is relevant to the gradual strengthening of the territorial integrity norm: "The advantage to be derived from stealing from one another was giving way to the greater advantage of stable commercial relations." Nadelmann 1990, 487.

CONCLUSION

The decline of successful wars of territorial aggrandizement during the last half century is palpable. In fact, there has not been a case of successful territorial aggrandizement since 1976. Furthermore, there have been important multilateral accords in support of the norm and frequent interventions by international organizations to force states to withdraw from foreign countries.

Clearly, a central source of the norm has been the industrialized world's fear that territorial revisionism could ignite a major war that would cause great human suffering. Several scholars have observed that this revulsion against the imposition of physical pain has been central to the strengthening of a variety of security and human rights regimes.[65] The experiences of the two world wars, a general understanding of territorial revisionism's encouragement of major wars, and a fear of nuclear weapons drove the development of the territorial integrity norm at key points in its multilateral legitimization. But one cannot dismiss the ideational element of democratic values among Western, and an increasing number of non-Western, countries. The Western democratic states were the driving force behind the norm in 1919, 1945, and 1975. A recent study on the CSCE highlights the impacts of democratic values on respect for interstate borders. According to Gregory Flynn and Henry Farrell, these values orient states to the peaceful settlement of disputes and respect for the territory and institutions of other countries.[66] They also stress that democratic countries place respect for states' territorial integrity before self-determination for ethnic communities because this strategy best realizes their two values of self-governance and freedom from violence – or liberty and order. They note that "the norm of [national] self-determination was not only subordinated to the norm of inviolability of borders; it was also effectively removed as an independent principle of international relations in Europe separable from the norm of democracy."[67] In other words, for most Western liberals, self-determination means self-governance for the peoples of juridical territorial states.

Wars of territorial aggrandizement since 1945 have, for the most part, concerned developing states' dissatisfaction with the boundaries

---

[65] Finnemore and Sikkink 1999, 267–68.

[66] Flynn and Farrell 1999.

[67] Flynn and Farrell 1999, 527 and passim. On the change in Western international practices that flow from the application of liberal democratic values, see also Adler 1998.

they inherited from the colonial powers; but these quarrels are largely coming to an end. On the whole, what is remarkable is the degree of support for the territorial order by developing countries. At the heart of their support have been their fear of territorial aggrandizement based on conflicting treaties, overlapping ethnic groups, and their military weakness; but the leverage of the Western states has also had a major impact in assuring respect for the norm. If the Western states had not backed the territorial status quo in the developing world, a good number of territorial aggressions would have succeeded, and the commitment of the developing states to the territorial integrity norm would have probably declined markedly.

One should not discount the contribution of economic trends in the strengthening of the territorial integrity norm, especially in recent decades. Of great import is the significance of a stable territorial order to the operation of the increasingly interdependent international economy: "The globalizing economy requires the backing of territorially based state power to enforce its rules."[68] At the same time there is no indication that economic discourses and economic motivations sustained the emergence of the norm – especially in the wake of the two world wars. In fact, while these economic trends have reduced states' perceptions of benefits and increased states' perceptions of costs of territorial aggrandizement, they do not account for why states are so strongly opposed to territorial aggressions by other states.

There is not a simple answer to why the territorial integrity norm has emerged as a central pillar of the international order. Different reasons were key for two major groupings of states, and the coincidence of several factors seems to have been crucial to their backing. These key factors have wrought a major change in the international territorial order. Boundaries have not been frozen, but states have been effectively proscribed from altering them by force. The multistate political and security order is clearly stronger than many political observers think in that the society of states has largely eliminated what scholars have identified as the major source of enduring rivalries and the frequency and intensity of warfare.[69]

* * *

[68] Cox 1996, 278.
[69] See Holsti 1991; Goertz and Diehl 1992; Vasquez 1993; Huth 1996; and Hensel 1999.

PART V

TREATY DESIGN AND DYNAMICS

13

Why Are Some International Agreements Informal?

Charles Lipson

"Verbal contracts," Samuel Goldwyn once said, "aren't worth the paper they're written on." Yet informal agreements and oral bargains suffuse international affairs. They are the form that international cooperation takes in a wide range of issues, from exchange rates to nuclear weapons. Take monetary affairs, for instance. Except for the regional European Monetary System, there have been no formal, comprehensive agreements on exchange rates since the downfall of the Bretton Woods system in 1971. A prolonged effort to resurrect the pegged-rate system failed, although new treaties were drawn up and duly signed. Private financial markets simply overwhelmed these official efforts, and central bankers eventually conceded the point. The one comprehensive agreement since then, concluded in 1976 in Jamaica, merely ratified a system of floating rates that had emerged unplanned. For the past fifteen years, monetary arrangements have been a succession of informal agreements of indefinite duration, most recently the Plaza Communiqué and the Louvre Accord, designed to cope with volatile currency movements.[1] The Bretton Woods system itself depended on such agreements in its declining years. It was held together by the tacit

For their comments and suggestions, I thank Ed Mansfield, David Spiro, Charles Kupchan, Jack Snyder, and other participants in the Seminar on International Political Economy at Columbia University. I am also grateful to Douglas Baird, Anne-Marie Burley, Dale Copeland, Scott Leuning, Duncan Snidal, Stephen Walt, and other colleagues in the Program on International Politics, Economics, and Security (PIPES) at the University of Chicago.
[1] See Yoichi Funabashi, *Managing the Dollar: From the Plaza to the Louvre* (Washington, D.C.: Institute for International Economics, 1988); and Peter B. Kenen, *Managing Exchange Rates* (London: Routledge, 1988). Kenen reproduces key portions of the Plaza Communiqué (22 September 1985) and the Louvre Accord (22 February 1987) on p. 50.

agreement of European central banks not to convert their major dollar holdings into gold. The system fell apart when Germany and France abandoned that commitment. They did so because they believed that the United States had abandoned its own (tacit) commitment to restrain inflation and to avoid large current account deficits. Put another way, the U.S. formal pledge to convert dollars into gold at $35 per ounce – the very heart of the Bretton Woods system – was sustained only by silent agreements that America would not be called upon to do so.[2]

Such informal agreements are vital in security relationships as well. America's relations with the Soviet Union have relied heavily on unspoken understandings. These tacit relationships are crucial for two reasons. First, the Americans and Soviets *** made very few direct treaty commitments, and fewer still in key areas of national security. Second, for much of the postwar period, each side was openly hostile to the other and outspoken in denying the value and even the legitimacy of cooperation. The rhetoric went much further at times, challenging the adversary's right to govern at home, its basic security interests abroad, and its trustworthiness in diplomatic dealings. For all that, the United States and Soviet Union have generally framed their basic security policies in more prudent and cautious terms. The U.S. decision to pursue containment rather than "rollback," even at the height of Cold War tensions, was a tacit acknowledgment of the Soviet sphere of influence in Eastern Europe. When popular uprisings broke out during the 1950s, the United States did nothing – nothing to aid resistance movements in Germany, Poland, and Hungary and nothing to deter their forcible suppression. *** Paul Keal has termed such policies the "unspoken rules" of superpower diplomacy.[3]

---

[2] See John Williamson, *The Failure of World Monetary Reform, 1971–1974* (New York: New York University Press, 1977); and Kenneth W. Dam, *The Rules of the Game: Reform and Evolution in the International Monetary System* (Chicago: University of Chicago Press, 1982). For a counterargument focusing on U.S. domestic politics rather than on the breakdown of international commitments, see Joanne Gowa, *Closing the Gold Window: Domestic Politics and the End of Bretton Woods* (Ithaca, N.Y.: Cornell University Press, 1983).

[3] See Paul Keal, *Unspoken Rules and Superpower Dominance* (London: Macmillan, 1983). Some diplomatic efforts were made to articulate the rules, but they did little in themselves to clarify expectations. In 1972, as the strategic arms limitation talks (SALT I) were concluded, Nixon and Brezhnev signed the Basic Principles Agreement. It sought to specify some key elements of the superpowers' relationship and thereby facilitate the development of detente. The product was vague and ambiguous. Worse, it seemed to indicate – wrongly – U.S. agreement with the Soviet position on peaceful coexistence and competition in other regions. Alexander George calls these elements "a pseudoagreement." For the text of the agreement, see *Department of State Bulletin*, 26 June 1972,

Unspoken rules are not the only kinds of informal arrangements between the superpowers. In the case of strategic arms limitations, both the Americans and the Soviets publicly announced that they would continue to observe the first SALT treaty after it expired in October 1977. The principal aim was to sustain a climate of cooperation while SALT II was being negotiated. *** The unratified treaty was observed informally even during the Reagan administration's major arms buildup. Both sides restricted specific categories of long-range nuclear weapons to meet SALT II limitations, despite the absence of any formal agreement to do so.

The Reagan administration always claimed that its nuclear policies were unilateral and voluntary. Yet it devoted considerable attention to possible Soviet "violations" of what was, after all, a nonexistent treaty.[4] These violations were important because President Reagan always stated that U.S. arms restraints depended on Soviet reciprocity and progress toward a new arms treaty.[5] Reagan repeatedly criticized the Soviets on both counts but in practice continued to observe SALT limits until well after the expiration date of the proposed treaty. The agreement was tacit, but no less an agreement for that.

---

pp. 898–99. For an analysis, see Alexander George, "The Basic Principles Agreement of 1972," in Alexander L. George, ed., *Managing U.S.–Soviet Rivalry: Problems of Crisis Prevention* (Boulder, Colo.: Westview Press, 1983), pp. 107–18.

[4] In 1984, in a confidential report to Congress, President Reagan cited in detail Soviet noncompliance with numerous arms control agreements. Reagan's accompanying message stated that "violations and probable violations have occurred with respect to a number of Soviet legal obligations and political commitments in the arms control field." SALT II violations were included, and the reference to "political commitments" alludes to them. These criticisms were expanded in another report, issued in 1985. The Soviets rejected these charges and made counterclaims regarding U.S. violations. Relevant documents are cited by Notburga K. Calvo-Goller and Michael A. Calvo in *The SALT Agreements: Content-Application-Verification* (Dordrecht, Netherlands: Martinus Nijhoff, 1987), pp. 318 and 326 ff.

[5] President Reagan did restate the U.S. commitment not to undercut SALT II in June 1985, some six months before the unratified treaty would have expired. U.S. policy, however, was always contingent on reciprocal Soviet adherence. On that point, Reagan was sharply critical: "The United States has not taken any actions which would undercut existing arms control agreements. The United States has fully kept its part of the bargain; however, the Soviets have not . . . . Certain Soviet violations are, by their very nature, irreversible. Such is the case with respect to the Soviet Union's flight-testing and steps toward deployment of the SS-X-25 missile, a second new type of ICBM [intercontinental ballistic missile] prohibited by the unratified SALT II agreement. Since the noncompliance associated with the development of this missile cannot be corrected by the Soviet Union, the United States reserves the right to respond in a proportionate

Informal accords among states and transnational actors are not exceptional. The scale and the diversity of such accords indicate that they are an important feature of world politics, not rare and peripheral. The very informality of so many agreements illuminates basic features of international politics. It highlights the continuing search for international cooperation, the profusion of forms it takes, and the serious obstacles to more durable commitments.

All international agreements, whether formal or informal, are promises about future national behavior. To be considered genuine agreements, they must entail some reciprocal promises or actions, implying future commitments. Agreements may be considered informal, to a greater or lesser degree, if they lack the state's fullest and most authoritative imprimatur, which is given most clearly in treaty ratification.

The informality of agreements varies by degrees, along two principal dimensions. The first is the government level at which the agreement is made. A commitment made by the head of state (an executive agreement) is the most visible and credible sign of policy intentions short of a ratified treaty. In important matters, commitments by lower-level bureaucracies are less effective in binding national policy. They are simply less constraining on heads of state, senior political leaders, and other branches of government, partly because they lack a visible impact on national reputation. The second dimension is the form, or means, by which an agreement is expressed. It may be outlined in an elaborate written document, or it may involve a less formal exchange of notes, a joint communiqué, an oral bargain, or even a tacit bargain.[6] Written agreements allow greater attention to detail and more explicit consideration of the contingencies that might arise. They permit the parties to set the boundaries of their promises, to control them more precisely, or to create deliberate ambiguity and omissions on controversial matters. At the other end of the spectrum – most informal of all – are oral and tacit agreements. Their promises are generally more ambiguous and

---

manner at the appropriate time." See the President's statement of 10 June 1985, quoted in *Weekly Compilation of Presidential Documents*, vol. 21, no. 24, 17 June 1985, pp. 770–71.

[6] It is worth noting that all of these distinctions are ignored in international law. Virtually all international commitments, whether oral or written, whether made by the head of state or a lower-level bureaucracy, are treated as "binding international commitments." What is missing is not only the political dimension of these agreements, including their status as domestic policy, but also any insight into why states choose more or less formal means for their international agreements.

less clearly delimited,[7] and the very authority to make and execute them may be in doubt.[8] If disputes later arise, it is often difficult to specify what was intended *ex ante*. Indeed, it may be difficult to show that there *was* an agreement.[9]

The interpretive problems are even more acute with tacit understandings and implicit rules that are not well articulated between the parties.[10] Are these arrangements cooperative agreements at all? That depends. They are *not* if they simply involve each actor's best strategic choice, given others' independent choices. This Nash equilibrium may produce order and predictability – that is, regular behavior and stable

---

[7] Tacit and oral agreements, by their very nature, do not specify promises in great detail and rarely spell out contingencies or remedies. Consider, for example, the informal cooperation between friendly intelligence agencies such as the U.S. Central Intelligence Agency and Israel's Mossad. Besides exchanging information, both sides engage in unacknowledged spying on each other. But what are the limits? What violates the informal agreement, and what differentiates serious violations from "normal cheating"? To clarify these issues and to encourage regular cooperation, the United States and Israel have signed informal accords, beginning with a secret agreement in 1951. Even so, such agreements are necessarily incomplete, sometimes making it difficult to differentiate cheating from permissible activity. *** See Wolf Blitzer, *Territory of Lies: The Exclusive Story of Jonathan Jay Pollard – The American Who Spied on His Country for Israel and How He Was Betrayed* (New York: Harper & Row, 1989), p. 163; and Dan Raviv and Yossi Melman, *Every Spy a Prince: The Complete History of Israel's Intelligence Community* (Boston: Houghton Mifflin, 1990), pp. 77 ff.

[8] The State Department's 1981 statement, for example, that the United States "would not undercut" the unratified SALT II treaty if the Soviets reciprocated is an informal commitment. To international lawyers, its status is clear-cut. The State Department has unambiguously committed the United States by using the standard diplomatic language of obligation to a treaty pending ratification. But what about the domestic political status of that promise? The debate within the Reagan administration raged for another year before the President publicly ratified the State Department position. Even then, the Congress and courts need not be bound by these executive branch statements.

[9] Recognizing these limitations on oral bargains, domestic courts refuse to recognize such bargains in many cases, thereby creating a powerful incentive for written contracts. There is no such incentive to avoid oral bargains in interstate agreements.

[10] According to Downs and Rocke, "A state bargains tacitly with another state when it attempts to manipulate the latter's policy choices through its behavior rather than by relying on formal or informal diplomatic exchange." Actions, not diplomatic words, are the crucial form of communications, and their aim is joint, voluntary cooperation rather than outright coercion. Downs and Rocke's contribution is to show how imperfect information affects states' strategic choices and may produce inadvertent arms races. Their focus is on uncertain estimates of others' strategies, preferences, and specific actions (either completed or intended), and not on the ambiguous meaning of tacit agreements and other informal bargains. See the following works of George W. Downs and David M. Rocke: "Tacit Bargaining and Arms Control," *World Politics* 39 (April 1987), p. 297; and *Tacit Bargaining, Arms Races, and Arms Control* (Ann Arbor: University of Michigan Press, 1990), p. 3.

expectations – without cooperation.[11] Genuine tacit cooperation involves something more. It is based on shared expectations that each party can improve its own outcome if its strategic choices are modified in expectation of reciprocal changes by others.[12] Shared "understandings" can arise in either case. They are not a unique marker of cooperative agreements. What distinguishes cooperation, whether tacit or explicit, are the subtle forms of mutual reliance and the possibilities of betrayal and regret.

The central point here is not taxonomic, presenting definitions of tacit arrangements and other informal bargains simply to classify them. The goal is to understand how different kinds of agreements can be used to order international relationships. The means of international cooperation are frequently informal, and it is important to explore their rationale, uses, and limitations. At the same time, we should not mistake all shared understandings for voluntary, informal bargains.

Informality is best understood as a device for minimizing the impediments to cooperation, at both the domestic and international levels. What are the impediments? And what are the advantages of informal agreements in addressing them? First, informal bargains are more flexible than treaties. They are willows, not oaks. They can be adapted to meet uncertain conditions and unpredictable shocks. "One of the greatest advantages of an informal instrument," according to a legal counselor in Britain's Foreign Office, "is the ease with which it can be amended."[13] Although treaties often contain clauses permitting renegotiation, the process is slow and cumbersome and is nearly always impractical. This point can be put in another, less obvious way: informal agreements make

---

[11] See Jon Elster's discussion of "the two problems of social order," in *The Cement of Society: A Study of Social Order* (Cambridge: Cambridge University Press, 1989), chap. 1. Elster's key distinction is between regular behavior patterns and cooperation. He distinguishes five main varieties of cooperation: helping others, voluntarily bearing costs of externalities, physical collaboration in joint ventures, mutual agreements to transfer rights (private orderings), and conventional equilibria (in which no party can improve its outcome by unilaterally deviating). In this article, my discussion of international cooperation focuses only on reciprocal contractual exchanges, which involve future performance and where the possibility of profitable defection might arise.

[12] In tacit cooperation, one party in effect takes a chance in the expectation that another will simultaneously take an equivalent chance, leaving both better off. Neither party takes such chances when it maximizes unilaterally and independently. Stable expectations can arise in either case, based upon stable Nash equilibria. It is important not to exaggerate the scale of international cooperation by calling all shared expectations "cooperation." They may be nothing more than unilateral maximizing.

[13] Anthony Aust, "The Theory and Practice of Informal International Instruments," *International and Comparative Law Quarterly* 35 (October 1986), p. 791.

fewer informational demands on the parties. Negotiators need not try to predict all future states and comprehensively contract for them. Second, because informal arrangements do not require elaborate ratification, they can be concluded and implemented quickly if need be. In complex, rapidly changing environments, speed is a particular advantage.

Finally, informal agreements are generally less public and prominent, even when they are not secret. This lower profile has important consequences for democratic oversight, bureaucratic control, and diplomatic precedent. Informal agreements can escape the public controversies of a ratification debate. They can avoid the disclosures, unilateral "understandings," and amendments that sometimes arise in that open process. Because of their lower profile, they are also more tightly controlled by the government bureaucracies that negotiate and implement the agreements and less exposed to intrusion by other agencies. Agencies dealing with specific international issues, such as environmental pollution or foreign intelligence, can use informal agreements to seal quiet bargains with their foreign counterparts, avoiding close scrutiny and active involvement by other government agencies with different agendas.

The lower profile and the absence of formal national commitment also mean that informal agreements are less constraining as diplomatic precedents. They do not stand as visible and general policy commitments, as treaties so often do. In all these ways, the most sensitive and embarrassing implications of an agreement can remain nebulous or unstated for both domestic and international audiences, or even hidden from them.

Yet all of these diplomatic benefits come at a price, and sometimes a very high one. The flexibility of informal agreements also means that they are more easily abandoned. Avoiding public debates conceals the depth of national support for an agreement. Ratification debates can also serve to mobilize and integrate the multiple constituencies interested in an agreement. These policy networks of public officials (executive, legislative, and bureaucratic) and private actors sustain agreements during the implementation stage. Joint communiqués and executive agreements sidestep these basic democratic processes. This evasion typically means that the final agreements are less reliable for all participants.

These costs and benefits suggest the basic reasons for choosing informal agreements:

(1) the desire to avoid formal and visible pledges,
(2) the desire to avoid ratification,
(3) the ability to renegotiate or modify as circumstances change, or

(4) the need to reach agreements quickly.

Because speed, simplicity, flexibility, and privacy are all common diplomatic requirements, we would expect to find informal agreements used frequently. Because the associated costs and benefits vary in different circumstances, we would also expect to find a distinct pattern of formal and informal agreements. Finally, we would expect to find various types of informal agreements used to meet particular needs.

This article examines the strengths and weaknesses of informal agreements. It is an inquiry into the neglected institutional constraints on international cooperation – and the imperfect devices to overcome them. It considers the basic choices between treaties and informal instruments, as well as the choices among different kinds of informal arrangements, all of which can be used to express cooperation among states. Finally, it asks what these varied forms of cooperation can tell us about the more general impediments to international agreement. The aim here is to use the *choice of forms of agreement* to explore some problems of rational cooperation in international affairs and particularly their contextual and institutional dimensions.

SELF-HELP AND THE LIMITS OF INTERNATIONAL AGREEMENT

When states cooperate, they can choose from a wide variety of forms to express their commitments, obligations, and expectations. The most formal are bilateral and multilateral treaties, in which states acknowledge their promises as binding commitments with full international legal status. At the other extreme are tacit agreements, in which obligations and commitments are implied or inferred but not openly declared, and oral agreements, in which bargains are expressly stated but not documented. In between lie a variety of written instruments to express national obligations with greater precision and openness than tacit or oral agreements but without the full ratification and national pledges that accompany formal treaties. These informal arrangements range from executive agreements and nonbinding treaties to joint declarations, final communiqués, agreed minutes, memoranda of understanding, and agreements pursuant to legislation. Unlike treaties, these informal agreements generally come into effect without ratification and do not require international publication or registration.

Although these agreements differ in form and political intent, legal scholars rarely distinguish among them. The dominant view is that international agreements, whatever their title, are legally binding upon the signatories, unless clearly stated otherwise. Thus, informal agreements, if they contain explicit promises, are conflated with treaties. They are rarely studied directly, except for the curiosity of "nonbinding" agreements such as the Helsinki Final Act.[14]

This distinction between agreements that legally bind and agreements that do not is a traditional one. It is central to the technical definition of treaties codified in the Vienna Convention on the Law of Treaties. Article 26 states that treaties are "binding upon the parties" and "must be performed by them in good faith."[15] Similarly, texts on international law emphasize the binding nature of treaties and, indeed, a wide range of other international agreements.[16]

The implicit claim is that international agreements have a status similar to domestic contracts, which are binding and enforceable. This claim is seriously misleading. It is a faulty and legalistic characterization of international agreements in practice and is also a poor guide to why states sometimes use treaties and other times use informal means to express agreements. Although international agreements are contracted commitments, any simple analogy to domestic contracts is mistaken for several reasons. First, in domestic legal systems, binding agreements are adjudicated and enforced by courts, backed by the instruments of state power. *** Courts can hold parties responsible for their promises, whether those promises were originally intended as contracts or not, and can settle their meaning.[17] When parties discuss compliance after agreements have been signed, they bargain in the shadow of law and judicial enforcement.

---

[14] See, for example, Oscar Schachter, "The Twilight Existence of Nonbinding International Agreements," *American Journal of International Law* 71 (April 1977), pp. 296–304; Michael J. Glennon, "The Senate Role in Treaty Ratification," *American Journal of International Law* 77 (April 1983), pp. 257–80; and Fritz Münch, "Non-Binding Agreements," in *The Encyclopedia of Public International Law*, vol. 7 (Amsterdam: North-Holland, 1984), pp. 353–57. The one general (and quite valuable) legal treatment of informal agreements is "The Theory and Practice of Informal International Instruments" by Anthony Aust, a practitioner in the British Foreign Office.

[15] The Vienna Convention on the Law of Treaties was opened for signature on 23 May 1969 and entered into force on 27 January 1980, after ratification by thirty-five nations. See UN document A/CONF. 39/27, 1969.

[16] See, for example, Lord McNair, *The Law of Treaties* (Oxford: Clarendon Press, 1961); and Taslim Elias, *The Modern Law of Treaties* (Dobbs Ferry, N.Y.: Oceana Publications, 1974).

[17] For a system of contract law to be effective, the parties cannot simply abandon their commitments unilaterally. Or, rather, they cannot abandon these commitments without facing legal penalties. Reflecting this understanding, the key disputes in contract law revolve around what constitutes a binding agreement and what constitutes an appropriate penalty for nonperformance. International legal scholarship largely avoids these fundamental issues, and it says all too little about related issues of renunciation, violation, and monitoring of agreements.

Whether the issue involves simple promises or complicated commercial transactions, the availability of effective, compulsory arbitration by courts supports and facilitates agreements. It does so, in the last resort, by compelling adherence to promises privately made or, more commonly, by requiring compensatory payment for promises broken.[18] Moreover, the prospect of such enforcement colors out-of-court bargaining.

* * *

There is no debate over the propriety of these judicial functions. They are crucial in complex capitalist economies in which independent agents work together by voluntary agreement. What legal scholars debate is not the propriety of enforcement power but its substantive content and the underlying principles that should govern damage awards when promises are broken.[19] ***

Whatever the standard for damages, it is clear that the courts offer political backing for the exchange of promises and, indeed, for the institution of promising in all its facets. Their role provides an important measure of protection to those who receive promises. It diminishes the tasks of self-protection, lowers the costs of transactions, and thereby promotes contractual agreements and exchange in general.

To lower the burdens of self-protection is not to eliminate them entirely. Using local courts to sustain agreements is often costly or impractical. The enforcement of contractual rights and obligations is imperfect. These costs and uncertainties raise the possibility that breaches of contract will go uncompensated or undercompensated. Knowing that, the parties must look to themselves for some protection against

---

[18] This backing for promises is qualified in at least two senses. First, it leaves aside the expense and opportunity costs of using the courts (some of which may be recovered in the final judgment). Second, it assumes that the contested promises can somehow be demonstrated to the satisfaction of a third party. For oral promises, this may be a difficult hurdle, as Goldwyn noted.

[19] Fried and Atiyah represent opposite poles in this debate. Fried argues that the common law of contracts is based on the moral institution of promising, rather than on commercial exchange. To sustain this institution, the recipients of broken promises should be awarded their expectations of profit. Atiyah argues that court decisions have moved away from this strict emphasis, which arose in the nineteenth century, and returned to an older notion of commercial practice, which limits awards to the costs incurred in relying on broken promises. See Charles Fried, *Contract as Promise: A Theory of Contractual Obligation* (Cambridge, Mass.: Harvard University Press, 1981); Patrick S. Atiyah, *From Principles to Pragmatism* (Oxford: Clarendon Press, 1978); and Patrick S. Atiyah, *The Rise and Fall of Freedom of Contract* (Oxford: Clarendon Press, 1979).

opportunism.[20] It is also true that domestic courts do not become involved in contract disputes through their own independent initiatives. They are called upon by parties to the dispute – at the parties' own initiative, at their own cost, and at their own risk. In that sense, access to the courts may be seen as an adjunct to other forms of self-help. Like these other forms, it is costly and the results uncertain.

But the fact that self-help is common to all agreements does not eradicate the fundamental differences between domestic and international bargains. Hanging over domestic bargains is the prospect of judicial interpretation and enforcement, whether the disputes are settled in court or not.[21] There is simply no analogue for these functions in international agreements. Of course, the parties to an interstate dispute may, by mutual consent, seek judicial rulings or private arbitration. In multilateral treaties, states may also agree in advance to use procedures for dispute resolution.[22] These procedures may have teeth. They can raise the diplomatic costs of violations and ease the burdens of retaliation. But the punishments are also highly circumscribed. For the most part, they simply define and justify certain limited acts of self-enforcement or retaliation. At most, they may force a violator to withdraw from an agreement or a multilateral organization, giving up the benefits of participation.[23]

[20] The courts themselves require some efforts at self-protection. Once a contract has been breached, for instance, the "innocent" party is expected to take reasonable actions to minimize the damages and cannot win awards that cover a failure to do so. For the efficiency implications of this legal doctrine, see Anthony Kronman and Richard Posner, *The Economics of Contract Law* (Boston: Little, Brown, 1979), pp. 160–61.

[21] See Robert H. Mnookin and Lewis Kornhauser, "Bargaining in the Shadow of the Law: The Case of Divorce," *Yale Law Journal* 88 (April 1979), pp. 950–97. Mnookin and Kornhauser also conclude that the impact of differing legal arrangements on divorce settlements cannot be specified with precision. They attribute that to a more general theoretical gap: a limited understanding of how alternative institutional arrangements can affect bargaining outcomes.

[22] These are often ad hoc procedures designed for a specific agreement. Their powers may be quasi-judicial, as in the dispute mechanisms of the General Agreement on Tariffs and Trade (GATT), or merely consultative, as in the procedures of the U.S.–Soviet Standing Consultative Commission, established in SALT I and SALT II. The presence of quasi-judicial bodies attached to specific agreements indicates, once again, the limits of international adjudication. And it points to the ad hoc means devised to manage the risks of international cooperation. See Richard B. Bilder, *Managing the Risks of International Agreement* (Madison: University of Wisconsin Press, 1981), pp. 56–61.

[23] A signatory always has the practical option of withdrawal, whether it is included as a legal option in the treaty or not. For legal analyses, see Arie E. David, *The Strategy of Treaty Termination: Lawful Breaches and Retaliations* (New Haven, Conn.: Yale University Press, 1975), pp. 203–16; and Herbert W. Briggs, "Unilateral Denunciation of Treaties: The Vienna Convention and the International Court of Justice," *American Journal of International Law* 68 (January 1974), pp. 51–68.

That can be punishment, to be sure, but it falls far short of the legal sanctions for violating domestic contracts. There, the rights of withdrawal are accompanied by external enforcement of damages, usually based on disappointed expectations of profit. The fact that *all* agreements contain some elements of self-protection and some institutions for private governance should not obscure these basic differences between domestic and international bargains.[24]

Domestic legal systems not only aid in enforcing contracts but also set effective boundaries on the scope and nature of private agreements. Statutes and court rulings limit the private, voluntary ordering of relationships. A significant portion of criminal law, for example, is devoted specifically to punishing certain categories of private agreements, from prostitution and gambling to the sale of illicit drugs. The rationale is that larger public purposes should override the immediate parties' own desires: their bargains should be barred or constrained. Civil laws governing rent control, usury, insider trading, cartel price-fixing, homosexual marriage, and indentured servitude are all directed at preventing private bargains, for better or for worse.[25] Such restrictions and the rules governing them are central elements of domestic legal systems.

Similarly, the law can restrict the *form* of agreements. One clear-cut and prominent example is the U.S. Statute of Frauds, which requires that certain agreements be put in writing. ***

Again, there are simply no equivalent restrictions on either the form or substance of international agreements. The domain of *permissible* international agreements is simply the domain of *possible* agreements.[26]

---

[24] There have been proposals, based on efficiency grounds or libertarian principles, that private agents play a much larger role in enforcing domestic laws and contracts and that they be compensated by bounties, paid either by violators or the state. These proposals cannot be applied to international agreements without significant modification, since they ultimately envision authoritative judicial interpretation and enforcement. See Gary S. Becker and George J. Stigler, "Law Enforcement, Malfeasance and Compensation of Enforcers," *Journal of Legal Studies* 3 (January 1974), pp. 1–18; Gary S. Becker, "Crime and Punishment: An Economic Approach," *Journal of Political Economy* 76 (March–April 1968), pp. 169–217; and George J. Stigler, "The Optimum Enforcement of Laws" *Journal of Political Economy* 78 (May–June 1970), pp. 526–36.

[25] As Mnookin and Kornhauser point out in their study of divorce laws, "A legal system might allow varying degrees of private ordering upon dissolution of the marriage. Until recently, divorce law attempted to restrict private ordering severely." See Mnookin and Kornhauser, "Bargaining in the Shadow of the Law," pp. 952–53.

[26] There is one restriction worth noting on the legal form of international agreements. The World Court will only consider agreements that have been formally registered with the United Nations. If the World Court were a powerful enforcement body, this restriction would influence the form of major agreements.

This absence of restraint is not due simply to the lack of an international legislature and executive (though surely they are absent). It is due equally to the absence of an effective system of adjudication. One major limitation on prohibited domestic bargains, aside from any direct penalties, is that illicit bargains are not enforced by courts. This restricts such bargains by making them more costly to execute. To implement illegal contracts requires special precautions and sometimes entails the establishment of a broader set of institutional arrangements: a criminal enterprise.[27]

These high costs of self-enforcement and the dangers of opportunism are important obstacles to extralegal agreements. Indeed, the costs may be prohibitive if they leave unsolved such basic problems as moral hazard and time inconsistency. The same obstacles are inherent features of interstate bargaining and must be resolved if agreements are to be concluded and carried out. Resolving them depends on the parties' preference orderings, the transparency of their preferences and choices (asymmetrical information), and the private institutional mechanisms set up to secure their bargains.[28] It has little to do, however, with whether an international agreement is considered "legally binding" or not. In domestic affairs, on the other hand, these legal boundaries make an enormous difference – the difference between selling contraband whiskey in Al Capone's Chicago and selling the same product legally ten years later.

In international affairs, then, the term "binding agreement" is a misleading hyperbole. To enforce their bargains, states must act for themselves. This limitation is crucial: it is a recognition that international politics is a realm of contesting sovereign powers. For that reason, it is misleading to understand treaties (as international lawyers typically do) in purely formal, legal terms, as instruments that somehow bind states to their promises. It is quite true that treaties incorporate the language of formal obligation, chiefly phrases such as "we shall" and "we undertake," together with specific commitments. Such conventional diplomatic language is a defining feature of modern treaties. But that language cannot accomplish its ambitious task of binding states to their promises. This

---

[27] Criminal organizations such as the Mafia can be understood partly as an institutional response to the problems of providing criminal services when the bargains themselves are illegal. For a fascinating economic study of such institutional arrangements, see Peter Reuter, *Disorganized Crime: Illegal Markets and the Mafia* (Cambridge, Mass.: MIT Press, 1983).

[28] On the mechanisms of private governance, see Oliver R. Williamson, *The Economic Institutions of Capitalism: Firms, Markets, Relational Contracting* (New York: Free Press, 1985).

inability is an inherent limitation on bargaining for international co-operation. It means that treaties, like all international agreements, must be enforced endogenously.

WHAT DO TREATIES DO?

If treaties do not truly bind, why do states use that language? Why frame agreements in that form? The chief reason, I think, is that states wish to signal their intentions with special intensity and gravity and are using a well-understood form to do so. The decision to encode a bargain in treaty form is primarily a decision to highlight the importance of the agreement and, even more, to underscore the durability and significance of the underlying promises. The language of "binding commitments," in other words, is a diplomatic communication aimed at other signatories and, often, at third parties. In the absence of international institutions that permit effective self-binding or offer external guarantees for promises, treaties use conventional forms to signify a seriousness of commitment. By making that commitment both solemn and public, the parties indicate their intention, at least, to adhere to a particular bargain.

The effect of treaties, then, is to raise the political costs of noncompliance. That cost is raised not only for others but also for oneself. The more formal and public the agreement, the higher the reputational costs of noncompliance. The costs are highest when the agreement contains specific written promises, made publicly by senior officials with the state's fullest imprimatur. States deliberately choose to impose these costs on themselves in order to benefit from the counterpromises (or actions) of others. Given the inherent constraints of international institutions, these formal pledges are as close as states can come to precommitment – to a contractual exchange of promises. In short, one crucial element of treaties is that they visibly stake the parties' reputations to their pledges.[29] The loss of credibility (because of deliberate violations) is a real loss, although it is certainly *not* always a decisive one, in terms of policy

---

[29] If a state already has a poor reputation for keeping its promises, then it risks little in staking that reputation on other agreements, and its pledges will fail to convince future partners without special efforts (such as bonds, hostages, or collateral) and careful monitoring, all designed to minimize reliance on "trust." That does not rule out treaties, but it suggests that they may be disingenuous and cannot be relied upon. Stalin and Hitler, for example, found their pact useful because it produced immediate gains for each: the division of Eastern Europe. The incorporation of the new territories also postponed a confrontation between the two. The pact was useful for these immediate and simultaneous gains, not for any future promises of cooperation it held out.

calculus.[30] Informal agreements are generally less reliable and convincing precisely because they involve less of a reputational stake.[31] The stakes are diminished either because the agreements are less public (the audience is narrower and more specialized) or because high-level officials are less directly involved.

In a world of imperfect information, where others' current and future preferences cannot be known with certainty, reputation has value. As a result, it can be used as a "hostage" or bond to support contracts. Because breaking a contract or even appearing to do so degrades reputation, it produces a loss of reputational capital. The threat of such loss promotes compliance, although it cannot guarantee it. Whether it succeeds depends on (1) the immediate gains from breaking an agreement, (2) the lost stream of future benefits and the rate of discount applied to that stream, and (3) the expected costs to reputation from specific violations.[32]

Not all violations discredit equally.[33] First, not all are witnessed. Some that are seen may be considered justifiable or excusable, perhaps because others have already violated the agreement, because circumstances have changed significantly, because compliance is no longer feasible, or because the contracted terms appear ambiguous. Thus, memory, inference, and context – social learning and constructed meaning – all matter. Second, not all actors have a reputation worth preserving. Some simply do not have much to lose, whether their violations are visible or not. Moreover, they may not choose to invest in reputation, presumably because the costs of building a good name outweigh the incremental

---

[30] Of course, commitments may be cast aside, no matter how formal, as Saddam Hussein did when he declared Iraq's border agreement with Iran "null and void" in 1981. The agreement, reached in 1975 in Algiers, stated that "land and river frontiers shall be inviolable, permanent and final." There is a cost to discarding such an agreement unilaterally, even if that cost seems remote at the time. It virtually rules out the ability to conclude useful agreements on other border disputes. See United Nations, *Yearbook of the United Nations, 1981*, vol. 35 (New York: United Nations, 1985), pp. 238–39. See also Iran, Ministry of Foreign Affairs, Legal Department, *A Review of the Imposed War* (Tehran: Ministry of Foreign Affairs, 1983), including the text of the 1975 treaty, the treaty addendum, and Iran's interpretation.

[31] In this sense, secret treaties are similar to informal agreements.

[32] In other words, if the future is highly valued, there can be an equilibrium in which the (current discounted) value of a reputation exceeds any short-run gains from taking advantage of it. If the prospective gains from reputation are sufficiently large, then it also pays to invest in reputation. See David M. Kreps, *A Course in Microeconomic Theory* (Princeton, N.J.: Princeton University Press, 1990), p. 532.

[33] J. Mark Ramseyer, "Legal Rules in Repeated Deals: Banking in the Shadow of Defection in Japan," *Journal of Legal Studies* 20 (January 1991), p. 96.

stream of rewards.[34] Sovereign debtors, for example, value their reputation least when they do not expect to borrow again.[35] Alternatively, actors with poor reputations (or little track record) may choose to invest in them precisely to create expectations about future performance. If these expectations can produce a stream of rewards and if the future is highly valued, it may be rational to make such investments.[36] Thus, the value of reputation lost depends on the visibility and clarity of both promises and performance, on the value of an actor's prior reputation, and on the perceived usefulness of reputation in supporting other agreements.

Compliance with treaties, as I have noted, is specifically designed to be a salient issue, supported by reputation. Unfortunately, the hostage of reputation is not always strong support. Some states foresee little gain from enhanced reputation, either because the immediate costs are too high or the ongoing rewards are too little, too late. They may sign treaties cynically, knowing that they can violate them cheaply. Others may sign treaties in good faith but simply abandon them if their calculations about future rewards change. Finally, some states may invest heavily to demonstrate the credibility of their promises, to show that they are reliable partners, unswayed by short-term gains from defection.[37] The general importance of reputation, in other words, does not eliminate the problem of multiple equilibria. Just as there can be economic markets with some sellers of high-quality goods and some sellers of

---

[34] Again, the shadow of the future is crucial. If future rewards are sharply discounted, then it pays to exploit prior reputation (to disinvest) to reap short-term rewards.

[35] Elsewhere, I have shown that sovereign debtors in the nineteenth century moved to settle their old defaults when they contemplated seeking new loans. Creditors had the greatest bargaining leverage at precisely these moments. See Charles Lipson, *Standing Guard: Protecting Foreign Capital in the Nineteenth and Twentieth Centuries* (Berkeley and Los Angeles: University of California Press, 1985), p. 47. See also Carlos Marichal, *A Century of Debt Crises in Latin America: From Independence to the Great Depression, 1820–1930* (Princeton, N.J.: Princeton University Press, 1989), pp. 122–23.

[36] The short-term price of reputation may either be foregone opportunities or direct expenditures, such as fixed investments that are most valuable within a specific bilateral relationship. Williamson has explored the use of such fixed investments to make credible commitments in *The Economic Institutions of Capitalism*.

[37] The United States made such an investment in reputation in the late 1970s, after its credibility as leader of the North Atlantic Treaty Organization (NATO) was damaged by the neutron bomb affair. The problem arose after the Carter administration first supported and then opposed NATO's deployment of new antitank weapons, equipped with enhanced radiation warheads or neutron bombs. Key European leaders had already declared their support publicly, at considerable political cost, and now they had to reverse

shoddy goods, both of them rational, there can be diplomatic environments in which some states are reliable treaty partners and some are not.[38]

Reputation, then, can contribute to treaty self-enforcement if not ensure it. Self-enforcement simply means that an agreement remains in force because, at any given moment, each party believes it gains more by sustaining the agreement than by terminating it. That calculation includes all future benefits and costs, appropriately discounted to give their present value.[39] Enhancing a reputation for reliability is one such benefit. It is of particular value to governments engaged in a range of international transactions requiring trust and mutual reliance. Of course, other costs and benefits may outweigh these reputational issues.[40] The key point, however, is that reputation can be used to support international cooperation and has important implications for its form. The choice of a formal, visible document such as a treaty magnifies the reputational effects of adherence and buttresses self-enforcement.

Nations still can and do break even their most formal and solemn commitments to other states. Indeed, the unscrupulous may use treaty

course. After the crisis died down, the Carter administration proposed another approach to nuclear modernization: Pershing II missiles. The administration then held fast (as did the Reagan administration) in support of its new plan. It did so despite a rising tide of public protest abroad and wavering support from European leaders, especially the Germans, who had initially proposed the modernization. According to Garthoff, "The principal effect of the neutron weapon affair was to reduce Western confidence in American leadership in the alliance, and later to lead the United States to seek to undo that effect by another new arms initiative for NATO . . . The Carter administration itself felt it needed to compensate for its handling of the neutron decision. It sought to do so by responding boldly to a perceived European concern through exercising vigorous leadership . . . . Doubts about the military necessity or even desirability of deploying new [long-range tactical nuclear force] systems were overwhelmed by a perceived political necessity within the alliance." See Raymond L. Garthoff, *Detente and Confrontation: American–Soviet Relations from Nixon to Reagan* (Washington, D.C.: Brookings Institution, 1985), pp. 853 and 859.

[38] Firms can guarantee quality by offering warranties. But what guarantees the warranty? The answer for expensive items may be the threat of litigation. But for less expensive items, it is simply the firm's reputation. "The hostage for performance," according to Rubin, "must be in the familiar form of a quasirent stream [either of profits or return on capital]. In either case, the price of the product must be above marginal cost, and the difference must be high enough so that cheating by the firm does not pay." See Paul Rubin, *Managing Business Transactions: Controlling the Cost of Coordinating, Communicating, and Decision Making* (New York: Free Press, 1990), p. 147.

[39] L. G. Telser, "A Theory of Self-Enforcing Agreements," *Journal of Business* 53 (January 1980), pp. 27–28.

[40] Thus, a single agreement can be self-enforcing, even if it is divorced from any reputational concerns. Conversely, even when reputational issues are salient, a treaty may break down if other costs are more important.

commitments as a way of deceiving unwary partners, deliberately creating false expectations or simply cheating when the opportunity arises. (Informal agreements are less susceptible to these dangers. They raise expectations less than treaties and so are less likely to dupe the naive.) But states pay a serious price for acting in bad faith and, more generally, for renouncing their commitments. This price comes not so much from adverse judicial decisions at The Hague but from the decline in national reputation as a reliable partner, which impedes future agreements.[41] Indeed, opinions of the World Court gain much of their significance by reinforcing these costs to national reputation.

Put simply, *treaties are a conventional way of raising the credibility of promises by staking national reputation on adherence.* The price of noncompliance takes several forms. First, there is loss of reputation as a reliable partner. A reputation for reliability is important in reaching other cooperative agreements where there is some uncertainty about compliance.[42] Second, the violation or perceived violation of a treaty may give rise to specific, costly retaliation, ranging from simple withdrawal of cooperation in one area to broader forms of noncooperation and specific sanctions. Some formal agreements, such as the General Agreement on Tariffs and Trade (GATT), even establish a limited set of permissible responses to violations, although most treaties do not. Finally, treaty violations may recast national reputation in a still broader and more dramatic way, depicting a nation that is not only untrustworthy but is also a deceitful enemy, one that makes promises in order to deceive.

This logic also suggests circumstances in which treaties – and, indeed, *all* international agreements – ought to be most vulnerable. An actor's reputation for reliability has a value over time. The present value of that reputation is the discounted stream of these current and future benefits. When time horizons are long, even distant benefits are considered valuable now. When horizons are short, these future benefits are worth little,[43] while the gains from breaking an agreement are likely to be more

---

[41] A poor reputation impedes a state's future agreements because the state cannot use its reputation as a credible and valuable "performance bond."

[42] "Reputation commands a price (or exacts a penalty)," Stigler once observed, "because it economizes on search." When that search must cover unknown future behavior, such as a partner's likelihood of complying with an agreement, then reputations are particularly valuable. See George Stigler, "The Economics of Information," *Journal of Political Economy* 69 (June 1961), p. 224.

[43] This discount rate refers only to the present value of known future benefits. It assumes perfect information about future payoffs. Greater risk or uncertainty about future benefits can also affect their present value.

immediate and tangible. Thus, under pressing circumstances, such as the looming prospect of war or economic crisis, the long-term value of a reputation for reliability will be sharply discounted. As a consequence, adherence to agreements must be considered less profitable and therefore less reliable.[44] This points to a striking paradox of treaties: they are often used to seal partnerships for vital actions, such as war, but they are weakest at precisely that moment because the present looms larger and the future is more heavily discounted.[45]

This weakness is sometimes recognized, though rarely emphasized, in studies of international law. It has no place at all, however, in the law of treaties. All treaties are treated equally, as legally binding commitments, and typically lumped together with a wide range of informal bargains. Treaties that declare alliances, establish neutral territories, or announce broad policy guidelines are not classified separately. Their legal status is the same as that of any other treaty. Yet it is also understood, by diplomats and jurists alike, that these three types of treaty are especially vulnerable to violation or renunciation. For this reason, Richard Baxter has characterized them as "soft" or "weak" law, noting that "if a State refuses to come to the aid of another under the terms of an alliance, nothing can force it to. It was never expected that the treaty would be 'enforced.'"[46]

* * *

The real point is to understand how *** perceptions of mutual advantage can support various kinds of international cooperation and how different legal forms, such as treaties, fit into this essentially political

---

[44] This logic should apply to all agreements lacking effective third-party enforcement, from modern warfare to premodern commerce. For an application of this approach to medieval economic history, see John M. Veitch, "Repudiations and Confiscations by the Medieval State," *Journal of Economic History* 46 (March 1986), pp. 31–36.

[45] Of course, states often do go to war alongside their long-time allies. My point is that if the costs are high (relative to longer-term reputational issues), their decision will be guided largely by their calculus of short-term gains and losses. That determination is largely independent of alliance agreements and formal treaties of mutual support. Knowing that, states facing war are reluctant to count too heavily on prior commitments, however formal or sincere, by alliance partners. By the same token, opponents have considerable incentives to design coalition-splitting strategies by varying the immediate costs and stakes to individual coalition members. This debate over long-term reputation versus short-term costs figured prominently in the British cabinet's debate over commitments to France before World War I.

[46] See Baxter, "International Law in 'Her Infinite Variety,'" p. 550. See also Ignaz Seidl-Hohenfeldern, "International Economic Soft Law," *Recueil de cours* (Collected Courses of the Hague Academy of International Law), vol. 163, 1979, pp. 169–246.

dynamic. The environment of contesting sovereign powers does not mean, as realist theories of international politics would have it, that cooperation is largely irrelevant or limited to common cause against military foes.[47] Nor does it mean that conflict and the resources for it are always dominant in international affairs. It does mean, however, that the bases for cooperation are decentralized and often fragile. Unfortunately, neither the language of treaties nor their putative legal status can transcend these limitations.

RATIONALES FOR INFORMAL AGREEMENTS

Speed and Obscurity

What we have concentrated on thus far are the fundamental problems of international agreements. Treaties, like less formal instruments, are plagued by difficulties of noncompliance and self-enforcement. These potential problems limit agreements when monitoring is difficult, enforcement is costly, and expected gains from noncompliance are immediate and significant. The traditional legal view that treaties are valuable because they are binding is inadequate precisely because it fails to comprehend these basic and recurrent problems.

To understand the choice between treaties and informal agreements, however, we need to move beyond the generic problems of monitoring, betrayal, and self-enforcement. Imperfect information and incentives to defect apply to all kinds of international bargains; they do not explain why some are framed as joint declarations and some as treaties. We therefore need to consider more specific properties of informal and formal agreements, along with their particular advantages and limitations.

To begin with, treaties are the most serious and deliberate form of international agreement and are often the most detailed. As such, they

---

[47] Realists consider cooperation important in only one sphere: military alliances. "In anarchy, states form alliances to protect themselves," says Walt. "Their conduct is determined by the threats they perceive." Although such alliances are important, they are simply considered the by-products of a world fundamentally characterized by conflict and the contest for relative gains. As Grieco bluntly puts it, "States are predisposed toward conflict and competition, and they often fail to cooperate even when they have common interests." See Stephen M. Walt, *The Origins of Alliances* (Ithaca, N.Y.: Cornell University Press, 1987), p. x; and Joseph M. Grieco, *Cooperation Among Nations: Europe, America, and Non-Tariff Barriers to Trade* (Ithaca, N.Y.: Cornell University Press, 1990), p. 4.

are the slowest to complete.[48] After the diplomats have finally left the table, the agreement must still win final approval from the signatories. That usually means a slow passage through the full domestic process of ratification. The process naturally differs from country to country, but in complex governments, and especially in democracies with some shared powers, gaining assent can be time-consuming.[49] If the executive lacks a secure governing majority or if the legislature has significant powers of oversight, it can take months. It also opens the agreement and the silent calculus behind it to public scrutiny and time-consuming debate.

For controversial treaties, such as the ones ceding U.S. control over the Panama Canal, ratification can be very slow and painful indeed. * * * Even when agreements are much less contentious, the machinery of ratification can grind slowly.[50] * * *

It is little wonder, then, that governments prefer simpler, more convenient instruments. It is plain, too, that executives prefer instruments that they can control unambiguously, without legislative advice or consent. But there are important domestic constraints, some rooted in constitutional prerogatives, some in legal precedent, and some in the shifting balance of domestic power. To cede control of the Panama Canal, for instance, the President had no choice but to use a treaty. His authority to conduct

[48] Adelman emphasizes the slowness of negotiating formal agreements, especially major agreements with the Soviets. The Limited Test Ban Treaty (1963) took eight years to complete; the Non-Proliferation Treaty (1968) took more than three years; and the SALT I agreement (1972) took more than two years. The SALT II agreement (1979) took seven years and still failed to win Senate ratification. See Kenneth Adelman, "Arms Control With and Without Agreements," *Foreign Affairs* 63 (Winter 1984–85), pp. 240–63.

[49] The slowness and difficulty of ratifying complex agreements and the problems of adapting to meet changing circumstances often lead states to choose less formal mechanisms. The United States and European Community (EC) have made exactly that choice to deal with their conflicts over "competition policy" and antitrust. The two sides "have abandoned the idea of drawing up a special treaty on competition issues," such as mergers and acquisitions, according to the *Financial Times*, "because it would be too complicated, and would involve obtaining the approval of both the U.S. congress and EC member states. Instead, they discussed more flexible arrangements providing for a better exchange of information, regular meetings and discussions on current cases, and a means of settling disputes." See *Financial Times*, 17 January 1991, p. 6.

[50] See "Treaty on Extradition and Mutual Assistance in Criminal Matters Between the United States of America and the Republic of Turkey, with Appendix, Signed June 7, 1979, Entered into Force January 1, 1981," in *United States Treaties and Other International Agreements*, vol. 32, part 3 (Washington, D.C.: Government Printing Office, 1986), pp. 3111 ff.

foreign affairs is broad, but not broad enough to hand over the canal and surrounding territory to Panama without Senate approval.[51] ***

Aside from extradition, which bears directly on the civil rights of accused criminals, the courts rarely affect the form of international agreements. That is true even for U.S. courts, which are normally quite willing to review political decisions. They try to avoid direct involvement in foreign policy issues and hold to this narrow line even when larger constitutional questions arise. They have done little, for instance, to restrict the widespread use of executive agreements, which evade the Senate's constitutional right to give "advice and consent" on formal treaties.[52]

Despite the courts' reluctance to rule on these issues, informal agreements do raise important questions about the organization of state authority for the conduct of foreign affairs. Informal agreements shift power toward the executive and away from the legislature. In recent decades, the U.S. Congress responded by publicly challenging the President's right to make serious international commitments without at least notifying the Senate. It also disputed the President's control over undeclared foreign conflicts by passing the War Powers Resolution.[53]

*   *   *

To summarize, then, informal agreements are often chosen because they allow governments to act quickly and quietly. These two rationales are often intertwined, but each is important in its own right, and each is sufficient for choosing informal means of international cooperation.

Uncertainty and Renegotiation

Informal agreements may also be favored for an entirely different reason: they are more easily renegotiated and less costly to abandon than treaties.

[51] Just what agreements must be submitted as treaties remains ambiguous. It is a constitutional question, of course, but also a question of the political balance of power between the Congress and the President. At one point, President Carter's chief of staff, Hamilton Jordan, announced that Carter would decide whether the Panama Canal agreements were treaties or not. He "could present [the accords] to the Congress as a treaty, or as an agreement, and at the proper time he'll make that decision." Interview on "Face the Nation," CBS News, cited by Loch K. Johnson in *The Making of International Agreements: Congress Confronts the Executive* (New York: New York University Press, 1984), p. 141.

[52] The U.S. Constitution, Article II, Section 2, provides that the President "shall have power, by and with the Advice and Consent of the Senate, to make treaties, provided two-thirds of the Senators present concur." For a detailed study of the constitutional issues, see Louis Henkin, *Foreign Affairs and the Constitution* (Mineola, N.Y.: Foundation Press, 1972).

[53] See the War Powers Resolution, 87 Stat. 555, 1973; and 50 *United States Code* 1541–48, 1980.

This flexibility is useful if there is considerable uncertainty about the distribution of future benefits under a particular agreement. In economic issues, this uncertainty may arise because of a shift in production functions or demand schedules, the use of new raw materials or substitute products, or a fluctuation in macroeconomic conditions or exchange rates. These changes could sabotage national interests in particular international agreements. The consequences might involve an unacceptable surge in imports under existing trade pacts, for example, or the collapse of producer cartels. In security affairs, nations might be uncertain about the rate of technological progress or the potential for new weapons systems. By restricting these innovations, existing arms treaties may create unexpected future costs for one side.[54] Such developments can produce unexpected winners and losers, in either absolute or relative terms, and change the value of existing contractual relations. Put another way, institutional arrangements (including agreements) can magnify or diminish the distributional impact of exogenous shocks or unexpected changes.

States are naturally reluctant to make long-term, inflexible bargains behind this veil of ignorance. Even if one state is committed to upholding an agreement despite possible windfall gains or losses, there is no guarantee that others will do the same. The crucial point is that an agreement might not be self-sustaining if there is an unexpected asymmetry in benefits. Such uncertainties about future benefits, together with the difficulties of self-enforcement, pose serious threats to treaty reliability under conditions of rapid technological change, market volatility, or changing strategic vulnerabilities. The presence of such uncertainties and the dangers they pose for breach of treaty obligations foster the pursuit of substitute arrangements with greater flexibility.

States use several basic techniques to capture the potential gains from cooperation despite the uncertainties. First, they craft agreements (formal or informal) of limited duration so that all participants can calculate their risks and benefits under the agreement with some confidence. Strategic arms treaties of several years' duration are a good example. Second, they include provisions that permit legitimate withdrawal from commitments under specified terms and conditions.[55] In practice, states can *always* abandon their international commitments, since enforcement is so costly and problematic. The real point of such treaty terms, then, is to

---

[54] For one model of how technical innovations could complicate treaty maintenance, see Downs and Rocke, *Tacit Bargaining, Arms Races, and Arms Control,* chap. 5.

[55] David, *The Strategy of Treaty Termination.*

lower the general reputational costs of withdrawal and thereby encourage states to cooperate initially despite the risks and uncertainties. Third, they incorporate provisions that permit partial withdrawal, covering either a temporary period or a limited set of obligations. GATT escape clauses, which permit post hoc protection of endangered industries, are a well-known example.[56] Finally, states sometimes frame their agreements in purely informal terms to permit their frequent adjustment. The quota agreements of the Organization of Petroleum Exporting Countries (OPEC) do exactly that. While the OPEC agreements are critically important to the participants and are central to their economic performance, they are framed informally to permit rapid shifts in response to changing market conditions. Once again, the form of agreements is *not* dictated by their substantive significance.

* * *

At the other end of the spectrum, in terms of formality, lie arms control treaties with detailed limitations on specific weapons systems for relatively long periods. They, too, must confront some important uncertainties. They do so principally by restricting the agreement to verifiable terms and a time frame that essentially excludes new weapons systems. The institutional arrangements are thus tailored to the environment they regulate.

Modern weapons systems require long lead times to build and deploy. As a result, military capacity and technological advantages shift slowly within specific weapons categories. With modern surveillance techniques, these new weapons programs and shifting technological capacities are not opaque to adversaries. The military environment to be regulated is relatively stable, then, so the costs and benefits of treaty restraints can be projected with some confidence over the medium term.

Given these conditions, treaties offer some clear advantages in arms control. They represent detailed public commitments, duly ratified by national political authorities. Although an aggrieved party would still need to identify and punish any alleged breach, the use of treaties raises the political costs of flagrant or deliberate violations (or, for

---

[56] Article XIX of the GATT covers safeguards. It permits the Contracting Parties to offer emergency protection to industries disrupted by imports. See Marco Bronckers, *Selective Safeguard Measures in Multilateral Trade Relations: Issues of Protectionism in GATT, European Community, and United States Law* (Deventer, Netherlands: Kluwer, 1985); and Peter Kleen, "The Safeguard Issue in the Uruguay Round: A Comprehensive Approach," *Journal of World Trade* 25 (October 1989), pp. 73–92.

that matter, unprovoked punishment). It does so by making disputes more salient and accessible and by underscoring the gravity of promises. * * *

Following this logic, most arms control agreements have been set out in treaty form. Whether the subject is nuclear or conventional forces, test bans or weapons ceilings, American and Soviet negotiators always aimed at formal documents with full ratification. Discussions during a summit meeting or a walk in the woods may lay the essential ground-work for an arms agreement, but they are *not* agreements in themselves.[57]

Over the history of superpower arms control, only the tacit obser-vance of SALT II could be classified as a major informal agreement. * * * Perhaps these tacit arrangements and encoded signals were the most that could be salvaged from the failed treaty.

SALT II, in its informal guise, actually survived beyond the expira-tion date of the proposed treaty. Like most arms control agreements, it had been written with a limited life span so that it applied in predictable ways to existing weaponry, not to new and unforeseen developments. Time limits like these are used to manage risks in a wide range of interna-tional agreements.[58] They are especially important in cases of superpower arms control, in which the desirability of specific agreements is related both to particular weaponry and to the overall strategic balance. As the military setting changes, existing commitments become more or less de-sirable. Arms control agreements must cope with these fluctuating bene-fits over the life of the agreement.

The idea is to forge agreements that provide sufficient benefits to each side, when evaluated at each point during the life of the agreement, so that each will choose to comply out of self-interest in order to perpetuate the treaty.[59] This self-generated compliance is crucial in superpower arms

---

[57] Note, however, that if the discussions pertained to domestic bargains, a court might interpret these "agreements in principle" as contractually binding, depending on the level of detail and the promissory language. Once again, the absence of effective international courts matters.

[58] Bilder, *Managing the Risks of International Agreement,* pp. 49–51.

[59] Raymond Vernon, writing on foreign investments, has shown the dangers of violating this approach. Even if an agreement provides significant benefits to both sides, it may provide those benefits to one side immediately and to the other much later. Such agreements are vulnerable to noncompliance in midstream, after one side has already received its benefits. This is one element of Vernon's "obsolescing bargain." It is a variant of Hobbes's critique of covenants, in which one side performs its side of the bargain first. See Raymond Vernon, *Sovereignty at Bay: The Multinational Spread of U.S. Enterprises* (New York: Basic Books, 1971). On the general logic of self-sustaining agreements, see Telser, "A Theory of Self-Enforcing Agreements," pp. 27–44.

control. Given the relative equality of power, U.S.–Soviet military agreements are not so much enforced as observed voluntarily. What sustains
them is each participant's perception that they are valuable and that
cheating would prove too costly if it were matched by the other side or
if it caused the agreement to collapse altogether. To ensure that treaties
remain valuable over their entire life span, negotiators typically try to
restrict them to known weaponry and stockpiles. That translates into
fixed expiration dates.[60]

When agreements stretch beyond this finite horizon, signatories may
be tempted to defect as they develop new and unforeseen advantages
or become more vulnerable to surprise defection, issues that were not
fully anticipated when the agreement was made. The preference orderings that once supported cooperation may no longer hold. * * *

* * *

All of these issues refer to the detailed regulation of slow-changing
strategic environments. Although the issues are crucial to national defense, they are not so sensitive diplomatically that the agreement itself
must be hidden from view. Cooperative arrangements in such issues, according to the arguments presented here, are likely to be in treaty form.

HIDDEN AGREEMENTS

When security issues must be resolved quickly or quietly to avoid serious
conflict, then less formal instruments will be chosen. If the terms are
especially sensitive, perhaps because they would humiliate one party or
convey unacceptable precedents, then the agreement itself may be hidden
from view.[61] The most dangerous crisis of the nuclear era, the Cuban missile crisis, was settled by the most informal and secret exchanges between
the superpowers. The overriding aim was to defuse the immediate threat.
That meant rapid agreement on a few crucial issues, with implementation
to follow quickly. These informal exchanges were not the prelude to
agreement, as in SALT or ABM negotiations; they *were* the agreement.

The deal to remove missiles from Cuba was crafted through an
exchange of latters, supplemented by secret oral promises. During the

---

[60] This allows negotiators to make reasonable calculations about the various parties' *ex
post* incentives to defect during the life of the agreement.

[61] In modern international politics, these hidden agreements are informal because ratification is public and the treaties are registered with the United Nations. In earlier international systems, however, neither condition applied and secret treaties were possible.

crisis, the Soviets had put forward a number of inconsistent proposals for settlement. President Kennedy responded to the most conciliatory: Premier Khrushchev's latter of 26 October 1962. The next day, Kennedy accepted its basic terms and set a quick deadline for Soviet counter-acceptance. The essence of the bargain was that the Soviets would remove all missiles from Cuba in return for America's pledge not to invade the island. The terms were a clear U.S. victory. They completely overturned the Soviet policy of putting nuclear missiles in the Western Hemisphere. The Soviets got nothing publicly. They were humiliated.

U.S. acceptance of the bargain was set out in diplomatic messages sent directly to Khrushchev. President Kennedy also sent his brother Robert to speak with Soviet Ambassador Anatoly Dobrynin, to convey U.S. acceptance and to add several points that were too sensitive to include in any documentation, however informal.[62] * * *

* * *

The bargains that ended the Cuban missile crisis were all informal, but their motives and their degree of informality differed. The key decisions to remove missiles from Cuba in exchange for a pledge of noninvasion were informal because of time pressure. They were embodied in an exchange of messages, rather than in a single signed document, but at least the key points were in writing. The removal of outdated Turkish and Italian missiles was also part of the overall bargain – an essential part, according to some participants – but it was couched in even more informal terms because of political sensitivity. The sensitivity in this case was America's concern with its image as a great power and, to a lesser extent, with its role in NATO. This kind of concern with external images is one reason why informal agreements are used for politically sensitive bargains: they can be hidden.

Once again, there are costs to be considered. If a hidden agreement is exposed, its presence could well suggest deception – to the public, to allies, and to other government agencies. Even if the agreement does stay hidden, its secrecy imperils its reliability. Hidden agreements carry little information about the depth of the signatories' commitments, poorly bind successor governments, and fail to signal intentions to third parties. These costs are clearly exemplified in the secret treaties between Britain and France before World War I. They could do nothing to deter Germany, which did not know about them. Moreover, they permitted the signatories

---

[62] Raymond L. Garthoff, *Reflections on the Cuban Missile Crisis*, revised ed. (Washington, D.C.: Brookings Institution, 1989), pp. 86–87.

to develop markedly different conceptions about their implied commitments as allies.[63]

Hidden agreements carry another potential cost. They may not be well understood inside a signatory's own government. On the one hand, this low profile may be a valuable tool of bureaucratic or executive control, excluding other agencies from direct participation in making or implementing international agreements. On the other hand, the ignorance of the excluded actors may well prove costly if their actions must later be coordinated as part of the agreement. When that happens, hidden agreements can become a comedy of errors.

One example is the postwar American effort to restrict exports to the Soviet bloc. To succeed, the embargo needed European support. With considerable reluctance, West European governments finally agreed to help, but they demanded secrecy because the embargo was so unpopular at home. As a result, the U.S. Congress never knew that the Europeans were actually cooperating with the American effort.[64] In confused belligerence, the Congress actually passed a law to cut off foreign aid to Europe if the allies did not aid in the embargo.[65]

This weak signaling function has another significant implication: it limits the value of informal agreements as diplomatic precedents, even if the agreements themselves are public. This limitation has two sources. First, informal agreements are generally less visible and prominent, and so they are less readily available as models. Second, treaties are considered better evidence of deliberate state practice, according to diplomatic convention and international law. Public, formal agreements are

---

[63] In 1906, the British Foreign Minister, Sir Edward Grey, discussed the dilemmas posed by these expectations. The entente agreements, signed by a previous British government, "created in France a belief that we shall support [the French] in war. . . . If this expectation is disappointed, the French will never forgive us. There would also I think be a general feeling that we had behaved badly and left France in the lurch. . . . On the other hand the prospect of a European war and of our being involved in it is horrible." See document no. 299, in G. P. Gooch and Harold Temperley, eds., *British Documents on the Origin of the War, 1898–1914*, vol. 3 (London: His Majesty's Stationery Office, 1928), p. 266.

[64] Although the State Department did try to persuade Congress that Western Europe was aiding the embargo, its efforts were in vain. Quiet reassurances from the State Department were distrusted by a hard-line, anticommunist Congress, which saw them as self-serving maneuvers to preserve diplomatic ties. See Michael Mastanduno, "Trade as a Strategic Weapon: American and Alliance Export Control Policy in the Early Postwar Period," in G. John Ikenberry, David A. Lake, and Michael Mastanduno, eds., *The State and American Foreign Economic Policy* (Ithaca, N.Y.: Cornell University Press, 1988), p. 136.

[65] See Mutual Defense Assistance Control Act of 1951 ("Battle Act"), 82d Congress, 1st sess., 65 Stat. 644.

conventionally understood as contributing to diplomatic precedent. Precisely for that reason informal agreements are less useful as precedents and more useful when states want to limit any broader, adverse implications of specific bargains. They frame an agreement in more circumscribed ways than a treaty. Discussions between long-time adversaries, for instance, usually begin on an informal, low-level basis to avoid any implicit recognition of wider claims. Trade relations may also be conducted indirectly, using third-party entrepôts, to avoid any formal contract relationships between estranged governments.

* * *

*** In this case and in many others, informal agreements are useful because they facilitate cooperation on specific issues while constraining any wider implications regarding other issues or third parties. They permit bounded cooperation.[66]

THE STATUS OF TACIT AGREEMENTS

We have concentrated, until now, on informal bargains that are openly expressed, at least among the participants themselves. The form may be written or oral, detailed or general, but there is some kind of explicit bargain.

Tacit agreements, on the other hand, are not explicit. They are implied, understood, or inferred rather than directly stated.[67] Such implicit arrangements extend the scope of informal cooperation. They go beyond the secrecy of oral agreements and, at times, may be the only way to avoid serious conflict on sensitive issues. Such bargains, however, are all too often mirages, carrying the superficial appearance of agreement but not its substance.

The unspoken "rules" of the Cold War are sometimes considered tacit agreements.[68] The superpowers staked out their respective spheres of

---

[66] Because informal extradition arrangements are ad hoc, they are easily severed. That is a mixed blessing. It means that extradition issues are directly implicated in the larger issues of bilateral diplomacy. They cannot be treated as distinct, technical issues covered by their own treaty rules. For example, the bloody suppression of popular uprisings in 1989 in the People's Republic of China blocked prisoner exchanges and made trade and investment ties politically riskier.

[67] This definition is based on the second meaning of "tacit" in *The Oxford English Dictionary*, 2d ed., vol. 17 (Oxford: Clarendon Press, 1989), p. 527.

[68] See Keal, *Unspoken Rules and Superpower Dominance*; and Friedrich Kratochwil, *Rules, Norms and Decisions* (Cambridge: Cambridge University Press, 1989), chap. 3.

influence and did not directly engage each other's forces. Yet they made no explicit agreements on either point. In the early years of the Cold War, the United States quietly conceded de facto control over Eastern Europe to the Soviets. The policies that laid the basis for NATO were designed to contain the Soviet Union, both diplomatically and militarily, but nothing more. They made no effort to roll back the Soviet army's wartime gains, which had been converted into harsh political dominion in the late 1940s. America's restraint amounted to a spheres-of-influence policy without actually acknowledging Moscow's regional security interests. This silence only confirmed the Soviets' worst fears and contributed to bipolar hostilities.

In the bitter climate of the early Cold War period, however, no U.S. official was prepared to concede the Soviets' dominance in Eastern Europe. Earlier conferences at Yalta and Potsdam had seemed to do so, but now these concessions were pushed aside, at least rhetorically.[69] While Democrats reinterpreted these agreements or considered them irrelevant because of Soviet violations, Republicans denounced them as immoral or even treasonous.[70] Backed by these domestic sentiments, U.S. foreign policy was couched in the language of universal freedoms, conceding nothing to the Soviets in Eastern Europe.[71] In practice, however, the United States tacitly accepted Soviet control up to the borders of West Germany.

How does tacit acceptance of this kind compare with the informal but explicit bargains we have been considering? They are quite different in principle, I think. The most fundamental problem in analyzing so-called

[69] A few international lawyers argued that the Yalta and Potsdam agreements were binding treaty commitments. The U.S. State Department did publish the Yalta Agreement in the *Executive Agreements Series* (no. 498) and in *U.S. Treaties in Force* (1963). In 1948, Sir Hersch Lauterpacht said that they "incorporated definite rules of conduct which may be regarded as legally binding on the States in question." The British and American governments explicitly rejected that view. In 1956, in an aide-mémoire to the Japanese government, the State Department declared that "the United States regards the so-called Yalta Agreement as simply a statement of common purposes by the heads of the participating governments and . . . not as of any legal effect in transferring territories." See *Department of State Bulletin*, vol. 35, 1956, p. 484, cited by Schachter in "The Twilight Existence of Nonbinding International Agreements," p. 298 n. See also L. P. L. Oppenheim, *Peace*, vol. 1 of H. Lauterpacht, ed., *International Law: A Treatise*, 7th ed. (London: Longmans, Green, 1948), p. 788, section 487.

[70] The one major exception among U.S. politicians was former vice president Henry Wallace, representing the left wing of the Democratic party. Wallace openly stated that the Soviets had legitimate security interests in Eastern Europe and should not be challenged directly there. His views were widely denounced in both parties and won few votes.

[71] Arthur M. Schlesinger, Jr., "Origins of the Cold War," *Foreign Affairs* 46 (Autumn 1967), pp. 22–52.

tacit bargains lies in determining whether any real agreement exists. More broadly, is there some kind of mutual policy adjustment that is (implicitly) contingent on reciprocity? If so, what are the parties' commitments, as they understand them? Often, what pass for tacit bargains are actually policies that have been chosen unilaterally and independently, in light of the unilateral policies of others. There may be an "understanding" of other parties' policies but no implicit agreements to adjust these policies on a mutual or contingent basis. Each party is simply maximizing its own values, subject to the independent choices made or expected to be made by others. What looks like a silent bargain may simply be a Nash equilibrium.

This is not to say that tacit bargains are always a chimera. Each party can adjust its policies on a provisional basis, awaiting some conforming adjustment by others. *** The problem, as George Downs and David Rocke have shown, is that states may not always know when others are cooperating or defecting and may not know what their intentions are.[72] One state may then punish others for noncompliance or defections that are more apparent than real and thus begin a downward spiral of retaliation. Such imperfect knowledge does not prevent tacit cooperation, but it does suggest serious impediments and risks to tacit bargaining, the need for more "fault tolerant" strategies, and the potential gains from more explicit communication and greater transparency.

In ongoing diplomatic interactions in which each side continually responds to the other's policies and initiatives, it may also be difficult to distinguish between tacit bargains and unilateral acts. One side may consider its own restraint part of an implicit bargain, while the other considers it nothing more than prudent self-interest. In the early Cold War, for instance, the United States could do nothing to reverse Soviet control in Eastern Europe without waging war. There was little to be gained by providing substantial aid to local resistance movements. Their chances for success were slim, and the dangers of escalation were significant. Any U.S. efforts to destabilize Soviet control in Eastern Europe would have markedly increased international tensions and raised the dangers of U.S.–Soviet conflict in central Europe. Under the circumstances, American policy was restrained. More aggressive action in Eastern Europe was deterred by the risks and poor chances of success, not by the implied promise of some reciprocal restraint by the Soviets. There was a learning process but no tacit bargain.

[72] See the following works by Downs and Rocke: "Tacit Bargaining and Arms Control"; and *Tacit Bargaining, Arms Races, and Arms Control.*

In any case, most tacit bargains are hard to identify with confidence. By their very nature, implicit agreements leave little trace. Moreover, what may appear to be implicit agreements are often explicable as outcomes of more narrowly self-interested unilateral policies. Given these difficulties, one valuable approach to uncovering tacit bargains is to examine the reactions and discourse surrounding possible "violations." Tacit bargains, like their more explicit counterparts, are based on the reciprocal exchange of benefits. Breaking the terms of that exchange is likely to be given voice. There will be talk of betrayal and recriminations, words of regret at having extended generous but uncompensated concessions. There ought to be some distinctive recognition that reasonable expectations and inferences, built up during the course of joint interactions, have been breached. Thus, there is regret and not merely surprise.[73]

*   *   *

The dangers of misunderstanding are certainly not unique to tacit agreements. They lurk in all contracts, even the most formal and detailed. But the process of negotiating written agreements does offer a chance to clarify understandings, to agree on joint interpretations, to draft detailed, restrictive language, and to establish mechanisms for ongoing consultation, such as the U.S.–Soviet Standing Consultative Commission. Tacit agreements, by definition, lack these procedures, lack this detail, and lack any explicit understandings.

These limitations in tacit agreements are not always a drawback. If the agreement covers only a few basic points, if the parties clearly understand the provisions in the same way, and if there are no individual incentives to betray or distort the terms, then some key defects of tacit bargains are irrelevant. Some coordination problems fit this description. They involve tacit agreement among multiple participants who cannot communicate directly with one another.[74]

Unfortunately, the hard issues of international politics are different. They involve complicated questions without salient solutions, where national interests are less than congruent. Any commitments to cooperate need to be specified in some detail.[75] The agreements themselves are not

---

[73] In *The Cement of Society*, Elster makes this distinction between regret and surprise and relates it to two forms of order. Departures from regularized, predictable behavior give rise to surprise. Unreciprocated cooperation produces regret.

[74] Edna Ullmann-Margalit, *The Emergence of Norms* (Oxford: Clarendon Press, 1977).

[75] This does not rule out deliberate vagueness on some issues as part of a larger, more detailed settlement. Cooperation is not comprehensive, and some issues have to be finessed if any agreement is to be reached.

so simply self-sustaining. If cooperation is to be achieved, the terms must be crafted deliberately to minimize the risks of misunderstanding and noncompliance.

CHOOSING BETWEEN TREATIES AND INFORMAL AGREEMENTS

Because tacit bargains are so limited, states are reluctant to depend on them when undertaking important projects. They want some clear, written signal that an agreement has been reached and includes specific terms. When a state's choice of policies is contingent on the choices of others, it will prefer to spell out these respective choices and the commitments they entail and will want to improve information flows among interdependent actors. These requirements can be met by either a formal treaty or an informal agreement, each with its own generic strengths and weaknesses. Each is more or less suited to resolving specific kinds of international bargaining problems.

These differences mean that actors must choose between them for specific agreements. However, they may also complement each other as elements of more inclusive bargains. The treaty commitments that define NATO, for instance, are given their military and diplomatic significance by a stream of informal summit declarations that address contemporary alliance issues such as weapons modernization, arms control, and Soviet policy initiatives.

Informal agreements, as I have noted, are themselves quite varied, ranging from simple oral commitments to joint summit declarations to elaborate latters of intent, such as stabilization agreements with the International Monetary Fund (IMF). Some of the most elaborate are quite similar to treaties but with two crucial exceptions. The diplomatic status of the promises is less clear-cut, and the agreements typically do not require elaborate ratification procedures. They lack, to a greater or lesser extent, the state's fullest and most authoritative imprimatur. The effects on reputation are thus constrained, but so is the dependability of the agreement.

States equivocate, in principle, on their adherence to these informal bargains. They are often unwilling to grant them the status of legally binding agreements. But what does that mean in practice, given that *no* international agreements can bind their signatories like domestic contracts can? The argument presented here is that treaties send a conventional signal to other signatories and to third parties concerning the *gravity* and *irreversibility* of a state's commitments. By putting reputation at stake, they add to the costs of breaking agreements or, rather, they do so if a signatory values reputation. Informal agreements are typically more elusive on these counts.

These escape hatches are the common denominators of informal agreements, from the most elaborate written documents to the sketchiest oral agreements. The Helsinki Final Act, with its prominent commitments on human rights, is otherwise virtually identical to a treaty. It includes sixty pages of detailed provisions, only to declare that it should not be considered a treaty with binding commitments.[76] At the other extreme are oral bargains, which are the most secret, the most malleable, and the quickest to conclude. Like their more elaborate counterparts, they are a kind of moral and legal oxymoron: an equivocal promise.

The speed and simplicity of oral bargains make them particularly suited for clandestine deals and crisis resolution. But for obvious reasons, states are reluctant to depend on them more generally. Oral agreements can encompass only a few major points of agreement; they cannot set out complicated obligations in any detail. They are unreliable in several distinct ways. First, it is difficult to tell whether they have been officially authorized and whether the government as a whole is committed to them. Second, they usually lack the visibility and public commitment that support compliance. Third, to ensure implementation in complex bureaucratic states, oral agreements must be translated into written directives at some point.[77] Sincere mistakes, omissions, and misunderstandings may creep in during this translation process with no opportunity to correct

[76] The Helsinki Final Act, formally known as the Final Act of the Conference on Security and Cooperation in Europe, was concluded in 1975 and signed by thirty-five states. On the one hand, the states declared their "determination to act in accordance with the provisions contained" in the text. On the other hand, these were not to be the binding commitments of a treaty. The text plainly said that it was not eligible for registration with the United Nations, as a treaty would be. Several democratic states, led by the United States, declared at the time that this document was not a treaty. "There does not appear to be any evidence that the other signatory states disagreed with this understanding," according to Schachter. The result is a curious contradiction: a nonbinding bargain. It juxtaposes elaborate "commitments" with a claim that they are not to be registered, as a treaty would be. The point, clearly, is to exempt the provisions from the legally binding status of treaty commitments. For an interesting analysis of the Helsinki agreement and its ambiguous status in international law, see Schachter, "The Twilight Existence of Nonbinding International Agreements," p. 296. The text of the Helsinki Final Act can be found in *International Legal Materials*, vol. 14, 1975, pp. 1293 ff.

[77] This translation of oral agreements into writing is required by the U.S. State Department's regulations implementing the Case Act. See "International Agreement Regulations," 22 *Code of Federal Regulations*, part 181; and 46 *Federal Register*, 13 July 1981, pp. 35917 ff.

them before an interstate dispute emerges. Last, but most important of all, it is easier to disclaim oral bargains or to recast them on favorable terms. Nobody ever lost an argument in the retelling, and oral bargains have many of the same properties. Perhaps this is what Sam Goldwyn had in mind when he said that verbal contracts were not worth the paper they were written on.[78]

Putting informal agreements into writing avoids most of these problems. It generally produces evidence of an intended bargain. What it still lacks is the depth of national commitment associated with treaties. That is the irreducible price of maintaining policy flexibility.

Informal agreements are also less public than treaties, in two ways. First, because states do not acknowledge them as fundamental, self-binding commitments, they are less convincing evidence of recognized state practices. They are thus less significant as precedents. For example, informal agreements on trade or extradition are no proof of implicit diplomatic recognition, as a formal treaty would be. These limitations mean that informal agreements are more easily restricted to a particular issue. They have fewer ramifications for collateral issues or third parties. They permit cooperation to be circumscribed. Second, informal agreements are more easily kept secret, if need be. There is no requirement to ratify them or to enact them into domestic law, and there is no need to register them with international organizations for publication. For highly sensitive bargains, such as the use of noncombatants' territory in guerrilla wars, that is a crucial attribute.[79]

Treaties, too, can be kept secret. There is no inherent reason why they must be made public. Indeed, secret treaties were a central instrument of

---

[78] There is a nice irony here. Goldwyn's disparaging comments about oral agreements are themselves probably apocryphal. He regularly mangled the English language, and quotes like this were often attributed to him, whether he said them or not. The murky origins of this quotation underscore a fundamental problem with oral bargains. How can third parties ever ascertain who really promised what to whom? Goldwyn himself gave one answer to that question: "Two words: im possible." See Carol Easton, *The Search for Sam Goldwyn* (New York: William Morrow, 1976), pp. 150–51; and Arthur Marx, *Goldwyn: A Biography of the Man Behind the Myth* (New York: Norton, 1976), pp. 8–10.

[79] States on the borders of a guerrilla war are vital allies to the protagonists. They offer a secure launching pad for military operations and a secure site for communications and resupply. If their role becomes too open and prominent, however, the bordering states could be brought directly into the fighting as protagonists themselves. This is clearly a delicate relationship. It is best managed by informal agreements, usually secret ones, such as those reached by the United States and Laos during the Vietnam War. See Johnson, *The Making of International Agreements*, p. 68.

balance-of-power diplomacy in the eighteenth and nineteenth centuries.[80] But there are powerful reasons why secret treaties are rare today. The first and most fundamental is the rise of democratic states with principles of public accountability and some powers of legislative oversight. Secret treaties are difficult to reconcile with these democratic procedures. The second reason is that ever since the United States entered World War I, it has opposed secret agreements as a matter of basic principle and has enshrined its position in the peace settlements of both world wars.

The decline of centralized foreign policy institutions, which worked closely with a handful of political leaders, sharply limits the uses of secret treaties. Foreign ministries no longer hold the same powers to commit states to alliances, to shift those alliances, to divide conquered territory, and to hide such critical commitments from public view. The discretionary powers of a Bismarck or Metternich have no equivalent in modern Western states. Instead, democratic leaders rely on informal instruments to strike international bargains in spite of domestic institutional restraints. That is precisely the objection raised by the U.S. Congress regarding war powers and executive agreements.

When leaders are freed from such institutional restraints, they can hide their bargains without making them informal. They can simply use secret treaties and protocols, as Stalin and Hitler did in August 1939 when they carved up Eastern Europe.[81] * * *

Aside from these protocols, secret pacts have rarely been used for important interstate projects since World War I. That partly reflects the

---

[80] The importance of secret treaties in European diplomacy was underscored when Woodrow Wilson tried to abolish the practice after World War I. Clemenceau and Lloyd George "said emphatically that they could not agree never to make a private or secret diplomatic agreement of any kind. Such understandings were the foundation of European diplomacy, and everyone knew that to abandon secret negotiations would be to invite chaos. To this [Colonel] House replied . . . that there was no intention to prohibit confidential talks on delicate matters, but only to require that treaties resulting from such conversations should become 'part of the public law of the world.'" Quoted by Arthur Walworth in *America's Moment: 1918 – American Diplomacy at the End of World War I* (New York: Norton, 1977), p. 56.

[81] See "Treaty of Non-Aggression Between Germany and the Union of Soviet Socialist Republics, August 23, 1939, Signed by Ribbentrop and Molotov," document no. 228 in United Kingdom, Foreign Office, *The Last Days of Peace, August 9 – September 3, 1939*, series D, vol. 7 of *Documents on German Foreign Policy, 1918–1945* (London: Her Majesty's Stationery Office, 1956), pp. 245–46. The volume provides official translations of documents from captured archives of the German Foreign Ministry and the Reich Chancellery.

war experience itself and partly reflects America's rise to global prominence. While the war was still being fought, Leon Trotsky had published the czarist government's secret treaties. They showed how Italy had been enticed into the war (through the London treaty) and revealed that Russia had been promised control of Constantinople. The Allies were embarrassed by the publication of these self-seeking agreements and were forced to proclaim the larger principles for which their citizens were fighting and dying.[82]

Woodrow Wilson had always wanted such a statement of intent. He argued that this was a war about big issues and grand ideals, not about narrow self-interest or territorial aggrandizement. He dissociated the United States from the Allies' earlier secret commitments and sought to abolish them forever once the war had been won. At the Versailles peace conference, where Wilson stated his Fourteen Points to guide the negotiations, he began with a commitment to "open covenants . . . openly arrived at." He would simply eliminate "private international understandings of any kind [so that] diplomacy shall proceed always frankly and in the public view."[83]

These Wilsonian ideals were embodied in Article 18 of the League of Nations Covenant and later in Article 102 of the United Nations (UN) Charter. They provided a means for registering international agreements and, in the case of the UN, an incentive to do so. Only registered agreements could be accorded legal status before any UN affiliate, including the International Court of Justice. This mixture of legalism and idealism could never abolish private understandings, but it did virtually eliminate secret treaties among democratic states. Informal agreements live on as their closest modern substitutes.

---

[82] Trotsky's release of the secret documents was shrewd and effective. There was a strong, sustained reaction against secret diplomacy, mainly in the Anglo-Saxon countries. Wilson himself was politically embarrassed. Either his wartime allies had not told him of their earlier bargains or they had told him and he had kept the secret, despite his principled attacks on secret diplomacy. See Mario Toscano, *An Introduction to the History of Treaties and International Politics,* vol. 1 of *The History of Treaties and International Politics* (Baltimore, Md.: Johns Hopkins University Press, 1966), pp. 42 and 215; and James Joll, *Europe Since 1870,* 2d ed. (Harmondsworth, UK: Penguin Books, 1976), p. 233.

[83] Wilson's war aims were stated to a joint session of Congress on 8 January 1918. When European leaders later challenged this commitment to open covenants, Wilson announced that he would never compromise the "essentially American terms in the program," including Point One. See Edward M. House, *The Intimate Papers of Colonel House,* vol. 4, ed. by Charles Seymour (London: Ernest Benn, 1928), pp. 182–83.

CONCLUSION: INTERNATIONAL COOPERATION
BY INFORMAL AGREEMENT

The varied uses of informal agreements illuminate the possibilities of international cooperation and some recurrent limitations. They underscore the fact that cooperation is often circumscribed and that its very limits may be fundamental to the participants. Their aim is often to restrict the scope and duration of agreements and to avoid any generalization of their implications. The ends are often particularistic, the means ad hoc. Informal bargains are delimited from the outset. More often than not, there is no intention (and no realistic possibility) of extending them to wider issues, other actors, longer time periods, or more formal obligations. They are simply not the beginning of a more inclusive process of cooperation or a more durable one.

These constraints shape the form that agreements can take. Interstate bargains are frequently designed to be hidden from domestic constituencies, to avoid legislative ratification, to escape the attention of other states, or to be renegotiated. They may well be conceived with no view and no aspirations about the longer term. They are simply transitory arrangements, valuable now but ready to be abandoned or reordered as circumstances change. The diplomatic consequences and reputational effects are minimized by using informal agreements rather than treaties. Informal agreements may also be chosen because of time pressures. To resolve a crisis, the agreement may have to be struck quickly and definitively, with no time for elaborate documents.

Because informal agreements can accommodate these restrictions, they are common tools for international cooperation. States use them, and use them frequently, to pursue national goals by international agreement. They are flexible, and they are commonplace. They constitute, as Judge Richard Baxter once remarked, a "vast substructure of intergovernmental paper."[84] Their presence testifies to the perennial efforts to achieve international cooperation and to its institutional variety. Their form testifies silently to its limits.

---

[84] Baxter, "International Law in 'Her Infinite Variety,'" p. 549.

14

The Politics of Dispute Settlement Design: Explaining Legalism in Regional Trade Pacts

James McCall Smith

In recent years two parallel trends have emerged in the organization of international trade. The first development is the rise of regionalism, with a host of new integration initiatives drawn along geographical lines. * * * The second is a distinct but less widespread move toward legalism in the enforcement of trade agreements. To an unusual extent trading states have delegated to impartial third parties the authority to review and issue binding rulings on alleged treaty violations, at times based on complaints filed by nonstate or supranational actors. Separately, the two trends have garnered scholarly attention * * *. The intersection of these two trends, however, remains little examined.

Few comparative studies of institutional form, across different trade accords, have been undertaken. This is curious, for regional trade pacts exhibit considerable variation in governance structures. Moreover, questions of institutional design – which constitute a dimension of bargaining distinct from the substantive terms of liberalization – have proven contentious in recent trade negotiations, underscoring their political salience.[1] The creation of supranational institutions in regional trade accords has direct implications for academic debates regarding sovereignty,

---

[1] Mexico threatened to walk away from the North American Free Trade Agreement (NAFTA) over the inclusion of sanctions in the side accords. See *International Trade Reporter*, 18 August 1993, 1352. Canada risked its 1988 pact with the United States through its insistence on "binding" dispute settlement. See Hart 1994, 260–63, 301–302.

For helpful comments I would like to thank the editors of *IO*, three anonymous reviewers, John Barton, Martha Finnemore, James Foster, Geoffrey Garrett, Kurt Gaubatz, Judith Goldstein, Miles Kahler, Stephen Krasner, Derek Scissors, Susan Sell, Lee Sigelman, Paul Wahlbeck, and Beth Yarbrough.

globalization, and interdependence. Nevertheless, research on this particular issue remains scarce. * * *

Addressing this gap, I focus on a specific aspect of governance in international trade: the design of dispute settlement procedures. In particular, I investigate the conditions under which member states adopt legalistic mechanisms for resolving disputes and enforcing compliance in regional trade accords. Some pacts are diplomatic, requiring only consultations between disputing states, but others invest standing judicial tribunals with the authority to issue prompt, impartial, and enforceable third-party rulings on any and all alleged treaty violations. To account for these variable levels of legalism, I offer a theory of trade dispute settlement design based on the domestic political trade-off between treaty compliance and policy discretion. The chief implication of this theory highlights the importance of economic asymmetry, in interaction with the proposed depth of integration, as a robust predictor of dispute settlement design. This framework helps explain otherwise puzzling delegations of authority by sovereign states to supranational judiciaries, linking variation in institutional design to domestic political factors conventionally ignored by traditional systemic theories of international relations. * * *

At issue in this study is the nature of *ex ante* institutional design, not the record of *ex post* state behavior. During trade negotiations, governments stand, in part, behind a veil of ignorance with regard to future implementation of the treaty and future disputes. The question I investigate involves the type of dispute settlement mechanism, given this uncertainty, the signatory states agree to establish. In advance of actual integration, it is difficult to distinguish sincere commitments from symbolic ones. Even the most successful regional initiative, the European Union, has weathered crises of confidence in its uneven movement toward a single market.[2] Without evaluating the extent to which integration has proceeded, I seek to explain the design of the institutions within which that process unfolds. I examine the institutional structure of the general game, not the outcome of specific disputes, which depend on strategic interactions and highly contextual international and domestic political variables. * * *

Nevertheless, I do assert that legalism tends to improve compliance by increasing the costs of opportunism. Legalistic mechanisms alter the cost-benefit calculus of cheating by increasing the probability of detection, resolving conflicts of interpretation, and endorsing commensurate

[2] Tsoukalis 1993, 14–45.

sanctions or making rulings directly applicable in domestic law. [Even] the most legalistic of mechanisms may not guarantee treaty compliance by sovereign states willing to defy its rulings. * Likewise, the least legalistic of pacts may give rise to highly successful integration. * Legalism is thus neither a necessary nor a sufficient condition for full compliance, but it does influence compliance by providing rulings of violation that are viewed as credible and legitimate by the community of member states. This information at a minimum increases the reputational costs of noncompliance, potentially jeopardizing opportunities for future international cooperation on issues of relevance to the domestic economy.[3]

In the first section I introduce the dependent variable, levels of legalism, by identifying specific institutional features that render one dispute settlement mechanism more or less legalistic than another. Next I sketch the elements of a theory of dispute settlement design, defining the basic trade-off and how it varies. Subsequent sections delimit the data set of regional trade agreements, summarize the principal characteristics of their dispute settlement mechanisms, and evaluate the explanatory leverage of my analytical framework ***.

DEFINING THE SPECTRUM: FROM DIPLOMACY TO LEGALISM

Discussions of dispute settlement in international and comparative law texts present the universe of institutional options as a standard set that ranges from direct negotiation at one extreme to third-party adjudication at the other.[4] Which features of institutional design determine the level of legalism along this spectrum? The first question is whether there is an explicit right to third-party review of complaints regarding treaty application and interpretation. A handful of agreements provide only for consultations and perhaps mediation or conciliation, which implies a very low level of legalism in that the disputing parties retain the right to reject any proposed settlement lawfully – the hallmark of a diplomatic system.[5] These pacts are identical in effect to treaties that offer an arbitral process but require explicit consent from all parties to the dispute, including the defendant, before the arbitration proceeds [– and to treaties where member countries that are not directly involved in the dispute control access to the arbitration process.] ***

---

[3] Maggi 1996.
[4] See Malanczuk 1997, 273–305; Merrills 1991; and Shapiro 1981.
[5] Diverse examples include the 1969 Southern African Customs Union; the 1983 ANZCERTA; and the 1992 Central European Free Trade Agreement.

Where there is an automatic right to third-party review, the second issue concerns the status in international law of rulings that result from the dispute settlement process. The question is whether arbitral or judicial rulings and reports are formally binding in international legal terms. *** If the disputants can lawfully ignore panel recommendations or sabotage panel reports by lobbying political allies, the system is less legalistic than mechanisms whose third-party rulings directly and irreversibly create an international legal obligation.

The next question concerns third parties – in particular, the number, term, and method of selecting arbitrators or judges in each treaty. At the diplomatic end of the spectrum are mechanisms that call for the appointment of ad hoc arbitrators to address a particular dispute. *** At the legalistic end are treaties that create a standing tribunal of justices who rule collectively on any and all disputes during extended terms of service. Even in the absence of explicit stare decisis, decisions made by a standing tribunal are likely to be more consistent over time – and thus more legalistic – than rulings by ad hoc panels whose membership changes with each dispute. [Most] agreements lie between these two poles. What varies is the extent to which disputants are able to angle strategically for sympathetic or biased judges. With a standing tribunal, the parties have little if any influence over the composition of the court after its initial establishment. With arbitrators selected ad hoc by the disputants, however, each party may be free to name nearly half the panel. Some arbitration mechanisms include innovative procedures that help enhance the impartiality of the panel ***.

A fourth question is which actors have standing to file complaints and obtain rulings. The tradition in international law has long been that only sovereign states have full international legal personality, according states an almost exclusive right to conclude international agreements and to bring claims regarding treaty violations. Most trade accords reflect this tradition by allowing only member states to initiate disputes. In some instances, however, standing is defined more expansively to allow treaty organizations – such as a secretariat or commission, which may have a bureaucratic interest in the treaty's effective implementation – to file official complaints against member countries for some failure to comply.[6] In other agreements even private individuals or firms, whose economic interests are most directly at stake in the context of trade policy, have

---

[6] In the Andean Pact, the Junta – a panel of three technocrats who administer the treaty – has standing to file complaints of noncompliance against member states. The European Union Commission enjoys similar powers.

standing to file complaints and require a ruling. *** Where individuals have standing, they can bring cases in one of two ways: directly, by filing a complaint with the tribunal; or indirectly, by requesting a domestic court to seek a preliminary ruling from the tribunal on any issue of relevance to the treaty. *** In general, the more expansive the definition of standing, the more legalistic the dispute settlement mechanism. When treaty organizations and private parties can file complaints, alleged violations are likely to be more frequent than if standing is accorded only to states, whose multiple diplomatic considerations make them reluctant to pursue certain cases.

Finally, there is the question of remedies in cases of treaty violation. The most legalistic alternative is to give direct effect in domestic law to dispute settlement rulings made at the international level.[7] Where rulings are directly applicable, government agencies and courts have a binding obligation under national law to abide by and enforce their terms. In most instances direct effect creates a right of action in national courts, allowing individuals or independent agencies to invoke the treaty and file suit against the government for disregarding its international commitments.[8]

*** [Another] remedy is the authorization of retaliatory trade sanctions. Permission to impose sanctions is granted only to the complaining state, not to the community of member states for collective action. This type of decentralized enforcement system has deep roots in international law ***. For several reasons, sanctions are not always viewed as an effective remedy in international trade,[9] but other things being equal treaties that provide for sanctions are more legalistic than those with no remedy at all ***. The specific way in which sanctions are authorized is relevant. Some accords *** require approval from a political body ***. Agreements that empower the arbitral panel or tribunal to authorize or prescribe sanctions directly are less subject to political interference and thus more legalistic.

---

[7] The question of direct effect may depend as much on domestic constitutional norms as on the terms of the treaty. *** I confine my analysis to explicit treaty provisions, assuming that reciprocal treaties should not provide for direct effect where domestic constitutional norms preclude it. ***

[8] The existence of a private right of action may also depend as much on domestic law as on specific treaty provisions. Again I restrict my analysis to the terms of the treaty. Some agreements ignore or confuse the issue, but others are clear.

[9] Even if carefully designed, sanctions impose costs on the sanctioning country as well as on the defendant. Moreover, a system of sanctions systematically favors larger, less trade-dependent states, which are able to implement and withstand retaliatory measures with less economic dislocation than smaller, more open countries. For a general critique of sanctions, see Chayes and Chayes 1995.

TABLE 14.1. *Institutional Options in Dispute Settlement Design*

Treaty provision	More diplomatic	<————>	More legalistic
Third-party review	None	Access controlled by political body	Automatic right to review
Third-party ruling	Recommendation	Binding if approved by political body	Directly binding obligation
Judges	Ad hoc arbitrators	Ad hoc panelists drawn from roster	Standing tribunal of justices
Standing	States only	States and treaty organs	States, treaty organs, and individuals
Remedy	None	Retaliatory sanctions	Direct effect in domestic law

Also relevant is whether the treaty provides any guidelines or potential limits on the level of sanctions that is approved. Mechanisms that offer a blanket authorization are less legalistic than those that apply certain norms regarding the appropriate level and sectoral composition of sanctions. * * *

Table 14.1 summarizes the key features of institutional design that make a dispute settlement system more or less legalistic. This list is not comprehensive, since other issues – such as the presence or absence of deadlines or the extent to which arbitrators and judges have relevant legal expertise – can push an agreement toward one end of the spectrum or the other. * With these basic indicators, however, it is possible to categorize individual pacts. Even though the features in Table 14.1 are in theory independent of one another, they tend to cluster in practice, suggesting a hierarchical ordering of four dimensions: third-party review, third-party ruling, judges, and standing. The first question is whether the treaty provides for independent third-party review. Among pacts with some system of review, the next issue is whether rulings are directly binding in international law. Among pacts with binding rulings, those with standing tribunals are more legalistic than those with ad hoc arbitrators. Finally, tribunals with jurisdiction over claims by individuals, treaty organs, and states alike are more legalistic than those accessible only by states. In terms of remedy, the most legalistic pacts provide rulings with direct effect in national law, but the presence or absence of sanctions – though still significant – is a less meaningful indicator of legalism, with unilateral measures always available to states seeking to enforce third-party rulings in the decentralized international system. The basic issue is how effectively a given dispute settlement mechanism is able to produce impartial, consistent, and legally binding third-party rulings on any and all alleged treaty violations.

THE ARGUMENT

When negotiating a trade pact, governments must decide how legalistic its dispute settlement mechanism will be. In making this choice, political leaders confront a trade-off between mutually exclusive goals. On the one hand, they care about compliance with the agreement, the value of which depends on the extent to which other parties honor their commitments. The more legalistic the dispute settlement mechanism they design, the higher the likely level of compliance. On the other hand, they also care about their own policy discretion – and the less legalistic the mechanism, the greater their discretion to craft policies that solidify domestic support.[10] * * *

Policy Discretion

International trade agreements pose a familiar dilemma for national political leaders motivated to remain in power.[11] Among the principal determinants of any executive's or ruling party's popularity is the state of the economy.[12] One way political leaders seek to increase growth and create jobs is to negotiate reciprocal trade agreements, which almost as a rule produce net welfare benefits.[13] The political dilemma lies in the distribution of costs and benefits. Although benefits outweigh costs in the aggregate, for consumers and producers they are diffuse, or shared in small amounts by numerous individuals, whereas costs are concentrated. In political terms, concentrated costs imply organized opposition from adversely affected groups in import-competing sectors.

* * *

This generic problem of trade liberalization – diffuse net benefits, concentrated costs – is a factor in the political calculus of dispute settlement design. Political leaders cannot perfectly anticipate which groups will bear the heaviest costs of adjustment. During the negotiations, they

---

[10] Yarbrough and Yarbrough pose a trade-off between rigor and the opportunity for derogations that parallels the one I have drawn between treaty value and policy discretion; See Yarbrough and Yarbrough 1997, 148–49; and Smith 1995.

[11] On the political economy of trade, see Schattschneider 1935; Pastor 1980; and Magee, Brock, and Young 1989.

[12] See Kieweit and Rivers 1984; and Alesina and Rosenthal 1995.

[13] Wolf 1987.

propose specific exemptions or side payments for sectors that are clearly vulnerable to import competition.[14] The substantive terms of a treaty, which establish the depth and pace of liberalization, usually reflect such concerns. But political leaders realize that liberalization will impose concentrated costs they cannot foresee. As a result, they want to retain the discretion to respond in the future to uncertain demands for relief from injured groups.[15] Under a legalistic dispute settlement system, political leaders who provide import protection *ex post* run the risk of provoking complaints from foreign trade partners that could lead to rulings of violation, with attendant reputational costs and perhaps sanctions.

In disputes over nontariff barriers, legalistic dispute settlement also threatens to compromise the autonomy of domestic officials across a range of general regulations, from health and safety standards to environmental, antitrust, and procurement policies. *** In recent decades, *** the principal obstacles to open trade have been nontariff barriers, domestic regulations that discriminate against foreign producers, [which dominate the agendas of contemporary trade negotiations.] The politics of regulation is not unlike the political economy of trade: the marginal impact of regulatory policy on small, organized groups is often disproportionately large compared to its impact on the general, unorganized public. This characteristic increases its salience to officials seeking to remain in power, *** who may now face unprecedented complaints from foreign governments alleging unfair regulatory barriers to trade. If the merits of these complaints are judged in legalistic dispute settlement procedures, the policy discretion of political leaders may be constrained – and in areas where the domestic political stakes, given mobilized interest groups, are high.

* * *

Treaty Compliance

If legalistic trade dispute settlement poses such a clear domestic political threat, why would trade negotiators ever consider, much less adopt, any binding procedures? The answer lies in the benefits generated by dispute settlement mechanisms that improve government compliance and instill business confidence. The very procedures that constrain the policy autonomy of public officials, giving rise to political risks, also improve the economic value of the treaty, yielding domestic political benefits. If those

---

[14] See Destler 1986; Destler and Odell 1987; Goldstein 1993; and Pastor 1980.
[15] Downs and Rocke 1995, 77.

benefits are sufficiently large, they may offset the potential costs of policy constraints, making legalistic dispute settlement an attractive institutional option.

There are several ways in which legalistic dispute settlement is likely to enhance the level of compliance with international trade agreements. When implementing reciprocal liberalization, trading states confront problems of motivation and information.[16] Each state knows its partners may be motivated at times to violate their treaty commitments in order to provide protection to domestic groups. Each state also knows that with the prevalence and complexity of nontariff barriers, it may be difficult to generate information about every instance of defection by its partners. These transaction costs may prevent states from achieving mutually beneficial gains from exchange. [International] institutions arise in part to mitigate such costs by providing information about violations and in some instances by enforcing commitments.[17]

Formal dispute settlement procedures serve these very functions. As official forums where complaints are filed and judged, dispute settlement mechanisms play an important role in monitoring treaty violations, helping to offset problems of information. As independent bodies with the authority to endorse sanctions against offenders, dispute settlement mechanisms also help enforce treaty commitments, mitigating problems of motivation. Trading states realize that agreements are valuable only if compliance with their terms is high. *** The more legalistic the mechanism – in other words, the more effectively and impartially it identifies violations and enforces third-party rulings – the higher the likely level of government compliance.[18]

In addition to monitoring and enforcing compliance, dispute settlement procedures also serve to define compliance, clarifying the meaning of the treaty in disputes over how to interpret its terms. [Dispute] settlement operates in this respect as a type of relational contract.[19] Because the parties to a trade agreement cannot foresee all possible contingencies, they find it very difficult *ex ante* to define compliance. The accord they negotiate is inevitably incomplete; it does not specify how the parties are to behave under all possible circumstances. As circumstances change, conflicts of interpretation may arise. To avoid such conflicts, parties agree in

---

[16] See Yarbrough and Yarbrough 1990; and Milgrom and Roberts 1992.

[17] Keohane 1984.

[18] Economists have sought to demonstrate the benefits of third-party trade dispute settlement with formal models. See Maggi 1996; and Kovenock and Thursby 1994.

[19] Milgrom and Roberts 1992, chap. 5.

relational contracts to assign rights and responsibilities to define compliance, a role that trade accords often confer on impartial third parties.[20]

Finally, legalistic dispute settlement also improves the expected value of reciprocal trade pacts through its impact on the behavior of private traders and investors. For political leaders to realize fully the benefits of liberalization, private sector actors must believe that having committed specific assets to production for (or sales in) foreign markets, they will not be denied access to that market. Traders and investors are risk-averse with respect to decisions about investment, production, and distribution involving assets that are highly specific – in other words, assets that are costly to convert to other uses.[21] Other things being equal, they prefer minimum uncertainty, prizing a stable policy environment in which to assess alternative business strategies.[22] Legalistic dispute settlement serves as an institutional commitment to trade liberalization that bolsters the confidence of the private sector, reducing one source of risk. The private sector thus increases the volume of trade and investment among the parties, amplifying the macroeconomic – and, in turn, political – benefits of liberalization.

* * *

Assessing the Trade-off

Political leaders negotiating the design of dispute settlement always confront this tension between policy discretion and treaty compliance. The trade-off between these objectives is universal, but not uniform. Different governments assess it in dissimilar ways. And the weight a specific government assigns to each objective changes in different settings, as does the probability that its preferred mechanism will be adopted. In specifying the dimensions of variance, it is helpful to distinguish two stages in the process of dispute settlement design. The first is national preference formation; the second, international bargaining.[23]

[20] See Garrett and Weingast 1993; and Weingast 1995.
[21] Not all assets, obviously, are specific. For a discussion, see Frieden 1991, 434–40, who builds on the pioneering work of Oliver Williamson. Williamson 1985.
[22] Not all firms prefer stable, liberal trade policy to the prospect of future protection. Firms close to insolvency or in sectors with low productivity are likely to prefer trade policy discretion – and the increased probability of protection – to legalistic dispute settlement.
[23] This distinction follows Moravcsik 1993, 480–82.

The level of legalism preferred by a particular government in a specific trade negotiation depends on several factors. The first is the extent to which its economy depends on trade with other signatories to the accord. The more trade-dependent the economy, measured as the ratio of intra-pact exports to gross domestic product (GDP), the more legalistic the dispute settlement mechanism its government will tend to favor. Legalistic dispute settlement is more valuable politically where trade with prospective partner countries accounts for a larger share of the domestic economy.

A second source of dispute settlement preferences is relative economic power. The more powerful the country in relative terms, the less legalistic the dispute settlement mechanism its government will favor. This hypothesis derives from the distinction between rule-oriented and power-oriented dispute settlement.[24] Rule-oriented systems resolve conflicts by developing and applying consistent rules to comparable disputes, enabling less powerful parties to win independent legal rulings that may be costly for more powerful parties to ignore. For small countries, the benefits of such rulings may outweigh the costs of diminished policy discretion. In power-oriented systems, parties resolve disputes through traditional diplomatic means of self-help, such as issue-linkage, hostage taking, and in particular the threat of retaliatory sanctions.[25] These strategies systematically favor more powerful countries, which tend to favor pragmatism over legalism. A telling measure of relative economic power within regional trade accords is each country's share of total pact GDP. The larger the country's economy in relative terms, the more influence it is likely to wield as the destination of imports from other signatories. Larger economies also tend to be less dependent on exports, giving their leaders diplomatic leverage in trade disputes.[26]

A third factor shaping dispute settlement preferences is the proposed depth of liberalization. Trade agreements come in a variety of forms, and the type of agreement at hand influences the type of dispute settlement system favored by member governments. In particular, the more ambitious the level of proposed integration, the more willing political leaders should be to endorse legalistic dispute settlement. One reason is that deeper integration promises to generate larger net economic gains.[27] A second

---

[24] For discussions of this distinction, which is also cast as "pragmatism" versus "legalism," see Dam 1970, 3–5; Hudec 1971, 1299–1300, 1304; and Jackson 1979.

[25] Yarbrough and Yarbrough 1986.

[26] Alesina and Wacziarg 1997.

[27] The same logic applies to the breadth of trade pacts: where coverage is comprehensive, excluding no major export sectors, political leaders are more likely to endorse legalism than in pacts that exempt significant sectors.

consideration is that legalism, viewed from a functional perspective, may be the most appropriate institutional design for the resolution of disputes in the process of deep integration, which includes coverage of complex nontariff barriers to trade and common regulatory regimes. *

Together these simple measures – intrapact trade dependence, relative economic power, and depth of liberalization – provide a way of specifying dispute settlement preferences *ex ante*. To specify outcomes, one must also identify which country's preferences – given divergent ideal points on the Pareto frontier of trade cooperation[28] – should prevail at the bargaining stage. Like most international treaty negotiations, trade talks require consensus. In the presence of a unanimity rule, the design of dispute settlement is likely to be only as legalistic as the signatory that most values policy discretion and least values treaty compliance will allow. The lowest common denominator drives the institutional outcome when all parties have a unit veto.

In trade negotiations, one proxy for legalism's lowest common denominator is intrapact economic asymmetry. Its utility lies in the fact that larger economies stand to gain less, in proportional terms, from regional liberalization than smaller economies. Within a given agreement, the largest economies – defined in terms of aggregate GDP – traditionally represent the most valuable potential markets for intrapact exports.[29] Larger economies also are less dependent on and less open to trade – with openness measured either in terms of policy measures or as the ratio of trade to GDP – than smaller economies.[30] [The] benefits of openness to trade, measured in terms of the impact on per capita GDP growth rates, diminish as aggregate GDP increases.[31] [Hence] the relative value of liberalization – and, by implication, of legalistic dispute settlement – is usually lower to larger economies than to smaller economies. The signatory state with the largest economy, therefore, is most likely to wield the unit veto that determines the level of legalism in a given agreement.

---

[28] Krasner 1991.

[29] For this observation to hold, per capita income levels should be comparable across member countries. Most regional trade pacts between 1957 and 1995 have been exclusively among either developed or developing countries, with NAFTA as the first of few exceptions.

[30] Alesina and Wacziarg report a strong negative correlation between country size and openness to trade. Alesina and Wacziarg 1997. This finding is robust across multiple measures of both variables, but of particular relevance to this study is their analysis of size based on the log of aggregate GDP.

[31] Alesina, Spolaore, and Wacziarg 1997.

This analysis leads one to expect less legalistic dispute settlement in accords between parties whose relative economic size and bargaining leverage are highly unequal. In pacts where a single member country is much larger than its partners – in other words, where intrapact economic asymmetry is high – the regional hegemon, whose economy stands to gain least from trade liberalization, has little incentive to risk its policy discretion on behalf of improved treaty compliance. Moreover, this hegemon also has the bargaining leverage to impose its preference for a pragmatic, power-oriented system, under which it can more effectively use unilateral trade measures. In other words, size matters – and significant disparities in relative economic position augur poorly for legalism. Legalistic dispute settlement is expected only in accords among parties whose relative size and bargaining leverage are more symmetric. In settings of low economic asymmetry – provided the proposed liberalization is sufficiently deep – all member governments have an incentive to improve treaty compliance through the use of impartial third parties. Given their comparable economic power *ex ante*, no signatory stands to lose bargaining leverage *ex post* from the transition to a legalistic system. The projected gains from liberalization must be significant, however, if political leaders are to compromise their policy discretion. If the level of integration is not ambitious – or if the pact exempts crucial export sectors – officials may very well reject legalism even in settings of low asymmetry.

* * *

THE DATA SET

Among advanced industrial and developing countries alike, regional trade integration has been a persistent feature of the world economy in recent decades. Counts vary, but no fewer than sixty regional trade arrangements, established through formal treaties, have come into being since 1957.[32] ***

Despite the general trend toward formal economic integration, these trade pacts differ on many dimensions[: size, members' level of economic development, the scope or depth of liberalization, levels of compliance, and durability.]

---

[32] In 1994 the International Monetary Fund compiled a list of more than sixty-eight regional agreements. An earlier study listed thirty-four existing and nineteen prospective arrangements. See IMF 1994; and de la Torre and Kelly 1992.

With such a diverse set of possible cases, it has been necessary to apply certain criteria to ensure comparability. In this study there are no restrictions on the number of signatories, though I do exclude GATT and the World Trade Organization – which stand alone as the world's only multilateral trade institutions ***. Similarly, there are no categorical restrictions on the type of agreement, with free trade areas, customs unions, common markets, and economic unions all represented. Finally, to minimize selection bias, the data set includes both successful and failed pacts. *** Despite these inclusive rules, trade agreements that failed to meet one or more of the following requirements did not qualify for this study.

First, liberalization must be reciprocal. Concessions need not be strictly equivalent or simultaneous. *** But at least among some core signatories, reciprocal market access must be the rule. ***

Second, liberalization must be relatively comprehensive in scope. Universal free trade, with no sectoral exceptions at all, is by no means required. Still, coverage of at least merchandise trade must in principle be broad. ***

Third, the trade pacts must have been signed between January 1957 and December 1995. Negotiations that did not produce specific liberalization commitments by the end of 1995 are excluded. Pacts in which implementation was at that point incomplete but in which liberalization had begun are incorporated. ***

Table 14.2 lists the sixty-two trade agreements that met these criteria. It also lists the year in which each treaty was signed and all member governments, identifying those governments that were not among the original signatories by indicating their years of accession in parentheses. Countries that signed but later withdrew from the agreement are noted, as are their years of departure. Appendix B lists the treaties from the relevant time period that failed to meet one of the first two criteria listed earlier, as well as those whose texts were for various reasons unavailable. As Table 14.2 suggests, one potential problem in the data set is a lack of independence among certain cases. There are four clusters of agreements, one in the Americas and three in Europe, within which the timing and terms of the accords are rather similar. So as not to exacerbate this problem, I exclude treaties that were later encompassed or superceded by subsequent agreements; examples include the Canada–U.S. Free Trade Agreement and various bilateral pacts between the EC and individual European Free Trade Association (EFTA) countries, almost all of which were replaced either by accession to the EC or by membership in the European Economic Area (EEA).

TABLE 14.2. *Data Set of Selected Regional Trade Agreements, 1957–95*

Pact	Year signed	Members[a]
AFTA (ASEAN Free Trade Area)	1992	Indonesia, Malaysia, Philippines, Singapore, Thailand, Brunei, Vietnam (1995), Laos (1997), Burma (1997)
Andean Pact	1969	Bolivia, Colombia, Ecuador, Peru, Venezuela (1973) (Chile withdrew in 1976)
ANZCERTA (Australia–New Zealand Closer Economic Relations Trade Agreement)	1983	Australia, New Zealand
Baltic Free Trade Agreement	1993	Estonia, Latvia, Lithuania
CACM (Central American Common Market)	1960	El Salvador, Guatemala, Honduras, Nicaragua, Costa Rica (1963) (Honduras withdrew in 1970 but rejoined in 1990)
CARICOM (Caribbean Community)	1973	Antigua and Bermuda, Barbados, Belize, Dominica, Grenada, Guyana, Jamaica, Montserrat, Saint Kitts and Nevis, Saint Lucia, Saint Vincent and the Grenadines, Suriname (1995), Trinidad and Tobago (Bahamas is a member of the Community but not of the Common Market)
CEAO (West African Economic Community) (dissolved in 1994)	1973	Benin, Burkina Faso, Ivory Coast, Mali, Mauritania, Niger, Senegal
CEEC (Central and East European Country) Pacts (5)		
Bulgaria–Czech Republic Free Trade Agreement	1995	Bulgaria, Czech Republic

(continued)

TABLE 14.2 *(continued)*

Pact	Year signed	Members[a]
Bulgaria–Slovak Republic Free Trade Agreement	1995	Bulgaria, Slovak Republic
Hungary–Slovenia Free Trade Agreement	1994	Hungary, Slovenia
Romania–Czech Republic Free Trade Agreement	1994	Romania, Czech Republic
Romania–Slovak Republic Free Trade Agreement	1994	Romania, Slovak Republic
CEFTA (Central European Free Trade Agreement)	1992	Czech Republic, Hungary, Poland, Slovakia, Slovenia (1996), Romania (1997)
Chile and Mexico Pacts (9)		
Chile–Bolivia Free Trade Agreement	1993	Chile, Bolivia
Chile–Canada Free Trade Agreement	1995	Chile, Canada
Chile–Colombia Free Trade Agreement	1993	Chile, Colombia
Chile–Ecuador Free Trade Agreement	1994	Chile, Ecuador
Chile–Venezuela Free Trade Agreement	1991	Chile, Venezuela
Mexico–Bolivia Free Trade Agreement	1994	Mexico, Bolivia
Mexico–Chile Free Trade Agreement	1991	Mexico, Chile
Mexico–Costa Rica Free Trade Agreement	1994	Mexico, Costa Rica
Group of Three Free Trade Agreement	1994	Colombia, Mexico, Venezuela

Pact	Year signed	Members[a]
CIS (Commonwealth of Independent States)	1993	Russia, Armenia, Azerbaijan, Armenia, Belarus, Georgia, Kazakhstan, Kyrgyzstan, Moldova, Tajikistan, Turkmenistan, Uzbekistan (Ukraine is a full member of the CIS but an associate member of the Economic Union)
COMESA (Common Market for Eastern and Southern Africa)	1993	Angola, Burundi, Comoros, Djibouti, Eritrea, Ethiopia, Kenya, Lesotho, Madagascar, Malawi, Mauritius, Mozambique, Namibia, Rwanda, Somalia, Sudan, Swaziland, Tanzania, Uganda, Zaire (1994), Zambia, Zimbabwe (Seychelles signed the treaty but does not participate)
EAC (East African Community) (collapsed in 1977; dissolved in 1984)	1967	Kenya, Tanzania, Uganda
EC (European Community)	1957	Austria (1995), Belgium, Denmark (1973), Finland (1995), France, Germany, Greece (1981), Ireland (1973), Italy, Luxembourg, Netherlands, Portugal (1986), Spain (1986), Sweden (1995), United Kingdom (1973)
EC Associations (12)		
EC–Bulgaria Association Agreement	1993	EC, Bulgaria
EC–Cyprus Association Agreement	1972	EC, Cyprus
EC–Czech Republic Association Agreement	1991	EC, Czech Republic

(continued)

TABLE 14.2 *(continued)*

Pact	Year signed	Members[a]
EC–Estonia Free Trade Agreement	1994	EC, Estonia
EC–Hungary Association Agreement	1991	EC, Hungary
EC–Poland Association Agreement	1991	EC, Poland
EC–Romania Association Agreement	1993	EC, Romania
EC–Slovak Republic Association Agreement	1991	EC, Slovak Republic
EC–Turkey Customs Union	1963	EC, Turkey
EC–Latvia Free Trade Agreement	1994	EC, Latvia
EC–Lithuania Free Trade Agreement	1994	EC, Lithuania
EC–Malta Association Agreement	1970	EC, Malta
EC–Israel Free Trade Agreement	1995	EC, Israel
ECOWAS (Economic Community of West African States) (revised in 1993)	1975	Benin, Burkina Faso, Cape Verde, Gambia, Ghana, Guinea, Guinea-Bissau, Ivory Coast, Liberia, Mali, Mauritania, Niger, Nigeria, Senegal, Sierra Leone, Togo
EEA (European Economic Area)	1992	EC, Iceland, Liechtenstein, Norway (Swiss voters rejected the EEA in 1992; Austria, Finland, and Sweden joined EC in 1995)
EFTA (European Free Trade Association)	1960	Iceland (1970), Liechtenstein (1991), Norway, Switzerland (United Kingdom and Denmark withdrew in 1973; Portugal in 1986; Austria, Finland (1986), and Sweden in 1994)

Pact	Year signed	Members[a]
EFTA Agreements (12)		
EFTA–Bulgaria Agreement	1993	EFTA, Bulgaria
EFTA–Czech Republic Agreement	1992	EFTA, Czech Republic
EFTA–Estonia Agreement	1995	EFTA, Estonia
EFTA–Hungary Agreement	1993	EFTA, Hungary
EFTA–Israel Agreement	1992	EFTA, Israel
EFTA–Latvia Agreement	1995	EFTA, Latvia
EFTA–Lithuania Agreement	1995	EFTA, Lithuania
EFTA–Poland Agreement	1992	EFTA, Poland
EFTA–Romania Agreement	1992	EFTA, Romania
EFTA–Slovak Republic Agreement	1992	EFTA, Slovak Republic
EFTA–Slovenia Agreement	1995	EFTA, Slovenia
EFTA–Turkey Agreement	1991	EFTA, Turkey
GCC (Gulf Cooperation Council)	1981	Bahrain, Kuwait, Oman, Qatar, Saudi Arabia, United Arab Emirates
Mano River Union	1973	Liberia, Sierra Leone, Guinea (joined after 1974)
MERCOSUR (Common Market of the South)	1991	Argentina, Brazil, Paraguay, Uruguay (Chile and Bolivia are associate members)
NAFTA (North American Free Trade Agreement)	1992	Canada, Mexico, United States

(continued)

TABLE 14.2 *(continued)*

Pact	Year signed	Members[a]
OECS (Organization of East Caribbean States)	1981	Antigua and Bermuda, Dominica, Grenada, Montserrat, Saint Kitts and Nevis, Saint Lucia, Saint Vincent and the Grenadines
SACU (Southern African Customs Union)	1969	Botswana, Lesotho, Namibia, South Africa, Swaziland
U.S.–Israel Free Trade Agreement	1985	Israel, United States
UDEAC (Central African Customs and Economic Union)	1964	Cameroon, Central African Republic, Chad, Republic of Congo, Gabon, Equatorial Guinea

[a] Dates in parentheses indicate years of accession for member states that were not among the original signatories. Countries that signed but later withdrew from the agreement are also noted, as are their years of departure.

OVERVIEW OF REGIONAL DISPUTE SETTLEMENT

In this segment I summarize the level of legalism in each of the regional trade pacts in the data set. The basic features of dispute settlement in each pact are highlighted in Table 14.3, which draws on the treaty texts listed in Appendix A. Related agreements in Europe and the Americas are aggregated; within each group, dispute settlement provisions are identical in every important respect. I include two observations for EFTA, whose membership changed significantly over time (see Table 14.2) and whose 1960 dispute settlement system was transformed with the creation of the EEA in 1992. *** In this respect, EFTA is an exception to the rule. There are a handful of other agreements whose dispute settlement procedures changed over time – namely the Andean Pact, Central American Common Market (CACM), Common Market of the South (MERCOSUR), AFTA, and a few bilateral EFTA agreements. Unlike EFTA, however, these cases have not undergone radical changes in membership or in other variables of interest to this study. As a result, I report and evaluate their most recent dispute settlement design (citations for the relevant agreements are listed in Appendix A).

Table 14.3 underscores the dramatic extent of institutional variation in the data set. Its final column organizes the agreements into five clusters

TABLE 14.3. *Levels of Legalism in Dispute Settlement Design*[a]

| | Treaty provision | | | | |
	Third-party review	Third-party ruling	Judges	Standing	Remedy	Level of legalism
Pact						
ANZCERTA	None	—	—	—	—	None
Baltic FTA	None	—	—	—	—	None
CEEC Pacts (5)	None	—	—	—	—	None
CEFTA	None	—	—	—	—	None
EEA	None – unless by mutual consent to ECJ on EC law	—	—	—	—	None
EFTA agreements with Czech Republic, Hungary, Poland, Romania, Slovak Republic, and Turkey	None	—	—	—	—	None
Mano River Union	None	—	—	—	—	None
SACU	None	—	—	—	—	None
UDEAC	None	—	—	—	—	None
AFTA	Yes – automatic	Not binding (ministers "consider" report in vote)	Ad hoc – roster	States only	Compensation, sanctions (only by vote of Council)	Low

(continued)

351

TABLE 14.3 *(continued)*

			Treaty provision			
Pact	Third-party review	Third-party ruling	Judges	Standing	Remedy	Level of legalism
CARICOM	Yes – automatic	Not binding (Council "may" vote to recommend)	Ad hoc – roster	States only	Sanctions (only by vote of Council)	Low
EFTA 1960	Yes – but only by majority vote of Council	Not binding (Council "may" vote to recommend)	Ad hoc	States only	Sanctions (only by vote of Council)	Low
GCC	Yes – but only by vote of Council	Not binding (panel issues recommendation to Supreme Council)	Ad hoc – roster	States only	None	Low
U.S.–Israel Pact	Yes – automatic	Not binding (merely a conciliation report)	Ad hoc	States only	Sanctions ("any appropriate measure")	Low
Chile and Mexico Pacts[b] (9)	Yes – automatic	Binding	Ad hoc – roster	States only	Sanctions (if prescribed or authorized)	Medium
EC associations (12)	Yes – but risk of deadlock at panel formation	Binding	Ad hoc	States and EC	None	Medium
EC-Israel Pact	Yes – but risk of deadlock at panel formation	Binding	Ad hoc	States and EC	None	Medium

EFTA agreements with Bulgaria, Israel, Estonia, Latvia, Lithuania, and Slovenia	Yes – automatic	Binding	Ad hoc	States only	None	Medium
MERCOSUR	Yes – but only after three preliminary reviews	Binding	Ad hoc – roster	States only	Sanctions	Medium
NAFTA	Yes – automatic (except in side accords, where two of three states must approve review)	Chap. 20 general disputes: not binding (contrary settlement or compensation allowed) Chap. 19 unfair trade law and Chap. 11 investment disputes: binding Side accords on labor and environment: binding	Ad hoc – roster	Chap. 20: states only Chap 11: individuals only Chap. 19 and side accords: states and individuals	Chap. 20: sanctions Chap. 11 and Chap. 19: direct effect Side accords: fines (direct effect for Canada)	Medium
OECS	Yes – automatic	Binding	Ad hoc – roster	States only	None	Medium

(continued)

TABLE 14.3 (continued)

Pact	Third-party review	Third-party ruling	Judges	Standing	Remedy	Level of legalism
	Treaty provision					
CEAO	Yes – automatic	Binding	**Standing tribunal**	States only	None	High
CIS	Yes – but jurisdiction limited	Binding	**Standing tribunal**	States only	None	High
EAC	Yes – automatic	Binding	**Standing tribunal**	States only	None	High
ECOWAS	Yes – automatic	Binding	**Standing tribunal**	States and treaty organs	Sanctions (imposed by heads of state)	High
Andean Pact	Yes – automatic	Binding	Standing tribunal	**States, treaty organs, and individuals**	Direct effect, sanctions (prescribed by tribunal)	Very High
CACM	Yes – automatic	Binding	Standing tribunal	**States, treaty organs, and individuals**	Direct effect	Very High
COMESA	Yes – automatic	Binding	Standing tribunal	**States, treaty organs, and individuals**	Sanctions (prescribed by tribunal)	Very High
EC	Yes – automatic	Binding	Standing tribunal	**States, treaty organs, and individuals**	Direct effect	Very High
EFTA 1992	Yes – automatic	Binding	Standing tribunal	**States, treaty organs, and individuals**	Direct effect	Very High

[a] Boldface indicates the distinguishing features of cases at levels above and below medium legalism.

[b] Several of the Chilean and Mexican pacts also include investor-state dispute mechanisms, rather like Chapter 11 of NAFTA.

Sources: See Appendix A.

that capture basic differences in the level of legalism. To define these categories, I start with the most basic question: whether a treaty provides any system of independent third-party review of disputes. For eighteen treaties, the answer is no, and they thus constitute the lowest level of legalism: none.[33] At the next level, with low legalism, are five agreements with dispute settlement mechanisms whose rulings are not binding in international law. These pacts nominally provide a system of third-party review but hold it hostage to decisions by political bodies, often a council of ministers, or in the case of the U.S.–Israel accord treat its rulings as mere recommendations.[34]

The midpoint of the sample – medium legalism – includes a diverse set of thirty-one agreements that provide for some version of standard international arbitration, offering states an automatic right to binding rulings by ad hoc arbitrators. Within this category there is variation regarding remedies, since a few pacts provide for sanctions. The only agreements with multiple dispute settlement procedures – NAFTA and several pacts signed by Chile and Mexico – also fall into this category. NAFTA includes at least five distinct mechanisms for different issue areas ***.[35] The mechanism most relevant to this study, Chapter 20 for general disputes, might qualify NAFTA at the level of low legalism because its rulings are not legally binding: compensatory payments can substitute for compliance, and disputants can reach a settlement contrary to the terms of a panel ruling after it has been issued. However, NAFTA's innovative procedures for unfair trade law and investment disputes – which include binding rulings and standing for individuals – push the agreement in the direction of legalism. Without any standing tribunal, the combination of these mechanisms arguably leaves NAFTA at the level of medium legalism. Many of the Chilean and Mexican pacts incorporate a version

---

[33] Inclusion of the EEA in this category may be controversial. Technically, all member states of both EFTA and the EC have access to highly legalistic tribunals for the resolution of disputes regarding issues of EC law, which the EEA extends to EFTA. Nevertheless, this option applies only to disputes among EFTA states before the EFTA Court or among EC states before the European Court of Justice. For disputes *between* the EC and EFTA, neither group has automatic access to third-party review. By common consent, questions of interpretation of EC law may be referred to the European Court of Justice, but EFTA states have no direct access. Their complaints go instead to the EEA Joint Committee for bilateral consultations between the EC Commission and the EFTA states "speaking with one voice." The original EEA draft proposed an EEA Court, but the European Court of Justice struck it down as an usurpation of its exclusive authority over EC law. See Bierwagen and Hull 1993, 119–24.

[34] Azrieli 1993, 203–205.

[35] For details on NAFTA's different mechanisms, see Smith 1995.

of NAFTA's mechanism for investment disputes. Although this procedure grants standing to individuals, it is limited in scope to rules on investment and relies on ad hoc arbitrators, which keep the Chilean and Mexican pacts within this category.

At the level of high legalism are four agreements that establish a standing tribunal to issue binding rulings on cases brought by states. Although in other respects these pacts resemble standard arbitration, the appointment of judges to a permanent court implies a significant step in the direction of legalism. These agreements create supranational institutions whose judges are likely to issue consistent legal rulings in developing their treaty jurisprudence. In practice, these four accords are among the most poorly implemented in the data set. Both the East African Community (EAC) and the West African Economic Community (CEAO), in fact, have been formally dissolved. The Economic Community of West African States (ECOWAS) Community Court of Justice awaits the realization of trade commitments in that largely dormant economic area, while the jurisdiction of the Commonwealth of Independent States (CIS) Economic Court appears to be severely restricted even among the CIS signatories that have endorsed it.[36]

There is a sizable leap toward legalism at the final level. All five agreements with very high legalism expand the definition of standing beyond member states to include both treaty organs and private individuals. With the exception of COMESA, they also give the rulings of standing tribunals direct effect in national law. To a significant extent, the judicial bodies envisaged for the CACM, Andean Pact, EFTA 1992, and COMESA draw on the model of the European Court of Justice. For example, all five tribunals have the authority, on request, to issue preliminary rulings to national courts, which can serve to broaden the access of individuals to supranational judicial review. On encountering questions of treaty interpretation, domestic judges may or may not exercise this option, but the preliminary question procedure has helped forge important links between the European Court of Justice and national judiciaries in Europe.[37]

* * *

---

[36] Very little information is available, but reports suggest that the jurisdiction of the CIS Economic Court has lawfully been refused by Kazakhstan. Three CIS members have not recognized it, and others have ignored its rulings. See "CIS Court Dismisses Moldova Claim for Kazakh Grain," *Reuter European Business Report*, 6 February 1997; and "CIS Economic Court to Be in Session," *TASS*, 7 July 1997.

[37] See Stone Sweet and Brunell 1998; and Mattli and Slaughter 1996.

MEASURING ASYMMETRY AND PROPOSED INTEGRATION

To test my argument on the trade-off between treaty compliance and policy discretion, I must find summary statistics that describe the level of economic asymmetry and proposed depth of integration within each regional trade arrangement. Measuring GDP asymmetry in trade pacts is not unlike measuring the level of industry concentration – or market share asymmetry – in different sectors of the economy. A standard measure for industrial concentration in economics is the Herfindahl-Hirschman index (HH), which equals the sum of the squared market shares of the firms in a given industry. In a situation of pure monopoly, the index is $(1.0)^2 = 1.00$. Where two firms divide the market evenly, $HH = (0.5)^2 + (0.5)^2 = 0.50$.

In its traditional form, this index is not an ideal measure of intrapact GDP asymmetry. In the two-firm example, a score of 0.50 – which is very high by antitrust standards – for me represents a situation of perfect symmetry if derived from a bilateral pact where the two countries have identical GDP shares. Yet the same index score could reflect a situation of high asymmetry in a pact with six signatories where the GDP shares are as follows: $HH = (0.68)^2 + (0.17)^2 + (0.10)^2 + (0.02)^2 + (0.02)^2 + (0.01)^2 = 0.50$. To correct for this problem, I subtract from the Herfindahl-Hirschman index what the index would be in a situation of perfect economic symmetry, where all signatories to a trade accord have identical shares of the total pact GDP. Given the nature of summed squares, this baseline of perfect symmetry always equals 1 divided by the number of signatories (N). By subtracting it, I obtain a new measure (P) that describes the proportional asymmetry of each pact. It captures the distance of each pact from symmetry: the further a pact is from that baseline, the higher the index. In the two-signatory example P would be zero, indicating perfect symmetry, but in the six-signatory example it would be much higher: $P = 0.50 - (1/6) = 0.33$.

To define this proportional asymmetry index in more formal terms,

$$P = \Sigma x_i^2 - 1/N \text{ for all } i$$

where x_i = each member's share of total pact GDP, such that $\Sigma x_i = 1$.

Among alternative indicators of inequality, P is related to variance measures. In fact, P is formally equivalent to N times the variance of income shares.[38] In other words, P represents the sum of the squared

---

[38] The variance of a given sample (Var) is the average squared deviation of data points from their sample mean, which for income shares that sum to one is by definition $1/N$: Var $(x) = (1/N) \cdot \Sigma(x_i - 1/N)^2$.

TABLE 14.4. *The Proportional Asymmetry Index of Intrapact GDP Shares*

Asymmetry	Pact	Year	GDP shares (x)	N	P	P/MAX
Low	Mano River Union	1973	.52, .48	2	.0007	.001
	EAC	1967	.38, .34, .28	3	.005	.007
	Romania–Czech Republic	1994	.545, .455	2	.004	.008
	Chile–Colombia	1993	.55, .45	2	.005	.010
	Bulgaria–Slovak Republic	1995	.57, .43	2	.011	.021
	COMESA	1993	.11, .10, .10, .08, .07, .07, .06, .06, .06, .06, .05, .05, .04 and below	22	.023	.024
	Baltic FTA	1993	.45, .31, .23	3	.025	.037
	OECS	1981	.26, .22, .14, .12, .12, .10, .05	7	.032	.037
	Chile–Venezuela	1991	.61, .39	2	.024	.048
	CACM	1960	.38, .23, .19, .12, .08	5	.053	.067
	AFTA	1992	.34, .27, .14, .13, .12, .01	6	.068	.082
	EFTA 1992	1992	.27, .26, .20, .14, .12, .01, .002	7	.073	.085
	Andean Pact	1969	.34, .28, .27, .07, .04	5	.072	.089
	CEAO	1973	.38, .19, .14, .09, .08, .08, .05	7	.076	.089
	EC	1957	.36, .33, .18, .07, .06, .003	6	.113	.136
	Romania–Slovak Republic	1994	.69, .31	2	.069	.138
High	UDEAC	1964	.47, .16, .14, .13, .09, .01	6	.124	.149
	CEFTA	1992	.53, .23, .17, .07	4	.112	.149
	Hungary–Slovenia	1994	.74, .26	2	.118	.235
	Chile–Ecuador	1994	.77, .23	2	.134	.268
	CARICOM	1970	.48, .31, .09, .05, .02, .01 and below	12	.252	.275
	Bulgaria–Czech Republic	1995	.79, .21	2	.162	.325

	Year	GDP shares (x_i)	N		
EFTA 1960	1960	.63, .12, .07, .05, .05, .04, .02	7	.281	.328
MERCOSUR	1991	.65, .32, .02, .01	4	.278	.371
GCC	1981	.67, .14, .11, .04, .03, .01	6	.313	.376
Group of Three	1994	.75, .13, .12	3	.261	.392
ECOWAS	1975	.72, .07, .05, .04, .02 and below	15[a]	.458	.491
ANZCERTA	1983	.88, .12	2	.293	.586
CIS	1993	.79, .06, .05, .04, .01 and below	11	.540	.594
Mexico–Chile	1991	.89, .11	2	.311	.622
Chile–Canada	1995	.89, .11	2	.311	.622
Chile–Bolivia	1993	.89, .11	2	.311	.622
NAFTA	1992	.87, .08, .05	3	.430	.645
EEA	1992	.91, .09	2[b]	.338	.676
EFTA Agreements (mean)	Various	.96, .04	2[b]	.421	.841
Mexico–Costa Rica	1994	.98, .02	2	.458	.916
Mexico–Bolivia	1994	.99, .01	2	.472	.944
SACU	1970	.984, .007, .005, .004	4	.718	.957
EC–Israel	1995	.99, .01	2[b]	.479	.958
U.S.–Israel	1985	.99, .01	2	.487	.974
EC Associations (mean)	Various	.99, .01	2[b]	.490	.980

Note: Shares of GDP may not sum to 1 or match the index scores exactly because of rounding.
GDP shares = members' GDP shares (x_i) (in current $US) in reported year.
$P = \Sigma x_i^2 - 1/N$ for all i where x_i is member i's share of total pact GDP such that $\Sigma x_i = 1$.
$MAX = 1 - 1/N$, the upper bound of P for each pact.
N = number of members at the time the agreement was signed.
[a] GDP data for Guinea were unavailable.
[b] Member states of the EC and/or EFTA act collectively as a unit in a bilateral governance structure.
Sources: World Bank (various years); OECD (various years); and *UN Statistical Yearbook* (various years).

deviation of individual GDP shares from their sample mean. One disadvantage is that the upper bound (MAX) of P, which is equivalent to $1 - 1/N$, varies with the number of signatories. To control for differences in the maximum value of P, I use the ratio of the proportional asymmetry index to its range (P/MAX).

To estimate the level of asymmetry within each accord, I use aggregate GDP figures denominated in U.S. dollars at current exchange rates. Where possible the index uses data from the year in which the treaty was signed.[39] For all cases, the index incorporates only countries that signed the accord at the time of its creation or reinvigoration; it excludes member states that later acceded and includes any that later withdrew. [EFTA] is the only pact to have duplicate entries. *** Other agreements that underwent various changes over time *** hardly shifted in terms of asymmetry and thus have one entry from the year of their establishment. *

Using these guidelines, Table 14.4 ranks and organizes the sixty-three data points into two categories, low and high, based on the level of economic asymmetry within each pact. The rank order of the pacts derives from their P/MAX scores, which are listed from low to high. To facilitate comparisons, Table 14.4 reports the underlying GDP shares of signatories to each agreement in descending order ***. These GDP shares make evident the intuitive appeal of this ordering, but with a small sample size and categorical dependent variable it is also necessary to draw a line between low and high asymmetry. Although this P/MAX index captures the level of asymmetry across all signatories, my theoretical approach suggests that the relative size of the largest members may be more important than the distribution of shares among smaller economies. The reason is that two or three symmetrically positioned regional powers that depend heavily on access to each others' markets may endorse a legalistic system even if the gap in size between them and their neighbors is substantial.[40] By focusing on the relative size of the largest signatories, one can define a threshold between high and low asymmetry that conforms to the rank order in Table 14.4. For bilateral pacts, if the larger country's share of GDP exceeds 70 percent, asymmetry is high, as it is in

---

[39] The two exceptions are the 1973 CARICOM and the 1969 SACU, both of which reflect GDP data from 1970.

[40] For an argument along these lines regarding the critical role of the United States and the European Union in the legalistic dispute settlement reforms of the Uruguay Round of GATT, see Smith 1998.

multilateral pacts where the GDP share of the largest signatory is more than twice that of the next largest. * * *

Like asymmetry, the proposed level of integration is a key variable that requires a metric. An adapted version of the traditional concept of stages of integration seems best able to capture the basic differences between shallow and deep initiatives. In a study of regional trade pacts, the International Monetary Fund labeled agreements as belonging to one of four categories.[41] At the shallow end of integration arrangements are free trade areas, which remove tariff and certain nontariff barriers * * *. More ambitious are customs unions, which in addition to free trade aim to establish harmonized external tariffs * * *. Common markets aim to guarantee freedom of movement not only for goods and services but also for factors of production such as capital and labor. And at the deepest level of liberalization are economic unions, which are common markets whose member states harmonize certain macroeconomic and regulatory policies.

Along the continuum of these four stages of integration, there is a fundamental break between customs unions and common markets. Free trade areas and customs unions focus on removing barriers to the cross-border movement of goods (and, at times, services), with an emphasis on tariffs and quantitative restrictions. Common markets and economic unions aim for a much higher level of integration, including the free movement of labor and capital and the harmonization of economic policies. * * * Free trade areas and customs unions indicate low integration, whereas common markets and economic unions signify high integration. This typology reflects the proposed level of integration in each agreement, not the extent of actual policy implementation.

With indicators for both asymmetry and integration, it is possible to generate a third independent variable that represents their interaction. This interaction term, of course, reflects my principal hypothesis – which is that legalism is most likely where asymmetry is low and proposed integration is high. * * * Table 14.5 below summarizes all three variables for each agreement.

ASYMMETRY, PROPOSED INTEGRATION, AND LEGALISM

Tables 14.6, 14.7, and 14.8 summarize the relationship between legalism and each of the three independent variables in turn: asymmetry, proposed

[41] IMF 1994, 90.

TABLE 14.5. *Legalism, Asymmetry, and Proposed Level of Integration*

Legalism	Pact	Asymmetry	Integration	Interaction
None or low	SACU	High	High – common market	High
	UDEAC	High	High – economic union	High
	ANZCERTA	High	High – common market[a]	High
	EEA	High	High – common market	High
	CARICOM	High	High – common market	High
	GCC	High	High – common market	High
	EFTA–Israel	High	Low – free trade area	Zero
	EFTA–Bulgaria	High	Low – free trade area	Zero
	EFTA–Estonia	High	Low – free trade area	Zero
	EFTA–Latvia	High	Low – free trade area	Zero
	EFTA–Lithuania	High	Low – free trade area	Zero
	EFTA–Slovenia	High	Low – free trade area	Zero
	Hungary–Slovenia	High	Low – free trade area	Zero
	Bulgaria–Czech Republic	High	Low – free trade area	Zero
	U.S.–Israel	High	Low – free trade area	Zero
	EFTA 1960	High	Low – free trade area	Zero
	Baltic FTA	Low	Low – free trade area	Zero
	CEFTA	Low	Low – free trade area	Zero
	Romania–Czech Republic	Low	Low – free trade area	Zero
	Bulgaria–Slovak Republic	Low	Low – free trade area	Zero
	Romania–Slovak Republic	Low	Low – free trade area	Zero
	Mano River Union	Low	Low – customs union	Zero
	AFTA	Low	Low – free trade area	Zero
Medium	MERCOSUR	High	High – common market	High
	EC–Israel	High	Low – free trade area	Zero
	EC Associations (12)	High	Low – free trade areas[b]	Zero
	EFTA–Czech Republic	High	Low – free trade area	Zero

Legalism	Pact	Asymmetry	Integration	Interaction
	EFTA–Poland	High	Low – free trade area	Zero
	EFTA–Hungary	High	Low – free trade area	Zero
	EFTA–Romania	High	Low – free trade area	Zero
	EFTA–Slovak Republic	High	Low – free trade area	Zero
	EFTA–Turkey	High	Low – free trade area	Zero
	NAFTA	High	Low – free trade area	Zero
	Chile–Ecuador	High	Low – free trade area	Zero
	Group of Three	High	Low – free trade area	Zero
	Mexico–Chile	High	Low – free trade area	Zero
	Chile–Canada	High	Low – free trade area	Zero
	Chile–Bolivia	High	Low – free trade area	Zero
	Mexico–Costa Rica	High	Low – free trade area	Zero
	Mexico–Bolivia	High	Low – free trade area	Zero
	OECS	Low	Low – customs union	Zero
	Chile–Colombia	Low	Low – free trade area	Zero
	Chile–Venezuela	Low	Low – free trade area	Zero
High or very high	CIS	High	High – economic union	High
	ECOWAS	High	High – common market	High
	CEAO	Low	High – economic union	Low
	COMESA	Low	High – common market	Low
	EAC	Low	High – common market	Low
	CACM	Low	High – common market[c]	Low
	Andean Pact	Low	High – common market	Low
	EC	Low	High – economic union	Low
	EFTA 1992	Low	High – common market	Low

[a] IMF (1994) codes ANZCERTA as a free trade area, but because it has achieved labor mobility, full coverage of services, and a competition policy, it is much more like a common market or, given the extent of legal harmonization, an economic union. See Kahler 1995, 109–11.

[b] The EC–Turkey agreement is a customs union.

[c] IMF (1994) codes the CACM as a customs union. The members had accomplished little more than a customs union at that point, but the aim of the treaty – as the name implies – is clearly to establish a common market.

Sources: For treaty type, see IMF 1994, app. I; and WTO 1995.

TABLE 14.6. *Legalism and Asymmetry*[a]

Level of legalism	Level of economic asymmetry		Total
	Low	High	
High or very high			9
	CACM	*CIS*	
	Andean Pact	*ECOWAS*	
	EC		
	EFTA 1992		
	COMESA		
	CEAO		
	EAC		
Medium			31
	OECS	MERCOSUR	
	Chile–Colombia	Mexico Pacts (4)	
	Chile–Venezuela	Chile–Bolivia	
		Chile–Canada	
		Chile–Ecuador	
		NAFTA	
		EC–Israel	
		EC Associations (12)	
		EFTA–Czech Republic	
		EFTA–Poland	
		EFTA–Hungary	
		EFTA–Romania	
		EFTA–Slovak Republic	
		EFTA–Turkey	
Low or none			23
	Baltic FTA	CARICOM	
	Romania–Czech Republic	U.S.–Israel	
	Bulgaria–Slovak Republic	EFTA 1960	
	Romania–Slovak Republic	EFTA–Israel	
	AFTA	EFTA–Bulgaria	
	Mono River Union	EFTA–Estonia	
		EFTA–Latvia	
		EFTA–Lithuania	
		EFTA–Slovenia	

Level of legalism	Level of economic asymmetry		Total
	Low	High	
		EEA	
		CEFTA	
		Hungary–Slovenia	
		Bulgaria–Czech Republic	
		SACU	
		UDEAC	
		ANZCERTA	
		GCC	
Total	16	47	63

Note: $P\,(\chi^2\{2\} > 17.08) = 0.000$.
   Fisher's exact $= 0.000$.
   Cramer's $V = 0.52$.
[a] Cases that lie off the predicted diagonal at high and low levels of legalism are shown in italics.

integration, and their interaction. To facilitate analysis of the small sample in this study, I collapse the five levels of legalism into three rows. ***

With a simplified dependent variable, it is possible to use chi-squared tests of statistical significance. For all three independent variables, the null hypothesis of independence can be rejected with very high levels of confidence ($p < .01$), suggesting a significant relationship to legalism.[42] To estimate the strength of that relationship, I also report Cramer's V, which for all three tables is relatively large ($V > .5$). The direction of each variable's effect on legalism is as expected: negative for asymmetry, positive for proposed integration, and negative for their interaction, reflecting the impact of asymmetry where proposed integration is high. ***

The first hypothesis to evaluate is whether levels of asymmetry and legalism are inversely related, given the preferences and negotiating leverage of regional hegemons. In its strongest form, the implication is that highly legalistic forms of dispute settlement should not occur in highly asymmetric settings. The evidence supports this claim, as shown in Table 14.6. Among the forty-seven cases of high asymmetry, there are only two examples of highly legalistic dispute settlement. All five pacts

[42] Given a sample size of sixty-three cases, the low expected frequencies of certain cells imply that the use of Pearson's chi-squared may be inappropriate. The reduced sample in Table 14.8 is especially problematic. For this reason I also report Fisher's exact, a more conservative test designed for small samples.

TABLE 14.7. *Legalism and Integration*

Level of legalism	Level of proposed integration		Total
	Low	High	
High or very high			9
	None	CACM	
		Andean Pact	
		EC	
		EFTA 1992	
		CIS	
		COMESA	
		CEAO	
		EAC	
		ECOWAS	
Medium			31
	OECS	MERCOSUR	
	Chile and Mexico Pacts (9)		
	NAFTA		
	EC–Israel		
	EC Associations (12)		
	EFTA–Czech Republic		
	EFTA–Poland		
	EFTA–Hungary		
	EFTA–Romania		
	EFTA–Slovak Republic		
	EFTA–Turkey		
Low or none			23
	U.S.–Israel	*CARICOM*	
	AFTA	*EEA*	
	Mano River Union	*SACU*	
	Romania–Czech Republic	*ANZCERTA*	
	Bulgaria–Czech Republic	*GCC*	
	Romania–Slovak Republic	*UDEAC*	
	Bulgaria–Slovak Republic		
	Hungary–Slovenia		
	EFTA 1960		
	EFTA–Israel		
	EFTA–Bulgaria		

Level of legalism	Level of proposed integration		Total
	Low	High	
	EFTA–Estonia		
	EFTA–Latvia		
	EFTA–Lithuania		
	EFTA–Slovenia		
	CEFTA		
	Baltic FTA		
Total	47	16	63

Note: P ($\chi^2\{2\} > 34.49$) = 0.000.
    Fisher's exact = 0.000.
    Cramer's V = 0.74.
[a] Cases that lie off the predicted diagonal at high and low levels of legalism are shown in italics.

with very high legalism are also cases of low asymmetry. And both anomalies with high legalism, the CIS and ECOWAS *** [– within which Russia and Nigeria, respectively, are dominant – at this point remain far from effective implementation, suggesting potential tension between the structure of political power in these accords and their institutional design.[43]]

Where asymmetry is low, high levels of legalism are expected only where the proposed level of integration is high. The evidence supports this claim as well. Six potentially anomalous cases italicized in Table 14.6 combine low asymmetry with low or no legalism, but all six treaties – four of which are among formerly socialist countries in Europe – aim to establish no more than a free trade area or customs union. Despite conditions of symmetry that might permit the adoption of rule-oriented dispute settlement, in these pacts governments have opted for relatively diplomatic systems. If they commit to deeper liberalization in the future, member states might endorse more legalistic dispute settlement. ***

A second test is for a positive relationship between the level of proposed integration and legalism, which the evidence generally confirms, as shown in Table 14.7. The majority of cases with low or high legalism fall on the

[43] The CIS Economic Court, for example, has yet to be given effective powers. President Lukashenka of Belarus has proposed reforming the CIS tribunal on the model of the European Court of Justice. See *BBC Summary of World Broadcasts* SU/D3168/D, 6 March 1998. In ECOWAS, very little progress has been made on liberalization. See "Ecobank Boss Deplores Rivalry in ECOWAS," *Panafrican News Agency*, 6 March 1999.

TABLE 14.8. *Legalism and the Interaction of Asymmetry and Integration*[a]

Level of legalism	Interaction of economic asymmetry and proposed integration		Total
	Low	High	
High or very high			9
	CACM	*CIS*	
	Andean Pact	*ECOWAS*	
	EC		
	EFTA 1992		
	COMESA		
	CEAO		
	EAC		
Medium	None	MERCOSUR	1
Low or none	None		6
		CARICOM	
		EEA	
		SACU	
		UDEAC	
		ANZCERTA	
		GCC	
Total	7	9	16

Note: $P (\chi^2\{2\} > 9.68) = 0.008$.
   Fisher's exact $= 0.004$.
   Cramer's $V = 0.78$.
[a] Cases where the interaction term is zero have been omitted to capture the impact of asymmetry where proposed integration is high. Cases that lie off the predicted diagonal at high and low levels of legalism are shown in italics.

predicted diagonal. No mere free trade agreements or customs unions have embraced the concept of binding rulings by a standing tribunal of justices. Only where the level of proposed integration is high, in the form of a common market or economic union, have highly legalistic mechanisms been endorsed. Nevertheless, no fewer than six cases lie at the intersection of ambitious integration and low or no legalism. In all six agreements, the signatories have embraced the prospect of deep integration but rejected binding third-party review. In the EEA, Southern African Customs Union (SACU), Australia–New Zealand Closer Economic Relations Trade Agreement (ANZCERTA), and Gulf Cooperation Council (GCC), member states have even managed to achieve considerable market

TABLE 14.9. *Ordered Probit Regression of Legalism*

Variable	Coefficient	Standard error
Proposed integration	3.203**	0.682
Economic asymmetry	1.067*	0.484
Interaction	−5.604**	1.483
Number of observations	63	
Log likelihood	−49.59	
Chi-squared	26.16	
Significance	0.000	

** $p < .01$, two-tailed test.
* $p < .05$, two-tailed test.

integration in the absence of highly legalistic institutions – in three of these cases without any system of third-party review at all.

These anomalous combinations of high integration and low legalism share one telling attribute: all six treaties shown in italics in Table 14.6 are cases of high asymmetry. This structural attribute – through its impact on the domestic political economy of trade – appears to be one of the principal reasons these deep integration initiatives have not adopted correspondingly legalistic dispute settlement mechanisms.[44] * * *

The most robust predictor of dispute settlement design seems to be the interaction of asymmetry and proposed integration. Where the level of proposed integration is relatively low – implying a value of zero for the interaction term – not a single treaty has approved a permanent court, as noted in Table 14.7. By excluding those cases, Table 14.8 highlights the impact of asymmetry where proposed integration is high. In this subset of sixteen common markets and economic unions, the multiplicative interaction term assumes the value of the asymmetry index. Where asymmetry is high, legalism is unlikely to be high even in cases where the proposed integration is deep. At high values of the interaction term, as Table 14.8 indicates, very few treaties endorse binding third-party review. The CIS and ECOWAS again stand out as exceptions. Among cases with low asymmetry, legalism is likely to be high only where policy goals are ambitious and the potential value of liberalization is considerable. As

44 * * * Predictably, the main obstacle to institutional reform in MERCOSUR is Brazil, by far the largest signatory. During negotiations for a permanent dispute settlement mechanism, Brazil rejected proposals by Uruguay and Argentina for a more legalistic system. See Pastori 1994, 4–7; and O'Neal Taylor 1996, 874–75.

Table 14.8 reveals, where the interaction term is low – the most favorable conditions for legalism, according to this framework – all seven treaties have endorsed standing tribunals.

The dramatic impact of this interaction appears also in an ordered probit regression of legalism. Table 14.9 summarizes the results of this statistical test, which uses asymmetry and the interaction term as continuous variables that range from zero to 1, capturing more variation than the preceding tabular analysis. Proposed integration (low = 0; high = 1) and legalism (none or low = 0; medium = 1; high or very high = 2) remain categorical variables. Despite the small sample size, which is not ideal for maximum likelihood estimation, * both integration and the multiplicative interaction term exhibit highly significant and strong effects on legalism.[45] These effects, moreover, are in the predicted direction. The coefficient of the interaction term is the largest in magnitude, indicating the decisively negative relationship of asymmetry to legalism where the level of proposed integration is high. *

This simple analytical framework, tested with basic indicators of GDP concentration and treaty type, successfully accounts for thirty of the thirty-two cases at the more extreme levels of legalism, where the implications of the theory are clearest. * * *

* * *

CONCLUSION

In this article I offer a political theory of dispute settlement design in international trade. My aim is to demonstrate and account for significant variation in the level of legalism across different regional accords. With a dual emphasis on economic asymmetry and the proposed depth of integration, I predict the extent to which trading states will delegate judicial review authority to impartial third parties. My central assertion is that in drafting governance structures for international trade, political leaders weigh the benefits of improved treaty compliance against the costs of diminished policy discretion. To make this judgment, they assess their

---

[45] In maximum likelihood analysis of small samples, positive findings of significance may be more reliable than negative results. Hart and Clark report that in probit models of binary dependent variables, the risk of false positive findings does not change appreciably as sample size decreases. Hart and Clark 1999. They conclude that "the likelihood that small samples will induce Type I errors is small," in contrast to the substantial risk of false negative findings.

economic stake in intrapact trade; their relative economic power vis-à-vis other parties to the accord; and the depth or intensity of the proposed liberalization. Thanks to their market size and lesser dependence on trade, relatively large countries tend to prefer less legalism than their smaller counterparts. Because treaties require unanimity, the institutional preferences of larger countries tend to prevail in negotiations, defining the lowest common denominator.

The implications of this approach – chief among which is that legalistic mechanisms are unlikely where asymmetry is high or integration is shallow – stand up to empirical scrutiny against a sizable set of more than sixty regional trade agreements. In almost every pact with high asymmetry, legalism is absent – even, in contrast to functional accounts, where integration is deep. Where asymmetry is low, legalism occurs only where at least a common market, and not just free trade or a uniform external tariff, is the ultimate policy objective. * * *

Seen from a broad perspective, this theory of trade dispute settlement design ostensibly relies on a hybrid of neoliberal institutionalist logic and structural realist indicators of relative economic power. Unlike those systemic approaches, however, it is grounded in a political calculation of costs and benefits in the domestic arena, not in expectations about absolute or relative gains internationally. Political leaders in this model are not primarily focused on overcoming market failures or improving their defensive positions in an anarchic international system, however germane such considerations may be to the decision to pursue economic integration in the first instance. Given a regional trade initiative, negotiations over dispute settlement design in my view are driven by domestic political concerns. Without delving into the particulars of comparative politics, my analytical framework connects generic domestic political incentives to issues of international institutional design, * * * bridging the steadily receding divide between comparative and international political economy. *

* * *

[My] account privileges the moment of institutional creation, when member states negotiate and establish a system for the resolution of disputes. This moment need not coincide with the signing of the initial treaty. In a few pacts, such as the CACM, MERCOSUR, and AFTA, member states adopted or amended their permanent dispute settlement mechanisms well after their commitments to liberalize trade. Like asymmetry and the depth of integration, dispute settlement designs may change over time, with one blueprint substituted for another as in EFTA. Within the parameters of that design, at every level of legalism, a range of behavioral outcomes – from frequent use to utter irrelevance – are possible. Nevertheless, outcomes still remain subject to boundary conditions established by the institutional blueprint of each treaty, rendering the basic design itself worthy of investigation.

APPENDIX A: SOURCES FOR TREATY TEXTS

The date following the treaty title indicates the year the treaty was published. The original signing date for each treaty can be found in Table 14.2.

AFTA (ASEAN Free Trade Area). 1992. *International Legal Materials* 31:506.

Protocol on Dispute Settlement Mechanism, available from the ASEAN Secretariat or online at <http://www. asean.or.id/economic/dsm.htm>.

Andean Pact. 1979. Treaty Creating the Court of Justice of the Cartagena Agreement. *International Lega Materials* 18:1203.

Statute of the Court of Justice of the Cartagena Agreement, available from the Organization of American States or online at <http://www.sice.oas.org/trade/junac/tribunal/cartage2.stm>.

ANZCERTA (Australia–New Zealand Closer Economic Relations Trade Agreement). 1983. *International Legal Materials* 22:945.

Baltic Free Trade Agreement. Available from the foreign ministries of member states.

CACM (Central American Common Market). 1994. *Basic Documents of International Economic Law* 2:529.

Statute of the Central American Court of Justice. 1995. *International Legal Materials* 34:921.

CARICOM (Caribbean Community). 1974. *United Nations Treaty Series* 946:17. New York: UN.

CEAO (West African Economic Community). 1981. *United Nations Treaty Series* 1257:362. New York: UN.

CEEC (Central and East European Country) Pacts. Available online at <http://www.wto.org/wto/online/ddf.htm>.

CEFTA (Central European Free Trade Agreement). 1995. *International Legal Materials* 34:3.

Chile and Mexico Pacts. Available from the Organization of American States or online at <http://www.sice.oas.org/trade.stm>.

CIS (Commonwealth of Independent States). 1995. *International Legal Materials* 34:1279.

COMESA (Common Market for Eastern and Southern Africa). 1994. *International Legal Materials* 33:1067.

EAC (East African Community). 1967. *International Legal Materials* 6:932.

EC (European Community). Agreement Establishing the European Economic Community and Protocol on the Statute of the Court of Justice of the EEC. 1958. *United Nations Treaty Series* 298:11, 147. New York: UN.

EC Associations. Available in *Official Journal of the European Communities*, or online at <http://europa.eu.int/eur-lex/en/>.

EC–Israel. 1996. *Official Journal of the European Communities* 39:1–11.

ECOWAS (Economic Community of West African States). 1975. *International Legal Materials* 14:1200. Revised Treaty. 1996. *International Legal Materials* 35:660.

Protocol A/P.1/7/91 on the Community Court of Justice. 1996. *Revue Africaine de Droit International et Compare* 8:228.

EEA (European Economic Area). 1993. *Common Market Law Reports* 29:1247.

EFTA (European Free Trade Association). 1960. *United Nations Treaty Series* 370:5. New York: UN.

EFTA. 1994. *Official Journal of the European Communities* 37:1–83.

EFTA Associations. Available online at <http://www.efta.int/docs/EFTA/Legal-Texts/FTAs/FTAdefault.htm>.

GCC (Gulf Cooperation Council). 1987. *International Legal Materials* 26:1131.

Mano River Union. 1974. *United Nations Treaty Series* 952:264. New York: UN.

MERCOSUR (Common Market of the South). 1991. *International Legal Materials* 30:1041. Protocol of Brasilia for the Settlement of Disputes. 1997. *International Legal Materials* 36:691. Ouro Preto Protocol, available from the Organization of American States or online at <http://www.sice.oas.org/trade/mrcsr/ourop/index.stm>.

NAFTA (North American Free Trade Agreement). 1993. *International Legal Materials* 32:605.

OECS (Organization of East Caribbean States). 1981. *International Legal Materials* 20:1166.

SACU (Southern African Customs Union). 1973. *United Nations Treaty Series* 860:69. New York: UN.

U.S.–Israel. 1985. *International Legal Materials* 24:654.

UDEAC (Central African Customs and Economic Union). 1964. *International Legal Materials* 4:699.

APPENDIX B: EXCLUDED REGIONAL ECONOMIC AGREEMENTS, 1957–95

This list draws largely on de la Torre and Kelly 1992; IMF 1994; and WTO 1995. These sources also include pacts that were superceded by subsequent agreements included in Table 14.2 or listed here.

Nonreciprocal Agreements

U.S. Caribbean Basin Initiative

EC Lomé Conventions with African, Caribbean, and Pacific States

EC Cooperation Agreements with Algeria, Egypt, Jordan, Lebanon, Morocco, Syria, and Tunisia

EFTA Cooperation Agreements with Albania, Egypt, and Tunisia

1976 Australia–Papua New Guinea Trade and Commercial Relations Agreement

1980 South Pacific Regional Trade and Economic Agreement

1991 CARICOM–Venezuela Agreement

1991 CARICOM–Colombia Agreement

Cooperation or Framework Agreements

1976 Economic Community of the Great Lakes Countries
1980 Latin American Integration Association
1983 Economic Community of Central African States
1984 Indian Ocean Commission
1985 Economic Cooperation Organization
1985 South Asian Association for Regional Cooperation (signed limited preferential trade pact in 1993)
1989 Asia Pacific Economic Cooperation Forum
1991 African Economic Community
1992 Southern African Development Community (signed free trade agreement in 1996)
1992 Black Sea Economic Cooperation Project
1994 Association of Caribbean States
1994 Free Trade Area of the Americas

Unavailable Agreements

1961 Borneo Free Trade Area
1962 African Common Market
1964 Arab Common Market
1975 Bangkok Agreement
1989 Arab Maghreb Union
1991 Thailand–Lao People's Democratic Republic Trade Agreement
1992 Slovak Republic–Czech Republic Customs Union
1993 Slovenia–Czech Republic Free Trade Agreement
1993 Slovenia–Slovak Republic Free Trade Agreement
1994 Kazakhstan–Kyrgyz Republic–Uzbekistan Customs Union
1994 Economic and Monetary Community of Central Africa (renewal of moribund 1964 UDEAC)
1994 West African Economic and Monetary Union (successor to dissolved 1973 CEAO)

15

Loosening the Ties that Bind: A Learning Model of Agreement Flexibility

Barbara Koremenos

* * *

*** Existing international agreements are testament to states' willingness and ability to cooperate despite the international anarchy in which they find themselves. Given the difficulties of cooperation under anarchy documented in the recent international relations literature, understanding how states manage to bring about the formal cooperation embodied in international agreements is of both theoretical and practical interest.

States can make agreements more desirable in prospect and more robust in practice by varying their provisions for duration and renegotiation. These provisions help states account for the uncertain economic, political, and technological contexts in which agreements are made and (ideally) kept.

* * *

Nevertheless, the issues of duration and renegotiation have been almost completely ignored in the political science literature on international relations. They have been wholly neglected in theoretical studies of international cooperation, and there has been surprisingly little discussion of these issues from an empirical point of view. In fact, although some discussions of individual agreements cover the issues of duration and renegotiation for the agreement in question, no work exists that attempts

I thank Jeffrey Smith, James Fearon, Andrew Kydd, James Morrow, Charles Glaser, Duncan Snidal, George Bunn, Richard Bilder, Brian Portnoy, Scott Mosier, T. Clifton Morgan, Alan Stam, Jack Child, and workshop participants at University of Chicago (PIPES), the Brookings Institution, and the Merriam Lab of the University of Illinois, Champagne-Urbana. The comments of editors Peter Gourevitch and David Lake and those of three anonymous referees greatly improved this article.

to account for or even describe the observed patterns and variation in agreement duration and renegotiation.[1]

* * *

What I am attempting essentially is to bring theory – in particular, formal international relations theory – to international law. I argue that uncertainty in the international environment – uncertainty that is of varying forms and degrees across issue contexts – leads states to choose particular duration and renegotiation provisions. These provisions, in turn, affect whether or not states conclude international agreements and whether or not they renege on them.[2]

This study is the first theoretical work to address the nominal (that is, negotiated) length of international agreements.[3] My theoretical work takes as its departure the economic theory of contracts, since agreements are essentially contracts between states, with the key difference that there is no external authority available to enforce them. The economic literature on contract duration formalizes the key trade-off in choosing contract duration between the benefit associated with spreading the (assumed) fixed cost of contracting over additional periods and the loss associated with staying for additional periods in a suboptimal contract.[4] This basic insight is helpful but insufficient to explain the range of duration and renegotiation provisions present in even the small set of agreements I consider here.

My theory identifies key factors affecting the choices of duration and renegotiation provisions in these agreements. The two most important factors are the degree of agreement uncertainty (formally, the variance of the distribution of gains from an agreement) and the degree of noise in the environment (formally, the variance of confounding variables whose effect on outcomes may be confused with that of an agreement). The greater the agreement uncertainty, the more likely states will want to limit the duration

---

[1] One exception is Bilder, who surveys a number of techniques that states can use to help themselves manage the risks of international agreements. Bilder 1981. He identifies and devotes two pages to the technique of "Limiting the Duration of the Agreement." Also, Grieco mentions issues of agreement durability in his concluding chapter (see fn. 22 below). Grieco 1990.

[2] Moreover, I would argue that renegotiation clauses (as well as other forms of flexibility provisions like escape clauses) help reconcile the tension between two doctrines of international law: *rebus sic stantibus* and *pacta sunt servanda* (treaties should be performed in good faith).

[3] Two recent studies by Gaubatz and Bennett examine realized durations of alliances using hazard-rate models. See Gaubatz 1996; and Bennett 1997. These studies ignore the fact that many agreements are initially concluded with a finite duration. They therefore conflate planned agreement terminations with those resulting from a violation of the agreement.

[4] The three main papers are Gray 1978; Dye 1985; and Harris and Holmstrom 1987.

of the agreement and incorporate renegotiation. The factor working against renegotiation is noise. The greater the noise, the more difficult it is to learn how an agreement is actually working; hence incorporating limited duration and renegotiation provisions becomes less valuable.

The model provides a framework within which to discuss the Nuclear Non-Proliferation Treaty (NPT). I describe the basic features of the agreement and summarize the available information about how the parties themselves framed the duration and renegotiation issues while negotiating the agreement. * * *

The remainder of this article is organized as follows. In the second section I develop a formal model in which an agreement characterized by uncertainty may be renegotiated to incorporate new information. The uncertainty is related to the division of gains under the agreement, with the parties resolving this uncertainty over time as they gain experience with the agreement. This form of uncertainty corresponds to the uncertainty experienced by the parties to the international agreement I discuss in detail in the third section. * * * In the fifth section I offer conclusions.

MODEL: LEARNING ABOUT THE WORKINGS OF AN AGREEMENT

* * *

In this model an agreement is like an experience good in which a complete knowledge of the effects of the good is gained only by using it. Over time, by observing the outcomes obtained under the agreement and attempting to distinguish the once-and-for-all effects of the agreement from the normal period-to-period fluctuation in outcomes, the parties come to learn with increasing precision the true distribution of benefits created by the agreement.[5]

---

[5] There are other forms of uncertainty, and, importantly, states respond to these with alternative flexibility provisions. For example, in the context of economics agreements, the uncertainty is often persistent; states cannot learn once and for all about the division of gains from an agreement because that division is subject to repeated shocks. In such a case, states may follow the example of the G5 finance ministers and have a *series* of finite-duration agreements with renegotiation in between. Koremenos 1999. In a recent study I consider the same environment but with a large number of parties. Koremenos 2000. In such a case renegotiation costs may be prohibitive (since they rise with the number of parties). Hence parties may choose to establish an institution (like the IMF) empowered to adjust the terms of the agreement in response to the repeated shocks. Bordo and Kydland's work on escape clauses during the gold standard addresses a different type of uncertainty: political shocks, such as wars and banking panics. Bordo and Kydland 1995 and 1996. Such uncertainty leads states to incorporate "suspension" mechanisms instead of "adjustment" mechanisms. Downs and Rocke and Rosendorff and Milner consider similar models in a trade context. See Downs and Rocke 1995; and Rosendorff and Milner [2002].

How can states make use of what they learn about the distribution of gains from the agreement? They may choose to make their initial agreement of finite duration, and then "re"negotiate a new agreement when the first one comes to a close. If they do so, they can use the information they have gained through their experience under the agreement to realign the division of gains in the renegotiated agreement. Under certain conditions (made precise below) this planned renegotiation and realignment reduces *ex ante* uncertainty and thereby raises the expected utility of the parties. Put another way, careful selection of the duration and renegotiation provisions allows the parties to conclude efficient agreements (ones that increase the size of the pie available to the parties) that otherwise might fail because of distributional problems.

Of course, states may also be uncertain about the absolute level of gains from a potential agreement. In this analysis I focus solely on distributional uncertainty. My justification is both theoretical and empirical. Uncertainty about the absolute level of gains is probably at least as pervasive as distributional uncertainty. However, what would make absolute uncertainty interesting from the viewpoint of cooperation theory is if its presence precluded any agreement at all. In other words, are there many cases in which there was substantial uncertainty about whether an agreement would produce a net gain and hence in which provisions for limited duration and renegotiation made cooperation possible? The one issue area for which absolute uncertainty might play such a role is the environment. Nonetheless, in that issue area, questions of distribution also loom large.[6] In any event, the distribution question seems at least as important empirically and much more interesting theoretically.[7]

Assumptions

The following assumptions underlie the model:

States care about the future – that is, their discount factor is not zero.
States are risk averse.
There is uncertainty about future states of the world.

---

[6] For example, writing about the Convention on Biological Diversity, Raustiala argues that the convention "addressed three (linked) central concerns: the conservation of biodiversity, the promotion of sustainable use, and the equitable sharing of benefits. It is this latter objective, with its clear redistributive implications, that was and remains the cause of much debate." Raustiala 1997, 491.

[7] See also fn. 12 below.

The costs of making agreements completely contingent are sufficiently
large that the parties do not ever choose to do so.[8]

There are costs to negotiating (and renegotiating) agreements.

There are costs to reneging on agreements.

States have shared *a priori* beliefs about the information they do not
possess, and they revise their beliefs according to Bayesian logic as
their interactions evolve.[9]

* * *

Consider the role each assumption plays. If states did not care about
the future, they would not bother to conclude agreements. If states were
not risk averse, they would always conclude indefinite agreements in order
to avoid paying renegotiation costs and would not care *ex ante* about how
much the distribution of gains might differ from that originally agreed
upon. If there were no uncertainty about future states of the world, there
would be no additional information to incorporate through renegotiation, and all agreements would be indefinite in order to economize on
renegotiation costs. If agreements could be made perfectly contingent on
the realized state of the world, states would do so and thereby save on
renegotiation costs by eliminating the need for renegotiation. If negotiation and renegotiation were costless, states would renegotiate every time
new information arrived, and all agreements would be of short duration.
If reneging were costless, states would renege often (assuming renegotiation costs were not too high) and would be less likely to adopt finite-
duration agreements. Instead, they would use reneging as a form of
contingent renegotiation within indefinite-duration agreements.

Basics of the Model

There are two prospective parties to the agreement. In the absence of an
agreement, each party obtains an outcome every period. This outcome
depends on the particular context, but it could represent something like
GNP or some measure of military security. Each party has an expectation
about what its outcome will be every period – for example, state 1 expects
its GNP to be $1 trillion. This is the party's base outcome. Of course, the
actual outcome will rarely, if ever, correspond exactly to the base. The

---

[8] For a justification of this assumption in the context of the economics literature on incomplete contracts, see the discussion in Hart and Holmstrom 1987.

[9] In Knightian terms, the parties face *risk*, not *uncertainty*.

actual outcome will consist of the base plus or minus some amount. For example, state 1's actual GNP might be $0.9 trillion or $1.1 trillion. I refer to this unanticipated variation as the outcome shock or noise.

I assume the agreement yields a total gain that is known at the time the agreement is concluded. What is not known at that time is how this gain will accrue to the two parties in practice. I assume that the parties can set the expected value of the two shares in the initial agreement.

The division of the gain agreed upon in the initial agreement reflects the relative bargaining power of the two parties. For example, suppose that states 1 and 2 have equal bargaining power and they conclude a joint research venture that will result in a total profit of $25 billion. What cannot be known in advance is exactly how whatever technology emerges from the venture will benefit industry in each of the two states. Initially, each state invests an equal amount, and the parties set the expected gain to be the same for both states, $12.5 billion.

The basic problem facing the parties to an agreement in this model is to sort out the effects of the agreement from other random fluctuations in outcomes. For example, suppose that, after the joint venture is concluded, state 1's GNP is $1.05 trillion. How can state 1 know how much (if any) of the $50 billion increase in GNP results from the joint venture and how much results from an agricultural boom spawned by favorable weather? The answer is that it cannot know exactly, but it can learn over time.

The states face a choice between an agreement of indefinite duration and one finite-duration agreement followed by an agreement of indefinite duration. In the simple two-period case I consider formally, the choice becomes one two-period agreement with no renegotiation or two one-period agreements with renegotiation in between to realign the distribution of gains.

Renegotiation takes place whenever a finite-duration agreement comes to an end. Thus the reservation outcome for both parties in the renegotiation consists of the no-agreement outcome. Essentially, the parties are in the same situation with renegotiation as in the original negotiation except that they have learned something about the realized distribution of gains from the agreement in the interim. Once the parties choose an indefinite-duration agreement, no further renegotiation takes place.

I assume that if and when the parties renegotiate the agreement, they incorporate an adjustment factor that makes the expected gain to each of the parties the same as it was in the original agreement. This adjustment factor takes account of the information gained about the realized value of the distribution of gains during the periods since the original agreement was concluded.

For example, suppose that, after a number of years, states 1 and 2 learn that state 1's industry is actually reaping significantly more benefits from the research venture than state 2's industry. If the parties originally agreed to a finite-duration agreement followed by renegotiation, then when they renegotiate at the end of the initial agreement, they will adjust the investment schedule so that state 1 invests more and state 2 invests less. This change will roughly bring the actual distribution of gains in line with what was expected when the agreement was first concluded. Assuming that the same expected division of gains is the result of every renegotiation is another way of saying that the relative bargaining power of the two parties is assumed to be constant over time.

In general, we would expect the bargaining power of the two states to change over time as their economic fortunes change. In particular, we might expect the realized division of gains under the agreement to affect the bargaining power of the two states if and when an agreement is renegotiated. Thus rather than returning to the initial expected division of gains in the renegotiated agreement, the states would agree to a new expected division of gains that would be more favorable to the party whose realized gain exceeded its original expected gain. Adding changes in bargaining power to the model in this form increases the variance of the outcomes conditional on renegotiation because the renegotiation no longer tries to undo completely the difference between the expected and realized gain. This, in turn, enlarges the set of cases in which no renegotiation would be chosen by risk-averse states.

I do not incorporate the effects of changes in bargaining power into the model for four reasons. First, and most important, given that the duration problem has been wholly neglected in the literature thus far, I choose to focus exclusively on it and keep other elements of the context (including the bargaining component) as simple as possible.[10] Second, allowing changes in bargaining power does not affect the comparative statics presented later. It changes the location of the cutpoint at which parties switch from one form of agreement to another, but the general

---

[10] This is especially important given that bargaining theory has not yet produced results that are robust. For example, results reported by Fearon disappear as soon as the war of attrition model is replaced with a Rubinstein alternating-offers model. Fearon 1998. Moreover, even within particular models, results depend greatly on very specific assumptions, such as the time between offers.

comparative static results remain.[11] Third, in some cases the resources affected by the agreement in question are small relative to GNP so that the actual effect of the realized division of gains under the agreement on the parties' bargaining power would be small. Fourth, for pairs of states involved in multiple agreements, the agreement shocks will tend to average out, so that the states' relative bargaining power remains roughly the same.

In the context of international relations, there is no external authority available to enforce agreements. In other words, states can renege. In this model, reneging is equivalent to abandoning the agreement. I assume that parties that renege suffer a cost. I also assume that the parties can negotiate a new agreement in the period following the abandonment of the old.

Hence the basic intuition of my model is that the parties will integrate planned renegotiation into international agreements when the value to them of reducing the *ex ante* variance of the outcome stemming from agreement uncertainty is large relative to the cost of renegotiating. This reduction in *ex ante* variance is achieved by realigning the division of gains at the time of the renegotiation to be closer to the original division by incorporating an adjustment factor into the agreement. Note that the adjustment factor is chosen by the parties within the model; it is not a parameter of the model for which comparative static results can be obtained. Put differently, it is an endogenous and not an exogenous variable.

Notation

Formally, assume that there are two prospective parties to the agreement, $n = 1, 2$. Let their outcomes in each period t in the absence of the agreement be given by

$$Y_{1,t} = b_1 + u_{1,t}$$

$$Y_{2,t} = b_2 + u_{2,t},$$

where the outcome $Y_{n,t}$ depends on the particular context but could represent something like GNP, where b_1 and b_2 are the expected values of the outcome measure, and where $u_{1,t}$ and $u_{2,t}$ represent variation in the outcome over time, independent of the agreement – noise. I assume that

---

[11] I elaborate this point later.

$u_{1,t}$ and $u_{2,t}$ have mean zero and are independently and identically distributed across periods and across parties with probability density function $f(u)$. Without loss of generality, I normalize b_1 and b_2 to zero.

With respect to the agreement, let the total gain from the agreement be a fixed amount g, known to both parties.[12] Denote the expected values of the shares determined in the bargaining process by m for party 1 and by $(g - m)$ for party 2. I assume that the actual realization $(m + \varepsilon)$ is a random variable with probability density function $h(m + \varepsilon)$ where $E(m + \varepsilon) = m$. Thus in the presence of the agreement, the outcomes of the two parties in period t are given by

$$Y_{1,t} = m + \varepsilon + u_{1,t}$$
$$Y_{2,t} = g - (m + \varepsilon) + u_{2,t},$$

with associated expected values

$$E(Y_{1,t}) = m$$
$$E(Y_{2,t}) = g - m.^{[13]}$$

Note that ε has no t subscript because it represents the one-time agreement uncertainty. It is drawn at the time an agreement is concluded and stays the same after that. In contrast, the u's, which represent the outcome shocks or noise, do have t subscripts, as new u's are drawn for both parties each period. Thus the u's embody persistent noise.

Initial negotiation costs are k_1. Renegotiation costs are k_2. The adjustment factor incorporated into the agreement at the renegotiation stage is a, and the cost paid by parties that renege is c.

---

[12] The simplifying assumption of a fixed, known g can be relaxed without changing any implications of the model. A more general model would make g random, with the parties then facing the more difficult problem of untangling both the total gain and the distribution of gains from the normal noise in the outcome. With a random g, agreements might be concluded in which the expected value *of g ex ante* was positive but the realized value was negative. This provides an additional motivation for having a finite-duration agreement. Instead of renegotiating, the parties will simply not conclude additional agreements if they learn that g is probably negative. In many agreement contexts, states clearly care about both the distribution of gains and the total gain. I have chosen to focus here on the distribution of gains in the interest of parsimony. None of the comparative statics in my model depend on the assumption of a fixed g, but allowing g to be a random variable would substantially increase the notational burden and the formal complexity of the model.

[13] Note that without period-specific shocks, determining the value of ε would take only a single period. With only a single common shock, $u_t = u_{1,t} = u_{2,t}$, the exact value of ε could be determined in two periods.

In sum, states are often unsure about how agreements will work in practice. The difference between how they expect an agreement to work and how it actually works is represented by ε, the random component of the distribution of gains from the agreement. The parties know the distribution from which ε is drawn but must learn about the particular value of ε for their agreement. The variance of the distribution from which ε is drawn represents their degree of agreement uncertainty.

In each period, each of the two parties to an agreement receives some outcome Y. In the absence of an agreement, the outcome consists of a known base b and a period-specific random component u. Since the parties know b, in the absence of an agreement they can figure out u.

When there is an agreement, the situation changes. The outcome Y now consists of three components: b, u, and either $(m + \varepsilon)$ or $g - (m + \varepsilon)$. The terms involving ε represent the gains from the agreement. Like u, these terms are random. Unlike u, these terms are fixed; they do not vary from period to period. The basic problem facing the parties is to sort out the effects of the agreement, ε, from the normal noise in the outcome, u. Over time, the parties can learn about the value of $(m + \varepsilon)$ or $(m - \varepsilon)$ realized under the agreement. That is, over time they can distinguish the effect of the agreement on their outcomes from the period-to-period variation due to u.

Two-Period Game

For simplicity, I assume throughout that the parties have identical utility functions and bargaining power and that the agreement yields a positive gain. The bargaining outcome in both periods is exogenous and satisfies the Nash bargaining solution.[14]

Timeline

At the beginning of period 1, the two parties, $n = 1, 2$, play a Nash demand game in which they choose the expected division of gains. The parties' Nash demand game strategies consist of $\{m_n : m_n \in [0, g]\}$. If $m_1 = m_2$ and $m_n \in [0, g]$, the parties continue the negotiations. In all other cases, the parties conclude no agreement.

If the parties continue the negotiations, they then enter the agreement-type choice stage wherein each party must choose among the following: no

---

[14] This cooperative solution corresponds to the Rubinstein alternating-offers noncooperative solution when δ is close to 1. See Osborne and Rubinstein 1990.

agreement (*NA*); one two-period agreement, which is the analog of a nonrenegotiated agreement (*NR*); and two one-period agreements, the analog of a renegotiated agreement (*R*). If both parties choose *NR*, the parties enter into a nonrenegotiated agreement. If both parties choose *R*, the parties enter into a renegotiated agreement. Otherwise, the parties conclude no agreement (*NA*). Note that nine possible strategy profiles can result at this stage, {*NA, NR, R*} × {*NA, NR, R*}, and only two, (*NR, NR*) and (*R, R*), result in an agreement.

Next, nature draws $u_{1,1}$ and $U_{2,1}$ and if there is some form of agreement, ε. The outcomes for period 1, $Y_{1,1}$ and $Y_{2,1}$, are observed by both players.

If the parties concluded a two-period agreement in the first period, then at the beginning of period 2 they choose whether to abide by the duration provision stipulated in the agreement. Similarly, if the parties agreed to two one-period agreements with renegotiation in between, they must decide whether to proceed with the renegotiation.

If the parties negotiated a one-period agreement in the initial period and elect to proceed with renegotiation, or if one party reneges on a two-period agreement, the parties negotiate a new agreement. They play a Nash demand game in which they choose the expected division of gains, where their action set again consists of $\{m_n^*:m_n^* \in [0, g]\}$. If $m_1^* = m_2^*$ and $m_n^* \in [0, g]$, the parties conclude a one-period agreement. Otherwise, the parties conclude no agreement.

Next, nature draws $u_{1,2}$ and $u_{2,2}$. At this point the parties receive their payoffs, and the game ends.

Equilibrium
The equilibrium concept employed is perfect Bayesian equilibrium. I employ an incomplete-information solution concept because, even though the preferences of both parties are common knowledge, there is uncertainty about the physical consequences of any concluded agreement. This gets translated as uncertainty regarding preferences over possible agreements. In this particular setup, each party is the "opposite type" from the other; as each party learns about its own type, it also learns about the other's type. We can think of party 1 as type $+\varepsilon$ and party 2 as type $-\varepsilon$. Additionally, I impose the following restriction: The set of punishment used by the parties (that is, the costs a party pays after reneging) must be renegotiation-proof. Appendix A provides a characterization of an equilibrium of the game.

Comparative Statics

I focus here on the two most important implications of my model. Both have to do with the effects of changing the amount and type of uncertainty faced by the parties to an agreement. First, consider the effects of changes in the degree of agreement uncertainty, represented by the variance of ε (the shock to the distribution of gains under the agreement):

Hypothesis 1: All else equal, for risk-averse parties an increase in agreement uncertainty (the variance of ε) increases the value of renegotiation and therefore makes the parties more likely to choose a renegotiated agreement (two one-period agreements) than a nonrenegotiated agreement (one two-period agreement).[15]

To see the intuition here, it helps to think of the effect of an increase in the variance of the agreement shock ε in two ways: absolutely and relative to the variance of the noise, u. To see the absolute effect, consider the special case where the variance of the noise, u, is zero. In this special case, an increase in the degree of agreement uncertainty would still increase the value of renegotiation. The more variable the agreement shocks, the more that risk-averse states gain in expected utility from being able to undo them through renegotiation.

To see the relative effect, return to the general case where the variance of u is not zero. In the general case, states can learn more about the realized value of ε when it is more easily distinguished from u. Increasing the variance of ε while holding the variance of u constant does just that – it makes it easier to distinguish the agreement shock from the noise. Put somewhat differently, increasing the variance of ε relative to that of u makes the first-period outcomes more informative about ε. Because renegotiation is more valuable when states have better information about the realized value of ε at the time they renegotiate, an increase in the variance of ε again increases the value of renegotiation.

Now consider the effect of an increase in the degree of agreement uncertainty on whether states choose to conclude any agreement. For risk-averse parties, any increase in the variance of the outcomes under the agreement reduces the expected utility (at the time of the decision whether to conclude an agreement) under either type of agreement relative to no agreement. This is obvious in the case of a nonrenegotiated agreement, but it is also the case for a renegotiated agreement, since the adjustment mechanism does not undo the effects of the agreement shocks in every state of the world. Note, however, that as long as the distribution of the

---

[15] It also makes it more likely that the parties will choose no agreement at all.

agreement shock is such that the probability that a state actually loses from an agreement is zero, the parties will always choose some form of agreement as long as the negotiation costs are not too large.

The second important implication of my model concerns the effects of changes in the variance of *u*, the factors outside the agreement ("noise" in this context) that affect the outcome of interest:

Hypothesis 2: All else equal, for risk-averse parties an increase in noise (the variance of *u*) decreases the value of renegotiation and therefore makes the parties more likely to choose a nonrenegotiated agreement (a two-period agreement) than a renegotiated agreement (two one-period agreements).

The intuition here concerns the value of renegotiating at the end of the first period. As the noise increases, the amount of information the first-period outcomes provide about the value of ε decreases. The less information the parties have about ε, the less value they place on being able to reset the division of gains under the agreement, and therefore the less value they place on renegotiating. In other words, an increase in the noise decreases the information content of the first-period realizations, with the result that the parties learn less about the true value of the agreement shock. This, in turn, means that the parties cannot do as good a job of realigning the distribution of gains, which decreases the (*ex ante*) value of renegotiation.[16] Note that this is precisely the reverse of what happens under hypothesis 1 when the relative variance of ε increases.

Figures 15.1 and 15.2 illustrate the two comparative static hypotheses using simulated choices from a discretized version of the two-period model. In the simulations, the base outcome, *b*, is set to 20.[17] The gain from the agreement, *g*, is set equal to 8 and is assumed to be divided equally in expectation between the two parties so that $m = 4$. I fix the values of the discount factor δ at 0.9; and the costs of negotiation, renegotiation, and reneging, k_1, k_2 and c, at 1.0, 0.5, and 1.0, respectively. I use a cube root utility function (that is, the utility from a given outcome is its cube root), which implicitly sets the level of risk aversion for the parties. ***

---

[16] Note that in addition to its effect on the relative attractiveness of a renegotiated agreement, an increase in the variance of *u* tends to decrease the expected utility associated with every agreement-type choice (including no agreement) for risk-averse parties by increasing the variance of the realized outcomes.

[17] I use a positive base value to ensure that the utility associated with each possible realization is always positive. This ensures that I can calculate utility values even with utility functions such as the cube root. I could change the base value to some larger number, such as 100 or 1,000, without changing any of the substantive results. Recall that in the model the base is normalized to zero.

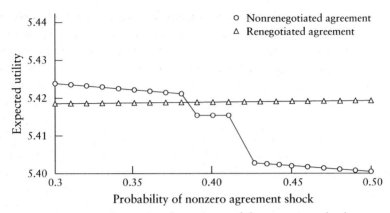

FIGURE 15.1. Increasing the variance of the agreement shock.

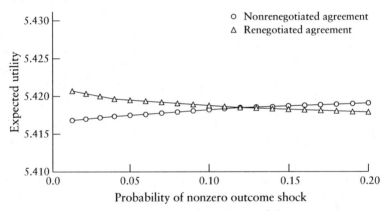

FIGURE 15.2. Increasing the variance of the noise.

Conditional on these values for the utility function and the model parameters, I calculate the utility of each state for a large number of values for the variances of the noise in the base outcome, u, and the one-time agreement shock, ε. In each case, I assume that u_1, u_2, and ε take on the values of -2, 0, or 2.

In Figure 15.1, I illustrate the effects of increasing the variance of the agreement shock, ε. I start with probabilities of $(0.3, 0.4, 0.3)$ for the three values of ε and then symmetrically increase the probabilities of the two nonzero values until I end up with probabilities of $(0.5, 0.0, 0.5)$. In other words, I increase the likelihood that the parties will receive a nonzero agreement shock. The probability of each nonzero value is shown on the horizontal axis of the figure. The probabilities for u remain constant at $(0.3, 0.4, 0.3)$ for all of the cases in Figure 15.1. The two lines in Figure 15.1 trace out the expected utility for both parties (they are identical) associated with a nonrenegotiated agreement (the line with the circles), and a renegotiated agreement (the line with the triangles) ***.[18] Thus moving from left to right in the figure shows the effects on the expected utilities of the different agreement types of an increase in the degree of agreement uncertainty, holding the noise constant. It can be seen that initially the states receive a higher expected utility from a nonrenegotiated agreement (one two-period agreement) but that as the variance of ε increases, the expected utility of a renegotiated agreement (two one-period agreements) eventually comes to dominate.[19] As a result, the states in my model change their agreement-type choice when the degree of agreement uncertainty exceeds a certain level.[20]

Figure 15.2 does the same thing, but this time allowing the probabilities of the values of u to vary from $(0.0, 1.0, 0.0)$ to $(0.2, 0.6, 0.2)$ while holding the probabilities of the values of ε constant at $(0.3, 0.4, 0.3)$. As you move to the right, which represents an increase in the degree of noise because the probabilities of the nonzero values are increasing, the states' preferences change from wanting to have a renegotiated agreement (two one-period agreements) to wanting to have a nonrenegotiated agreement (one two-period agreement).[21] This reflects the decreasing value of renegotiation as the variance of u increases, which causes u to

---

[18] Figures 15.1 and 15.2 both omit the value of no agreement. In each case it always lies between 5.1 and 5.2. In Figure 15.1 it is flat since it is unaffected by the variance of ε. In Figure 15.2 it declines with the variance of u.

[19] The sudden drops in the expected utility of the nonrenegotiated agreement in Figure 15.1 result from states deciding to renege in particular states of the world when the variance of the agreement shock reaches a certain level.

[20] If the bargaining power of the parties were affected by the realized distribution of gains as discussed earlier, this would reduce the expected utility of a renegotiated agreement for all values of the variance of the agreement shock. This, in turn, would lead the two lines in Figure 15.1 to cross to the right of where they do now, implying that the states would choose not to renegotiate in some cases where they otherwise would have.

[21] The fact that the expected utility associated with a nonrenegotiated agreement is increasing in the variance of the outcome shock (the noise) over most of the range shown in Figure 15.2 may seem puzzling given that the states are risk-averse. This pattern results from the effect of the variance of the noise on the probability of states of the world in which one state reneges and imposes on the other state a cost larger than the benefit it gets from doing so. As the variance of the noise increases, these states of the world become less likely. Over this range, the positive effect of reducing the probabilities of these states of the world on the overall expected value outweighs the negative effect of the increasing variance in outcomes.

"drown out" the information about ε implicit in the parties' first-period outcomes. In other words, as the environment becomes noisier, it is harder for states to learn.[22]

Up to this point, I have considered a two-period version of my model solely for simplicity in exposition and analysis. The real world, of course, has more than two periods. A more general version of my model lengthens the time horizon to infinity. The basics of the analysis stay the same, but states now may face two choices. The first is an agreement-type choice between no agreement, one infinite-duration agreement, and one finite agreement followed by an infinite-duration agreement. If states choose to renegotiate the agreement, they must then make a second choice regarding the timing of the renegotiation. The degree of noise in the environment will determine the optimal timing, with more noise leading to a longer period before renegotiation so that the parties have more time to learn about the true distribution of gains. This case of a finite-duration agreement followed by renegotiation and an indefinite-duration agreement is of particular interest because the NPT adopts this form.

NUCLEAR NON-PROLIFERATION TREATY

* * *

This case study makes the following points. First, it reveals the empirical importance of this structure of duration and renegotiation provisions. The NPT is arguably one of the more important international agreements of this century. An understanding of its provisions necessarily informs any

---

[22] It is important to note that the implications of my model are consistent with certain neorealist views of international cooperation. While my model incorporates neoliberal assumptions (that is, states care about absolute gains), incorporating the neorealist assumption that states care about relative gains would actually *enlarge* the set of cases for which states would choose to incorporate renegotiation provisions into their international agreements. In fact, Grieco states that "If two states are worried or uncertain about relative achievement of gains, each will prefer a less durable cooperative arrangement, for each will want to more readily be able to exit from the arrangement in the event that gaps in gains favor the other." Grieco 1990, 228. (I thank an anonymous referee for pointing me to this passage in Grieco's work.) In terms of Figure 15.1, adding in concerns about relative gains would lower the expected value of a nonrenegotiated agreement and raise the value of a renegotiated agreement. These movements result from the fact that concerns about relative gains magnify the utility gains and losses associated with any given departure from the agreed-upon division of gains. The net result is that the lines in Figure 15.1 would then cross to the left of where they do in a world where states care only about absolute gains, which means that adding in concerns about relative gains *increases* the set of cases in which the states choose to renegotiate.

analysis of its successes and failures and also contributes to the effective design of future agreements.

Second, at an even more basic level, the case demonstrates the importance that the parties to major international agreements assign to duration and renegotiation provisions. They spend time debating them during the negotiation process, they implicitly (and sometimes explicitly) recognize the trade-off captured by my model, and they choose these provisions in a way that my model shows to make sense.

Third, the case study provides an example of how to operationalize the key variables in the model. The variables in the model, like many variables considered by political scientists more generally, are more difficult to operationalize than, for example, earnings are for an economist. The case pays particular attention to operationalizing the distribution of gains from the agreement and the uncertainty that initially surrounded this distribution.

Fourth, the case study demonstrates that my model provides a powerful framework for organizing and systematizing discussions of the duration and renegotiation provisions of international agreements. By identifying the key variables that determine these provisions, it guides the investigator in sifting through what is, in the case of the NPT, a very large volume of information. It also highlights key areas on which the parties disagreed and shows how the solutions they chose solved the problems they faced.

Background and Substance of the Agreement

The NPT was signed in 1968 and entered into force in 1970 for a period of twenty-five years. In 1995 the parties to the treaty reconvened and decided to extend the treaty indefinitely. The NPT arose out of fears on the part of the existing nuclear-weapon states (NWS) during the early Cold War era that the spread of nuclear weapons to a substantial number of additional countries would be both dangerous and destabilizing. As Thomas Graham recounts, "In 1968, the United States Atomic Energy Commission foresaw a world that might have as many as twenty-eight nuclear powers. The danger that such a world would pose cannot be overstated." Quoting a Swiss official, he continues, "Between two nuclear powers it's a game of chess, among four, it's bridge, among a dozen, it would be poker, roulette, or any of those games controlled by chance."[23] In response to this concern, the United States and the Soviet Union,

[23] Graham 1989, 662.

along with a number of other countries, undertook to establish a treaty prohibiting the further proliferation of nuclear weapons.

The treaty has the following main provisions: Article 1 prohibits NWS from transferring nuclear explosives to any recipient regardless of whether that recipient is a party to the NPT and from otherwise assisting a nonnuclear-weapon state (NNWS) in developing such weapons. Article 2 places obligations on the NNWS not to receive or manufacture nuclear explosive devices. Article 3 requires that the signatories negotiate either individually or collectively full-scope safeguards agreements with the International Atomic Energy Association (IAEA). Articles 4 and 5 provide reassurance to the NNWS that they will be able to enjoy the peaceful uses of nuclear energy and nuclear explosions without discrimination, that is, the NWS are obliged to provide both technological and material assistance to the NNWS. Article 6 demands progress by the existing nuclear powers on controlling the arms race.[24]

Duration and Renegotiation: The Role of Uncertainty

Choosing the duration and renegotiation provisions of the NPT provoked an intense debate. The treaty negotiations lasted from 1962 to 1968. As late as 1967, the United States and the Soviet Union (the original drafters of the treaty) were pressing for a treaty with an unlimited duration, whereas the Germans and the Italians were emphasizing the impossibility of accepting such a duration. Because of their uncertainty about the distribution of gains that would result from the NPT, many NNWS mirrored Germany and Italy in being wary about tying their hands for an unlimited period in an uncertain world.

First, uncertainties surrounded the security consequences of the treaty. The NNWS felt great uncertainty about the effort that the NWS would put into nuclear disarmament.[25] Closely related to this is a paradox inherent in the text of the NPT. If the NWS really did reduce their nuclear stockpiles as Article 6 commits them to do, the extended deterrence they provide to their NNWS allies would become less credible,

---

[24] Treaty on the Non-Proliferation of Nuclear Weapons 1968.
[25] A broader formal model of duration and renegotiation choice in the NPT could include NWS effort as an unobserved variable and actual arms reductions as an observed variable increasing in effort but not completely determined by it. The NNWS, which might condition their willingness to extend the treaty on observed disarmament, would then essentially be in a principal-agent relationship with the NWS.

and these states would have a stronger incentive to join the nuclear club.[26] In regard to the nonnuclear NATO countries, George Bunn and Charles N. Van Doren note that the "countries that were most advanced in civilian nuclear technology and that relied on an alliance with the United States to deter possible attack by the Soviet Union spoke out . . . against an NPT of longer duration than their alliances might turn out to be."[27] Jenson content-analyzed speeches made during a 1968 UN General Assembly debate on the proposed treaty in an effort to ascertain and categorize reservations. He reports that 62 percent of the speakers expressed concern regarding security guarantees, wondering how NNWS would be protected under the NPT.[28]

Another source of uncertainty about the distribution (and level) of security benefits under the NPT centered on which countries would end up participating in the regime. The overall level of gains increases with the number of countries that join, and the distribution of gains depends heavily on the geographic distribution of signators.

Second, the NNWS were concerned about the effect of the NPT on their economic prosperity and on their technological development. They were apprehensive that the treaty might restrict their ability to make peaceful use of nuclear energy. The treaty would have to draw a line between the use of nuclear energy for peaceful, civilian purposes and the use of nuclear energy for military purposes. Much uncertainty existed among the NNWS about whether this line could be effectively drawn and what the distributional effects would be of drawing it. Speaking before the Bundestag in 1967, Foreign Minister Brandt declared that his "government and others are also seeking to insure that the nonproliferation treaty does not further widen the already existing technological gap between the nuclear powers and the non-nuclear countries."[29]

Many potential NPT members also worried about how economically costly the IAEA monitoring would turn out to be. George Quester details concerns raised by the Japanese nuclear power industry about the potential costs associated with the extensive on-site monitoring required by the NPT, including the possibility of shutting down plants in order to

---

[26] See, for example, the discussion in Smith 1987.

[27] Bunn and Van Doren 1992, 5. These NNWS did not propose making the NPT duration contingent on the continued membership of the United States in NATO. This suggests that the barriers to contingency in agreements that are often invoked in theory are also present in fact.

[28] Jenson 1974, 2.

[29] U.S. Arms Control and Disarmament Agency 1967, 49.

allow verification of nuclear fuel information. Quester also notes that many states (including Japan) worried that "the IAEA inspectorate may become imperiously bureaucratic, demanding greater access even where no increase whatsoever is thereby achieved in safeguards reliability . . . due to personal vanity, institutional imperialism, or excessive legalism."[30] These concerns affect both the distribution and level of gains given concerns that the IAEA would be dominated by those NWS whose experts performed the inspections; those states could vary the inspection costs to suit their political and economic agenda.

Another area of uncertainty about the distribution of economic gains concerned the NPT's failure to fully address the relationship between parties to the NPT who supply nuclear technology and NNWS not party to the treaty who purchase it. The NNWS that joined the treaty worried that NNWS not party to the treaty would be able to obtain nuclear technology with fewer restrictions than signatory NNWS.

The potential decline of the U.S. commercial nuclear industry added still another source of uncertainty. As Roger K. Smith notes, this decline was expected, but it would have been difficult to know in advance when other suppliers would emerge and who they would be.[31] These changes would affect states on both sides of the market for peaceful nuclear technology.

Third, uncertainties surrounded the political benefits and costs that would result from such an agreement. Because the NPT would make the NNWS importers of peaceful nuclear technology, they were uncertain about whether this situation would give the NWS political leverage they could exploit. A similar concern was expressed about fuel supplies. Moreover, the effect of treaty adherence on the political power and prestige of the NNWS was uncertain. Prestige might follow from the acquisition of nuclear weapons or it might follow instead from a state's willingness to accede to the treaty. As Lloyd Jensen states: "If there is general acceptance of the NPT, the few states refusing to join are likely to be just that much more criticized." Only time would tell how universal the treaty (and the norm embodied in it) would become.[32]

Other political concerns revolved around specific regional issues. According to Quester, Italy worried that European unification would "be impossible once the NPT has endorsed France and Britain as nuclear states

[30] Quester 1973, 105, 212.
[31] Smith 1987.
[32] Jensen 1974, 38.

and relegated Germany and Italy permanently to the position of non-weapons status."[33] That is, Italy worried that the distribution of gains from the NPT would skew the distribution of power in Europe in ways that would make European integration difficult if not impossible. On the other side of the globe, Japan had concerns over how the NPT would affect its ability to react to a broader U.S. withdrawal from Southeast Asia in the wake of the Vietnam War.

In sum, the parties to the NPT faced substantial uncertainty at the time of its inception about its effects on their security and on their economic and political well being. Some of this uncertainty, such as that surrounding how many countries would eventually join the regime, concerned the overall level of gains from the agreement. However, much of the political and security uncertainty, and all of the economic uncertainty, concerned the distribution of gains (and possibly losses) from the NPT. For example, conditional on any given number of countries joining the regime, which specific countries joined had large effects on the distribution of security gains from the agreement. In the economic realm, concerns about how well peaceful uses of nuclear power could be separated from military ones, competition in the market for peaceful nuclear power technology, and IAEA inspection costs are all distribution.

This kind of uncertainty is the cornerstone of hypothesis 1. In this case, the agreement shock, ε, can be broken down into three components: security, economic, and political. All three are characterized by high variance.[34]

Additionally, it is important to note that many aspects of the uncertainty about the distribution of gains from the NPT were of the one-time character that underlies my model. For example, to the extent that the advent of the NPT set in motion a transition to a stable equilibrium in terms of membership in the regime, all that states have to do is to wait and find out what that equilibrium will be to determine the realized distribution of gains. Similarly, once a stable set of institutions arises to govern the transfer of peaceful nuclear technology by members to nonmember NNWS, the

---

[33] Quester 1973, 7.

[34] Hypothesis 1 is essentially a comparative static result, which cannot be tested with this case study. The case study does, however, show the plausibility of the model. Later, I briefly compare the NPT to the Outer Space Treaty for which the variance of the agreement shock was arguably low. Additionally, hypothesis 1 is put forth as a conjecture in the Rational Designs project (Koremenos, Lipson, and Snidal [2001]) and is the most strongly supported conjecture among the eight case studies.

member NNWS can determine the effect of this aspect of the NPT on their economic well being.

Duration and Renegotiation: The Compromise

The Italian representative to the negotiating committee, Roberto Caracciolo, proposed a "certain flexibility in the provisions of the treaty relating to duration, amendments, and the right of withdrawal"; reacting to Article 7 of the draft treaty, which called for a treaty of unlimited duration, he stated that, "it is not the lot of man, to pledge eternity. Moreover, if we look back across our thousands of years of history, we see very few noninstitutional treaties that have simply survived the vicissitudes of one generation, let alone achieved immortality. Therefore we fear that to affirm a principle so remote from reality may introduce into the treaty an element of weakness rather than of strength."[35] Reacting to this same article, a Swiss aide-memoire stated that "to subscribe to such a commitment seems hardly conceivable in a field where development is as rapid and unpredictable as that of nuclear science and its technical, economic, political, and military implications." Consequently, it would be preferable that the treaty should be concluded for a definite period, at the end of which a review conference would decide about its renewal.[36]

The states that favored an unlimited duration argued that if the parties knew for certain that the treaty would end on a specified date in the future, they would feel pressure to obtain nuclear weapons by that date, thereby undermining the treaty. Furthermore, they argued that it was important that the treaty be guaranteed a life-span of sufficient length to enable it to serve as a foundation upon which other nuclear disarmament measures could be built.

The parties began the path toward compromise when Caracciolo submitted the following to replace the "unlimited duration" paragraph in the draft treaty: "This treaty shall have a duration of X years and shall be renewed automatically for any party which shall not have given, six months before the date of expiry of the treaty, notice of its intention to cease to be party to the treaty." He stated that "the proposed amendment could be regarded as an acceptable compromise between the idea of unlimited duration and that of a fixed term. It provides that the treaty

---

[35] U.S. Arms Control and Disarmament Agency 1967, 527–29.
[36] Ibid., 573.

shall always remain in force for those who do not denounce it, and at the same time allows those who are not satisfied with its operation to withdraw after a certain number of years."[37] A month later the Italian amendment was revised: "The present treaty shall have a duration of X years. It shall be automatically extended for terms equal to its initial duration for those governments which, subject to six months notice, shall not have made known their intention to withdraw."[38]

The final resolution of the duration and renegotiation issues was a compromise between the Soviet and U.S. desires for an indefinite-duration agreement and the preferences of the NNWS for a finite learning period during which they could determine whether the agreement as it worked in practice was in their interest. As Bunn and Van Doren explain, "The Italian proposal for a specific period, plus successive automatic renewals, was the most detailed and the most important before the American and Soviet co-chairmen when they drafted the present language of Article 10.2." They continue: "What the Co-Chairmen drafted – the present Article 10.2 – called for an extension conference after 25 years to decide whether to extend the Treaty 'indefinitely . . . or for an additional fixed period or periods.' It thus accepted the basic Italian idea of a first period of years at the end of which there would be an opportunity for renewal. To the Italian option for an indefinite number of consecutive renewal periods, the drafters added other options, including indefinite renewal and one fixed period."[39]

The drafters also altered the renewal mechanism proposed by the Italians. Instead of individual notices of intentions to withdraw (and therefore automatic subsequent withdrawal), the duration issue would be decided at a multilateral extension conference after twenty-five years.

Why did the NWS and NNWS have different preferences over duration? This can easily be explained within the context of my model. It is reasonable to assume that the distribution of possible values of the agreement shock ε was skewed. Specifically, there was virtually no chance that the NWS could "lose big" from the NPT. The worst that could happen for them would be to find out that nuclear weapons had no use and hence were a complete waste of resources. In contrast there was a chance that the NNWS could "lose big" from adhering to an agreement that demanded they forsake nuclear weapons in a world in which other

[37] Ibid., 529.
[38] Bunn and Van Doren 1991, 7.
[39] Ibid., 7–8.

states – both members and nonmembers of the NPT – possessed them. Such a skewed distribution would imply different preferences over duration even if the expected gains of the NWS and NNWS were equal.[40]

Resolving the Uncertainty Through Learning

The sources of economic, political, and security outcomes are ambiguous. For example, if a state experiences a low growth rate in a given year, the role played by its decision not to develop its own nuclear industry may not be immediately apparent. The costs and benefits of nuclear energy as a source of power were quite uncertain in the late 1960s and early 1970s. Hence it would take time for states to sort out the effects of the NPT on their well being from those of other factors. Put another way, the level of noise (the cornerstone of hypothesis 2) is high.

If my model is relevant to this case, we should see evidence that the states involved did indeed initiate learning processes to help them distinguish the value of the agreement shock from the noise in the environment. Again, the real world is seldom two periods, and the NPT context is no exception. The multiperiod variant of hypothesis 2 addresses both the incidence and the timing of renegotiation.[41]

The parties to the NPT planned review conferences every five years at which they could cooperatively take stock of how the treaty was working in practice. This interval was chosen in part because it would take approximately that long to produce arms control agreements. Referring to the Third Review Conference, Hon. Lewis A. Dunn, of the U.S. Arms Control and Disarmament Agency, stated:

The main task at the Review Conference will be an article-by-article review of the operation of the Treaty. Woven throughout that review and ensuing debate there will be five major questions. First, has the Treaty strengthened the security of the parties by helping prevent the further spread of nuclear explosives? Second, how well has the Treaty facilitated cooperation in the peaceful uses of nuclear energy? Third, what has been done to bring the nuclear arms race to an end? Fourth, what can realistically be done to strengthen the NPT? And most important of all, weighing each of these considerations, has the NPT been a success?[42]

---

[40] For simplicity, the formal model and the simulations presented in the second section assume the agreement shock, ε, has a symmetric distribution. Importantly, there is nothing in the model that precludes the agreement shock from having a skewed distribution.

[41] Koremenos 1999.

[42] U.S. House of Representatives 1985, 65.

The evidence indicates that the uncertainty about many aspects of the true distribution of gains persisted years after the NPT was signed. At the 1980 Review Conference, the debate centered on Article 4 (which focuses on technological exchange) and Article 6 (which focuses on arms control). Disagreements between the NWS and the NNWS regarding how these Articles were working in practice prevented the conference participants from agreeing on and hence issuing a final document. In other words, given the level of noise, the parties had not yet been able to determine the true distributional effects of the NPT. By 1985, much more of the uncertainty surrounding Article 4 had been resolved, as the following statement by Dunn illustrates:

Since the 1980 Review Conference:

- all new or amended agreements for cooperation with non-nuclear weapon states entered into by the United States have been with parties to the NPT or the Treaty of Tlatelolco;[43]
- virtually all US exports of enriched uranium . . . were to NPT parties; . . .
- all of US-funded IAEA "Footnote A" (extrabudgetary) technical assistance projects – 111 projects for more than $4.5 million – have been for developing country Non-Proliferation Treaty parties.[44]

Essentially, the passage of time resolved much of the uncertainty over the distribution of economic gains from the NPT. Regarding the issue that raised so many concerns during the original negotiations, the parties successfully separated the civilian and military uses of nuclear technology so that trade in legitimate nuclear materials flourished under the NPT within a network of IAEA safeguards agreements. In practice, there has not been discrimination against the NNWS regarding technological progress in nuclear energy. With respect to Article 5, which addresses the issue of peaceful nuclear explosions, by the mid-1970s, it was determined by the NWS that the anticipated benefits from such explosions were not forthcoming.

Furthermore, over the two-and-a-half decades following the signing of the NPT, the parties witnessed the development of alternative suppliers of nuclear technology, such as France and Germany. Taken together, these developments represented the stabilization of the regime regarding

---

[43] The Treaty of Tlatelolco establishes Latin America as a nuclear weapons–free zone.
[44] U.S. House of Representatives 1985, 69–70.

the distribution of peaceful nuclear technology to NNWS. Under the regime that eventually emerged, it was clear that the NNWS that joined the NPT would not suffer economic harm along this dimension.[45]

In addition to the concerns that played a major role at the review conferences, many other aspects of the uncertainty surrounding the distribution of gains from the NPT were largely or completely resolved during the initial trial period: In terms of security, the NPT greatly reduced the spread of nuclear weapons compared with what would likely have occurred without it. During the trial period, membership in the NPT increased to the point of being almost global.

In terms of the distribution of political gains (and losses), it became clear that concerns that the NPT would prevent European integration were groundless. What turned out to matter for European integration was not Britain's bombs but Germany's GNP. Time also rendered moot Japan's worries about its ability to react to a broad U.S. pullout from Asia.

In 1995 after four review conferences, the 163 parties to the treaty gathered in New York to decide whether the NPT would continue in force indefinitely or be extended for an additional fixed period or periods. Interviews with conference participants suggest that essentially all of the parties came to the conference favoring extension, a fact that itself provides powerful evidence of learning. Debate centered on whether extension would be indefinite or for a series of twenty-five-year periods.[46] In the end, a consensus resolution extended the NPT indefinitely. The NWS had gained what they expected to in terms of maintaining their power and influence (as Panofsky and Bunn note, "possession of nuclear weapons and permanent membership in the UN Security council remain identical"),[47] and the NNWS had learned how the NPT worked for them in practice.

* * *

---

[45] Nye presents additional examples of learning and uncertainty resolution in his discussion of policies relating to the nuclear fuel cycle and attempts to control aspects of the cycle related to nuclear weapons development. Nye 1981.

[46] The interviews appear in Welsh 1995. The debate regarding the extension provision was largely among the NNWS, since the NWS all favored indefinite extension. Ultimately, the Canadian argument that indefinite duration would cause the NWS "to be permanently held accountable to Article VI on disarmament" carried the day.

[47] Panofsky and Bunn 1994, 9.

CONCLUSION

The credibility of commitments in the face of uncertainty requires a trade-off between flexibility and constraint. I focus on a particular form of uncertainty – a one-shot uncertainty surrounding the division of gains from an agreement – and on a particular kind of flexibility – the combination of limited duration followed by a single renegotiation.

Some might argue that we do not observe much reneging on international agreements empirically and draw the implication that pretty much any duration and renegotiation provisions would do in a given context. In my model, this is clearly false. I calculate the lost utility from failure to choose the optimal provisions. In the case of small deviations, the lost utility takes the form of unrealized potential gains from the agreement. In the case of large deviations, it takes the form of reneging or failure to initiate the agreement at all. Empirically, a selection process similar to that described by George Downs, David Rocke, and Peter N. Barsoom regarding state compliance in international agreements is at work with respect to duration and renegotiation provisions.[48] The reason we do not observe much reneging in actual agreements is in part because their duration and renegotiation provisions have been chosen in ways that act to minimize this costly behavior. For example, the reason we do not observe agreements failing because of uncontrollable economic circumstances is that agreements in areas subject to such disruptions will tend to be of short duration – short enough that states experiencing sudden losses will stay with the agreement until it is renegotiated rather than renege.

My analysis also responds to some recent game-theoretic work in international relations. James D. Fearon points out a weakness in current theories of international cooperation that focus primarily on the enforcement of international agreements while ignoring the bargaining that generates the agreements in the first place. Fearon's model integrates the bargaining over the terms of an agreement into the cooperation problem. This formulation reveals that the same shadow of the future that allows self-enforcing agreements also makes reaching an agreement more difficult by increasing the distributional effects of the selection of the initial equilibrium.[49]

[48] Downs, Rocke, and Barsoom 1996.
[49] Fearon 1998. Fearon's work as well as Morrow's show how distributional differences can undermine cooperation in significant ways. Morrow 1994. These works are in part a response to Grieco and Krasner, who have rightly argued that neoliberals tend to emphasize enforcement issues and ignore distributional issues. See Grieco 1988; and Krasner 1991.

I provide a theoretical justification for the fact that states often integrate planned renegotiation into international agreements. Building in renegotiation at the start reduces the distributional impacts of the initial equilibrium selection but does not reduce the shadow of the future that supports enforcement of the agreement as a whole since violations in the initial period can still be punished by noncooperation in future periods. Of course, allowing renegotiation adds the possibility that one party may drop out at the end of a particular finite-duration contract. Indeed, in the case of the International Coffee Agreement, the United States did just that. Nonetheless, if the probability of continuation is sufficiently high, finite-duration contracts linked by renegotiation may represent the real-world solution to Fearon's theoretical dilemma.

Finally, my analysis extends the neoliberal international relations literature beyond its current focus on the general issue of how cooperation can emerge. Both Robert Axelrod and Kenneth Oye suggest devices such as lengthening the shadow of the future, practicing reciprocity, and improving recognition capabilities; Stephen D. Krasner looks at the role of international regimes in promoting and maintaining cooperation; and Robert O. Keohane argues that regimes reduce the transactions costs associated with international cooperation.[50] This literature has opened up the central questions of international politics. It has done so, however, only by moving well away from any detailed analysis of specific institutional arrangements or questions of institutional design. In other words, this literature has failed to investigate the precise mechanisms through which cooperation can emerge.[51] There is no inherent reason, however, why the broader political issues cannot be considered simultaneously with the specific institutional arrangements designed to address them in ways that illuminate both the broader relationships and the institutionalization itself. My goal in investigating duration and renegotiation provisions has been to deepen our understanding of international cooperation by asking about specifics.

[50] See Axelrod 1984; Oye 1986; Krasner 1983; and Keohane 1984.
[51] Likewise, the tools of game theory have been directed mainly at abstract questions that emphasize cooperation rather than institutional design as the dependent variable.

16

Driving with the Rearview Mirror: On the Rational Science of Institutional Design

Alexander Wendt

How can social scientists best contribute to the design of international institutions? Presumably our value lies in producing knowledge about design that those designing institutions need but do not have. But what kind of knowledge is that? What should a science of institutional design be "about?"

As a discipline international relations (IR) has barely begun to think about institutional design. Anarchy makes the international system among the least hospitable of all social systems to institutional solutions to problems, encouraging actors to rely on power and interest instead. * * * Skeptics may be right that all this activity is unimportant but policymakers apparently disagree. And that in turn has left IR with less to say to them than it might have. By bracketing whether institutions matter and turning to the problem of institutional design, therefore, this volume takes an important step toward a more policy-relevant discourse about international politics.

The articles in this volume deserve to be assessed on their own terms, within the particular rationalist framework laid out in Barbara Koremenos, Charles Lipson, and Duncan Snidal's introduction. That framework highlights collective-action problems and incomplete information as impediments to institutional design. * * * However, offering an internal critique of the Rational Design project from any rationalist perspective is not something I am particularly qualified or inclined to do, nor was it the charge given to me when I was generously invited to contribute. From the start

For their helpful comments on a draft of this article, I am grateful to two anonymous reviewers, the *IO* editors, Michael Barnett, Deborah Boucoyannis, Martha Finnemore, Peter Katzenstein, and especially Jennifer Mitzen.

the editors deliberately set aside a number of "nonrationalist" arguments in order to see how far they could push their approach to the problem. The purpose of soliciting this comment was to get an outside perspective.

Actually, I am not that qualified or inclined to make a fully external critique either. Although some epistemological issues will come up, I share the volume's commitment to social science, and while I doubt that rationalism can tell us everything, I certainly think it can tell us a lot.[1] Additional insights about institutional design might emerge by rejecting social science or rationalism altogether, but I shall not do so here. However, in the space between a purely internal and purely external critique I hope to raise some fairly fundamental questions about the approach. ***

I shall raise two main concerns, one more external than the other. The first is the volume's neglect of alternatives to its explanation of institutional designs. At base, the theory of rational design is that states and other actors choose international institutions to further their own interests.[2] This amounts to a functionalist claim: actors choose institutions because they expect them to have a positive function.[3] Alternatives to this hypothesis come in at least two forms, both associated with "sociological" or "constructivist" approaches to institutions.[4]

On the one hand, alternatives could be rival explanations, where the relationship to the theory of rational design is zero-sum; variance explained by one is variance not explained by the other. At first glance it might seem hard to identify plausible rivals. One is tempted to say, Of course actors design institutions to further their interests – what else would they do? But in fact there are some interesting rivals, both to the proposition that institutions are rationally chosen and to the proposition that they are designed. I discuss each in turn and argue that neglect of these alternatives makes it more difficult to assess the volume's conclusions. ***

On the other hand, "alternatives" could refer to explanations that do not contradict rational-design theory but embed it within broader social or historical contexts that construct its elements (preferences, beliefs, and so on). Whereas the question with rival explanations is one of variance explained, the issue here is one of "causal depth."[5] Even if states choose rationally, this may be less interesting than the underlying structures that

---

[1] See Wendt 1999; and Fearon and Wendt forthcoming.

[2] Koremenos, Lipson, and Snidal [2001], 762.

[3] On functionalism in design theory and its alternatives, see especially Pierson 2000b.

[4] For good introductions to this extensive literature, see Powell and DiMaggio 1991; Hall and Taylor 1996; and March and Olsen 1998.

[5] Wilson 1994.

make certain choices rational in the first place. It is on such structures that sociological and constructivist approaches to institutions typically focus. * * *

* * *

Despite its focus on alternative explanations, this first critique remains internal in the sense that it assumes, with the Rational Design project, that the question we are trying to answer about institutional design is an explanatory one: Why do institutions have the features they do? However, part of what makes the problem of institutional design interesting, in my view, is that it raises further questions which go beyond that explanatory concern. In particular, the term *design* readily calls up the policy-relevant question, What kind of institutions should we design? * * * [Given] that this volume focuses on a theoretic issue with important policy implications, it seems useful in this essay to reflect on how the gap between positive and normative could be narrowed further.

Bridging this gap depends, I shall argue, on recognizing the epistemological differences between the kinds of knowledge sought in the scientific and policy domains, which stem from different attitudes toward time. Positive social scientists are after "explanatory" knowledge, knowledge about why things happen. This is necessarily backward-looking, since we can only explain what has already occurred * * *. Policymakers, and institutional designers, in contrast, need "making" or "practical" knowledge, knowledge about what to do. This is necessarily forward-looking, since it is about how we should act in the future. As Henry Jackman puts it, "we live forwards but understand backwards."[6] The former cannot be reduced to the latter. Knowing why we acted in the past can teach us valuable lessons, but unless the social universe is deterministic, the past is only contingently related to the future. Whether actors preserve an existing institution like state sovereignty or design a new one like the EU is up to them. * * *

Practical knowledge may nevertheless interact in interesting ways with explanatory knowledge. To show this, in the last third of this article I briefly discuss two domains of inquiry about institutional design not addressed in this volume. The first is institutional effectiveness. * * * The second domain is the specifically normative one. What values should we pursue in institutions? * * *

Positive and normative inquiries are, of course, in many ways distinct, but a science of institutional design that deals only with the former

[6] Jackman 1999.

will be incomplete and useful primarily for "driving with the rearview mirror." The larger question I want to raise here, therefore, is an epistemological one – what should count as "knowledge" about institutional design? In social science we often assume that knowledge is only about explaining the past. Institutional design is an issue where the nature of the problem – making things in the future – may require a broader view ***.

ALTERNATIVES TO RATIONAL DESIGN

Given the question, What explains variation in institutional design? it is clear that rational-design theory provides some leverage. But how much leverage? It is difficult to say until we make lateral comparisons to its rivals and vertical comparisons to deeper explanations. Thus, assuming that the phrase "rational design" is not redundant, I break the volume's hypothesis down into two parts, that institutions are chosen rationally and that they are designed.

Alternatives to "Rational"

*** Rationality can be defined in various ways.[7] In rational-choice theory it refers to instrumental or "logic of consequences" thinking:[8] Actors are rational when they choose strategies that they believe will have the optimal consequences given their interests. *** This is a subjective definition of rationality in that a rational choice is not what will actually maximize an actor's pay-offs (we might call this an "objective" view of rationality), but what the actor thinks will do so. ***

If for a single actor rational action is what subjectively maximizes its interests, then when there are multiple actors, as in international politics, a rationally chosen institution will be one that solves their collective-action problem ***. *** Collective-action problems, in short, are subjective at the group level, in that they are constituted by a shared perception of some facts in the world as (1) being a "problem" (versus not), (2) requiring "collective action" (versus not), and (3) having certain features that constitute what kind of collective-action problem it is (coordination, cooperation, security, economic, and so on). These understandings are only partly determined by objective facts in the world ***. They are also constructed by a communicative process of

---

[7] See especially Hargreaves-Heap 1989.
[8] Jackman 1999.

interpreting what that world means and how and why designers should care about it.[9] ***

***

What are the alternatives to the hypothesis that states choose subjectively rational institutions? One, of course, is that states knowingly choose institutions that will defeat their purposes, but that does not seem very plausible. We have to look elsewhere for interesting alternatives. I discuss two.

The Logic of Appropriateness

One alternative is that states choose institutional designs according to the "logic of appropriateness":[10] Instead of weighing costs and benefits, they choose on the basis of what is normatively appropriate. *** In international politics there are many examples of decision making on appropriateness grounds. An example I have used before is what stops the United States from conquering the Bahamas, instrumental factors or a belief that this would be wrong?[11] One can construct an "as if," cost-benefit story to explain nonconquest, but I doubt this is the operative mechanism; it is more likely that U.S. policymakers see this as illegitimate. A more difficult and thus interesting example is provided by Nina Tannenwald's study of the "nuclear taboo," which suggests that even when instrumental factors weighed in favor of using nuclear weapons, as in the Vietnam War, U.S. decision makers refrained on normative grounds.[12] The way such a logic ultimately works is through the internalization of norms. As actors become socialized to norms, they make them part of their identity, and that identity in turn creates a collective interest in norms as ends in themselves.[13] The result is internalized self-restraint: actors follow norms not because it is in their self-interest, but because it is the right thing to do in their society. ***

The Bahamas and nuclear taboo examples highlight the fact that the logic of appropriateness has usually been used in IR to explain *compliance* with regimes.[14] *** However, design is a different question from compliance, to which it is less obvious that logics of appropriateness are directly relevant.

---

[9] Kratochwil 1989.
[10] March and Olsen 1998.
[11] Wendt 1999, 289–90.
[12] Tannenwald 1999.
[13] Wendt 1999.
[14] The Meyer School being an important exception.

Nevertheless, there are at least three ways in which normative logics might be rivals to rational explanations of institutional design. One is by supplying desiderata for institutions that make little sense on consequentialist grounds. A norm of universal membership, for example, operates in many international regimes. Why do landlocked states have a say in the Law of the Sea, or Luxembourg a vote in the EU? It is not obvious that the answers lie in the enforcement and distributional considerations emphasized by the Rational Design framework. Or consider the norm that Great Powers have special prerogatives. Without reference to this idea, it is hard to explain the inclusion of Russia in the Group of Eight, or to make sense of debates about the future of the UN Security Council. The norm that the control of international institutions should be democratic is also gaining strength. The Rational Design framework proposes that designs for institutional control reflect degrees of uncertainty and asymmetries of contribution, yet in debates about how to fix the "democratic deficit" in the EU and other international organizations such cost-benefit considerations seem less salient than questions of legitimacy and principle.[15] *** And so on. These possibilities do not mean that rational factors are not also operative in regime design, but they do suggest the story may be more complicated than a pure consequentialism would allow.

A second, converse, way in which logics of appropriateness may constitute rival hypotheses is by taking design options that might be instrumentally attractive off the table as "normative prohibitions."[16] *** [One] might expect a purely rational regime for dealing with "failed states" to include a trusteeship option, but because of its association with colonialism, this is unacceptable to the international community. Finally, norms about what kinds of coercion may be used in different contexts may also factor into regime design. Military intervention to collect sovereign debts was legitimate in the nineteenth century,[17] but it is hard to imagine this being done today. *** A true test of rational-design theory would include *all* instrumentally relevant options, not just those that are normatively acceptable.

Finally, logics of appropriateness can affect the modalities used to design institutions, which as a result may be historically specific. ***

In at least three ways, then, logics of appropriateness may help structure international institutions. These possibilities do not mean that

---

[15] See, for example, Pogge 1997; and Dryzek 1999.
[16] Nadalmann 1990.
[17] Krasner 1999.

consequentialism is wholly absent. But insofar as our objective is to assess variance explained, the logic of appropriateness suggests that rival factors may be important as well.

* * *

On Uncertainty

In addition to instrumental thinking, rationality as understood in this volume relies on a particular, and contested, way of handling uncertainty. As the editors point out, a focus on uncertainty is one of the Rational Design project's significant departures from earlier rationalist (and non-rationalist) scholarship on international institutions.[18] Since uncertainty is intrinsic to social life, and especially to institutional design – which tries to structure an otherwise open future – addressing it can make IR more realistic and policy-relevant. However, the Rational Design framework seems to treat the nature of uncertainty as unproblematic and ends up with a conceptualization that effectively reduces it to risk. This assertion may seem wrong, since the editors say they are adopting the "standard terminology in using the term *uncertainty* instead of *risk*," [19] but the premise of this terminology is that the two are equivalent. That there is an important distinction between risk and uncertainty has been known at least since Frank Knight's classic 1921 work[20] and the distinction is used in some rationalist scholarship today, even elsewhere by Snidal himself.[21] But in most orthodox economics and formal theory the two are conflated, and it is to this literature that this volume seems most indebted. In contrast, heterodox Austrian and post-Keynesian economists vigorously uphold Knight's distinction and indeed base much of their critique of mainstream economics on its failure to do so.[22] * * *

"Risk" describes a situation in which some parameters of the decision problem, such as other actors' preferences or beliefs, are not known for certain, but – importantly – all the possibilities are known and can be assigned probabilities that add up to 1. The utility of different courses of action is then weighted by these probabilities, leading to the formalism of expected-utility theory. A key implication of risk is that even though actors

---

[18] Also see Koremenos 2001.
[19] Koremenos, Lipson, and Snidal 2001, 779.
[20] Knight 1921.
[21] For example, Abbott and Snidal 2000, 442.
[22] The literature here is extensive. See, for example, Davidson 1991; Vercelli 1995; and Dequech 1997.

cannot be certain about the outcomes of their choices, they can at least see well-defined (if still probabilistic) relationships between ends and means, so that they can calculate precisely the chances of achieving their goals with different strategies.[23] Choose *A*, and there is a given chance that payoff *X* will occur; choose *B*, another chance; and so on. This is significant because it means there is always a clear and principled answer to the question, What is the rational thing to do?

*** [Uncertainty] exists when an actor does not know all the possibilities in a situation, cannot assign probabilities to them,[24] or those probabilities do not sum to unity. To distinguish it from the standard view, uncertainty in this heterodox tradition is often qualified with adjectives like "strong," "hard," "genuine," or "structural." *** [Where] there is genuine uncertainty, the clear (if probabilistic) relationship between ends and means breaks down, so that optimal behavior may not be distinguishable from sub-optimal. If optimality is no longer calculable, then what is instrumentally rational is no longer well defined.

This suggests a rival hypothesis about how rational actors should behave. On the orthodox view, actors facing incomplete information should continually adjust their beliefs and strategies in response to changing estimates of the situation. The importance of such updating is reflected in the volume's conjectures about the effects of uncertainty on rational design, namely that institutions should maximize flexibility and individual control. In contrast, Ronald Heiner argues on heterodox grounds that actors facing genuine uncertainty may be better off *not* trying to optimize, because they are not competent to grasp the true problem and so are prone to make mistakes and have regrets.[25] On his view, in other words, in situations of genuine uncertainty expected-utility theory may actually be a poor guide to "rational" behavior. Instead, actors should do just the opposite of what that theory recommends: follow simple, rigid rules and avoid continually updating expected values. Heiner argues further that most people in the real world understand this, since their behavior is much more stable than would be expected if they were constantly optimizing. Under conditions of genuine uncertainty, it is our willingness to *depart* from the optimizing standard that is the "origin of predictable behavior."[26] In the context of institutional design, therefore, the rational

---

[23] Beckert 1996, 819.
[24] Which may presuppose a nonsubjectivist view of probability.
[25] Heiner 1983.
[26] Ibid.

action may be to *minimize* flexibility and control rather than to maximize them.

*** [The] inferences drawn in the empirical articles about how "uncertainty" should play out concretely seem generally persuasive, and so it is not clear that the heterodox view would lead to different conclusions. Yet some interesting questions remain. In particular, one wonders whether the apparent empirical strength of the volume's treatment of uncertainty is related to the fact that five of its eight articles concern the economic issue-area.[27] One might expect this domain to have relatively weak logics of appropriateness, and so actors will have little incentive to bind themselves to inflexible rules over which they lack individual control. *** However, in issue-areas where logics of appropriateness are stronger, like human rights or perhaps the environment, the heterodox view may be a better guide to "rational" design. In the face of (genuine) uncertainty in these domains states may prefer to define rigid criteria of acceptable behavior rather than maintain the conditions for optimizing their individual interests. On this continuum the security issue-area may occupy an interesting middle ground: in some respects a domain of pure rational self-interest where the volume's conjectures should apply, in others one of deep if limited norms, like those embodied in Just War theory and prohibitions on the use of chemical and biological weapons, which seem harder to square with a desire to maintain flexibility and control.[28] In short, the possibility that the meaning of rational behavior under (genuine) uncertainty varies by issue-area seems worth pursuing. ***

* * *

Alternatives to "Design"

In the preceding section I mapped some of the contrast space implied by "rationality" as a determinant of institutional variation. Although there will be some overlap, doing the same for "design" will put the volume in different relief.

* * *

Thinking about rational design as essentially equivalent to rational choice is also useful for mapping contrasts to the design hypothesis.

---

[27] Of the remainder, one (Mitchell and Keilbach) does not address uncertainty much at all, and another (Kydd) does so in a somewhat idiosyncratic way due to the problem being addressed.

[28] On the chemical weapons case, see Price 1995.

Intuitively the idea that designs are choices has three implications: (1) designers exist prior to designs, (2) designs are intended, and (3) designers have some freedom of action. Each points to alternative explanations, some rivals to rational-design theory and some with greater causal depth. I take these up in turn.

No Designer?

Are institutional designers causes or effects of their designs? On one level the answer must clearly be causes. Institutions do not come out of the blue but are designed by people. However, on another level we can also see the reverse logic at work, with designers being constructed by designs. To that extent, perhaps more is going on in institutional design than the rationalist lens captures.[29] Designers could be constructions of designs in two ways, causally and constitutively.

First, institutional designs today may play a causal feedback role in constructing the actors who make designs tomorrow. This could occur on three levels. As Koremenos, Lipson, and Snidal briefly note, one level would be institutional designs that expand the set of members who make up the subsequent designing actor. In their example of the EU, enlargement choices made in the past affected who is making enlargement choices today, and this will affect who makes choices in the future.[30] A second kind of feedback on actors occurs when institutions affect designers' identities and interests. NATO is a good example: Even if its original design reflected the self-interests of its members, over time they arguably have come to identify with the institution and thus see themselves as a collective identity, valuing NATO as an end in itself rather than just as a means to an end.[31] *** And third, institutional designs may affect actors by changing their beliefs about the environment. *** Such feedback effects may not be intended at the moment of initial design, but the longer our time horizon, the more likely they will occur. Over time, designs cause designers as much as designers cause designs.

The rationalist approach can also be turned around in a second, more constitutive way by adopting a "performative" model of agency. On this view, associated especially with post-modernism,[32] there is an important

---

[29] For further discussion of this idea, see Wendt 1999, chap. 7.

[30] Koremenos, Lipson, and Snidal 2001, 778.

[31] See Risse-Kappen 1996; and Williams and Neumann 2000.

[32] See especially Ashley 1988; Campbell 1998; and Weber 1998. For critical discussion, see Laffey 2000.

sense in which actors do not preexist actions, but rather are instantiated as particular kinds of subjects at the moment of certain performances. To the extent that they are not separable, actors cannot be said to *cause* institutional designs, but are instead constituted by them.[33] In international politics the institution of sovereignty provides perhaps the most fundamental example. By acting as the members of sovereign states are expected to act – defending their autonomy, privileging their citizens over foreigners, recognizing the rights of other states to do likewise, and, now, engaging in practices of international institutional design – certain groups of individuals constitute themselves as the corporate actors known as "sovereign states," which have particular powers and rights in international politics. *** Since this process is continuous, state identity is always an ongoing accomplishment, not ontologically given.[34]

* * *

This ongoing process of constructing modes of subjectivity matters for at least three reasons.

First, it is part of what is "going on" in institutional design, and therefore a complete understanding of the latter must address it. Doing this would enable us to embed the rational explanation within a larger historical process in which institutional designers are themselves at stake in their practices.

Second, institutional design creates and reproduces political *power* – since in making choices designers are constituting themselves and others as subjects with certain rights – and as such studying the construction of designers by designs matters normatively. Designing a POW regime helps legitimate the right of states to make war and thus kill members of other states; designing a trade regime helps legitimate states' right to protect private property even if this conflicts with justice; and so on. "We" might want states to have those powers, but then again we might not; and our preference may depend on who is included, and excluded, in this "We." Constituting states and their members as the bearers of sovereign rights is an intensely political issue, and so bracketing it in favor of an assumption of given state subjectivity de-politicizes the design of international institutions to that extent. Calling attention to the effects of designs on designers is a way to ensure the power of the latter remains accountable rather than being taken for granted.

[33] For discussion of this distinction, see Wendt 1998 and 1999, 77–88.
[34] Ashley 1988.

Finally, this issue raises questions about rationality. If part of what institutional designers are doing is choosing future designers, how do we assess the rationality of the choices they make today? The Rational Design framework defines rationality relative to a given conception of Self. This is fine for certain purposes, but what do we do if the Self will change as a result of our choices? Do we factor in the preferences of future, as yet nonexisting, designers, and if so, which ones and at what discount rate?[35] Attending to alternatives to the assumption that designers are given in design choices would push these important questions to the fore.

No Intentionality?

A second assumption implied by the Rational Design framework is that the features of international institutions are chosen intentionally, by a conscious or deliberate process of calculation. At first glance it is hard to see what a plausible alternative to this would be, since human beings are not automatons. As such, there will always be *some* intentionality in the process by which institutions are created. However, this does not mean we can automatically conclude that institutions are intended. In social theory a long and sometimes fierce battle has been waged by proponents of a rival, "evolutionary" explanation of institutions, especially Friedrich Hayek and his intellectual descendants, against the design approach (which ironically they term "constructivism").[36] The intensity of the resistance stems not only from a theoretical disagreement about what explains institutions but also from the perceived political implications of those explanations. Evolutionists argue that in fact it is very difficult to intend institutions, and that failure to recognize this has led to over-confidence and some of the most catastrophic design failures in history, namely communism and fascism.[37] As an alternative to "constructivism" they favor trusting instead to processes of trial-and-error learning and natural selection, which operate like an "invisible hand" behind the backs of rational actors. ***

Proponents of the evolutionary approach do not necessarily deny that people are intentional beings, that we make rational choices, or even that we should tinker with existing institutions. Many would best be described as "rationalists" themselves. Their concern is rather that

---

[35] For suggestive treatments of these issues, see MacIntosh 1992; and Stewart 1995.

[36] No relation to "constructivism" in IR. For introductions to this debate, see Hayek 1973; Ullmann-Margalit 1978; Prisching 1989; Hodgson 1991; and Vanberg 1994.

[37] See especially Hayek 1973; and Scott 1998.

even though we may be able to modify institutions incrementally to better realize our ends, the limits of human knowledge and cognitive capacity are so profound that we should not think we can intend successful institutions *up front*. Even the most deliberately created institutions, like the U.S. Constitution, have been amended repeatedly since their founding. Each amendment to the Constitution was certainly intended at the time it was adopted, but in what sense is the result of those changes intended, and who was doing the intending? Perhaps the Founders, whose "original intent" has guided the evolution of the Constitution, and who also consciously created a mechanism for amending it. But it would be odd to say that the Founders "designed" today's Constitution, since they could not have anticipated the changes that have been made; in many respects it is clearly an *un*intended consequence of earlier choices. The assumption that institutional designs are intended, therefore, is ambiguous about whether it refers to the discrete changes made at each step of the way, or to the development over time of the overall structure. Intentionality at the local or micro-level is fully compatible with no intentionality at the global or macro-level. * * *

Uncertainty is central to the Hayekian argument, and so the Rational Design project's focus on this factor would seem to put it squarely on the evolutionist side of this debate. Yet the introduction and two of the empirical articles make claims that confuse the issue. Specifically, Koremenos, Lipson, and Snidal argue that even institutions that have evolved very incrementally can be explained by the theory of rational design if their rules have periodically been the object of conscious choice.[38] Their example is sovereignty, the features of which today are the result of many changes made intentionally to the original Westphalian rules. Rational-design theory may shed light on some of the micro-level causes of these changes, but do the editors mean to suggest that sovereignty as we know it today was "intended" in 1648, or that all the individual designers of sovereignty since 1648 add up to a single, trans-historical designer? Presumably not, but in that case then the structure of sovereignty today would require an *additional*, nonintentional explanation. Similarly, Mattli argues that the development of international private arbitration can be explained by an evolutionary process whose outcome is equivalent to what would have been achieved by a direct effort at rational design.[39] That may be true, but how

---

[38] Koremenos, Lipson, and Snidal 2001, 766.
[39] Mattli 2001, 923–24.

is it evidence for rational-design theory? The latter assumes rational actors; evolutionary arguments, in contrast, require no such assumption. The decentralized, unintended process Mattli describes is precisely what evolutionists see as a *rival* to design explanations; it is the structure of the evolutionary process, not the choices at each step of the way, that explains the overall outcome. Finally, in response to the criticism that decision makers may not understand the design problem and as such need to figure things out incrementally, Mitchell and Keilbach suggest that a "trial-and-error process of design, though taking longer, is no less rational or purposive."[40] This again seems to conflate the intentionality of micro-decisions with the intentionality of the macro-result.

Perhaps what these authors are getting at goes back to their functionalism: If, over time, actors make intentional changes to an institution such that the overall result is functional, we can say it was "designed." Yet this seems to introduce a new understanding of "functionalism" from the one underpinning this volume. If micro-intention equals macro-intention, we seem to be saying that subjective rationality equals objective (or "trans-historically subjective") rationality. But that cannot be right. Incremental changes may cause institutions to evolve in an objectively functional way, but that evolution is more a behind-the-backs process than a purposive one, and as such would have to be explained by the *structures* in which intentional agents are embedded, not their intentions themselves.[41] If we continue with functionalist imagery, therefore, it may be useful to distinguish two variants: "intentional" functionalism, where outcomes are explained by the expected results of intentional action, and "invisible hand" functionalism, where beneficial outcomes are explained by structural features of a system. Rational-design theory as currently formulated would not explain the latter.

* * *

No Choice?

Finally, "design" seems to imply that designers have the freedom to act otherwise, that their designs are "choices." To be interesting this needs to be more than just an existential freedom. Assuming free will, human beings always have the trivial ability to "just say no," even if this means they will be shot. The claim needs instead to be that actors have *genuine* choices to

---

[40] Mitchell and Keilbach 2001, 906.
[41] For good discussions of these issues, see Ullmann-Margalit 1978; and Jackson and Pettit 1992.

make, especially if we are going to use the aesthetic term *design*, which suggests a creative expression of inner desire, where the designer could have done things differently but chose not to.

Some philosophers have questioned whether rational-choice theory is compatible with genuine choice, arguing that its model of man is mechanical and deterministic, reducing actors to unthinking cogs in the juggernaut of Reason.[42] *** Rather than pursue this argument, however, I will take at face value the assumption that institutional designers make choices, and focus on how they might be prevented from doing so by structural constraints. The potential effects of such constraints are captured by two alternative explanations, path dependency and teleology.

The implications of path dependency for functional theories of institutional design have been explored in detail by Paul Pierson ***.[43] Especially when institutions are created piecemeal rather than *ex nihilo*, would-be designers may face a substantial accumulation of existing norms and practices. Such historical structures facilitate elaboration of existing norms through a logic of "increasing returns,"[44] and inhibit adopting norms that would undo them. *** Whether for consequentialist or normative reasons, therefore, actors may be constrained by existing structures from making ideally rational choices and as such get locked into a path of institutional "design" that effectively takes away their choice in the matter. ***

The path-dependency perspective suggests a second alternative to the assumption of choice: the teleological view that institutional designers are really just working out the details of some "central animating idea."[45] This could be interpreted in two ways. One version is that the evolution of institutional designs is driven in a counter-rational direction by the unfolding logic of foundational normative principles like equality, democracy, or sovereignty. *** If the EU continues its current (if halting) institutional evolution in the direction of a federal as opposed to unitary state, for example, then in retrospect one could argue that its core commitment to the principle of state sovereignty contained within it the seeds of the outcome (a federal state being more compatible with sovereignty than a unitary one). At the moment of each decision in this evolution actors might have the freedom to make choices, but in the end, at the macro-level, the overall result was pre-ordained. This brings us back to the earlier

---

[42] See Wendt 1999, 126, and the references cited there.
[43] Pierson 2000b; see also Pierson 2000a.
[44] Ibid.
[45] This alternative is raised by Robert Goodin. Goodin 1996, 26.

discussions about the relationship between designs and designers, and design versus evolution. If designers are merely implementing the logic of norms, what really is doing the causal work here: agents or structures? * * *

However, there is another way to spin a teleological explanation that parallels the volume's functionalist approach, suggesting that the two accounts might be compatible. One could imagine a teleological explanation that took as its central animating idea not substantive principles like sovereignty or democracy, but the principle of instrumental rationality itself.[46] * * *

In summary, because the Rational Design project does not engage in a dialogue with alternative explanations, it is difficult to assess fully its own explanation of institutional design. * * *

BROADENING THE SCIENCE OF INSTITUTIONAL DESIGN

Up to this point I have taken as given that the question we are trying to answer about international institutional design is the positive social science one: What explains the choice of designs? In the rest of this article I raise two questions that are not asked in this volume – about institutional effectiveness and normative desirability – and as such my discussion turns more purely external. * * * [Part] of what makes the issue of institutional design compelling is that it does raise big questions beyond the explanatory one. These form another kind of contrast space, the mapping of which will help put the project further into perspective. * * *

Let us assume that we want to contribute to institutional design in the real world to be "policy-relevant." * * * What should social scientists do to make our study of this issue as useful as possible? In short, what should count as "knowledge" about institutional design?

To answer this it is useful to step back and ask, what kind of "problem" is institutional design? What do we need our knowledge *for*?[47] There is no single answer, but any satisfactory one should recognize first that making institutions is about what we should do in the future. In contrast, explaining institutions is about what we did in the past. By identifying constraints, explanations of the past may provide some insight into the future, but the connection is not straightforward. Consider the implications if rational-design theory were a perfect, 100 percent true explanation of past institutional designs. In that case it would reveal laws of human

---

[46] Cf. Meyer et al. 1997; and Boli and Thomas 1999.
[47] Cf. Wendt 2001.

behavior with which we can predict institutional choices in the future. That kind of knowledge is great for social scientists, but how does it help institutional designers? They do not need a theory to tell them what they are already going to do. Ironically, rational-design theory seems like it would be more policy-relevant if it were false, since then it could be used normatively to persuade decision makers to be more rational next time. * * *

From a practical perspective, in other words, it is not clear what the "problem" is to which rational-design theory is the solution. In fairness, this is not unique to this theory: any theory, rationalist or constructivist, that only explains past choices will be of limited value in making future ones. This stems from a basic assumption of positive social science: that the universe is causally closed and deterministic, and so there must be some set of causes or laws that explains why we had to do what we did. To be sure, the complexity of the social world is such that we can rarely know these laws with certainty, and thus our knowledge will usually be probabilistic rather than deterministic. But this is typically viewed as an epistemological constraint, not an ontological one. I suspect few positive social scientists would say that social life is *inherently* nondeterministic in the way that quantum mechanics suggests micro-physical reality is; * probabilistic laws are simply a function of the limits of our knowledge in a complex world. It is hard to see where human freedom and creativity come into such an ontologically closed picture, except in the "error term." In contrast, the basic premise of real-world design is that the future is open, that we have genuine choices to make, that voluntarism rather than determinism rules the day. This openness means that the question of what will happen tomorrow is to a great extent fundamentally normative rather than positive. * * *

In short, there is an irreducible ontological and epistemological gap between explaining institutions and making them, rooted in their different orientations toward time * * *.[48] Interestingly, this gap between backward- and forward-looking thinking is implicit in E. H. Carr's characterization of the difference between "realism" and "utopianism."[49] As is well known, Carr criticized pure utopianism for "ignor[ing] what was and what is in contemplation of what should be," and thus as being too voluntaristic and dangerous.[50] However, Carr's critique was ultimately

---

[48] On the difference between prediction and forecasting, which are rooted in explaining, and "making" as ways of thinking about the future, see Huber 1974.

[49] Carr [1939] 1964.

[50] Ibid., 11.

not of utopianism per se, but of utopianism untempered by an appreciation for constraints. In his view pure realism was also problematic because it was deterministic and sterile, unable to do anything more than reconcile us fatalistically to the evils of the world. As a result, "sound political thought and sound political life will be found only where *both* have their place."[51] Which one should be emphasized at a given time depends on historical conditions. While sometimes "realism is the necessary corrective to the exuberance of utopianism, ... in other periods utopianism must be invoked to counteract the barrenness of realism."[52] With the Cold War over, the international community can once again contemplate the utopian side of life, and this volume brings welcome rigor to that impulse. Yet the way it has posed its central question seems still caught up in a realist mentality, oriented toward explaining rather than making, determinism rather than voluntarism.

*** The different temporalities of explaining and making mean there will always be a gap between a science of the past and a policy for the future. If we want to drive forward rather than just see where we have been, therefore, we need kinds of knowledge that go beyond the causes of institutional design, and we need two in particular: knowledge about institutional effectiveness and knowledge about values.

Institutional Effectiveness

Functionalism assumes that actors will choose those institutional designs that they believe will most efficiently serve their interests. As such, the criterion for whether or not an institution is a rational choice is subjective (at the level of the group), namely that it helps them solve their perceived collective-action problem. ***

However, institutions are designed to solve problems in the world, and therefore we will also want to know how well they fit or match the reality toward which they are directed. If institutions perform as their designers expected, there is no problem. Functionalism would then correspond to a Dr. Pangloss situation, the best of all possible worlds. But what if designers' expectations turn out later to have missed the mark? What if an institution has unintended negative consequences of sufficient magnitude that had these been known in advance designers would have made different choices? In short, what if design features are not, in fact,

[51] Ibid., 10; emphasis added.
[52] Ibid.

functional? In that case institutional choices might have been rational in the subjective sense, but in the objective sense, a mistake.

Of course, what is objectively rational can only be known after the fact and so is not fully available to us. However, by studying institutional effectiveness we can gain some relevant foreknowledge. * * *

In particular, understanding institutional effectiveness helps us make the future in at least two ways. One is by enhancing the objective accuracy with which design problems are defined, and the quality of our means-end calculations. Here we can see a partial dependence of making on explaining/predicting: to be successful the former depends in part on being able to do the latter. For example, knowing how well different institutions work might enable us to choose better between what Philip Pettit calls "deviant-centered" and "complier-centered" designs.[53] To that extent such research would nicely complement this volume's agenda.

However, understanding effectiveness could also have a second, more rival impact. What if it turns out that institutions designed according to the criterion of maximizing expected utility frequently have significant negative unintended consequences, so that the gap between what seems functional and what really is functional is often large? In some of these cases it might still be best to try to maximize expected utility, in the hopes of getting as close to the optimal outcome as we can. But in other cases, according to the "theory of the second best" we might be better off not doing so and adopting some other decision rule instead.[54] If learning that we are often very poor at predicting design outcomes leads us to approach design in a new way, then the effectiveness problematique would not complement the Rational Design project's research program so much as reconstitute its central concept, rationality. Research into the causes of design choices might then be led to ask a new question, Why do states make such *ir*rational choices?

* * *

Normative Desirability

Perhaps even more important than knowledge about what works is knowledge about what is right and wrong. After all, institutions are created to advance certain values, and so we cannot design anything until

---

[53] Pettit 1996.
[54] On the design implications of the theory of second best, see Goodin 1995; and Coram 1996.

we know what values we should pursue. This knowledge is not considered part of social science as conventionally understood, so some might argue that its production should not take place in IR but over in political theory and normative IR. There is something to this; a division of labor between positive and normative theory is often useful. However, with respect to real-world institutional design their separation is problematic. Given the futural and open-ended character of this problem, a science of design will be more useful if it addresses the relationship between positive and normative in a systematic way.

Assuming that the empirical support for this volume's conjectures holds up, how should we evaluate this result normatively? Is it *good* that the designers of international institutions are "rational?" Not necessarily – that depends on what their designs are for. The possibility that the institutions set up by the Nazis or Imperial Japanese were rational does not mean they should be repeated. However, from the perspective of the Rational Design framework this normative relativity is not a problem because it defines rationality as purely instrumental. Rationality has to do with means, not ends, and as such does not *itself* have normative content.

The belief that instrumental rationality has no normative content suggests two points. First, note that this belief treats as exogenously settled many of the most important questions about international institutional design, namely about the constitution of ends. (1) Who should be the designer? In most cases states are the designers. Is this a good thing? What about those affected by international institutions? (2) What values should states pursue in their designs? Wealth? Power? Justice? (3) For whom should states pursue these values? Nations? Civilizations? Humanity? (4) What should be their time horizon? Should states care about future generations, and if so at what discount rate? (5) Should institutional designs focus on outcomes or procedures? In sum, what constitutes "the good" in a given situation to which designers should be aspiring? All of these normative questions are intensely political, and their answers will strongly condition how design problems are defined. There are still interesting normative questions left once ends are decided (some distributional questions, for example), but it is hard not to feel that by the time this volume's rational designers begin their deliberations much of the politics is over.

Second, is it so clear that instrumental rationality has no normative content? One way to raise doubts would be to invoke Jurgen Habermas's concept of communicative rationality, which Thomas Risse sees as an alternative both to rationalism's logic of consequences and the logic of appropriateness emphasized by constructivists.[55] According to Habermas, strategic (a form of instrumental) rationality and communicative rationality exhibit different "orientations toward action," the former being oriented toward success, the latter toward achieving consensus or understanding. An important feature of this difference is that implicit within it are different relationships between Self and Other, which in this case could be one designer to another, or to consumers. Instrumental rationality positions the Other as an object to be manipulated in order to realize the interests of the Self. In this case Self and Other position each other as separate individuals, and power and interest will drive their interaction. Communicative rationality, in contrast, positions Self and Other not as distinct objects but as members of the same community, "team,"[56] or "We." In this case power and individual interest do not matter (or as much), and instead deliberation, persuasion, and the force of the better argument take over. To that extent the difference between the two rationalities may seem to be one of process rather than outcome, which the Rational Design framework seeks to bracket.[57] However, it matters here because (1) it suggests that acting in an instrumentally rational way is itself a *constitutive choice* about who actors are going to be, which brings us back to the question of performativity discussed earlier,[58] and as such (2) it is a choice that may have normative consequences, distinct from those of the ends that action seeks to realize. ***

*** It is certainly desirable that institutional designers know how to calculate, but one would also hope they have wisdom, judgment, and an understanding of the good. These are qualities that a rigid separation of positive and normative theory will do little to cultivate.

CONCLUSION

A complete, policy-relevant science of institutional design will provide knowledge that answers at least three questions: How and why have design choices been made in the past? What works? And what goals should we pursue? The Rational Design project represents an important step toward answering the first. It addresses the second only implicitly, through the functionalist assumption that states will understand subjectively what is objectively rational. About the third this volume is silent.

---

[55] Risse 2000.
[56] On "thinking like a team," see Sugden 1993.
[57] Koremenos, Lipson, and Snidal [2001], 781.
[58] On different design rationalities as constitutive choices, see Dryzek 1996.

* * *

One can fairly ask whether a science that combined all three questions would really be a "science." It probably would not be on conventional understandings of that term. However, one lesson I took away from this volume is that, if we are to make social science relevant to the problems of institutional design facing real-world decision makers (and us, their consumers), we need to broaden our conception of social science to integrate positive and normative concerns – to develop a "practical" understanding of social science, in both its everyday and philosophical senses. Different images of a practical social science can be found in work inspired by Aristotle, Dewey, Buchanan, and Habermas.[59] But with the partial exception of Habermas, these traditions have made little impact on IR, which continues not only to maintain a high wall between positive and normative concerns but also to actively marginalize the latter.

One reason for this marginalization is probably the strong influence of positivism on our discipline, but it has received further impetus from the long theoretical dominance of realism.[60] If international politics is condemned to be a realm of eternal conflict, then the future cannot be different from the past, and normative concerns can be dismissed as "fantasy theory."[61] The third question that a practical science of institutional design should answer – What values should we pursue? – does not come up, since we have no value choices to make. The best we can hope to do is survive, and for that all we need is a positive social science, one that looks to the past to guide our journey "back to the future."[62] In such a closed and deterministic universe the idea of institutional "design" is irrelevant.

Yet this volume's premise is that states do design international institutions, that these choices matter, and (presumably) that social scientists should try to help make them better. As such, its premise is at least implicitly one of voluntarism and an open future, where things do not have to be done as they have in the past. To fully realize the potential of this premise, however, we need to think harder about the nature of the design problem, its differences from our traditional social scientific

---

[59] See Salkever 1991; Cochran 1999; Buchanan 1990; and Linklater 1998, respectively. Given its rationalist basis, the absence of the Buchanan tradition in this volume, as represented in the journal Constitutional Political Economy, is particularly noteworthy.

[60] For a classic discussion, see Wight 1966.

[61] Schweller 1999.

[62] Mearsheimer 1990.

concern with explanation, and the implications for the kind of knowledge we seek to produce. Driving may be difficult when it is dark outside, but a science that tries to see the road ahead by using only the rearview mirror makes little sense, especially if we are building the road as we go along. The Rational Design project has performed a valuable service for IR by raising such an interesting problem. Having done so, the hope is that it will lead eventually to a more forward-looking, practical social science.

17

The Dynamics of International Law: The Interaction of Normative and Operating Systems

Paul F. Diehl, Charlotte Ku, and Daniel Zamora

* * *

International law provides the framework for political discourse among members of the international system. The framework does not guarantee consensus, but it does foster the ongoing discourse and participation needed to provide conceptual clarity in developing legal obligations and gaining their acceptance. In playing this role, international law performs two different functions. One is to provide mechanisms for cross-border interactions, and the other is to shape the values and goals these interactions are pursuing. We call the first set of functions the "operating system" of international law, and the second set the "normative system."[1]

The purpose of this article is to describe the basic components of the operating and normative systems as a conceptual framework for analyzing and understanding international law. We also explore, in a preliminary fashion, the interaction of these two systems, specifically the conditions under which operating system changes occur in response to normative changes. We present a number of theoretical arguments and illustrate them by reference to the norm prohibiting genocide and the subsequent steps taken by states to change international legal rules so that this norm could influence state behavior.

* * *

[1] Ku and Diehl 1998.

*** [Most] scholarship has been devoted to how norms arise,[2] with special attention to the moral character of the norm and how it becomes accepted broadly by the international community. Such scholarship has not often paid attention to the ways in which the international community has sought to ensure that such norms actually influence state behavior. Either this was assumed to be a tautology (some argue that behavior modification is an essential component of a norm)[3] or dismissed as a fundamentally different question. Our analysis seeks to assess whether particular factors will likely help or hinder a norm's effectiveness.

More broadly, our analysis answers the call[4] to bridge international legal and international relations theories. Although not exclusively concerned with international regimes,[5] our analysis has implications for how regimes are designed and what mechanisms exist for their maintenance. As Slaughter et al.[6] indicate, "effective regime design requires a theory of why states cooperate through institutional arrangements and why those arrangements might not succeed." We hope to offer insights on when states will build institutional as well as other mechanisms to ensure that regime norms are not empty ideals. In effect, operating system provisions become a necessary part of the legal regime in a given issue area. Thus understanding how normative change prompts operating system change could be a major component of understanding the development and, ultimately, the effectiveness of international regimes.

* * *

INTERNATIONAL LAW AS OPERATING AND NORMATIVE SYSTEMS

International law's existence today as a collection of rules, prescriptions, and aspirations governing the conduct of states seems well established. Yet there seems to be a vacuum of inquiry into the relationship between the structures and processes of international law and its normative content. Our study examines this by stepping away from the traditional approaches of sources, hierarchy, or functions of international law toward a concern with dynamics or change in international law. Our approach is to look at international law as a package of related activities that

[2] For example, Klotz 1995; and Finnemore 1996.
[3] Goertz and Diehl 1992.
[4] Slaughter, Tulumello, and Wood 1998; Beck 1996.
[5] For a review, see Hasenclever, Mayer, and Rittberger 1997.
[6] Slaughter, Tulumello, and Wood 1998, 385.

are both structural and directive at the same time. We identify the two threads as operating (structural) and normative (directive). We chose the word "operating" as one would conceive of a computer's operating system. It is the basic platform upon which a system will operate. When the computer operating system (for example, Microsoft Windows) functions to allow the use of specific word processing programs, spreadsheets, or communications software, there is little direct consideration given to that system by the user. Similarly, the operating system of international law provides the signals and commands that make multiple functions and modes possible, and when functioning, often requires little conscious effort. * * *

Operating System

The dual character of international law results from its Westphalian legacy in which law functions among, rather than above, states and in which the state carries out the legislative, judicial, and executive functions that in domestic legal systems are performed by separate institutions. The operating system of international law therefore functions in some ways as a constitution does in a domestic legal system – by setting out the consensus of its constituent actors (primarily states) on distribution of authority and responsibilities for governance within the system. Legal capacity can be expressed and recognized in terms of rights and duties, and is a major portion of constitutions. Nevertheless, constitutions also provide more. Dahl[7] identified a number of items that constitutions generally specify, several of which are also specified by international law. These include competent decisions, accountability, and ensuring stability, to name a few.

In order for the operating system to maintain vibrancy and resiliency, and to ensure the stability necessary for orderly behavior, the operating system must provide for a dynamic normative system that facilitates the competition of values, views, and actors. It does so by applying the constitutional functions as described above when including new actors, new issues, new structures, and new norms. Who, for example, are the authorized decision makers in international law? Whose actions can bind not only the parties involved, but also others? How does one know that an authoritative decision has taken place? When does the resolution of a conflict or a dispute give rise to new law? These are the questions that the operating system answers. Note, in particular, that where the operating system may be associated with formal structures, not all

---

[7] Dahl 1998.

operating system elements are institutional. For example, the Vienna Convention on Treaties entails no institutional mechanisms, but does specify various operational rules about treaties and therefore the parameters of lawmaking.

The operating system has a number of dimensions or components, typically covered in international law textbooks, but largely unconnected with one another. Some of the primary components include the following:

1. Sources of Law. These include the system rules for defining the process through which law is formed, the criteria for determining when legal obligations exist, and which actors are bound (or not) by that law. This element of the operating system also specifies a hierarchy of different legal sources. For example, the operating system defines whether United Nations (UN) resolutions are legally binding (generally not) and what role they play in the legal process (possible evidence of customary law).

2. Actors. This dimension includes determining which actors are eligible to have rights and obligations under the law. The operating system also determines how, and the degree to which, those actors might exercise those rights internationally. For example, individuals and multinational corporations may enjoy certain international legal protections, but those rights might only be asserted in international forums by their home states.

3. Jurisdiction. These rules define the rights of actors and institutions to deal with legal problems and violations. An important element is defining what problems or situations will be handled through national legal systems as opposed to international forums. For example, the Convention on Torture (1985) allows states to prosecute perpetrators in their custody, regardless of the location of the offense and the nationality of the perpetrator or victim, affirming the "universal jurisdiction" principle.

4. Courts or Institutions. These elements create forums and accompanying rules under which international legal disputes might be heard or decisions might be enforced. Thus for example, the Statute of the International Court of Justice (ICJ) provides for the creation of the institution, sets general rules of decision making, identifies the processes and scope under which cases are heard, specifies the composition of the court, and details decision-making procedures (to name a few).

Our conception of an operating system clearly overlaps with some prior formulations, but is different in some fundamental ways. Regime theory[8] refers to decision-making procedures as practices for making and implementing collective choice, similar to "regulative norms,"[9] which lessen transaction costs of collective action. Although these may be encompassed by the international law operating system, our conception of the latter is broader. The operating system is not necessarily issue-specific but may deal equally well (or poorly) with multiple issues – note that the ICJ may adjudicate disputes involving airspace as well as war crimes. Regime decision-making procedures are also thought to reflect norms, rules, and principles without much independent standing.

Hart[10] developed the notion of "secondary rules" to refer to the ways in which primary rules might be "conclusively ascertained, introduced, eliminated, varied, and the fact of their violation conclusively determined."[11] This comports in many ways with our conception of an international legal operating system. Yet Hart views secondary rules (his choice of the term "secondary" is illuminating) as "parasitic" to the primary ones. This suggests that secondary rules follow in time the development of primary rules, especially in primitive legal systems (to which international law is sometimes compared). Furthermore, secondary rules are believed to service normative ones, solving the problems of "uncertainty," "stasis," and "inefficiency" inherently encountered with normative rules.

Our conception of an international legal operating system is somewhat different. For us, the operating system is usually independent of any one norm or regime and, therefore, is greater than the sum of any parts derived from individual norms and regimes. The operating system in many cases, after its creation, may precede the development of parts of the normative system, rather than merely reacting to it. In this conception, the operating system is not merely a maid-servant to the normative system, but the former can actually shape the development of the latter. For example, established rules on jurisdiction may restrict the development of new normative rules on what kinds of behaviors might be labeled as international crimes. Neither is the operating system as reflective of the normative system as Hart implies it to be. The operating system may develop some of its configurations autonomously from specific norms, thereby serving political as well as legal needs (for example, the

---

[8] Krasner 1982.
[9] Barnett 1995.
[10] Hart 1994.
[11] Ibid., 94.

creation of an international organization that also performs monitoring functions). In the relatively anarchic world of international relations, we argue that this is more likely than in the domestic legal systems on which Hart primarily based his analysis.

*** [The] operating system has a greater "stickiness" than might be implied by Hart's formulations. The operating system may be more resistant to change and not always responsive to alterations in the normative system or the primary rules. It is this formulation that suggests, and makes interesting, our concern with how operating system change follows or not from normative change. This is not merely a matter of moving from a primitive legal system to a more advanced one (as Hart would argue), but of considering how adaptive the two systems are to each other. Finally, our formulation sees effective norm development as dependent on the operating system or the structural dimension. A failure to understand this dependence may stall or obstruct a norm's effectiveness. Again, the metaphor of the computer operating system may be useful as the failure of the operating system to adequately support a specific software application will slow down or render inoperable features of that application for the user.

The evolution of the operating system in all of the areas enumerated above has been toward expansion – in the number of actors, in the forms of decision making, and in the forums and modes of implementation. Although international law remains principally a body of rules and practices to regulate state behavior in the conduct of interstate relations, much of international law now also regulates the conduct of governments and the behavior of individuals within states, and may address issues that require ongoing transnational cooperation. Human rights law is an example of the normative system regulating behavior within states. Such human rights law, however, may configure elements of the operating system in that the human rights granted may convey legal personality onto individuals, thereby rendering them capable of holding or exercising legal rights. ***

[Participants] in the international legal process today include more than 190 states and governments, international institutions created by states, and elements of the private sector – multinational corporations and financial institutions, networks of individuals, and NGOs. ***

There has also been an expansion in the forms of law. This has led to thinking about law as a continuum "ranging from the traditional international legal forms to soft law instruments."[12] This continuum

---

[12] Chinkin 1989; see also Weil 1983.

includes resolutions of the UN General Assembly, standards of private organizations such as the International Standards Organization, and codes of conduct developed in international organizations,[13] such as the code of conduct on the distribution and use of pesticides adopted by the Food and Agriculture Organization in 1985. The concept of a continuum is useful because these modes are likely not to operate in isolation, but rather to interact with and build on each other. ***

The forums and modes for implementation have also expanded. *** Although international law still relies on domestic legal and political structures for implementation, the international community has also created new international institutions and recognized transnational legal processes that have over time become recognized forums in which to engage in decision making, interpretation, and recently even the prosecution of individuals on the basis of violations of international law.[14] Not only do representatives of states continue to meet to make law, but they also meet routinely in international settings to ensure its implementation and compliance (for example, CSCE follow-up meetings after the Helsinki accords in 1975). ***

*   *   *

The Normative System

We choose the word normative to describe the directive aspects of international law because this area of law functions to create norms out of particular values or policies. Using a different set of analogies, we could imagine "normative" processes as quasi-legislative in character, as they mandate particular values and direct specific changes in state and other actors' behaviors. References to the term "norms" abound in the study of international relations, and it is not always clear what is conveyed by a particular construction. In the regimes literature,[15] norms and principles (for example, orthodox versus embedded liberalism in trade) are broader philosophies of how states and other actors should behave. Although they tend to be issue-specific (for example, addressing trade or human rights), regime norms are not generally defined at the microlevel (for example, precise changes in rules governing certain human rights

[13] Charney 1993.
[14] See Ku and Borgen 2000.
[15] Krasner 1982.

violations). In this sense, they are similar to what Barnett[16] refers to as "constitutive norms." Our conception of norms is on the one hand narrower and more precise. We focus only on normative elements that have a legally binding character, analogous to the idea of rules in the regime literature. Because we are interested in the international legal system, we are not concerned with acts of "comity" or with so-called "soft law," which might be appropriate subjects for a broader inquiry of international norms. On the other hand, we have a deeper conception of norms that goes beyond broad general principles to include specific elements about behavior. That is, our normative system is concerned with particular prescriptions and proscriptions, such as limitations on child labor.

Our conception of a normative system is similar to what Hart[17] defines as primary rules that impose duties on actors to perform or abstain from actions – but there is an important difference. Hart sees primary rules as the basic building blocks of a legal system, logically and naturally preceding the development of what we define as the operating system components. For Hart, a primitive legal system can be one with developed rules, but without substantial structures to interpret or enforce those rules. We see a more developed international legal system where norms may exist without specific reference to the operating system but cannot function without using the operating system's mechanisms. Nevertheless, the normative system may remain somewhat autonomous from the operating system and may even lag behind in its development.

In defining the normative system, the participants in the international legal process engage in a political and legislative exercise that defines the substance and scope of the law. Normative change may occur slowly with the evolution of customary practices, a traditional source of international law. Yet in recent historical periods, normative change has been precipitated by new treaties (for example, the Nuclear Non-Proliferation Treaty) or by a series of actions by international organizations (for example, UN Special Commission activities in Iraq).* Nevertheless, the establishment of international legal norms is still less precise and structured than that in domestic legal systems, where formal deliberative bodies enact legislation.

In contrast to the general terms associated with topics of the operating system (for example, jurisdiction or actors), the topics of the normative system are issue-specific, and many components of the system refer to subtopics within issue areas (for example, the status of women within

---

[16] Barnett 1995.
[17] Hart 1994.

the broader topic area of human rights). Many of these issues have long been on the agenda of international law. Proscriptions on the use of military force have their roots in natural law and early Christian teachings on just war. Many normative rules concerning the law of the sea (for example, seizure of commercial vessels during wartime) also have long pedigrees in customary practice. Yet recent trends in the evolution of the normative system represent expansions in its scope and depths. Some current issue areas of international legal concern, most notably with respect to human rights and the environment, have developed almost exclusively over the past fifty years. Furthermore, within issue areas, legal norms have sought to regulate a wider range of behaviors; for example, international law on the environment has evolved beyond simple concerns of riparian states to include concerns with ozone depletion, water pollution, and other problems.

* * *

The effectiveness of the normative system, * * * depends largely on the operating system, the mechanisms and processes that are designed to ensure orderly processes and compliance with those norms and to bring about change if problems signal a need for change. The normative system may facilitate compliance in isolation from the operating system by "compliance pull."[18] Compliance pull is induced through legitimacy, which is powered by the quality of the rule or the rule-making institution. Still, "primary rules, if they lack adherence to a system of validating secondary rules, are mere ad hoc reciprocal arrangements."[19] Compliance pull may exist under such circumstances, but it will be considerably weaker than if secondary rules (related to the operating system) are present. Note that we are speaking of more than compliance concerns in dealing with norms. Regime theory has typically assumed that it is the desire to improve the efficiency of interstate interactions (for example, by reducing transaction costs) that drives the adoption of normative rules. Our view is that states adopt normative rules largely to promote shared values in the international system. Rule adoption and institution creation (largely operating system changes) may be helpful in implementation and in reducing transaction costs, but are not a necessary element or purpose of normative change.

* * *

[18] Franck 1990.
[19] Ibid., 184.

CORRELATES OF OPERATING SYSTEM CHANGE

* * * We argue that the operating system does not necessarily optimally support the normative system. One major question * * * arises from this conceptual framework: How does change in the normative system affect the operating system? Our theoretical argument specifies several necessary conditions for normative change to produce operating system change, with other factors essentially operating as limiting conditions or veto points. * * *

There are some assumptions and caveats underlying our analysis below. First, we focus on operating system changes that succeed normative change. This is not to say that the reverse is not possible or that the process is not recursive. Obviously, both processes occur, but we want to isolate and examine the "norms produce structural changes" process as a first step in understanding the complex interaction. Thus because we take norms as a given, their genesis (including the influences of structure) is outside the scope of this study. Second, we assume that the international legal operating system is somewhat "sticky," and thereby has an inertial resistance to change. Thus the operating system is not merely a reflection of the normative system and does not necessarily move in synchronous fashion with alterations in the latter.

* * *

The Necessity of Necessity

The operating system for international law only changes in response to necessity. That is, one might anticipate operating system change only when the status quo system cannot handle the requirements placed on it by the adoption of new normative standards. There is also the assumption, of course, that states actually want to implement normative provisions, rather than let them linger with largely symbolic effects.

Some of the logic underlying the necessity requirement is related to the contractualist model of international regime formation.[20] In this model, states cooperate and build institutions to lessen the "transaction costs" associated with the negotiation, monitoring, and enforcement of agreements. In particular, regimes are designed to mitigate the latter sanctioning problems that arise at the international level when seeking to ensure that states follow certain prescriptions. Thus such approaches to

[20] Keohane 1984.

regime formation focus on the efficiency of new structural arrangements. Necessity goes beyond simple efficiency bases, however, and stresses that the operating system must change to give effect to new standards. Thus necessity assumes that some actions must be completed (an inherent increase in efficiency), but it does not presuppose that the operating system change will necessarily be the most efficient arrangement, and therefore may fall short of rationalist expectations. The contractualist approach to regimes recognizes that institution creation is not done in a vacuum, but rather in the context of past efforts and institutional experiences. Thus the status quo becomes an important reference point for potential regime alterations. With respect to our concern with the international law operating system, extant system arrangements vis-à-vis new norms become critical. Accordingly, there seem to be three separate elements of necessity that may precipitate changes in the operating system: insufficiency, incompatibility, and ineffectiveness.

When legal norms are completely *de novo,* and therefore dissimilar to existing norms, it is likely that the legal operating system does not possess relevant provisions to deal with them. When the operating system is therefore insufficient to give effect or regulate relations surrounding the new norm, changes might be expected to occur in that operating system to accommodate the new rules. An example of such change would include the construction of a committee for regulating the observance of a new environmental law, similar to the creation of UN's Commission on Sustainable Development following the Conference on Environment and Development in 1992.

Related to the insufficiency of current operating arrangements is their incompatibility vis-à-vis alterations in legal prescriptions. The extant operating system in international law may not simply be inadequate to deal with new norms, it may be contrary to them. At that point, some reconciliation is necessary. For example, holding national leaders responsible for torture or other crimes (Convention on Torture) creates new norms but is incompatible with notions of sovereign immunity[.] *** Exceptions to foreign sovereign immunity may need to be created for the operating system to be consonant with these new agreements and the legal norms embedded within them.

A third variation of the necessity argument concerns ineffectiveness. Unlike insufficiency, which presupposes the complete absence of relevant operating arrangements, the ineffectiveness variation finds operating mechanisms present, but not well designed to meet the challenges presented by the new or modified norm. Thus some specific changes in the operating system are needed that specifically reflect the new norm. For example, compliance mechanisms based on reciprocity may be largely ineffective with respect to emerging norms in areas such as human rights. There, the violation of legal standards by one state has little commensurate effect on the probability that other states will also violate the law (and thereby impose costs on the original violator). Indeed, reciprocity concerns may undermine compliance as states implicitly cooperate *not* to sanction one another for such violations. This is illustrated by UN member countries' refusal to denounce human rights atrocities committed by their neighbors.

Although we argue that some necessity is required for operating system change, we leave the question of what proposed changes appear on the international agenda and which actors press for those changes as exogenous. At this stage, we believe that proposals for change are always available in the marketplace of ideas. This is consistent with public policy analyses postulating that there are always "solutions" present in the system, but these solutions must wait for the right conditions before they are seriously considered or adopted. Many of those proposals will arise and be promoted by a concatenation of actors in the international policy process. These would most prominently include states with a direct interest in facilitating operating system change (for example, coastal states seeking compliance with pollution rules), epistemic communities, and other policy entrepreneurs (for example, international lawyers) as well as international governmental organizations and NGOs. The major point in this section, however, is that the efforts of these actors to propose or champion operating system change will fail unless necessity considerations prevail.

The Impetus of Political Shocks

There is inherent inertia in any political system, and international law has been characterized as changing more glacially than other legal systems. Accordingly, we posit that some significant impetus must be present before the operating system adjusts to the normative change. That impetus must come from a significant political shock.[21] Political shocks can be discrete events, such as world wars, acts of terrorism, or horrific

---

[21] The notion of political shocks producing significant environmental change has been adopted by scholars of American public policymaking drawing heavily from biological models of punctuated equilibrium. See Baumgartner and Jones 1993. For an application to international relations phenomena, see Diehl and Goertz 2000.

human rights abuses. Shocks might also appear as significant processes, such as global democratization, that extend over a period of time. All political shocks, however, represent dramatic changes in the international political environment, which in turn facilitate changes in the international legal operating system. Of course, the type of political shock one might expect to see will vary according to the issue area in question. For example, a shift away from the gold standard might be expected to affect international economic law rather than human rights law. This is in contrast to the traditional view of international law as a slowly evolving body of rules, traditionally articulated by customary law, which almost by definition presupposes gradualist change.

Political shocks can have a number of effects on international relations and thereby facilitate operating system change. First, political shocks may radically reorder relations between states, such that previous impediments to cooperation are removed. Previous animosities or divisions may give way to alliances between former enemies. * * * Operating system change may not have been possible previously because of disputes between states or restrictions imposed by the international environment. A change in that environment may break down the barriers to the adoption of new policies – or new legal structures or provisions. Second, political shocks may place issues or policies on the global agenda and thereby prompt the community of states to take action on them. For example, some human rights concerns only become salient issues following catastrophic violations. Thus even though operating system change may be needed, there may be no action until the issue becomes salient. We know from numerous studies of public policy that while a multitude of problems exist, only a subset receives government action, often at the impetus of dramatic events or changes in the political environment (for example, a new government). We envision that international political shocks perform a similar agenda-setting function with respect to the international legal system.

Political shocks may have the effect of changing the normative and operating system simultaneously or sequentially. That is, an initial political shock may prompt a normative change (for example, restrictions on the use of military force after World War I), and this may include corresponding changes in the operating system (for example, the creation of the League of Nations and its provisions for dealing with aggression). In contrast, the operating system change may not result from the same shock as that which prompted the initial normative change. Thus it may take another shock, potentially many years later, for the operating system to be altered. Thus our model recognizes that normative and operating change may not be coterminous and provides a specification of the process under which this might happen. As conceptualized, political shocks provide the necessary, but not always sufficient, conditions for operating system change. That is, not every political shock will produce an operating system change; some shocks will occur with little or no after-effects.

Although we see operating system change flowing from requirements of necessity and spurred on by political shocks, two factors may limit or stifle operating system change even under those conditions: the opposition of leading states and domestic political factors.

The Role of Leading States

Among the most prominent theoretical schools in international relations is hegemonic stability theory.[22] According to this approach, typically applied to international economics, a system leader and its preferences define and shape the interactions that occur within the international system. The hegemon also subsidizes the provision of public goods to enhance the stability of the system. The leading state must have the capacity and the willingness to produce the resources or infrastructure necessary for the smooth operation of the system. The United States (following, in some conceptions, Great Britain) has fulfilled that role for the world since 1945.

If one were to adopt some hegemonic version of operating system change, then such change would only occur when it was the self-interest of the hegemon and when that state took the lead in facilitating the change. This leading role may mean providing the public goods necessary for norm compliance. Yet we are hesitant to adopt the hegemonic stability model as an explanation for international legal change. The model has come under intense criticism[23] and even one of those who helped formulate it acknowledges the limited empirical support it has received.[24] Furthermore, Keohane[25] also admits that a hegemon is neither necessary nor sufficient for cooperation, and by implication, therefore, for operating system change.

Despite these limitations, there is good reason to consider revised and more modest elements of the hegemonic stability idea as relevant for

[22] See Kindleberger 1973; and Keohane 1980.
[23] See more recently, Pahre 1999.
[24] Keohane 1984.
[25] Ibid.

international legal change. That hegemonic stability theory is inadequate or incorrect does not mean that the behavior of leading states is unimportant. Whether in creating law or institutions or in developing general standards of behavior (that is, custom), the history of international law has predominantly been written by Western states, and in particular, the major powers. In arguing that leading states can arrest or inhibit operating system change, however, we break from hegemonic stability models in several ways. First, we do not confine ourselves to the influence of one leading state, but instead focus on several powerful states. No one state has been able to impose its will on the international legal system. Furthermore, the identity of leading states has often varied by issue area; for example, leading naval powers have exercised a disproportionate share of the power in shaping the law of the sea.

Second, we differ in our emphasis on the operating system, as opposed to hegemonic stability's preoccupation with norm development. Some scholars[26] have argued that normative change may only arise with the active support of the hegemon. Our concern here is not with the origins of normative change, but rather its consequences for the operating system. Yet a hegemonic view of norm origination seems to suggest that operating system change would automatically follow from the original normative change. Thus normative and operating changes stem from the same cause. Nevertheless, we deviate from this perspective. We can conceive of circumstances in which norms arise outside the purview of leading states in the world. As Sikkink[27] notes, hegemonic views of norms have great difficulty accounting for the rise of human rights and other norms. Moreover, interpretive[28] and other approaches[29] make compelling cases for the role of nonstate actors in norm formation. Yet it may be the case that norms can arise without the support of, or even with active opposition from, leading states in the system.

Nevertheless, leading states may be the major actors determining whether norms are reflected in the actors, jurisdictional requirements, and institutions that make up the operating system. Even if we accept that norm origination requires the consent of the leading states in the system, it is conceivable that such states may still choose to block operating system changes. Support for normative change may largely be for

---

[26] Ikenberry and Kupchan 1990.
[27] Sikkink 1998.
[28] Klotz 1995.
[29] Keck and Sikkink 1998.

symbolic reasons (for example, the adoption of the Universal Declaration of Human Rights), but without substantive impact. Leading states may support human rights norms, for example, while also opposing individual standing before international courts and other operating changes that would facilitate the observance of the norm. If leading states benefit from the status quo, they may be worse off under an operating system change and move to prevent that change;[30] this circumstance may be true for many states, but leading states have the power to protect their interests.

Third and most critically, we see the power of leading states as residing in their ability to block, rather than impose, operating system change. In this way, leading states can act much as the "Big Five" do in the UN Security Council: a veto can prevent action, but no state can compel the adoption of a particular policy. The enforcement of normative rules largely depends on the willingness of leading states to bear the costs of enforcement.[31] Yet strong states have incentives to resist delegating authority to new institutions, one component of the operating system. Strong states bear greater sovereignty costs associated with such delegation.[32] Furthermore, such leading states may have to bear disproportionate burdens in providing the public goods associated with operating system change; the prevalence of free riding and the unwillingness of leading actors to bear those costs may be sources of barriers to policy change.[33]

Thus assessing the preferences of leading states is vital to determining whether and to what extent operating system change occurs. How such operating system change might affect the strategic and economic interests of those states is an important consideration. Equally important are the costs of such change borne by the leading states vis-á-vis the private benefits accrued to those actors. We argue that change will likely *not* occur in the operating system when such an alteration threatens the self-interest of the dominant states or is actively opposed by one or more of those states. If this change does occur, however, the change will prove to be sufficiently minimal and ineffective so as not to challenge the interests of the dominant states. The necessity of consent from the dominant state(s)

---

[30] Alston 2000.
[31] Goldstein et al. 2000.
[32] Abbott and Snidal 2000.
[33] Alston 2000.

can, therefore, be seen as a condition that needs to be achieved before any effective operating system change takes place.

Domestic Political Influences

Domestic political concerns may act as intervening factors that affect the outcomes of operating system change. In contrast, some operating system changes require that domestic legal systems be altered. For example, norms against political torture or child marriage necessitate appropriate changes in the domestic legal systems of treaty signatory states. Indeed, any non-self-executing agreement requires some type of domestic political action to give it effect. This goes beyond the ratification process, which may be essential to norm creation. Rather, it involves making changes to domestic legal systems to accommodate the new international norm. This might involve providing remedies for norms within domestic legal institutions, altering jurisdictional rules, or changing the legal standing of individuals or groups to bring claims.

State leaders may be placed in the position of conducting "two-level" games,[34] one with international adversaries and the other with domestic constituencies. Domestic constituencies offer a potential veto point at which operating system change can be stifled. Even a sincere leader may not be able to deliver on promises to enact domestic legal reforms. An insincere leader may actually support the creation of an international norm but move to block the necessary changes in his/her state's legal system for domestic political purposes. Such action permits a principled stance abroad, and a politically popular or necessary position at home. For example, the People's Republic of China signed the Covenant on Civil and Political Rights but has given little indication that it will incorporate many of the treaty's protections into its domestic laws. Beyond leadership incentives, domestic interest groups may seek to block national implementation of international normative changes when their political or economic interests may be harmed by such implementation. For example, labor and manufacturing groups in the United States have sought to weaken the adoption of domestic regulatory mechanisms that give effect to international environmental agreements.

Thus international legal changes with a domestic component will be less likely to be adopted than those without this characteristic. One might also presume that operating system changes requiring domestic

[34] Evans, Jacobson, and Putnam 1993.

action will take longer than those without this restriction, if only because domestic legislative processes are an additional hurdle to operating system change. Operating system change with a domestic political component may also be incomplete or inefficient, given that such changes must be adopted by nearly 190 different states; it might be expected that not all of them will adopt such changes or at least will do so in different ways and to different degrees.

* * *

ILLUSTRATING THE INTERACTION BETWEEN THE OPERATING AND THE NORMATIVE SYSTEMS: THE CASE OF THE GENOCIDE NORM

* * *

Genocide is selected as the issue area for illustration in large part because of the breadth of acceptance for the norm in the world community. Unlike many other areas of human rights, such as economic well-being, there is less controversy concerning the idea that genocide is wrong.[35] This legal issue area provides us with an opportunity to view operating system change for a norm in which consensus appears broad and strong, among the purest cases for analysis. In contrast, norms on the use of force have historically been more controversial. Another important consideration in selecting genocide is that it deals with behavior at both international and domestic levels. Genocide law is primarily focused on the treatment of individuals within state borders, but changes in statutory limitations and jurisdictional rights for the prosecution of crimes such as genocide have had an equally important impact on enforcing human rights norms at the international level. Although some may argue that the genocide norm has distant roots in natural law, its development and accompanying operating system changes are almost exclusively post–World War II phenomena. Thus genocide provides us with a case of norm adoption, much similar to those in international environmental law, that developed in the modern era and represents the new wave of international lawmaking. This issue area allows us to more closely examine a narrow time period, a more manageable task in this limited space than perusing an expansive period such as that covering the development of the law of the sea.

[35] We, of course, recognize that there is some controversy over the specific provisions of the genocide norm, as reflected in some states' initial reluctance to sign the Genocide Convention or the reservations they attached to their acceptance.

We explore genocide by first identifying major normative and operating system changes in the period under study. Yet we do not consider only actual operating system changes. Rather, we also consider instances in which operating system change did *not* occur in some areas or was merely proposed in the wake of a normative change. *** [This] involves properly identifying the normative and operating system changes, specifying their causal sequence, and searching for the major factors suggested by the approach. Although there are a number of changes in this issue area, for space and illustration purposes we describe only three, which are among the central components of the operating system: jurisdiction, institutions, and actors.

The Genocide Norm

That the systematic killing of national, ethnic, racial, or religious groups – genocide – was against international law was probably established before World War II. Indeed, some international and national court cases (for example, *Reservations to the Convention on the Prevention and Punishment of Genocide,* 1951) explicitly make this argument. Nevertheless, the genocide norm was solidified and extended (the prohibition of genocide no longer being confined to wartime) in 1946 with the adoption of UN General Assembly Resolution 96, and codified in the Convention on the Prevention and Punishment of the Crime of Genocide (1948). Before this time, there were few legal structures with which to deal with genocide. States had to rely on diplomatic protest or armed intervention (something not recognized under international law at the time) as mechanisms to punish those who committed genocide. After World War II, genocide has clearly been recognized as contrary to international law. Yet most of the debate surrounding the adoption of the Genocide Convention, and throughout the 1950s, concentrated on refining the definition of genocide and the groups that might be subsumed under the definition.[36] That is, prospective changes in international law dealt more with the normative system than the operating one.

The Genocide Convention has now passed its fiftieth birthday and is generally regarded as a symbolic triumph of international human rights consensus in a world of cultural and political diversity. Yet it is equally regarded as a failure in its ability to prevent genocide or to punish those responsible. A review of the international law of genocide over the past

[36] Kader 1991.

fifty-plus years reveals a mixed bag of operating system changes designed to give the treaty effect, as well as many missed opportunities to revise the operating system toward that same end. Clearly, most analysts regard the operating system for genocide as weak and largely ineffective.[37]

Jurisdiction

Article VI of the Genocide Convention lays out the jurisdictional limits for the prosecution of individuals suspected of genocide. The primary basis of jurisdiction is the territorial principle, whereby criminals are prosecuted according to where the offenses allegedly took place; territorial jurisdiction is not necessarily exclusive as criminals might also be prosecuted under the nationality or passive personality principles depending on national laws. That article of the treaty recognizes the jurisdiction of an international penal tribunal, assuming one has been created and accepted by the relevant states. Most notable is the absence of provisions for universal jurisdiction,[38] whereby any state having the defendant(s) in custody could conduct a genocide trial. Of course, universal jurisdiction for genocide may exist based on customary law, rather than the Genocide Convention; some national court decisions (for example, *Attorney General of Israel v. Eichmann*, 1961) have taken this position, although it is far from certain that this is widely accepted.

During the past fifty years, there has not been much change in jurisdiction provisions for genocide. The recent war crimes tribunals for the former Yugoslavia and for Rwanda both include provisions for concurrent jurisdiction between national courts and the tribunals, but international courts are given primacy. Part of establishing territorial jurisdiction involved creating domestic legislation to make genocide a crime (as provided in Article V). Yet years later, very few states have incorporated the necessary provisions in their own legal codes. Largely, the operating system for criminal acts has undergone little dramatic change with the adoption of the Genocide Convention. What best explains these circumstances?

Necessity for operating system change seems to be present. That necessity does not, however, derive from incompatibility. States may have chosen the territorial principle for genocide because that was the most widely accepted basis for establishing jurisdiction for other crimes. Rather,

---

[37] See Lippman 1998; and American Society of International Law 1998 for a historical retrospective on genocide law.

[38] Part of what Van Schaack (1997) calls the convention's "blind spot."

necessity comes more from the insufficiency and ineffectiveness of the operating system to give effect to the genocide norm. As no permanent tribunal existed ***, implementing genocide norms would fall to national courts. Although there has been a recent upsurge in national courts dealing with international human rights issues,[39] relying on national courts has proven ineffective historically. The expectation that states would prosecute their own leaders or elites, perhaps for crimes authorized by the state, is highly dubious. Only when those guilty of genocide are the losers in a war and the friendly regime is overthrown can one expect national courts to do the job, as was the case for some war crimes cases in Rwanda.[40] The other possibility is some type of occupation government that would prosecute those accused of genocide. Even then, note that a special "international" tribunal was used to try Nazi war criminals at Nuremberg rather than going through German courts. Given the character of the crime and the likely perpetrators, ineffectiveness was an impetus for operating system change and the move toward universal jurisdiction. Universal jurisdiction is not merely necessary to ensure prosecution of criminals; its presence may actually serve to make national courts work better. The option of "international" prosecution may create incentives for domestic courts to prosecute, lest the prosecution occur outside of the control of national authorities.[41]

As we argued above, necessity is not enough to prompt operating system change as political shocks must be present to spur action. That condition was present in the genocide case, although not until decades after the initial adoption of the Genocide Convention. Various political shocks, including those directly relevant to genocide, took place in the period following the adoption of the Genocide Convention. These included mass killings in Cambodia, acts of genocide in Rwanda, and ethnic cleansing in Bosnia. These crises and the calls to hold individuals accountable did indeed prompt calls for changes in the international legal system. Yet despite the inadequacy of the operating system and the presence of political shocks, only minimal operating system change with respect to jurisdiction took place: recent ad hoc war crimes tribunals have had primacy over national courts in jurisdiction, but only within those defined areas and frameworks. The reason may lie in the opposition of leading states to, and the absence of domestic political incentives for,

---

[39] Ratner and Abrams 1997.
[40] Ferstman 1997.
[41] Dunoff and Trachtman 1999.

universal jurisdiction, which identifies factors that could block change. It is also the case that other operating system changes rendered the need for universal jurisdiction moot.

The United States and other leading powers, such as Great Britain, opposed a universal jurisdiction provision for the Genocide Convention.[42] The fear was that other states would try U.S. and British citizens, for example, for crimes allowable under national law or directed by the government. Such opposition was enough to prevent expansion of jurisdiction after World War II, and the opposition of leading states continues today. In addition, most states have been unwilling to change national laws unilaterally so as to permit prosecution of crimes that took place outside of their jurisdiction and by aliens. There are few domestic political incentives for states to adopt such enabling legislation; after all, none of its citizens may have been directly affected by the crime. Furthermore, there are significant risks that one's own citizens would be unduly subject to foreign courts if other states followed suit; that is, significant sovereignty costs might accrue to the creation of universal jurisdiction rules. Overall, the expectations of the model are fulfilled. The basic conditions for international legal change have been present, but such change has been arrested by opposition of leading states as well as domestic political conditions not conducive to the change.

* * *

Institutions

As much of the contemporary debate over genocide has focused on compliance mechanisms, it is perhaps not surprising that the most profound changes, proposed and actually implemented, center on institutions designed to ascertain and punish violations. It is in this part of the operating system that the most changes have been contemplated, although the number and scope of those implemented are considerably less.

At the birth of the Genocide Convention, extant institutions were assumed to bear the primary burden for monitoring compliance with the norm and dealing with violations. In part, this may be a function of the available institutions for these purposes, but there was also significant opposition to proposed new structures. The convention itself contains provisions (Article VIII) that "Any Contracting Party may call upon the competent organs of the United Nations to take such action under the

---

[42] See LeBlanc [1991] on the United States and the Genocide Convention.

Charter of the United Nations as they consider appropriate for the prevention and suppression of acts of genocide ...."[43] The UN was just beginning to create the operating mechanisms to deal with human rights violations. The Commission on Human Rights was the logical UN organ to deal with the problem of genocide, and certainly other organs, such as subcommittees dealing with the treatment of minorities, would have also been appropriate. Of course, threats to international peace and security stemming from and involving genocide could be handled by the Security Council. Article IX of the convention also provided for referral of disputes to the ICJ.

Although genocide was to be handled within UN institutions, there were various proposals for a permanent international criminal court. Indeed, such ideas date back to the earlier years of the century, but opposition from some major states killed those proposals. Although there were already precedents for ad hoc tribunals (Nuremburg and Tokyo) stemming from World War II, support in the international community was not strong enough to create a permanent court.

It soon became obvious that UN human rights mechanisms were inadequate to deal with human rights violations in general, and with genocide in particular. Throughout the next forty years, various proposals for special committees or courts dealing with genocide were suggested, although never adopted. Seemingly recognizing the futility of pursuing these ideas, the international community began to create alternatives both within and outside the international legal system. The failure to make changes within the operating system has led some scholars and diplomats to suggest that the normative system be altered in ways that enhance enforcement. For example, there has been an attempt to legitimize the norm of humanitarian intervention – that states could militarily intervene in the affairs of other states for the purposes of redressing human rights violations or humanitarian emergencies.[44] Although not fully accepted, this type of intervention would provide a mechanism to deal with genocidal acts, one that is only appropriate if supranational mechanisms are lacking. * * *

The 1990s have seen renewed activity in terms of institutional changes in the operating system. Clearly, the UN system has been more intimately involved in genocide issues as the Security Council, ICJ, and other organs have dealt with the conflicts in Rwanda and the former Yugoslavia. Yet this

[43] Convention on the Prevention and Punishment of the Crime of Genocide. UN6AOR Res. 260A (III), 9 December 1948, Article VIII.

[44] Chopra and Weiss 1992.

level of activity is perhaps still below what might have been envisioned or hoped for at the time the Genocide Convention was adopted. More significantly, specific institutions have been created to deal with genocide. The UN created a war crimes tribunal in 1993 to address the conflict in Bosnia and surrounding territories and then adopted a similar tribunal a year later in response to the Rwandan civil war. Yet both of these courts were ad hoc, with their scopes limited to particular incidents. Only in 1998 did the proposal for a permanent ICC finally receive support from a broad cross-section of states. * * *

The critical questions here are (1) why has the international community not been more successful in creating institutions to deal with genocide? and (2) what accounts for the recent flurry of activity in this issue area? Although it is clear that the theoretical operation of UN institutions remained compatible with the genocide norm, it soon became evident that such institutions proved inadequate and ineffective in practice. By the 1950s, it was evident that UN agencies would not be able to meet the requirements for norm compliance for a range of human rights, not the least of which was genocide. At that point, the push for an operating system change would be renewed or in some cases would begin. Yet it was more than four decades before such a necessity was addressed. In large part, it was the political shocks of the 1990s that brought proposals for an international criminal court back to the international agenda.

The movement toward an ad hoc, and now one permanent, court to handle genocide and other concerns lies in the political shocks of the last decade. Indeed, policymakers explicitly cite such shocks as prerequisites for such occurrences. The UN sees the genocidal acts in Yugoslavia and Rwanda as the triggering events * while others cite the end of the Cold War as the facilitating condition. * In any case, it did appear that a dramatic change in the political environment was necessary for a revival of the international criminal court idea. Either a rearrangement of political coalitions or shocking the conscience of civilized nations (or perhaps both) provided the necessary impetus.[45]

The conditions were then ripe for an operating system change in the form of new institutions, just as they were ripe for moving toward universal jurisdiction. Yet the international legal system adapted in the direction of the former, rather than the latter, largely because the

---

[45] Of course, previous acts of genocide in Cambodia did not spur new action. As a necessary condition, political shocks may not always produce operating system change, even in the presence of other conditions. * * *

behavior of the leading states and the domestic political factors did not loom as large as impediments to change.

The United States initially opposed the creation of an international criminal court. Other important states, such as Great Britain, were also reluctant to support such an initiative. Consequently, while the idea of such a court persisted, it did not start on the road to becoming a reality until recently. This, together with the absence of political shocks, helps explain why few institutional changes were evident in the operating system over an extended period. Although the United States has not led the charge for an international criminal court, it has not actively opposed its creation in recent years; indeed, the Clinton administration supported the general concept of the ICC.[46] U.S. opposition has related more to certain provisions for the court, and the United States has sought changes in the ICC treaty before becoming a party. Thus this position is not equivalent to active and unequivocal opposition. Indeed, the United States has also been a leader in pushing for the ad hoc war crimes tribunals that might be considered predecessors to the permanent court. In addition, only seven states opposed the Rome Conference resolution supporting the court, and virtually all of Western Europe, as well as Russia, voted in favor. Furthermore, except for some opposition among Republican representatives in the U.S. Congress and segments of the U.S. military, the creation of such a supranational institution does not necessarily raise issues of domestic legal changes that might block or dilute its implementation.[47] There is also less perceived risk that national citizens will be dragged before an international criminal court if a state, such as the United States, does not ratify the ICC treaty or attaches significant reservations to its adherence.[48] There are few such assurances that personnel would be sheltered from foreign courts under a system that permitted universal jurisdiction. Despite a lengthy lag time after the adoption of the normative change, however, operating system change in the form of ad hoc tribunals and the ICC still occurred.

---

[46] President Bill Clinton signed the treaty before leaving office, but ratification prospects are uncertain given significant opposition in the U.S. Senate and less support of the institution by President George W. Bush.

[47] Except perhaps with respect to extradition; the lack of agreements with some neighboring states on handing over suspects to the war crimes tribunal for the former Yugoslavia has created some "safe havens" for war crimes suspects.

[48] That perception may be misguided, as some legal opinions suggest that U.S. military personnel may be subject to the ICC whether the United States ratifies the treaty or not.

Subjects/Actors in International Law

Identifying the actors who have rights and responsibilities is a major element of the international law operating system. Traditionally, public international law has assigned most of these rights and responsibilities to states, although there is a more recent trend toward raising the status of individuals, groups, and organizations.[49] The Genocide Convention holds individuals directly responsible for genocidal acts (Article IV), with no ability to hide behind the veil of the state, consistent with the emerging operating system change and the Nuremburg precedent. Other than piracy and a few other concerns, such international crimes are unusual when the norm is to hold states responsible. Yet the Genocide Convention has few provisions for state responsibility, even though one might expect many acts of genocide to be committed by individuals acting on orders from state authorities. Article IX provides for referral of disputes over interpretation, application, or fulfillment of the Convention to the ICJ. Yet this avenue has rarely been pursued. Despite efforts of some NGOs, signatory states were unwilling to press a case concerning Khmer Rouge killings in Cambodia, and a case involving Pakistan and India was withdrawn after a negotiated agreement between the two states. Only the case brought by Bosnia-Herzegovina against Yugoslavia (*Bosnia and Herzegovina v. Yugoslavia, Serbia, and Montenegro,* ongoing) has directly fallen under this provision of the treaty. The ICJ has recognized its jurisdiction over the case based on Article IX, but almost a decade after the original filing, a final ruling has yet to be made as of this writing.

The major question is why the operating system, at least with respect to genocide, concentrated on individual responsibility to the neglect of state responsibility. The inertia of the extant system provides some explanation. Individual responsibility for genocidal acts could fit quite comfortably with the prevailing territorial and nationality jurisdiction principles, prevalent in the international legal system for criminal behavior and reiterated in Article VI of the Genocide Convention. To rely exclusively on state responsibility would have been inconsistent with extant operating system practice. State responsibility is usually handled on the diplomatic level and through claims commissions (note the agreement between the United States and Germany on compensation to Holocaust victims and their families) or international courts. Imputing individual responsibility only makes sense if there are proper legal mechanisms for trying

[49] Arzt and Lukashuk 1995.

individuals suspected of genocide; yet the operating system still lacks the evidentiary standards and extradition to make this process efficient.[50] Because many of the perpetrators would be committing genocide at the behest of the state, holding states *and* individuals responsible would seem necessary. The provision for ICJ intervention in state disputes over genocide proved to be inadequate in the long run, given that many states accepted the Genocide Convention only with reservations that lessened the likelihood that Article IX on ICJ referral would ever be operative.

The shock of World War II and the Holocaust shaped not only the normative system changes that were to occur, but also the operating system changes. The experience at Nuremburg probably led drafters of the convention to emphasize individual responsibility given the frequent claims of Nazi officers that they were only following orders and the absence of any real state to hold responsible (note that both Germany and Japan had occupation governments). Yet subsequent acts of genocide in Cambodia and elsewhere, shocks in and of themselves, did not produce any further operating system changes with respect to state responsibility. Whether the genocidal acts in Rwanda and Yugoslavia will prompt further changes in actor responsibility is an open question and may depend on the disposition of the ongoing cases at the ICJ. Thus political shocks do provide some purchase in understanding operating system change, although they are suggestive of more change than actually occurred in recent times.

The focus on individual responsibility may be partly accounted for by reference to U.S. policy, as well as that of its allies and some other leading states. After World War I, the United States opposed individual responsibility for war crimes but switched positions at the time of the Genocide Convention, thus removing an obstacle to system change. Still, the United States resisted new powers to hold states accountable for actions. It was feared that the United States could be hauled in the courts of another country, representing a potential threat to the idea of sovereign immunity. This is a fear shared by many other states, including the People's Republic of China. The United States did not ratify the convention, even with its narrow focus, until the late 1980s, again indicating that it was reluctant to grant sweeping powers under the convention. Indeed, U.S. reservations with respect to the compulsory jurisdiction of the ICJ led to the dismissal of Yugoslavian claims against it for NATO actions in Kosovo; U.S. allies also sought to exclude ICJ action based on jurisdictional grounds. Accordingly, there is opposition among leading states

---

[50] Ratner and Abrams 1997.

to redressing the inadequacies of ICJ supervision of state behavior, and indeed those states have relied on that inadequacy. Domestic political opposition, especially in the United States, has prevented any further expansion of legal powers to act against states accused of genocide. The UN Security Council remains the primary multilateral mechanism to punish state perpetrators of genocide (and other threats to international peace and security); the Security Council is also the organ empowered to give effect to ICJ judgments. The major power veto and the general limitations of that organization prevent it from playing a major role. With respect to genocide, states have been reluctant to implement national legislation to bring other sovereign states before their own courts, fearing reciprocal consequences for their actions.

CONCLUSION

In this article, we present a new conceptualization of the international legal system, focusing on it as both an operating system and as a normative system. Our conception fundamentally challenges traditional ones in international law and international relations. Unlike previous works that suggest a symmetry between normative and operating systems, we argue that the operating system does not always respond to normative changes, and this may account for suboptimal legal arrangements.

There are many theoretical questions that follow from the framework embodying a normative and operating system. We briefly outline one of those in this article, namely how the operating system changes. In doing so, we seek to address the puzzle of why operating system changes do not always respond to alterations in the normative sphere. A general theoretical argument focuses on four conditions. We argue that the operating system only responds to normative changes when response is "necessary" (stemming from incompatibility, ineffectiveness, or insufficiency) to give the norm effect, and when the change is roughly coterminous with a dramatic change in the political environment (that is, "political shock"). We also argue, however, that opposition from leading states and domestic political factors might serve to block or limit such operating system change. These arguments were illustrated by reference to three areas of the operating system as they concern the norm against genocide. Clearly, a more complete model could include other factors, including those specific to the normative issue area involved.

* * *

PART VI

LAW AND LEGAL INSTITUTIONS

18

Europe Before the Court: A Political Theory of Legal Integration

Anne-Marie Slaughter [Burley] and Walter Mattli

European integration, a project deemed politically dead and academically moribund for much of the past two decades, has reemerged as one of the most important and interesting phenomena of the 1990s. The pundits are quick to observe that the widely touted "political and economic integration of Europe" is actually neither, that the "1992" program to achieve the single market is but the fulfillment of the basic goals laid down in the Treaty of Rome in 1958, and that the program agreed on for European monetary union at the Maastricht Intergovernmental Conference provides more ways to escape monetary union than to achieve it. Nevertheless, the "uniting of Europe" continues.[1] Even the self-professed legion of skeptics about the European Community (EC) has had to recognize that if the community remains something well short of a federal state, it also has become something far more than an international organization of independent sovereigns.[2]

An unsung hero of this unexpected twist in the plot appears to be the European Court of Justice (ECJ). By their own account, now confirmed by both scholars and politicians, the thirteen judges quietly

* * *

[1] The reference is to the title of Haas's magisterial study of early integration efforts focused on the European Coal and Steel Community. See Ernst B. Haas, *The Uniting of Europe* (Stanford, Calif.: Stanford University Press, 1958).

[2] See, for example, Robert Keohane and Stanley Hoffmann, "Conclusions: Community Politics and Institutional Change," in William Wallace, ed., *The Dynamics of European Integration* (London: Pinter, 1990), pp. 280–81.

working in Luxembourg managed to transform the Treaty of Rome (hereafter referred to as "the treaty") into a constitution. They thereby laid the legal foundation for an integrated European economy and polity. * Until 1963 the enforcement of the Rome treaty, like that of any other international treaty, depended entirely on action by the national legislatures of the member states of the community. By 1965, a citizen of a community country could ask a national court to invalidate any provision of domestic law found to conflict with certain directly applicable provisions of the treaty. By 1975, a citizen of an EC country could seek the invalidation of a national law found to conflict with self-executing provisions of community secondary legislation, the "directives" to national governments passed by the EC Council of Ministers. And by 1990, community citizens could ask their national courts to interpret national legislation consistently with community legislation in the face of undue delay in passing directives on the part of national legislatures.

The ECJ's accomplishments have long been the province only of lawyers, who either ignored or assumed their political impact. * Beginning in the early 1980s, however, a small coterie of legal scholars began to explore the interaction between the Court and the political institutions and processes of the EC. However, these approaches do not explain the *dynamic* of legal integration. Further, they lack microfoundations. They attribute aggregate motives and interests to the institutions involved to illustrate why a particular outcome makes theoretical sense, but they fail to offer a credible account of why the actual actors involved at each step of the process might have an *incentive* to reach the result in question.

On the other side of the disciplinary divide, political scientists studying regional integration in the 1950s and 1960s paid, surprisingly, little attention to the role that supranational *legal* institutions may play in fostering integration.[3] Even more puzzling is that much of the recent literature on the EC by American political scientists continues to ignore the role courts and community law play in European integration.[4]

We seek to remedy these deficiencies by developing a first-stage theory of the role of the Court in the community that marries the insights of legal scholars in the area with a theoretical framework developed by

[3] A noteworthy exception is Stuart Scheingold, *The Rule of Law in European Integration* (New Haven, Conn.: Yale University Press, 1965). Other early works on the Court will be discussed below.

[4] The one major exception, discussed below, is Geoffrey Garrett, "International Cooperation and Institutional Choice: The European Community's Internal Market," *International Organization* 46 (Spring 1992), pp. 533–60. ***

political scientists. We argue that the legal integration of the community corresponds remarkably closely to the original neofunctionalist model developed by Ernst Haas in the late 1950s. * By legal integration, our dependent variable, we mean the gradual penetration of EC law into the domestic law of its member states. This process has two principal dimensions. First is the dimension of formal penetration, the expansion of (1) the types of supranational legal acts, from treaty law to secondary community law, that take precedence over domestic law and (2) the range of cases in which individuals may invoke community law directly in domestic courts. Second is the dimension of substantive penetration, the spilling over of community legal regulation from the narrowly economic domain into areas dealing with issues such as occupational health and safety, social welfare, education, and even political participation rights.[5] Cutting across both these categories is the adoption of principles of interpretation that further the uniformity and comprehensiveness of the community legal system.

We find that the independent variables posited by neofunctionalist theory provide a convincing and parsimonious explanation of legal integration. We argue that just as neofuctionalism predicts, the drivers of this process are supranational and subnational actors pursuing their own self-interests within a politically insulated sphere. * The distinctive features of this process include a widening of the ambit of successive legal decisions according to a functional logic, a gradual shift in the expectations of both government institutions and private actors participating in the legal system, and the strategic subordination of immediate individual interests of member states to postulated collective interests over the long term.

Law functions as a mask for politics, precisely the role neofunctionalists originally forecast for economics. The need for a "functional" domain to circumvent the direct clash of political interests is the central insight of neofunctionalist theory. This domain could never be completely separated from the political sphere but would at least provide a sufficient buffer to achieve results that could not be directly obtained in the political realm. Law *** is widely perceived by political decision makers as "mostly technical," and thus lawyers are given a more or less free hand to speak for the EC Commission, the EC Council of Ministers and the national governments. * The result is that important political outcomes are debated

---

[5] A quantitative illustration of the growing importance of community law is the number of cases referred to the ECJ by domestic courts. The number jumped from a low of nine in 1968 to a high of 119 in 1978.

and decided in the language and logic of law. Further, although we make the case here for the strength of neofunctionalism as a framework for explaining *legal* integration – an area in which the technicality of the Court's operation is reinforced by the apparent technicality of the issues it addresses – the principle of law as a medium that both masks and to a certain extent alters political conflicts portends a role for the Court in the wider processes of economic and even political integration.

This specification of the optimal preconditions for the operation of the neofunctionalist dynamic also permits a specification of the political *limits* of the theory, limits that the neofunctionalists themselves recognized. The strength of the functional domain as an incubator of integration depends on the relative resistance of that domain to politicization. Herein, however, lies a paradox that sheds a different light on the supposed naiveté of "legalists." At a minimum, the margin of insulation necessary to promote integration requires that judges themselves appear to be practicing law rather than politics. Their political freedom of action thus depends on a minimal degree of fidelity to both substantive law and the methodological constraints imposed by legal reasoning. In a word, the staunch insistence on legal realities as distinct from political realities may in fact be a potent political tool.

The first part of this article [focuses the inquiry on the more specific question of explaining legal integration and offers a brief review of the principal elements of neofunctionalist theory. The second part details the ways in which the process of legal integration as engineered by the Court fits the neofunctionalist model.] *** The final part returns to the larger question of the relationship between the ECJ and the member states and reflects on some of the broader theoretical implications of our findings.

* * *

A RETURN TO NEOFUNCTIONALISM

An account of the impact of the Court in terms that political scientists will find as credible as lawyers must offer a political explanation of the role of the Court from the ground up. It should thus begin by developing a political theory of how the Court integrated its own domain, rather than beginning with legal integration as a fait accompli and asking about the interrelationship between legal and political integration. The process of legal integration did not come about through the "power of the law," as the legalists implicitly assume and often explicitly insist on. Individual actors – judges, lawyers, litigants – were involved, with specific identities, motives, and objectives. They interacted in a specific context and through specific processes. Only a genuine political account of how they achieved their objectives in the process of legal integration will provide the basis for a systematic account of the interaction of that process with the political processes of the EC.

Such an account has in fact already been provided, but it has never been applied to the Court as such. It is a neofunctionalist account.

Neofunctionalism in historical perspective: a theory of political integration

The logic of political integration was first systematically analyzed and elaborated by Ernst Haas in his pioneering study *The Uniting of Europe*.[6] This work and a collection of later contributions[7] share a common theoretical framework called neofunctionalism. Neofunctionalism is concerned with explaining "how and why nation-states cease to be wholly sovereign, how and why they voluntarily mingle, merge, and mix with their neighbors so as to lose the factual attributes of sovereignty while acquiring new techniques for resolving conflicts between themselves."[8] More precisely, neofunctionalism describes a process "whereby political actors in several distinct national settings are persuaded to shift their loyalties, expectations, and political activities towards a new and larger center, whose institutions possess or demand jurisdiction over the pre-existing national states."[9]

As a theory of European integration, neofunctionalism was dependent on a set of highly contingent preconditions: a unique constellation of

---

[6] See Haas, *The Uniting of Europe*.

[7] See in particular the following works by Ernst Haas: "International Integration: The European and the Universal Process," *International Organization* 15 (Summer 1961), pp. 366–92; *Beyond the Nation-State* (Stanford, Calif.: Stanford University Press, 1964); "Technocracy, Pluralism, and the New Europe," in Stephen Graubard, ed., *A New Europe?* (Boston: Houghton Mifflin, 1964) reprinted in Joseph Nye, *International Regionalism* (Boston: Little, Brown, 1968), pp. 149–79 (our citations refer to this latter version); and "The Study of Regional Integration: Reflection on the Joy and Anguish of Pretheorizing," *International Organization* 24 (Autumn 1970), pp. 607–46. See also Ernst B. Haas and Phillipe Schmitter, "Economic and Differential Patterns of Political Integration: Projections About Unity in Latin America," *International Organization* 18 (Autumn 1964), pp. 705–37.

[8] Haas, "The Study of Regional Integration," p. 610.

[9] Haas, "International Integration," p. 366. See also, Haas, *The Uniting of Europe*, p. 12.

exogenous historical, international, and domestic variables. For present purposes, however, the principal contribution of neofunctionalist theory is its identification of the functional categories likely to be receptive to integration and its description of the actual mechanics of overcoming national barriers within a particular functional category *after the integration process has been launched.*

Neofunctionalism as a theory of the integration process: overcoming national barriers

The actors: circumventing the state

The primary players in the integration process are above and below the nation-state. Actors *below* the state include interest groups and political parties. Above the state are supranational regional institutions. These supranational institutions promote integration, foster the development of interest groups, cultivate close ties with them and with fellow-technocrats in the national civil services, and manipulate both if necessary.

The Commission of the European Communities, for example, has the "power of initiative."[10] To have its proposals accepted by the Council of Ministers, the commission forges behind-the-scene working alliances with pressure groups. As its policymaking role grows, interest groups coalesce across national boundaries in their pursuit of communitywide interests, thus adding to the integrative momentum. Note that these groups need not be convinced "integrationists." The very existence of the community alters their situation and forces them to adjust.[11]

What role is there for governments? According to neofunctionalism, government's role is "creatively responsive."[12] As holders of the ultimate political power, governments may accept, sidestep, ignore, or sabotage the decisions of federal authorities. Yet, given their heterogeneity of interests in certain issue-areas, unilateral evasion or recalcitrance may prove unprofitable if it sets a precedent for other governments.[13] Thus governments may either choose to or feel constrained to yield to the pressures of converging supra- and subnational interests.

---

[10] Stuart A. Scheingold and Leon N. Lindberg, *Europe's Would-be Polity* (Englewood Cliffs, N.J.: Prentice-Hall, 1970), p. 92.

[11] Ibid., p. 78.

[12] We borrow this expression from Reginald Harrison, *Europe in Question: Theories of Regional International Integration* (London: Allen and Unwin, 1974), p. 80.

[13] Haas, *The Uniting of Europe*, p. xiv.

The motives: instrumental self-interest

One of the important contributions of neofunctionalism is the introduction of an unambiguously utilitarian concept of interest politics that stands in sharp contrast to the notions of unselfishness or common goods that pervades functionalist writing.[14] Assumptions of good will, harmony of interests, or dedication to the common good need not be postulated to account for integration. Ruthless egoism does the trick by itself.[15] As Haas puts it, "*The 'good Europeans' are not the main creators of the . . . community;* the process of community formation is dominated by nationally constituted groups with specific interests and aims, willing and able to adjust their aspirations by turning to supranational means *when this course appears profitable.*"[16] The supranational actors are likewise not immune to utilitarian thinking. They seek unremittingly to expand the mandate of their own institutions to have a more influential say in community affairs.

The process: incremental expansion

Three related concepts lie at the very core of the dynamics of integration: functional spillover, political spillover, and upgrading of common interests.

Functional spillover * is based on the assumption that the different sectors of a modern industrial economy are highly interdependent and that any integrative action in one sector creates a situation in which the original goal can be assured only by taking further actions in related sectors, which in turn create a further condition and a need for more action, and so forth.[17] This process is described by Haas: "Sector

---

[14] Haas, *Beyond the Nation-State*, p. 34.

[15] This idea points to an affinity of neofunctionalism with rational choice theories. Self-interest need not be identical with selfishness. The happiness (or misery) of other people may be part of a rational maximizer's satisfaction.

[16] Haas, *The Uniting of Europe*, p. xiv, emphasis added.

[17] Leon Lindberg, *The Political Dynamics of the European Economic Integration* (Stanford, Calif.: Stanford University Press, 1963), p. 10. We follow George's suggestion of strictly distinguishing those two types of spillover. See Stephen George, *Politics and Policy in the European Community* (Oxford: Clarendon Press, 1985), pp. 16–36. George also offers a compelling illustration of functional spillover. He argues that the removal of tariff barriers will not in itself create a common market. The fixing of exchange rates also is required in order to achieve that end. But, the surrender of control over national exchange rates demands the establishment of some sort of monetary union, which, in turn, will not be workable without the adoption of central macroeconomic policy coordination and which itself requires the development of a common regional policy, and so forth (pp. 21–22).

integration . . . begets its own impetus toward extension to the entire economy even in the absence of specific group demands."[18]

Political spillover describes the process of adaptive behavior, that is, the incremental shifting of expectations, the changing of values, and the coalescing at the supranational level of national interest groups and political parties in response to sectoral integration. It is crucial to note that neofunctionalism does not postulate an automatically cumulative integrative process. Again, in Haas's words, "The spillover process, though rooted in the structures and motives of the post-capitalist welfare state, is far from automatic,"[19] and "Functional contexts tend to be autonomous; lessons learned in one organization are not generally and automatically applied in others, or even by the same group in a later phase of its life."[20] In other words, neofunctionalism identifies certain linkage mechanisms but makes no assumptions as to the inevitability of actor response to functional linkages.

Upgrading common interests is the third element in the neofunctionalist description of the dynamics of integration. It occurs when the member states experience significant difficulties in arriving at a common policy while acknowledging the necessity of reaching some common stand to safeguard other aspects of interdependence among them. One way of overcoming such deadlock is by swapping concessions in related fields. In practice, the upgrading of the parties' common interests relies on the services of an institutionalized autonomous mediator.[21] This institutionalized swapping mechanism induces participants to refrain from vetoing proposals and invites them to seek compromises, which in turn bolster the power base of the central institutions.

The context: nominally apolitical

The context in which successful integration operates is economic, social, and technical.[22] Here Haas seems to accept a key assumption of the predecessor to his theory, functionalism, which posits that functional cooperation must begin on the relatively low-key economic and social

---

[18] Haas, *The Uniting of Europe*, p. 297.
[19] Haas, "Technocracy, Pluralism, and the New Europe," p. 165.
[20] Haas, *Beyond the Nation-State*, p. 48.
[21] "The European executives [are] able to construct patterns of mutual concessions from various policy contexts and in so doing usually manage to upgrade [their] own powers at the expense of the member governments." Haas, "Technocracy, Pluralism, and the New Europe," p. 152.
[22] Ibid.

planes. In David Mitrany's words, "Any political scheme would start a disputation, any working arrangement would raise a hope and make for confidence and patience."[23] However, economic and social problems are ultimately inseparable from political problems. Haas thus replaced the dichotomous relationship between economics and politics in functionalism by a continuous one: "The supranational style stresses the indirect penetration of the political by way of the economic because *the 'purely' economic decisions always acquire political significance in the minds of the participants.*"[24] "Technical" or "noncontroversial" areas of cooperation, however, might be so trivial as to remain outside the domain of human expectations and actions vital for integration.[25] The area must therefore be economically important and endowed with a high degree of "functional specificity."[26]

A NEOFUNCTIONALIST JURISPRUDENCE

The advent of the first major EC crisis in 1965, initiated by De Gaulle's adamant refusal to proceed with certain aspects of integration he deemed contrary to French interests, triggered a crescendo of criticism against neofunctionalism. The theory, it was claimed, had exaggerated both the expansive effect of increments within the economic sphere and the "gradual politicization" effect of spillover.[27] Critics further castigated neofunctionalists for failing to appreciate the enduring importance of nationalism, the autonomy of the political sector, and the interaction between the international environment and the integrating region.[28]

Neofunctionalists accepted most of the criticism and engaged in an agonizing reassessment of their theory. The coup de grace, however, was Haas's publication of *The Obsolescence of Regional Integration Theory*,

---

[23] David Mitrany, *A Working Peace* (Chicago: Quadrangle Books, 1966), p. 99. Besides Mitrany's work, see also James Patrick Sewell, *Functionalism and World Politics*, (Princeton, N.J.: Princeton University Press, 1966); Ernst Haas, *Beyond the Nation-State*, especially chaps. 1–4; and Claude, *Swords into Plowshares*, especially chap. 17.

[24] Haas, "Technocracy, Pluralism, and the New Europe," p. 152, emphasis added.

[25] Haas, "International Integration," p. 102.

[26] Ibid., p. 372.

[27] Joseph Nye, "Patterns and Catalysts in Regional Integration," *International Organization* 19 (Autumn 1965), pp. 870–84.

[28] See Stanley Hoffmann, "Obstinate or Obsolete? The Fate of the Nation-State and the Case of Western Europe," *Daedalus* 95 (Summer 1966), pp. 862–915; Stanley Hoffmann, "Discord in Community: The North Atlantic Area as a Partial System," reprinted in Francis Wilcox and Henry Field Haviland, eds., *The Atlantic Community: Progress and Prospects* (New York: Praeger, 1963).

in which he concluded that researchers should look beyond regional integration to focus on wider issues of international interdependence.[29]

With the benefit of greater hindsight, however, we believe that neofunctionalism has much to recommend it as a theory of regional integration. Although it recognizes that external shocks may disrupt the integration process,[30] it boasts enduring relevance as a description of the integrative process *within a sector*. The sector we apply it to here is the legal integration of the European Community.

The creation of an integrated and enforceable body of community law conforms neatly to the neofunctionalist model. In this part of the article we describe the phenomenon of legal integration according to the neo-functionalist categories set forth above: actors, motives, process, and context. Within each category, we demonstrate that the distinctive character-istics of the ECJ and its jurisprudence correspond to neofunctionalist prediction. We further show how the core insight of neofunctionalism – that integration is most likely to occur within a domain shielded from the interplay of direct political interests – leads to the paradox that actors are best able to circumvent and overcome political obstacles by acting as non-politically as possible. Thus in the legal context, judges who would advance a pro-integration "political" agenda are likely to be maximally effective only to the extent that they remain within the apparent bounds of the law.

Actors: a specialized national and supranational community

On the supranational level, the principal actors are the thirteen ECJ judges, the commission legal staff, and the six advocates-general, official members of the Court assigned the task of presenting an impartial opinion on the law in each case. Judges and advocates general are drawn from universities, national judiciaries, distinguished members of the community bar, and national government officials.[31] Judges take an oath to decide cases inde-pendently of national loyalties and are freed from accountability to their home governments by two important facets of the Court's decision-making process: secrecy of deliberation and the absence of dissenting opinions.

---

[29] Ernst B. Haas, *The Obsolescence of Regional Integration Theory* (Berkeley: University of California Press, 1975). See also Ernst B. Haas, "Turbulent Fields and the Theory of Regional Integration," *International Organization* 30 (Spring 1976), pp. 173–212.

[30] Haas and Schmitter, "Economic and Differential Patterns of Political Integration," p. 710.

[31] For a cross-section of the résumés of both judges and advocates general, see L. Neville Brown and Francis Jacobs, *The Court of Justice of the European Communities* (London: Sweet and Maxwell, 1977), pp. 33–48.

A quick perusal of the Treaty of Rome articles concerning the ECJ suggests that the founders intended the Court and its staff to interact primarily with other community organs and the member states. Articles 169 and 170 provide for claims of noncompliance with community obligations to be brought against member states by either the commission or other member states. Article 173 gives the Court additional jurisdiction over a variety of actions brought against either the commission or the council by a member state, by the commission, by the council, or by specific individuals who have been subject to a council or commission decision directly addressed to them.

Almost as an afterthought, Article 177 authorizes the Court to issue "preliminary rulings" on any question involving the interpretation of community law arising in the national courts. Lower national courts can refer such questions to the ECJ at their discretion; national courts of last resort are required to request the ECJ's assistance. In practice, the Article 177 procedure has provided a framework for links between the Court and subnational actors – private litigants, their lawyers, and lower national courts.[32] From its earliest days, the ECJ waged a campaign to enhance the use of Article 177 as a vehicle enabling private individuals to challenge national legislation as incompatible with community law. The number of Article 177 cases on the Court's docket grew steadily through the 1970s, from a low of 9 in 1968 to a high of 119 in 1978 and averaging over 90 per year from 1979 to 1982.[33] This campaign has successfully transferred a large portion of the business of interpreting and applying community law away from the immediate province of member states.[34]

As an additional result of these efforts, the community bar is now flourishing. Groups of private practitioners receive regular invitations to visit the Court and attend educational seminars. They get further encouragement and support from private associations such as the International Federation for European Law, which has branches in the member states that include both academics and private practitioners.

---

[32] It may seem odd to characterize lower national courts as subnational actors, but as discussed below, much of the Court's success in creating a unified and enforceable community legal system has rested on convincing lower national courts to leapfrog the national judicial hierarchy and work directly with the ECJ. See Mary L. Volcansek, *Judicial Politics in Europe* (New York: Peter Lang, 1986), pp. 245–67; and John Usher, *European Community Law and National Law* (London: Allen and Unwin, 1981).

[33] Hjalte Rasmussen, *On Law and Policy in the European Court of Justice : A Comparative study in Judicial Policymaking* (Dortrecht: M. Nijhoff, 1986), p. 245.

[34] The Court's rules allow member states to intervene to state their position in any case they deem important, but this provision is regularly underutilized.

Smaller practitioners' groups connected with national bar associations also abound.[35] The proliferation of community lawyers laid the foundation for the development of a specialized and highly interdependent community above and below the level of member state governments. The best testimony on the nature of the ties binding that community comes from a leading EC legal academic and editor of the *Common Market Law Review*, Henry Schermers. In a recent tribute to a former legal advisor to the commission for his role in "building bridges between [the Commission], the Community Court and the practitioners," Schermers wrote,

Much of the credit for the Community legal order rightly goes to the Court of Justice of the European Communities, but the Court will be the first to recognize that they do not deserve all the credit. Without the loyal support of the national judiciaries, preliminary questions would not have been asked nor preliminary rulings followed. And the national judiciaries themselves would not have entered into Community law had not national advocates pleaded it before them. For the establishment and growth of the Community legal order it was essential for the whole legal profession to become acquainted with the new system and its requirements. Company lawyers, solicitors and advocates had to be made aware of the opportunities offered to them by the Community legal system.[36]

In this tribute, Schermers points to another important set of subnational actors: community law professors. These academics divide their time between participation as private consultants on cases before the court and extensive commentary on the Court's decisions. In addition to book-length treatises, they edit and contribute articles to a growing number of specialized journals devoted exclusively to EC law.[37] As leading figures in their own national legal and political communities, they play a critical role in bolstering the legitimacy of the Court.

Motives: the self-interest of judges, lawyers, and professors

The glue that binds this community of supra- and subnational actors is self-interest. In the passage quoted above, Schermers speaks of making

---

[35] See Brown and Jacobs, *The Court of Justice of the European Communities*, pp. 180–181.

[36] Henry Schermers, "Special Foreword," *Common Market Law Review*, no. 27, 1990, pp. 637–38.

[37] Prominent examples include *The Common Market Law Review*, *The European Law Review*, *Yearbook of European Law*, *Legal Issues of European Integration*, *Cahier de Droit Européen*, *Revue trimestrielle de Droit Européen*, and *Europarecht*. A vast number of American international and comparative law journals also publish regular articles on European law.

private practitioners aware of the "opportunities" offered to them by the community legal system. The Court largely created those opportunities, providing personal incentives for individual litigants, their lawyers, and lower national courts to participate in the construction of the community legal system. In the process, it enhanced its own power and the professional interests of all parties participating directly or indirectly in its business.

Giving individual litigants a personal stake in community law

The history of the "constitutionalization" of the Treaty of Rome, and of the accompanying "legalization" of community secondary legislation, is essentially the history of the direct effect doctrine. And, the history of the direct effect doctrine is the history of carving individually enforceable rights out of a body of rules apparently applicable only to states. In neofunctionalist terms, the Court created a pro-community constituency of private individuals by giving them a direct stake in promulgation and implementation of community law. Further, the Court was careful to create a one-way ratchet by permitting individual participation in the system only in a way that would advance community goals.

The Court began by prohibiting individuals from seeking to annul legal acts issued by the Council of Ministers or the EC Commission for exceeding their powers under the Treaty of Rome. As noted above, Article 173 of the treaty appears to allow the council, the commission, the member states, and private parties to seek such an injunction. In 1962, however, the Court held that individuals could not bring such actions except in the narrowest of circumstances.[38] A year later the Court handed down its landmark decision in *Van Gend & Loos,* allowing a private Dutch importer to invoke the common market provisions of the treaty directly against the Dutch government's attempt to impose customs duties on specified imports.[39] *Van Gend* announced a new world. Over the explicit objections of three of the member states, the Court proclaimed:

the Community constitutes a *new legal order* . . . for the benefit of which the states have limited their sovereign rights, albeit within limited fields, and *the subjects of which comprise not only Member States but also their nationals.* Independently of the legislation of the Member States, Community law *therefore*

---

[38] See Case 25/62, *Plaumann & Co. v. Commission of the European Economic Community, European Court Reports (ECR),* 1963, p. 95. See also Hjalte Rasmussen, "Why is Article 173 Interpreted Against Private Plaintiffs?" *European Law Review,* no. 5, 1980, pp. 112–27.

[39] Case 26/62, *N.V. Algemene Transport & Expeditie Onderneming Van Gend & Loos v. Nederlandse Administratie der Belastingen, ECR,* 1963, p. 1.

not only imposes obligations on individuals but it also intended to confer upon them rights which become part of their legal heritage. These rights arise not only where they are expressly granted by the Treaty, but also by reason of obligations which the Treaty imposes in a clearly defined way upon individuals as well as upon the Member States and upon the institutions of the Community.[40]

The Court effectively articulated a social contract for the EC, relying on the logic of mutuality to tell community citizens that since community law would impose new duties of citizenship flowing to an entity other than their national governments, which had now relinquished some portion of their sovereignty, they must be entitled to corresponding rights. Beneath the lofty rhetoric, however, was the creation of a far more practical set of incentives pushing toward integration. Henceforth importers around the community who objected to paying customs duties on their imports could invoke the Treaty of Rome to force their governments to live up to their commitment to create a common market.

The subsequent evolution of the direct effect doctrine reflects the steady expansion of its scope. Eric Stein offers the best account,[41] charting the extension of the doctrine from a "negative" treaty obligation to a "positive" obligation[42]; from the "vertical" enforcement of a treaty obligation against a member state government to the "horizontal" enforcement of such an obligation against another individual[43]; from the application only to treaty law to the much broader application to secondary community legislation, such as council directives and decisions.[44] After vociferous protest from national courts,[45] the Court did balk temporarily at granting horizontal effect to community directives – allowing individuals to enforce obligations explicitly imposed by council directives on member states against other individuals – but has subsequently permitted

---

[40] Ibid., p. 12, emphasis added.

[41] See Eric Stein, "Lawyers, Judges, and the Making of a Transnational Constitution," *American Journal of International Law* 75 (January 1981), pp. 1–27.

[42] Case 57/65, *Alfons Lütticke GmbH v. Hauptzollamt Saarlouis*, ECR, 1986, p. 205.

[43] See Case 36/74, *B.N.O. Walrave and L.J.N. Koch v. Association Union Cycliste Internationale*, ECR, 1974, p. 1405; and Case 149/77, *Gabrielle Defrenne v. Societe Anonyme Belge de Navigation Aerienne Sabena*, ECR, 1978, p. 1365.

[44] See Case 9/70, *Franz Grad v. Finanzamt Traunstein*, ECR, 1970, p. 825; and Case 411/74, *Yvonne Van Duyn v. Home Office*, ECR, 1974, p. 1337.

[45] *Bundesfinanzhof*, decision of 25 April 1985 (VR 123/84), Entscheidungen des Bundesfinanzhofes, vol. 143, p. 383 (noted by H. Gerald Crossland, *European Law Review*, 1986, pp. 476–79). The decision was quashed by the *Bundesverfassungsgericht* (the German Constitutional Court) in its decision of 8 April 1987 (2 BvR 687/85), [1987] *Recht der Internationalen Wirtschaft* 878. See also the *Cohn Bendit* case, *Conseil d'Etat*, 22 December 1978, Dalloz, 1979, p. 155.

even these actions where member governments have failed to implement a directive correctly or in a timely fashion.[46]

Without tracking the intricacies of direct effect jurisprudence any further, it suffices to note that at every turn the Court harped on the benefits of its judgments for individual citizens of the community. In *Van Duyn*, for instance, the Court observed: "A decision to this effect (granting direct effect to community directives) would undoubtedly strengthen the legal protection of individual citizens in the national courts."[47] Conversely, of course, individuals are the best means of holding member states to their obligations. "Where Community authorities have, by directive, imposed on Member states the obligation to pursue a particular course of conduct, the useful effect of such an act would be weakened if individuals were prevented from relying on it before their national courts and if the latter were prevented from taking it into consideration as an element of Community law."[48]

The net result of all these cases is that individuals (and their lawyers) who can point to a provision in the community treaties or secondary legislation that supports a particular activity they wish to undertake – from equal pay for equal work to a lifting of customs levies – can invoke community law and urge a national court to certify the question of whether and how community law should be applied to the ECJ. When litigants did not appear to perceive the boon that had been granted them, moreover, the Court set about educating them in the use of the Article 177 procedure.[49] The Court thus constructed a classically utilitarian mechanism and put it to work in the service of community goals. Citizens who are net losers from integrative decisions by the council or the commission cannot sue to have those actions declared ultra vires. But citizens who stand to gain have a constant incentive to push their governments to live up to paper

---

[46] See Case 152/84, *Marshall v. Southampton and South West Hampshire Area Health Authority (Teaching)*, *Common Market Law Review*, vol. 1, 1986, p. 688; and Case 152/84, *ECR*, 1986, p. 737. On the relationship between *Marshall* and *Marleasing*, see Hjalte Rasmussen, "The Role of the Court in the European Community: Towards a Normative Theory of Interpretation of Community Law," *University of Chicago Legal Forum*.

[47] *Van Duyn*, p. 1342.

[48] *Ibid.*, p. 1348. For a discussion of more recent cases in which the Court explicitly has carved out individual rights in the enforcement of community directives, see Deirdre Curtin, "Directives: The Effectiveness of Judicial Protection of Individual Rights," *Common Market Law Review*, vol. 27, 1990, pp. 709–39.

[49] Mancini describes this process in great detail; see G. Federico Mancini, "The Making of a Constitution for Europe," *Common Market Law Review*, vol. 26, 1989, pp. 605–6. See also Pierre Pescatore, *The Law of Integration*, (Leyden : Sijthoss, 1974), p. 99; and Rasmussen, *On law and Policy in the European Court of Justice*, p. 247.

commitments.[50] As Haas argued in 1964, a successful international organization can achieve "growth through planning . . . only on the basis of stimulating groups and governments in the environment to submit new demands calling for organizational action."[51]

Courting the national courts

The entire process of increasing the use of the Article 177 procedure was an exercise in convincing national judges of the desirability of using the ECJ. Through seminars, dinners, regular invitations to Luxembourg, and visits around the community, the ECJ judges put a human face on the institutional links they sought to build.[52] Many of the Court's Article 177 opinions reenforced the same message. It was a message that included a number of components designed to appeal to the self-interest primarily of the lower national courts. It succeeded ultimately in transforming the European legal system into a split system, in which these lower courts began to recognize two separate and distinct authorities above them: their own national supreme courts, on questions of national law, and the ECJ, on questions of European law. Judge Mancini explains quite candidly that the ECJ needed the "cooperation and goodwill of the state courts."[53]

Shapiro expresses surprise at the willingness of lower national courts to invoke Article 177 against the interests of their own national supreme courts, noting that lower court judges "must attend to their career prospects within hierarchically organized national judicial systems."[54]

---

[50] More prosaically, but no less effectively for the construction of a community legal system, the Article 177 procedure offers "clever lawyers and taticians . . . the possibility of using Community law to mount challenges to traditional local economic restrictions in a way which may keep open a window of trading opportunity whilst the legal process grinds away." In a word, delay. See L. Gormley, "Recent Case Law on the Free Movement of Goods: Some Hot Potatoes," *Common Market Law Review*, vol. 27, 1990, pp. 825–57.

[51] Haas, *Beyond the Nation-State*, p. 128.

[52] Rasmussen describes a "generous information campaign," as a result of which a steadily increasing number of national judges traveled to the *Palais de Justice*, at the ECJ's expense, for conferences about the court and the nature of the Article 177 procedure. See Rasmussen, *On Law and Policy in the European Court of Justice*, p. 247.

[53] Mancini, "The Making of a Constitution for Europe," p. 605. In this regard, Mary Volcansek offers an interesting discussion of the various "follow-up mechanisms" the ECJ employed to further an ongoing partnership with the national courts, including positive feedback whenever possible and gradual accommodation of the desire occasionally to interpret community law for themselves. See Volcansek, *Judicial Politics in Europe*, pp. 264–66.

[54] Martin Shapiro, "The European Court of Justice," in Alberta M. Sbragia, ed., *Europolitics: Institutions and Policymaking in the New European Community* (Washington, D.C.: Brookings Institution, 1991), p. 127.

Weiler offers several explanations, beginning with the legitimacy of ECJ decisions conferred by the national prestige of individual judges and the precise reasoning of the opinions themselves. He ultimately concludes, however, that the "legally driven constitutional revolution" in the EC is "a narrative of plain and simple judicial empowerment."[55] And further, that "the E.C. system gave judges at the lowest level powers that had been reserved to the highest court in the land." For many, "to have de facto judicial review of legislation . . . would be heady stuff."[56]

Perhaps the best evidence for this "narrative of empowerment" comes from the ECJ itself. Many of the opinions are carefully crafted appeals to judicial ego. In *Van Gend & Loos* itself the Belgian and Dutch governments had argued that the question of the application of the Treaty of Rome over Dutch or Belgian law was solely a question for the Belgian and Dutch national courts. The ECJ responded by announcing, in effect, that the entire case was a matter solely between the national courts and the ECJ, to be resolved without interference from the national governments. When the Belgian government objected that the question of European law referred by the national court could have no bearing on the outcome of the proceedings, the ECJ piously responded that it was not its business to review the "considerations which may have led a national court or tribunal to its choice of questions as well as the relevance which it attributes to such questions."[57] In this and subsequent direct effect cases the ECJ continually suggested that the direct effect of community law should depend on judicial interpretation rather than legislative action.[58]

Finally, in holding that a national court's first loyalty must be to the ECJ on all questions of community law,[59] the Court was able simultaneously to appeal to national courts *in their role* as protectors of individual

---

[55] Joseph Weiler, "The Transformation of Europe," *Yale Law Journal* 100 (June 1991), p. 2426.

[56] Ibid. Anecdotal evidence also suggests that lower national courts who refer questions to the ECJ save themselves the work of deciding the case themselves and simultaneously protect against the chance of reversal.

[57] *Van Gend & Loos*, p. 22.

[58] See, e.g., *Lütticke*, p. 10, where the ECJ announced that the direct effect of the treaty article in question depends solely on a finding by the national court; see also Case 33/76 *Rewe-Zentralfinanz Gesellschaft and Rewe-Zentral AG v. Landwirtschaftskammer für das Saarland*, ECR, 1989, p. 1998; and Case 45/76 *Comet BV v. Produktschap voor Siergewassen*, ECR, 1976, pp. 2052–53.

[59] Case 106/77, *Amministrazione delle Finanze dello Stato v. Sirnmenthal S.p. A.* [1978] ECR 629.

rights – a very effective dual strategy.[60] Such argumentation simultaneously strengthens the force of the Court's message to national courts by portraying the construction of the European legal system as simply a continuation of the traditional role of European courts and, indeed, liberal courts everywhere: the protection of individual rights against the state. At the same time, as discussed above, the Court strengthens its own claim to perform that role, building a constituency beyond the Brussels bureaucracy.

Reciprocal Empowerment

This utilitarian depiction of the integration process must include the ECJ itself. It is obvious that any measures that succeed in raising the visibility, effectiveness, and scope of EC law also enhance the prestige and power of the Court and its members, both judges and advocates general. In addition, however, by presenting itself as the champion of individual rights and the protector of the prerogatives of lower national courts, the ECJ also burnishes its own image and gives its defenders weapons with which to rebut charges of antidemocratic activism. Rasmussen points out that the encouragement to use Article 177 procedure meant that the Court visibly sided with "the little guy," the underdog against state bureaucracies, "the 'people' against the 'power-elite'."[61] Strikingly enough, this is a characterization with which Judge Koenrad Lenaerts essentially concurs.[62]

The empowerment of the ECJ with respect to the national courts is more subtle. While offering lower national courts a "heady" taste of power, the ECJ simultaneously strengthens its own legal legitimacy by making it appear that its own authority flows from the national courts. It is the national courts, after all, who have sought its guidance; and it is the national courts who will ultimately *decide* the case, in the sense of issuing an actual ruling on the facts. The ECJ only "interprets" the relevant provision of community law, and leaves it for the national court to apply it to the facts of the case. In practice, of course, the ECJ frequently offers a virtual template for the subsequent lower court decision.[63] But, the all-important fiction is preserved.

---

[60] *Ibid.*, p. 643.

[61] Rasmussen, *On Law and Policy in the European Court of Justice*, p. 245.

[62] See Koenrad Lenaerts, "The Role of the Court of Justice in the European Community: Some Thoughts About the Interaction Between Judges and Politicians," *University of Chicago Legal Forum*.

[63] For a number of specific examples, see Ulrich Everling, "The Court of Justice as a Decisionmaking Authority," *Michigan Law Review* 82 (April/May 1984), pp. 1299–1301.

Finally, the empowerment of the ECJ simultaneously empowers all those who make their living by analyzing and critiquing its decisions. Here community law professors and their many assistants join with members of the community bar to form a communitywide network of individuals with a strong stake in bolstering the Court's prestige. On the most basic level, the growing importance of community law translates into a growing demand for professors to teach it and hence, funding for chaired professorships.[64] The holders of these chairs are likely, in turn, to aspire to become judges and advocates general themselves, just as many current judges and advocates general are likely to return to the professoriate when their terms expire. This is a neofunctionalist interest group par excellence.

Process

As discussed above, the neofunctionalist description of the actual process of integration focused on three major features: functional spillover, political spillover, and upgrading of common interests. All three dynamics are clearly present in the building of the EC legal system.

Functional spillover: the logic of law

Functional spillover presupposes the existence of an agreed objective and simply posits that the jurisdiction of the authorities charged with implementing that objective will expand as necessary to address whatever obstacles stand in the way. This expansion will continue as long as those authorities do not collide with equally powerful countervailing interests. Alternatively, of course, one objective might conflict with another objective. Such limits define the parameters within which this "functionalist" logic can work.

In the construction of a community legal system, such limits were initially very few, and the functional logic was very strong. Judge Pierre Pescatore has attributed the ECJ's success in creating a coherent and authoritative body of community law to the Court's ability – flowing from the structure and content of the Treaty of Rome – to use "constructive methods of interpretation."[65] One of the more important of those

---

[64] The "Jean Monnet Action," a program of the European Commission, has recently created fifty-seven new full-time teaching posts in community law as part of a massive program to create new courses in European integration.

[65] Pescatore, *The Law of Integration*, pp. 89–90.

methods is the "systematic method," drawing on "the various systematic elements on which Community law is based: general scheme of the legislation, structure of the institutions, arrangement of powers . . . , general concepts and guiding ideals of the Treaties. Here is a complete 'architecture,' coherent and well thought out, *the lines of which, once firmly drawn, require to be extended.*"[66] Interpretation according to the systematic method means filling in areas of the legal structure that logically follow from the parts of the structure already built.

A well-known set of examples confirms the power of this functional logic as applied by the ECJ. After *Van Gend & Loos,* the next major "constitutional" case handed down was *Costa v. Enel,* which established the supremacy of community law over national law. In plain terms, *Costa* asserted that where a treaty term conflicted with a subsequent national statute, the treaty must prevail. Predictably, Judge Federico Mancini justifies this decision by reference to the ruin argument.[67] He argues further, however, that the supremacy clause "was not only an indispensable development, it was also a logical development."[68] Students of federalism have long recognized that the clash of interests between state and federal authorities can be mediated in several ways: either (1) by allowing state authorities to implement federal directives at the time and in the manner they desire, or (2) by allowing both state and federal authorities to legislate directly, which entails formulating guidelines to establish a hierarchy between the two. On this basis, Mancini (and Eric Stein before him) points out that *because* the Court had "enormously extended the Community power to deal directly with the public" in *Van Gend & Loos,* it now became logically necessary to insist that community law must prevail over member state law in cases of conflict.[69] In short, the "full impact of direct effect" can only be realized "in combination with" the supremacy clause.[70]

The evolution of community law also has manifested the substantive broadening typical of functional spillover. EC law is today no longer as dominantly economic in character as in the 1960s.[71] It has spilled

---

[66] Ibid., p. 87, emphasis added.

[67] Mancini, "The Making of a Constitution for Europe," p. 600.

[68] Ibid.

[69] Ibid., p. 601.

[70] This is the way Joseph Weiler describes the supremacy cases, again tacitly emphasizing a necessary logical progression. See Weiler, "The Transformation of Europe," p. 2414.

[71] Neil Nugent, *The Government and Politics of the European Community* (Durham, N.C.: Duke University Press, 1989), p. 151.

over into a variety of domains dealing with issues such as health and safety at work, entitlements to social welfare benefits, mutual recognition of educational and professional qualification, and, most recently, even political participation rights.[72] Two notable examples are equal treatment with respect to social benefits of workers, a field developed almost entirely as a result of Court decisions,[73] and the general system of community trademark law – again formed entirely by the Court's case law.[74] In both areas the Court gradually extended its reach by grounding each new decision on the necessity of securing the common market.

Political spillover: "transnational incrementalism"

The neofunctionalists argued that integration was an adaptive process of gradually shifting expectations, changing loyalties, and evolving values.[75] In trying to explain why member states responded positively to the Court's legal innovations, Joseph Weiler writes: "it is clear that a measure of transnational incrementalism developed. Once some of the highest courts of a few Member States endorsed the new constitutional construct, their counterparts in other Member States heard more arguments that those courts should do the same, and it became more difficult for national courts to resist the trend with any modicum of credibility."[76]

Beyond the Court's specific machinations, however, law operates as law by shifting expectations. The minute a rule is established as "law," individuals are entitled to rely upon the assumption that social, economic, or political behavior will be conducted in accordance with that rule. The creation and application of law is inherently a process of shifting expectations. A major function of a legal rule is to provide a clear and certain standard around which expectations can crystallize.

---

[72] See "Council Directive on Voting Rights for Community Nationals in Local Elections in Their Member States of Residence," *Official Journal*, 1988, C 256/4, and Amended Proposal, *Official Journal*, 1989, C 290/4.

[73] For further reading, see Paul Leleux, "The Role of the European Court of Justice in Protecting Individual Rights in the Context of Free Movement of Persons and Services," in Eric Stein and Terrence Sandalow, eds., *Courts and Free Markets*, vol. 2 (Oxford: Clarendon Press, 1982), pp. 363–427.

[74] Henry Schermers, "The Role of the European Court of Justice in the Free Movement of Goods," in Eric Stein and Terrence Sandalow, eds., *Courts and Free Markets*, vol. 1, pp. 222–71.

[75] See Haas, "International Integration," p. 366; and Haas, *The Uniting of Europe*, p. 12.

[76] Weiler, "*The Transformation of Europe*," p. 2425.

As long as those actors to which the Court's decisions are directed – member state governments, national courts, and individuals – accept one decision as a statement of the existing law and proceed to make arguments in the next case from that benchmark, they are shifting their expectations. This is precisely the process that court watchers, even potentially skeptical ones, have identified. Hjalte Rasmussen demonstrates that even governments overtly hostile to the Court's authority do not seek to ask the Court to overturn a previous ruling but rather accept that ruling as a statement of the law and use it as a point of departure for making arguments in subsequent cases. After reviewing an extensive sample of briefs submitted to the Court by member governments, Rasmussen was unable to find even one instance in which a member state suggested that a prior precedent be overruled.[77]

This finding is particularly striking given that states do often strongly object to a proposed interpretation or application of a particular legislative term in its briefs and arguments *prior* to a particular decision.[78] * * *

Upgrading common interests

For the neofunctionalists, upgrading common interests referred to a "swapping mechanism" dependent on the services of an "institutionalized autonomous mediator." The Court is less a mediator than an arbiter and has no means per se of "swapping" concessions. What it does do, however, is continually to justify its decisions in light of the common interests of the members as enshrined in both specific and general objectives of the original Rome treaty. The modus operandi here is the "teleological method of interpretation," by which the court has been able to rationalize everything from direct effect to the preemption of member state negotiating power in external affairs in every case in which the treaty grants internal competence to community authorities.[79] All are reasoned not on the basis of specific provisions in the treaty or community secondary legislation but on the accomplishment of the most elementary community goals set forth in the Preamble to the treaty.

According to Judge Pescatore, the concepts employed in the teleological method include "concepts such as the customs union, equality of

---

[77] Rasmussen, *On Law and Policy in the European Court of Justice*, pp. 275–81.

[78] As is now widely recognized, Belgium, Germany, and the Netherlands all filed briefs strongly objecting to the notion of direct effect in *Van Gend & Loos*. None subsequently suggested revisiting that decision.

[79] Case 22/70, *Commission of the European Communities v. Council of the European Communities*, ECR, 1971, p. 363.

treatment and non-discrimination, freedom of movement, mutual assistance and solidarity, economic interpenetration and finally economic and legal unity as the supreme objective."[80] He goes on to cite two examples from early cases concerning the free movement of goods and the customs union. He points out that "formulas" such as describing the customs union as one of the "foundations of the Community," the role of which is "essential for the implementation of the Community project . . . have been repeated and developed in very varied circumstances since this first judgment."[81]

Rhetorically, these formulas constantly shift the analysis to a more general level on which it is possible to assert common interests – the same common interests that led member states into the community process in the first place. French sheepfarmers might fight to the death with British sheepfarmers, but the majority of the population in both nations have a common interest in "the free movement of goods." "Upgrading the common interest," in judicial parlance, is a process of reasserting long-term interest, at least as nominally perceived at the founding and enshrined in sonorous phrases, over short-term interest. In the process, of course, to the extent it succeeds in using this method to strengthen and enhance community authority, the Court does certainly also succeed in upgrading its own powers.

Context: the (apparent) separation of law and politics

The effectiveness of law in the integration process – as Haas predicted for economics – depends on the perception that it is a domain distinct and apart from politics. Shapiro has argued, for instance, that the Court, aided and abetted by its commentators, has derived enormous advantage from denying the existence of policy discretion and instead hewing to the fiction, bolstered by the style and retroactivity of its judgments. An absolute division between law and politics, as between economics and politics, is ultimately impossible. Nevertheless, just as Haas stressed that overt political concerns are less *directly* engaged in economic integration, requiring some time for specific economic decisions to acquire political significance, so, too, can legal decision making function in a relative political vacuum. Although the political impact of judicial decisions will

---

[80] Pescatore, *The Law of Integration*, p. 88.
[81] *Ibid.*, p. 89.

ultimately be felt, they will be more acceptable initially due to their independent nonpolitical justification.

The importance of undertaking integration in a nominally nonpolitical sphere is confirmed by the underlying issues and interests at stake in the nascent debate about judicial activism in the community. As periodic struggles over the proper balance between judicial activism and judicial restraint in the United States have demonstrated, assertions about the preservation of the legitimacy and authority necessary to uphold the rule of law generally have a particular substantive vision of the law in mind.[82] In the community context, the response to Rasmussen's charge of judicial activism reveals that the substantive stakes concern the prospects for the Court's self-professed task, integration. In heeding widespread advice to maintain a careful balance between applying community law and articulating and defending community ideals, the Court is really pre-serving its ability to camouflage controversial political decisions in "technical" legal garb.

Maintaining the Fiction

The European legal community appears to understand the importance of preserving the Court's image as a nonpolitical institution all too well. The dominant theme in scholarship on the Court in the 1970s and 1980s was reassurance that the Court was carrying out its delicate balancing act with considerable success.[83] Rasmussen describes a widespread refusal among community lawyers and legal academics to criticize the Court on paper. The consensus seems to be that overt recognition of the Court's political agenda beyond the bounds of what "the law" might fairly be said to permit will damage the Court's effectiveness.[84] Commenting on the same phenomenon, Shapiro has observed that the European legal community

---

[82] See, for example, Martin Shapiro, "The Constitution and Economic Rights," in M. Judd Harmon, ed., *Essays on the Constitution of the United States* (Port Washington, N.Y.: Kennikat Press, 1978), pp. 74–98.

[83] See F. Dumon, "La jurisprudence de la Cour de Justice. Examen critique des methodes d'interprétation" (The jurisprudence of the ECJ. Critical study of methods of interpre-tation) (Luxembourg: Office for Official Publications of the European Communities, 1976), pp. 51–53; A.W. Green, *Political Integration by Jurisprudence* (Leiden: Sijthoff, 1969), pp. 26–33 and 498; Clarence Mann, *The Function of Judicial Decision in European Economic Integration* (The Hague: Martinus Nijhoff, 1972), pp. 508–15; Scheingold, *The Rule of Law in European Integration*, pp. 263–85; and Stein, "Lawyers, Judges, and the Making of a Transnational Constitution," passim.

[84] For a discussion of "the oral tradition" of criticism that European scholars refuse publicly to acknowledge, see Rasmussen, *On Law and Policy in the European Court of Justice*, pp. 147–48 and 152–54.

understands its collective writings on the Court as a political act designed to bolster the Court. By denying the existence of judicial activism and thus removing a major potential locus of opposition to the Court, they promote an institution whose pro-community values accord with their own internalized values.[85]

The Court itself has cooperated in burnishing this nonpolitical image. Pescatore set the tone in 1974, contending that the first reason for the "relative success of Community case law" is "the wide definition of the task of the Court as custodian of law."[86] And certainly the Court has carefully crafted its opinions to present the results in terms of the inexorable logic of the law. To cite a classic example, in the *Van Gend & Loos* decision, in which the Court single-handedly transformed the Treaty of Rome from an essentially nonenforceable international treaty to a domestic charter with direct and enforceable effects, it cast its analysis in the following framework: "To ascertain whether the provisions of an international treaty extend so far in their effects it is necessary to consider the spirit, the general scheme, and the wording of those provisions."[87]

Judge Mancini recently has continued this tradition in his description of the Court's success in winning over national judges. Referring to the ECJ's "courteously didactic" method, Mancini ultimately attributes the rise of the Article 177 procedure to the "cleverness" of his colleagues not in devising political strategies but in fashioning the law in such a way that its autonomous power and ineluctable logic would be clear to the benighted national judges. He seems astonishingly candid, observing, with an insider's wink: "The national judge is thus led hand in hand as far as the door; crossing the threshold is his job, but now a job no harder than child's play."[88] In fact, however, his "revelations" amount to a story about the power of law, thus continuing the Court's proud tradition of insisting on the legal-political divide.

Mancini also has joined with other judges, most notably Ulrich Everling, in public penance to reassure concerned onlookers that the Court was very aware of the need for prudence. By the early 1980s, responding to simmering criticism, Judge Everling published several articles announcing that much of the foundational work in establishing

---

[85] Martin Shapiro, "Comparative Law and Comparative Politics," *Southern California Law Review* 53 (January 1980), p. 542.

[86] Pescatore, *The Law of Integration*, p. 89.

[87] *Van Gend & Loos.*

[88] Mancini, "The Making of a Constitution," p. 606.

the Treaty of Rome as a community constitution was done and that the Court could now afford to take a lower political profile. In 1989 Judge Mancini applauded the work of the Court to date but noted that the political relaunching of the community embodied in the SEA and the progress of the 1992 initiative toward a genuine common market would now permit the Court essentially to confine its activities to the more purely legal sphere.[89]

Transforming the political into the legal

Court watchers have long understood that the ECJ uses the EC Commission as a political bellwether. In any given case, the ECJ looks to the commission's position as an indicator of political acceptability to the member states of a particular result or a line of reasoning.[90] From the Court's own perspective, however, the chief advantage of following the commission is the "advantage of objectivity," resulting from the commission's supranational perspective.[91] In neofunctionalist terms, the Court's reliance on what Pescatore characterizes as "well-founded information and balanced legal evaluations," as "source material for the Court's decisions" allows it to cast itself as nonpolitical by contrasting the neutrality and objectivity of its decision-making processes with the partisan political agendas of the parties before it.

Relatively less attention has been paid to the role of the commission in depoliticizing potentially inflammatory disputes among the member states. Judge Pierre Pescatore credits the procedure set forth in Article 169 (whereby the *commission* initiates an action against a member state for a declaration of default on a community legal obligation) with defusing the potential fireworks of an Article 170 proceeding, in which one state would bring such a charge directly against another.[92] By allowing default proceedings to be initiated by "an institution representative of the whole, and hence objective both by its status and by its task," this device "permits the Member States more easily to accept this process of control over their Community behavior and the censure which may arise for them from the judgments of the Court."[93] Against this

---

[89] Ibid., pp. 612–14.
[90] The classic study documenting this proposition is Eric Stein, "Lawyers, Judges, and the Making of a Transnational Constitution," p. 25. Out of ten landmark cases, Stein found only two in which the Court had diverged from the Commission.
[91] Pescatore, *The Law of Integration*, p. 80.
[92] Ibid., pp. 80–82.
[93] Ibid., p. 82.

backdrop, it is of signal importance that the Court itself actively and successfully encouraged the increased use of the Article 169 procedure.[94]

This perspective reveals yet another dimension of the Court's encouragement of the Article 177 procedure. The increased use of Article 177 shifted the vanguard of community law enforcement (and creation) to cases involving primarily *private* parties. It thus further removed the Court from the overtly political sphere of direct conflicts between member states, or even between the commission and member states. The political implications of private legal disputes, while potentially very important, often require a lawyer's eye to discern. Following Haas's description of economic integration, Article 177 cases offer a paradigm for the "indirect" penetration of the political by way of the legal.

Law as a mask

The above discussion of context reveals that the neofunctionalist domain is a domain theoretically governed by a distinct set of nonpolitical objectives, such as "the rule of law" or "economic growth and efficiency," and by a distinctive methodology and logic. These characteristics operate to define a purportedly "neutral" zone in which it is possible to reach outcomes that would be impossible to achieve in the political arena. Neofunctionalists also insisted, however, that this neutral zone would not be completely divorced from politics. On the contrary, "economic" – or, in our case, "legal" – decisions inevitably would acquire political significance. This gradual interpenetration was the mechanism by which economic integration might ultimately lead to political integration.

The key to understanding this process is that even an economic decision that has acquired political significance is not the same as a "purely" political decision and cannot be attacked as such. It retains an independent "nonpolitical" rationale, which must be met by a counterargument on its own terms. Within this domain, then, contending political interests must do battle by proxy. The chances of victory are affected by the strength of that proxy measured by independent nonpolitical criteria.

From this perspective, law functions both as mask and shield. It hides and protects the promotion of one particular set of political objectives against contending objectives in the purely political sphere. In specifying this dual relationship between law and politics, we also uncover a striking paradox. Law can only perform this dual political function to the extent it is accepted as law. A "legal" decision that is transparently "political," in

---

[94] See Rasmussen, *On Law and Policy in the European Court of Justice*, pp. 238–40.

the sense that it departs too far from the principles and methods of the law, will invite direct political attack. It will thus fail both as mask and shield. Conversely, a court seeking to advance its own political agenda must accept the independent constraints of legal reasoning, even when such constraints require it to reach a result that is far narrower than the one it might deem politically optimal.

In short, a court's political legitimacy, and hence its ability to advance its own political agenda, rests on its legal legitimacy. This premise is hardly news to domestic lawyers. It has informed an entire school of thought about the U.S. Supreme Court.[95] It also accords with the perception of ECJ judges of how to enhance their own effectiveness, as witnessed not only by their insistence on their strict adherence to the goals of the Treaty of Rome but also by their vehement reaction to charges of activism. Mancini again: "If what makes a judge 'good' is his awareness of the constraints on judicial decision-making and the knowledge that rulings must be convincing in order to evoke obedience, the Luxembourg judges of the 1960s and 1970s were obviously *very* good."[96]

What is new about the neofunctionalist approach is that it demonstrates the ways in which the preservation of judicial legitimacy shields an entire domain of integrationist processes, hence permitting the accretion of power and the pursuit of individual interests by specified actors within a dynamic of expansion. Moreover, the effectiveness of "law as a mask" extends well beyond the ECJ's efforts to construct a community legal system. To the extent that judges of the European Court do in fact remain within the plausible boundaries of existing law, they achieve a similar level of effectiveness in the broader spheres of economic, social, and political integration.

[CONCLUSION]

* * *

In his most recent article, Weiler depicts much of the "systemic evolution of Europe" as the result of the self-created and internally sustained power of law. Shapiro made a similar point in the article in which he first threw down the gauntlet to community legal scholars to take account of the larger

---

[95] The most notable proponents of this approach to American judicial politics were Justice Felix Frankfurter and his intellectual protégé Alexander Bickel. See Alexander Bickel, *The Supreme Court and the Idea of Progress* (New York: Harper and Row, 1970).

[96] Mancini, "The Making of a Constitution for Europe," p. 605, emphasis original.

political context in which the Court was acting. He concluded that the legalist analysis might ultimately be the more "politically sophisticated one" on the ground that "legal realities are realities too."[97] Rasmussen would agree, although he fears that legal realities are likely to be overborne by political realities as a result of a loss of judicial legitimacy. This position might be described as the "sophisticated legalist" position – one that recognizes the existence of countervailing political forces but that nevertheless accords a role for the autonomous power of law.[98]

The neofunctionalist approach integrates that insight with a carefully specified theory of the individual incentives and choices facing the servants of law and a description of the processes whereby they advance their own agenda within a sheltered domain. Thus, although we agree with Weiler's conclusion, we go far beyond his general claim that the power of law within the community emanates from the "deep-seated legitimacy that derives from the mythical neutrality and religious-like authority with which we invest our supreme courts."[99] The power flows from a network of strongly motivated individuals acting above and below the state. To enhance and preserve that power, they must preserve and earn anew the presumed legitimacy of law by remaining roughly faithful to its canons.

In conclusion, neofunctionalism offers a genuine political theory of an important dimension of European integration. It is a theory that should be equally comprehensible and plausible to lawyers and political scientists, even if European judges and legal scholars resist it for reasons the theory itself explains. Previously, those who would argue for the force of the law had to forsake "political" explanations, or at least explanations satisfactory to political scientists. Conversely, most of those seeking to construct a social scientific account of the role of the Court typically have eschewed "fuzzy" arguments based on the power of law. We advance a theory of the interaction of law and politics that draws on both disciplines, explaining the role of law in European integration as a product of rational motivation and choice. Lawyers seeking to offer causal explanations, as well as political scientists trying to explain legal phenomena, should be equally satisfied.

---

[97] Shapiro, "Comparative Law and Comparative Politics," pp. 540–42.

[98] It should be noted here that Volcansek has integrated similar arguments into a more comprehensive political theory about the impact of ECJ judgments on national courts, arguing for the importance of "legitimacy and efficacy" as one of four factors determining the nature of that impact. See Volcansek, *Judicial Politics in Europe*, pp. 267–70.

[99] Weiler, "The Transformation of Europe," p. 2428.

19

The European Court of Justice, National Governments, and Legal Integration in the European Union

Geoffrey Garrett, R. Daniel Kelemen, and Heiner Schulz

* * *

The growth of European law has been central to the broader process of European integration. The accretion of power by the European Court of Justice (ECJ) is arguably the clearest manifestation of the transfer of sovereignty from nation-states to a supranational institution * * * in modern international politics * * *. The ECJ is more similar to the U.S. Supreme Court than to the International Court of Justice or the dispute panels of the North American Free Trade Agreement (NAFTA) and the World Trade Organization (WTO). The Court interprets European Union (EU) treaties as if they represent a de facto constitution for Europe and exercises judicial review over laws and practices within member states. The ECJ is thus in the business of declaring extant national laws and the behavior of national governments "EU-unconstitutional." Even more significantly from the standpoint of conventional international relations, member governments often abide by such decisions.

There are two perspectives on the evolution and operation of Europe's remarkable legal system. The legal autonomy approach argues that the ECJ has been able to push forward its European integration agenda against

We gratefully acknowledge the helpful comments of Carsten Albers, Karen Alter, Lisa Conant, Christian Joerges, John Odell, Susanne Schmidt, participants of GAAC Young Scholars' Institute, three anonymous reviewers, and the editors of *International Organization*. We would particularly like to thank Anne-Marie Slaughter for her detailed critique of an earlier version of this paper. Garrett and Schultz acknowledge the financial support, respectively, of the Reginald Jones Center of the Wharton School and the Gottlieb Daimler- and Karl Benz-Foundation.

the interests of some member states.[1] According to this view, national governments paid insufficient attention to the Court's behavior during the 1960s and 1970s when the Court developed a powerful set of legal doctrines and co-opted the support of domestic courts for them. By the time member governments finally realized that the ECJ was a powerful actor in the 1980s, reining in the Court's power had become very difficult.

In contrast the political power approach argues [that governments from EU member states] have not been *** victims of European legal integration ***.[2] From this perspective the member governments have given the ECJ autonomy to increase the effectiveness of the incomplete contracts the governments have signed with each other (that is, the EU treaty base). In turn the judges of the ECJ realize that their power is ultimately contingent on the acquiescence of member states and hence are reticent to make decisions of which governments disapprove.

Notwithstanding rhetorical characterizations of the ECJ either as "master" or as "servant," proponents of each view agree on one common assumption: the ECJ is a strategic actor that is sensitive to the preferences of EU member governments. ***

[We follow suit] by presenting a game theoretic analysis of the strategic environment affecting interactions between the Court and national governments in the EU. This yields three empirically testable hypotheses. *** First, the greater the clarity of ECJ case law precedent, the lesser the likelihood that the Court will tailor its decisions to the anticipated reactions of member governments. Second, the greater the domestic costs of an ECJ ruling to a litigant member government, the lesser the likelihood that the government will abide by an ECJ decision that adversely affects its interests (and hence, *** the lesser the likelihood that the Court will make such "adverse" decisions).

Our third hypothesis brings in the reactions of governments other than the litigant in a particular case. Governments that are subject to adverse decisions can engage in unilateral noncompliance. However, they can also press for the passage of new *** EU legislation *** or even revision of the EU treaty base ***. Noncompliance may reduce the costs of an adverse decision, but it is less likely to constrain the future

---

[1] See *** Burley and Mattli 1993; *** Slaughter, Stone, and Weiler 1997; Stein 1981; and Weiler 1991.

[2] See Cooter and Drexl 1994; Garrett 1992; Garrett 1995a; and Garrett and Weingast 1993.

behavior of the ECJ than is secondary legislation. Treaty revisions are clearly even more constraining on the Court. But legislation and treaty revisions demand more coordination on the part of member governments. [We thus hypothesize] that the greater the activism of the ECJ and the larger the number of member governments adversely affected by it, the greater the likelihood that responses by litigant governments will move from individual noncompliance to coordinated retaliation. Conversely, of course, the specter of coordinated responses will make the ECJ more reticent to make adverse decisions.[3]

It should be clear from these hypotheses that the ECJ may face conflicting incentives. [In order to maintain its legitimacy, the Court will seek to avoid making decisions that it anticipates governments will defy.] In order to maintain its status as an independent arbiter, however, the Court must *** minimize the appearance of succumbing to political pressures from interested parties. Avoiding member government defiance may call for one decision; maintaining legal consistency may demand a very different one. In making its rulings, the ECJ must weigh the consequences of both courses of action. [It] is in those cases where the Court is cross-pressured that conflict with governments is likely to break out.

*** Until now the protagonists in the legal politics debate have sought to support their own arguments with selective citation of illustrative cases. We strive to do better. ***

* * *

Our case selection strategy seeks to capture the analytic benefits of focusing on adverse ECJ decisions that prove ex post to be controversial (that is, eliciting government responses), but to do so while minimizing the costs of [this inherent] selection bias. We have chosen to analyze broad streams of controversial ECJ case law where the Court repeatedly confronts similar legal principles but in different contexts. This allows us to test *** our three hypotheses by holding the legal principles constant ***.

We focus on three lines of cases ***. The first involves bans on agricultural imports, where ECJ decisions stood on the front line in the battle between the conflicting trade liberalization and agricultural protection agendas of the EU. The second set of cases involves the application of principles of equal treatment of the sexes to occupational pensions – one of the most controversial areas of ECJ activism in recent years because of

---

[3] These two statements may seem mutually inconsistent, but they are not in the context of iterated games and incomplete information.

its enormous financial implications. Finally, we analyze Court decisions pertaining to state liability for the violation of EU law. These last cases arguably represent the Court's most important constitutional decisions since the early 1970s concerning the relationship between EU law and national sovereignty.

Empirical analysis of these lines of cases lends broad-based support to each of our three hypotheses. * * *

The article is divided into three sections. In the first section we present our game theoretic understanding of the strategic interactions between the ECJ and member governments. In the second section we outline our three hypotheses regarding the impact of ECJ precedent, domestic conditions, and EU coalitions on the behavior of litigant governments and the Court. In the third section we examine the empirical utility of our arguments against lines of cases concerning trade liberalization, equal treatment of the sexes, and state liability.

THE LEGAL POLITICS GAME IN THE EUROPEAN UNION

Asserting that ECJ decision making is strategic is no longer controversial * * *.[4] The Court's preferences regarding how EU law should be interpreted often differ from those of member state governments * * *.

* * * We analyze the ECJ–litigant government interaction as a repeated noncooperative * * * game * * * in which actors discount the future at a reasonable rate (see Figure 19.1). * [The] ECJ moves first by ruling on the legality of an existing national law or practice with respect to European law (embodied in EU treaties, directives, regulations, and decisions made pursuant to the treaties or previous Court decisions).[5] If the Court decides that the national law or practice is consistent with EU law, the status quo is not disturbed ("conciliation" between the ECJ and the relevant government results in payoffs of C_c and G_c, respectively).[6]

If, however, the ECJ rules against an extant national law or practice, the adversely affected member government must choose whether to abide by the ruling. Acceptance entails changing national practices or laws to conform with the decision or compensating the party that has suffered

---

[4] See Burley and Mattli 1993; Mattli & Slaughter 1995; and Weiler 1991.

[5] In practice, of course, numerous steps take place prior to the Court's decision (including previous plays of the government–ECJ game). Perhaps the most important of these that we do not analyze is the referral of cases to the ECJ by national courts – the *preliminary judgments* procedure of Article 177 of the Treaty of Rome. * * *

[6] For definition of terms, see Figure 19.1.

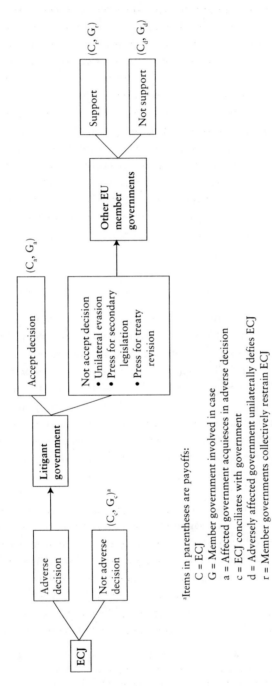

FIGURE 19.1. *The legal politics game*

losses as a result of them (payoffs from such "acquiescence" are C_a, G_a). If the government chooses not to abide by the decision, it has three ways to respond. The government may engage in overt or concealed evasion of the decision, it may press for new EU legislation to overturn the decision, or it may call for changes in the constitutional foundations of the Court by proposing revisions to the EU treaty base.

The final part of the stage game concerns the reactions of the remaining EU member governments to the decision by one of its members not to accept an ECJ decision. If the other governments support their colleague by "restraining" the ECJ (through new legislation or treaty revisions), the resulting payoffs to the Court and the adversely affected government are C_r and G_r. If the other governments do not support nonacceptance, the adversely affected member government will have to engage in isolated "defiance" (C_d, G_d).

This is the end of the stage game, but the process continues with the next Court decision. The Court's strategic choice is the same: it must decide whether to interpret EU law in a way that adversely affects a member government. In the second round, however, the Court takes into account the information it gained in the previous play of the game ***. The government that plays in the second iteration of the game may be the same as in the first round, or it may be different. After the second decision and reaction by the litigant government and by other EU members, the actors update their information, and the stage game is played again. The indefinite repetition of this process determines the evolution of the EU legal system.

In the stage game, the basic preference ordering of the ECJ (assuming that prima facie legal grounds justify an adverse decision) can be described by the following inequality:

$$C_a > C_d > C_c > C_r \qquad (1)$$

The ECJ has a clear institutional interest in extending the scope of Community law and its authority to interpret it. * The best way for the Court to further this agenda is through the gradual extension of case law (that is, the replacement of national laws by ECJ decisions as the law of the land ***). [One] can think of the conciliation outcome (for which the Court's payoff is C_c) as maintaining the status quo: the ECJ does not expand the scope of its case law, but its authority is not questioned by government defiance.[7] From the Court's perspective, situations in which

---

[7] It is important to remember here that the ability of the ECJ to engage in judicial review of legislation is not guaranteed by the founding treaties of the EU. ***

it makes adverse decisions that the relevant government accepts are clearly preferable to the status quo ($C_a > C_c$). However, if an adverse ECJ decision results in other EU governments rallying around in support of the litigant government to restrain the Court, *** this would be a worse outcome for the ECJ than maintaining the status quo. *** As a result, $C_c > C_r$.

The Court's preferences are less clear-cut regarding the situation in which an adverse ruling is not followed by the litigant government, but that government's position is not supported by its colleagues (C_d). The Court would clearly prefer that the litigant government accept its adverse decision (that is, $C_a > C_d$); the worst outcome for the ECJ would be where a government's nonacceptance of an adverse decision is supported by the other EU governments ($C_d > C_r$). But how should the Court compare isolated defiance with maintenance of the status quo? We believe that, in general, $C_d > C_c$. Our reasoning is that at least one EU member state (tacitly) approves of the Court's decision (in cases where unanimity is required to restrain the Court), or a substantial minority (under qualified majority voting). Even though having even a single government flout its authority is a matter of concern for the ECJ, this would likely be outweighed by the implicit support of the decision by other member governments. Nonetheless, it should be pointed out that our analysis does not depend on $C_d > C_c$ (see the next section). ***

We now consider the basic preference order of the litigant member government in the stage game, which we assume to be generally expressed by the following inequality:

$$G_c > G_r > G_a > G_d \qquad (2)$$

[We] assume the EU member governments support a powerful system of EU law in which the ECJ faithfully implements the governments' intentions as laid out in the EU treaty base. * Governments understand that having a well-defined rule of law fosters mutually beneficial economic exchange. But it is very difficult *** to write complete contracts (in the case of the EU, treaties). Delegating authority to the ECJ is thus essential to the efficient functioning of the rule of law in Europe ***. Any time a member government rejects an ECJ decision, this not only undermines the legitimacy of the EU legal system, but also threatens to earn for the government a reputation as an actor that does not play by the rules. By contrast, when member states comply with an adverse ruling, they strengthen the EU legal [system.] The more a member government benefits from the economic exchanges made possible by the rule of law in Europe, the greater its respect for ECJ decisions.

At the same time, adverse decisions will always be costly to governments ***. As a result, the status quo is the best outcome for the litigant government (G_c). Once the Court makes an adverse decision, however, the litigant government would most prefer the situation in which it does not accept the decision *** and where it is supported by the other EU member governments through new legislation or a treaty revision that restrains the ECJ (that is, $G_r > G_a$). Finally, we assume that the worst outcome for a litigant government is isolated defiance of an adverse ECJ decision (C_d). *** As was the case with the Court's preference order, however, our analysis would be unaffected if we were to assume that governments might prefer isolated defiance to acceptance (that is, $G_d > G_a$) – for example, by virtue of placing a very heavy weight on sovereignty ***.

We have now described the preference orders of the ECJ and litigant governments in the legal politics stage game. The equilibrium outcome in the stage game depends on the behavior of the EU member governments that are not party to the case at hand. If they support the litigant government, *** the ECJ would not make an adverse decision, since the litigant government would not abide by the ruling ***. If, on the other hand, the other governments decide not to act, the ECJ would rule against the litigant government, which in turn would accept the decision ***. Moreover, changes in the legislative rules of the EU will also affect the behavior of the ECJ and litigant governments. [The] use of qualified majority voting makes collective resistance easier and more likely. This suggests that court activism should have decreased since the ratification of the Single European Act in 1987. ***

* * *

ECJ PRECEDENT, DOMESTIC POLITICS, AND EU COALITIONS

If the theoretical framework presented in the preceding section is to provide us with analytic leverage over the actual jurisprudence of the ECJ, it must generate comparative statics results that relate differences in the specific circumstances of a case to variations in outcomes (both case law and government reactions to decisions). We begin this task by discussing the factors that will influence the preferences of the ECJ and member governments as the dynamics of the legal politics game unfold over time with respect to lines of case law.

The ECJ

[Legal] precedent greatly concerns the ECJ. * All independent judiciaries are expected to make decisions based on legal principles. Although the foundations for such principles are often enshrined in constitutions (or treaties in the case of the EU), they are invariably modified in case law where courts assert powers or interpretations that are not transparent in such foundational documents. If a court's jurisprudence were to change frequently from case to case ***, however, the court would surely lose legitimacy. This is because a court's claim to power ultimately rests on its image as an impartial advocate for "the law." ***

This argument suggests that from the standpoint of the ECJ, a tension will often exist between the desire not to make judgments that adversely affect the interests of member governments and the importance of legal consistency. Avoiding member government defiance may call for one verdict; following precedent may dictate another. Can we put a metric on the costs of inconsistency for the ECJ? The simple answer is that these costs are a function of the clarity of existing precedent. Where there are more conflicting cases on the books or where the treaties of the EU are more ambiguous on a given point of law (for example, Articles 30 and 36 concerning "free movement"), the costs of inconsistency will be lower. * More generally:

H1: The greater the clarity of EU treaties, case precedent, and legal norms in support of an adverse judgment, the greater the likelihood that the ECJ will rule against a litigant government.

This hypothesis suggests that the Court's ceteris paribus preference ordering outlined in inequality (1) should be modified to take into account the clarity of legal precedent. *** Consider a scenario in which case law precedent is transparent and dictates that the ECJ should take an adverse decision against a member government. * The effects of this change on the first part of the game tree in Figure 19.1 are clear. Unambiguous precedent increases the attractiveness to the ECJ of taking an adverse decision that the litigant government subsequently accepts (that is, the gap between C_a and C_c would increase). *** Clear precedent should also increase the utility the Court would derive from the isolated defiance outcome relative to the situation in which the litigant government's defiance is supported by other ECJ governments (thus, the gap between C_d and C_r would increase).

But what if the Court prefers an outcome in which its (precedent-driven) decision ultimately leads the member governments collectively to restrain the ECJ to the scenario in which the Court does not make an adverse decision in the first place and hence does not provoke an inter-governmental reaction (that is, if $C_r > C_c$)? This change in the Court's preferences would have a dramatic impact on the legal politics game. *** Irrespective of how the litigant government and its other EU colleagues behaved, the Court would still rule the extant national law or practice illegal. In this extreme case, the litigant government would face a clear choice between accepting the decision (G_a) and trying to enlist the support of the other member governments to restrain the Court (G_r). The litigant government's preferred outcome (G_c) would no longer be feasible. Clearly, litigant governments will always prefer G_r to G_a, but restraint can only be achieved with the support of other member governments (we discuss the conditions that make this more likely with respect to H3). ***

The Litigant Government

The international preferences of national governments over foreign policy no doubt contain both internal and external elements. For some, government preferences are largely a function of the constellation of do-mestic interests,[8] perhaps conditioned by the institutional structure of national polities.[9] But observers of the EU often suggest that sovereignty concerns are preeminent for at least some member governments ***. These two views can be integrated by arguing that governments typically value sovereignty because they view it as a pre-requisite for winning in domestic politics.[10] ***

With respect to domestic factors, the short-termism inherent in democratic politics means that distributive politics will generally tend to dominate the incentives to increase aggregate prosperity. ECJ decisions often threaten to impose heavy costs on segments of the economy – for example, by overturning national laws that act as nontariff barriers supporting specific sectors. Other Court decisions may harm the agendas of feminist, environmental, or other interest groups. For governments, the operative question is the importance of these groups to their reelec-tion efforts. ***

But ECJ decisions may also have deleterious consequences for na-tional governments in a more direct sense – for example, by imposing

---

[8] See Frieden 1991; and Frieden and Rogowski 1996.
[9] Garrett and Lange 1995.
[10] Powell 1991.

new responsibilities on the state or by reducing tax receipts. Finally, the potential for governments to be held liable for the violation of EU law increases the threat that the Court could impose sanctions itself – for example, through orders to compensate citizens and firms that have suffered due to the violation. Our intent here is not to develop a detailed algorithm for weighting these various factors. * Rather, we only wish to propose the following hypothesis:

H2: The greater the domestic costs of an ECJ ruling to a litigant government, the lesser the likelihood that the government will abide by an adverse ECJ decision.

*** The simplest consequence of H2 is that the gap between G_c and all other outcomes would increase with the greater costs to the government of an adverse decision. That is, the desirability to the litigant government of the Court's not taking an adverse decision would rise. H2 also implies that the payoff gap between collective restraint of the ECJ (G_r) and accepting adverse decision (G_a) would increase ***.

The pivotal issue, however, concerns how the litigant government's domestic circumstances would affect its utility comparison between G_a and defying the ECJ in isolation (G_d). If the government is sufficiently concerned about the domestic costs of an adverse decision, then $G_d > G_a$. As was the case for the Court's decisional calculus, this would give the litigant government a dominant strategy in cases where the ECJ makes an adverse decision. The government would not accept the decision, irrespective of whether it thought other member governments would support its defiance. ***

Other Member Governments

* * *

The most decisive way that member governments can restrict ECJ activism without violating the basic tenets of the EU legal system is to revise EU treaties. Although this has occasionally been done (see our discussions of the Barber protocol in the next section), the threshold to such constitutional revision is very high – unanimity among the EU member governments and subsequent ratification by national parliaments, national referendums, or both.

An easier path for restraining legal activism is the passage of new EU legislation to counteract the effects of ECJ decisions. *** [Since] the mid-1980s much legislation requires only the support of a qualified majority in the Council, significantly reducing the obstacles to passage. *

Clearly, however, an inverse relationship exists between the ECJ-restraining power of these strategies and their ease of implementation. Secondary legislation is relatively easy to pass, but it cannot be guaranteed to rein in the Court's activism in a given area. The ECJ could simply respond by arguing that its interpretation is consistent with the EU treaty base, and that the new legislation is not. Treaty revision is much harder to achieve, but it is the ultimate constraint on the Court (which views itself as the protector of the treaties).

When should we expect the EU governments collectively to seek to restrain ECJ activism? Two conditions stand out. First, the greater the importance of a particular case to more member governments, the greater the likelihood that they will collectively support a litigant government seeking to defy an adverse judgment. Second, the greater the number of cases within a similar branch of the law that the Court adversely decides, the greater the likelihood of a collective response to constrain the ECJ. ***

Thus our third hypothesis is:

H3: The greater the potential costs of a case, the larger the number of governments potentially affected by it, and the larger the number of adverse decisions the ECJ makes in similar areas of the law, the greater the likelihood that the EU member governments will respond collectively to restrain EU activism.

The effects of variations in EU-wide support for litigant governments on the legal politics game are straightforward. The greater the probability of a collective restraint response to adverse ECJ decisions, the lesser the weight that the Court and the litigant government should attach to the pair of payoffs C_d, G_d. Indeed, if both actors were to attach zero probability to this outcome, the strategic dynamics of the legal politics game would change considerably. The litigant government would know that its defiance would be supported by its EU colleagues. It would thus not accept any adverse decision by the ECJ because it could always do better by pressing for new secondary legislation or treaty revisions (because $G_r > G_a$). In turn the ECJ would not make an adverse decision in the first place, because conciliating the litigant government is better for it than inciting a collective act of restraint ($C_c > C_r$).

A STRATEGIC HISTORY OF ECJ CASE LAW

The preceding two sections have developed a simple framework for analyzing EU legal politics and a set of hypotheses about the dynamics of ECJ–litigant government interactions. This section assesses how well our theory and hypotheses fit the actual history of ECJ jurisprudence, using three lines of cases: nontariff barriers to agricultural trade, equal treatment of the sexes, and state liability for the violation of EU law.

Import Bans on Agricultural Products

The 1958 Treaty of Rome demanded as part of the effort to create a common market that extant trade quotas among member states be abolished during a transitional period ending on 31 December 1969 (Articles 8 and 32). The treaty spelled out a detailed timetable for the progressive elimination of these quotas (Article 33). The treaty also required that the establishment of a Common Agricultural Policy among the member states (Article 38 (4)) accompany the development of the common market. Thus domestic deregulation was combined with deregulation at the EU level * * *.

By the end of the transition period, however, member states had not established common policies for a few agricultural products. In the 1970s the ECJ heard a series of cases concerning the effect of the Rome treaty on these products. The *Charmasson* case involved a requested annulment of a quota for banana imports imposed by the French government on 28 October 1969.[11] *Charmasson* argued that the quota violated the timetable set forth in Article 33 for eliminating quantitative restrictions to trade. The French government contended that because a national marketing organization for bananas was already in place in 1958, Article 33 did not apply. * * *

The ECJ decided that the existence of a national marketing organization could preclude the application of Article 33 and made it clear that the French quota scheme could be viewed as such a national organization. The Court added, however, that such marketing organizations could suspend the application of Article 33 only during the transitional period. After 31 December 1969 Article 33 would have to be applied, regardless of whether or not the member states had established a communitywide marketing organization.

* * * The contradictions between a free-trade article (Article 33) and the agricultural provisions (Articles 38–46) gave the ECJ leeway in interpreting the Rome treaty. The Court made a bold pro-integration interpretation by ruling that national marketing organizations could not stand in the way of free trade after the end of the transition period. * * * The French government opposed this interpretation and, given the domestic

---

[11] Case 48/74, *Mr. Charmasson v. Minister for Economic Affaires and Finance* [1983] ECR 1383.

sensitivity of the banana sector, was likely to defy the ECJ (consistent with H2). * The likelihood of immediate French defiance, however, was somewhat tempered by the Court's use of the classic *Marbury v. Madison* technique. The ECJ decided for the French government in the case at hand, while establishing a principle that the government opposed (Article 33 would be applied after the end of the transitional period). Nonetheless, the French government was likely to oppose the dissolution of its banana marketing organization.

Why did the Court make such a pro-integration ruling, knowing that it would likely provoke French defiance? Consistent with H3, the fact that the ECJ had little reason to expect a collective response from the member governments was likely [very important.] Given the divisive nature of banana politics in the EU, and because few other products had not yet been incorporated into the Common Agricultural Policy, a treaty revision was most unlikely. *** A more probable collective response was that the ruling would spur the member states to create a common marketing organization for bananas (which is what the Court wanted).

The *Charmasson* precedent was subsequently tested in a dispute over potatoes. In the *Potato* case, the Commission challenged the United Kingdom's national market organization ***.[12]

The precedent established in *Charmasson* made it more likely that the ECJ would rule against the United Kingdom in the *Potato* case – as eventually transpired. ***

The next development in this line of ECJ jurisprudence was the *Sheep Meat* case, in which the French government claimed that it should be allowed to maintain its national market organization for mutton.[13] *** The French government asserted that in the period between the abolition of its national rules and the establishment of EU rules, domestic producers would be unfairly disadvantaged in competition with British producers who were subsidized by their government.[14] *** The French government also declared that it would continue banning imports regardless of the Court's decision. * Nonetheless, the Court held that the French sheep meat regime had to be discontinued. This decision sparked what came to be known as the "sheep meat war." France refused to comply with the Court's ruling, declaring that it would do nothing until a common market organization for sheep meat was established. *

---

[12] Case 231/78, *Commission v. UK* [1979] ECR 1447.
[13] Case 232/78, *Commission v. France* [1979] ECR 2729.
[14] Rasmussen 1986, 339.

The domestic costs of the *Sheep Meat* decision led the French government to defy the ECJ (consistent with H2). Given the high cost of an adverse decision to French farmers and given the French government's open unwillingness to comply with an adverse decision the Court might have chosen not to rule against France. This was a case, however, where H1 and H3 dominated H2. On the one hand, the ECJ knew that if it violated its own clear and recent precedents under pressure from the French, it would lose legitimacy as an impartial arbiter in the eyes of other member governments. On the other hand, the Court had little reason to believe that the member governments would act collectively to oppose its decision. Overturning the decision would require unanimous member government support for a treaty revision, whereas at least one member government, the United Kingdom, was known to oppose the French position (as it was eager to export sheep meat to France). In this case, the cost of caving in to member government pressure apparently was higher to the Court than the cost of isolated French defiance.

The sheep meat dispute was ultimately resolved in the manner suggested by the French government – a common market organization for sheep meat was established at the Dublin meeting of the Council in May 1980. At the same meeting, in a clear reference to the *Sheep Meat* ruling, President Valéry Giscard d'Estaing of France suggested that the member states should jointly constrain the ability of the ECJ to make "illegal decisions." * Giscard suggested an institutional reform that would have given the "big four" member governments an additional judge on the Court (similar to Roosevelt's efforts to pack the Supreme Court with New Dealers in 1936). * Ultimately, however, no such changes were made.

In sum, this line of cases provides some support for each of our three hypotheses. The ECJ took advantage of the conflict between a free-trade provision (Article 33) and agricultural policy provisions (Articles 38–46) to establish a controversial precedent [(H1).] *** The conflict came to a head in the *Sheep Meat* case, and when push came to shove the French government was not prepared to back down given the high domestic costs of so doing (H2). The Court was willing to maintain its adversarial stance because it did not think that a restraining collective response from the member governments was likely (H3).

Equal Treatment of the Sexes

Article 119 of the Treaty of Rome states that men and women should receive equal pay for equal work. Pay is defined broadly (in ironically sexist language) as "the ordinary basic or minimum wage or salary and any other consideration, whether in cash or in kind, which the worker receives, directly or indirectly, in respect of his employment from his employer." This loose definition has prompted numerous ECJ cases concerning the benefits that fall under the rubric of Article 119 ***, particularly age pensions.

The first significant case was *Defrenne No. 1.*[15] The ECJ held that pensions paid under statutory (that is, publicly mandated) social security schemes did not constitute pay as defined in Article 119. *** In *Defrenne No. 2*, the ECJ declared that Article 119 had direct effect; individuals could rely on Article 119 in cases before national courts.[16] The Court applied a retrospective limitation to its judgment so that states would not have to answer to complaints regarding violations of Article 119 prior to the date of the *Defrenne No. 2* decision. This was expedient since it was clear that acting otherwise might have ran some national pension schemes into bankruptcy. * This decision left unanswered the question of whether Article 119 applied to occupational pensions.

Finally, in *Bilka* the Court declared that occupational pensions constituted pay under Article 119.[17] *** The ramifications of this decision were potentially enormous and extremely costly to employers. This seems inconsistent with H3 because the Court could have expected a collective restraining response from the EU member governments.

Indeed, the Council made a quick, if somewhat messy, effort at damage control. Two months after *Bilka* the Council passed a new directive on occupational pensions.[18] The directive gave occupational pension schemes until 1993 to comply with the equal treatment principle but exempted the use of sex-based actuarial assumptions and survivors' pensions from the equal treatment doctrine altogether. The directive also delayed the requirement to equalize pensionable ages. *

The ECJ moved next. In the *Barber* case the Court ruled that sex-based differences in pensionable ages violated Article 119 and had to be eliminated.[19] This decision was at odds with the Council's directive regarding pensionable ages and in effect overruled it. However, the Court

---

[15] Case 80/70, *Defrenne v. Belgium* [1971] ECR 445 at para. 6.
[16] Case 43/75, *Defrenne v. SABENA* [1976] ECR 455.
[17] Case 170/84, *Bilka Kaufhaus GmbH v. von Hartz* [1986] ECR 1607.
[18] Directive 86/378 OJ 1986 L225/40.
[19] Case 262/88, *Barber v. Guardian Royal Exchange* [1990] ECR I-1889.

reduced the potential tensions by limiting the retrospective application of the principles. * The Court's language was vague:

The direct effect of Article 119 of the Treaty may not be relied upon in order to claim entitlement to a pension with effect from a date prior to that of this judgment, except in the case of workers or those claiming under them who have before that date initiated legal proceedings or raised an equivalent claim under the applicable national law.

This could be interpreted in many ways. At the conservative extreme the Court's ruling might imply that only workers who joined occupational pension schemes after the date of the judgment are eligible for equal benefits. The liberal interpretation would be that the equal treatment principle applies to future pension payments for all workers regardless of when they joined. *

Why did the Court leave its retrospective limitation so ambiguous? One plausible interpretation is that the ECJ may have made a vague ruling in order to gauge the reaction of member governments. Their reaction was swift and decisive. The EU governments were extremely worried by the enormous financial implications of the *Barber* decision, and they reacted in the strongest possible way – through treaty revision. The governments added a protocol to the Maastricht Treaty that limited the application of the equal treatment principle to periods of work after the *Barber* judgment.[20]

The ECJ responded to the "Barber protocol" in the 1993 case *Ten Oever*.[21] In this case the Court was asked to clarify the retrospective limitation it had imposed in *Barber*. *** The Court *** affirmed the governments' preference as expressed in the protocol. In effect the Court's ruling said: "this is what we meant all along. The member governments did not overrule us; they simply helped us clarify a point."

In two subsequent cases, however, the ECJ behaved in ways that arguably challenged the Barber protocol. The *Vroege*[22] and *Fisscher*[23] cases concerned whether the retrospective limitation with regard to pensionable ages established in *Barber,* and affirmed in the protocol, also applied to the right to join occupational pension schemes. * The Court

---

[20] Treaty on European Union, Protocol No. 2 on Article 119.

[21] Case 109/91, *Ten Oever v. Stichting Bedrijfspensioenfonds voor het Glazenwassers- en Schoonmaakebedrijf* [1993] ECR I-4879.

[22] Case 57/93, *Vroege v. NCIV Instituut voor Volkshuisvesting BV and Stichting Pensioenfonds NCIV* [1994] ECR I-4541.

[23] Case 128/93, *Fisscher v. Voorhuis Hengelo BV and Stiching Bedrijfspensioenfonds voor de Detail- handel* [1994] ECR I-4583.

decided that the retrospective limitation in *Barber* applied only to equalization of pensionable ages and did not apply to the right to join pension schemes. Therefore, Vroege and Fisscher could date the right to join their pension schemes back to 8 April 1976, the date when Article 119 had been given direct effect in *Defrenne No. 2.* *

Ostensibly, these bold decisions circumscribed the applicability of the Barber protocol to the specific issue involved in the *Barber* case (differences in pensionable ages) when it was likely that the governments had intended the protocol to limit the retrospective application of Article 119 in general. But the ECJ provided member states with methods for limiting the financial consequences of these decisions. The Court held that women would have to pay their back-contributions in order to join the schemes retroactively – making it extremely unlikely that many would choose this option. More importantly, the ECJ allowed member states to maintain existing legislation limiting retrospective claims or to pass new laws to this effect. * Women are now entitled to receive equal treatment under pension schemes, but the full impact of this change will not be felt for years, when this generation of workers retires.

We can learn three important lessons from this line of cases about the interaction between the ECJ and the member governments. First, in instances where the potential domestic ramifications of adverse ECJ decisions are great member governments are unlikely to passively abide by Court decisions. This is completely consistent with H2.

Second, as H3 suggests, Court decisions with costly domestic ramifications for all member governments are likely to provoke collective responses to rein in the Court. * * * In this line of cases the ECJ was willing to circumvent secondary legislation passed by the Council. Once the governments clearly signaled their resolve through a treaty revision, however, the Court retreated.

Finally, this line of cases illustrates that the ECJ–member state game is not one of complete information. If it were, the Court would not have pushed so hard for an expansive interpretation of "equal pay" – because it would have known that this was universally unacceptable among EU member governments. In reality the Court did not anticipate the strength of government opposition. Thus it floated a series of trial balloons – in the form of open-ended decisions – designed to test the resolve of governments. Because the precedents established in these decisions were vague, they did not constrain the Court. Consistent with H1, the Court thus had room to modify its interpretation in subsequent judgments to accommodate member government preferences. * * *

State Liability for the Violation of EU Law

One of the central ways in which EU policy is made is through directives. These are pieces of secondary legislation that member governments are required to transpose into national law. This process, however, is plagued by a fundamental problem. Governments that do not approve of an EU directive (typically when passed by a qualified majority in the Council) may not transpose it into national law on time, may transpose it incorrectly, or may not transpose it at all. Moreover, until Maastricht, the EU treaties made no provision for sanctioning member states that failed to implement directives. Under Articles 169 and 170 of the Rome treaty, the Commission or other governments may take a member state to the ECJ for failing "to fulfill an obligation under this Treaty." If the Court finds the state to be in violation of a directive and that the relevant government failed to remedy the problem, the plaintiff can take the government back to the ECJ (Article 171). But governments that ignored ECJ rulings faced no penalties until the ratification of the Maastricht Treaty. *

The Court sought in a series of decisions to increase the effectiveness of EU directives, primarily by granting individuals legal recourse to them in national courts even if their government had failed to transpose them into national law (that is, the "direct effect" of directives). But direct effect did not apply to all directives, and member governments continued to evade their obligation to abide by them. Then in the landmark 1991 *Francovich* decision the ECJ ruled that governments must compensate individuals for the loss caused to them resulting from the nonimplementation of directives, even those without direct effect.[24] The implications of *Francovich* are still not clear; the Court has yet to establish a system of state liability for the violation of EU law. Here we speculate on the likely course of interaction between the ECJ and member governments that will determine the shape of such a system. * * *

History of Direct Effect

We begin by sketching briefly the thirty-year history of the Court's efforts to empower individuals with respect to EU law. In 1963 the Court decided that some EU provisions could have direct effect, conferring rights on individuals rather than simply imposing duties on governments.[25] The

[24] Joined cases C-6/90 and 9/90, *Francovich and Others v. Italy* [1991] ECR I-5357.
[25] Case 26/62, *Van Gend en Loos* [1963] ECR 1.

ECJ then decided in *Van Duyn* that direct effect applied, in principle, to directives.[26] This decision was subsequently clarified, stating that directives are only subject to direct effect when the deadline for national implementation has passed.[27]

In 1986 the Court ruled that private parties could sue only the state, not other private parties, for violating directives that have not been transposed into national law.[28] The Court's next decision then side-stepped the whole notion of direct effect. In *Marleasing* the Court ruled that where a directive had not been incorporated into national law, domestic courts had to interpret existing national law in light of that directive.[29] * * *

But the ECJ was not yet finished with the issue of conferring individual rights under EU directives. With the passage of the Single European Act and the spate of directives issued pursuant to it in order to complete the internal market, the Commission stepped up its proceedings against member governments with respect to the nonimplementation or "incorrect" implementation of directives. * The effectiveness of using Articles 169–171, however, was limited by the lack of enforcement provisions. As a result, disobedient governments simply refused to implement judgments. The best way to ensure real member government compliance with directives was for individuals to bring cases against their governments in national courts for violations of their rights under EU law. In *Francovich* the Court had the opportunity to make this possible.

The Francovich Ruling

Francovich concerned Italy's failure to implement a directive intended to ensure that employees received full payment of salary arrears if their employers became insolvent.[30] Even though the Commission brought a successful proceeding against Italy under Article 169, Italy still took no action to implement the directive.[31] Francovich and others, who were owed arrears of salary, then sued the Italian government. The case was ultimately referred to the ECJ.

---

[26] Case 41/74, *Van Duyn v. Home Office* [1974] ECR 1337.
[27] Case 148/78, *Ratti* [1979] ECR 1629.
[28] Case 152/84, *Marshall v. Southampton and South West Hampshire Area Health Authority (Teaching)* [1986] ECR 723.
[29] Case C-106/89, *Marleasing* [1990] ECR I-4135.
[30] Directive 80/987 OJ L283/23, 1980 ("Insolvency Directive").
[31] Case 22/87, *Commission v. Italy* [1989] ECR 143.

The Court held that the insolvency directive was not directly effective. *
It also ruled, however, that member governments are liable to compensate individuals for losses resulting from the nonimplementation of
a directive – even if the national legal systems do not permit such liability –
provided that three conditions are met. First, the directive must confer
rights on individuals. Second, these rights must be identifiable from the
provisions of the directive. Finally, a causal link must exist between the
breach of EU obligations by the national government and the loss suffered
by the individual.

Francovich thus represented a quantum leap in the Court's intervention inside member states because it asserted that individuals' claims to
damages from the violation of EU law did not depend on the doctrine of
direct effect. * The decision sent shock waves through European capitals.
Although *Francovich* concerned only a small number of limited claims,
the potential range of claimants and size of damages under the state
liability principle were virtually without limit.

The ECJ, however, did not address in *Francovich* the scope of the
state liability principle. A number of outstanding issues remained to be
resolved. Did the principle extend to cases where the Court ruled that
national implementing measures were inadequate? What about much
broader, and more vague, obligations under EU treaties? How far should
state liability go? What conditions should be established before states are
liable to pay damages?

How the ECJ answers these questions will ultimately determine the
impact of *Francovich*. An extensive interpretation by the Court would be
the capstone on more than thirty years of effort by the ECJ to expand and
entrench its authority. It is equally clear, however, that member governments will not passively accept such an interpretation. We now explore
the responses of member governments to *Francovich*.

Government Responses to Francovich

Earlier we sketched three possible responses by governments to adverse
ECJ decisions. The first – noncompliance by the litigant government – is
not at issue with respect to *Francovich* because the Italian government
has already accepted the decision. The other two collective responses –
statutory legislation and treaty revision – have been widely discussed by
member governments. Not surprisingly, the U.K. Conservative, government took the lead in trying to restrict the scope of *Francovich*. It claimed
that the question of state liability should be a matter of national law ***.

This would limit state liability to cases in which governments have shown "grave and manifest disregard" of their EU obligations – a very strict condition that is rarely fulfilled.[32] The British government also advocated a statute of limitations restricting damage payments to recent violations of EU norms.[33] Furthermore, it demanded that existing national laws be allowed to stand that limit the time span over which damages must be paid.[34]

The broader issue of constitutional (that is, treaty) limitations on the ECJ was widely discussed in the context of the 1996–97 Intergovernmental Conference. The U.K. government proposed that a qualified majority in the Council should be able to overturn ECJ decisions. *** A somewhat less controversial British proposal sought to restrict to the highest court in each member country the right to refer cases to the ECJ for "preliminary judgments" (Article 177 EC).[35] ***

As in so many other issues, however, British Conservatives were outliers in Europe. * Some members of the EU – most notably, France and Germany (along with their economic allies among the Benelux countries and Austria) – attach a greater positive weight to the presence of an effective legal system in Europe. These countries strongly support the EU legal system for at least two reasons. First, [they] are deeply committed to expanding European integration as a means of stabilizing geopolitics on the continent. Second, the economies of the northern core of the EU are those that benefit most from the removal of nontariff barriers to trade in the EU, and the ECJ has been a powerful actor in furthering this agenda. Thus these governments have strong incentives not to emasculate the ECJ, even in the face of an incendiary decision such as *Francovich*.

We are not saying that those member governments that generally support the rule of EU law should be expected to sit idly by and allow the ECJ to entrench the state liability principle. They were, however, reticent to follow the British lead of institutionalizing political

---

[32] Submission of the British government to the ECJ regarding *Factortame No. 3* (see later). ***

[33] See *Daily Mail*, 24 October 1995, 22; and *The Times*, 23 October 1995.

[34] For example, when the British government was recently ordered by the Court to change its prescription charge laws – a ruling that threatened to cost up to £500 million due to reimbursing all men between the ages of sixty and sixty-four for charges dating back five years – it cited a 1993 regulation applying a three-month time limit, reducing the overall costs of compliance with the ruling to £40 million; *Daily Mai*, 24 October 1995, 22.

[35] See *Financial Times*, 2 February 1995, 10; 3 April 1995, 17; 22 August 1995, 10; and *The Times*, 23 October 1995.

intervention in European law. The political consensus in the EU seems to support two objectives limiting the *Francovich* ruling. The first is to adopt restrictive criteria for establishing the liability of member states. The second is to circumscribe the retrospective application of all ECJ rulings, not only *Francovich,* and to allow existing national laws to stand that constrain the time span over which damages must be paid.[36]

Toward a System of State Liability for the Violation of EU Law

How should we expect the ECJ to react to this political environment? Given that the costs of *Francovich* to all member states are potentially enormous (H2, H3), and given that the exact nature of the precedent set in the case is unclear (H1), we anticipate that in the future the Court will voluntarily restrict the application of the state liability doctrine in ways desired by the bulk of member governments.

Four recent cases provide a preliminary test for our predictions. First, in *Brasserie du Pêcheur* a French brewing company sought damages from the German government for losses incurred when forced to stop exporting beer to Germany because its product did not comply with the German beer purity law (declared in violation of EU law by the ECJ in 1987).[37] Second, in *Factortame No. 3* a group of Spanish fishermen claimed damages from the British government for losses incurred as a result of the 1988 Merchant Shipping Act, ruled illegal by the ECJ in 1991.[38] Third, in *British Telecommunications* the plaintiff sought damages from the U.K. government for losses following the failure to implement appropriately a directive on procurement procedures for utilities.[39] Finally, in *Dillenkofer* a number of German tourists claimed damages from the German government for its failure to implement a 1990 EU directive on package tours.[40]

On 5 March 1996 the ECJ delivered its rulings in the *Brasserie du Pêcheur* and *Factortame* cases.[41] The ECJ reaffirmed the principle established in *Francovich.* It ruled that states have to pay damages if three conditions are met: (1) the violated EU law must confer rights on

---

[36] *The Times,* 23 October 1995.
[37] Case C-46/93.
[38] Case 48/93.
[39] Case C-392/93.
[40] Joined cases C-178/94, C-179/94, 188/90, 189/94, and 190/94.
[41] Joined cases C-46/93 and C-48/93, *Brasserie du Pêcheur* and *Factortame* [1996] ECR I-0000.

individuals, (2) the violation must be sufficiently serious, and (3) the damage must have been directly caused by the violation. The ECJ stated that a violation of EU law is "sufficiently serious" if it has persisted despite a court ruling or if it is clear in light of settled case law. The decisive test is whether the government has "manifestly and gravely" disregarded the limits of its discretion.

This formulation corresponds to the Court's interpretation of Article 215 EC, which governs the noncontractual liability of EU institutions. The ECJ left it to national courts to decide whether a violation of EU law is sufficiently serious. National courts must also decide on the level of damages. However, the ECJ ruled that damages must be no less than the compensation for similar claims under domestic law. The Court held that national liability laws apply as long as they do not make it "excessively difficult or impossible" to obtain effective compensation.

The ECJ ruled on the *British Telecommunications* case three weeks later.[42] The Court held that the conditions for establishing state liability set out in its 5 March decision also applied to cases where a government had incorrectly transposed a directive into national law. *** On 8 October 1996 the ECJ delivered its ruling in the *Dillenkofer* case.[43] The Court reaffirmed the conditions set out in *Brasserie du Pêcheur* and *Factortame* and ruled that the failure to take any measure to transpose a directive on time constituted a sufficiently serious violation of EU law.

The Court's reasoning in these cases follows in three important ways the prior proposals of national governments regarding limitations of the *Francovich* principle. First, the "manifest and grave" violations proviso is a very strict condition. *** Second, the Court held that only violations of clear and unambiguous provisions would give an automatic right to compensation ***. Third, the ECJ left it to national courts to adjudicate state liability cases according to national liability laws. The Court thus followed government demands that state liability should be a matter of national law, subject to a minimum EU standard based on the principles governing the liability of EU institutions.

These cases suggest that the ECJ is willing to tailor its state liability rulings in ways that the core member governments, especially France and Germany, wish. Nonetheless, a number of issues remain to be resolved. The fact that liability claims are to be adjudicated according to national

---

[42] Case 392/93, *British Telecommunications* [1996] ECR I-0000.

[43] Joined cases C-178/94, C-179/94, 188/90, 189/94, and 190/94, *Dillenkofer* [1996] ECR I-0000.

liability laws raises the question of the extent to which the Court will allow national statutes of limitation to stand. In most member states the state incurs liability only under very restrictive substantive and procedural conditions. * Thus national liability laws may provide member states with an effective shield from liability in most cases and with an effective cap on retrospective payments of damages. ***

CONCLUSION

The existing literature on legal integration in the EU poses a stark dichotomy between two views of ECJ–government interactions: the legal autonomy and political power perspectives. This article has developed a theoretical framework that is subtler and more balanced than either of these perspectives. Moreover, we have subjected our view to empirical tests that are much less vulnerable to the "sampling on the dependent variable" critique. Our theoretical framework generated three independent hypotheses about the strategic interactions between the Court and member governments. These hypotheses were then tested against a carefully selected set of cases in which we sought to hold constant as many factors – other than those of direct bearing on our hypotheses – as possible.

The starting point of our theoretical analysis is that the ECJ is a strategic actor that must balance conflicting constraints in its effort to further the ambit of judicial review in the EU. On the one hand, the Court's legal legitimacy is contingent on its being seen as enforcing the law impartially by following the rules of precedent. On the other hand, the Court cannot afford to make decisions that litigant governments refuse to comply with or, worse, that provoke collective responses from the EU governments to circumscribe the Court's authority. Understanding how these conflicting constraints function requires careful delineation of the legal and political conditions in particular cases.

The empirical analysis generated strong support for our three hypotheses. First, the greater the clarity of EU treaties, case precedent, and legal norms in support of an adverse judgment, the greater the likelihood that the ECJ will rule against litigant governments. Second, the greater the costs of an ECJ ruling to important domestic constituencies or to the government itself, the greater the likelihood that the litigant government will not abide by the decision. Third, the greater the costs of a ruling and the greater the number of EU member governments affected by it, the greater the likelihood that they will respond collectively to rein in EU activism – with new secondary legislation revisions of the EU treaty base.

So much for the normal science. *** The ECJ is manifestly neither master nor servant of EU member governments. As is more generally true with respect to scholarship on European integration, engaging in labeling debates – neofunctionalism versus intergovernmentalism, for instance – is unproductive. Instead, research should concentrate on deriving empirically testable propositions from logical theoretical arguments and then systematically evaluating them against the data. This article represents our attempt to do this in the context of the strategic interactions between the ECJ and EU member governments.

* * *

PART VII

OTHER SUBSTANTIVE AREAS OF INTERNATIONAL LAW

20

Scraps of Paper? Agreements and the Durability of Peace

Virginia Page Fortna

Why does peace sometimes last and sometimes fall apart? What, if anything, can be done to enhance the durability of peace in the aftermath of war? Some cease-fires fall apart within days or months, others hold for years, while others last indefinitely. Why, for example, did a cease-fire in the Arab-Israeli war in 1948 fail within three months, while the next one lasted for years? Why has peace so often faltered between India and Pakistan but held, despite ongoing tensions, between North and South Korea? Surprisingly little theoretical or empirical work has explored this important question.

States have devised a number of mechanisms to try to make it easier to maintain peace. These mechanisms are often implemented as part of a cease-fire agreement. States set up demilitarized zones, accept international peacekeeping missions, establish dispute resolution procedures, sign formal agreements, and undertake other steps to try to enhance the prospects for peace. Do these measures work? If so, why? This article begins to answer this question by analyzing the duration of peace after

Many friends and colleagues have given advice and comments on the larger project of which this paper is a part. In particular I would like to thank Scott Bennett, Nora Bensahel, Erik Bleich, Dan Drezner, Lynn Eden, Nisha Fazal, Jim Fearon, Wendy Franz, Erik Gartzke, Chris Gelpi, Doug Gibler, Hein Goemans, Amy Gurowitz, Lise Howard, Bob Jervis, Bob Keohane, Zeev Maoz, Lisa Martin, Dani Reiter, Don Rothchild, Evan Schofer, Curt Signorino, Jack Snyder, Al Stam, Celeste Wallander, Barb Walter, Suzanne Werner, and four anonymous reviewers. I am grateful also for research assistance from Carol St. Louis. This project would not have been possible without financial and intellectual support from the Olin Institute at Harvard University, the Center for International Security and Cooperation at Stanford University, and the Institute of War and Peace Studies at Columbia University.

international wars ending between 1946 and 1997. It draws on and develops theories of international cooperation to argue that measures
such as these help enemies overcome the cooperation problem inherent
in the aftermath of war. Students of international relations have long
drawn on contracting theory and the new economics of organization literature to examine how actors can achieve cooperation even as anarchy
makes it impossible to write enforceable contracts.[1] Scholarship in this
vein points to a number of ways in which cease-fire agreements might
influence the chances of maintaining peace. I argue that mechanisms
within agreements can make durable peace more likely by changing the
incentives to break a cease-fire, by reducing uncertainty about actions
and intentions, and by preventing accidental violations from triggering another round of fighting. If this argument is correct, the content of
cease-fire agreements should affect whether peace lasts. Individually and
collectively, these measures should be associated with more durable
peace, all else being equal.

Scholars of international relations in the realist tradition likely would
argue that cease-fire agreements and the measures within them are at
best epiphenomenal. In these scholars' view, agreements may reflect other
factors that affect durability, but arguments that they themselves shape
the chances for lasting peace are idealistic. In this view, agreements are
merely "scraps of paper." They are not binding in an anarchical system
and should have no independent effect on international behavior, least
of all on decisions about war and peace.[2] To test the effects of agreements on the durability of peace, one therefore needs to control for
other factors that affect the baseline prospects for peace. If, once these
variables are included, agreement mechanisms have no effect, then one
can conclude that agreements are only scraps of paper. If, however,
agreements matter even when the baseline prospects are accounted for,
this would support the argument that even deadly enemies can overcome
the obstacles to cooperation.

* * *

The first section of this article develops cooperation theory to explain
how specific mechanisms within cease-fire agreements might affect the

---

[1] See Coase 1988; Martin 1993; Moe 1984; Oye 1986; and Williamson 1985.
[2] This is akin to the argument that international institutions are epiphenomenal.
Mearsheimer 1994. See also Mearsheimer 2001. If agreements have no effect, however,
it is not clear why states bother to write them. Leeds, Long, and Mitchell 2000.

durability of peace. This argument suggests that measures such as the withdrawal of forces, creation of demilitarized zones, formal cease-fire agreements, peacekeeping, third-party guarantees, and dispute resolution procedures should help foster peace that lasts. The more of these measures implemented, the longer peace should last, all else being equal. This section also lays out the counterargument and explores other variables that might be expected to affect the baseline prospects for peace. * * * The second section describes the econometric model and the data set of cease-fires in international wars used to test these hypotheses. The findings, presented in the third section, show that agreements are not merely scraps of paper; rather, the implementation of specific mechanisms within cease-fire agreements can help make peace last. Strong agreements lead to more durable peace.

In this study I define peace merely as the absence of war. I do not distinguish between relations that become very friendly and those that remain acrimonious despite the absence of violence. Under my definition, North and South Korea have been at "peace" for half a century. Clearly, not all varieties of peace are equally desirable, nor does stability necessarily coincide with social justice. Nevertheless, most wars cause poverty, disease, and dislocation, and all entail the large-scale loss of human life. Repeated conflict only exacerbates these tragedies. This study not only indicates that states can overcome obstacles to maintaining peace in war-torn areas, but also identifies the most effective ways of doing so.

COOPERATION THEORY AND AGREEMENTS

Maintaining peace in the aftermath of war requires cooperation. Because war is costly, there is shared interest in avoiding renewed hostilities. This shared interest, however, does not automatically lead to peace. Recent belligerents have deeply conflicting interests and strong incentives to take advantage of each other.[3] They also have good reason to fear each other's intentions. Cooperation is therefore difficult to achieve. I argue that cease-fire agreements can foster cooperation in several ways, by changing incentives, by reducing uncertainty about actions and intentions, and by controlling accidental violations of the cease-fire.

This argument rests on three assumptions: (1) that states are rationally led [but not that they are unitary actors;] (2) that war is costly, and not desired for its own sake; and (3) that each ex-belligerent has incentives to

[3] Keohane 1984; Oye 1986.

take advantage of its opponent, or good reason to fear its opponent's intentions. I do not assume that both belligerents reach a cease-fire on equal footing.[4] There are usually winners and losers in war, and at least one side's acceptance of a cease-fire may have been "coerced." However, unless one side is completely eliminated in war, both sides can impose costs on each other, and the problem of cooperation maintains.[5]

* * *

Conflicting interests give belligerents an incentive to break the cease-fire in a bid to make unilateral gains on the battlefield. This is the familiar game of prisoner's dilemma. There may also be cases where neither side would prefer to attack, even unopposed. However, there is no easy way for actors to know this. In an atmosphere of deep mistrust in the aftermath of war, each side has good reason to fear attack from its opponent. Uncertainty and fear about the other's intentions can undermine cooperation even where perfect information would automatically yield a cooperative outcome. Security dilemma dynamics and their spirals of fear and hostility are especially likely among states who have recently engaged in mortal combat.[6] With communication channels severed during the war, and enemies likely to assume the worst about each other, incidents along the cease-fire line, even if accidental or the result of rogue forces, can reignite war. Peace is precarious.

A hypothetical case helps illustrate the obstacles to peace. Imagine two states that have just fought a war over a piece of territory (Israel and Syria in 1973, perhaps, or El Salvador and Honduras after the 1969 Football War). The war was costly and the two states would prefer not to fight again, but they would each like more of the disputed land, preferably all of it. Both believe it to be rightfully theirs, and domestically, occupation of any part of it by the enemy is seen as a travesty. The side that lost territory in the war has an incentive to try to win it back, and the side that gained may hope it can now claim more. Both sides therefore have incentives to try to encroach upon the other, or even to make a dramatic advance, to push the cease-fire line farther toward the other side.

---

[4] For the sake of simplicity, I discuss the problem of cooperation as involving only two states. A number of wars in this study have multiple belligerents. These are split into separate dyadic observations in the quantitative research discussed below.

[5] Kecskemeti 1964. The only case examined here in which one side was eliminated by the other is South Vietnam's fall to the North in 1975.

[6] Jervis 1978. In assurance games such as stag hunt, it is the grave payoff of being attacked and the difficulty of assessing intentions that makes cooperation risky.

Moreover, both states have good reason to fear encroachment or attack by the other. These fears have likely been exacerbated by leaders' inflammatory remarks for domestic consumption. Both sides will be particularly wary of military maneuvers, resupply efforts, or anything that might be a precursor to a new attack. When the fighting stopped, soldiers were likely left in close proximity to their enemies, facing each other "eyeball-to-eyeball" across the cease-fire line. The chance of troops firing across the line or of skirmishes as each side tries to improve its position is quite high. If irregular troops were involved in the fighting, or if command and control are somewhat loose, there may be incidents of unauthorized attacks or advances. In such a tense atmosphere of mistrust, with normal diplomatic channels cut, such small clashes can easily escalate. Whether through deliberate action, spirals of fear and preemption, or accident and involuntary defection, the probability of war erupting anew is high.[7]

Although both sides are better off with peace, they cannot simply declare peace and leave it at that. Their commitments to maintain peace are not credible.[8] An actor with hostile intentions has an incentive to say it will abide by the cease-fire so that its partner will cooperate and be "suckered" into letting down its guard and perhaps leaving itself vulnerable to attack. In international relations, of course, there is no external enforcement power to prevent actors from such cheating. This is the central problem of cooperation under anarchy in international relations.

So how do deadly enemies ever achieve peace? Cease-fire arrangements rely on reciprocity and mutual deterrence. Each side stops fighting in exchange for the other side doing the same. If either breaks the cease-fire, the other will respond in kind. It is the prospect of return fire that deters attack. This is so central to the notion of a cease-fire that it may seem quite obvious. However, for reciprocity and deterrence to work, several things must be true: the cost of reinitiating conflict must outweigh the incentives to attack; it must be easy to distinguish

---

[7] Reiter (1995) found preemption to be rare as the sole cause of war. But conflicts that start or escalate to war through preemption are most likely among deadly enemies, such as Israel and its Arab neighbors in 1967. Similarly, wars rarely start purely by accident, but escalating clashes, often at least partially the result of accidents or unauthorized action, can contribute to the spiral toward war. Such was the case between India and Pakistan in 1965, and arguably again in 1999. Escalating clashes led to the second war between China and Vietnam, and to serious fighting short of full-scale war between Honduras and El Salvador in 1976.

[8] For analyses of the problem of credible commitments as an obstacle to peace see Fearon 1995; and Walter 2001.

compliance from noncompliance; both sides must be reassured about each other's intentions, especially if there is a military advantage to striking first; and accidents must be prevented from triggering another war. These requisites suggest both the obstacles to peace and strategies for overcoming them.

Cease-fire agreements can employ three types of strategies to ensure that peace lasts: changing incentives by making it more costly to attack; reducing uncertainty about actions and intentions; and preventing or controlling accidental violations. These strategies suggest specific observable mechanisms, the effects of which are tested below.

Altering Incentives

* * * [There] are steps belligerents and the international community can take to increase the costs of an attack. These steps widen the bargaining space between belligerents and make another bout of war less likely. Adversaries can tie their own hands by physically constraining their ability to attack. Withdrawal of troops from the front line, creation of a demilitarized buffer zone, and arms control make remobilizing for war more difficult. These actions also make a successful surprise attack much less likely.

Belligerents may also be able to alter incentives by declaring their cease-fire formally. By signing a formal agreement, states invoke international law. Of course, with no higher authority to enforce it, international law is not binding in the way that domestic law is. International agreements can be broken, but breaking them risks losing international aid and military support, and legitimizes retaliation by the other side. Formal and public declaration of a cease-fire thus invokes international audience costs. *

Actors may also turn to outsiders to help them enforce a cease-fire. Commitment by a third party to guarantee the peace serves as a deterrent, again by raising the cost of noncompliance. An external guarantor takes on some of the responsibility for retaliation in the event of defection. The presence of peacekeeping troops interposed between forces may also serve as a physical and reputational buffer to ensure the cease-fire.

Reducing Uncertainty About Actions and Intentions

Agreements can reduce uncertainty by specifying the terms of a cease-fire. Marking the exact location of the cease-fire line provides a focal point that can help prevent "salami tactic" attempts to push the line to either side's advantage. Spelling out the rules of the cease-fire explicitly helps to define compliance and noncompliance, which serves to prevent misunderstandings and avoid unnecessary tension. The more specific the agreement, the less uncertainty there will be about what constitutes compliance.

Verification mechanisms can alleviate concerns about detecting aggressive moves by the opponent in time to respond. Monitoring may be less important in cease-fire agreements than other sorts of agreements, because states are likely to rely on national intelligence for warning of an attack, and it is difficult to hide aggression once it starts. However, neutral referees can play an important role in fostering stable peace. Because it is costly to be seen as the aggressor, states will try to blame the other side for any fighting that starts. Without neutral observers, claims of being the victim of aggression are not credible and there are bound to be disputes over "who started it." Monitors to investigate incidents and provide unbiased information on compliance are therefore important for distinguishing unprovoked aggression from legitimate retaliation. The international audience costs of breaking a cease-fire, therefore, often depend on impartial monitoring.

Physical constraints, audience costs, and third-party guarantees or peacekeeping efforts change belligerents' incentives, but also serve as important signaling devices that can reduce uncertainty about intentions. Willingness to accept measures that make war more costly is a credible signal of benign intent. States contemplating an attack will be less willing than those with nobler intentions to sign on to measures that increase the physical or political cost of fighting. Critics might argue that this concedes the point that agreements are epiphenomenal; only those who intend to abide by the cease-fire will agree to strong mechanisms, but it is the intentions, not the mechanisms, doing the causal work. This argument is unfalsifiable, as is there is no way to measure intentions a priori (if there were, international relations would be very different and war might not exist at all). But it also misses the point. Of course intentions matter. One of the ways in which agreements affect the durability of peace is by providing credible ways of signaling these intentions and overcoming the security dilemma.

In the abstract, there are two distinct causal pathways possible: one in which agreement mechanisms influence peace directly by constraining states or providing information, and another in which mechanisms simply signal intentions. However, the two pathways are not so easily distinguished in reality. As the literature on signaling and "cheap talk" suggests, if there are incentives to misrepresent, as there surely are among deadly enemies, signals are only credible if they are costly. For a state to limit its ability to wage war, or to open itself up to verification is costly, and therefore credible. That is, the indirect signaling function depends in large part on the more direct effects of agreement mechanisms. *

Controlling Accidents

Reciprocal strategies can be very vulnerable to accidents and misunderstandings. If troops stray over the cease-fire line, or fire accidentally, and the other side retaliates, the situation can quickly spiral back into full-blown war. If leaders do not exercise full control over their troops (or in some cases over civilians), rogue groups opposed to peace can easily upset it by violating the cease-fire and provoking retaliation.

Ongoing negotiations and dispute resolution procedures can alleviate this danger by preventing misunderstandings and providing a forum for resolving differences before a spiral of retaliation is triggered. However, because both sides have an incentive to blame violations on accidents or rogue factions, communication by itself may not always be credible.

Withdrawal of forces, buffer zones, and arms control can help prevent accidents and misunderstandings from occurring in the first place.[9] "Confidence-building measures" to regulate and make transparent behavior (such as military exercises) that is likely to cause tension can also prevent misunderstandings and alleviate suspicions. Cease-fire agreements often hold each state responsible for violations coming from its own territory, to prevent these violations from being used as an excuse for intentional defection. Agreements may also include concrete measures for internal control to deal with this problem of "involuntary defection."[10] In addition to acting as referees, international monitors investigate and mediate small clashes and disputes to keep them from escalating.

The theory put forth here is an institutionalist argument about mechanisms to overcome the obstacles to cooperation. I hypothesize that agreements can enhance the durability of peace by raising the cost of breaking a cease-fire, reducing uncertainty, and preventing and controlling accidents. While these three strategies for maintaining peace are

[9] On the role of arms control in providing stability, see Jervis 1993.

[10] For example, irregular forces were disarmed after the Football War between El Salvador and Honduras. The United Nations Emergency Force was given responsibility for pursuing *fedayeen* (guerrillas) in the Sinai after 1956.

presented separately, their functions are intimately connected, and specific mechanisms often serve several purposes. For example, monitoring by peacekeepers reduces uncertainty by ensuring that defectors will be caught. This also raises the cost of reinitiating war. In practice, much of peacekeepers' day-to-day work entails mediation and the prevention of small clashes from spiraling out of control. Physical constraints that alter the incentives for war also necessarily reduce fears of impending attack and reduce the likelihood of accidents. Belligerents' willingness to implement measures to tie their own hands and raise the cost of attack serves as a credible signal of commitment and thereby reduces uncertainty and makes accidents easier to control.

While analytically distinct, the strategies of raising costs, reducing uncertainty, and controlling accidents therefore overlap in practice. The strategies themselves cannot be observed directly. But the specific mechanisms discussed above can be observed and their effects tested empirically. I focus on the following measures: withdrawal of forces, establishment of demilitarized zones, arms control, measures to control potential rogue groups, third-party involvement, peacekeeping, confidence-building measures, dispute resolution procedures, the specificity of agreements, and whether agreements are formal or tacit.

I use the term "strength of agreement" to refer to the number and extent of the measures implemented as part of a cease-fire. Agreement strength varies from none, if a cease-fire takes place with no agreement or without implementing any of the measures listed above (as when the second war between China and Vietnam simply fizzled out with no real cease-fire agreement), to very strong if the agreement implements significant buffer zones, peacekeepers, confidence-building measures, is formal and very specific, and so on. (The agreements reached between Israel and Egypt after the Yom Kippur war, as well as the Korean Armistice, are examples.) If the cooperation theory spelled out here is correct, peace should last longer, ceteris paribus, the stronger the agreement implemented. Furthermore, each of the individual measures should be associated with more durable peace. Both together and separately, these mechanisms are hypothesized to increase the stability of peace.

Political Settlement

Altering incentives, reducing uncertainty, and controlling accidents are all rather apolitical strategies for avoiding war. But the political content of an agreement should also be important. Resolving the underlying issues of conflict, if it is possible, is a way of removing the reason to fight. Whether an agreement purports to settle the political issues over which the war was fought, rather than simply to stop hostilities, should affect stability. I focus on the more mechanical tools for maintaining peace, because settlement of the basic political issues, whether by agreement or by force, is quite rare in the post–World War II era. *** Nevertheless, when a settlement of substantive political issues is reached, whether imposed or agreed to, one should expect it to be associated with stable peace.

The Counterargument: Agreements Are Epiphenomenal, Merely "Scraps of Paper"

All else being equal, stronger agreements should lead to more durable peace. All else is not equal, however. The agreement aside, peace will be easier to maintain in some cases than in others. The counterargument to the hypothesis that agreements can foster peace is that when cooperation is relatively easy, parties will be able to draft strong agreements. These are the very cases in which peace will last in any case. Conversely, when cooperation is difficult and the chances of peace falling apart are high for other reasons, belligerents will be unable to conclude agreements that do anything more than paper over differences. According to this argument, agreements are merely epiphenomenal; they reflect other factors that determine the duration of peace but have no independent effect of their own.

*** [It] is thus crucial to control for other variables that might affect the baseline prospects for peace (the "degree of difficulty," as it were) to test accurately the effects of cease-fire agreements.[11] In the empirical tests below, I control for a series of factors that make peace more or less difficult to maintain, [including whether the war ended in a decisive military victory or a stalemate,[12] the cost of war, the belligerents' history of conflict before the war, whether the war threatened a state's very existence,[13] contiguity[14] changes in relative military capabilities, and democracy.[15]]

---

[11] Downs, Rocke, and Barsoom 1996.

[12] Wars that end with a victor-imposed regime change are particularly stable. Werner 1999. There are only a few such cases in the data examined here, however. Controlling for this variable by dropping these cases makes no change to the results presented.

[13] See Powell 1991; Fearon 1998; and Smith and Stam 2001. ***

[14] See Bremer 1992; and Hensel 2000.

[15] See Russett 1993; and Brown, Lynn-Jones, and Miller 1997. Leadership changes do not have a significant effect on the resumption of war. Werner 1999.

If the counterargument that cease-fire agreements are epiphenomenal is correct, the strength of agreements should have no bearing once these other factors are taken into account.

METHOD: MODEL AND DATA

The Econometric Model

This article examines the duration of peace; why some cease-fires fall apart quickly while others last longer. * * *

* * * Duration models (also known as hazard rate or survival time models), [such as the Weibull model used here,] estimate the effects of independent variables on the length of time something lasts, and the models can incorporate our uncertainty about how long the phenomenon, (in this case, peace,) will continue into the future [(i.e., the issue of censored data).][16]

The Cease-Fires Data Set

To test the hypotheses laid out above, I constructed a data set that includes information on cease-fires and how long they lasted; on the situation between the belligerents at the time of cease-fire (their history of conflict, the decisiveness of military victory, etc.) as well as changes over time (in relative capabilities, regime type, etc.); and detailed information on the nature and content of any agreement and peace mechanisms that accompanied or followed the cease-fire.

The data set covers cease-fires in international wars ending between 1946 and 1997. Each case is a cease-fire between a pair of principal belligerents in the Correlates of War Version 3 (COW) data set's list of interstate wars. I split multilateral wars from the COW data set into separate dyads and eliminated minor participants.[17] A cease-fire is defined as an end to or break in the fighting, whether or not it represents the end of the war. It need not be accomplished through an explicit agreement. COW wars in which fighting stopped and started again are divided into separate cases, one for each cease-fire. During the first Arab-Israeli

---

[16] [The findings are no different in a Cox proportional hazard model. The Weibull is preferred because it gives more precise estimates in a small data set like the one used here. Box-Steffensmeier and Jones 1997, 1435. For a technical explanation of duration models, see Greene 1993.]

[17] Defined as those contributing less than one-tenth the number of troops committed by the largest provider of troops.

war in Palestine, for example, there was a break in the fighting in 1948 in accordance with a United Nations (UN) Security Council resolution ordering a cease-fire. Three months later, the cease-fire failed when Israel launched an offensive to seize the Negev. Another cease-fire ended the war in 1949. I treat these as distinct cases. History tends to forget the failed cease-fires, focusing only on the ones that succeeded in ending the war. Breaking these into separate cases is therefore crucial to avoid selecting on the dependent variable.[18] Cease-fires range in length from two weeks (the first Turco-Cypriot cease-fire) to fifty years and counting (Korea).

Because wars that start and stop again are treated as separate observations, and because multilateral wars are split into dyads, not all of the cases in the data set are independent of one another. I correct for the statistical problem of autocorrelation by calculating robust standard errors,[19] but a substantive caveat should also be noted. Because the Arab-Israeli conflict has been both multilateral and oft-repeated, much of the data set thus consists of Middle East cases. Domination of the data set by one conflict raises issues of generalizability. However, in neither the quantitative work, nor related case-study research have I found significant differences between the Middle East cases and others that would skew results.[20]

There are forty-eight cease-fire cases in the data set. * * * Each of these cease-fires is a subject for which there are multiple observations over time, each of a year or less, for a total of 876 observations. This allows me to record changes in military capabilities over time, the arrival or departure of peacekeepers, or the fact that a new agreement has been reached implementing new measures. These are known as "time-varying covariates" in the duration analysis lingo. For each subject, the time spans run continuously to the start of a new war or the end of the data at the beginning of 1998. The duration model treats each subject as a history, focusing on whether peace survived each time period in the

---

[18] I used COW data on when states "left" and "reentered" the war, supplemented by my research, to determine these breaks in the fighting. It is possible that I have missed some very short-lived cease-fires. This selection bias should work against my own argument, however, as brief cease-fires are much more likely to be reported if accompanied by strong agreements than by weak ones.

[19] These are calculated using Huber's method, with cases clustered by conflict. All of the Arab-Israeli cases are one cluster, all of the India-Pakistan cases another, and so on. Cases are assumed to be independent between clusters but not necessarily within clusters.

[20] Where controlling for Arab-Israeli Cases made a significant difference in the results, it is discussed below.

history. Peace is considered to fail at the start of another COW war between the same two belligerents. The data set is censored at the end of 1997.[21] War resumes eventually in twenty-one cases ***.

Data on the various aspects of agreements come from my research on each case.[22] I investigated and coded the following aspects of agreements: the extent of withdrawal of forces, demilitarized zones, arms control measures, peacekeeping (whether a monitoring mission or a peacekeeping force, and whether the mission was new or was left over from a previous mission before the war broke out), third-party involvement in peacemaking or guarantees of the peace, the specificity of any agreement, whether it was formal or tacit, dispute resolution procedures, confidence-building measures, measures to control possible rogue action, and whether the political issues over which the war was fought were settled. ***

Not all of the cease-fires are accompanied by agreements, of course. The data set includes a number of cases in which fighting stopped with a unilateral withdrawal, in which war simply fizzled to an end with no explicit cease-fire, or in which fighting ended with the installation by one side of a "friendly" government for the other (as in Hungary in 1956). In such cases, the mechanisms under discussion here are coded as zero unless measures were implemented in the absence of an agreement.

Agreement strength is measured in two ways. One is simply an index of the mechanisms implemented, with a point for a demilitarized zone, another for arms control measures, half for a monitoring mission or one for an armed peacekeeping force, and so on. This measure is crude but has the benefit of being objective and replicable by others. It ranges from 0 to 10. The other is a more subjective coding of the extent of the measures implemented. This measure is a five-point scale ranging from none for cease-fires with no mechanisms *** to very strong for formal, detailed agreements with peacekeeping contingents, demilitarized zones, dispute resolution procedures, and so on ***. It is derived from a qualitative comparison of all of the cases in the data set.[23] The objective and subjective measures

---

[21] The North Vietnam–South Vietnam case is censored immediately because South Vietnam ceased to exist.

[22] Sources included references surveying international conflict in the postwar era (including Bercovitch and Jackson 1997; Brogan 1992; Butterworth 1976; Goldstein 1992; Miall 1992; and Tillema 1991), secondary sources on each conflict, and primary documents, including cease-fire agreement texts.

[23] Note that neither measure includes whether the agreement settled the political issues over which the war was fought, which I consider separately.

are highly correlated (.88). Using both helps ensure that the subjective coding is not biased and that the objective coding is fairly accurate.

Data on situational or control variables come from existing data sets. A dummy variable marks whether the war ended in a tie or in a military victory for one side. The COST OF WAR measure is based on battle deaths. HISTORY OF CONFLICT measures the extent to which the belligerents' shared past is marked by serious disputes. I include measures noting whether one side's very existence was threatened by the war, *** and whether belligerents are contiguous ***. Following Werner, I use the COW material capabilities data to measure changes in relative capabilities.[24] [Other control variables, including whether the fight was over territory, whether the war involved more than two states, and] measures of expected utility, were tested, but found to have no significant effect (results not shown).[25,26]

FINDINGS

Baseline Prospects for Peace

*** Table 20.1 shows the statistical results. Coefficients indicate the effect of variables on the hazard of war resuming. Positive coefficients indicate variables associated with peace that falls apart more quickly (a higher hazard of failing), and negative coefficients mark variables associated with more durable peace (a lower risk of another war). To give a sense of the relative size of effects, the right-hand column presents estimated hazard ratios for variables found to have a significant effect. Hazard ratios are interpreted relative to a baseline of one: a ratio of 0.50 indicates that the hazard is cut in half, while a ratio of 2.0 indicates a doubling of the risk of another war.

---

[24] [Werner 1999.] Because democratic dyads never fight, there are no cease-fires between democratic states, but some dyads become jointly democratic after a cease-fire is in place (for example, Britain and Argentina after 1983). Joint democracy may make peace more durable, but the finding depends largely on how one codes Cyprus during the extremely short-lived cease-fire in 1974. It is also called into question by the 1999 Kargil War between India and Pakistan (which occurs after the data used here are censored). For further discussion of these cases and the relationship between democracy and the durability of peace, see Fortna 2004, chap. 3. Here, I control for the possible effects of the democratic peace by dropping those few observations in which both states are democracies (based on Polity data) in some tests.

[25] Bueno de Mesquita and Lalman 1992.

[26] Coding details and the data are available online at <http://www.columbia.edu/~vpf4/scraps.htm>.

TABLE 20.1. *Agreement Strength (Weibull Estimates)*

Variables	1 Agreement strength (subjective measure)		2 Index of strength (objective measure)	
	Coefficient (RSE)	Hazard ratio	Coefficient (RSE)	Hazard ratio
AGREEMENT STRENGTH				
None	0.32 js (0.52)	1.38		
Very weak	0.40 js (0.38)	1.50		
Weak	(omitted category)			
Moderate	−0.83*** js (0.21)	0.43		
Strong	−1.70 js (1.50)	0.18		
INDEX OF AGREEMENT STRENGTH			−0.25*** (0.06)	0.78
TIE	3.53*** (0.61)	34.28	3.63*** (0.33)	37.58
COST OF WAR	−0.55*** (0.21)	0.58	−0.68*** (0.18)	0.50
HISTORY OF CONFLICT	0.90*** (0.31)	2.46	0.95*** (0.26)	2.59
EXISTENCE AT STAKE	2.10*** (0.31)	8.13	2.31*** (0.31)	10.10
CONTIGUOUS	1.38*** (0.44)	3.99	1.20*** (0.24)	3.31
CHANGE IN RELATIVE CAPABILITIES	0.82*** (0.20)	2.28	0.85*** (0.19)	2.33
Constant	−8.37*** (2.44)		−6.60*** (1.72)	
Shape parameter p	0.90 (0.08)		0.91 (0.06)	
N	727		727	
Subjects	47		47	
Log likelihood	−39.78		−40.62	

Note: Cases of joint democracy are dropped. Negative coefficients and hazard ratios <1 indicate decrease in risk of another war (increase in duration of peace). Positive coefficients and hazard ratios >1 indicate increase in risk of another war (decrease in duration of peace). RSE = robust standard errors, js = jointly significant.

*** $p \leq .01$.

** $p \leq .05$.

* $p \leq .10$. Two-tailed tests used.

[Consider first the control variables that shape the baseline prospects for peace.] Wars that end in a tie are much *** more likely to be repeated than those that end with a decisive victory for one side. More costly wars are followed by substantially more durable peace, all else being equal. Peace is significantly more fragile between belligerents with more acrimonious shared histories, and is almost six times more precarious when one side's existence is threatened by the conflict.[27] *** Neighboring states are [more likely] to fight again, but [note that] this finding is not always statistically significant.[28]

As Werner's argument would predict, changes in relative capabilities over time do seem to be associated with the resumption of war.[29] ***

*   *   *

These findings suggest that it will be much harder to maintain peace in a case like the 1948 cease-fire in the Arab-Israeli War – which took place without a clear victor, between states whose entire history was marked by violence, and with the very existence of one side at stake – than in a case such as the Falklands War, fought by states a long distance from each other with little previous history of militarized conflict, ending in a very lopsided victory for Britain, with a relatively low death toll.

*   *   *

Agreement Strength

[Turn now to our primary variables of interest, the measures of agreement strength at the top of Table 20.1.] *** The subjective coding of agreement strength is a categorical variable (none, very weak, weak, moderate, strong). Model 1 shows the comparison to the omitted middle category (weak). As expected, the strongest agreements yield the most durable peace, and moderately strong agreements perform better than

---

[27] The latter finding is driven largely, but not entirely, by the Arab-Israeli cases.

[28] While neighbors are more likely to fight in the first place, all of the states in these data have proven themselves to have both reason to fight and the ability to reach each other militarily. It is thus not surprising that the effects of contiguity are weaker for the resumption of war than for propensity to fight in the first place.

[29] [But it is not entirely clear from this finding which way the arrows run. Do changes in relative capabilities lead to war, or does war lead to changes in relative capability? For example, was the India-Pakistan war over Bangladesh caused by Pakistan's falling capabilities, or did the war, which severed Pakistan in two, cause our measures of capability to drop? A lagged measure of the change in relative capabilities has no positive effect on the risk of war, casting significant doubt on the finding that changes in relative capabilities cause peace to break down.]

weak ones. Compared to the median agreement (weak), moderate agreements reduce the risk of another war by an estimated 57 percent (as indicated by the hazard ratio of 0.43), and strong agreements reduce the hazard of failure by more than 80 percent. Very weak agreements are associated with the least durable peace, faring perhaps even worse than no agreement at all. But compared to the middle category, peace falls apart more quickly with both very weak and no agreements. These effects are jointly significant.[30]

The findings are even clearer if one uses the objective index of agreement strength (Model 2). The negative and statistically significant coefficient indicates that the stronger the agreement, the longer peace lasts, all else being equal. A unit increase in agreement strength is associated with about a 20 percent reduction in the risk of another war. Overall, I find fairly strong support for the hypothesis that the content of agreements matter. Even when one takes the baseline prospect for peace into account, stronger agreements lead to more durable peace.

* * *

Assessing Individual Peace Mechanisms

Although mechanisms to alter incentives, reduce uncertainty, and control accidents are effective in the aggregate, examining the effects of each peace mechanism individually is important to know how best to maintain peace. Tables 20.2 to 20.4 show the results of each mechanism in turn, controlling for the baseline prospects for peace. Unfortunately, the small data set and problems of multicolinearity mean it is not possible to test all of these measures simultaneously. Because many aspects of agreements are correlated, it is difficult to reach strong conclusions about which measures are most effective relative to each other. For each mechanism, I checked the results controlling for the other aspects of agreements that were highly correlated with the measure under consideration.[31] Including correlated aspects of agreements solves the omitted variable bias but introduces multicolinearity, which reduces the efficiency of the estimates. Note that while the trade-off between multicolinearity and omitted variable bias makes it difficult to assess precisely the relative merits of each aspect of agreements, it does not call into

---

[30] Joint significance is determined with F-tests using STATA's "test" command.

[31] Where findings are not robust to these changes in model specification, I note this in the discussion below.

TABLE 20.2. *Individual Peace Mechanisms (Weibull Estimates)*

Variables	Coefficient (RSE)	Hazard ratio	Coefficient (RSE)	Hazard ratio
WITHDRAWAL	−0.33 (0.75)	0.72		
DEMILITARIZED ZONES				
Partial	−0.83* (0.47)	0.43		
Full	−2.38** (1.03)	0.09		
ARMS CONTROL	0.45 (0.48)	1.57		
INTERNAL CONTROL				
Responsible			0.70 (0.78)	2.01
Concrete			0.28 (1.21)	1.32
THIRD-PARTY				
Mediation			1.33 (1.02)	3.79
Guarantee			−15.54*** (0.97)	0.000
TIE	3.47*** (0.32)	32.10	3.26*** (0.36)	26.04
COST OF WAR	−0.45** (0.19)	0.64	−0.85*** (0.21)	0.43
HISTORY OF CONFLICT	1.16*** (0.16)	3.20	0.56* (0.31)	1.75
EXISTENCE AT STAKE	1.85*** (0.65)	6.35	2.22*** (0.84)	9.16
CONTIGUOUS	0.76 (0.48)	2.13	1.68*** (0.45)	5.35
CHANGE IN RELATIVE CAPABILITIES	1.13*** (0.22)	3.09	0.66*** (0.18)	1.93
Constant	−7.49*** (2.64)		−6.07*** (2.32)	
Shape parameter p	0.76** (0.10)		0.83 (0.11)	
N	770		770	

Variables	Coefficient (RSE)	Hazard ratio	Coefficient (RSE)	Hazard ratio
Subjects	48		48	
Log likelihood	−46.07		−44.33	

Note: Negative coefficients and hazard ratios <1 indicate decrease in risk of another war (increase in duration of peace). Positive coefficients and hazard ratios >1 indicate increase in risk of another war (decrease in duration of peace).

RSE = robust standard errors.

*** $p \leq .01$.

** $p \leq .05$.

* $p \leq .10$.

Two-tailed tests used.

doubt the general finding that agreements matter in the construction of durable peace. The bias arises because the omitted agreement mechanisms also affect the durability of peace, contradicting the null hypothesis that agreements do not matter.

As Table 20.3 indicates, withdrawing forces from the cease-fire line may reduce the risk of another war, but not significantly so. Troops withdraw to the status quo ante in about one-third of the cases examined here, suggesting that the norm against taking (and keeping) territory by force is fairly strong. Failure to withdraw from land captured during war has often laid the seeds for another round of fighting (the continuing strife over territories occupied by Israel in 1967 being the best example). But returning to the prewar lines does not ensure peace. Israel and Egypt fought again after Israel withdrew from the Sinai in 1956, for example.

Demilitarized zones (DMZs) to separate troops help foster durable peace. Even partial or very limited zones can help reduce the danger of accidents and skirmishes (for example, the number of incidents between India and Pakistan dropped markedly when narrow DMZs were established after the first and second Kashmir wars), but this effect is only marginally significant. However, full DMZs (defined as those 2 km wide or more, running the full length of the cease-fire line) have a clear stabilizing effect, reducing the hazard of another war by about 90 percent. DMZs have contributed to peace between El Salvador and Honduras after the Football War, in Korea, and between Israel and Syria in the Golan Heights. Arms control measures have not reduced the likelihood of recurrent war.[32]

---

[32] The sign of the coefficient for arms control flip-flops depending on model specification.

TABLE 20.3. *Individual Peace Mechanisms (Weibull Estimates)*

Variables	All peacekeeping		New peacekeeping only	
	Coefficient (RSE)	Hazard ratio	Coefficient (RSE)	Hazard ratio
PEACEKEEPING				
Monitors	−1.10* (0.59)	0.33	−6.87*** (2.62)	0.001
Armed forces	−0.21 (0.80)	0.81	−7.29* (4.05)	0.001
TIE	3.79*** (0.47)	44.24	11.17** (4.50)	70898.3
COST OF WAR	−0.70*** (0.18)	0.50	−1.84* (1.10)	0.16
HISTORY OF CONFLICT	1.27*** (0.29)	3.56	7.38** (3.77)	1605.81
EXISTENCE AT STAKE	2.35*** (0.23)	10.50	7.66* (4.27)	2124.89
CONTIGUOUS	0.97** (0.40)	2.63	1.43** (0.69)	4.17
CHANGE IN RELATIVE CAPABILITIES	0.80*** (0.23)	2.23	−0.16 (0.37)	0.85
Constant	−5.78*** (1.88)		−15.18** (7.34)	
Shape parameter p	0.76* (0.11)		1.82 (1.18)	
N	770		593	
Subjects	48		37	
Log likelihood	−46.78		−16.67	

Note: Negative coefficients and hazard ratios <1 indicate decrease in risk of another war (increase in duration of peace). Positive coefficients and hazard ratios >1 indicate increase in risk of another war (decrease in duration of peace).
RSE = robust standard errors.
*** $p \leq .01$.
** $p \leq .05$.
* $p \leq .10$. Two-tailed tests used.

Nor have measures to establish internal control over potential rogue groups made peace more stable. A number of cease-fire agreements specify that each side is responsible for any hostile action coming from its territory. Such statements are not effective at making states rein in irregular forces; in fact these statements are more likely an indicator of a serious problem with rogue groups. In some cases (such as the Football War), there is evidence that concrete measures to disarm irregular forces can help cement peace. But in many cases, the problem has not been one of "involuntary defection" by rogue groups, but of the voluntary use of irregular forces to carry out covert aggression. This problem, especially prominent in India and Pakistan and in the Middle East, has not been effectively dealt with.

The effect of third parties on peace depends on their level of involvement. Outsiders often help mediate a cease-fire, as the United States did for Israel and Egypt in 1970 to end the War of Attrition, or as Iran did in Armenia and Azerbaijan in 1992. Third parties may also pressure client states to stop fighting, as in the Sinai War and the Iran-Iraq War. This level of involvement may help warring states reach a cease-fire to begin with, but it does not help them keep it. If anything, cease-fires reached with outside mediation appear to be more likely to break down quickly (the coefficient is positive but not significant). Explicit guarantees, though not terribly frequent, are much more successful. There are no cases of peace failing when an outside state has explicitly underwritten the cease-fire. Unlike in civil wars, such guarantees are not necessary[33] (there are many cases of durable peace without them), but they clearly help reduce the risk of another war.

Table 20.4 shows the effect of peacekeeping. The international community has sent monitors or armed peacekeepers to about two-thirds of the interstate cease-fires in the post–World War II era. These efforts have helped keep the peace, but the effectiveness of peacekeeping can be easily undermined. The presence of monitors appears to lengthen the duration of peace.[34] However, the presence of armed peacekeepers does not have a statistically significant effect. A look at peacekeeping's record suggests an important difference between missions deployed at the time of the cease-fire, and those already in place before the war broke out. More than half of peacekeeping's failures (that is, cases where peacekeepers were present and war resumed) were those of missions deployed long before the cease-fire. In many cases these missions were largely inactive and had been discredited by their earlier failures. The

---

[33] Walter 2001.
[34] This finding is not as strong when the Arab-Israeli conflict is controlled for. Deploying a larger number of peacekeepers seems to reduce the risk of another war, but this effect is not statistically significant (results not shown).

TABLE 20.4. *Individual Peace Mechanisms (Weibull Estimates)*

Variables	Coefficient (RSE)	Hazard ratio	Coefficient (RSE)	Hazard ratio
CONFIDENCE-BUILDING MEASURES	−0.18 (2.11)	0.83		
SPECIFICITY	−0.04*** (0.01)	0.96		
DISPUTE RESOLUTION				
Ongoing mediation			1.84*** (0.49)	6.27
Joint commission			−16.69*** (0.81)	0.000
FORMAL AGREEMENT			−0.69 (0.57)	0.50
TIE	3.57*** (0.33)	35.36	2.24*** (0.28)	9.35
COST OF WAR	−0.25 (0.28)	0.78	−0.31* (0.16)	0.73
HISTORY OF CONFLICT	0.52*** (0.13)	1.69	0.68*** (0.18)	1.97
EXISTENCE AT STAKE	3.24*** (0.57)	25.49	1.98*** (0.47)	7.21
CONTIGUOUS	1.93*** 0.28	6.89	1.16*** (0.27)	3.20
CHANGE IN RELATIVE CAPABILITIES	1.53*** (0.09)	4.63	1.08*** (0.18)	2.94
Constant	−12.18*** (2.73)		−10.49*** (2.95)	
Shape parameter *p*	1.08 (0.17)		1.07 (0.27)	
N	757		770	
Subjects	47		48	
Log likelihood	−37.64		−37.36	

Note: Negative coefficients and hazard ratios <1 indicate decrease in risk of another war (increase in duration of peace). Positive coefficients and hazard ratios >1 indicate increase in risk of another war (decrease in duration of peace).

RSE = robust standard errors.

*** $p \leq .01$.

** $p \leq .05$.

* $p \leq .10$. Two-tailed tests used.

UN Force in Cyprus (UNFICYP) had been deployed in 1964 to help keep peace between Turkish and Greek Cypriots in an internal conflict. It could do nothing to prevent military action by Turkey in 1974, nor was its presence effective in maintaining a cease-fire in the midst of the Turco-Cypriot War. Both the UN Truce Supervision Organization (UNTSO) in the Middle East and the UN Military Observer Group (UNMOGIP) in Kashmir were effective in the early years of their deployments, but after more bouts of fighting – in 1956 and especially 1967 in the Middle East, and in 1965 in Kashmir – these missions were rendered useless. Both missions remain in place today, but are inactive.

If one drops cases in which peacekeeping contingents were already deployed before the war (for example, keeping the first Arab-Israeli cease-fire when UNTSO was first established but dropping subsequent cases in which UNTSO is the only peacekeeping mission), one can see that new peacekeeping missions have been quite effective.[35] Of course, new peacekeeping missions are not foolproof, or there would never be old missions discredited by their failure to keep peace. But there is a large and statistically significant difference between cease-fires overseen by a fresh set of international peacekeepers and those without the benefit of peacekeeping.[36]

The jury is still out on the effectiveness of confidence-building measures, because they are relatively rare. The risk of another war appears to be lower in cases where measures such as notification of troop rotations or hotlines between military commanders have been implemented (see Table 20.4). But these measures have been employed in only a few cases, making it is possible that this finding is merely an artifact of the data.

I examined two types of dispute resolution between belligerents: that provided by ongoing third-party mediation after a cease-fire has been reached;[37] and joint commissions made up of representatives from both states in the war. The former is not an effective dispute resolution tool; in fact it is associated with peace that is significantly more likely to break down quickly. But joint commissions such as those set up after the

---

[35] Note that because almost all of the omitted cases are wars that ended with a decisive victory but were repeated, the hazard ratio for the variable tie is highly exaggerated.

[36] This finding contradicts the conclusions of Diehl, Reifschneider, and Hensel 1996; however, the results they report in Table 20.4 suggest that both active and operational involvement by the UN reduce the risk of another dispute.

[37] As opposed to mediation to reach a cease-fire, which was examined above.

Korean War, between Ethiopia and Somalia in 1988, or between El Salvador and Honduras in 1980, have been much more successful. The history of the armistice commissions between Israel and its Arab neighbors suggests that willingness to work within such a forum can provide an important signal of intentions. These commissions worked well in their early years to settle disputes over land use and fishing and farming rights, as well as to handle small incidents between soldiers. Conversely the breakdown of these regimes both signaled and contributed to increasing hostility on both sides.[38]

All else being equal, the more specific the cease-fire agreement, the longer peace tends to last. More specific agreements also tend to implement other measures to keep peace, but the finding that specificity reduces the hazard of another war holds up even when these other measures are controlled for. The most detailed agreements, such as the Korean Armistice and the Israeli-Egyptian peace agreement, have been followed by lasting peace. Cases of medium detail (China-India, the Gulf War, and the two Kashmir Wars, for example) have had mixed success, and the much less detailed agreements (for example, the Six Day War and the first Turco-Cypriot cease-fire) have tended to fail quickly. Demarcating the exact location of the cease-fire line put a halt to efforts on both sides to push for slight advantages in the early days of each cease-fire between India and Pakistan.[39] Of course, deliberate attacks cannot be stopped by specifying the location of the cease-fire line, but defining compliance can clearly help prevent skirmishing as both sides try to improve their positions.

Peace tends to last longer after formal agreements than after tacit or unilaterally declared cease-fires, all else being equal, but the difference is not significant statistically, nor terribly robust to different model specifications. Concern about international audience costs often plays a role in states' decisions about whether, when, and how to fight each other. India and Pakistan, for example, have both tried hard not to appear as the aggressor in their repeated wars, using proxy forces rather than regular troops to initiate hostilities.[40] These two states have also fought in

---

[38] For the history of these Military Armistice Commissions, see Azcárate 1966; Khouri 1963; and Kinsolving 1967.

[39] See UN document S/6710 and addenda, various dates 1965–66.

[40] Pakistan sent Azad Kashmir forces across the cease-fire line in 1965, successfully laying the blame for the war on India's retaliation. India learned the lesson and sponsored the Mukti Bahini insurgency in East Pakistan (Bangladesh) in 1971.

places where their formal agreement left loopholes, as on the Siachen Glacier in the early 1980s.[41]

However, formalizing a cease-fire may not be crucial for invoking international audience costs. The general norm against aggression means that costs may be paid even for breaking an informal cease-fire. The international reaction has often been muted, either by great powers turning a blind eye for strategic reasons (especially during the Cold War), or by a UN reluctant to threaten its impartiality by naming an aggressor.[42] Formalism may, therefore, not be the best way to test for the role of international audience costs.

In sum, arms control, third-party mediation, and attempts to control irregular forces have not helped maintain peace, and may in fact be associated with especially fragile peace. Confidence-building measures, formalizing an agreement, and withdrawal of forces may help, but the evidence to support their role is unclear. The most effective tools for maintaining peace in the aftermath of war are demilitarized zones, explicit third-party guarantees, peacekeeping, joint commissions for dispute resolution, and making the cease-fire specific.

Political Settlement

Not surprisingly, political agreement on the issues over which the war was fought leads to very durable peace (see Table 20.5). In fact, there are no cases in the wars examined here in which both sides agreed explicitly to a political settlement and war later resumed. But, as mentioned earlier, such settlement is quite rare in the post–World War II period. Only three wars led to an explicit agreement on the basic dispute over which the war was fought: the Yom Kippur War between Israel and Egypt; the Iran-Iraq War, in which Iraq conceded the Shatt al'-Arab waterway to secure its flank with the outbreak of the Gulf War; and the Gulf War itself, in which Iraq formally renounced its claim to Kuwait when it surrendered.[43] Wars that end leaving the basic issues unsettled, as in

---

[41] Lamb 1991, 325–26. The cease-fire line is not marked on the glacier, both because the territory is so inhospitable, and because specifying a terminus would require agreement on the disputed border with China.

[42] A blatant example of this was the UN's decision not to blame Pakistan for its role in starting the 1965 war with India. For Secretary General U Thant's rationale, see UN document S/6651 (3 September 1965), 7.

[43] In a few other cases, belligerents eventually settled their political conflict many years after the war ended, as Israel and Jordan did in 1994.

TABLE 20.5. *Political Settlement (Weibull Estimates)*

Variables	Coefficient (RSE)	Hazard ratio
POLITICAL SETTLEMENT	-15.34^{***} (1.02)	0.000
Imposed	-15.57^{***} (0.99)	
Agreed	2.94^{***} (0.47)	0.000
TIE	-0.66^{***} (0.18)	18.89
COST OF WAR	0.91^{***} (0.23)	0.52
HISTORY OF CONFLICT	1.55^{***} (0.45)	2.49
EXISTENCE AT STAKE	0.68^{*} (0.36)	4.73
CONTIGUOUS	0.81^{***} (0.24)	1.97
CHANGES IN RELATIVE CAPABILITIES	-4.96^{**} (2.50)	2.25
Constant	0.72^{*} (0.14)	
Shape parameter p	770	
N	48	
Subjects	-46.39	
Log likelihood		

Note: Negative coefficients and hazard ratios <1 indicate decrease in risk of another war (increase in duration of peace). Positive coefficients and hazard ratios >1 indicate increase in risk of another war (decrease in duration of peace).
RSE = robust standard errors.
*** $p \leq .01$.
** $p \leq .05$.
* $p \leq .10$. Two-tailed tests used.

the Korean Armistice, have been the norm rather than the exception. Even if one includes settlements imposed unilaterally by a decisive victor (but without official acceptance by the defeated side, as in the Falklands), settlement is rather rare.[44] This de facto category also appears to be quite

[44] The basic issue of the war has been settled unilaterally in eight wars (nine dyads) in these data: Russia-Hungary, China-India, Vietnam (North versus South), India and Pakistan in 1971, the second round of the Turco-Cypriot War, Uganda-Tanzania, the Falklands War, and the second part of the Azeri-Armenian War.

stable. None of these imposed settlements have failed.[45] Not surprisingly, settling the underlying political issues is the best way to ensure peace. But this advice is not particularly useful for most belligerents. When the underlying issues remain disputed, it is the other mechanisms examined in this study that can be used to maintain peace.

* * *

CONCLUSION

Are some war-torn areas simply doomed to repeated conflict and warfare, or is there something that can be done to improve the chances for peace? The findings of this article warrant optimism. Peace is hard to maintain among deadly enemies, but mechanisms implemented in the context of cease-fire agreements can help reduce the risk of another war. Peace is precarious, but it is possible. Agreements are not merely scraps of paper, their content affects whether peace lasts or war resumes.

The job of building peace is harder in some cases than in others. It is more difficult when wars end in stalemates, when states' previous history is riddled with conflict, and when war can threaten the very existence of one side. It seems to be harder for neighbors, but it is easier when states have just fought a very deadly war, giving a greater incentive to avoid further bloodshed.

But given these givens, states can act to improve the chances for peace. I have focused on measures that: alter incentives by raising the cost of an attack either physically or politically; reduce uncertainty by specifying compliance, regulating activities that are likely to cause tension, providing credible signals of intention; or help prevent or manage accidents from spiraling back to war. Do these measures help encourage durable peace? I find that, in general, they do. All else being equal, peace lasts longer when stronger agreements, implementing more of these measures, are in place. A counterargument suggests that strong agreements are only associated with durable peace because they are implemented in the easy cases. But the effects of agreements do not wash out when the baseline prospects for peace are controlled for.

While some international relations scholars might be surprised to learn that states can institute measures to overcome the obstacles to peace, practitioners probably know this already. For them, the value of this

---

[45] The imposed settlement between India and Pakistan in 1971 failed when they fought again in 1999 after our point of censoring.

research is in its lessons about which mechanisms work better than others. Because these measures are often implemented in conjunction with each other, one cannot reach conclusions about this that are as strong as one might like. But the history of cease-fires over the past half-century suggests that creating buffer zones between opposing armies is quite effective. Making the terms of the cease-fire, including the location of the cease-fire line, as specific as possible is also important, as is setting up joint commissions to discuss the inevitable conflicts and misunderstandings that arise in the aftermath of fighting. Confidence-building measures, formal agreements, and withdrawal of forces do not hurt, but the evidence that these measures help is less clear-cut.

For their part, outsiders interested in helping belligerents maintain peace can improve its chances by providing an explicitly stated guarantee of the cease-fire, and by deploying international monitors or troops as peacekeepers. But third parties should be aware that mediation to reach a cease-fire may be counterproductive in the long run. Peacekeeping can easily become discredited. Leaving a mission in place after it has failed does little to bolster the prospects for peace.

That states can implement measures to reduce the risk of another war raises the question of whether they can do more to prevent war breaking out in the first place. If demilitarized zones or peacekeeping can help maintain peace after war, can they do so beforehand? Obviously one cannot answer this question definitively without a wider study, but at least in theory, the measures discussed above should be effective pre-emptively. The challenge is likely to be in convincing states to implement them. It is normal, and therefore politically more acceptable, to take measures to ensure peace in the aftermath of war. Giving up territory to create a buffer zone or allowing international peacekeepers to infringe on their sovereignty before hostilities break out, of course, is more difficult.

Whether or not the measures examined here can help prevent war in the first place, I have shown that measures to reduce uncertainty, alter incentives, and manage accidents can help maintain peace in the hardest cases – among deadly enemies with strong incentives to take advantage of each other and in an atmosphere of deep mistrust. Maintaining peace is difficult, but even bitter foes can and do institute measures to avoid another war. Creating a durable peace requires work, but it is possible.

21

In the Shadow of Law or Power? Consensus-Based Bargaining and Outcomes in the GATT/WTO

Richard H. Steinberg

* * *

International organizations use one or a combination of three types of decision-making rules for most non-judicial action: "majoritarian" (decisions are taken by a majority vote of member states, and each member has one vote); "weighted voting" (decisions are taken by a majority or super-majority, with each state assigned votes or other procedural powers in proportion to its population, financial contribution to the organization, or other factors); or "sovereign equality." Organizations with these latter rules – which are rooted in a notion of sovereign equality of states derived from natural law theory and later adopted by positivists and others – formally negate status, offer equal representation and voting power in international organizations, and take decisions by consensus or unanimity of the members.[1] Organizations like the Association of Southeast Asian Nations (ASEAN), Conference on Security and Cooperation in Europe (CSCE), the Executive Committee of the International Monetary Fund (IMF), the GATT/WTO,[2] Common Market of the South, Mercado Comun del Sur (MERCOSUR), North Atlantic Treaty Organization (NATO), Organization for Economic Cooperation and Development (OECD), and many specialized agencies of the United Nations (UN), including the UN Development Program (UNDP) and the

* * *

[1] See Vattel 1852; Dickinson 1920, 51–55, 95–99, 335; Kelson 1944, 209; and Riches 1940, 9–12.

[2] GATT/WTO refers to both the General Agreement on Tariffs and Trade (GATT), and its successor, the World Trade Organization (WTO).

Executive Committee of the UN High Commission on Refugees (UNHCR), usually have taken decisions only with the consensus or unanimous support of member states. These organizations employ a host of procedures (described below) that purport to respect the sovereign equality of member states.

While sovereign equality decision-making rules are used widely in international organizations, the operation of those rules – how states behave in practice under them and the consequences of that behavior – is not well understood. Consensus decision making at the GATT/WTO and related procedural rules, which are based on the sovereign equality of states, raise three related questions about the relationship between state power and international law.

The first question is most striking. Why would powerful entities, like the EC[3] and the United States, support a consensus decision-making rule in an organization like the GATT/WTO, which generates hard law? There have been recent efforts to redefine the distinction between hard and soft law and to argue that soft law may be effective or might transform into hard law.[4] But conventionally the distinction has turned on whether or not the public international law in question is mandatory or hortatory; most public international lawyers, realists, and positivists consider soft law to be inconsequential.[5] Realists have long argued that – empirically – powerful countries permit majoritarianism only in organizations that are legally competent to produce only soft law, which poses little risk that powerful states would be bound by legal undertakings they might disfavor.[6] In contrast, in hard law organizations, structural realists, neoclassical realists, and behavioralists with realist sympathies have suggested that there must be a direct relationship between power, voting rules, and outcomes.[7] Yet in organizations with consensus decision-making rules, weaker countries have formal power to block the legislation of important hard law that would reflect the will of powerful countries. Structural realism would predict the collapse of organizations

---

[3] EC is used to refer to the European Community, the European Economic Community, or both. The European Economic Community was "seated" at GATT meetings from about 1960. Jackson 1969, 102. With conclusion of the Maastricht Treaty in 1992, the name changed from European Economic Community to European Community, which then became a member of the WTO at its inception in 1995.

[4] See, for example, Raustiala and Victor 1998; and Abbott and Snidal 2000.

[5] See Hart 1961, 77–96; and Simma and Paulus 1999, 304.

[6] See Riches 1940, 297, 894; Morgenthau 1978, 327; Zamora 1980; and Krasner 1983b.

[7] See Krasner 1983a; and Morgenthau 1978, 325–28.

with decision-making rules that can be used to stop powerful countries from getting their way – or a change in those rules, which structural realism treats as brittle.[8] Some modified structural realists have tried to explain exceptions to the expectation that decision-making rules would reflect underlying power, using institutional or sociological arguments.[9] However, mixing sociology and realism in this manner is theoretically degenerative,[10] and offers no prediction of when to expect rules to deviate from power or power to overtake institutional inertia.

The problem is solved partly by observing that the EC and the United States have dominated bargaining and outcomes at the GATT/WTO from its early years,[11] despite adherence to consensus decision-making. Yet that solution is only partial, as it suggests two more questions: How have the EC and the United States dominated GATT/WTO outcomes in the face of a consensus decision-making rule? And if such powerful states dominate GATT/WTO decision making, why have they bothered to maintain rules based on the sovereign equality of states, such as the consensus decision-making rule?

This article answers those questions, explaining how consensus decision making operates in practice in the GATT/WTO legislative context[12] and why the consensus rule has been maintained. First, the paper conceptualizes two modalities of bargaining – law-based and power-based – synthesizing previous work on these frameworks, giving them context in the GATT/WTO, and providing empirical examples of both forms of bargaining at the GATT/WTO. When GATT/WTO bargaining is law-based, states take procedural rules seriously, attempting to build a consensus that is Pareto-improving, yielding market-opening contracts that are roughly symmetrical. When GATT/WTO bargaining is power-based, states bring to bear instruments of power that are extrinsic to rules (instruments based primarily on market size), invisibly weighting[13] the decision-making process and generating outcomes that are asymmetrical and may not be Pareto-improving.

Second, the history of recent multilateral trade rounds is analyzed, identifying stages of rounds in which GATT/WTO legislative decision

---

[8] Krasner 1999.
[9] Krasner 1985, 29.
[10] See Popper 1959; Kuhn 1962; and Lakatos 1970, 173–80.
[11] Curzon and Curzon 1973.
[12] The analysis does not attempt to explain bargaining in the judicial context.
[13] Elizabeth McIntyre used this term in reference to U.S. power in the Havana Charter negotiations, but she did not elaborate the concept. McIntyre 1954, 491.

making has been primarily law-based and in which it has been primarily power-based. Since at least as far back as the Dillon Round, trade rounds have been launched through law-based bargaining that has yielded equitable, Pareto-improving contracts designating the topics to be addressed. In contrast, to varying degrees, rounds have been concluded through power-based bargaining that has yielded asymmetrical contracts favoring the interests of powerful states. The agenda-setting process (the formulation of proposals that are difficult to amend[14]), which takes place between launch and conclusion, has been dominated by powerful states; the extent of that domination has depended upon the extent to which powerful countries have planned to use their power to conclude the round.

Next, the paper explains why powerful countries have favored maintaining sovereign equality decision-making rules instead of adopting a weighted voting system, and why they carried them forward into the WTO. Analysis of the consensus decision-making process and interviews with GATT/WTO negotiators show that the rules generate information on state preferences that makes it possible to formulate legislative packages that favor the interests of powerful states, yet can be accepted by all participating states and generally considered legitimate by them.

This article concludes that the GATT/WTO consensus decision-making process is organized hypocrisy in the procedural context. Sociologists and political scientists have recently identified organized hypocrisy as patterns of behavior or action that are decoupled from rules, norms, scripts, or rituals that are maintained for external display.[15] The procedural fictions of consensus and the sovereign equality of states have served as an external display to domestic audiences to help legitimize WTO outcomes. The raw use of power that concluded the Uruguay Round may have exposed those fictions, jeopardizing the legitimacy of GATT/WTO outcomes and the decision-making rules, but weaker countries cannot impose an alternative rule. Sovereign equality decision-making rules persist at the WTO because invisible weighting assures that legislative outcomes reflect underlying power, and the rules help generate a valuable information flow to negotiators from powerful states. While theory suggests several potential challenges to the persistence of these patterns of bargaining and outcomes at the WTO, limits on transatlantic power pose the most serious challenges.

---

[14] See Tsebelis 1994; and Garrett and Tsebelis 1996.
[15] See Brunsson 1989, 7, 168; March 1994, 197–98; Meyer et al. 1997; and Krasner 1999.

BARGAINING AND OUTCOMES IN THE GATT/WTO:
TWO MODALITIES

Two meta-theoretical traditions help conceptualize bargaining and outcomes in the GATT/WTO: bargaining in the shadow of law and bargaining in the shadow of power. Empirically, legislative bargaining at the GATT/WTO usually takes one or a combination of these two forms.

Bargaining in the Shadow of Law: Contracting for Consensus at the GATT/WTO

In a law-based approach, bargaining power in international organizations is derived from substantive and procedural legal endowments. Decision-making rules determine voting or agenda-setting power, which shapes outcomes.

* * *

Sovereign Equality Decision-Making Rules at the GATT/WTO

To understand how law-based bargaining works in the GATT/WTO legislative context, it is crucial to know the procedural rules used there. In all plenary meetings of sovereign equality organizations, including the GATT/WTO, diplomats fully respect the right of any member state to: attend; intervene; make a motion; take initiatives (raise an issue); introduce, withdraw, or reintroduce a proposal (a legal text for decision) or amendment; and block the consensus or unanimous support required for action.[16] A consensus decision requires no manifested opposition to a motion by any member present.[17] If an empowered state representative fails to object to (or reserve a position on, or accept with qualification – for example, *ad referendum)* a draft at a formal meeting where it is considered, that state may be subjected to an argument that it is estopped by acquiescence from any subsequent objection to the draft.[18]

GATT decisions were not always taken by consensus. The GATT 1947 provided for voting: each contracting party had one vote, and no nation or class of nations was given formally superior voting power. The

---

[16] Schermers and Blokker 1995, 475–506.
[17] M'bow 1978.
[18] See Schwarzenberger 1957, 51, 95, 608–26; Bowett 1957; MacGibbon 1958, 476–80, 501–504, and Blackhurst 2001, 8.

General Agreement required different majorities of the Contracting Parties[19] for approval of different types of actions. ***

But GATT/WTO decision-making practice has differed from these formal requirements. From 1948 to 1959, the GATT often used an informal version of consensus decision making instead of formal voting. At least as early as 1953, and on several occasions thereafter, the chairman took a sense of the meeting instead of resorting to a vote. Since 1959, virtually all GATT/WTO legislative decisions (except on accessions and waivers) have been taken by consensus.[20]

The most common explanation for development of the consensus practice at the GATT is rooted in the *en masse* accession of developing countries beginning in the late 1950s. If a bloc of developing countries had formed, constituting a super-majority of the Contracting Parties, then that bloc might have been able to assume many of the legislative functions of the organization; would surely have been able to assume all of the administrative and judicial functions; and through its judicial power might have been able to legislate new obligations, even if all the industrialized countries stood together in opposition.[21] In that context, U.S. policymakers considered alternative voting rules, but rejected them for reasons ultimately related to the Cold War.[22] *** By the late 1950s, many in the U.S. Congress and State Department were concerned about the geopolitical alignment of developing countries, a concern that became even more pronounced in the trade context after Soviet efforts to strengthen the UN Conference on Trade and Development (UNCTAD) in the early 1960s. *** U.S. policymakers thought it would be impossible to reach agreement on a weighted voting formula and expand the GATT into a broad-based organization that could attract and retain developing countries. *** Finally, since the late 1940s, some U.S. trade negotiators had considered formal weighting unnecessary in light of influence over voting that was rooted in the underlying power of the United States.[23]

When the WTO was established, consensus decision making was not only retained, but was adopted as the formally preferred method of

---

[19] In this article, Contracting Parties refers to governments, acting jointly or in their individual capacities, that were applying the provisions of the GATT between 1948 and 1994.

[20] See Patterson and Patterson 1994; and Porges 1995.

[21] See Jackson 1969, 123–28; Porges 1995, 2; and Schermers and Blokker 1995, 514.

[22] This analysis is based on telephone interviews and conversations with Walter Hollis, Washington, D.C., December 1985; Richard Matheison, Washington, D.C., November 1989; and corroborating authorities cited below.

[23] Wilcox 1972, 195–97.

decision making: Article IX of the Agreement Establishing the World Trade Organization requires that only "where a decision cannot be arrived at by consensus, the matter shall be decided by voting." It defines consensus the same way it had been defined in GATT practice since 1959: a decision by consensus shall be deemed to have been taken on a matter submitted for consideration if no signatory, present at the meeting where the decision is taken, formally objects to the proposed decision. If there were recourse to voting in the WTO, Article IX provides that decisions would be taken by majority, two-thirds, or three-fourths vote – depending on the type of measure. But there has been no voting at the WTO.

Law-Based Bargaining at the GATT/WTO

Deductions from consensus or unanimity decision-making rules suggest that legislation will be Pareto-improving, obliging the "organ to seek a formula acceptable to all,"[24] since legislation that would make any state worse off would be blocked by that state. Moreover, the rules permit weak countries to block positive-sum outcomes that they deem to have an inequitable distribution of benefits. Experimental economics, and legal applications of it, have suggested that individuals will often decline acceptance of a positive-sum package if the benefits are distributed inequitably.[25] Equity has been, of course, a persistent international theme, particularly in postwar economic organizations, and developing countries have often blocked consensus in the GATT/WTO on grounds that a proposal did not sufficiently address their special and differential needs.

Bargaining and outcomes at the GATT/WTO have frequently assumed this pattern. The consensus-based decision to launch the Kennedy Round offers a simple example. In November 1961, as the Dillon Round was ending, the Contracting Parties decided by consensus to establish a new committee on tariff reductions and permit existing committees to continue addressing agriculture and less-developed country (LDC) preferences, respectively. Over the next year, however, no progress was made in any of the committees, with the committee on LDC preferences deadlocked along North-South lines. In late 1962, the U.S. government shifted its position on LDC preferences, declaring that a successful round would require simultaneous negotiation of the topics being considered in all three committees. On that basis, a consensus was reached to schedule a Ministerial Meeting in early 1963. In May 1963, the Ministers launched

[24] Riches 1940, 15.
[25] See Davis and Holt 1993; and Korobkin 2000.

the round, adopting by consensus a set of conclusions and recommendations embodying issues of interest to all Contracting Parties, and a resolution to establish a Trade Negotiations Committee composed of representatives of all participating countries.[26] The round was launched only after the developed countries agreed to include in the negotiations issues that had the potential to make all countries – including developing countries – better off.

Bargaining in the Shadow of Power: Invisible Weighting at the GATT/WTO

In contrast to the law-based approach, realists see most legislative bargaining and outcomes in international organizations as a function of interests and power.[27] Diplomatic memoirs and works by lawyers who have been employed in international organizations are replete with stories of using state power to achieve desired outcomes from international organizations.[28] *** This work suggests that it is possible for powerful states to simultaneously respect procedural rules and use various practices to escape the constraints on power apparently intrinsic to those rules.

Relative Market Size as an Underlying Source of Bargaining Power at the GATT/WTO

While measuring power is notoriously difficult, in trade negotiations, relative market size offers the best first approximation of bargaining power. Most political scientists suggest that governments treat foreign market opening (and associated increases in export opportunities) as a domestic political benefit and domestic market opening as a cost.[29] Hence, for example, the greater the export opportunities that can be attained, the greater the domestic political benefit to the government of the country attaining them. Market opening and closure have been treated as the currency of trade negotiations in the postwar era.[30]

Whether trade bargaining takes the form of mutual promises of market opening, threats of market closure, or a combination of both, larger, developed markets are better endowed than smaller markets in trade

---

[26] Conclusions and Resolutions adopted on 21 May 1963, in General Agreement on Tariffs and Trade, *Basic Instruments and Selected Documents: 12th Supplement* (1964), 36–48 (hereafter GATT BISD).

[27] See Morgenthau 1940; Krasner 1983a,b; and Schachter 1999.

[28] See Kennan 1972, 24; and Wilcox 1972, 195–97.

[29] See Schattschneider 1935; Bauer, de Sola Pool, and Dexter 1963; and Putnam 1988.

[30] See Hirchman 1945; Waltz 1970; and Krasner 1976.

negotiations. The proportionate domestic economic and political impact of a given absolute change in trade access varies inversely with the size of a national economy. Larger national economies have better internal trade possibilities than smaller national economies. A given volume of trade liberalization (measured in dollar terms, for example) offers proportionately more welfare and net employment gain to smaller countries than to larger ones. The political implication is that a given volume of liberalization offers proportionately less domestic political benefit to the government delivering it in the larger country. * * *

Conversely, in negotiations entailing threats of trade closure, a threat of losing a given volume of exports is a relatively less potent tactic when used against a larger country than when used against a smaller one. Hence, it is well established that developed economies with big markets have great power in an open trading system by virtue of variance in the relative opportunity costs of closure for trading partners.[31]

* * *

While market size is generally a good indicator of trade bargaining power, the possibility of linkage across issue areas potentially limits its usefulness. The value of market size as an approximation of trade bargaining power is diminished to the extent that states are willing to use non-trade sources of leverage. * * * While the extent of linkage across issue areas has been a subject of theoretical and empirical debate for decades, regime theory suggests that, within a particular regime, bargaining can usually be best understood as confined to the particular issue area addressed by the regime.[32] Moreover, most empirical analyses of postwar trade policy have suggested that potential military or financial leverage has not been used in trade negotiations.[33] * * *

Using market size as a measure of trade bargaining power, the EC and the United States are the world's greatest powers. As rough indicators, consider that in 1994 (the year the Uruguay Round was closed) retained merchandise imports into the EC and the United States accounted for approximately 40 percent of all retained merchandise imports in the world,[34] and that the EC-U.S. combined 1994 gross domestic product (GDP) represented nearly half the world's total GDP.[35] By this measure,

---

[31] Krasner 1976.
[32] Haas 1980.
[33] See Krasner 1976; Cohen 1985; and Hoekman 1989.
[34] World Trade Organization 1995, 26, table II.3.
[35] See Central Intelligence Agency 1995; and World Trade Organization 1995, 54, table III.30.

the combined power of the EC and the United States is enormous in the trade context. And to the extent that the EC and the United States can cooperate, they wield great influence in multilateral trade negotiations.[36]

Power Tactics at the GATT/WTO: Asymmetrical Contracting and Coercion

It is useful to think of a range of power tactics that influence outcomes in the GATT/WTO. First, powerful states may contract asymmetrically, generating consensus support for outcomes that are skewed in their favor. When aimed at an individual state, this contracting may be considered a "side-payment." * * *

Second, and more important than asymmetrical contracting for understanding GATT/WTO bargaining and outcomes, weaker states may be coerced by powerful states into consensus support of measures skewed in their favor. By threatening to make weaker states worse off, coercion may generate consensus for an outcome that makes powerful states better off and weaker states worse off,[37] or that is Pareto-improving but with benefits distributed in favor of powerful states. * * *

When aimed at a group of states – and in its most potent form – coercion takes the form of a threat to exit[38] the organization that is unable to achieve consensus. In some cases, exit involves moving (or threatening to move) the issue to another organization where powerful countries are more likely to get their way. For example, in the early 1980s, when the EC and the United States were unable to attain the required majority in the World Intellectual Property Organization for broader intellectual property protection, they moved the issue to the GATT, where they were able to conclude the Trade-Related Aspects of Intellectual Property Rights (TRIPs) Agreement in 1994.[39] In other cases, the exit tactic may involve simply ignoring the deadlocked organization and creating a new organization that will become a source of future legal benefit in the issue area. * * *

In still another variant, the exit tactic involves withdrawing from the deadlocked organization, stepping into anarchy, and reconstituting a new organization under different terms. As shown below, this is the means by which the EC and the United States closed the Uruguay Round.

[36] Steinberg 1999.
[37] Gruber 2001.
[38] Hirschman 1970, 21–29.
[39] Beier and Schricker 1989.

TRADE ROUNDS AS CYCLES BOUNDED BY LAW-BASED AND POWER-BASED BARGAINING: LAUNCHING, AGENDA SETTING, AND CLOSING TRADE ROUNDS

Trade negotiating rounds are the means by which the vast proportion of GATT/WTO law has been legislated. Bargaining in the Tokyo and Uruguay rounds is analyzed here to understand the extent to which bargaining in trade rounds has been law- or power-based. These most recent trade rounds are most likely to exemplify a representative range of law- and power-based bargaining, largely because prior to 1970 the GATT was dominated by an "anti-legal" culture that began to melt away in the late 1960s and did not completely collapse until the early 1980s.[40]

As shown below, the extent to which negotiations in trade rounds have been law- or power-based has depended on the stage of the round and geostrategic context. Trade rounds may be analyzed in three overlapping stages: launching, informal agenda setting, and closing. Generally, power has been used more overtly as rounds have proceeded from launch to conclusion, with the extent of coercion used in closing the Tokyo Round constrained by the Cold War context.

Launching Trade Rounds through Law-Based Bargaining

The easiest way to launch a round has been to attain consensus on a vague mandate for negotiation that includes virtually all initiatives offered by any member. This approach has enabled all parties to believe that the round could result in a Pareto-improving and equitable package of outcomes, with domestic political liabilities from increased import competition offset by foreign market opening. Negotiators typically haggle over alternative ways to frame issues and objectives in the mandate, but – to reach consensus – the less prejudice in the mandate, the better. In some rounds, there have been one or two issues that simply could not appear in the mandate because of domestic political constraints. But typically, a consensus on the draft negotiating mandate has been blocked until virtually all topics of interest to members have been included, and until the language has been sufficiently vague so as not to prejudice the outcome of negotiations in a manner that any country might oppose. From the perspective of powerful countries, invisible weighting could be used at later stages. Moreover, only at later stages, after years of negotiations, will powerful countries have enough information on state

---

[40] See Hudec 1988; and Price 1992.

preferences to fashion a package of asymmetric outcomes that they can be confident will be accepted by weaker countries. Hence, bargaining to launch trade rounds has been law-based.

In preparing to launch each of the last five rounds, there has been a North-South split over the pace, form, or structure of liberalization. Each time, the developing countries have demanded a mandate for negotiations that would include special and differential treatment. Developed countries have initially resisted including developing country initiatives in the decision to launch. But the legal power of developing countries to block a consensus has led to the inclusion of their initiatives in the consensus decisions to launch the Dillon, Kennedy, Tokyo, Uruguay, and Doha rounds.

* * *

Informal Agenda Setting in the Shadow of Closure

Many have argued that in legislative settings where authority to set the agenda (that is, formulate proposals that are difficult to amend) rests with a formally specified agent, the process of agenda setting explains outcomes better than plenary voting power.[41] In contrast, in organizations based on sovereign equality, the agenda-setting function is performed informally, largely by the coordinated action of the major powers and a secretariat that is strongly influenced by them.

The GATT/WTO agenda-setting process has three overlapping stages: (1) carefully advancing and developing *initiatives* that broadly conceptualize a new area or form of regulation; (2) drafting and fine-tuning *proposals* (namely, legal texts) that specify rules, principles, and procedures; and (3) developing a *package* of proposals into a "final act" for approval upon closing the round, which requires the major powers to match attainment of their objectives with the power they are willing and able to use to establish consensus. The agenda-setting process involves iteratively modifying proposals in minor ways (for example, providing a derogation, floor, or phase-in),[42] fulfilling unrelated or loosely related objectives of weaker countries (that is, promising side-payments), and adjusting the package that will constitute the final act. After being launched, the work of trade rounds has taken place on a formal basis in proposal-specific working

---

[41] See, for example, Baron and Ferejohn 1989; Garrett and Tsebelis 1996; and Moravcsik 1998, 67–77.

[42] On use of these techniques in the EC, see Esty and Geradin 1997, 550–56.

groups, negotiating committees, the Trade Negotiations Committee, the GATT Council, special sessions of the Contracting Parties, and occasional ministerials. But important work takes place on an informal basis in caucuses, the most important of which are convened and orchestrated by the major powers. The process has historically operated in the shadow of the coercive power of the EC and the United States.

Most initiatives, proposals, and alternative packages that evolve into documents presented for formal approval have usually been developed first in Brussels and Washington, discussed informally by the transatlantic powers, then in increasingly larger caucuses (for example, Quad countries, G-7, OECD), and ultimately in the "Green Room." Green Room caucuses consist of twenty to thirty-five countries that are interested in the particular text being discussed and include the most senior members of the secretariat, diplomats from the most powerful members of the organization, and diplomats from a roughly representative subset of the GATT/WTO's membership. The agenda for most important formal meetings – round-launching ministerials, mid-term reviews, and round-closing ministerials – has been set in Green Room caucuses that usually take place in the weeks preceding and during those meetings. The draft that emerges from the Green Room is presented to a formal plenary meeting of the GATT/WTO members and is usually accepted by consensus without amendment or with only minor amendments.[43]

The EC and the United States have dominated advancing initiatives at the GATT/WTO for at least forty years.[44] Both weak and powerful countries may advance initiatives, and they may be included in the ministerial declaration that launches a round. But initiatives from weak countries have a habit of dying: after launching the Tokyo and Uruguay rounds, powerful countries often blocked a consensus to advance initiatives by weak countries when they were introduced for formal action in the relevant negotiating committee.[45] Moreover, weak countries are

---

[43] See Winham 1989, 54; Blackhurst 1998; and WTO General Council, Chairman's Statement, Internal Transparency and the Effective Participation of Members, 17 July 2000.

[44] Curzon and Curzon 1973.

[45] For example, while the declarations that launched both the Tokyo and Uruguay rounds called for "Tropical Products" liberalization and "special and differential treatment" for developing countries, most developing country initiatives in these areas died in the relevant negotiating groups, and the results in these areas disappointed developing countries. Winham 1986. In the Uruguay Round, developing country initiatives and proposals in the TRIPs negotiating group were "dead on arrival." Interview with Emery Simon, Washington, D.C., April 1994.

usually excluded from the initial informal caucuses at which powerful countries discuss with each other their important initiatives.[46]

Powerful countries have also dominated proposal development. Successful proposals have usually been drafted first in the capitals of powerful countries – Brussels or Washington. They have then been discussed informally in caucuses of the major powers, and then in other caucuses that include some less powerful countries.[47] In the Tokyo and Uruguay rounds, after the mid-term review, proposals and frameworks for negotiation that had been discussed informally in caucuses were then introduced into the formal working group meetings. *** Weaker countries rarely tabled draft texts. Tabled texts typically contained unbracketed language that all countries could accept and bracketed language representing alternative formulations favored by different groups of countries. The bracketed language became the subject of detailed negotiation in working groups and – ultimately – in the Green Room prior to and during ministerials.

Simultaneous with initiative and proposal development, powerful countries have considered the package of proposals that should be included in the final act for approval upon conclusion of a round. The package has changed depending largely on how the proposals were shaping up and how much coercion was to be exercised by powerful countries.

The secretariat has usually facilitated this process and has often engaged directly in it by tabling proposals or a package as its own. The secretariat's bias in favor of great powers has been largely a result of who staffs it and the shadow of power under which it works. ***

The End of the Day: Power-Based Bargaining in Closing Trade Rounds – and the Cold War Context as a Constraint

In closing a round, the EC and the United States must employ invisible weighting if they are to achieve an asymmetrical outcome. The decision about how much power to use to facilitate a desired outcome in a particular issue area may be linked to interests in another issue area or to geostrategic context. At the end of both the Tokyo and Uruguay rounds, there was temptation to resort to exit. Both rounds included an

---

[46] Winham 1986. This is typical in consensus-based organizations. Schermers and Blokker 1995, 501–502.

[47] This process is typical in consensus-based organizations. See M'bow 1978; and Schermers and Blokker 1995, 502.

ambitious set of nearly completed agreements covering topics that went far beyond the traditional tariff-cutting protocols of earlier years. Reaching consensus on such an ambitious package would be difficult if only contracting could be used. Yet U.S. trade negotiators ultimately decided not to exit in closing the Tokyo Round and to instead contract through law-based bargaining. In the Uruguay Round, they made the opposite decision, choosing to coerce by exiting the GATT and reconstituting the system. The difference in choices is attributable ultimately to the Cold War context: U.S. policymakers, particularly in the Department of State, maintained a trade policy-security policy contextual linkage that constrained the U.S. use of power in concluding the Tokyo Round;[48] this linkage did not operate in closing the Uruguay Round.

Closing the Tokyo Round

In the summer of 1978, as the Tokyo Round was about to close, [several developing country leaders] argued that the GATT decision-making rules endowed the developing countries with substantial leverage in determining the final shape of the Tokyo Round codes. They reasoned that the codes being negotiated on dumping, subsidies, and customs valuation could be considered interpretations of the GATT, which would therefore require support by a consensus of the Contracting Parties. Moreover, these developing countries offered an interpretation that the benefits of those codes had to be provided to all GATT Contracting Parties on an MFN basis, in accordance with GATT Article I, because they constituted interpretations of GATT Articles VI, XVI, and XXIII. Finally, the GATT secretariat could not provide services to administer a code without a consensus of the Contracting Parties. In August 1978, the legal department of the UNCTAD secretariat prepared a memorandum that synthesized this legal analysis.[49] * * *

The Tokyo Round outcome reflected the success of this legal strategy: the developing countries received all of the rights to the subsidies code and the anti-dumping code, but they were not obligated to sign or

---

[48] This argument is based on authorities cited below and interviews or conversations in Washington, D.C., in either December 1985, November 1989–February 1990, or July 2000, with Walter Hollis, Richard Matheison, Peter Murphy, and Doug Newkirk (who worked at STR at the close of the Tokyo Round), and Chip Roh and Jerry Rosen (who worked at the Department of State during that period).

[49] Legal and Procedural Questions on the Conclusion of the MTN, Memorandum From the UNCTAD Secretariat, 21 August 1978, UNCTAD Doc. MTN/CB.14.

otherwise abide by the obligations contained in those agreements.[50] The developed countries had objected strenuously to what they characterized as a "free ride" for the developing countries. But in a legal bind, the developed countries acquiesced: the decision of the Contracting Parties on administration of the subsidies code and the antidumping code obtained the necessary consensus by reflecting the commitment to apply them on an MFN basis.[51] * * *

U.S. trade negotiators were disturbed by these outcomes, which many thought could have been avoided by the use of more potent bargaining tactics. * * * Some special Trade Representative (STR) negotiators wanted to break the developing countries' law-based leverage by threatening to create an alternative preferential regime, proposing to move all or part of the negotiations to the OECD and concluding the round as something akin to a GATT-Plus package. In 1974, when the round was just beginning, the Atlantic Council had proposed establishment of a GATT-Plus regime. The plan provided that the EC, the United States, and most industrialized countries would deepen trade liberalization among themselves, extending the benefits of the arrangements only to those willing to undertake the obligations.[52] The result would have been a two-tiered global trade regime, which would quietly pressure the developing countries into liberalizing or otherwise facing the trade and investment diversion associated with the more liberal GATT-Plus regime.[53]

The approach was controversial within the STR's office, but the U.S. State Department killed it. * * * The State Department was strongly opposed on the grounds that such an action risked hardening the "UNCTADization" of the GATT, diplomatic spillovers into other

[50] As of 1990, only thirteen of the more than seventy-five developing country Contracting Parties to the GATT had accepted the subsidies code, and only fifteen had accepted the anti-dumping code. Multilateral Trade Negotiations: Status of Acceptances of Protocols, Agreements and Arrangements (as at 7 December 1990), GATT Doc. L/6453/Add. 8, 10 December 1990.

[51] Action By the Contracting Parties on the Multilateral Trade Negotiations, 28 November 1979, and Differential and More Favourable Treatment, Reciprocity and Fuller Participation of Developing Countries, Decision of 28 November 1979, in GATT BSID *26th Supplement*, (1980), 201, 203–205. The United States Congress did not faithfully implement the international commitments: U.S. law accorded the injury test in countervailing duties cases only to "countries under the [Subsidies Code] Agreement." Tariff Act of 1930, as amended by Section 101 of the Trade Agreements Act of 1979. As a result of this contravention, the Executive Branch had to compensate several countries, including India, with a package of commercial concessions.

[52] Atlantic Council 1976.

[53] Hufbauer 1989. See generally, Viner 1950.

international organizations, and disturbance of diplomatic relations with developing countries more broadly – all of which were undesirable in the Cold War context in which the United States did not want to alienate developing countries.[54] *** With State Department opposition, it was apparent to STR negotiators that the Trade Policy Committee could not reach the consensus required to support a formal diplomatic threat of exit.[55]

*** When it became apparent to the developing countries, in spring 1979, that the transatlantic powers would ultimately not exercise power to force them on board, the Tokyo Round was closed with law-based bargaining, yielding a final package that gave developing countries a free ride on many agreements.

Closing the Uruguay Round: The Single Undertaking[56]

In contrast, by the time USTR negotiators settled on a plan for concluding the Uruguay Round, the Cold War had ended and the State Department had dropped its opposition to an overt use of power.

Since the beginning of the Uruguay Round negotiations, most developing countries had stated their intention not to sign on to the agreements on TRIPs, TRIMs, or the General Agreement on Trade in Services (GATS). U.S. negotiators considered developing country acceptance of these agreements crucial to U.S. interests and to Congressional support of a final package. Moreover, the EC and the United States were concerned that the developing countries would use their leverage under the

---

[54] This analysis is consistent with arguments by others that U.S. Cold War policy sought to avoid alienating developing countries and so led to their free-riding. See Krasner 1976; and Gilpin 1981.

[55] Without such a consensus, U.S. law on and practice in the interagency trade policy process would have required a Presidential decision on the matter. See Section 242 of the Trade Expansion Act of 1962, as amended, 19 U.S.C 1801; amended by P.L. 93–618; and 40 Fed. Reg. 18419, 28 April 1975. STR officials were unwilling to take the matter to the President.

[56] The analysis in this section is based on interviews or conversations with several European, U.S., and GATT/WTO Secretariat officials, including Julius Katz, Washington, D.C., August–December 1990, and March 1995; Horst Krenzler, Los Angeles, September 1999; and Warren Lavorel, Washington, D.C., August–December 1990, and Geneva, March 1995; and several U.S. government documents, including the following memoranda (on file with author): Memorandum to UR Negotiators and Coordinators, Preliminary Legal Background on Ending the Uruguay Round, From USTR General Counsel, 1 December 1989; Memorandum for Ambassador Warren Lavorel and Ambassador Rufus Yerxa, A Single Protocol for Concluding the Round, From USTR General Counsel and Deputy General Counsel, 20 July 1990; and Memorandum for General Counsel's Office, Options for Concluding the Round, 13 August 1990.

consensus tradition of the GATT to block the secretariat from servicing those agreements unless they were applied to both signatories and non-signatories on an MFN basis.

In late spring of 1990, USTR negotiators decided to try to build a U.S. government consensus on what some at USTR referred to internally as "the power play," a tactic that would force the developing countries to accept the obligations of all the Uruguay Round agreements. The State Department supported the approach and, in October 1990, it was presented to EC negotiators, who agreed to back it. The plan was later to be characterized as the single undertaking approach to closing the round. Specifically, as embodied in the Uruguay Round Final Act, the Agreement Establishing the WTO contains "as integral parts" and "binding on all Members": the GATT 1994; the GATS; the TRIPs Agreement; the TRIMs Agreement; the Subsidies Agreement; the Anti-dumping Agreement; and every other Uruguay Round multilateral agreement. The Agreement also states that the GATT 1994 "is legally distinct from the General Agreement on Tariffs and Trade, dated 30 October 1947 . . ." After joining the WTO (including the GATT 1994), the EC and the United States withdrew from the GATT 1947 and thereby terminated their GATT 1947 obligations (including its MFN guarantee) to countries that did not accept the Final Act and join the WTO. The combined legal/political effect of the Final Act and transatlantic withdrawal from the GATT 1947 would be to ensure that most of the Uruguay Round agreements had mass membership rather than a limited membership.

GATT Director-General Arthur Dunkel agreed to embed the plan in the secretariat's draft Final Act, which was issued in December 1991. From that time forward, it remained in all negotiating drafts, enabling the transatlantic partners to more completely dominate the agenda-setting process in the Uruguay Round than in the Tokyo Round.

MAINTAINING SOVEREIGN EQUALITY RULES TO GENERATE INFORMATION ABOUT THE INTERESTS OF ALL STATES

As shown below, at the GATT/WTO, powerful states have used invisible weighting to define not only substantive rules, but also future decision-making rules. Powerful countries could choose either weighted voting or sovereign equality rules to achieve asymmetric outcomes. But sovereign equality rules are more likely than weighted voting to confer legitimacy on those outcomes. Whether or not that legitimacy sticks, sovereign equality rules are more useful than weighted voting in generating information that is crucial to agenda setting dominated by powerful states, and that can lead to a package acceptable to all states.

International legislative outcomes generated from a consensus-based system may enjoy more legitimacy than those from a weighted voting system.[57] *** The legitimizing effect of sovereign equality rules on outcomes may be particularly pronounced for domestic audiences, as opposed to trade negotiators who have witnessed invisible weighting first-hand.

The asymmetry of outcomes derived through invisible weighting risks undermining the legitimacy of the outcomes and the decision-making rules. Yet developing countries do not determine what the decision-making rules will be. Powerful states have preferred sovereign equality rules to weighted voting in the GATT/WTO because they provide incentives and opportunities for collecting the information necessary for a successful agenda-setting process. Several political scientists have shown how international organization secretariats[58] and non-governmental organizations (NGOs)[59] may collect and transmit information that leads to efficiency in policymaking – or influence over it.[60] Law scholars have shown how alternative deliberative procedures in business organizations, among appellate judges, between litigants, and in other organizations may be used to generate efficiency-enhancing information.[61] The task of a powerful country negotiator in GATT/WTO agenda setting is to develop a final act that will maximize fulfillment of her country's objectives, given the power that her country can use to attain consent from all states – a process that one WTO official has described as "filling the boat to the brim, but not overloading it."[62] The agenda setters from powerful states must have good information about each country's preferences, the domestic politics behind those preferences, and risk tolerances – across all of the topics that might be covered – to understand potential zones of agreement on a package acceptable to all.[63] To be most useful, the available information must be sincere and not provided for strategic purposes (that is, not for purposes of yielding

---

[57] See Zamora 1980; and Gold 1972, 201.

[58] See Keohane 1983 and 1984.

[59] Raustiala 1997.

[60] See Haas 1989; and Bernauer 1995.

[61] See Charny 1997; Bainbridge 1998; and Caminker 1999.

[62] Telephone interview with Warren Lavorel, Geneva, March 1995.

[63] Kenneth Arrow has argued that welfare-maximizing decision making by consensus requires that each party have information about every other party's preferences, whereas authority decision making requires only that the decision maker have information about every party's preferences. Arrow 1974, 69.

an outcome that would make the information provider better off than if he or she had provided sincere information).[64]

The GATT/WTO secretariat can at best transmit incomplete information for use in agenda setting. Generally, large, branching hierarchies like the GATT/WTO secretariat are unlikely to promote complete information generation and transmission.[65] Moreover, the GATT/WTO secretariat usually lacks authority or political power to force a revelation of state preferences, and states are often reluctant to rely on the secretariat to transmit information that may be crucial to explaining their negotiating objectives and domestic political constraints, efforts aimed at shaping perceptions of the bargaining zone. ***

Under the consensus rule, diplomats from powerful states have incentives to obtain accurate information on the preferences of weaker states: they need to understand those preferences if they are to fashion a substantive package and design legal-political maneuvers that will lead to outcomes acceptable to all. In contrast, a weighted voting scheme can, under certain circumstances, permit a handful of powerful states to routinely determine outcomes without considering the interests of weaker states. *** Some commentators have suggested that the Executive Committee of the IMF adopted an informal consensus decision-making rule because use of its formal weighted voting rules had led to a pattern of exclusionary decision making, limited information generation, and outcomes that disregarded weaker country interests.[66]

Conversely, under the consensus rule, diplomats from weaker states have opportunities and incentives to provide information on preferences to powerful states. If weaker states perceive that the information they provide will be taken into account by the major powers in their agenda-setting work, then weaker states have an incentive to offer detailed information about their preferences. Even if many weaker states perceive that some of their preferences will be ignored, they would have difficulty sustaining a cooperative strategy of obstructing the information-gathering process because of wide variance in their interests across issue areas, and defensive and offensive incentives to provide the information.[67] A weak country that tries to resist the agenda-setting process by withholding information on its preferences risks suffering a *fait*

---

[64] See Charny 1997; and Caminker 1999.
[65] Bainbridge 1998, 1036.
[66] See M'bow 1978, 898; Schermers and Blokker 1995, 514; and Gold 1972, 195–200.
[67] Stein 1993.

accompli in the form of a final package that does not take into account its interests; such a final package instead would take into account the interests of other weak states that do provide information.

Moreover, in some circumstances, sovereign equality procedures may help generate important information by forcing a revelation of sincere state preferences. Powerful countries offer initiatives, proposals, amendments, or "non-papers" not only in the hope of hearing a favorable response but also as a "probe" intended to engender an informative response. Whenever a probe is tabled, a state opposed to any part of it must block consensus or that state risks an argument that it is estopped by acquiescence from subsequently opposing the text.[68] The consequences of an argument of estoppel by acquiescence range from the persuasive to the peremptory according to the circumstances.[69] Hence, failure to block consensus by a participating state may sometimes be a non-strategic transmission of information implying a sincere unwillingness to oppose it.

While consensus-blocking could be strategic, insincerity carries risks of retributive behavior by other diplomats and loss of trust in future deliberations.[70] Moreover, the reliability and accuracy of diplomatic statements opposing a proposal made in Geneva are often investigated by the intelligence services of powerful countries or by their diplomats stationed in the capital of the country whose representative made the statement. *** Thus state responses to specific initiatives, proposals, and amendments tabled by powerful countries – the act of opposing or not opposing a consensus, associated explanations, and offers of amendments – generate information for refinement by agenda setters, part of a progressive and iterative dynamic of information generation and proposal refinement.

* * *

Interviews with EC and U.S. diplomats who discussed alternative decision-making rules for the WTO confirm that legitimacy and information generation for drafting agreements acceptable to all were important reasons they decided to maintain consensus decision making – indeed to formalize it in the Agreement Establishing the WTO.[71] ***

---

[68] On estoppel by acquiescence, generally, see the discussion above corresponding to n. 31.

[69] See MacGibbon 1958, 502; and Bowett 1957.

[70] Charny 1997, 17.

[71] Interviews or conversations with Ambassador Julius Katz, Washington, D.C., August–December 1990 and March 1995; Horst Krenzler, Los Angeles, September 1999; Ambassador Warren Lavorel, Washington, D.C., August–December 1990, and via telephone to Geneva, March 1995; and others from the European Commission and USTR.

* * *

CONCLUSION: THE ORGANIZED HYPOCRISY OF CONSENSUS DECISION MAKING – AND ITS LIMITS

GATT/WTO decision-making rules based on the sovereign equality of states are organized hypocrisy in the procedural context.[72] The transatlantic powers have simultaneously dominated GATT/WTO legislative bargaining outcomes and supported the consensus decision-making rule – and related rules – that are based on the sovereign equality of states. The GATT/WTO decision-making rules have allowed adherence to both the instrumental reality of asymmetrical power and the logic of appropriateness of sovereign equality.[73] Trade rounds may be launched by law-based bargaining, but powerful states have dominated agenda setting, and rounds have been concluded in the shadow of power – to varying degrees. GATT/WTO sovereign equality decision-making rules and processes help generate crucial information for powerful states to use in the invisible weighting process, and have helped legitimize GATT/WTO bargaining and outcomes for domestic audiences. Instead of generating a pattern of Pareto-improving outcomes deemed equitable by all states, GATT/WTO sovereign equality decision-making rules may be combined with invisible weighting to produce an asymmetric distribution of outcomes of trade rounds.

Distributive Consequences

In the Tokyo Round, transatlantic capacity combined with uncertainty about whether the EC and the United States might opt for a preferential regime to yield an outcome that has been criticized as ignoring the interests of developing countries[74] – even though contextual issue-linkage attributable to the Cold War dampened U.S. willingness to coerce a more highly asymmetrical outcome. The raw use of power to close the Uruguay Round via the single undertaking best exemplifies transatlantic domination of the GATT/WTO, despite the sovereign equality decision-making rules there. *** [It] is hard to argue that developing countries uniformly enjoyed net domestic political benefits from the

---

[72] Krasner has concluded that Westphalian sovereignty is organized hypocrisy. Krasner 1999. Sovereign equality decision-making rules are corollaries of Westphalian sovereignty. See Dickinson 1920, 335; Riches 1940, 9–12; Kelson 1944, 209; and Remec 1960, 56.

[73] March and Olsen 1998.

[74] See, for example, Winham 1986, 375–79, 387–88.

nontariff agreements: they assumed new obligations in the TRIPs and TRIMs agreements, the GATS, and the Understanding on Balance-of-Payments Provisions of the GATT 1994 – which most long opposed; they gained nothing of significance from the revised subsidies and anti-dumping agreements; and they were required to assume the obligations of those two agreements – in contrast to the Tokyo Round codes, which had voluntary membership. And while the Textiles Agreement provides for elimination of quotas on textiles and apparel, it is heavily back-loaded and U.S. tariff peaks of around 15 per cent on those products were not eliminated. Most developing countries got little and gave up a lot in the Uruguay Round[75] – yet they signed on.

* * *

This analysis does not suggest that developing countries have not benefited from GATT/WTO participation or from liberalization more broadly. But as measured by their own objectives going into the last two rounds, their complaints about the shortcomings of the outcomes of those rounds, and informed by the analysis above, it is hard to conclude that developing country negotiators are – on the whole – nearly as pleased as their EC and U.S. counterparts with negotiating outcomes at the GATT/WTO. And it appears that some developing country negotiators now consider their countries worse off as a result of the Uruguay Round agreements than they were under the status quo ante.

Limits on the Organized Hypocrisy of Consensus Decision Making at the GATT/WTO

Is this pattern of bargaining and outcomes likely to be sustained over time? The Doha Round was recently launched in a familiar pattern, and the Doha Ministerial Declaration states that the negotiation will be closed through a single undertaking. Yet theory suggests several potential limits to invisible weighting at the WTO and to the organized hypocrisy of sovereign equality decision making, more broadly.

Several possibilities suggested by theory seem unlikely to materialize in the short run. One possibility is that the principle of sovereign equality could take on a life of its own, precluding any political action that contradicts it. Just as norms limit realist regimes theory,[76] they could

---

[75] See Ramakrishna 1998; Srinivasan 1998, 99–101; and Oloka-Onyango and Udagama 2000.

[76] Krasner 1983b.

limit invisible weighting. While theory suggests this possibility, process-tracing, memoirs, interviews, and secondary histories of the GATT/WTO offer no evidence that normative considerations have thus far precluded the eventual equilibration of outcomes with power that is explained by invisible weighting.

Another possibility is that GATT Contracting Parties and WTO members have been willing to use sovereign equality rules – and have not deadlocked the organization – only because they have agreed implicitly to move together in an embedded neoliberal[77] direction. *****

Still another possibility is that even when powerful states identify a common interest to pursue in negotiations with weaker countries, cooperation problems between major powers could inhibit their effective use of power tactics and their domination of agenda setting, resulting in outcomes that do not reflect the common interests of powerful states. Game theoretical analyses have suggested, from the earliest work on the subject, that serious cooperation problems will exist in multi-party negotiations.[78] Failure to employ collaborative solutions to cooperation problems (for example, sequencing or packaging issues) has at times constrained the effective use of power tactics and agenda setting by the transatlantic powers.[79] But the packaging of topics in trade rounds as the usual *modus operandi* of GATT/WTO legislation has generally solved this cooperation problem.

Finally, substantial transaction costs of exit could constrain use of the most potent forms of coercion.[80] There was little financial cost in exiting from the GATT and creating the WTO. While there may have been some political costs, these seem relatively low. The organized hypocrisy heuristic suggests that exposure of the mismatch between behavior (on one hand) and norms, scripts, or rituals (on the other) can engender disorder. Such disorder may be characterized by: social or political tension between those adversely affected by the behavior and those perpetrating it; a breakdown or collapse in operation of the norms, scripts, or rituals; or demands to reform them. Typically, these problems are remedied by new norms, scripts, or rituals – these may simply constitute new fictions or reinforce old ones.[81]

[77] Ruggie 1983.
[78] von Neumann and Morgenstern 1947, 220–37.
[79] Steinberg 1999.
[80] See generally, Hirschman 1970 on barriers to exit.
[81] Brunsson 1989.

Consistent with these expectations, since conclusion of the Uruguay Round, developing country negotiators have organized to demand procedural reforms to ensure an inclusive and transparent negotiating process. *** There have been ongoing, contentious discussions in the WTO about increasing the internal transparency of its decision-making process. *** But there is no reason to believe that the putative remedy – a hortatory commitment to increased internal transparency – will fundamentally change agenda setting or invisible weighting at the WTO. Even if developing countries understand exactly why and how the WTO decision-making process leads to asymmetrical outcomes, the analysis above shows there is little they can do about it.

The most plausible contemporary constraints on invisible weighting at the WTO are related to the limits of transatlantic trade power. If power continues to disperse in the WTO, invisible weighting by Brussels and Washington will become more difficult. Expanded membership has been diffusing power in the GATT/WTO. Moreover, many developing countries tried to cooperate with each other in closing the Tokyo Round, in blocking the launch of the Uruguay Round, and in efforts to shape the launch of the Doha Round. Sustained cooperation among developing countries – which until now has proven difficult – could further empower them. EC-U.S. cooperation could become insufficient to drive outcomes, requiring the addition of new powers to the inner core of countries that drive the organization, making cooperation within that inner core more difficult. This would favor more law-based bargaining at the WTO – dampening the flow of outcomes there, but making the pattern more symmetric.

Simultaneously, many newer issues on the WTO agenda seem to require solutions based on institutional changes to national legal, economic, and political systems that will not easily be realized and are exposing the limits of raw trade bargaining power. The apparent incapacity of most developing countries to implement the TRIPs agreement exemplifies the problem. Adding investment, environmental regulation, and competition policy to the trade agenda will magnify the limits of power.

Finally, it is possible that geostrategic context will emerge again as a constraint on the raw use of trade power by Europe and the United States. Just as the Cold War dampened U.S. willingness to exit the GATT or to formally threaten doing do, so may the war against terrorism – or the next geostrategic imperative.

22

The Legalization of International Monetary Affairs

Beth A. Simmons

Sovereign control over money is one of the most closely guarded national prerogatives.[1] Creating, valuating, and controlling the distribution of national legal tender is viewed as an inherent right of a nation-state in the modern period. Yet over the course of the twentieth century, international rules of good monetary conduct have become "legalized" in the sense developed in this volume. This historic shift took place after World War II in an effort to bolster the confidence that had been shattered by the interwar monetary experience.[2] If the interwar years taught monetary policymakers anything, it was that economic prosperity required credible exchange-rate commitments, open markets, and nondiscriminatory economic arrangements. International legalization of monetary affairs was a way to inspire private actors to once again trade and invest across national borders.

*** The Bretton Woods institutions involved only three international legal obligations regarding the conduct of monetary policy. The best known of these was to establish and maintain a par value, an obligation that was formally eliminated by the Second Amendment to the International

[1] Cohen 1998.
[2] See Eichengreen 1992; and Simmons 1994.

Thanks to William Clark and Brian Pollins, the editors of *International Organization* and this special volume, and two anonymous reviewers for very helpful comments. I would like to acknowledge the extremely helpful research assistance of Zachary Elkins and Conor O'Dwyer, who assisted with data management and analysis; Becky Curry, who assisted with the legal research; and Aaron Staines, Maria Vu, and Geoffrey Wong, who assisted with data collection and entry. I would also like to thank the Archives of the International Monetary Fund for access to documents. All errors remain my own.

Monetary Fund's (IMF) Articles of Agreement in 1977. But two other obligations remain: to keep one's current account free from restrictions, and to maintain a unified exchange-rate system. The first requires that if a bill comes due for imports or an external interest payment, national monetary authorities must make foreign exchange available to pay it. The second proscribes exchange-rate systems that favor certain transactions or trade partners over others. IMF members can voluntarily declare themselves bound by these rules (Article VIII status) or they can choose to maintain, though not augment, the restrictions that were in place when they joined the IMF (a form of grand-fathering under Article XIV).

My premise is that legalization of international monetary relations helps governments make credible policy commitments to market actors. As I will argue, the central mechanism encouraging compliance is the desire to avoid reputational costs associated with reneging on a legal obligation. As Kenneth Abbott and Duncan Snidal suggest in this volume, legalization is a tool that enhances credibility by increasing the costs of reneging. The hard commitments enclosed at Bretton Woods were thought to be necessary because the soft arrangements of the interwar years had proved useless. Governments have used commitment to the rules contained in the Articles of Agreement as a costly commitment to stable, liberal external monetary policies. This does not mean that compliance is perfect, but it is enhanced when other countries comply and when governments have a strong reputation for respecting the rule of law. * * *

* * *

THE INTERNATIONAL MONETARY SYSTEM BEFORE 1945: NATIONAL LAWS AND INTERNATIONAL "UNDERSTANDINGS"

The Nineteenth-Century Gold Standard

* * *

Although the gold standard certainly had a clear legal basis, there was nothing international about the legal structure on which it rested. It was, at most, a decentralized system of regulatory harmonization.[3] To access international capital and trade, other countries had an incentive to follow Britain onto gold. So in 1871 the German Empire made gold its standard (even though this required Germany to hold much more gold in reserve

---

[3] See, for example, the description by the MacMillan Committee on Finance and Industry, Cmd. 3897, HMSO 1931, as reprinted in Eichengreen 1985, 185–99.

than did Britain). Switzerland and Belgium followed in 1878. France adopted the gold standard but restricted convertibility when the franc was weak. The Austro-Hungarian gulden floated until the passage of (what was purported to be) gold standard legislation in 1891. In 1900 the United States declared gold as the "standard unit of value," which put the country officially on the gold standard (though silver coins still circulated). None of these national decisions involved the international community in their making. ***

Nor was this system managed through international legal arrangements. Even if one does not accept the traditional description of balance-of-payments adjustment under the classical gold standard as fully "automatic," its cooperative aspects knew no international legal guidelines. *** This decentralized system of harmonized national rules seemed to provide a good degree of stability – at least for international traders and investors at the industrialized core of the system.[4] As long as investors were confident that the system would be maintained,[5] there was little reason to design an elaborate international legal structure for its maintenance.

The Interwar Years

World War I disrupted not only the economic relationships but also the domestic political and social stability that underlay the confidence in the gold standard.[6] As a result, the interwar years were a "largely unsuccessful groping toward some form of organizational regulation of monetary affairs."[7] Increasingly, the major governments turned to negotiated agreements that had the feel of "soft law" as described by Abbott and Snidal. *** In 1922 the governments of the major European countries met in Genoa to agree informally to the principles of a gold exchange standard, which would economize on gold by encouraging smaller financial centers to hold a portion of their reserves in foreign exchange rather than gold. Although this agreement did in fact have an important impact on the composition of reserves, it was at most a soft admonition to economize gold holding. ***

---

[4] Ford 1985.
[5] Eichengreen writes extensively about the confidence that investors had in the prewar gold standard. Eichengreen 1992.
[6] Simmons 1994.
[7] Dam 1982, 50.

Virtually every important exchange-rate decision made in the interwar years was made unilaterally. On 21 September the British government implemented the Gold Standard (Amendment) Act of 1931, suspending payments of gold against legal tender and officially leaving the gold standard. Even as multilateral negotiations were in progress, the Roosevelt administration unilaterally imposed exchange controls and an export embargo.[8] Even when governments tried to coordinate their actions, diplomatic declarations were chosen over legal commitments. The Gold Bloc, formed in July 1933 among the governments of Belgium, France, Switzerland, and the Netherlands to cooperate to defend existing parities, was a "soft" legal arrangement created by declaration and communiqué, rather than a formal treaty. When France left the gold standard, for domestic reasons leaders needed multilateral cover and sought it in the form of the "Tripartite Agreement" of 1936. This agreement was the loosest of arrangements, in which Britain, the United States, and France issued separate declarations rather than sign a single document. Without mentioning devaluation, France announced the "readjustment" of its currency, while promising, as far as possible, to minimize the disturbance of such action on the international exchanges. ***

That governments tried at all to coordinate their monetary choices during this period had much to do with the growing incentives governments faced after World War I to externalize their problems of economic adjustment. The international monetary system was still dependent on national law, but the nature of the national rules had changed. Certainly governments could no longer passively accept internal adjustments in the face of mounting political demands to manage the economy. In contrast to the nineteenth century, during the 1930s a number of countries claimed to be on a "gold standard" even though gold had little to do with the money supply and hence held no implications for internal adjustment.[9] Once the national rules no longer commanded respect for internal adjustments, governments were increasingly faced with the need for international rules to put limits on external adjustments. Efforts to formalize international monetary relations arose from the need for credible limits on external adjustment.

---

[8] Presidential Proclamations 2039 (6 March 1933) and 2040 (9 March 1933); Executive orders 6111 (20 April 1933) and 6260 (28 August 1933). Cited in Dam 1982, 47, 55.

[9] In the United States it was illegal after 1933 (Exec. order 6260) for a resident to hold gold coins or bullion. Sterilization funds in both the United States and Great Britain further severed the relationship between gold flows and international monetary policy.

THE IMF AND INTERNATIONAL MONETARY LAW: TOWARD
THE FORMALIZATION OF "RULES OF GOOD CONDUCT"

The legalization of international monetary relations burgeoned after World War II.[10] In rejecting the less formalized arrangements of the past century and establishing for the first time a public international law of money,[11] negotiators from the United States and the United Kingdom were consciously choosing an international legal framework to enhance the system's credibility. Moreover, the IMF was to be, among other things, a fund, the purpose of which was to extend loans to members in balance-of-payments trouble. *** The IMF was created by a multilateral treaty arrangement, by which signatories agree to pay in subscriptions in exchange for voting and drawing rights. *** With the entry into force of the IMF's Articles of Agreement, money – like activity on the seas and diplomatic relations among states – was drawn under the system of public international law and became newly subject to its broader norms and principles.[12]

Fixed Exchange Rates: The Rise and Fall of Legalization

The Articles of Agreement set forth two primary regulatory goals that reflected lessons drawn from the interwar years: governments should be obligated to peg exchange rates and to remove exchange controls and discriminatory practices that affected current transactions. *** Controls that were once under the sovereign control of national governments now had to be justified to the international community and were collectively condoned only to the extent necessary "to carry out a purpose contributing to general prosperity."[13] In short, in the postwar monetary system, public international law was to be used as it had been for decades in trade relations: to help facilitate the international exchange of goods and services by providing for currency convertibility in open, free, and legal markets.

The international community thus explicitly recognized for the first time that exchange rates were properly a matter of international concern. To become a member of the IMF, a country had to communicate a "par

---

[10] The expression "rules of good conduct" is used by Gold 1965, passim.

[11] Gold 1984a, 801. A French plan was offered at the beginning of the postwar monetary negotiations. Although it played no direct role, it did indicate the French preference for agreement among the "principal nations" somewhat analogous to the Tripartite Agreement. The French plan saw an international institution as optional. Dam 1982, 76.

[12] Gold 1980, 5. Nonetheless, legal treatments of these obligations are surprisingly few. See generally Denters 1996, 16–20.

[13] From the White Plan. Horsefield and De Vries 1969, 3:64.

value" for its currency by direct or indirect reference to gold. This might involve minor negotiations with the IMF staff, but it basically established par values very close to those prevailing just prior to membership. Members then had an obligation to maintain that par value within the margins prescribed in the articles.[14] Members were required, without exception, to consult with the IMF before making a change in their initial or subsequent par values; failing to do so constituted a breach of a legal obligation. And although the IMF could not propose a change in a member's par value, by using its resources it could influence a member's decisions to adopt a particular par value. In short, "the authority over exchange rates granted to the Fund by the original articles was unprecedented in international law."[15]

* * *

Remaining Monetary Obligations: Article VIII

Despite the softening of legal obligations with respect to the system of par values, governments who are members of the IMF do retain two important obligations in the conduct of their external monetary policy. Both of these are contained in Article VIII of the Articles of Agreement, which spells out the general obligations of members. These rules prohibit restrictions on the making of payments and transfers for current international transactions; they also prohibit multiple currency practices without the approval of the IMF itself.[16] Article VIII section 2(a) provides that governments must make foreign exchange available for goods, services, and invisibles.[17] By agreeing to this standard, governments obligate themselves to make available to their citizens foreign exchange to settle all legal international transactions (it remains up to the

[14] Art IV, sec. 4. Furthermore, Art. IV, sec. 2 provided that "no member shall buy gold at a price above par value plus the prescribed margin, or sell gold at a price below par value minus the prescribed margin." A central bank could not enter into any gold transaction with another central bank other than at par without one or the other violating the articles.

[15] Gold 1988, 48.

[16] Art. VIII, sec. 2, para. (a), and sec. 3. Member states are, however, permitted to maintain or impose exchange restrictions under certain conditions: (1) if they are necessary to regulate international capital movements (art. VI, sec. 3); (2) with the approval of the IMF (art. VIII, sec. 2 (a)); (3) if the IMF has declared a currency "scarce" (art. VII, sec. 3 (b)); and (4) if the exchange restrictions were effective at the time the state became a member of the IMF (art. XIV, sec. 2).

[17] The restriction applies only to payments and transfers for current international transactions. The IMF articles explicitly permit the regulation of international capital movements (Art. VI, sec. 3).

government to determine which are legal).[18] They also agree to refrain from delaying, limiting, or imposing charges on currency transfers if these have the effect of inhibiting or increasing the costs of making payments.[19] Interestingly, this provision appears to be the only part of the Bretton Woods Agreements that constitutes an obligation of member states toward their own residents.[20]

Multiple currency practices that establish different rates of exchange have always been prohibited by the Articles of Agreement. Article VIII section 3 creates a hard legal obligation to avoid such practices,[21] which were viewed as a threat to the original parity rule, potentially discriminatory, and always distortionary. As with the restrictions in section 2, the IMF could, however, approve temporarily such practices, which can serve to soften the proscription in the short run. Multiple currency practices were rampant after World War II: about a third of all the countries involved in the Bretton Woods negotiations had multiple currency systems in place. As late as 1971, a major member, France, introduced a multiple exchange-rate system. The United Kingdom also maintained a separate investment rate as late as 1979.

Why were rules forbidding these practices considered necessary? For two general reasons: Governments may want to support developmental objectives that favor certain kinds of imports over others based on established state priorities.[22] More often, however, governments use exchange controls and multiple currency practices as one among a variety of methods to deal with balance-of-payments problems.[23] For either purpose, they may require exporters to surrender foreign currencies received in export sales to government authorities, at governmentally determined rates.[24] In turn, importers are required to obtain foreign currency from the governmental authority or authorized bank. Such systems

---

[18] See Executive Board Decision 1034 (60/27), 1 June 1960, para. 1, *Selected Decisions of the International Monetary Fund and Selected Documents*, 11:259 (Washington, D.C.: IMF). See also Horsefield and de Vries 1969, 3:260.

[19] Edwards 1985, 391 (see fn. 39 for original documentary sources); and Horn 1985, 295.

[20] Boehlhoff and Baumanns 1989, 108.

[21] Art. VIII, sec. 3 says: "No member shall engage in, or permit any of its fiscal agencies referred to in Article V, Section 1 to engage in, discriminatory currency arrangements or multiple currency practices . . . except as authorized under this agreement or approved by the Fund."

[22] See, for example, India and Article VIII, 11 July 1955, S424, Transitional Arrangements, Article VIII Country Studies (Washington, D.C.: IMF Archives).

[23] See Edwards 1985, 381–32; and Gold 1988, 255.

[24] Edwards 1985, 391. Surrender requirements are not prohibited, because surrender in itself is not considered to be an impediment to the making of payments. Gold 1984a, 813.

allow for foreign currency rationing or import discrimination in which foreign currency is made available (or available at favorable rates) for some goods or some transactions but not others.[25]

The IMF has always viewed such systems of control as dangerous substitutes for economic adjustment and inhibitions to the development of free foreign exchange markets. However, because many of the IMF's founding members could not immediately achieve full convertibility at unified rates, Article VIII obligations are made voluntarily. Upon joining the IMF, new members can avail themselves of "transitional" arrangements, under Article XIV, which in effect "grandfather" practices that were in place on their accession to the Articles of Agreement.[26] Even so, Article XIV countries are expected to withdraw restrictions when they are no longer needed for balance-of-payments reasons[27] and are required to consult annually with the IMF about retaining restrictions inconsistent with Article VIII.[28] In the course of these consultations the IMF tries to persuade members gradually to move from "transitional" practices – foreign exchange rationing, multiple exchange rates, foreign exchange licensing systems – to the IMF's traditional approach: reduction of domestic inflation, comprehensive fiscal reform, devaluation if necessary, and simplification of exchange restrictions to remove their tax and subsidy effects. Once these fundamentals are in place the IMF usually urges the Article XIV country to commit itself to Article VIII status.[29]

---

[25] Edwards 1985, 382. A very comprehensive system of exchange controls might prohibit residents to transfer the state's currency to nonresidents, except with the state's permission on a case-by-case basis, or prohibit residents to hold foreign currencies except with the state's permission.

[26] Art. XIV, sec. 2. An Art. XIV country can also adapt its restrictions without the need for IMF approval. But an Art. XIV country cannot introduce new restrictions without approval, adapt multiple currency practices without IMF approval, nor maintain restrictions that the member cannot justify as necessary for balance-of-payments reasons. See Horsefield and De Vries 1969, 1:248–59.

[27] Art. XIV, sec. 2.

[28] Art. XIV, sec. 3.

[29] Ideally, the IMF wants the removal of restrictions to coincide with the assumption of Art. VIII obligations, though it has recognized that this might not always be possible and that waiting for the complete removal of every last restriction would only serve to delay the making of such a commitment. See Article VIII and Article XIV, memo prepared by Irving S. Friedman, Exchange Restrictions Department, 24 May 1955, S424, Transitional Arrangements, Art. VIII and XIV, September 1954–55, (IMF Archives). In a few cases, developing countries that were not in an especially strong position to accept Art. VIII had no restrictions in place, and the IMF urged them to go ahead and commit, since they had nothing to "grandfather" under Art. XIV. See Haiti, memo from H. Merle Cochran to Irving S. Friedman, 30 October 1953, C/Haiti/424.1, Trans. Arrange., Members' Intent

LEGAL COMMITMENT: EXPECTATIONS AND EVIDENCE

But why should a government voluntarily assume Article VIII obligations? And why should it continue to comply with them? After all, the
articles specify neither a time period nor a set of criteria for ending the
transitional period.[30] And although the IMF encourages countries they
believe are in a position to do so to make an Article VIII commitment, the
IMF does not provide direct positive or negative incentives for doing
so.[31] Nor does it directly "enforce" these obligations.[32] It does publish
data on states' policies from which one can infer compliance ***. The
executive board can also "approve" restrictions (or not) and has done so
as an accompaniment to adjustment programs it is supporting. But the
consequences of nonapproval are questionable, since the board does not
generally make its decisions public.[33] The executive board can declare a
member ineligible to use the IMF's resources if the member "fails to fulfill
any of its obligations" under the articles,[34] and noncompliance sometimes
does interrupt drawings under standby and extended arrangements.[35]

to Use (IMF Archives); and Letter, Ivar Rooth, M.D., to Jose Garcia Ayber, Governor of
the Central Bank of the Dominican Republic, 1 August 1953, C/Dominican Republic/
424.1, Trans. Arrange., Members' Intent to Use (IMF Archives). These countries often
turn out to be long-term noncompliers.

[30] Horsefield and De Vries 1969, 2:225. The IMF staff discussed on various occasions the
imposition of time limits for the removal of restrictions and the unification of exchange
rates, but rejected them as impractical. Article VIII and Article XIV, memo prepared by
Irving S. Friedman, 24 May 1955, S 424, Trans. Arrange. (IMF Archives). There were also
debates over the IMF's legal authority to declare an end to the transitional period.
Furthermore, there were debates in the early period about exactly what "transitional"
referred to. Extract, Executive Board Informal Session 54/2, 19 November 1954, S424,
Trans. Arrange. (IMF Archives).

[31] However, sometimes countries in fairly tenuous balance-of-payments positions who were
willing to accept Art. VIII obligations were provided standby arrangements. For example,
see Costa Rica (1965), Executive Board Minutes, EBM/65/7, 29 January 1965, C/Costa
Rica/424.1, Trans. Arrange., Members' Intent to Use (IMF Archives).

[32] In 1948, the executive board explicitly disapproved France's multiple exchange-rate
practice and declared France ineligible to use IMF resources, invoking Art. IV, sec. 6 sanctions. The sanction failed to induce France to adopt a unitary rate. The use of sanctions
was perceived as a failure and never invoked again. Dam 1982, 132.

[33] Although the board is not barred from publishing reports that communicate the board's
views, doing so requires a two-thirds majority of the total voting power to make this
decision. Gold 1979, 153.

[34] Art XV, sec. 2 (a).

[35] According to Gold, "All standby arrangements include a uniform term on measures
that directly or indirectly affect exchange rates. Under this term a member is precluded
from making purchases under an arrangement if at any time during the period of
the arrangement the member: 'i. imposes [or intensifies] restrictions on payments and
transfers for current international transactions, or ii. introduces [or modifies] multiple

But, in fact, the IMF has used these formal remedies very sparingly. Noncompliers rarely have to worry about retaliation directly from the IMF, since members that vote for some kind of punishment may be concerned about drawing a retaliatory vote in the future. The IMF is much more likely to use persuasion than to apply a remedy for continued noncompliance.[36]

* * *

Governments therefore face something of a dilemma: there are costs to being the first to liberalize (including the possibility of direct balance-of-payments pressures), but there are also costs to lagging too far behind international or regional norms. Governments have keenly felt this dilemma in formulating their policies regarding Article VIII. The major Western European countries, for example, assumed Article VIII obligations in unison, since "None of the six countries wanted to move in advance of the other, and all of them preferred to come under Article VIII at the same time as the United Kingdom."[37] A similar decision was made by the African franc zone countries three and a half decades later. * * * In discussions of the timing of Article VIII acceptance with the IMF, Peru's prime minister "agreed Peru should not jump out ahead of the others, but ... definitely does not want to 'miss the boat.'"[38] These concerns are

currency practices, or iii. concludes bilateral payments agreements which are inconsistent with Art. VIII, or iv. imposes [or intensifies] import restrictions for balance of payments reasons.'" Gold 1988, 466.

[36] Gold 1979, 185.

[37] Implementation of Article XIV and Article VIII Decision, minutes of staff visit to the United Kingdom, 22 July 1960, S424, Trans. Arrange., Move to Article VIII Mission, minutes of meetings (IMF Archives). The IMF archives contain ample evidence that no European power wanted to pay the potential costs of being the first mover, yet none wanted to lag a decision by other countries in the region. Thus, "The French policy with regards to restrictions depends on the policy followed by other European countries, especially Great Britain. It might even be said in large measure it is conditioned by that policy." F. A. G. Keesing, 1 July 1955. S424, Trans. Arrange., Art. VIII Country Studies (IMF Archives). For a similar position by the Netherlands, see Netherlands and Article VIII. 23 June 1955, S424, Trans. Arrange., Art. VIII Country Studies (IMF Archives). On the United Kingdom's unwillingness to move alone, see memo from Rooth to E. M. Bernstein, 20 May 1955, S424, Trans. Arrange., Art. VIII and XIV, Sept. 1954–55 (IMF Archives). On the incentives for a general snowball effect within Europe, see memo from F. A. G. Keesing, 13 May 1955, S424, Trans. Arrange., Art. VIII and XIV, 1954–55 (IMFArchives).

[38] Memo from Jorge del Canto to Per Jacobsson, IMF Managing Director, 23 September 1960, C/Peru/ 424.1, Trans. Arrange., Members' Intent to Use (IMF Archives). Peru was basically free from all restrictions in 1960, and IMF staff members wondered whether they should be encouraged to assume Art. VIII obligations as soon as possible or wait and go with the Europeans. In a hand written note in the margins, Per Jacobsson wrote, "No. It would not profit Peru to move first – more advantageous to be 'drawn by movement' with others." Memo from Jorge del Canto to Per Jacobsson, 17 May I960, C/Peru/424.1 (IMF Archives).

understandable if legal commitment is viewed as a way to reassure markets in a competitive economic environment. Although there may be few incentives to liberalize first, governments need to be cognizant of the signal they may be sending by refusing to commit, especially when other countries with whom they might compete for capital or trade have done so.

If a legal commitment to Article VIII is a way to improve access to capital and trade by in effect raising the costs of interfering in foreign exchange markets, then we should expect commitment to be influenced by two factors: (1) a basic ability to comply (which is necessary for a credible commitment), and (2) the commitment decisions of other countries (which avoids the costs of being the first to move and reduces the costs of lagging).

We should also consider a set of plausible control variables that could reveal a spurious correlation with these hypothesized relationships. I am not suggesting that a credible commitment is the only reason a government would commit to Article VIII but investigating whether it stands up to a range of plausible alternatives. The first is a straightforward argument based on domestic demands: commitment is likely to be a function of domestic policy demands, just like any other aspect of foreign economic policymaking.[39] *** Article VIII provides a right of access to foreign exchange for residents and nonresidents, and demands for such a right are likely to be greater in countries where trade is an important part of the national economy. ***

The IMF staff, in their discussions of who was ready to commit, clearly recognized the incentives that trade dependence created. Indonesia was deemed unlikely to commit, for example, because "The restrictive system is somewhat peripheral to the broad economic issues in which the public are interested: foreign trade is only 6% of GDP. And non-nationals control the major industries" (jute and tea).[40] On the other hand, when Guyana made the Article VIII commitment, the executive board noted explicitly that "Guyana was one of those very few developing countries in the world whose imports and exports, taken separately, were larger than 50 per cent of GNP, and this necessarily meant that the country was

---

[39] The literature linking foreign economic policymaking to domestic political demands is vast. Most of this work concentrates on demands for trade protection. See, for example, Aggarwal, Keohane, and Yoffie 1987; Alt et al. 1996; Destler and Odell 1987; Goodman, Spar, and Yoffie 1996; McKeown 1984; Milner 1988; and Rogowski 1989. For works on financial and monetary policy, see Simmons 1994; and Frieden 1991.

[40] Indonesia and Article VIII, 14 July 1955, S424, Trans. Arrange., Art. VIII Country Studies (IMF Archives).

highly vulnerable to swings both in capital and in trading magnitudes." Trade dependence made Guyana a good candidate for Article VIII but also implied a possible need for IMF assistance should liberalization prove destabilizing. A standby arrangement was considered simultaneously.[41]

Furthermore, we might expect that the demand for guaranteed foreign exchange access is most likely to be addressed by a democratic regime. The political organization around this issue area is likely to be that of civil society versus the state: on the one hand, it is difficult to conceive of a private interest that would organize to actively oppose free access to foreign exchange. On the other hand, the concentrated rents go to the government, as the dispenser of limited access to hard currency. If one of the primary characteristics of democracy is the extent to which it empowers civil demands vis-à-vis the state, and if it is also true that these demands are likely to favor those who want free access to foreign exchange, then we should expect democratic governance to be positively associated with the acceptance of Article VIII.

It is also important to control for the institutional incentives provided by the IMF for those who commit: An early inducement for countries to choose Article VIII status was the fact that multilateral surveillance applied only to Article XIV countries until the Second Amendment (revisions to Article IV) extended mandatory surveillance to the entire IMF membership.[42] Prior to 1977, governments willing to announce acceptance of Article VIII obligations could actually avoid multilateral surveillance.[43] *** Thus until 1977, members faced a perverse incentive to accept Article VIII obligations: the commitment gave them the ability to avoid discriminatory and potentially humiliating surveillance and formal board review. We can hypothesize that the acceptance rate was therefore higher, all else being equal, before 1977 than after.

Finally, controlling for time is appropriate in this analysis. One important reason is that countries may have been reluctant to commit to Article VIII in the early years of the IMF because it was unclear just how the executive board would interpret the obligation. Countries clearly did not want to commit and then be surprised that the executive board

---

[41] Guyana – Acceptance of Obligations of Article VIII, Sections 2, 3, and 4, Initial Par Value, and Stand-by Arrangement, 13 February 1967, EMB/67/10, C/Guyana/424.1, Trans. Arrange., Members' Intent to Use (IMF Archives).

[42] James 1995, 773, 775.

[43] Gold 1983, 474–75. Consultations with Art. VIII countries were established in 1960 but were completely voluntary. Horsefield and De Vries 1969, 2:246–47.

considered them in breach of their obligation.[44] As time went on, this kind of uncertainty could be expected to wane through approval decisions and executive board clarification.

* * *

Before proceeding to more complicated analyses, it is useful to make a visual inspection of the data. The data set used is a panel of 138 countries. The only criterion for their inclusion was membership in the IMF by 1980. Of these countries, we have time varying and case varying data for 110 countries that have chosen Article VIII status since 1966. Using yearly observations for these countries, it is useful to construct a Kaplan-Meier "survival function" that describes the period of transition prior to making an Article VIII commitment (see Figure 22.1).[45]

One fact becomes obvious from this visual representation of the data: the "transitional" regime could in fact last a long period of time for a number of countries. The Kaplan-Meier function estimates about a 25 percent chance of accepting Article VIII status in the first twenty-four years of IMF membership, a 50 percent chance within thirty-five years, and about a 75 percent chance after fifty years. Clearly, many countries have been in no rush to commit legally to keeping their current account free from restrictions.

What affects the rate at which governments make the commitment? Table 22.1 presents the findings of the Cox proportional hazard estimation for a combination of variables discussed earlier. (Note that ratios of more than 1 indicate an increase in the rate of Article VIII acceptance, and ratios of less than 1 indicate a reduction in the rate of acceptance. Thus the null hypothesis is that the hazard ratio is not significantly different from 1.) Consider first the ability to comply, which I argue is essential

[44] For example, the United Kingdom did not want the stigma of a board decision that they maintained an illegal multiple currency practice as a result of what the United Kingdom considered a legitimate way to control capital movements. Implementation of Article XIV and Article VIII Decision, minutes of staff visit to the United Kingdom, 27 July 1960, S424, Trans. Arrange., Move to Art. VIII Mission (IMF Archives). Uncertainty over board interpretation inhibited early commitment. Generally, see Policy Aspects of the Article VIII and Article XIV Problem, 21 October 1954, S424, Trans. Arrange., Art. VIII and XIV, 1954–55 (IMF Archives).

[45] The literature usually terms the event of interest a "failure" and the time elapsed until its occurrence as "survival" regardless of the substantive problem modeled. Proponents of international openness and free markets would in this case view "survival" analysis as "transition" analysis, and an Art. VIII commitment as a "success"; those who favor closer government management of markets might agree that the customary appellations are in fact more apt.

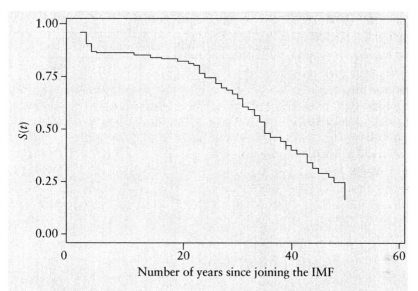

Note: The Kaplan-Meier estimator for maintaining Article XIV status beyond time t is the product of the probability of maintaining this status in time t and the perceding periods:

$$S(t) = \prod_{j=t0}^{t}\{(nj - dj)/nj\}$$

where n represents those cases that neither accepted Article VIII status nor were censored, and d represents the number of acceptances during the time period.

	Country-years at risk	Incidence rate	Number of countries	Survival time		
				25%	50%	75%
Total	3,125	.01999	110	24	35	50

FIGURE 22.1. *The Kaplan-Meier survival function: Duration of Article XIV status over time.*

for a credible commitment. My expectation is that countries are more unlikely to make Article VIII obligations when their payments are volatile and they tend toward deficit. In the models developed here, balance-of-payments levels (the average balance of payments for the period as a whole) are interacted with balance-of-payments volatility.[46] This

---

[46] Reserve levels and volatility, as well as terms of trade volatility, were also analyzed, but because the results were insignificant they are not reported here.

TABLE 22.1. *Influences on the Rate of Article VIII Acceptance*

	Rate of Article VIII acceptance (hazard ratios)			
	Model 1	Model 2	Model 3	Model 4
Average balance of payments	—	—	1.364** (.145)	1.352** (.180)
Balance-of-payments volatility	—	—	.390** (.170)	.400* (.205)
Balance-of-payments (volatility*mean)	—	—	.887** (.035)	.891** (.046)
Universality	1.073*** (.015)	1.330*** (.092)	1.385*** (.111)	1.553*** (.386)
Regional norm	1.030*** (.005)	1.043*** (.009)	1.045*** (.010)	1.040*** (.010)
Surveillance	.608 (.289)	.047*** (.042)	.041*** (.047)	.061** (.087)
Openness	1.009*** (.003)	1.015*** (.003)	1.018*** (.004)	1.018*** (.005)
Democracy	—	1.078* (.050)	1.081* (.044)	1.079* (.044)
Year	—	—	—	.904 (.199)
N	1,988	1,757	1,754	1,754
Time "at risk"	2,517.97	2,296.98	2,294.98	2,294.98
Log likelihood	−182.45	−93.39	−90.15	−89.96
χ^2	132.12	75.63	66.09	74.76
Prob. $> \chi^2$	0.00	0.00	0.00	0.00

Note: Table shows estimated hazard rates using a Cox proportionate hazard model with time varying covariates. Robust standard errors are in parentheses.
*** $p > |Z| = .01$.
** $p > |Z| = .05$.
* $p > |Z| = .10$.

specification is meant to distinguish volatility effects conditional on whether the balance-of-payments position is relatively strong or weak. The results displayed in Table 22.1 show that, as anticipated, balance-of-payments volatility reduces the proportional hazard rate substantially. In model 3, it reduces the rate by $(1 - .390)$, or .610, when mean deficits are equal to zero. Substantively, volatility is very likely to reduce the rate at which countries accept Article VIII obligations. Also as expected, countries that have better balance-of-payments positions are more likely to accept Article VIII obligations (36.4 percent more likely for every percentage point of balance of payments as a proportion of gross domestic product, GDP, according to model 3). Interestingly, the negative effects of volatility may be slightly greater in countries with better payment positions on average, as indicated by the statistically significant but substantively small impact of the interaction term. These findings about the balance of payments support the hypothesis that countries that are more capable of compliance are more likely to commit. The commitment is, in turn, more likely to be credible.

The next two variables, "universality" and "regional norm," are meant to test the proposition that taking on an obligation is likely to be contingent on similar actions by others. "Universality" is the proportion of all IMF members who have accepted Article VIII status, and "regional norm" is the proportion of countries within each subregion (as defined by the World Bank) that have done so. (All variable measures and sources are discussed in the data appendix.) Both of these variables have a large and positive influence on the acceptance rate. According to model 3, for example, every 1 percent increase in the proportion of IMF members accepting Article VIII increases the likelihood of acceptance by 38.5 percent. Similarly, a 1 percent increase in the regional proportion of Article VIII adherents increases a country's likelihood of acceptance by 4.1 percent. This translates into a 49 percent increase for every 10 percent increase in regional accession.[47] Clearly, as the number of countries who accept Article VIII increases, there is a greatly increased chance that an uncommitted government will do so. Note that this impact is significant even if we control for time ("year" in model 4). We can be fairly confident, then, that the universality and regional norms variables evaluated here do not simply reflect the fact that adherents increase over time. What most influences the acceptance rate is not time, but the proportion of adherents. This finding is consistent with the incentives of the competitive economic environment in which governments declare their legal adherence to Article VIII.

Domestic political demands that flow from trade-openness also have an important impact on the acceptance rate. Openness to the international trade system raises the proportional hazard rate significantly. According to model 3, every one point increase in imports plus exports as a proportion of GDP increases the likelihood of Article VIII acceptance by 1.8 percent. This could account for a 67 percent difference in acceptance probability for countries with trade profiles as different

---

[47] Which is calculated by raising the estimated hazard ratio to the tenth power.

as, say, Malaysia (imports plus exports totaling approximately 80 percent of GDP for the period under consideration) and the Philippines (where the corresponding figure is about 50 percent).[48] Certainly, the demands of importers and exporters have much to do with the government's willingness to commit. Interestingly, whether or not a country was democratic only marginally affected the decision, if at all. In the improbable event that a country transformed itself from a complete nondemocracy to a highly democratic society, the possible impact on the probability of accepting Article VIII would only be about 19 percent. Our confidence in this effect barely reaches standard levels of significance, however.[49]

There is also evidence that institutional incentives have made a big difference in Article VIII acceptance. "Surveillance" here is a dummy variable that takes on a value of zero prior to 1977 and 1 thereafter. Once surveillance has been extended to all countries – not just those availing themselves of the Article XIV transitional regime – the impact has been to reduce drastically the probability of accepting Article VIII, as we expected, though our confidence in this result is reduced somewhat by the exclusion of democracy as an independent explanation. The hazard ratio indicates that once the surveillance advantage of Article VIII states was removed, countries were anywhere from 40 percent to as much as 96 percent less likely to accept Article VIII status, other conditions held constant. The end of discriminatory surveillance seems to have mattered greatly to governments' willingness to commit. On the other hand, the simple passage of time had little effect. This could be because the uncertainty regarding obligations that motivated the inclusion of this variable was highly concentrated in the very earliest years of the IMF. There is little reason to believe that time itself accounts for changes in the rate of commitment.

The evidence suggests that governments are more likely to commit to Article VIII status when the commitment is credible and when other countries, especially countries in their own region, have done so as well. Although other factors influence the decision to commit, these results are consistent with the use of legal commitments as a signal to markets of a serious intent to maintain open and nondiscriminatory foreign exchange markets.

---

[48] Calculated in this case by raising the estimated hazard ratio to the twenty-ninth power.

[49] Subtracting the polity scores on autocracy from those on democracy, yielding a scale from −10 to 10, does not significantly alter this general conclusion.

WHO COMPLIES? EXPLAINING THE COMPLIANCE DECISION

* * *

If legalization is an attempt to make a commitment more credible, then governments should resist violating international law because they want to preserve their reputations as law abiding. The incentive for such a reputation in the monetary area is clear: governments want to convince markets that they provide a desirable venue for international trade and investment. Investors and suppliers seeking opportunities for international commerce should prefer to do business with firms in countries that provide a more certain legal framework with respect to the nondiscriminatory fulfillment of international contracts. Although there is no central enforcement of this obligation, the desire to avoid reputational costs should motivate compliance.

The question is, when will reputational costs have their greatest impact? My first hypothesis is that costs are greatest when a violator is an outlier among comparable countries. That is, rule violation is most costly when comparable countries manage to continue to comply. On the one hand, the more competitors are willing to comply, the greater the pressure for any one country to comply, even in the face of economic pressure to protect the national economy through restrictions or multiple exchange rates. On the other hand, if it is common for Article VIII countries in the region to disregard their commitment, this should increase the probability that any given country in that region will decide against compliance. Rampant violation makes it difficult for markets to single out any one violator for "punishment." Thus, we should expect compliance to be positively influenced by what other countries choose to do.

Consider next characteristics of the domestic polity itself. Several analysts have implied that compliance with international legal commitments is much more prevalent among liberal democracies, pointing to the constraining influence exercised by domestic groups who may have interests in or a preference for compliant behavior.[50] In this view participatory politics might put pressure on the government to comply, especially in the case where noncompliance involves curtailing the rights of residents to foreign exchange (it is less clear how this argument relates to the choice to implement or maintain a unified exchange-rate system). Others have argued that the most important characteristic of liberal democracy when it comes to international compliance is its strong domestic commitment

---

[50] See Young 1979; and Schachter 1991. See also Moravcsik 1997.

to the rule of law. *** In essence, these are affinity arguments: they seem to suggest that domestic norms regarding limited government, respect for judicial processes, and regard for constitutional constraints[51] "carry over" into the realm of international politics. They rest on an intuitively appealing assumption that policymakers and lawmakers are not able to park their normative perspectives at the water's edge.[52]

There are other reasons, however, to expect the rule of law to be associated with Article VIII compliance. Countries respecting the rule of law have a strong positive reputation for maintaining a stable framework for property rights. Markets expect them to maintain their commitments, and to undermine this expectation would prove costly. Countries that score low with respect to the rule of law do not have much to lose by noncompliance; erratic behavior is hardly surprising to investors and traders. I use an indicator for the rule of law that is especially appropriate to test the market's assessment of the reputation for rule of law: a six-point scale published by a political risk analysis firm expressly to assess the security of investments.[53] The scale represents the willingness of citizens peacefully to implement law and adjudicate disputes using established institutions. Higher scores on this six-point measure indicate the presence of such institutional characteristics as a strong court system, sound political institutions, and provisions for orderly succession. Low scores reflect an increased use of extra-legal activities in response to conflict and to settle disputes.

Since I have argued that the purpose of legalization is to make more credible monetary commits, that compliance is market enforced, and that markets prefer certainty in the legal framework, the comparison between the participatory characteristics of democracy and rule-of-law regimes should be especially telling. We have little reason to expect that democracy alone provides the stability that economic agents desire; on the contrary, popular participation along with weak guarantees for fair enforcement of property rights can endanger these rights. Clearly, these two variables are positively correlated (Pearson correlation = .265), but they are certainly conceptually distinct and may have very different effects on the

---

[51] "International law is not unlike constitutional law in that it imposes legal obligations on a government that in theory the government is not free to ignore or change." Fisher 1981, 30. Constitutional constraints most often rest on their shared normative acceptance, rather than on the certainty of their physical enforcement, providing another possible parallel to the international setting.

[52] See Risse-Kappen 1995b; and Lumsdaine 1993.

[53] See Knack and Keefer 1995, 225.

decision to comply with Article VIII obligations. Thus we are able directly to compare two regime characteristics that are often conflated: democracy with its participatory dimensions on the one hand and the rule of law with its emphasis on procedural certainty on the other. Monetary compliance should therefore be conditioned by (1) compliance by other countries in the region, and (2) a country's reputation for respecting the rule of law. Participatory democracy is expected to have no effect.

The central explanation for compliance should revolve around these reputational factors. Still, it is important to control for other factors that could influence the compliance decision. Consistent with the reputational argument, it may be more costly for a country that is highly dependent on world trade to violate Article VIII. Certainly, retaliation would be more costly to nationals of such a country. Second, it is plausible that countries defending a fixed exchange rate might find it more difficult to maintain Article VIII obligations; countries that had shifted to more flexible regimes would not be under the same pressure to conserve foreign exchange for purposes of defending the currency's peg.[54] Third, use of the IMF's resources could provide an incentive to comply. Pressure from the IMF should be especially strong when countries are in need of a loan. Fourth, it may be the case that compliance is enhanced by the nesting of the Article VIII regime within a broader regime of free trade. Membership in the General Agreement on Tariffs and Trade (GATT) might encourage a country to maintain free and nondiscriminatory foreign exchange markets.[55] Finally, compliance may simply become easier with the passage of time. Thus the following control variables provide a small sample of other factors that could encourage compliance: (1) positive economic conditions,

---

[54] The board clearly recognized this was the case: "It was quite evident that flexible rates made it easier for a country to eliminate payment and trade restrictions. This made the fact that several European countries were now accepting the obligations of Art VIII on the basis of a fixed parity all the more significant." Peru's currency was still fluctuating. Executive board minutes, 8 February 1961, EBM/61/4., p. 15, C/Peru/424.1, Trans. Arrange., Members' Intent to Use (IMF Archives).

[55] Indeed, the date of GATT's entry into force was conditioned on the acceptance of Art. VIII, sec. 2, 3, and 4 obligations by the contracting parties to the GATT. According to a memo circulated among the staff of the IMF, "The date of entry into force of the revised [GATT] rules concerning discrimination and quantitative restrictions is linked specifically to the date at which the obligations of Article VIII, Sections 2, 3, and 4 of the Fund Agreement become applicable to such contracting parties as are members of the Fund, the combined foreign trade of which constitutes at least 50 per cent of the aggregate foreign trade of all contracting parties." Article VIII and Article XIV, memo prepared by Irving S. Friedman, 24 May 1955 (IMF Archives).

(2) a high degree of trade dependence, (3) flexible exchange rates, (4) use of IMF resources, (5) membership in the GATT, and (6) the passage of time.

In this case the compliance decision is modeled using logistical regression (logit), with the dependent variable taking on a value of 1 for the presence of restrictions or multiple exchange rates and zero for the absence of both. (Since we are analyzing only Article VIII countries, each instance of restrictions or multiple-rate systems is also a case of apparent noncompliance.) Because the data consist of observations across countries and over time, with a strong probability of temporal dependence among observations, a logit specification is used that takes explicit account of the nonindependence of observations.[56] The results are reported in Table 22.2.

One of the most important findings of this analysis is, again, the clustering of compliance behavior within regions. Article VIII countries are much more likely to put illegal restrictions on current account or use illegal multiple exchange-rate regimes if other countries in the region are doing so. The impact of regional behavior is substantial: the difference between a region with no violators compared to one with nearly all violators increased the probability of noncompliance by 79 percent. Could this be the result of common economic pressures sweeping the region? This explanation cannot be completely ruled out, but it is rendered less likely by the range of economic variables included in the specification. The inclusion of various measures of current account difficulty and GDP growth failed to wash out apparent regional convergence. Compliance decisions are apparently not being made on the basis of economic conditions alone, but with an eye to standards of regional behavior. The most obvious reason for this concern would be reputational consequences in a competitive international economic environment.

The domestic political variables tell an interesting story about regime characteristics. In contrast to theories of international behavior that concentrate on the law consciousness of democracies, the evidence presented here suggests that, in this set of countries, democracy may be associated with a greater tendency to violate the country's international monetary obligations.[57] Substantive interpretation of the coefficients

---

[56] Beck, Katz, and Tucker 1998. A counter vector was employed using the STATA routine made available on Richard Tucker's Web site at <http://www.fas.harvard.edu/~rtucker/papers/grouped/grouped3.html>. Three cubic splines were included in the analysis but are not reported here.

[57] This conclusion is not significantly altered by the use of the combined democracy-autocracy variable.

TABLE 22.2. *Influences on the Decision to Violate Article VIII Obligations*

Explanatory variables	Model 1	Model 2	Model 3	Model 4
Constant	−17.8***	−17.13***	−17.3***	−17.9***
	(4.75)	(4.88)	(4.89)	(4.77)
Rule of law	−.340***	−.346***	−.272**	−.333***
	(.020)	(.119)	(.133)	(.120)
Democracy	.017*	.016	.018*	.018*
	(.010)	(.010)	(.010)	(.010)
Regional noncompliance	5.57***	5.47***	5.21***	5.45***
	(.554)	(.540)	(.567)	(.553)
Balance of payments/GDP $(t − 1)$	−.030**	−.031**	−.029**	−.030**
	(.013)	(.013)	(.013)	(.012)
Balance-of-payments volatility	.753***	.794***	.793***	.716***
	(.257)	(.262)	(.276)	(.266)
Change in GDP	−.055*	−.057*	−.056*	−.055*
	(.032)	(.032)	(.033)	(.031)
Openness	−.014***	−.014***	−.014***	−.014***
	(.003)	(.003)	(.003)	(.003)
Year	.198***	.188***	.186***	.203***
	(.051)	(.053)	(.052)	(.052)
Flexible exchange rates	—	.270	—	—
		(.404)		
Use of fund resources	—	—	.601	—
			(.404)	
GATT member	—	—	—	−.377
				(.334)
N	593	593	593	593
Wald χ²	(11)	(12)	(12)	(12)
	207.63	207.04	215.52	220.2
Prob. > χ²	0.000	0.000	0.000	0.000
Log likelihood	−137.7	−137.4	−136.6	−137.3

Note: The dependent variable is an apparent Article VIII violation, either a restriction on current account or multiple exchange-rate system. This analysis covers Article VIII countries only. Logit coefficients are reported with correction for nonindependence of observations. Robust standard errors are in parentheses. Estimation includes three cubic splines, which are not reported here.

*** $p > |Z| = .01$.
** $p > |Z| = .05$.
* $p > |Z| = .10$.

reveals a highly asymmetrical impact; however, a move from zero to 5 on the democracy scale increases the chances of violating a commitment by only 2.89 percent, whereas a move from 5 to 10 on that scale increases the probability of violating by 10.8 percent. Why this might be so is not difficult to understand. A rich literature in political economy suggests that a potential cost of democracy is that the public does not always fully anticipate the consequences of its aggregate demands. For example, if democracies allow for macroeconomic policies that exhibit an inflationary bias,[58] participatory politics may complicate the international compliance problem. However, a strong domestic commitment to the rule of law contributed positively to Article VIII compliance. Again, the impact is somewhat asymmetrical for values on the explanatory variable. A move from 1 to 3 on the six-point rule-of-law scale reduced the probability of violating Article VIII by 17.7 percent, whereas a move from 4 to 6 reduced the probability of violating by about 4 percent. The effect of the rule of law is understandable in light of the argument about uncertainty and reputation: governments that have invested heavily in a reputation for respecting the rule of law – one aspect of which is protecting property rights – have a lot to lose by reneging on their international obligations.

None of the control variables affects these findings. As anticipated, a weakening balance of payments, as well as higher volatility, contributes to violation, as does a worsening business cycle. Governments of more open economies work hard to abide by their obligation of policy openness, consistent with our expectation. Surprisingly, compliance with these obligations does not improve over time; if anything, violations worsen over the years when other variables in the model are held constant. Flexible exchange rates, GATT membership, and the use of IMF resources may be important institutional contexts for international economic relations, but they do not systematically affect the compliance decision.

CONCLUSIONS

The legalization of some central aspects of the international monetary regime after World War II allows us to examine the conditions under which law can influence the behavior of governments in the choice of their international monetary policies. Historically, this policy area has been devoid of international legal rules. The classical gold standard did

---

[58] See the review of this literature in Keech 1995.

not depend on international legal commitments for its reputed stability. "Soft" international legal commitments began to develop only in the interwar years, largely in response to markets' shattered confidence in the ability of governments to maintain the commitments they had made unilaterally in the previous period. Driven by the need to limit the externalization of macroeconomic adjustment costs, some governments sought international commitments as a way to enhance certainty and reassure markets. However, these commitments were in the softest possible form and did little to constrain behavior or encourage the confidence of economic agents.

The Bretton Woods agreement brought to an end the unbridled national legal sovereignty over monetary affairs. They hardly represent the triumph of legalization over market forces, however, as attested to by the breakdown of the original legal obligation to defend a par value system. Legal obligations cannot stifle market forces: capital mobility has made fixed rates very nearly unmanageable, treaty arrangements to the contrary notwithstanding. The end of the legal obligation to defend pegged rates is a clear reminder that legalization cannot be viewed in teleological terms. Obligations that increasingly frustrate major players as market conditions change are not likely to remain obligations for long.

* * *

Legalization is one way governments attempt to make credible their international monetary commitments. The evidence shows that governments are hesitant to make international legal commitments if there is a significant risk that they will not be able to honor them in the future. The hazard models of the rate of acceptance of Article VIII indicate that commitment is associated with conditions that one can reasonably anticipate will make compliance possible. Balance-of-payments weakness and volatility could and did delay the acceptance of obligations for openness significantly. Furthermore, economic downturns and unanticipated balance-of-payments difficulties were associated with noncompliance among Article VIII countries. However, both the archival evidence and the quantitative analysis presented here suggest that governments wanted to be relatively sure they could comply before they committed legally to the open foreign exchange regime. Legal commitment was part of a strategy to make a credible commitment to maintain a liberal foreign exchange regime.

Among Article VIII countries, two regime effects had clear consequences for compliance. Surprisingly for those who view the international behavior of democracies as somehow distinctive with respect to law and obligation, the more democratic the Article VIII country, the more likely it may have been ($p = .10$) to place restrictions on current account. On the other hand, regimes that were based on clear principles of the rule of law were far more likely to comply with their commitments. This finding indicates that rules and popular pressures can and apparently sometimes do pull in opposite directions when it comes to international law compliance. There is no reason to think, based on these findings, that democracy itself is a positive influence on the rule of law in international relations. On the contrary, there is more reason to associate compliance with the extent to which the polity in question respects institutional channels for mediating domestic conflict and protecting property rights than with a participatory or competitive political system. Some analysts have argued that this finding can be understood as a normative constraint on foreign policy choice. But it is also consistent with rational market incentives, since rule-of-law regimes have more to lose reputationally than do capricious regimes in the event of a legal violation.

One of the most interesting findings of this research has been the evidence that commitment and compliance are related to the commitment and compliance patterns beyond one's own borders. The hazard model clearly indicates that the breadth of acceptance influenced acceptance by uncommitted governments. Both worldwide and regional acceptance of Article VIII status had this effect, even when controlling for time. Furthermore, the pervasiveness of restrictions within a region has a negative effect on the compliance decision among Article VIII countries. It is impossible to know from these associational effects, of course, exactly what kinds of mechanisms might be at play in such a relationship. I have argued that these kinds of regional and universal effects likely reflect the strategic nature of implementing restrictions: punishment by economic agents and retaliation or other pressures by trading partners, for example, may be minimal where restrictions are common (since it is prohibitively costly to punish everyone). Those who offer more normative explanations of state behavior might interpret this pattern as an example of the importance of regional norms of appropriate behavior. Or perhaps it is simply the case that although governments feel some moral obligation to obey the law, their willingness to comply breaks down as others abandon the rules at will. Although these tests cannot distinguish these distinct explanations, the ability to document a degree of contingent compliance provides a basis for disentangling the possible mechanisms in future research. What we can say is that compliance and commitment are likely influenced, for whatever reason, by the actions taken by other members of the international system.

This research has broader implications for the study of legalization and compliance with international legal obligations. It shows that legalization as a tool for commitment is limited by economic conditions and market forces. International monetary legalization can be characterized by an inverted "J" pattern: legalization was nonexistent under the classical gold standard and soft during the interwar years. It peaked between 1946 and 1971, when treaty obligations regulated the central relationship among currencies, and now involves definite obligations over a more limited range of policies. Much of the behavior that constitutes international monetary relations remains completely outside of legalized relationships, especially rules and practices with respect to the provision of liquidity.[59]

Rather than debating whether compliance is pervasive or minimal,[60] my purpose here has been to examine the conditions under which compliance is likely. The study of international law compliance is rife with problems of conceptualization and measurement,[61] but in this case it has been possible to match a treaty obligation with authoritative assessments of behavior over time for a large number of countries and to match the suggested mechanisms with contextual archival materials. The evidence taken together points to law as a hook for making a credible commitment, with compliance largely "enforced" by the anticipation of reputational consequences.

[59] Art. VII, sec. 2 empowered the IMF to borrow from a member but also provided that no member should be obliged to lend to the IMF. Thus the General Agreement to Borrow was negotiated by the managing director and representatives of the signatory countries outside normal IMF channels. Reminiscent of the Tripartite Agreement, it was enshrined as a series of identical letters among participating countries. Swaps are also soft arrangements created by central banks and operating through the Bank of International Settlements. These were developed completely outside of the IMF framework. Dam 1982, 150. Nor are IMF standby arrangements a contract in the legal sense. Failure to carry out the performance criteria in the letter of intent is not a breach of any agreement and certainly not a breach of international law. All the "seal of approval" effects come despite the nonlegal nature of this commitment. The Executive board's decision of 20 September 1968 explicitly concerns the nonlegal status of standby arrangements. Gold 1979, 464–66.

[60] On this point, compare Chayes and Chayes 1993 and 1995 and Henkin 1979 with Downs, Rocke, and Barsoom 1996.

[61] These issues are discussed in Simmons 1998.

23

Constructing an Atrocities Regime: The Politics of War Crimes Tribunals

Christopher Rudolph

* * *

*** From the notorious "killing fields" of Cambodia to recent evidence of brutality in Sierra Leone, the grizzly nature of ethnic and other identity-oriented conflict incites horror, outrage, and a human desire for justice.

In response to reports of atrocities in Bosnia, Kosovo, and Rwanda the international community established ad hoc international war crimes tribunals to investigate crimes and prosecute perpetrators.[1] Successive efforts have been made to expand the atrocities regime by forming a permanent tribunal, the International Criminal Court (ICC). *** Proponents support international tribunals not only as a means of holding perpetrators of atrocities accountable but also as a mechanism of peace by establishing justice and promoting reconciliation in war-torn regions. Former U.S. Secretary of State Madeline Albright proposed that, "In the end, it is very difficult to have peace and reconciliation without justice."[2]

*** I seek to identify and analyze the myriad political and procedural obstacles to establishing an effective atrocities regime by examining humanitarian norms, the strategic interests of powerful states, and bureaucratic factors. *** I argue that although liberal humanitarian ideas have

[1] Another is being established for Sierra Leone pursuant to S.C. Res. 1315, UN SCOR, UN Doc. S/RES/1315 (2000).

[2] *Los Angeles Times*, 19 October 1999, A6.

I thank Arthur Stein; Kenneth Abbott; Gary Jonathan Bass; the editors of *IO*, Peter Gourevitch and David Lake; and two anonymous referees for their extremely helpful and constructive comments. The generous financial support of the Institute for the Study of World Politics, Washington, D.C., and the UCLA Graduate Division is gratefully acknowledged.

created the demand for political action, the process of dealing with brutality in war has been dominated by *realpolitik* – that is, furthering the strategic interests of the most powerful states. However, by understanding the political interests and procedural obstacles involved, the international community can make institutional adjustments in the design and implementation of an atrocities regime to bridge the gap between *idealpolitik* and *realpolitik*. ✳✳✳

✳✳✳ Historically, warfare has been viewed as consistent with the laws of nature. Hugo Grotius, in his seminal work *De Jure Belli ac Pacis Libri Tres (The Law of War and Peace)*, provides vivid accounts of wartime brutality consistent with norms of the time, citing Hellenic, Roman, and Biblical texts. Moreover, though Grotius includes some limitations on what was permissible in war, they would certainly be considered barbaric by modern liberal sensibilities. These norms permitted, for example, the killing or injuring of all who were in the territory of the enemy, including women, children, captives, and those whose surrender had not been accepted.[3] Rather than focusing on the *jus in bello*, Grotius is in fact more concerned with notions of the *jus ad bello*.[4]

In matters involving acts of war and treatment of a nation's citizenry, the dominant norm in the modern period is deference to national sovereignty. In fact, "prior to 1945, no principle of international law was more widely revered in practice than the idea of 'domestic jurisdiction' on matters relating to human rights."[5] Since the Holocaust, however, there has been tremendous interest in promoting human rights and creating more stringent standards of international conduct, including during armed conflicts, that is consistent with these evolving ideas.[6] What explains the dramatic turn in the 1990s toward legalization? What drives the process of forming and applying the regime in given cases? ✳✳✳

IDEAS, INTERESTS, AND INSTITUTIONS

✳✳✳ [Kenneth Abbott] suggests that, "IR helps us describe legal institutions richly, incorporating the political factors that shape the law; the interests, power, and governance structures of states and other actors;

---

[3] Grotius [1925] 1962, 641–62.

[4] *Jus in bello* focuses on conduct in war and the protection of civilians during armed conflict (crimes of war), whereas *jus ad bello* refers to acceptable justifications for the resort to armed force (the just war). See Christopher 1994.

[5] Beres 1988, 124.

[6] See Sikkink 1993 and 1998; and Finnemore 1996.

the information, ideas, and understandings on which they operate; [and] the institutions within which they interact."[7] Although the movement to establish a universal atrocities regime *** is predicated on the international community's desire to strengthen norms of human rights and justice, it is fraught with political obstacles and differing views on how to negotiate this complicated normative and strategic terrain. ***

Within the domain of IR theory, *** [realists] generally argue that in a world of asymmetrical power distribution with no international body to exert pressure, "logics of consequences dominate logics of appropriateness."[8] *** Realists predict that powerful states will not accept a regime that significantly undermines its ability to respond to perceived security threats. Moreover, they would predict that both the forms such institutions take and the application of their jurisdictions in particular cases will thus reflect the interests and relative power of the states involved. *** In contrast to realists, constructivists reject this notion that state interests are static and centered only on material factors; they suggest that such factors explain neither state behavior regarding human rights nor humanitarian intervention.[9] Regarding the creation of war crimes tribunals, constructivists would argue that evolving liberal ideas and concern for human rights explain outcomes and that analysis should focus on these variables in explaining regime formation. Ideas and norms produce outcomes either through "path dependence" or international socialization and gain strength as they become increasingly embedded, producing an *idealpolitik* to complement *realpolitik*.[10]

Bridging the gap between these two points of view, liberal institutionalism suggests that the proclivity for conflict in the anarchic international system can be overcome through carefully designed institutions whose purpose is international cooperation.[11] States engage in international regimes and abide by international treaties to realize gains contingent on cooperation, and states may forgo short-term gains to obtain long-term objectives. In the case of the emerging atrocities regime, these goals

---

[7] Abbott 1999, 362.

[8] See Krasner 1999, 51; see also Morgenthau 1985; and Carr 1961.

[9] See Finnemore 1996; Goldstein and Keohane 1993; Katzenstein 1996; Sikkink 1993; and Wendt 1992 and 1999.

[10] On "path dependence," see Weber 1920; Goldstein and Keohane 1993; and Meyer, Boli, and Thomas 1987. On international socialization, see Bull 1977; and Watson 1992.

[11] See Abbott and Snidal 1998; Axelrod 1984; Axelrod and Keohane 1985; Keohane and Martin 1995; Oye 1986; and Stein 1990. On regime theory, see Hasenclever, Mayer, and Rittberger 1997; and Krasner 1983.

clearly are attempts to alleviate political and identity-based conflict *** and to produce compliance (that is, deterrence).[12] *** Applied to the case of war crimes tribunals, this perspective suggests that success hinges on regime design and the strength of the resulting institution.[13] The central tension here is between "hard" and "soft" law.[14] Those who favor hard law in international legal regimes argue that it enhances deterrence and enforcement by signaling credible commitments, constraining self-serving auto-interpretation of rules, and maximizing "compliance pull" through increased legitimacy.[15] Those who favor soft law argue that it facilitates compromise, reduces contracting costs, and allows for learning and change in the process of institutional development.[16] *** Institutionalists would predict that a well-structured atrocities regime will not only hold orchestrators of genocide and crimes against humanity accountable but also deter future atrocities and help to alleviate tensions in sensitive regions prone to egregious acts of violence.

I begin my analysis with three cases where tribunals were successfully established: Bosnia, Rwanda, and Kosovo. These cases show the strong link between political challenges and legal (and procedural) challenges, especially when strategic interests of powerful states are not at stake. Whereas the case of Bosnia reveals the political obstacles to initially establishing an international legal regime, the cases of Rwanda and Kosovo illustrate both the dynamic process of legalization and the effects of institutional learning; they also reveal the limited deterrent capability of the atrocities regime – at least in the early stages of its development. I then examine two cases where tribunals were not successfully established: Cambodia and East Timor. I also examine the case of the ICC, which continues to be marked by difficulties in achieving great power support. These difficulties show how power and strategic interests dominate regime formation; they also point to the need for a "softening"

---

[12] On "legalization," see Abbott et al. 2000.

[13] Keohane 1997, 501. Oran Young identifies three types of regimes: spontaneous, negotiated, and imposed. While constructivists might focus on "spontaneous" orders, liberal institutionalists would examine the factors at play as the elements of a new regime are negotiated, as I do here. Young 1983, 98–101.

[14] Kenneth Abbott and Duncan Snidal define "hard" legalization as legally binding obligations characterized by high degrees of obligation, precision, and delegation, and define "soft" legalization as a more flexible manifestation characterized by varying degrees along one or more of these same dimensions. Abbott and Snidal 2000.

[15] See Abbott and Snidal 2000; and Franck 1990.

[16] Abbott and Snidal 2000; on flexibility and learning in international agreements, see Koremenos 1999.

of the legalization process if political obstacles are to be successfully overcome. ***

THE ICTY IN BOSNIA

The case of the International Criminal Tribunal for the former Yugoslavia (ICTY) illustrates the political difficulties associated with establishing an international legal regime where the strategic interests of powerful states are not directly at stake ***. This case is especially salient given international lawyers' initial desires to form a regime based on hard law, that is, one that could transcend *realpolitik* by eliminating distinctions between powerful states and weak states (equality under the law) and could challenge long-held notions of sovereignty. There are legal obstacles to creating hard law in an institution built on internationalism and attempting to bring together states with very disparate legal foundations. The case of the ICTY reveals the relevance of realism in explaining tribunal action and the process of institutionalization. Although norms and ideas of human rights prompt calls for state action in cases of genocide and war crimes, the case of the ICTY illustrates how the strategic interests of powerful states (through the UN Security Council) shape the process of institutionalization and its use.

*   *   *

In the early stages of the war in Yugoslavia (1990–91), the international community seemed intent on preserving the territorial integrity of the country and was hesitant to become entangled in a turbulent region that had ignited World War I.[17] *** One of the first events to prompt decisive international action was the discovery of atrocities at the Omarska detention camp near Prijedor. On 2 August 1992 *New York Newsday* reported that Bosnian Muslims held at the camp were being slaughtered by their Serbian guards. Moreover, subsequent reports likened conditions in the camp to Nazi concentration camps.[18] Similar conditions were alleged at another camp at Trnopolje. Television coverage worldwide showed striking images of men with protruding rib cages, recalling for viewers images of inmates freed from concentration camps at the close of World War II.[19] The similarity between events in

---

[17] Germany's early recognition of Croatia and Slovenia conspicuously went against the European consensus regarding the Balkan conflict. See Crawford 1994.

[18] Gutman 1993.

[19] Neier 1998, 135.

Nazi Germany and contemporary Bosnia served to cultivate close associations with World War II and its lessons. Considerations of the "Munich analogy" necessitated some kind of intervention.[20]

Further prompting analogies to Nazi-era crimes against humanity was the program of "ethnic cleansing" being undertaken in Bosnia. Before this program was initiated, the population in the Prijedor municipality of northwestern Bosnia, for example, was 112,470, of which 44 percent were Muslim, 42.5 percent were Serbian, 5.6 percent were Croat, 5.7 percent were of mixed ethnicity, and 2.2 percent were "other."[21] By June 1993, figures released by the Serbian media showed that the number of Muslims living in Prijedor had declined from 49,454 to 6,124; and the number of Croats from 6,300 to 3,169; but the number of Serbs had increased from 47,745 to 53,637.[22] An international consensus developed that Serbs were the principal instigators of wartime atrocities; however, those who were to investigate the situation would find it more complex than it appeared at the time. Cedric Thornberry noted that "all three sides were responsible for appalling developments in Bosnia. The actions of some of the Croats of western Herzogovina rivaled in barbarity those of Serb chieftains of eastern Bosnia, and what was done to the Muslims of Mostar by Croats was perhaps as bad as the Serb shelling of the mainly Muslim parts of Sarajevo."[23] While documented atrocities demanded international humanitarian intervention, the political and strategic complexities involved provided an unappealing scenario for the international community. Some observers drew an analogy between Bosnia and the Vietnam War, and pundits considered the Balkan crisis a conflict that presented a "slippery slope" for all who dared to involve themselves.

*** Torn between the ethical desire to promote human rights and the tactical and political challenges of intervention, the creation of a UN tribunal represented a palatable compromise. As one analyst noted, "It was a way to do *something* about Bosnia that would have no political cost domestically."[24]

Using its authority under Chapter VII of the UN Charter, the Security Council passed the resolution to create the ICTY for the purpose of prosecuting four clusters of offenses: (1) Grave breaches of the 1949 Geneva

---

[20] Ibid., 136–37.
[21] Ibid., 138.
[22] Ibid., 139.
[23] Thornberry 1996, 79.
[24] Neier 1998, 129.

Conventions (Art. 2), (2) violations of the laws or customs of war (Art. 3), (3) genocide (Art. 4), and (4) crimes against humanity (Art. 5).[25] * * *

The first challenge of the ICTY was to establish guidelines for fairness within its institutional structure, considered by international lawyers to be a key component of its legitimacy. As one ICTY prosecutor remarked, "If the tribunal is necessary . . . to bring a sense of justice to the victims, and thereby undercut the hopeless cycle of revenge, then it is imperative that everything the tribunal does be fair to the accused and conducted according to the highest standards of due process."[26] Hence, there has been a strong push to make the body truly "international," though the influence of the UN Security Council is omnipresent. Judges are nominated and elected by the member states of the UN General Assembly, but the list of nominees must first be approved by the UN Security Council.[27] Moreover, the chief prosecutor – a key figure in the adjudication process – is appointed exclusively by the Security Council on the recommendation of the Secretary General, rather than being nominated by the General Assembly, as is the case for judges. * * *

The tribunal's legal jurisdiction poses another challenge. According to currently accepted notions of international humanitarian law, war crimes are limited to situations of international armed conflict.[28] Moreover, while the ICTY may prosecute breaches of the 1949 Geneva Convention, its jurisdiction is limited to "grave breaches." As one legal analyst noted, "A 'grave breach' can only be committed against a person protected by the Convention; that is, only a person of a nationality different from that of the perpetrator."[29] Therefore, the grave breach clause does not cover, for example, the slaughter or rape of a Bosnian Muslim by a Bosnian Serb. While international legal sovereignty was granted to Croatia, facilitating adjudication by making the domestic/international line more distinct, less clear are cases involving Kosovo and Rwanda because the conflict was between rival ethnic groups and no such sovereignty has been granted. These crucial issues of jurisdiction were brought up by the defense in the case of Dusko Tadic, a former official at the Omarska prison camp. However, the court ruled that although Article 2

---

[25] ICTY Fact Sheet, 16 September 1999, available at <http://www.un.org/icty/glance/fact.htm>.

[26] Schrag 1995, 194.

[27] The roster of judges is diverse, though nationals of the permanent members of the Security Council comprise nearly 30 percent of the presiding judges.

[28] Morris and Scharf 1995, 391.

[29] Scharf and Epps 1996, 651.

of the Geneva Convention applies only to international conflicts, Article 3 applies to war crimes whether or not combatants are from different countries, adding that "the distinction between interstate wars and civil wars is losing its value as far as human beings are concerned."[30]

* * *

The most pressing challenge the ICTY faces is apprehending and detaining defendants. At Nuremberg most surviving instigators of Hitler's "final solution" were apprehended by the Allies and detained for trial. The ICTY began with no defendants in custody. The problem this presents is clear: "The ad hoc tribunal for former Yugoslavia has itself to arrange the capture of those it is to try. For this crucial element in the procedure it will be totally dependent on the assistance of belligerent and third states."[31] This challenge is further compounded by the tribunal's prohibition on trials in absentia, a component of the institutional structure intended to bolster fairness of the proceedings; however, as Theodor Meron noted, "without *in absentia* trials, the tribunal is left with few options. The international community has given the tribunal strong rhetorical support, but little aid in enforcement."[32] Consequently, the tribunal initially tried those having little political power or significance, since those masterminding wartime atrocities were better able to elude apprehension. Thus, as one analyst remarked, "the securing of the attendance of the accused war criminal may be random, ineffectual, and arbitrary."[33]

Such obstacles, though initially daunting, have not been insurmountable. As of 1 March 2001, thirty-five defendants were awaiting trial in the ICTY detention unit, and twelve cases had been concluded through the appeals stage. *** The *** arrest of Slobodan Milosevic by Yugoslav police on 1 April 2001 and subsequent extradition to The Hague on 28 June 2001 certainly represents a milestone for the tribunal regime. Milosevic is the first head of state to face trial at the tribunal.

The ICTY's experience in the Balkans reveals not only the legal and procedural difficulties in designing a regime to combat atrocities but also the influence of powerful states during the process of institutionalization. While vivid images from Balkan prison camps recalled memories

---

[30] *Prosecutor v. Tadic*, IT-94-1-AR72, P77 (1995).
[31] Fox 1993, 194.
[32] Meron 1997, 4.
[33] Fox 1993, 196.

of the Holocaust and engendered public calls for action, powerful states used the ICTY as a means to respond to such calls in a politically inexpensive way. Moreover, once the international community decided to establish an ad hoc tribunal, the influence of the UN Security Council was omnipresent in key aspects of its design, in particular, its jurisdiction and the appointment of judges and the chief prosecutor. These same factors are also evident in the application of the atrocities regime in Rwanda.

GENOCIDE IN RWANDA

In 1994 the atrocities regime was extended to Rwanda.[34] This case is instructive for two reasons: it illustrates how the interests of the great powers affect the process of regime formation, and, perhaps more importantly, it demonstrates that negotiating the political terrain between "hard" and "soft" law is a dynamic process involving degrees of institutional learning. Given the scope and magnitude of the atrocities committed in Rwanda and the procedural, bureaucratic, and budgetary obstacles involved in developing an effective tribunal, this case illustrates the need for institutional flexibility. Moreover, because the tribunal in Rwanda followed the precedent set by the ICTY, this case allows us to assess the regime's broader goals: deterrence and national reconciliation.

Violence plagued Rwanda for most of the late 1980s and early 1990s, and on 6 April 1994 the plane carrying Juvénal Habyarimana, president of Rwanda, and Cyprien Ntaryamira, president of Burundi, was shot down over Kigali, Rwanda. Ethnic Hutus immediately blamed Tutsi rebels of the Rwandan Patriotic Front, and within minutes after the crash soldiers of the presidential guard began hunting down Tutsis and indiscriminately killing all they encountered. Aid workers estimated that as many as 500,000 Tutsis were killed in the month after the assassination.[35] More than three-quarters of the Tutsi population in Rwanda are estimated to have been killed.[36] Another estimate suggests that in April, May, and June 1994 more than half of Rwanda's population of 7.5 million people were either killed or displaced.[37] As was the case in the early stages of ethnic conflict in the former Yugoslavia, Western governments were reluctant to intervene for fear of casualties. ***

---

[34] An excellent historical account of the tragedy in Rwanda can be found in Des Forges 1999.
[35] *Time*, 16 May 1994, 57.
[36] Kuperman 2000, 101.
[37] *Time*, 13 June 1994, 36.

While military intervention was not forthcoming after the events of April and May 1994,[38] the UN Security Council created the International Criminal Tribunal for Rwanda (ICTR) on 8 November 1994. Its jurisdiction is time specific – that is, it covers only the period from 1 January 1994 to 31 December 1994; its scope is limited to those events temporally proximate to the assassination of President Habyarimana. To promote consistency between the two ad hoc tribunals – considered crucial to establishing a clear precedent and consistent legal norms – Article 12 of the statute specifies that the appeals chamber of the ICTY will also serve as the appeals chamber for cases brought before the ICTR. Moreover, to encourage consistency in investigations and prosecutorial strategy Article 15 specifies that the chief prosecutor of the ICTY will also serve as the chief prosecutor of the ICTR.

That the basic structure of the ICTY was implemented in another atrocities scenario speaks to its success in being perceived as an appropriate policy option in cases where massive human rights violations have occurred. By 22 February 2001 forty-four suspects were being held at the UN detention facility in Arusha, Tanzania.[39] The ICTR was initially more successful than the ICTY in detaining high-profile defendants, including former military commanders and political leaders * * *.[40] Yet the ICTR faces many of the same political and procedural challenges as the ICTY.

Although it can be argued that the war in Bosnia and Croatia was an international conflict stemming from international legal recognition granted to the separatist republics, this was clearly not the case in Rwanda. However, by ruling that Article 3 of the Geneva Convention applies to both interstate and intrastate conflict, the ICTY opened the door to international adjudication of internal conflicts, such as that in Rwanda.[41] The normative importance of this precedent cannot be overstated, for it clearly expands the jurisdiction of the tribunal and applies international law to issues that traditionally have deferred to national sovereignty.[42] While this precedent certainly aids the ICTR in trying suspected war criminals in Rwanda, this expansion of jurisdiction may become a significant obstacle to a working international criminal court, since powerful states have expressed concern about an international court that seeks to expand its authority.

---

[38] See Des Forges 1999; and Kuperman 2000.
[39] <http://www.ictr.org>.
[40] LCHR 1997, 2.
[41] *Prosecutor v. Tadic*, IT-94-1-AR72 (1995).
[42] Meron 1995.

The limited temporal jurisdiction applied to the ICTR is also a point of contention that initially threatened cooperation between the tribunal and the Rwandan government. In fact the Rwandan government opposed the establishment of the tribunal as articulated in the Security Council's resolution, even though it initially solicited Security Council action.[43] The Rwandan ambassador to the United States explained, "the government of Rwanda regarded the dates set for the *ratione temporis* competence of the international tribunal for Rwanda . . . as inadequate. The genocide which the world witnessed in April 1994 had been the result of a long period of planning during which pilot projects for extermination had been successfully tested before this date."[44] Reports of massacres and ethnic violence taking place in 1991–93 were documented by several agencies, including the Special Rapporteur of the UN (May 1993). Because of this, the Rwandan government proposed that the tribunal's jurisdiction be extended back to 1 October 1990, a proposal ultimately rejected by the Security Council. While the Security Council's decision clearly helps to expedite the adjudication process by limiting its investigation, Rwandan representatives have countered that this will severely curtail its ability to achieve domestic reconciliation: "An international tribunal which refused to consider the causes of the genocide . . . cannot be of any use to Rwanda because it will not contribute to eradicating the culture of impunity or creating a climate conducive to national reconciliation."[45] Here we see acute political tension between the need for expediency in the adjudication process and the need for domestic cooperation and holistic efforts to deal with the causes of the conflict.

According to the tribunal statute, the ICTR's jurisdiction has primacy over national courts, and it may request national courts to defer to it at any stage of ongoing proceedings.[46] Clearly, for such transfers to take place, cooperation with state authorities is imperative. In addition Article 9 of the statute conforms to the principle of *non bis in idem*.[47] These two principles are clearly at odds when national court proceedings are underway or have been completed. In cases where an ongoing national trial is not impartial or independent, jurisdiction is to be transferred to the ICTR; however, the ICTR's rules of procedure and evidence

---

[43] *New York Times*, 29 December 1994, A1.
[44] Bakuramutsa 1995, 645.
[45] Ibid., 646.
[46] ICTR statute, Art. 8(2). Similar jurisdictional primacy is codified in Art. 9.
[47] *Non bis in idem* refers to prohibitions against trying defendants twice for the same crime(s), often referred to as "double jeopardy."

offer no clear guidelines for doing this, nor do they specify who is to make such decisions. Moreover, the primacy of the ICTR's jurisdiction over that of the national courts also pays little heed to the cultural elements of local legal norms, an element that may be crucial to the tribunal's goal of achieving national reconciliation and alleviating ethnic tensions. The ICTR is authorized to impose a maximum sentence of life imprisonment, whereas the Rwandan national courts may impose the death penalty for those found guilty of capital crimes. Rwandan diplomats have expressed the common belief that those tried by the tribunal "would get off more lightly than ordinary Rwandans who faced the death penalty in local courts."[48] The provisions prohibiting double jeopardy leave the national courts no recourse when the tribunal's decisions are seen as unjust. According to Rwandan legal sensibilities, the ICTR does not offer an adequate range of sentencing options to distinguish top-level planners from those who carried out the plans. Because it is possible that those who devised and organized the genocide may escape capital punishment (if tried by the tribunal) but those who simply carried out the orders may not (if tried by domestic courts), such incongruities may not be conducive to national reconciliation in Rwanda.[49] This perceived incongruity was also cited by the Rwandan government as a reason they could not support the tribunal; instead, Rwanda established the Organic Law on the Organization of Prosecutions for Offenses Constituting the Crime of Genocide or Crimes Against Humanity Committed Since October 1, 1990.[50] These new national laws, to be adjudicated in the national courts, classify suspects into four categories according to degree of culpability – leaders and organizers are subject to the death penalty, whereas those accused of lesser crimes may be eligible for reduced penalties in exchange for a complete confession, a guilty plea, and an apology to victims.[51]

* * *

Further hindering the ICTR's ability to foster national reconciliation is the tribunal's lack of relevance to the Rwandan population. While the statute identifies neutrality and independence as institutional imperatives – largely because Security Council members believed the tribunal's neutrality was essential for reconciliation – neutrality may in fact work against

[48] Bakuramutsa 1995, 648.
[49] Bakuramutsa 1995. See also *New York Times,* 2 November 1994; and *International Herald-Tribune,* 9 November 1994.
[50] Available online at <http://www.rwandemb.org/prosecution/law.htm>.
[51] As specified in Art. 2, 5, and 14–16.

reconciliation. "The structural distance of the ICTR from the Rwandan social process makes it very difficult for the ICTR's work to be relevant and even more unlikely that its work will address the root causes of the genocide."[52] This "social distance" takes place at several levels. The tribunal convenes in Arusha, Tanzania, not in Rwanda. This location, though chosen to promote neutrality, instead separates the proceedings from the people they were intended to help. Moreover, "there is a disconnection between the ICTR trials and the internal social process. Not only the physical distance, but the way in which the ICTR has operated and publicized its efforts does not involve the population in any real sense."[53] While the government-operated radio station provides limited coverage of trial proceedings, there are no television broadcasts outside the capital city, and few Rwandans understand the legal procedures and proceedings.

From the outset, the relationship between the largely Tutsi government of Rwanda and the ICTR has been, in the words of one analyst, "frosty."[54] While simple logistics give the ICTR a strong incentive to limit the duration of its legal jurisdiction – in August 1999 Rwandan detention facilities held over 124,000 prisoners awaiting legal procedure[55] – this limitation may profoundly affect the tribunal's success in establishing reconciliation among the Rwandan population. Other analysts counter that other forces are at play: "Those [temporal] limits were the product of a highly political process within the Security Council and reflect diplomatic concerns. Broader jurisdiction for the ICTR could well have led to inquiries that would have embarrassed either the UN as a whole or particular permanent members of the Security Council."[56] Yet dealing with a war crimes scenario as vast as that encountered by the ICTR often poses a dilemma: Limiting the scope of the investigation and trials may impede justice by not holding all of the guilty accountable for their actions and reduce the tribunal's success in achieving reconciliation in Rwanda (and elsewhere); however, a more expansive role burdens an already over-extended institution and may significantly affect its ability to quickly resolve cases. * * *

---

[52] Howland and Calathes 1998, 161.
[53] Ibid., 155.
[54] *New York Times*, 21 November 1997, A10.
[55] *Deutsche Presse-Agentur*, 13 August 1999.
[56] Alvarez 1999, 397.

THE ICTY IN KOSOVO

Further application of the tribunal system became necessary in 1999 as ethno-nationalist warfare broke out between ethnic Albanian nationalist forces and the Serbian army. While initial casualties were light by international standards, numbering some 2,500, accusations of renewed "ethnic cleansing" by Serbian forces surfaced after the failure of the Rambouillet talks and subsequent NATO air strikes. Reports of mass graves, torture, rape, and executions of ethnic Albanians poured out of Kosovo as quickly as the thousands of refugees who left their homeland under duress; calls for war crimes investigations were nearly concurrent with NATO action. On 29 September 1999 it was announced that the ICTY's jurisdiction under its original statute would be extended to Kosovo. Like the case of Rwanda, this case sheds light on whether the tribunal's actions in Bosnia had any effect on deterrence and national reconciliation. It not only addresses a conflict that occurred after a tribunal action elsewhere but also allows us to assess whether fear of adjudication affects the decisions of political and military leaders. In this case many of those accused of atrocities had already been named as perpetrators in the Bosnian conflict. The re-application of the atrocities regime to the volatile situation in the Balkans also brings to the surface the public's perception of tribunal action, that is, whether decollectivization of guilt can promote national reconciliation and peace. On both accounts, the case of ICTY action in Kosovo is not encouraging.

To gain "institutional momentum" during the Bosnia investigations, the ICTY actively pursued investigations against defendants at all levels of culpability. Most of the defendants and detainees in the Bosnia trials were at the lower rungs of command and control, yet they were considered important for establishing procedural norms and precedent. Functional considerations have prompted the tribunal to pursue exceptionalism, focusing investigations on successful prosecution of the significant players. One court official noted, "As far as I'm concerned, [the tribunal] simply can't try every Tom, Dick, and Harry."[57] The tribunal prosecutor added, "It is clear that the OTP [Office of the Prosecutor] ICTY has neither the mandate, nor the resources, to function as the primary investigative and prosecutorial agency for all criminal acts committed on the territory of Kosovo."[58] While there are tactical benefits to prosecuting low-level

[57] *Los Angeles Times,* 27 August 1999, A5.
[58] Statement by Carla del Ponte, 29 September 1999. Available online at <http://www.un.org/icty/pressreal/p437-e.htm>.

perpetrators, most analysts have stressed that the ICTY's deterrence value hinges ultimately on its ability to successfully prosecute those at the highest levels.[59]

The Kosovo case is also very useful in analyzing the tribunal's ability to shape state action, since the conflict in Kosovo followed two tribunals that successfully tried war crimes cases. Clearly, the evidence emerging from Kosovo – mass graves, witness accounts of summary executions of civilians, torture – suggest that Serbs were clearly undeterred by the presence of the ICTY. This was documented by Cedric Thornberry, who in his dealings with those involved in war crimes atrocities observed that

> Our interlocutors plainly were skeptical that the "international community" would do anything. In Belgrade and Zagreb, they usually preserved the diplomatic niceties and kept straight faces, but often the sneer around the table was nearly audible. In less sophisticated circles, when we spoke directly with those we knew had been the instigators and warned them that justice would some day come, the local establishment and its forces of law and order often snickered aloud.[60]

Similar attitudes were also evident during hearings on Rule 61 held in The Hague in July 1996 (discussed later); a witness testified that Ratko Mladic scoffed openly at NATO's inability to protect the Muslims in Srebenica in July 1995, an event that occurred two years after the ICTY was created.[61] Clearly, the desired effect of adjudication, to deter war crimes, has been significantly hampered by the difficulty of arresting suspects, especially during the tribunal's early period. Even prosecutors in The Hague agree that "the only true deterrents . . . are not investigations but arrests."[62] Yet members of the international community seem to have little desire to take the tactical risks involved in apprehending the high-level perpetrators currently indicted.[63] After the Dayton Accords brought the conflict in Bosnia to a close, the NATO

---

[59] See Scharf 1997, 219, 225; Alvarez 1999; and Morris 1997.

[60] Thornberry 1996, 77.

[61] Guest 1996, 80.

[62] *New York Times*, 15 September 1999, A3.

[63] A detailed plan to capture Radovan Karadzic, called "Operation Amber Star," was completed in April 1997 and involved several hundred French and U.S. commandos. When advised of the plan, President Clinton wanted French forces to spearhead the raid; however, Jacques Chirac was reluctant to assume such a "high risk" position for fear of reprisals against French troops in the region. Likewise, Clinton and British Prime Minister Tony Blair were reluctant because of concerns over potential casualties, and so the plan was never executed. *Time*, 10 August 1998, 68–70.

implementation force (IFOR) was given extremely cautious instructions for dealing with indicted war criminals.[64] Initial operating procedures authorized IFOR troops to arrest those they encountered but did not permit IFOR to seek them out.[65] ***

In an effort to increase the deterrence value of the tribunal, given the difficulties involved in arresting indicted war criminals, the ICTY established Rule 61 (under Art. 15 of the statute), which provides for a "super-indictment" in certain instances. The purpose of this rule is to broaden world awareness of perpetrators' actions without violating the mandate forbidding trials in absentia. It allows the indictment and all supporting evidence to be submitted to the tribunal in an open court session. This may include examination of witnesses whose testimony becomes part of the record. Under the provisions of Rule 61, the prosecution may present highlights of the case in the absence of the accused, essentially for the media.[66] While the line between executing Rule 61 and prohibiting absentia trials is rather thin, the aim of the super-indictment is unmistakable: to ensure that those indicted will be considered international pariahs, even if they manage to elude arrest.[67] *** Rather than establishing closure through justice, these measures seem to be stop-gap attempts to provide some sense of "justice" to victims of war crimes until the guilty parties can be brought to trial. The question is, will such stop-gap measures provide the necessary deterrence and reconciliation to mitigate future transgressions of the *jus belli,* especially as time between transgression and adjudication becomes ever greater?

Although the slow pace of proceedings is understandable given the legal and logistical hurdles facing the ICTY, it may hinder both deterrence and national reconciliation.[68] In a recent news report, interviews revealed that many Serbs are avoiding responsibility for the ethnic hatred that drove the program of ethnic cleansing, and many deny that atrocities, such as those committed at Srebenica, ever really occurred.[69] In an

---

[64] IFOR was later renamed "Stabilization Force" (SFOR).

[65] See Meron 1997, 5; and Bass 2000.

[66] Thornberry 1996, 83.

[67] Scharf and Epps 1996, 649.

[68] One tribunal judge remarked that if Milosevic were turned over to the ICTY for trial, it would be three years before his case would find a place on the docket. See *Los Angeles Times,* 27 August 1999, A5. In a June 2000 report to the UN Security Council, it was estimated that it would take sixteen years to complete the ICTY's current caseload. See *Los Angeles Times,* 6 July 2000, A10.

[69] *Los Angeles Times,* 6 July 2000, A1, A10.

opinion poll published in June 1999 by the newsmagazine *Nin,* almost two-thirds of Serbs do not believe that the atrocities alleged in the tribunal proceedings occurred; instead they "emphasize the high price that Serbs are now paying."[70] This sense of "reversal" was well articulated by a Serb lawyer: "I didn't kill anyone, but an Albanian neighbor told me I would never be safe in Kosovo. I am a victim of their ethnic cleansing."[71] Others considered tribunal reports as nothing less than anti-Serb propaganda. Ethnic Albanians seem particularly sensitive to what they perceive as a whitewashing by the Serbian government. Pajazit Nushi, member of the Council for Defense of Human Rights and Freedoms in Pristina, notes, "Still, now, there is no single Serbian political voice that has condemned the crimes."[72] Moreover, the withdrawal of Serbian troops from Kosovo has been accompanied by acts of violent retribution by ethnic Albanians. One news account noted, "In the early days of NATO occupation, many Serbs who stayed [in Kosovo] were optimistic that they could forge a future with their Albanian neighbors. But a wave of retaliatory killings of Serbs by Albanians enraged by wartime atrocities has calcified emotions."[73] Time is certainly not assisting efforts to create a peaceful, multiethnic Kosovo, as new justifications for animosity between ethnic groups are kindled and old hatreds reinforced.

Clearly, the deterrence value of the emergent regime has been, to this point, quite weak, owing largely to the reluctance of the international community to aggressively pursue high-level perpetrators; however, the arrest of Milosevic and the possibility of his extradition for trial at the Hague tribunal leaves considerable room for optimism that the regime's deterrence power may dramatically increase. The case of ICTY action in Kosovo also illustrates the limitations of the atrocities regime in promoting national reconciliation in ethnically torn states. It remains to be seen whether the arrest of Milosevic will serve to disclose the truth of events that occurred during the Balkan conflict and promote national healing, or whether his arrest and extradition in response to Western pressure will further calcify animosities between ethnic groups in the region. The ability of the ICTY to obtain Milosevic's extradition is a crucial point in the development of a more viable atrocities regime.

---

[70] *Los Angeles Times,* 2 July 1999, A1.
[71] Ibid.
[72] *Los Angeles Times,* 10 October 1999, A1.
[73] Ibid., A30.

JUSTICE IN SOUTHEAST ASIA?

That the ICTY has not only survived but has served as a model for other ad hoc tribunals, including a permanent international criminal court, could indicate that war crimes adjudication is a successful policy tool. However, although the regime has overcome considerable procedural and structural obstacles in the Balkans and Rwanda, these obstacles remain formidable in other cases. In regions dominated by power politics, regime/norm development remains in the formative stage, especially in situations where powerful states have strong incentives *not* to become involved. Without the direct intervention by strong states and cooperation by governments in states where atrocities are alleged to have occurred, the atrocities regime lacks strength.

Cambodia

It has been estimated that more than a million Cambodians died from execution, torture, disease, or hunger from 1975 to 1979 under the Khmer Rouge regime; some estimates go as high as 2 million. Although it is unclear why a war crimes tribunal was not established earlier in the wake of such a profound human tragedy, the institutional momentum of the atrocities regime has prompted the UN to seek to establish a judicial mechanism for Cambodia. The failure to establish a tribunal earlier can be attributed to the interests of several Security Council member states and to the recalcitrance of the current Cambodian government.

At the time atrocities were committed a tribunal was not in the strategic interests of the United States; in the aftermath of the Vietnam War there was little incentive once again to become entangled in Southeast Asia's political quagmire. Moreover, in adjudicating charges of war crimes, information about U.S. secret bombings of Cambodia and other sensitive information could become part of the public record. William Dowell, UN correspondent for *Time,* suggests that many countries, including the United States, "have used the Khmer Rouge to pursue their own political interests in the region at one time or another, and all are reluctant to talk about their relationship with the Khmer Rouge."[74] This fear may be particularly acute for China, already dealing with image problems that complicate its bid for membership in the World Trade Organization. Given the current political climate, Beijing is understandably hesitant to have its role in supporting the Khmer Rouge regime exposed to the

[74] *Time,* 22 January 1999.

international community it wishes to engage.[75] While such reasons may discourage powerful governments from becoming involved, public demands for action in Cambodia have also been less acute than was the case for the Balkans or Rwanda. In the United States public desire for justice and accountability has been tempered by an equally compelling desire to "close the book" on the Vietnam era, reducing domestic demands for state action.

Domestic resistance is also an important factor in Cambodia. Initial UN attempts to establish a tribunal for Cambodia were met with little cooperation from the Cambodian government, especially Prime Minister Hun Sen. The UN has proposed several possible tribunal configurations, all of which display institutional adjustments stemming from the lessons learned in the Balkans and Rwanda. First, the UN wishes to try in a single trial only twelve former political and military leaders of the Khmer Rouge, thereby avoiding the protracted proceedings that plague other ad hoc tribunals currently in operation; however, the Cambodian government has expressed little interest. "We have no confidence in an international court of law," noted Hun Sen, showing concern that a trial may upset his fragile hold on power in Cambodia.[76] Hun Sen has been concerned that the scope of criminal culpability may make reconciliation through justice problematic in Cambodia. As one observer remarked, "justice itself seems a rusty chain that will only bloody anyone who tries to touch it. To try Khmer Rouge chieftains would be, in a sense, to prosecute the whole country."[77]

* * *

The case of Cambodia also illustrates the problem time poses when relying on adjudication to promote peace and reconciliation. Although there is no statute of limitations on tribunal indictments, human rights groups argue that because of the advanced age and poor health of many suspects, quick action to create a tribunal is imperative lest Cambodia lose its chance to bring Khmer Rouge leaders to justice.[78]

Indonesia and East Timor

In response to a successful referendum in September 1999 declaring East Timor's independence from Indonesia, pro-Indonesia militias mounted

[75] *South China Morning Post*, 25 August 1999, 14.
[76] *Time*, 22 March 1999, 56.
[77] *Time*, 16 August 1999.
[78] *New York Times*, 12 August 1999, A8.

a campaign of violence and intimidation throughout East Timor. *** In light of evidence of human rights abuses, the UN Commission for Human Rights (UNCHR) opened a special session that resulted in a resolution calling for a preliminary investigation into war crimes in East Timor, seen by many as the first step toward establishing a war crimes tribunal.[79] The resolution specifically refers to Security Council Resolution 1264, in which the Council "demanded that those responsible for such acts be brought to justice."[80] However, the government of Indonesia quickly rejected the UNCHR resolution, a move that denied UN investigators access to Jakarta's military files. During the special session of the UNCHR, the Indonesian representative dismissed the need for international intervention: "The Government last night had established a fact-finding commission to compile information on human-rights violations and bring the perpetrators to justice. It was important to ensure that this august body not do anything that would open old wounds and exacerbate problems in the territory."[81] Indeed, the Indonesian government's lack of cooperation makes the creation of a tribunal quite unlikely.

That tribunals were not established in Cambodia and Indonesia reflects two weaknesses in relying on international law to provide peace and reconciliation in war-torn regions: the need for cooperation, both internationally and in war-torn regions, and the hesitancy of the international community to intervene militarily. While ad hoc tribunals may be formed by fiat of the Security Council, the difficulties encountered by the ICTY show how lack of cooperation may stifle institutional effectiveness and regime development. Proponents of an international criminal court point to Cambodia and East Timor, where the atrocities regime appears beholden to the interests of the powerful, as evidence that such a permanent institution is necessary if a truly effective regime is to be established.

THE INTERNATIONAL CRIMINAL COURT

*** While the ICC is not a specific case of the application of a legal regime to an instance of genocide or crimes against humanity, examining its development is crucial to understanding the political challenges of expanding the existing ad hoc tribunal system to a more universal

[79] UNCHR Res. 1999/S-4/1.

[80] S.C. Res. 1264, UN Doc. S/RES/1264 (1999). See also S.C. Res. 1272, Art. 16, UN Doc. S/RES/1272 (1999), available online at <http://www.un.org/Docs/scres/1999/99sc1272.htm>.

[81] UN press release, HR/CN/99/67, 23 September 1999, 6.

atrocities regime. This case illustrates the tension between the need for great power support and the desire to establish a hard law regime that transcends power and political interests (that is, holds strong and weak states equally accountable). *** The ad hoc system employed in the existing atrocities regime is appealing to powerful states because it facilitates adjudication, yet control over its application in a given case remains with the Security Council. *** While the statute to create the ICC is an established fact, its power as part of the atrocities regime remains contested and indefinite, and its development is marked by concessions made to great power interests. This case suggests that if the atrocities regime is to gain widespread acceptance, the process of legalization will likely undergo "softening" in order to mitigate the political contracting costs of the new regime. As noted by Kenneth W. Abbott and Duncan Snidal, hardening the legal foundations of the atrocities regime is a sensitive and protracted process that may involve initially taking softer positions.[82]

Although President Clinton signed the Rome Statute on 31 December 2000 that created the ICC, the United States has long opposed several key components of the Rome Statute, opposition still expressed by the Bush administration.[83] The first involves the universal jurisdiction provisions as articulated in the statute that subject any state, signatory to the statute or not, to the court's jurisdiction.[84] ***

The United States was also concerned that the scope of crimes covered under the court's jurisdiction was overly broad. "Crimes of aggression," for example, is included, though no precise definition of "aggression" was agreed on during the drafting of the statute. ***

Another concern was the prosecutor's authority to investigate crimes even in cases where no state party had issued a complaint. Under Articles 13 and 15, the prosecutor may investigate crimes *proprio motu* based on information provided by parties within the court's jurisdiction.[85] U.S. negotiators wanted to limit the power to bring cases to the court to the Security Council, consistent with the precedent set by the ad hoc tribunals. Without this limitation, U.S. negotiators argued, members of the U.S. armed forces "would be subject to frivolous, politically motivated charges" that may hinder crucial peacekeeping missions in the future if there was a possibility of "malicious prosecution."[86] ***

---

[82] Abbott and Snidal 2000.
[83] *Los Angeles Times*, 15 February 2001, A4.
[84] Rome Statute, Article 4(2).
[85] Rome Statute, Article 13(c); 15(1).
[86] David 1999, 357.

Finally, the Clinton administration insisted on an exception for personnel involved in official military action. David Scheffer, U.S. ambassador-at-large for war crimes issues, stated that the United States wanted "a clear recognition that states sometimes engage in very legitimate uses of military force to advance international peace and security."[87] *** Critics, however, argue that exceptions would render the ICC an empty vessel. Richard Dicker, associate counsel for Human Rights Watch, argued that the exceptions favored by the United States represent "a loophole the size of the Grand Canyon that any rogue state would drive right through."[88]

*** One U.S. official remarked, "We have shown that the only way to get war criminals to trial is for the U.S. to take a prominent role. If the U.S. is not a lead player in the creation of this court, it doesn't happen."[89] While Clinton's signing of the Rome Statute was lauded by ICC proponents and human rights organizations, it may be more symbolic than instrumental. Articulating the Bush administration's stance at the UN, Secretary of State Colin Powell declared, "As you know, the United States . . . does not support the International Criminal Court. President Clinton signed the treaty, but we have no plans to send it forward to our Senate for ratification."[90] As normative considerations press for harder legalization in the emergent atrocities regime,[91] negotiating the political dimensions necessary to building institutional strength seems predicated on softening some aspects to gain the necessary international consensus. The evidence suggests that such softening measures have already taken place.

EVALUATING THE ATROCITIES REGIME

Formation

The evidence suggests that expanding liberal norms of state conduct and protecting human rights certainly explain the existence of tribunals in locales with little strategic or material importance. The proliferation of human rights norms is evident in current legal trends in both the United States and Europe.[92]

---

[87] Quoted in *Associated Press*, 14 August 1999, PM Cycle.
[88] Quoted in *Associated Press*, 14 August 1999, PM Cycle.
[89] *Time*, 27 July 1998, 46.
[90] *Los Angeles Times*, 2 February 2001, A4.
[91] For example, holding perpetrators of genocide, war crimes, and crimes against humanity accountable independent of political power and interests involved.
[92] Henkin 1990.

In the United States the term *human rights* was articulated in only 19 federal court cases prior to 1900; this number grew to 34 from 1900 to 1944, 191 from 1945 to 1969, 803 in the 1970s, 2000 times in the 1980s, and over 4000 times in the 1990s. In Europe the case load of the European Court of Human Rights jumped from 11 cases during 1959–73 to 395 cases during 1974–92.[93] ***

Exponential growth in the articulation of human rights norms is not only a function of what Oran Young termed "spontaneous regime development"; it is also being cultivated by nongovernmental human rights organizations and aided by growing media coverage, often generated by such groups as Human Rights Watch and Amnesty International.[94] In addition the emergent atrocities regime itself may be seen as a norm entrepreneur.[95] Once established, the tribunal articulates and reinforces norms of state conduct and may also apply direct pressure to states through calls for investigations or by releasing information to the media. Such pressures may be manifest at the systemic level, through states' desiring to avoid being labeled "pariahs" or "rogues" or simply through emulation.[96] In a world of interdependence, reputation is a valuable asset in maintaining positive relations with key partners.[97] Pressures may also follow a "bottom-up" path, especially in liberal democracies where public exposure can generate policy demands. Certainly, additional research is necessary to trace such demand-side questions and to identify the role of the tribunals themselves in generating demands for political action.

However, though these developments signal the evolution of norms to protect civilians during armed conflict, they may also be building norms that preclude military intervention at early stages of crises. The danger of relying on mechanisms that only respond *ex post facto* to atrocities is clearly evident in both Bosnia and Rwanda. Though cognizant of atrocities in Bosnia, "the major powers . . . backed away from significant armed intervention. Facing domestic criticism for allowing the slaughter to continue unchecked, some governments seemed to feel obliged to show that they were doing *something*. It was in this vacuum that the proposal for a tribunal advanced."[98] *** Although human rights norms may be strengthening, norms of military intervention (often necessary for

[93] See Jacobson 1996; and Lutz and Sikkink 2000.
[94] Young 1983, 98–99.
[95] I thank an anonymous *IO* reviewer for this important observation.
[96] Rosecrance 1999.
[97] See Chayes and Chayes 1995, 230; and Keohane 1997, 501.
[98] Neier 1998, 112.

successful atrocities adjudication) make action increasingly difficult to initiate. The same groups that lobby for adjudication and accountability are often the most vocal opponents of military intervention. Moreover, norms of intervention increasingly require multilateral rather than unilateral action for both operational (cost-sharing) and political (legitimacy) reasons.[99] Clearly, this has troubling implications for enforcement, for as the evidence presented here suggests, military intervention may be necessary in many cases for successful adjudication.

Application

Realist variables of power and interest best explain why tribunals may be established in some cases but not in others. Power and interest strongly influence a state's reluctance to establish a given ad hoc tribunal or be signatory to a comprehensive international legal regime. In the cases of Cambodia, East Timor, Chechnya, and Korea, great power nations were obviously reluctant to expose sensitive issues in a public arena, especially past or present collusion with despotic regimes (in the Cambodian case). In addition, strategic interests figure prominently in the reluctance of strong states to ratify the Rome Statute. Modern warfare often necessitates destroying "civilian" targets for military victory, and in general "collateral damage" from bona fide military missions has rarely been considered a violation of human rights, even by critics.[100] These military actions may further the overall good, even when the human cost is high; in other words, the "just war" may sometimes involve regrettable human costs that should not be prosecutable offenses under international law. The evidence presented here suggests that powerful states are reluctant to engage any regime that may *significantly* impede measures deemed necessary to achieving security. The dominance of the Security Council in decisions to establish ad hoc tribunals has been, to date, driven by state interests. While it can be argued that the Balkans and Rwanda offer no particularly salient security incentives, establishing tribunals was certainly not seen as threatening or compromising to great power interests.

* * *

[99] Finnemore 1986, 180–85.
[100] Donnelly 1998, 531. See also Morgenthau 1985, 253–60.

Expanded Goals and Institutional Adjustments

*** While evolving norms of human rights may initiate the construction of the atrocities regime in the first place, differentials in power and the interests of the most powerful states clearly shape the process of institutionalization. E. H. Carr suggested that, "The law is . . . the weapon of the stronger. . . . Law reflects not any fixed ethical standard, but the policy and interests of the dominant group in a given state at a given period." As such, "Politics and law are indissolubly intertwined."[101] This certainly applies to the case of war crimes adjudication. Iain Guest suggests that suspicions ran high, especially early in the tribunal's development, that the tribunal was serving as "a substitute, an alternative, to the kind of tough political action which would put an end to the ethnic cleansing that was taking place."[102] States find establishing a tribunal system appealing because it provides an economically and politically inexpensive means of responding to demands for international action; it enables states to commit at a level commensurate with their strategic interest in the region involved. From the standpoint of *realpolitik*, the regime is a success whether or not it succeeds in bringing justice or alleviating ethnic conflict. From the standpoint of *idealpolitik*, the measures of success – reducing human suffering, protecting human rights, and promoting regional stability – are certainly left wanting. Here we must assess the tribunal's success from another dimension – as a component of conflict management.

Theodor Meron offers the best articulation of the regime's more expansive and idealistic aims: "The great hope of tribunal advocates was that the individualization and decollectivization of guilt . . . would help bring about peace and reconciliation. . . . Another of the tribunal's objectives was deterrence of continued and future violations of the law."[103] For international lawyers the connection between a functioning legal regime and political order is clear: "There can be no peace without justice, no justice without law, and no meaningful law without a court to decide what is just and lawful under any given circumstance."[104] If peace is a function of law and justice, is an atrocities regime the panacea for the problem of ethnonationalist violence? Here, the current evidence is certainly not compelling. Effective deterrence requires three

---

[101]   Carr 1961, 176–77.
[102]   Quoted in Commission on Security and Cooperation in Europe 1996, 12.
[103]   Meron 1997, 6. See also Pejic 1998.
[104]   Ferencz 1980, 1.

elements – commitment, capability, and credibility.[105] The existence of war crimes tribunals and the successful prosecution of initial cases did little to curb actions in any of the cases examined. The record of U.S. and NATO intervention in ethnic conflicts over the past thirty years has been marked by very limited commitments, especially in cases where threats to U.S. interests were limited.[106] Because of the rather spotty record of the West regarding intervention and the formidable institutional obstacles facing the fledgling tribunal system, perpetrators of brutality have had little reason to take UN commitment seriously. In terms of capability, the United States has certainly possessed the power to apprehend war criminals and political despots indicted by the tribunal. However, the difficulty of apprehending such people came at an unacceptably high logistical and political cost, considering that a large-scale military commitment would be necessary and that to ensure stability such forces would need to remain for prolonged periods.[107] ***

Preliminary evidence does not seem to support notions that decollectivization of guilt through war crimes adjudication is, on its own, an effective means to achieving national reconciliation – seen as essential in dealing with ethnic or religious violence (identity-based conflict). In the former Yugoslavia, ethnic tensions remain high and are accompanied by sporadic violence and acts of retaliation on both sides.[108] While instrumentalists may argue that ethnic tensions are manipulated by actors to further material or political interests, the ability to generate group solidarity and ethnic blood-lust is certainly facilitated by a historical cycle of violence.[109] In this sense, ethnic violence is congruent with other forms of identity conflict, including religious wars, and groups have long endured cycles of violence and reprisal.[110] Decollectivizing guilt is a

---

[105] See Morgan 1977; George and Smoke 1974; Lebow and Stein 1990; and Spiegel and Wheling 1999, 497–500.

[106] See Callahan 1997, 187–199; and Harvey 1998.

[107] Chaim Kaufmann remarked that "such peaces last only as long as the enforcers remain." Once peacekeepers are removed from the situation, the artificially established balance of power shifts, an "ethnic security dilemma" arises, and the credibility of majority commitment not to exploit minority ethnic groups falters, threatening to renew the cycle of violence. See Kaufmann 1996,137; Posen 1993; and Fearon 1998.

[108] See *Los Angeles Times*, 25 March 2000, A5; and *Los Angeles Times*, 4 March 2001, A1, A9.

[109] Instrumentalist accounts also do not explain why ethnic and religious conflict tend to be so much more barbaric than other forms of conflict. Targeting of women and children and organized programs created to terrorize a population certainly carry no specific advantages to conventional conflict in attaining material gains. See Lake and Rothchild 1998a, 5–7; and Brown et al. 1997.

[110] Girard 1977, 24.

curative measure taken by the state to break this historical cycle. However, the effectiveness of such a strategy is contingent on detaining high-level perpetrators and, presumably, giving amnesty to those at lower levels (perhaps in return for admitting guilt, fully disclosing events, and testifying at trials of political and military leaders, as has occurred in truth and reconciliation proceedings elsewhere). Yet early precedent set by the tribunals runs an opposite course.

*　*　*

Decollectivizing guilt also does not provide a means of promoting tolerance by shaping ethnic and national identities. Social constructivists argue that ethnic identities are malleable and shaped by continually changing social contexts, yet none of the currently debated elements of ethnic conflict management incorporate a mechanism for "re-imagining" the sociopolitical community.[111] It would seem that some mechanism of social education should accompany decollectivization of guilt if the atrocities regime is to succeed within these more expansive agendas.

*　*　*

CONCLUSION

What lessons can be drawn from these initial developments in the atrocities regime? Realist factors have dominated the politics of war crimes adjudication, but the atrocities regime is in its infancy. To dismiss the efficacy of the atrocities regime at this stage is premature, and the evidence here suggests that its development is proceeding rapidly. From an institutionalist perspective, we can ask how the regime can be strengthened, and what lessons can be learned from the existing ad hoc tribunal system. IL analysts suggest that the strength of legal regimes centers on consistency (precedent) and legitimacy, on hard law.[112] Conversely, regime analysts, most notably in the field of international political economy, suggest that flexibility, rather than rigidity, increases regime strength.[113] Robert Keohane argues that "Institutions based on substantive rules have proven to be fragile entities," adding "flexibility and openness . . . may increase the usefulness of an international institution."[114] Flexibility is also important when the long-term impacts of

[111] Anderson 1983.
[112] See Franck 1990; Jackson 1984; and Trimble 1990.
[113] Krasner 1983.
[114] Kahler 1995, 137. See also Goldstein et al. 2000, 392.

the institution are uncertain, especially when state sovereignty and/or national security are involved.[115] The key to establishing an effective regime lies in squaring the circle between hard legalization and political flexibility and locating the regime within a comprehensive program of ethnic conflict management. On the first point, examining the cases as part of a dynamic political development suggests that steps are being taken to "soften" the legalization process – at least in the short run – in order to attain flexibility and minimize concerns about sovereignty and security. On the second point, the regime must be linked with other policy tools applicable to ethnic violence, including preventive diplomacy, foreign aid, international intervention, spatial separation and reconfiguring political spaces, and social education programs.[116]

War crimes adjudication also presents analytical challenges. A purely legalistic (IL) view cannot accurately explain many of the political dimensions involved in forming an atrocities regime nor can the highly macroscopic, analytical view of IR. The issues presented here suggest the need for a war crimes vocabulary and more mid-level theories for understanding war crimes tribunals and their use in establishing justice and promoting peace.[117] Clearly, to understand and inform the development of the atrocities regime, we need research that incorporates the overlap between IL and IR.[118] While researchers remain at the forefront of this agenda, promoting peace and ameliorating human suffering provide strong incentives for further analysis.

[115] Abbott and Snidal 2000.
[116] See Jentleson 1998; Kaufmann 1996; Lake and Rothchild 1998b; and Walter and Snyder 1999.
[117] I owe this important insight to an anonymous *IO* reviewer.
[118] See Goldstein et al. 2000; Keohane 1997; and Slaughter 1993.

24

The Origins of Human Rights Regimes: Democratic Delegation in Postwar Europe

Andrew Moravcsik

The fiftieth anniversary of the UN Universal Declaration on Human Rights marks an appropriate moment to reconsider the reasons why governments construct international regimes to adjudicate and enforce human rights. Such regimes include those established under the European Convention for the Protection of Human Rights and Fundamental Freedoms (ECHR), the Inter-American Convention on Human Rights, and the UN Covenant on Civil and Political Rights.

These arrangements differ from most other forms of institutionalized international cooperation in both their ends and their means. Unlike international institutions governing trade, monetary, environmental, or security policy, international human rights institutions are not designed primarily to regulate policy externalities arising from societal interactions across borders, but to hold governments accountable for purely internal activities. In contrast to most international regimes, moreover, human rights regimes are not generally enforced by interstate action. Although most arrangements formally empower governments to challenge one another, such challenges almost never occur. The distinctiveness of such regimes lies instead in their empowerment of individual citizens to bring suit to challenge the domestic activities of their own government. Independent courts and commissions attached to such regimes often respond to such individual claims by judging that the application of domestic rules or legislation violates international commitments, even where such legislation has been enacted and enforced through fully democratic

*** For an earlier version of this article with more detailed documentation, see Moravcsik 1998b.

procedures consistent with the domestic rule of law. Arrangements to adjudicate human rights internationally thus pose a fundamental challenge not just to the Westphalian ideal of state sovereignty that underlies realist international relations theory and classical international law but also – though less-frequently noted – to liberal ideals of direct democratic legitimacy and self-determination. The postwar emergence of these arrangements has rightly been characterized as the most "radical development in the whole history of international law."[1]

Consider, for example, the ECHR, established under the auspices of the Council of Europe and based in Strasbourg, France. The ECHR system is widely accepted as the "most advanced and effective" international regime for formally enforcing human rights in the world today.[2] Since 1953, when the ECHR came into force, it has sought to define and protect an explicit set of civil and political rights for all persons within the jurisdiction of its member states, whether those individuals are aliens, refugees, stateless persons, or citizens. It initially established a Commission on Human Rights to review petitions.[3] The Commission could investigate the case, seek to settle it, or forward it under certain circumstances to a court of human rights, whose decisions governments are legally bound to follow. Two optional clauses of the ECHR, Articles 25 and 46, were subsequently adopted by all member states; they permit individual and state-to-state petitions and recognize the compulsory jurisdiction of the court. Many European governments have subsequently incorporated the convention into domestic law, directly or indirectly. For these reasons, the ECHR Court is right to proclaim the convention "a constitutional document of European public order."[4]

Over the last half-century, analysts agree, the legal commitments and enforcement mechanisms entered into under the ECHR have established "effective supranational adjudication" in Europe. Compliance is so consistent that ECHR judgments are now, in the words of two leading

---

[1] See Humphrey 1974, 205, 208–209; Krasner 1995; and Falk 1981, 4, 153–83.

[2] Petitions could be judged admissible if they meet several criteria, most importantly the prior exhaustion of domestic remedies. Henkin et al. 1999, 551. In this article I am not concerned with purely rhetorical human rights documents, such as the UN Universal Declaration, but solely with enforceable commitments. Rights imply remedies, without which the former are of little utility. Unsurprisingly, hypocrisy in signing declarations without mechanisms for direct enforcement appears to be without significant cost, regardless of a country's domestic policies. ***

[3] See Janis, Kay, and Bradley 1995; Robertson and Merrills 1993; and van Dijk and van Hoof 1998. ***

[4] *Loizidou v. Turkey,* 310 Eur. Ct. *H.R.* (ser. A, 1995), 27.

international legal scholars, "as effective as those of any domestic court."[5] In hundreds of cases where an explicit decision has been taken or a "friendly settlement" reached – including matters of criminal procedure, penal codes and the treatment of prisoners, vagrancy legislation, civil codes, systems of legal aid fees and civil legal advice, the rights of illegitimate children, military codes, expropriation policies, systems of awarding building permits, treatment of the mentally ill, reformatory centers, wiretapping, and censorship of the press – governments have amended legislation, granted administrative remedies, reopened judicial proceedings, or paid monetary damages to individuals whose treaty rights were violated.[6] When the court recently ruled that exclusion of homosexuals from the British armed forces violated the ECHR, the British government immediately announced its intention to comply. * * * [7]

There is a real theoretical puzzle here. Why would any government, democratic or dictatorial, favor establishing an effective independent international authority, the sole purpose of which is to constrain its domestic sovereignty in such an unprecedentedly invasive and overtly non-majoritarian manner?

To answer questions such as this, political scientists tend to espouse either a realist or an ideational explanation for the emergence and expansion of formal human rights regimes. Democratic governments and transnationally active members of democratic civil societies either coerce other governments to accept human rights norms (the realist view) or persuade other governments to do so (the ideational view). Some scholars espouse both positions at once, arguing that powerful democracies are persuaded for essentially idealistic reasons to coerce others to respect human rights norms.

Such realist and ideational conjectures, though popular among scholars, rest on a remarkably thin empirical foundation. * * * Only the UN system – a notably weak regime – has been the subject of significant research, and this body of work focuses on rhetorical statements, such as the UN Declaration, rather than arrangements for adjudication and enforcement.[8] Such analyses, moreover, tend to accept uncritically the *ex post* conjectures of practitioners and commentators.

---

[5] Helfer and Slaughter 1997, 283, who draw on Shapiro 1981, 7, 26–36.
[6] Carter and Trimble 1995, 309.
[7] On domestic incorporation, see Polakiewicz and Jacob-Foltzer 1991; Drzemczewski 1983, 11–12; and Merrills 1993.
[8] For the best of these, see Morsink 1999.

This article contains the first systematic empirical test of competing theories of the establishment of formal international human rights regimes. It does so by examining the negotiations to establish the ECHR in 1949–50. I argue that the primary proponents of binding international human rights commitments in postwar Europe were neither great powers, as realist theory would have it, nor governments and transnational groups based in long-established liberal democracies, as the ideational account would have it. Although established democracies supported certain human rights declarations, *they allied with dictatorships and transitional regimes in opposition to reciprocally binding human rights enforcement* – a seldom-noted tendency for which realists and ideational theorists have no explanation. The primary proponents of reciprocally binding human rights obligations were instead the governments of newly established democracies.

This curious pattern is explicable only if we adopt a different theoretical starting point: the domestic political self-interest of national governments. Establishing an international human rights regime is an act of political delegation akin to establishing a domestic court or administrative agency. From a "republican liberal" perspective – one related to institutional variants of "democratic peace" theory as well as to the analysis of "two-level games" and public-choice theories of delegation – creating a quasi-independent judicial body is a tactic used by governments to "lock in" and consolidate democratic institutions, thereby enhancing their credibility and stability vis-à-vis nondemocratic political threats. In sum, governments turn to international enforcement when an international commitment effectively enforces the policy preferences of a particular government at a particular point in time against future domestic political alternatives.

I argue that governments will resort to this tactic when the benefits of reducing future political uncertainty outweigh the "sovereignty costs" of membership. It follows that "self-binding" is of most use to *newly established democracies,* which have the greatest interest in further stabilizing the domestic political status quo against nondemocratic threats. We should therefore observe them leading the move to enforce human rights multilaterally, whereas established democracies have an incentive to offer lukewarm support at best. In the case of the ECHR, this theoretical approach best explains the cross-national pattern of support for binding norms, the tactics governments employed, and the archival record of public rhetoric and confidential domestic deliberations.

The implications of this approach go well beyond postwar European human rights. The logic of "locking in" credible domestic policies through international commitments can be generalized to other human rights regimes – including the recent International Criminal Court – and unilateral human rights policies, not least the apparently anomalous behavior of the United States, as well as to other issue areas in world politics, regardless of whether their substantive content is "liberal." The latter include the stabilization of autocratic regimes under the Concert of Europe and Comintern, and the coordination of monetary and trade policies.

EXISTING THEORIES OF INTERNATIONAL HUMAN RIGHTS COOPERATION

Existing scholarship seeking to explain why national governments establish and enforce formal international human rights norms focuses on two modes of interstate interaction: coercion and normative persuasion. Respectively, these define distinctive "realist" and "ideational" explanations for the emergence of human rights regimes. ***

Interstate Power: "For Countries at the Top, This Is Predictable"

Realist theories of international relations, and thus of the origin of human rights regimes, stress the distribution of interstate bargaining power. Governments accept international obligations because they are compelled to do so by great powers, which externalize their ideology – a prediction that follows equally from hegemonic stability theory and conventional realist bargaining theory. * All governments seek to maintain full domestic sovereignty wherever possible. With governments uniformly skeptical of external constraints, the major limitation on cooperation is the cost of coercion or inducement, which is inversely proportional to the concentration of power. Establishment of a binding human rights regime requires, therefore, a hegemonic ("k") group of great powers willing to coerce or induce recalcitrant states to accept, adjust to, and comply with international human rights norms. The greater the concentration of relative power capabilities, the greater the pressure on recalcitrant governments and the more likely is an international regime to form and prosper.

Precise formulations of the realist argument vary. E. H. Carr, Hans Morgenthau, and other classical realists maintain that governments employ liberal ideology, including support for human rights, to justify the pursuit of geopolitical interest.[9] Jack Donnelly writes of the Inter-American

[9] See Carr 1946; and Morgenthau 1960.

Convention on Human Rights that "much of the explanation [for] the Inter-American human rights regime . . . lies in power, particularly the dominant power of the United States. . . . [It] is probably best understood in these terms. The United States . . . exercised its hegemonic power to ensure its creation and support its operation."[10] John Ruggie uncharacteristically takes a similar line when he conjectures that human rights regimes will be weaker than nuclear nonproliferation regimes, because the former are of less concern to the core superpower security interests.[11] Kenneth Waltz asserts that powerful nations invariably seek to impose their views on other nations: "Like some earlier great powers, we [the United States] can identify the presumed duty of the rich and powerful to help others with our own beliefs . . . England claimed to bear the white man's burden; France had its *mission civilisatrice*. . . . For countries at the top, this is predictable behavior."[12] Alison Biysk links acceptance of human rights norms to the pressure by international financial organizations such as the World Bank, backed by Western donor countries.[13] * * *

Normative Persuasion: "The Inescapable Ideological Appeal of Human Rights"

The most prominent ideational explanations for the emergence and enforcement of human rights regimes look to altruism and the persuasive power of principled ideas. Such explanations rest, to that extent, on what used to be termed "utopian" or "idealist" foundations. The essence of such explanations lies in the prominence of idealistic or altruistic motivations for spreading liberal values.[14] Governments accept binding international human rights norms because they are swayed by the overpowering ideological and normative appeal of the values that underlie them. "The seemingly inescapable ideological appeal of human rights in the postwar world," writes Donnelly, who espouses a wide range of theories, "is an important element in the rise of international human rights regimes."[15]

Ideational arguments differ most fundamentally from realist arguments in their reliance on a distinctive conception of interstate interaction. They explicitly reject choice-theoretic foundations and instead stress

[10] See Donnelly 1986, 625, also 637–38; and Ruggie 1983, 99.
[11] Ruggie 1983, 104.
[12] Waltz 1979, 200. See also Krasner 1992.
[13] Brysk 1994, 51–56.
[14] Keck and Sikkink 1998, chap. 1–3.
[15] Donnelly 1986, 638. On soft power, see Nye 1990.

the transformative power of normative moral discourse itself. In this view, a critical characteristic of political action in this area is that it is "principled" – that is, the altruistic and moral motives of actors have persuasive power in themselves. Accordingly, the most fundamental motivating force behind human rights regimes is not rational adaptation, let alone coercion, but transnational socialization – the "logic of appropriateness."[16] Many such explanations assert that transformations in actor identities occur though the impact of "principled" nongovernmental organizations (NGOs) on domestic and transnational opinion.[17] NGOs and publics within established democracies set up transnational networks, epistemic communities, and global discourses of human rights, dedicated to the advancement of a normative discourse of human rights. This in turn mobilizes domestic and transnational civil society at home and abroad, eventually socializing foreign and domestic leaders.[18]

Whence the ideological appeal of human rights? Some scholars look to human moral psychology, regional cultures, or salient historical events, but the most plausible explanation links support for international human rights protection to domestic democracy and commitment to the "rule of law."[19] In this view, which Thomas Risse terms "liberal constructivism," established democratic governments seek to extend their domestic values abroad and recognize others who do so. The more democratic they are, the more likely their espousal of human rights values.[20] Charles Kupchan and Clifford Kupchan conjecture that "states willing to submit to the rule of law and civil society are more likely to submit to their analogues internationally."[21] Similarly, Kathryn Sikkink points to the leading role of established democracies in promoting human rights, such as linking Scandinavian support for human rights enforcement to the salience of social democratic values in their domestic politics.[22] Thomas Franck asserts that compliance with international law is a function of the normative acceptance of international

---

[16] See Finnemore and Sikkink 1998; and Donnelly 1986.

[17] See Sikkink 1993; Risse-Kappen 1994; and Finnemore 1996.

[18] See, for example, Keck and Sikkink 1998; and Ramirez, Soysal and Shanahan 1997.

[19] Russett 1993. For alternative views, see Keck and Sikkink 1998; Sikkink 1993; Sieghart 1983, 26–27; and Ando 1992, 171–72. See also Donnelly 1986; Whitfield 1988, 31, also 28–31; and Drzemczewski 1983, 220.

[20] See Risse-Kappen 1996; and Moravcsik 1997. This view is related to the ideational variant of democratic peace theory, in which the democratic peace results from the tendency of liberal governments to externalize their domestic ideals. See Russett 1993.

[21] Kupchan and Kupchan 1991, 115–16.

[22] Sikkink 1993.

rules, which in turn reflects (among other things) their consistency with domestic values.[23] In sum, governments promote norms abroad because they are consistent with universal ideals to which they adhere; governments accept them at home because they are convinced doing so is "appropriate."

The desire to conform to shared ideas and norms of state behavior ("collective expectations about proper behavior for a given identity"), in this view, does not simply regulate state behavior, but constitutes and reconstitutes state identities.[24] Such theories explicitly distance themselves from explanations that rely on instrumental calculations about the establishment of legitimate domestic governance.[25] Two leading ideational theorists explicitly reject, for example, the argument I shall introduce later – namely, that governments support human rights regimes to advance partisan and public interest in preventing domestic violence and interstate warfare. In a striking historical conjecture, these analysts assert that in the 1940s and 1950s governments could not possibly have sought human rights regimes to preserve the "democratic peace" because such founding moments "came well before the emergence of the new social knowledge" that undemocratic regimes undermine peace – a collective belief they date to research by liberal international relations theorists in the early 1980s, led by Michael Doyle.[26] As we shall soon see, this equation of "social knowledge" with academic political science misstates the true origins of human rights regimes because it underestimates the ability of nonacademics to generate a widely accepted, factually grounded – and ultimately accurate – consensus about world politics.

The "New Orthodoxy": A Curious Convergence of Realism and Idealism

The study of human rights makes unlikely bedfellows. Although realist and ideational theories start from very different assumptions, their predictions about human rights tend to converge. Most existing analyses of human rights regimes rest on an uneasy synthesis of these two

[23] Franck 1988.

[24] Jepperson, Wendt, and Katzenstein 1996, 54.

[25] Finnemore and Sikkink 1998. Thomas Risse has sought to take this further by drawing on Habermasian normative theory as a basis for positive analysis. See Risse 2000.

[26] Keck and Sikkink 1998, 203. See also [fn. 53] and accompanying text in this article. Compare Helfer and Slaughter 1997, 331–35.

explanations. Realists cited earlier tend to argue that human rights norms are expressions of domestic values, not simply propagandists justifications for the pursuit of national security interests.[27] * * *

Many in both schools adopt what Robert Keohane has elsewhere termed the realist "fall-back" position: Public interest groups with idealistic values, perhaps transnationally organized, shape the underlying preferences of democratic great powers, which then deploy their preponderant power to construct and enforce international human rights norms. Idealism explains the position of great powers; realism explains the spread of norms.[28] In generalizing about human rights regimes, for example, Margaret Keck and Kathryn Sikkink focus extensively on the transcultural attractiveness of ideas and the density of transnational organization (ideational factors) *and* the vulnerability of targets to sanctions (a realist factor). As we have seen, they explicitly contrast this explanation, however, with an explanation that focuses on domestic institutional and material preconditions, which they reject outright (on theoretical, not empirical grounds) as at most only secondary.[29]

There is thus considerably more convergence in empirical predictions about the source of support for human rights regimes than broad theoretical labels might suggest (see Table 24.1). Most theories, whether realist or ideational, predict that governments, interest groups, and public opinion in established democratic states spearhead efforts to form and enforce international human rights regimes – and they induce, coerce, or persuade others to go join. Yet, as I discuss in more detail later, this is simply not the case. In postwar Europe, as in the UN during this period, established democracies consistently opposed reciprocally binding human rights obligations and neither coerced nor persuaded anyone else to accept them. Before moving on to the empirical analysis, it is therefore necessary to examine a third explanation for the formation of human rights regimes.

---

[27] Even if this were the case, the argument would not be entirely realist, since the claim that democratic governments are more likely to side with the West does not necessarily follow from realist theory. Even self-styled realists increasingly concede that societal preferences play an important, often determinant role in alliance formation. For a criticism of this type of realist degeneration, see Legro and Moravcsik 1999.

[28] Ruggie 1983, 98–99. On this sort of realist fall-back or two-step position more generally, see Legro 1996; Moravcsik 1997, 543; Keohane 1986, 183; and Legro and Moravcsik 1999.

[29] Keck and Sikkink 1998, 201–209.

TABLE 24.1. *Establishing Human Rights Regimes: Theories, Causal Mechanisms, and Predictions*

	Realism	Ideational theory	Republican liberalism
Motivations and tactics	Great powers employ coercion or inducement to unilaterally extend national ideals derived from national pride or geopolitical self-interest. Smaller states defend their sovereignty.	Altruistic governments and groups in established democracies seek to extend perceived universal norms. Less-democratic states are socialized or persuaded through existing transnational networks (the "logic of appropriateness").	Governments seek to prevent domestic oppression and international conflict through international symbols, standards, and procedures that secure domestic democracy. They are constrained by fear that domestic laws might be struck down. International agreement reflects convergent interests.
Predicted national preferences on compulsory commitments	Supporters are led by democratic great powers. The weaker the state, the less support we observe.	Supporters are led by societal groups and governments in the most democratic states. The less established the democracy, the less support we observe.	Supporters are led by newly established democracies. Established democracies accept only optional or rhetorical commitments. Nondemocracies oppose.
Predicted variation in cooperation	Greater concentration of power in the hands of great power democracies. More cost-effective coercion or inducement. More cooperation.	More attractive norms, more salient, more legitimate exemplars, and the more established the transnational networks. More powerful socialization effects. More cooperation.	More immediate threats to democracy. Greater desire to enhance domestic stability. More cooperation.

631

REPUBLICAN LIBERALISM: DEMOCRATIC PEACE AND
DOMESTIC COMMITMENT

If realist and ideational explanations view the motivations for establishing human rights regimes as involving international coercion or persuasion, a "republican liberal" explanation views them as resulting from instrumental calculations about domestic politics.[30] In general, republican liberal theories stress the impact of varying domestic political institutions – in particular, the scope and bias of political representation – on foreign policy. The most prominent among such theories include institutional explanations of the "democratic peace," yet the family of republican liberal theories offers a far wider range of potential explanations, subsuming theories of the role of cartelized elites and independent militaries in provoking war, and of interest group capture (or the countervailing delegation of authority to strong executives) in foreign economic policy.[31] In contrast to the idealist theories considered earlier, which assume that social actors are responsive to external socialization and often altruistically motivated, republican liberal theories assume that states are self-interested and rational in their pursuit of (varying) underlying national interests, which reflect in turn variation in the nature of domestic social pressures and representative institutions.[32]

---

[30] Liberal international relations theory focuses on state behavior driven by variation in the economic interests and conceptions of public goods provision on the part of societal groups, as well as by the nature of domestic political institutions. The republican liberal label is appropriate to international relations theory debates, though the concern about promoting democracy also has elements of ideational liberalism – the strand of liberal theory based on the tendency to promote domestic provision of public goods (national identity, political institutions, and legitimate economic redistribution) preferred by domestic actors. (This differs from idealist theory in the minimal role it accords altruism or transnational socialization.) On the ideational strand of liberal theory, see Moravcsik 1997; and Van Evera 1990. In American or comparative politics, such an explanation might be thought of as drawing on public-choice theory, institutionalist theory, constitutional theory, the theory of delegation, or theories of nested games.

[31] For a discussion on the full range of potential liberal explanations, see Moravcsik 1997.

[32] Liberal international relations theories assume that states behave as rational, unitary actors in the pursuit of their underlying preferences, though not in the definition of those preferences. Their theoretical distinctiveness lies in their consistent focus on variation in national preferences resulting from social pressures for particular material and ideational interests, as well as the way such interests are represented by state institutions. In this regard, institutional variants of democratic peace theory and theories of legislative-executive relations share common liberal theoretical assumptions. For an elaboration, see Moravcsik 1997; Doyle 1986; Russett 1993; Snyder 1991; Bailey, Goldstein, and Weingast 1997; Van Evera 1999; and Legro and Moravcsik 1999.

A useful republican liberal starting point for the problem at hand is to assume that international institutional commitments, like domestic institutional commitments, are self-interested means of "locking in" particular preferred domestic policies – at home and abroad – in the face of future political uncertainty. This presumption, which is not only consistent with republican liberalism but also draws on theories widely employed to explain domestic delegation to courts and regulatory authorities in American and comparative politics, treats domestic politics as a game in which politicians compete to exercise public authority.[33] Terry Moe observes that "most political institutions . . . arise out of a politics of structural choice in which the winners use their temporary hold on public authority to design new structures and impose them on the polity as a whole . . . . [Institutions are] weapons of coercion and redistribution . . . the structural means by which political winners pursue their own interests, often at the great expense of political losers."[34] Governments establish courts, administrative agencies, central banks, and other independent bodies as means by which the winners of political conflict seek to commit the polity to preferred policies. From this perspective, a rational decision to delegate to an independent body requires that a sitting government weigh two crosscutting considerations: *restricting government discretion* and *reducing domestic political uncertainty*.

Consider first the surrender of national discretion, which in the international context might be termed the *sovereignty cost* of delegation to an international authority. All other things equal, governments in power prefer to maintain short-term discretion to shape collective behavior or redistribute wealth as they see fit. They are therefore inherently skeptical of delegation to independent judges or officials, since there is always some "agency cost" to the operation of central banks, administrative agencies, courts, and other quasi-independent political authorities. Judges, in particular, may seek to negate government actions by nullifying them outright or by failing to enforce them effectively. ***

In the international realm, the defense of governmental discretion translates into the defense of national sovereignty. All other things equal, the "sovereignty cost" of delegating to an international judge is likely to be even greater than that of delegating to a domestic judge. One reason is that cross-national variation in the precise nature, scope, application, and enforcement of human rights is likely to be greater than domestic variation.

[33] Moe 1990.
[34] Ibid., 222, 213. ***

*** Particularly for nations without a constitutional court – again, Britain is a striking example – the procedure marks a significant innovation.[35] *** From this perspective, the defense of "national sovereignty" is, in part, a legitimate defense of national ideals, political culture, and even democratic practices – a problem of which the framers of post–World War II human rights documents (and their academic advisers) were quite aware.[36]

Why would a national government, democratic or not, ever accept such external normative and institutional constraints on its sovereignty? The answer lies in the second major consideration that enters into a government's decision whether to delegate to an independent political body: reducing political uncertainty. In the republican liberal view, politicians delegate power to human rights regimes, such as domestic courts and administrative agencies, to constrain the behavior of future national governments. As Moe explains, a politician must always calculate that "while the right to exercise public authority happens to be theirs today, other political actors with different and perhaps opposing interests may gain that right tomorrow."[37] To limit the consequences of this eventuality, government authorities may thus seek to "lock in" favored policies in such a way, thereby insulating them from the actions of future governments.

From this perspective, human rights norms are expressions of the self-interest of democratic governments in "locking in" democratic rule through the enforcement of human rights. By placing interpretation in the hands of independent authorities managed in part by foreign governments – in other words, by alienating sovereignty to an international body – governments seek to establish reliable judicial constraints on future nondemocratic governments or on democratically elected governments that may seek (as in interwar Italy and Germany) to subvert democracy from within. In the language of international relations theory, this "two-level" commitment "ties the hands" of future governments, thereby enhancing the credibility of current domestic policies and institutions.[38] Salient and symbolic international constraints serve as signals to trigger domestic, and perhaps also transnational and international, opposition to any breach of the democratic order. Thus

[35] Drzemczewski 1983, 11.
[36] McKeon 1949.
[37] Moe 1990, 227.
[38] Evans, Putnam, and Jacobson 1993.

democratic regimes seek to prevent political retrogression or "backsliding" into tyranny.

The decision of any individual government whether to support a binding international human rights enforcement regime depends, in this view, on the relative importance of these two basic factors: Sovereignty costs are weighted against establishing human rights regimes, whereas greater political stability may be weighted in favor of it. If we assume that the inconvenience governments face is constant (or randomly distributed), it follows that a country is most likely to support a human rights regime when its government is firmly committed to democratic governance but faces strong internal challenges that may threaten it in the future. Its willingness to tolerate *sovereignty costs* increases insofar as the costs are outweighed by the benefits of reducing *domestic political uncertainty.*

If the republican liberal view is correct, *the strongest support for binding human rights regimes should come not from established democracies but from recently established and potentially unstable democracies.* ***

*** Less obvious and in striking contrast to realist and idealist accounts *** is the prediction that dictatorships will be joined in opposition to binding commitments by well-established liberal democracies. By accepting binding obligations, governments in established democracies incur an increased, if modest, risk of de facto nullification of domestic laws without a corresponding increase in the expected stability of domestic democracy, since the latter is already high. Such governments have good reason – indeed, a democratically legitimate reason – to reject any reciprocal imposition of international adjudication and enforcement of human rights claims.

This is not to say that established democracies never have an incentive to support international human rights instruments. According to republican liberal theory, established democracies have an incentive to promote such arrangements for others – which may involve some small risk of future pressure on established democracies to deepen their commitment – in order to bolster the "democratic peace" by fostering democracy in neighboring countries.[39] This is most likely to occur when democratization is expected to pacify a potentially threatening neighbor or solidify opposition to a common nondemocratic enemy. In such cases, established democracies can be expected to support rhetorical declarations in favor

---

[39] Russett 1993. This argument is liberal rather than realist, since for realists the domestic governance of states should make no difference in the perception of threat, whereas for democratic peace theorists, it does.

of human rights and regimes with optional enforcement that bind newly established democracies but exempt themselves. Yet there is little reason to believe that this concern will outweigh domestic interests; thus they are likely to remain opposed to reciprocally enforceable rules.[40] Further observable implications concerning national tactics and confidential discussions are developed in the next section.

TESTING THE THEORIES: THE NEGOTIATION OF THE ECHR

What light does the negotiating history of the ECHR cast on the power of these three competing theories? The negotiation of the ECHR took place between 1949 and 1953 under the auspices of the Council of Europe. At the first session of the Council of Europe's Consultative Assembly in September 1949, its legal committee under the chairmanship of the Frenchman Pierre-Henri Teitgen recommended that an organization be created to ensure adherence to human rights in Europe. * * *

Realist, ideational, and liberal institutional theories all offer prima facie explanations for the general form and timing of the ECHR's establishment. For realists, this period marked the dawning of an "American century" and a moment in which the West became embroiled in a bipolar conflict with the Soviet Union. For ideational theorists, it immediately followed the Holocaust, a salient historical event of considerable moral force, and occurred immediately after the rise to salient Western leadership of two long-established democratic exemplars, the United States and the United Kingdom.[41] During the immediate postwar period, republican liberals might observe, a wave of new liberal democracies emerged (or reemerged) across Western Europe. Nondemocratic institutions were widely viewed as a source of both World War II and the Cold War, and, accordingly, the democratization of Germany, Italy, and other West European nations was seen as a guarantee against both a revival of fascism and the spread of communism.

To assess the relative importance of these three plausible theories, we therefore require more fine-grained evidence than a simple coincidence of timing or the existence of occasional public rhetorical justification.

---

[40] In theory, one might argue that the incomplete adherence of established democracies could be expected to undermine the international regime, which could in turn destabilize newly established democracies and thereby create threats to established democracies. Yet in practice the signaling function of international norms in any given country does not appear to depend on the adherence by others to enforcement clauses; certainly this conjecture seems to have played an unimportant role in British or European deliberations.

[41] For a more solidly grounded view, see Helfer and Slaughter 1997, 331–35.

I consider three types of evidence: the cross-national pattern of national positions, the process of international negotiation, and the direct documentary record of national motivations. * * *

Cross-National Variation in National Preferences

* * *

We can measure the willingness of governments to accept binding obligations by examining their position on two related elements of the institutional design of the ECHR – both essential to the future effectiveness of the regime.

- *Compulsory jurisdiction*: Should the regime mandate that member states recognize the jurisdiction of an independent international court, as opposed to a body of foreign ministers?
- *Individual petition*: Should the regime mandate that member states grant private individuals and groups standing to file cases?

Since both mandatory binding jurisdiction *and* individual petition are required to render a system of international human rights adjudication effective, a vote for both is defined as support for a reciprocally binding regime, whereas a vote against either marks opposition.[42] * * *

To investigate the relationship between democratic governance and support for binding regimes, we also require a measure of how stable a democracy is expected to be.[43] European political systems involved in the negotiations can be divided into three categories. The first category, "established democracies," contains those systems that had been continuously under democratic rule since before 1920 and remained so thereafter: Belgium, Denmark, Luxembourg, Netherlands, Norway, Sweden, Netherlands, and the United Kingdom. (Occupation is not coded

---

[42] Sikkink suggests a less satisfactory coding, one which conflates the domestic and external concerns of governments in such a way as to greatly exaggerate the relative importance of the latter. Sikkink 1993. In fact only a miniscule set of ECHR cases have been brought by one state against another. [Council of Europe 1975, IV/248–52, also 132ff, 242–96, also I/xxiv, 10–24, 296ff; passim, and V/68–70. By the time the member states negotiated individual petition, underlying positions were harder to make out, since it was becoming increasingly clear that such provisions will be optional.]

[43] Conventional political science measures of "democracy" are inappropriate, since such measures assess institutions' levels of democracy, not future expectations of democratic stability. The length of continuous democratic rule is a conventional measure in the literature on the democratic peace and elsewhere for the depth of commitment to democracy. See, for example, Russett 1993. * * *

as a suspension of domestic democracy, but the establishment of a non-democratic domestic regime is – for example, Vichy France) The second category, "new democracies," contains those that were firmly established during the negotiations and remained so thereafter, but only since a point between 1920 and 1950: Austria, France, Italy, Iceland, Ireland, and West Germany. The third category, "semidemocracies and dictatorships," contains the two governments that were not fully democratic by 1950, because of civil war or internal repression (and did not remain so thereafter), namely Greece and Turkey. Spain and Portugal, though not involved in the negotiations, also belong in this category.[44]

Turning to the findings, we see little evidence of the positive correlation between support for binding regimes and power or length of democratic rule predicted by realist and idealist theory. Instead, we observe the inverse-U-shaped relationship between the stability of democracy and support for binding human rights commitments predicted by republican liberal theory. Table 24.2 summarizes the findings. [New democracies] support binding human rights guarantees. In contrast, six of the seven established democracies join the four transitional governments and non-democracies in opposing one or both such guarantees (or, in the case of Luxembourg, abstaining). *** The correlation is so strong that even recategorization of borderline cases – France and Turkey, say – would not undermine the striking relationship.

A number of ad hoc conjectures suggested by historians, legal academics, and common intuition about postwar European politics also fall by the wayside. Opposition appears to be uncorrelated with the possession of colonies.[45] ***

Opposition is similarly uncorrelated with the existence of a strong domestic tradition of parliamentary sovereignty, as some analysts of Britain conjecture. Many strong supporters – France, Belgium, Italy, Germany, Austria, Iceland, and Ireland – shared an equally deep tradition of parliamentary sovereignty. Any imputation of causality from the correlation between *postwar* support for domestic judicial review and international enforcement of human rights (say, in the cases of Italy, Germany, and Austria), furthermore, is very likely to be spurious. *** It is far more plausible that these countries adopted both domestic *and* international judicial review because of a strong desire to bolster the democratic order ***. *** [The] establishment of domestic constitutional

---

[44] For a further discussion of this coding, see the notes to Table 24.2.
[45] This is the factor most often mentioned in the secondary literature.

TABLE 24.2. *Stability of Democratic Governance and National Positions on the European Convention on Human Rights*

	Unstable or nondemocracies (stable democracy not yet clearly established by 1950)	New democracies (continuous democracy only since a date between 1920 and 1950)	Established democracies (continuous democracy since a date before 1920)
Supports enforcement (individual petition and compulsory jurisdiction mandatory)	—	Austria, France, Italy, Iceland, Ireland, Germany[b]	Belgium[c]
Opposes enforcement (individual petition and/or compulsory jurisdiction optional or absent)	Greece,[a] Turkey [a] (Portugal,[d] Spain[d])	—	Denmark, Sweden, Netherlands, Norway, United Kingdom, Luxembourg[e]

[a] Greece and Turkey are characterized as unstable, whereas Austria, France, Italy, Iceland, Ireland, and Germany are characterized as new, because (1) it had been less than a year after conclusion of the bloody Greek civil war, and extra-legal measures were still in force; and (2) Greek and Turkish democracy were widely viewed as limited by the role of the military and incomplete judicial autonomy. It is also worth noting that both governments would subsequently slip back into dictatorship.

[b] Germany, not yet a member of the Council of Europe, did not have voting rights, but participated actively in the negotiations.

[c] Belgium initially hesitated, supporting the convention only with optional clauses, but then came to favor mandatory enforcement.

[d] Spain and Portugal, both dictatorships, were not members of the Council of Europe. Yet, in striking contrast to Germany (also not a member), they showed little independent interest in participating informally, nor were they invited to do so.

[e] In some the cases, Luxembourg abstained on, rather than opposed enforcement measures.

Subsequent data reanalysis revealed that Belgium should have been coded as "opposed" and Turkey as "democratic." This removes one anomaly but creates another. AMM [2005].

review, like the establishment of international human rights guarantees, is a postauthoritarian phenomenon. * * *

Republican liberal theory also seems to offer the most accurate account of the instrumental attitude governments adopted toward more detailed provisions of the ECHR. Should the convention create, governments asked themselves, an independent court, a quasi-judicial body of government representatives, or no central institution at all? Cleavages around this issue were similar to those around compulsory jurisdiction and individual petition, with opponents of effective enforcement opposing the court.[46] Governments favorable to binding human rights adjudication proposed that the members of the intermediary Commission on Human Rights be nominated by the court – a clear effort to render international institutions more independent – whereas more skeptical governments favored granting power of nomination to the intergovernmental Committee of Ministers.[47]

* * *

The Domestic and International Decision-Making Process

Realism, ideational theory, and republican liberalism also generate distinctive predictions about the tactics likely to be most salient in interstate negotiations. Realist theory, with its stress on interstate power and deep conflicts of interest, leads us to expect to observe attempts by great powers to coerce or bribe weaker states to change their policies. Ideational theory, by contrast, leads us to expect to observe attempts by governments or transnational groups in civil society to engage in transnational persuasion. Such persuasion may suffice in itself or may be a prelude to subsequent coercive tactics. For liberal theorists, by contrast, there is little reason to expect governments to alter their views on fundamental issues such as the nature of constitutional adjudication in light of threats, promises, or normative persuasion by other democratic governments. * * *

Published documents contain very little direct confirmation of either the realist or ideational predictions. No great power or long-standing democracy appears to have made threats or offered inducements to secure stronger commitments. The most important powers engaged in Western Europe at the time, the United States and the United Kingdom, were respectively absent or opposed. Ideational theorists might point out that the "European Movement," working through the Assembly of the Council of Europe, was engaged in transnational discussion and mobilization. Certainly many leading advocates of the convention were European federalists and viewed the ECHR as a step toward European integration.[48] Yet there is

---

[46] Council of Europe 1975, IV/248–50.
[47] Council of Europe 1975, 111/268–70.
[48] Some Jewish parliamentarians and law professors were also prominent and may have been influenced by their experiences and beliefs.

little evidence that a shared transnational discourse influenced the positions of parliamentary politicians in the assembly, let alone representatives of national governments. ***

Instead the preponderance of evidence concerning negotiating tactics confirms republican liberal predictions. Rather than seeking to coerce or persuade one another, or mobilizing groups in civil society, national governments conducted a classical international negotiation. Governments focused primarily on practical compromises that would assure that the system functioned to assure each state its preferred level of sovereign control. New institutions were modified to a compromise close to the lowest common denominator, with no government forced to accept immediate constraints on its own policies significantly greater than those it ideally sought. Where there was discord, optional clauses afforded governments flexibility. ***

Domestic Deliberation and Public Justification

The final type of evidence consists of the records of confidential deliberations and public justifications by national decision-makers, drawn from debates in the Parliamentary Assembly of the Council of Europe, negotiating sessions among the national governments, and the documentary record of confidential deliberations in one critical country where such documents are available, namely the United Kingdom. ***

*** Not a single piece of documentary evidence in the sources I have been able to consult supports the realist prediction that governments impose international human rights norms through threats of external coercion or inducement. At no point do we observe governments weighing the costs and benefits of coercion, concerning themselves with the distribution of power capabilities, or mentioning foreign or military aid.

There is slightly more evidence for the ideational view, but not enough to establish any confidence in its veracity. At most, NGOs and public opinion appear to have played a secondary, even insignificant, role.[49] The rhetoric of politicians in the European Assembly, as well as some interest groups, invoked moral considerations. Yet for the ideational theory to be confirmed, such statements must be designed to socialize or persuade national governments by appealing to respect for human rights as an end in itself, rather than as an instrument to promote

---

[49] For a similar conclusion regarding the abolition of the slave trade, see Kaufman and Pape 1999.

concrete ends of enduring interest to member governments – the prevention of tyranny, genocide, and aggression. There is no evidence of this; positions, as we have seen, do not change. * * *

The overwhelming bulk of the documentary evidence confirms instead the republican liberal account. By far the most consistent public justification for the ECHR, to judge from debates in the Council of Europe Constituent Assembly, was that it might help combat domestic threats from the totalitarian right and left, thereby stabilizing domestic democracy and preventing international aggression. (It is helpful to remember that both Hitler and Mussolini came to power, at least initially, by constitutional means.) Teitgen, the chief French advocate of the ECHR in the assembly, considered "Fascism, Hitlerism, and Communism" as the major postwar threats to democracy.[50] Governments, Teitgen argued, should seek to "prevent – before it is too late – any new member who might be threatened by a rebirth of totalitarianism from succumbing to the influence of evil, as has already happened in conditions of general apathy. It is not enough to possess freedom; positive action must be taken to defend it . . . . Would Fascism have triumphed in Italy if, after the assassination of Matteoti, this crime had been subjected to an international trial?"[51] Yet postwar human rights regimes were a response not simply to the recent fascist past but also to the prospect of a Communist future. The latter was mentioned just as often. In this period, we must recall, the French Communist Party enjoyed plurality electoral support. Teitgen spoke of the "abominable temptation" to "exchange . . . freedom for a little more bread."[52]

*** This *** refutes the conjecture – which, as we have seen, Sikkink and Keck treat as an essential piece of evidence for ideational theory – that few analysts before the 1980s could possibly have been aware of a link between democracy and peace. In many ways the democratic peace proposition, which dates from the eighteenth century, was a central tenet, arguably *the* central tenet, of postwar Western planning, as it had been in the thinking of Woodrow Wilson and other liberal statesmen a generation before.[53]

Yet domestic self-interest dominated. The most explicit justifications for the ECHR as a bulwark against future tyranny were advanced not

---

[50] Council of Europe 1975, I/40–42.
[51] Council of Europe 1975, I/192, 120, 64, also 60–64, for statements by others, I/66, 84, 120ff, 192–94, 276, 278–80, 292.
[52] Council of Europe 1975, I/40–42.
[53] Keck and Sikkink 1998, 203. Compare footnote 26. See Moravcsik 1992 and 1997.

by representatives from countries with the longest democratic heritage but, as republican liberal theory predicts, by those from newly established democracies. Among the most persistent advocates of this position were Italian and German representatives. *** A German representative went further, proposing a treaty obliging all member states to come to each other's aid, apparently with force, if domestic freedom were threatened.[54]

Yet the primary expectation was not that the regime would strengthen democracy by mobilizing intervention by foreign governments to enforce human rights norms, as realist and some ideational theory might lead us to expect. Nor did governments stress active transnational mobilization. Most participants appear to have felt that domestic politics would remain the primary site of enforcement – all members were to be democracies, at least formally – with international controls serving as an external signaling device to trigger an appropriate domestic response.[55] The ECHR was intended primarily to strengthen existing domestic institutions of judicial review, parliamentary legislation, and public action, not to supplant them. ***

*** The arrangement was primarily a means to prevent backsliding by new democracies. As Sir David Maxwell-Fyfe of the United Kingdom put it: "In answer to the criticism that, as signatories will be limited to democratic states the Convention is unnecessary . . . our plan has the advantage of being immediately practicable; it provides a system of collective security against tyranny and oppression."[56]

Unlike the UN system, the ECHR was designed to be enforceable – a goal, Maxwell-Fyfe argued, that was realistic only because all of its members already shared an essentially democratic political culture.[57]

[The United Kingdom is a critical case.] Opposition by the oldest and most firmly established democracy in Europe constitutes a particularly striking disconfirmation of realist and ideational theory.[58] The British, as we have seen, supported international declaratory norms but firmly

---

[54] Ibid., V/328–30, 336–40.
[55] Lester 1994, 4–5. See also Teitgen 1988, 482.
[56] Council of Europe 1975, I/120.
[57] See ibid., I/50–52; and Teitgen 1988, 488.
[58] The UK position was also viewed as decisive. See, for example, Paul-Henri Spaak, cited in Teitgen 1988, 478. Britain is also a country for which we have a wealth of reliable archival documents and oral histories. I have restricted myself here to materials found in published sources.

opposed any attempt to establish binding legal obligations, centralized institutions, individual petition, or compulsory jurisdiction.[59] * * *

What issues were raised in confidential British deliberations? The secondary literature on British human rights policy makes much of two British concerns: the fear that residents of British colonies and dependencies might invoke the ECHR, and aversion to European federalism. To judge from confidential discussions, however, neither appears to have been a dominant concern. * * * [Overall] there is surprisingly little discussion of colonial implications in the deliberations – certainly far less than purely of domestic considerations. Colonial Office concerns appear to have been isolated and intermittent. In any case, a colonial clause in the ECHR would limit any such claims, and consideration of such a clause did not blunt British opposition.[60] * * *

Confidential domestic deliberations suggest instead that British opposition reflected what A. Maxwell, permanent secretary to the Home Office, described as "grave apprehension about what might happen at home."[61] When the issue finally reached the Cabinet, the attention of ministers – after brief mention of colonial and economic concerns – seems to have focused on domestic application. Precisely as republican liberal theory predicts, the primary concern was not the vulnerability of the overall British record on human rights. As Parliamentary Secretary for Foreign Affairs Hector McNeil observed in a 1947 memo to Prime Minister Clement Atlee, Britain had an "extremely good record." British decision-makers appear sincerely to have believed that Britain would be less inconvenienced by reciprocal commitment than other member governments. The definition of rights in the convention was, so the Foreign Office memo to the Cabinet in 1950 concluded, "consistent with our existing law in all but a small number of comparatively trivial cases."[62]

* * *

[59] Marston 1993, 799–800.

[60] Marston 1993, 806–807, 809–10, 812, 816. In 1953 the British government voluntarily extended the Convention to the forty-two overseas territories for whose international relations they were responsible.

[61] Marston 1993, 813.

[62] Marston 1993, 811. With a lack of modesty about their domestic political institutions characteristic of this period, British officials and politicians also sometimes cited the need to set a good example for foreign countries as a reason for Britain to take an active role in the negotiations.

The specific issue cited most often by the government's legal authorities was the British policy toward political extremists. A ministerial brief referred to a "blank cheque" that would "allow the Governments to become the object of such potentially vague charges by individuals as to invite Communists, crooks, and cranks of every type to bring actions."[63] * * *

Yet it would be misleading to argue that British institutional idiosyncrasy *caused* British opposition. Every established democracy, after all, has its treasured idiosyncrasies, and British leaders sincerely believed that, as the cradle of rule-of-law governance, they would suffer least.[64] * * * For British decision-makers, the decisive point was not the nature of these concrete objections but *the utter absence in the British domestic context of any countervailing self-interested argument in favor of membership.*

The quaint scenarios of extremist threats raised by British officials demonstrate this. They arose not because extremist groups in Britain were particularly strong but because, in comparison with the Continent, they were so weak. Whereas French, German, and Italian officials viewed the ECHR as a check on the potential triumph of popular extremist parties, British officials saw it only as a hindrance to a defense of the political system against agitation by isolated individuals. British internal debates and external statements were utterly devoid of any recognition of the advantages of collective security against domestic extremists – advantages central to continental arguments for the ECHR. Whereas the French were concerned that the Communist Party might take power electorally and have to be checked by the ECHR, the British were concerned that isolated radicals might file suit under the ECHR. In this context, marginal inconveniences overridden elsewhere in the interest of bolstering democratic stability became fundamental obstacles to the acceptance of binding international human rights norms.

For these reasons, the British government long considered opposing the convention altogether. Yet, in the words of an internal Foreign

---

[63] Marston 1993, 806.

[64] It is possible they were wrong. One intriguing conjecture is that the longer a democratic form of government is in place, the more attached to its idiosyncrasies citizens and elites are likely to grow, and the further from the norm of international constitutionalism its practices are likely to become. Hence we would expect countries such as Britain, the Netherlands, Sweden, and the United States to become particularly attached to their idiosyncratic national systems. If correct, this would mean that established democracies not only reap fewer benefits from international human rights enforcement but also bear greater costs.

Office paper, "The alternative, namely refusal to become a party to a Convention acceptable to nearly all the remaining States of the Council of Europe, would appear to be almost indefensible . . . . Political considerations, both domestic and foreign, compel us now to bring ourselves to accept" an (optional) right of individual petition.[65] What blunted British opposition to any postwar European human rights regime was, above all, the fear of resurgent totalitarianism abroad that might pose an eventual military threat to the United Kingdom – precisely as republican liberal theory predicts.[66] This fear reflected not just a concern with a resurgence of Fascism, but also a turnaround in British foreign policy in 1948 in response to the perceived rise of the Communist threat in Western Europe. The West, the government argued, needed not only to maintain the military balance but also to strengthen continental democracies.

* * *

Having secured concessions, which essentially rendered the convention unenforceable in Britain, the cabinet unanimously accepted the desirability of signing it.

* * *

GENERALIZING THE ARGUMENT: HUMAN RIGHTS AND BEYOND

We have seen that the origins of the ECHR, the most successful international human rights adjudication and enforcement regime in the world today, lies not in coercive power politics or socialization to idealistic norms, as contemporary international relations theories predict. Instead its origins lie in self-interested efforts by newly established (or reestablished) democracies to employ international commitments to consolidate democracy – "locking in" the domestic political status quo against their nondemocratic opponents. This empirical finding has three broader implications for future research on domestic politics and international relations.

The Origin and Evolution of Human Rights Regimes

The first implication of the theoretical argument is that the tendency of states to enhance the credibility of domestic policies by binding themselves

---

[65] W. E. Beckett, Legal Advisor to the Foreign Office, April 1947 Foreign Office meeting, cited in Marston 1993, 798, 811, also 798–804.

[66] Note that this differs from the realist account in that the threat is not, in the first instance, a function of military power, but of political and ideological difference.

to international institutions may help explain the origins and evolution of human rights enforcement regimes more generally. In negotiations to create the Inter-American Convention on Human Rights, the UN Covenants, and the emergent African human rights system, we should expect to see a similar pattern of support from new democracies, suspicion from established democracies, and hostility from dictatorships.[67] In the following overview I highlight suggestive evidence and propose areas for future research.

The negotiation of the UN Covenant on Civil and Political Rights appears to illustrate the dynamics of democratic commitment. At the height of the Cold War, in the early 1950s, the most stable among modern democracies, including the United States and the United Kingdom, allied with authoritarian and totalitarian states like the Soviet Union, China, South Africa, and Iran, in opposition to the inclusion of compulsory, enforceable commitments. The alliance in favor of such commitments, as republican liberal theory predicts, included recently established democracies in continental Europe, Latin America, and Asia.

* * *

The positions of the established democracies in recent years concerning the creation of war crimes tribunals offer at least partial confirmation of republican liberal theory. Established democracies had little difficulty accepting tribunals with jurisdiction over the former Yugoslavia and Rwanda, where their own policies would not be implicated. Yet where commitments were (de facto) reciprocally binding – namely, in open-ended institutional commitments involving countries that actually engage in foreign intervention – established democracies, confident that they maintain adequate domestic safeguards against domestic atrocities, hesitated to accept international constraints. In the recent International Criminal Court negotiations, three established democracies with a recent history of intervention abroad (the United States, France, and Israel) posed the greatest difficulties. After fighting to dilute the obligations of the treaty, the United States and Israel joined China and highly repressive Middle Eastern and North African states in opposition, while France was the very last major power to lend its support to the treaty.[68]

---

[67] For an overview, see Robertson and Merrills 1996.

[68] For a general treatment of war crimes tribunals demonstrating the unwillingness of established democracies to pay high costs, see Bass 1999.

What about the development of human rights regimes over time? An understanding of major human rights regimes does not end with their founding. We have seen that the ECHR, like other major human rights instruments, created a number of optional clauses on individual petition and compulsory jurisdiction of the court. In some cases, early opponents of an enforceable convention remained exceptionally recalcitrant.[69] Yet over the subsequent five decades, all West European governments progressively adopted such clauses and in many cases incorporated the ECHR into domestic law.

Much of this accords with republican liberal theory. We observe a strengthening of commitments during and immediately after "democratic waves" – as hit Latin America and Central Europe during the 1990s. Such efforts are strongly favored by new democracies.[70] In Europe, the most important reform in the history of the ECHR, for example, was launched in the early to mid-1990s. "Protocol 11," opened for signature in May 1994, permits the ECHR Court to assume the functions of the commission and compels all new signatories to accept compulsory jurisdiction and individual petition – practices already universal among the original members. Leading legal academics argue that the most important impetus for Protocol 11 was "the widening . . . to include [states] that have had little domestic, much less international, experience in the legal protection of human rights."[71] The first three countries to ratify Protocol 11 were three transitional democracies: Bulgaria, Slovakia, and Slovenia. The governments of some new democracies in Central and East Europe were similarly quick to accept minority rights obligations as a means of locking in domestic democracy.[72] In the Americas, acceptance of compulsory jurisdiction by the Inter-American Court has occurred over the past two decades – a period in which domestic constitutional review also became nearly universal. In contrast,

---

[69] Sweden and the Netherlands are among the handful of countries that have been specifically ordered by the ECHR to allow more effective domestic judicial review of human rights claims; many have argued that Britain should be on the list as well. Lester 1994.

[70] Huntington 1991. Consider, however, former British colonies, which on gaining independence adopted explicit bills of rights and constitutional review – some on their own, some with the encouragement of the British government. Many were patterned after the European Convention, but the underlying impetus stems, republican liberal theory argues, from their status as emerging postauthoritarian democracies. Some of the most stable of these, such as those in the Caribbean, rejected international obligations.

[71] Janis, Kay, and Bradley 1995, 88–89, 113–18.

[72] See Manas 1996; and Wippman 1999.

human rights norms remain weak in those regions where new democracies are few, as in Africa or the Middle East.

Despite these important insights, however, the determinants of the evolution of human rights regimes are unlikely to be identical to the determinants of their founding and are therefore unlikely to be explained entirely by republican liberal theory. The ECHR deepened over a period during which European governments grew more confident about the stability of domestic democratic governance. Hence the theory advanced here cannot be the sole, or even the major, explanation for the subsequent deepening of the regime. A social process intervenes between original intent and ultimate evolution – a process, we have seen, of which governments were quite aware in 1950. British officials believed that the ECHR would alter domestic political arrangements so as to encourage the mobilization of new social demands for human rights enforcement. Republican liberal theory would suggest that such new demands reflect new opportunities for representation of social interests once a nation joins a regime; broader liberal theory would stress changes in social ideas and interests. Further research is required to clarify the precise dynamics of such long-term trends.[73]

Generalizing the Theory to Other Issue Areas

A second direction for future research is to extend the theory to cooperation in other issue areas. Despite the "republican liberal" label, the theoretical distinctiveness of the explanation advanced here is only incidentally connected to the liberal content of the philosophy embodied in human rights regimes. In other words, the argument is *theoretically* rather than substantively liberal.[74] Distinct to republican liberal theory is the decisive role of domestic political representation in world politics and, by extension, the possibility that international institutions, like their domestic counterparts, can enhance the credibility of domestic political commitments, thereby "locking in" current policies. Whether or not governments are "liberal," international institutions may "strengthen the state" domestically by expanding its domestic control over initiative, information, ideas, and institutions.[75] * * *

---

[73] Moravcsik 1995.
[74] Moravcsik 1997.
[75] Moravcsik 1994.

Under what general conditions should we expect to observe international commitments of this kind? Republican liberal theory suggests three conditions: (1) governments fear future domestic political uncertainty, (2) the position of the national government is supported by a consensus of foreign governments, and (3) international cooperation helps induce domestic actors to support the maintenance of current policies.

Where else in world politics might these three conditions be met? Two types of examples must suffice. Where nondemocratic governments cooperate to enhance their domestic credibility, a mirror image of human rights institutions may arise. Stephen David argues that "weak and illegitimate" leaders of developing countries often view internal enemies as more dangerous than external ones and are therefore likely to select international alliances that undermine domestic opponents.[76] The Holy Alliance is a nineteenth-century example of international cooperation designed to block the seemingly inevitable spread of domestic liberalism and nationalism – inside and outside its membership. ***

Further examples of efforts to use international regimes to bolster domestic policy credibility are found in international trade and monetary policy.[77] Mexico, for example, in exchange for its commitment to the North American Free Trade Area (NAFTA), gained relatively few economic concessions from the United States and Canada. This has led many analysts to argue that NAFTA should be seen less as a quid pro quo and more as a means of establishing the credibility of the Mexican commitment to trade and economic liberalization against the future potential of backsliding.[78] Mexican reform within NAFTA was just such a case where the three conditions were met: policy credibility was questionable, the consensus among foreign governments (the United States and Canada) was closer to the views of the domestic (Mexican) government than those of Mexican protectionists, and the costs of unilateral defection were perceived as large.

The process of European integration rested similarly on centralizing power in national executives, who consistently employed "foreign policy" decision-making institutions to handle issues traditionally decided in "domestic" forums.[79] *** In European monetary cooperation, weak-currency countries like France and Italy have been among the strongest

---

[76] David 1991.
[77] Rodrik 1989.
[78] For example, Haggard 1997.
[79] See Moravcsik 1994; and Goldstein 1996.

proponents of deeper exchange-rate cooperation – often with the intention of using external policy to stabilize domestic macroeconomic policy and performance ***, [– and deeper agricultural cooperation – both of which shifted the perceived costs of defection.[80]]

Realism and Idealism in International Relations Theory

The third and broadest implication of this analysis is that it counsels caution about the uncritical acceptance of certain ideational explanations for the emergence of international norms. Recent scholarship has been quick to assume that if realist (or regime) theory fails to explain international cooperation – say, in areas like human rights and environmental policy – the motivation for cooperation must lie in ideational socialization to altruistic beliefs. This assumption, once termed "idealist" or "utopian," seems plausible at first glance. ***

Yet scholars should not jump too quickly to the conclusion – as many recent studies of foreign aid, arms control, slavery, racism, and human rights invite them to do – that altruism must motivate the establishment of morally attractive international norms.[81] The tendency to jump to this conclusion demonstrates the danger of conducting debates about world politics around the simple dichotomy of realism versus idealism (or realism versus constructivism), as seems the current norm.[82] Presumptive evidence for the importance of altruistic or "principled" motivations vis-à-vis a realist account may melt away, as we have seen, as soon as the underlying theory is tested against more sophisticated rationalist, yet nonrealist (in this case, liberal) theories of self-interested political behavior. Moreover, to establish methodologically the existence of altruistic motivations and socialization processes, rather than alternative liberal theories, one must do more than cite public professions of idealism, document the actions of moral entrepreneurs, or invoke the desirability of the ultimate end. Talk and even mobilization are often cheap and often redundant or futile; accordingly, such evidence is often misleading.

---

[80] See Frieden 1993; Collins 1988; Moravcsik 1998a, chap. 4, 6; and Krugman 1994, 189–94.

[81] What drives cooperation is prior domestic institutional convergence. Hence the nature of domestic regimes is not an intermediate variable between fundamental socialization and state behavior but the critical variable that determines the nature of interdependence in the first place.

[82] This is a view ideational theorists are coming to accept. Finnemore and Sikkink 1998, 916–17.

Cross-national comparison and primary-source documentation of decision making are the critical tests.

In the case of the establishment of the ECHR, the proper theory and method reverses an idealist conclusion that might appear to offer a plausible alternative to realism.[83] What seems at first to be a conversion to moral altruism is in fact an instrumental calculation of how best to lock in democratic governance against future opponents – a practice hardly distinct from similar practices in the most pecuniary areas of world politics, such as trade and monetary policy. I am not denying, of course, that ideas and ideals matter in foreign policy; I am challenging only a particular idealist argument. Surely some domestic support for democratic governance may be ideological, even idealistic, in origin. But if we can learn a single lesson from the formation of the world's most successful formal arrangement for international human rights enforcement, it is that in world politics pure idealism begets pure idealism – in the form of parliamentary assemblies and international declarations. To establish binding international commitments, much more is required.

[83] For example, Legro and Moravcsik 1999.

25

Regime Design Matters: Intentional Oil Pollution and Treaty Compliance

Ronald B. Mitchell

Too many people assume, generally without having given any serious thought to its character or its history, that international law is and always has been a sham. Others seem to think that it is a force with inherent strength of its own. . . . Whether the cynic or sciolist is the less helpful is hard to say, but both of them make the same mistake. They both assume that international law is a subject on which anyone can form his opinions intuitively, without taking the trouble, as one has to do with other subjects, to inquire into the relevant facts.

—J. L. Brierly

Regime design matters.[1] International treaties and regimes have value if and only if they cause people to do things they would not otherwise do. *** [Whether] a treaty elicits compliance or other desired behavioral changes depends upon identifiable characteristics of the regime's

[1] This article summarizes the arguments made in Ronald B. Mitchell, *Intentional Oil Pollution at Sea: Environmental Policy and Treaty Compliance* (Cambridge, Mass.: MIT Press, forthcoming).

The research reported herein was conducted with support from the University of Oregon and the Center for Science and International Affairs of Harvard University. Invaluable data were generously provided by Clarkson Research Studies, Ltd. The article has benefited greatly from discussions with Abram Chayes, Antonia Chayes, William Clark, and Robert Keohane and from collaboration with Moira McConnell and Alexei Roginko as part of a project on regime effectiveness based at Dartmouth College and directed by Oran Young and Marc Levy. John Odell, Miranda Schreurs, David Weil, and two anonymous reviewers provided invaluable comments on earlier drafts of this article. The epigraph is from J. L. Brierly, *The Outlook for International Law* (Oxford: Clarendon Press, 1944), pp. 1–2.

compliance systems.² As negotiators incorporate certain rules into a regime and exclude others, they are making choices that have crucial implications for whether or not actors will comply.

For decades, nations have negotiated treaties with simultaneous hope that those treaties would produce better collective outcomes and skepticism about the ability to influence the way governments or individuals act. Both lawyers and political scientists have theorized about how international legal regimes can influence behavior and why they often do not.³ * * *

[Researchers interested in compliance] face two critical questions. First, given that power and interests play important roles in determining behavior at the international level, is any of the compliance we observe with international treaties the result of the treaty's influence? Second, if treaties and regimes can alter behavior, what strategies can those who negotiate and design regimes use to elicit the greatest possible compliance? This article addresses both these questions by empirically evaluating the international regime controlling intentional oil pollution. Numerous efforts to increase the regime's initially low levels of compliance provide data for comparing the different strategies for eliciting compliance within a common context that holds many important explanatory variables constant. The goal of the treaties underlying this regime has been to reduce intentional discharges of waste oil by tankers after they deliver their cargoes. Since the late 1970s, these treaties have established two quite different compliance systems, or "subregimes," to accomplish this goal. One has prohibited tanker operators from discharging oil in excess of specified limits. The other has required tanker owners to install expensive pollution-reduction equipment by specified dates. Treaty parties viewed both subregimes as equally legitimate and equally binding. * The two subregimes regulated similar behavior by the same nations and tankers over the same time period. The absence of differences in power and interests would suggest that compliance levels with the two subregimes would be quite similar. * According to collective action theory, these cases are among the least likely to provide support for the hypothesis that regime

---

² * * * [Oran Young,] *Compliance and Public Authority: A Theory with International Applications* (Baltimore, Md.: Johns Hopkins University Press, 1979), p. 3.

³ See, for example, Abram Chayes and Antonia Handler Chayes, "On Compliance," *International Organization* 47 (Spring 1993), pp. 175–205; Young, *Compliance and Public Authority*; Roger Fisher, *Improving Compliance with International Law* (Charlottesville: University Press of Virginia, 1981); and W. E. Butler, ed., *Control over Compliance with International Law* (Boston: Kluwer Academic Publishers, 1991).

design matters: subregime provisions required the powerful and concentrated oil industry to incur large pollution control costs to provide diffuse benefits to the public at large.[4] Indeed, the lower cost of complying with discharge limits would suggest that compliance would be higher with those limits than with equipment requirements.

*** [Violations] of the limits on discharges have occurred frequently, attesting to the ongoing incentives to violate the agreement and confirming the characterization of oil pollution as a difficult collaboration problem.[5] A puzzle arises, however, from the fact that contrary to expectation compliance has been all but universal with requirements to install expensive equipment that provided no economic benefits. *** [The] significant variance across subregimes can only be explained by specific differences in subregime design. *** [The] equipment subregime succeeded by ensuring that actors with incentives to comply with, monitor, and enforce the treaty were provided with the practical ability and legal authority to conduct those key implementation tasks. *** [The] regime elicited compliance when it developed integrated compliance systems that succeeded in increasing transparency, providing for potent and credible sanctions, reducing implementation costs to governments by building on existing infrastructures, and preventing violations rather than merely deterring them.

COMPLIANCE THEORY AND DEFINITIONS

Explaining the puzzle of greater compliance with a more expensive and economically inefficient international regulation demands an understanding of existing theories about *** compliance in international affairs. Realists have inferred a general inability of international regimes to influence behavior from the fact that the international system is

---

[4] Michael McGinnis and Elinor Ostrom, "Design Principles for Local and Global Commons," Workshop in Political Theory and Policy Analysis, Bloomington, Ind., March 1992, p. 21. Olson's argument that small groups supply public goods more often than large groups assumes that group members benefit from providing the good, which is not true in the oil pollution case; see Mancur Olson, *The Logic of Collective Action: Public Goods and the Theory of Groups* (Cambridge, Mass.: Harvard University Press, 1965), p. 34.

[5] See Arthur A. Stein, *Why Nations Cooperate: Circumstance and Choice in International Relations* (Ithaca, N.Y.: Cornell University Press, 1990); and Robert Axelrod and Robert O. Keohane, "Achieving Cooperation Under Anarchy: Strategies and Institutions," in Kenneth Oye, ed., *Cooperation Under Anarchy* (Princeton, N.J.: Princeton University Press, 1986).

characterized by anarchy and an inability to organize centralized enforcement. *** ["Considerations of power rather than of law determine compliance."[6]] *** Treaties are epiphenomenal: they reflect power and interests but do not shape behavior.

This view does not imply that noncompliance is rare ***. Although nations will violate rules whenever they have both the incentives and ability to do so, *** "the great majority of the rules of international law are generally observed by all nations."[7] For the realist, behavior frequently conforms to treaty rules because both the behavior and the rules reflect the interests of powerful states. More specifically, compliance [arises because:] (1) a hegemonic state *** induces other states to comply; (2) the treaty rules codify the parties' existing behavior or expected future behavior; or (3) the treaty resolves a coordination game in which no party has any incentive to violate the rules. ***

Treaty rules correlate with but do not cause compliance. Therefore, efforts to improve treaty rules to increase compliance reflect either the changed interests of powerful states or are misguided exercises in futility. The strength of this view has led to considerable attention being paid to whether rules influence behavior and far less being paid to design features that explain why one rule influences behavior and another does not.

In contrast, international lawyers and institutionalists contend that the anarchic international order need not lead *** to nations violating agreements whenever doing so suits them. Other forces – such as transparency, reciprocity, accountability, and regime-mindedness – allow regimes to impose significant constraints on international behavior under the right conditions.[8] Implicit in the institutionalist view is the assumption *** [that a given constellation of power and interests] leaves room for nations to choose among treaty rules that will elicit different levels of

---

[6] Hans Joachim Morgenthau, *Politics Among Nations: The Struggle for Power and Peace*, 5th ed. (New York: Alfred A. Knopf, 1978), p. 299. See also Kenneth Waltz, *Theory of International Politics* (Reading, Mass.: Addison-Wesley Publishing Co., 1979), p. 204; and Susan Strange, "Cave! Hic Dragones: A Critique of Regime Analysis," in Stephen D. Krasner, ed., *International Regimes* (Ithaca, N.Y.: Cornell University Press, 1983), pp. 337–54 at p. 338. For a contrasting view, see Young, *International Cooperation*, p. 62.

[7] Morgenthau, *Politics Among Nations*, p. 267.

[8] See, for example, Abram Chayes and Antonia Chayes, "Compliance Without Enforcement: State Behavior Under Regulatory Treaties," *Negotiation Journal* 7 (July 1991), pp. 311–30; Young, *International Cooperation*; Robert O. Keohane, "Reciprocity in International Relations," *International Organization* 40 (Winter 1986), pp. 1–27; and Krasner, *International Regimes*.

compliance. High compliance levels can be achieved even in difficult collaboration problems in which incentives to violate are large and on-going. * * * [Institutionalists] do not exclude the possibility that regimes, rather than mere considerations of power, [can cause] compliance.[9]

[Is behavior ever any different than it would have been without an agreement?] If we define "treaty-induced compliance" as behavior that conforms to a treaty's rules because of the treaty's compliance system, institutionalists view treaty-induced compliance as possible. * * * [Realists] see all compliance as "coincidental compliance," * * * behavior that would have occurred even without the treaty rules.

The debate between these theories highlights the demands placed on research that seeks to identify those design characteristics of a regime, if any, that are responsible for observed levels of compliance. I define compliance, the dependent variable, as an actor's behavior that conforms with an explicit treaty provision. Speaking of compliance with treaty provisions rather than with a treaty captures the fact that parties may well comply with some provisions while violating others. A study of "treaty compliance" would aggregate violation of one provision with compliance with another, losing valuable empirical information.[10] Restricting study to the explicit rules in a treaty-based regime allows the analyst to distinguish compliance from noncompliance in clear and replicable ways. Obviously, a focus on explicit rules ignores other potential mechanisms of regime influence, such as norms, principles, and processes of knowledge creation.[11] * * *

[This article differentiates] among three parts of any compliance system: a primary rule system, a compliance information system, and a noncompliance response system. The primary rule system consists of the actors, rules, and processes related to the behavior that is the substantive target of the regime. * * * [The] primary rule system determines the pressures and incentives for compliance and violation. The compliance

---

[9] See, for example, Louis Henkin, *How Nations Behave: Law and Foreign Policy* (New York: Columbia University Press, 1979), p. 47; Young, *International Cooperation*, p. 62; and Chayes and Chayes, "Compliance Without Enforcement," p. 31.

[10] At the extreme, if all parties violated treaty provision A and complied with treaty provision B, they could all be classified as in partial compliance, ignoring the important variance incompliance rates.

[11] See Haas, Keohane, and Levy, *Institutions for the Earth*; George W. Downs and David M. Rocke, *Tacit Bargaining, Arms Races, and Arms Control* (Ann Arbor: University of Michigan Press, 1990); Charles Lipson, "Why Are Some International Agreements Informal?" *International Organization* 45 (Autumn 1991), pp. 495–538; and Chayes and Chayes, "On Compliance," pp. 188–92.

information system consists of the actors, rules, and processes that collect, analyze, and disseminate information on instances of violations and compliance. [The] compliance information system * * * determines the amount, quality, and uses made of data on compliance and enforcement. The noncompliance response system consists of the actors, rules, and processes governing the formal and informal responses * * * employed to induce those in noncompliance to comply. * * * These categories provide the framework used in * * * this article to evaluate the oil pollution regime's sources of success and failure in its attempt to elicit compliance.

TWO SUBREGIMES FOR INTERNATIONAL OIL POLLUTION CONTROL

For most people, oil pollution conjures up images of tanker accidents such as that of the *Exxon Valdez*.[12] * * * [Although] oil from such accidents poses a concentrated but localized hazard to the marine environment, the waste oil traditionally generated during normal oil transport has posed a more diffuse but ubiquitous threat. After a tanker delivers its cargo, a small fraction of oil remains onboard, adhering to cargo tank walls. Ballasting and tank-cleaning procedures mixed this oil – averaging about 300 tons per voyage – with seawater, creating slops. These in turn were most easily and cheaply disposed of by discharging them overboard while at sea. * By the 1970s, the intentional discharges made on thousands of tanker voyages were putting an estimated million tons of oil into the oceans annually.[13] [The impact of these chronic but low-concentration discharges and that of accidents on seabirds and resort beaches have produced regular international efforts at regulation.] *

Intentional oil discharges were one of the first pollutants to become the subject of an international regulatory regime.[14] In the International

---

[12] The *Exxon Valdez* wrecked in Prince William Sound, Alaska, on 24 March 1989, [spilling thirty five-thousand tons of oil.]

[13] National Academy of Sciences, *Petroleum in the Marine Environment* (Washington, D.C. National Academy of Sciences, 1975). See also National Academy of Sciences and National Research Council, *Oil in the Sea: Inputs, Fates, and Effects* (Washington, D.C.: National Academy Press, 1985).

[14] For the history of oil pollution control from the 1920s through the 1970s, see Sonia Zaide Pritchard, *Oil Pollution Control* (London: Croom Helm, 1987); for a history from the 1950s through the 1970s, see R. Michael M'Gonigle and Mark W. Zacher, *Pollution, Politics, and International Law: Tankers at Sea* (Berkeley: University of California Press, 1979).

Convention for the Prevention of Pollution of the Seas by Oil (OILPOL) of 1954, nations addressed the coastal oil pollution problem by limiting the oil content of discharges made near shore.[15] [Numerous regulatory revisions have been negotiated] within diplomatic conferences sponsored by the Intergovernmental Maritime Consultative Organization (IMCO) or within its committees and those of its successor, the International Maritime Organization (IMO). By the late 1970s, the regime's major provisions, now contained in the International Convention for the Prevention of Pollution from Ships (MARPOL), consisted of restrictions on both tanker operations and tanker equipment that relied on quite different compliance systems.[16] Although rule-making has remained consistently international, governments and nonstate actors have played crucial roles in the implementation and enforcement of the regime: tanker owners and operators have been the targets of the regulations while maritime authorities, classification societies, insurers, and shipbuilders have monitored and enforced the regulations.

The Discharge Subregime

[MARPOL'S discharge subregime] evolved from the initial regulations of 1954. That agreement constituted a compromise between the United Kingdom – which wielded strong power in oil markets but had strong environmental nongovernmental organizations pushing it to reduce coastal pollution – and Germany, the Netherlands, the United States, and other major states that viewed any regulation as either environmentally unnecessary or as harmful to their *** shipping interests. Although the United Kingdom had sought to restrict tanker discharges throughout the ocean, the final agreement limited the oil content of discharges made within fifty miles of any coastline to 100 parts oil per million parts water (100 ppm). In 1962, the British pushed through an amendment

---

[15] "International Convention for the Prevention of Pollution of the Sea by Oil," 12 May 1954, *Treaties and Other International Agreements Series (TIAS)*, no. 4900 (Washington, D.C.: U.S. Department of State, 1954).

[16] See *International Convention for the Prevention of Pollution from Ships (MARPOL)*, 2 November 1973, reprinted in *International Legal Materials (ILM)*, vol. 12 (Washington, D.C.: American Society of International Law, 1973), p. 1319 (hereafter cited by abbreviation, volume, and year); and *Protocol of 1978 Relating to the International Convention for the Prevention of Pollution from Ships*, 17 February 1978, reprinted in *ILM*, vol. 17, 1978, p. 1546 (hereafter cited together as *MARPOL 73/78*).

applying this 100 ppm standard to discharges made by new tankers regardless of their distance from shore.

The principle underlying the 1962 amendment – that crude oil could float far enough that discharge zones would not effectively protect coastlines – had gained sufficient support by 1969 that nations agreed to limit discharges by all tankers throughout the ocean. The pressure to amend the 1954/62 agreement came from two different sources. On one side, the thirty-five million gallons of oil spilled by the grounding of the *Torrey Canyon* off Britain and France [in 1967] and growing environmentalism, especially in the United States, supported a push for stronger regulations.[17] The previously resistant United States replaced the United Kingdom as the leading activist state and especially sought to ensure that amendments would address the growing evidence of enforcement problems ***.

On the other side, oil companies rightly interpreted the 1962 amendments as a wake-up call that discharge standards would soon be replaced by expensive equipment requirements. In response, Shell Marine International developed and promoted an operational means by which tankers could reduce oil discharges without *** new equipment.[18] The load-on-top procedure (LOT) involved consolidating ballast and cleaning slops in a single tank, *** [decanting the water from beneath the oil,] and loading the next cargo on top of the remaining slops. The beauty of LOT was that it [wasted less cargo,] thereby advancing both [environmental and economic goals.] *** The problem was that normal operation of LOT produced discharges that exceeded the 100 ppm standard. If this criterion had remained in effect, tankers would have had to install expensive new equipment ***. With the support of France, the Netherlands, Norway, and the now less-activist United Kingdom, oil and shipping companies therefore also sought to amend the treaty. Oil companies considered LOT so effective that they wanted diplomats to scrap the 1954/62 zonal approach altogether. The pressures for greater environmental protection, however, led them to support the more limited objective of redefining the limits on discharges from the 100 ppm "content" criterion to one that could be monitored using existing onboard equipment.[19]

In a unanimously accepted compromise in 1969, more stringent and enforceable regulations were framed in terms that averted equipment

---

[17] M'Gonigle and Zacher, *Pollution, Politics, and International Law*, p. 100.

[18] J. H. Kirby, "The Clean Seas Code: A Practical Cure of Operation Pollution," in *Third International Conference on Oil Pollution of the Sea: Report of Proceedings, Rome 7–9 October 1968* (Winchester, England: Warren and Son, 1968), pp. 201–19.

[19] Kirby, "The Clean Seas Code," p. 206.

requirements. Within the fifty-mile near-shore zones, discharges could now only involve "clean ballast" that left no visible trace; outside the fifty-mile zones, discharges could not exceed 60 liters of oil per mile (60 l/m). Proponents argued that the clean ballast provision would improve enforcement by transforming any sighting of a discharge into evidence of a violation.[20] The more crucial change involved a new limit that total discharges not exceed one fifteen-thousandth of a tanker's capacity.[21] Although compliance with this standard required a tanker to reduce its average discharges by almost 98 percent, Shell's J. H. Kirby claimed that "any responsibly run ship, no matter how big, could operate" within these standards if it used LOT.[22] The low total discharge limit also allowed port authorities to assume that any tanker with completely clean tanks *** had violated the agreement.[23] These standards took effect in 1978 and remain in force today through their incorporation into the 1973 MARPOL agreement.

The Equipment Subregime

By the early 1970s, public concern was pushing environmental issues onto the international political scene with increasing frequency. The United Nations Conference on the Human Environment and negotiation of the London Dumping Convention in 1972 set the stage for a major overhaul of the OILPOL agreement. IMCO hosted a major conference in 1973 to negotiate the MARPOL treaty. Its goal was the replacement of OILPOL's rules with rules that would cover all major types of vessel-source marine pollution.

The U.S. government had become increasingly concerned that the ease with which tanker crews could violate discharge standards and the massive resources and diligence needed to detect violations were preventing effective mitigation of the growing oil pollution problem.[24] By 1972,

---

[20] Assembly resolution 391, IMCO/IMO doc. resolution A.391(X), 1 December 1977, Annex, par. 5. All document citations herein refer to IMCO/IMO documents housed in the IMO Secretariat library. ***

[21] *1969 Amendments to the International Convention for the Prevention of Pollution of the Sea by Oil,* 21 October 1969, reprinted in Bernd Ruster and Bruno Simma, eds., *International Protection of the Environment: Treaties and Related Documents* (Dobbs Ferry, N.Y.: Oceana Publications, 1975).

[22] Kirby, "The Clean Seas Code," p. 208.

[23] See Kirby, "The Clean Seas Code," pp. 200 and 209; and William T. Burke, Richard Legatski, and William W. Woodhead, *National and International Law Enforcement in the Ocean* (Seattle: University of Washington Press, 1975), p. 129.

[24] M'Gonigle and Zacher, *Pollution, Politics, and International Law,* p. 108.

Congress had adopted legislation that threatened to require all American tankers as well as all tankers entering U.S. ports to install expensive pollution-reducing equipment. The legislation included a proposal to require all large tankers to install double hulls to address accidental spills and segregated ballast tanks (SBT) to address intentional discharges. The SBT system involved arranging ballast tanks and associated piping such that ballast water could not come into contact with oil being carried as cargo. The system was expensive both in terms of capital and the reduction to cargo-carrying capacity. The United States sought international agreement to require SBT but threatened to require it unilaterally if necessary. Discharge requirements clearly were cheaper, more economically efficient, and "in theory ... a good idea."[25] However, environmental pressures and growing evidence that LOT was neither as widespread nor as effective as had been hoped led the United States and the United Kingdom to support rules that offered easier and more effective enforcement.

The largely U.S.-based oil companies initially opposed SBT requirements but eventually supported them as preferable to threatened U.S. unilateral rules. Many shipping states also reluctantly supported SBT requirements. They believed such requirements would avert an even more costly double bottom requirement. It was also fiscally acceptable: the combination of a recent building boom and the proposed language of the requirements meant that tanker owners would only have to incur the additional costs of SBT many years in the future and then only for large tankers. However, governments representing shipbuilding interests (France and Japan) and those representing independent tanker owners (Denmark, Germany, Greece, Norway, and Sweden) opposed the requirement.[26] By a vote of thirty to seven, the conference adopted a requirement for tankers over 70,000 tons built in 1980 and later to install SBT.

By 1977, a spate of accidents in the United States and continuing enforcement concerns led President Jimmy Carter to propose that SBT requirements be applied to all tankers, not just large new tankers.[27] Given (1) that the United States was again explicitly threatening unilateral action and (2) that the 1973 MARPOL agreement [had only been ratified

---

[25] See statements submitted by the U.S. delegation to the 13th Preparatory Session for an International Conference on Marine Pollution in 1973: IMCO/IMO doc. MP XIII/2(c)/5, 23 May 1972. ***

[26] M'Gonigle and Zacher, *Pollution, Politics, and International Law*, p. 114.

[27] Jacob W. Ulvila, "Decisions with Multiple Objectives in Integrative Bargaining," Ph.D. diss., Harvard University, 1979, appendix A1.1.

by three states,] IMCO called a second major conference in 1978. State positions reflected the fact that retrofitting existing tankers with SBT would reduce each tanker's (and the fleet's) cargo capacity by some 15 percent.[28] Greece, Norway, and Sweden saw this as a means to put scores of their laid up independent tankers back to work. However, most states saw SBT retrofitting as extremely expensive.[29] Just as the 1962 amendments had prompted LOT development, the 1973 MARPOL agreement prompted oil companies to perfect a technique known as crude oil washing (COW), which entailed spraying down cargo tanks with the cargo itself rather than with seawater. Operating COW equipment during cargo delivery transformed oil that otherwise would have been discharged as slops into usable delivered cargo, simultaneously reducing oil pollution and increasing cargo owner revenues. The industry proposal for COW as an alternative to SBT produced a compromise in which tankers built after 1982 had to install both SBT and COW, while existing tankers had to be retrofitted with either SBT or COW by 1985. The 1978 Protocol Relating to the International Convention for the Prevention of Pollution from ships was made an integral part of the 1973 MARPOL agreement. While MARPOL and its protocol, known collectively as MARPOL 73/78, did not enter into force until 1983, their standards regulated all new construction after 1979.

OBSERVED COMPLIANCE LEVELS

Available evidence demonstrates a wide divergence in levels of compliance under these two subregimes. During the same time period in which almost every tanker owner was retrofitting existing tankers and buying new tankers to conform with MARPOL's requirements for SBT and COW, large numbers of tanker operators continued to discharge oil well in excess of legal limits. ***

Violations of the clean ballast, 60 l/m, and total discharge standards in place since 1978 have been common. Oil company surveys from the 1970s show that neither oil company nor independent tankers reduced average discharge levels to the one fifteen-thousandth limit in any year between 1972 and 1977 (see Figure 25.1). Although oil company tankers

[28] See Sonia Z. Pritchard, "Load on Top: From the Sublime to the Absurd," *Journal of Maritime Law and Commerce* 9 (April 1978), pp. 185–224 at p. 194.

[29] For an excellent discussion of state positions during both the 1973 and 1978 conferences, see M'Gonigle and Zacher, *Pollution, Politics, and International Law,* pp. 107–42.

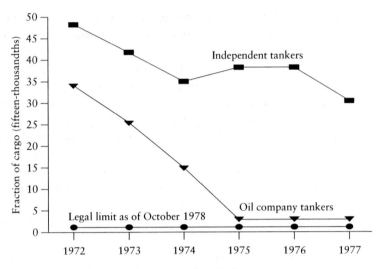

FIGURE 25.1. Average tanker discharges, 1972–77.

Source: U.S. Congress, House Committee on Government Operations, *Oil Tanker Pollution: Hearings Before the Subcommittee on Government Activities and Transportation, 18 and 19 July 1978,* 95th Congress, 2d sess., p. 322.

dramatically reduced average discharges in the early 1970s, discharges remained at three times the legal limit. The two-thirds of the fleet operated by independent oil transporters did far worse, with discharges that were thirty times the legal limit and that were not much below levels that a tanker practicing no pollution control would have produced.[30] The trends in these discharges suggest that few tankers complied with the limit after it took legal effect in 1978.[31]

Other evidence confirms the frequency of discharge violations. [National Academy of Sciences studies conducted in 1981 and 1989 assumed that significant fractions (50 percent and 15–20 percent, respectively) of the world's tanker fleet were violating the total discharge limit.[32]] Representatives of independent transporters [admitted] that tankers often

[30] See, for example, the estimate of 0.3 percent in James E. Moss, *Character and Control of Sea Pollution by Oil* (Washington, D.C: American Petroleum Institute, 1963), p. 47, and the estimate of 0.4 percent in IMCO/IMO doc. OP 1/21, 15 January 1965, of the Oil Pollution subcommittee. (Using note 30 as a guide, this indicates the only document issued relating to agenda item 21 at the 1st meeting of the subcommittee.)

[31] Unfortunately, oil companies discontinued the surveys after 1977. Personal communication from Arthur McKenzie, Tanker Advisory Center, New York, 1992.

[32] [IMCO/IMO doc. MEPC XVI/Inf.2, 4 November 1981. IMCO/IMO doc. MEPC 30/ Inf.13, 19 September 1990, p. 15.]

violate discharge limits * * *.[33] Studies of detected oil slicks and dead seabirds as well as [IMO violation reports] confirm that many tankers continue to discharge their slops at sea.[34]

[By contrast there is considerable evidence] that compliance with the equipment standards has been exceptionally high. By 1981, * * * new tankers were being built with SBT and existing tankers were being retrofitted with SBT and/or COW.[35] [National] and international studies and industry experts [assume] that all tankers comply with the equipment standards * * *.[36]

Analysis of previously unavailable data on equipment installed on large tankers supports these perceptions.[37] Among large tankers in the fleet at the end of 1991, 94 percent of tankers built in 1979 or earlier had installed SBT or COW as required, 98 percent of those built between 1980 and 1982 had installed SBT as required, and 98 percent of those built after 1982 had installed both SBT and COW as required. The figures not only confirm remarkably high compliance rates but also document that tankers of all nations, not merely those that supported the equipment requirements during negotiation, have complied.

---

[33] For example, "IMO, Tanker Owners Urge Increase in Facilities Accepting Oily Wastes," *International Environment Reporter*, 8 March 1989, p. 130.

[34] See, for example, C. J. Camphuysen, *Beached Bird Surveys in the Netherlands 1915–1988: Seabird Mortality in the Southern North Sea Since the Early Days of Oil Pollution* (Amsterdam: Werkgroep Noordzee, 1989); United States Coast Guard, *Polluting Incidents In and Around U.S. Waters* (Washington, D.C.: U.S. Department of Commerce, 1973 and 1975–86); N. Smit-Kroes, *Harmonisatie Noordzeebeleid: Brief van de Minister van Verkeer en Waterstaat* (Tweede Kamer der Staten-Generaal: 17–408) (Harmonization of North Sea policy: Letter from the Minister of Transport and Waterways; Lower House of Parliament) (The Hague: Government Printing Office of the Netherlands, 1988); IMCO/IMO doc. MEPC 21 /Inf. 8, 21 March 1985; and Second International Conference on the Protection of the North Sea, *Quality Status of the North Sea: A Report by the Scientific and Technical Working Group* (London: Her Majesty's Stationery Office, 1987), p. 14.

[35] Drewry Shipping Consultants, Ltd., *The Impact of New Tanker Regulations*, Drewry publication no. 94 (London: Drewry Shipping Consultants, Ltd., 1981), p. 25.

[36] See IMCO/IMO doc. MEPC 30/Inf.l3, 19 September 1990, p. 8; Second International Conference on the Protection of the North Sea, *Quality Status of the North Sea*, p. 57; Pieter Bergmeijer, "The International Convention for the Prevention of Pollution from Ships," paper presented at the 17th Pacem in Maribus conference, Rotterdam, August 1990, p. 12; and personal interview with E. J. M. Ball, Oil Companies International Marine Forum, London, 26 June 1991;

[37] The detailed statistics in Table 1 and Figure 2 were developed from an electronic version of Clarkson Research Studies, Ltd., *The Tanker Register* (London: Clarkson Research Studies, Ltd., 1991) generously provided by Clarkson Research Studies, Ltd.

[Both] international politics and private economics would lead us to expect higher compliance with the discharge standards, not the equipment standards. The discharge standards had been adopted unanimously. In contrast, several powerful nations opposed the equipment standards in both 1973 and 1978. Tankers seeking the economic benefits of conserving oil could have done so most cheaply by using the equipment-free option of LOT, not by installing COW or the even more expensive SBT. Indeed, in 1978, one analyst *** predicted that the enormous costs of SBT would make compliance "negligible."[38]

In short, the empirical evidence of higher compliance levels with the equipment subregime runs contrary to predictions based on a simple analysis of exogenous power and interests. How do we explain what appears to be a significant divergence between theory and observed outcomes? Was any of the observed compliance treaty-induced? If so, what elements of the equipment standards compliance system explain its greater success at eliciting compliance? ***

WAS COMPLIANCE TREATY-INDUCED?

[Before explaining these differences in compliance levels, we need to ensure they can be attributed to features of the subregimes.] *** Did tanker owners and operators act any differently than they would have in the absence of international regulations? The following accounting strongly suggests (1) that increased use of LOT owes more to economics than to international law, (2) that increased installation of COW equipment owes much to economics but also reflects the MARPOL regime's influences, and (3) that increased installation of SBT largely is due to MARPOL influences.

LOT

[The] 1969 rules had little to do with the observed increase in the use of LOT by tanker operators. A large share of tankers simply did not use LOT or comply with the discharge standards. The continuing noncompliance with discharge standards did not result from an inability to use

---

[38] Charles Odidi Okidi, *Regional Control of Ocean Pollution: Legal and Institutional Problems and Prospects* (Alphen aan den Rijn, The Netherlands: Sijthoff and Noordhoff, 1978), p. 34.

LOT – a noncomplex procedure that required no new equipment – but from insufficient incentives to use it.

The subregime itself produced few effective mechanisms for inducing operators to adopt LOT. [The] discharge subregime's compliance system failed to induce the monitoring and enforcement necessary to deter violations. The subregime's failure effectively to detect, identify, prosecute, and penalize violators left tanker operators' incentives to comply with it largely uninfluenced. * * *

Given the absence of these pathways for regime influence, it is not surprising to find that economic influences readily explain the pattern of LOT usage. A tanker operator's first-order incentives to use LOT depended on the costs of recovering waste oil, the value of that oil, and the ownership of the oil being transported. This last factor meant that oil companies had far greater incentives to adopt LOT than did independent transporters. The latter carry oil on charter to cargo owners and are paid for the amount of oil initially loaded, * * * not for the amount delivered. Therefore, discharging waste oil at sea costs the independent transporter nothing. * * * In contrast, operators that own their cargoes, as oil companies usually do[, could benefit by almost \$15,000 per trip.[39]]

The decrease in average discharges of oil company tankers in the 1970s and the absence of a similar decrease in discharges of independent tankers correlate more with these divergent incentives and with rising oil prices than with any treaty proscription. Oil companies' greater incentives to conserve oil explain why their average discharges were lower than those of independent tankers in 1972 and why they decreased discharges more rapidly after the 1973 oil price hikes (see Figure 25.1). If the regime * * * were influencing oil company behavior, these decreases should have occurred only after the total discharge limits took legal effect in 1978 * * *. The far smaller decrease in average discharge among independents reflects the fact that conserved oil had little value to them.

* * *

COW

The almost universal installation of COW equipment initially tempts one to conclude that compliance was treaty-induced. The contrast in rates

---

[39] The following discussion of the costs of LOT, COW, and SBT draws heavily on William G. Waters, Trevor D. Heaver, and T. Verrier, *Oil Pollution from Tanker Operations: Causes, Costs, Controls* (Vancouver, B.C.: Center for Transportation Studies, 1980).

of use of LOT and COW suggest that differences in the designs of the corresponding subregimes may be responsible, given that both methods allowed a tanker operator to reduce waste oil. However, closer evaluation reveals that here, too, economic factors played an important role, although not an exclusive one.

Like LOT, COW has economic as well as environmental benefits. COW's costs include those for the washing machines and the additional time and labor needed to wash tanks in port ***. As with LOT, the offsetting benefit of more delivered cargo accrues to the cargo owner. However, the tanker operator also benefits: the decrease in oil left onboard increases the tanker's effective cargo capacity and reduces [repair and maintenance costs. Saving about $9,000 per voyage.]

These economic incentives to adopt COW are [evident in the timing of its adoption.] *** [Many oil companies adopted cow in the mid-1970s, years after it became available but before the MARPOL deadline. Like LOT, this timing corresponds with the rising oil prices of the 1970s.]

The contrast to SBT *** also confirms the role of economics. The higher capital costs of SBT and the significant reduction to cargo-carrying capacity that SBT involved imposed a net cost per voyage on a tanker with SBT of $1,500 ***. A new tanker installing both COW and SBT, as required by MARPOL, faced costs of almost $8,000 per voyage. Owners of large tankers built before 1980, who were allowed to choose between SBT and COW, installed COW equipment on 89 percent of their tankers and SBT on only 36 percent. Owners also installed COW equipment on 95 percent of large tankers built between 1980 and 1982, even though MARPOL only required them to install SBT. ***

[If economics were the sole influence on behavior, however, we should expect companies to achieve the economic goal of conserving oil by the cheapest and most cost-effective means possible, that is, by LOT, not COW.] We should also expect to see the same divergence between the behavior of independent carriers and oil companies as we observed in the LOT case. Yet the 99 percent compliance rate attests to the fact that all tanker owners were installing COW. The adoption of COW more frequently than SBT does not imply that the subregime was ineffective, only that when the subregime left owners with alternatives, their choices were driven by costs. In contrast to clear flaws in the compliance system supporting discharge standards, *** the design of the compliance system supporting equipment requirements provided several means of successfully reducing both the incentives and ability of tanker owners to violate COW requirements. Thus, an interplay among economics and subregime characteristics appears to have been the source of widespread COW adoption.

SBT

Adoption of the SBT standard provides an unambiguous example of subregime influence on behavior. Unlike COW or LOT, tanker owners had no economic incentives to install this technology. SBT's additional piping and equipment added several million dollars to the cost of a new tanker, representing almost 5 percent of total cost.[40] Installing SBT also reduced cargo capacity * * *. Yet these costs provided no offsetting benefits * * *. [Supporters of SBT admitted that SBT would increase the cost of carrying oil by 15 percent;] some oil company estimates ran up to 50 percent.[41] As late as 1991, oil and shipping interests opposed mandatory SBT retrofitting as too expensive.[42]

[Observed SBT installations reflect effective treaty rules rather than economics.] [More] than 98 percent of those required to install SBT did so despite the significant costs involved. * * * [The timing of the increase in the number of tankers installing SBT seen in Figure 25.2 reinforces the conclusion that owners installed SBT only under the regulatory threat posed by the subregime's compliance system.] In short, ["If there were not a regulatory requirement, there would not be SBT."[43]] Within several years, the subregime had caused a radical change in tanker owner behavior.

One alternative explanation of SBT adoption deserves special attention. At least one analyst has claimed that hegemonic pressures exerted by the United States explain the success of MARPOL.[44] [Certainly SBT requirements were adopted because of explicit threats of unilateral U.S. regulation. Yet, this does not imply that subsequent behaviors results

[40] See Philip A. Cummins, Dennis E. Logue, Robert D. Tollison, and Thomas D. Willett, "Oil Tanker Pollution Control: Design Criteria Versus Effective Liability Assessment," *Journal of Maritime Law and Commerce* 7 (October 1975), pp. 181–82; and Charles S. Pearson, *International Marine Environmental Policy: The Economic Dimension* (Baltimore, Md.: The Johns Hopkins University Press, 1975), p. 98.

[41] See IMCO/IMO doc. MEPC V/Inf. 4, 8 March 1976, p. A18; and M'Gonigle and Zacher, *Pollution, Politics, and International Law,* p. 134.

[42] See IMCO/IMO doc. MEPC 31/8/5, 4 April 1991; and Osborne and Ferguson, "Technology, MARPOL, and Tankers," p. 6–2.

[43] Personal interview with Sean Connaughton, marine transportation analyst, American Petroleum Institute Washington, D.C., 8 April 1992.

[44] Jesper Grolin, "Environmental Hegemony, Maritime Community, and the Problem of Oil Tanker Pollution in Michael A. Morris, ed., *North–South Perspectives on Marine Policy* (Boulder, Colo.: Westview Press, 1988).

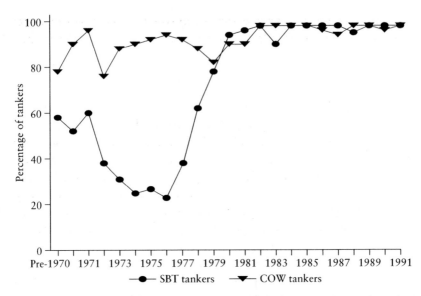

FIGURE 25.2. Percentage of tankers with segregated ballast tanks (SBT) and/or crude oil washing equipment (COW) onboard in 1991, by year of tanker construction.

Source: Electronic version of Clarkson Research Studies, Ltd., *The Tanker Register* (London: Clarkson Research Studies, Ltd., 1991), provided to the author.

from that same pressure.] The relevant question is, "Could the United States, through unilateral measures, have induced so many tanker owners to install SBT?" Available evidence suggests not.

While the United States wields tremendous diplomatic leverage, it wields nothing near hegemonic power in oil transportation markets. Since the United States became concerned about oil pollution in the late 1960s, it has been responsible for less than 5 percent of new tankers built, less than 7 percent of tanker registrations, and less than 20 percent of world oil imports.[45] Given SBT's high costs, oil transportation companies would have been more likely to respond to unilateral U.S. equipment requirements by installing SBT on a sufficient number of tankers to service the U.S. market than by installing it on all tankers. *** Indeed, in terms of power to control oil tankers, Japan – which opposed SBT

[45] See Lloyd's Register of Shipping, *Annual Summary of Merchant Ships Completed* (London: Lloyd's Register of Shipping, various years); Lloyd's Register of Shipping, *Statistical Tables* (London: Lloyd's Register of Shipping, various years); and United Nations, *Statistical Yearbook* (New York: United Nations, various years).

requirements in both 1973 and 1978 – consistently has controlled larger shares of tanker construction, tanker registration, and oil imports than the United States. ***

MECHANISMS OF INFLUENCE

Compliance with discharge standards via the use of LOT was largely an artifact of economic factors. Compliance with requirements for SBT and COW has been both higher and more clearly the result of the treaty. Rival explanations of economic influences and international political hegemony prove incapable of adequately explaining the observed outcomes. The equipment subregime succeeded at inducing reluctant tanker owners to spend considerable money on additional equipment that provided no economic benefit. ***

Which of the many differences between the two subregimes best explain the different levels of observed compliance? [The design of the equipment regime induced compliance by (1) eliciting monitoring and enforcement and (2) reducing opportunities for violation.]

Enhancing Transparency

The equipment subregime had one major advantage over the discharge subregime in its significantly higher transparency level. Violations of the SBT and COW requirements simply [were easier to observe.]

Consider the two compliance information systems. Both OILPOL and MARPOL required tanker captains to note discharges in record books and to make those books available to port authorities for inspection. This obvious reliance on self-incrimination made naval and aerial surveillance programs the more common means of detecting illegal discharges. The total discharge standard of one fifteen-thousandth of cargo capacity improved on this system by providing a criterion that could be monitored by tank inspections in port without relying on information supplied by the tanker captain. Practically speaking, these inspections were restricted to ports in oil-exporting states, since discharges occurred after delivery, on a tanker's return to port to load more cargo.

In contrast, the compliance information system for equipment standards relied on the fact that buying or retrofitting a tanker requires the knowledge and consent of at least three other actors: a builder, a classification society, and an insurance company. Agents in each of

these industries would know of a violation even before it was committed. MARPOL also required flag state governments, or classification societies nominated by them, to survey all tankers to ensure
compliance before issuing the required International Oil Pollution
Prevention (IOPP) certificate and to conduct periodic inspections
thereafter.[46] As part of the process of evaluating tankers to provide
insurers with the information needed to set rates, classification societies
regularly monitor compliance with international construction requirements ***.[47] Finally, MARPOL gave all port states the legal authority to
inspect a tanker's IOPP certificate and its equipment ***.

The equipment standards subregime made violations more transparent than violations in the discharge standards subregime in several ways.
To begin with, regulating the tanker builder–tanker buyer transaction
yielded a drastically reduced number of events to be monitored. While
several thousand tankers ply the world's oceans, they are owned, built, and
classified by only a few owners, shipyards, and classification societies. A
tanker making ten trips per year could violate the total discharge standard
three hundred times in its thirty-year life but could only violate the
equipment requirements once.

Equipment standards also required authorities to monitor fewer
locations ***. The discharge process standards – 100 ppm, clean ballast,
and 60 l/m – required patrols of wide areas of ocean to detect slicks that
often could not be linked with the responsible tanker. *** The addition of
total discharge limits allowed detection of violations while a tanker was
in an oil port, a procedure involving far fewer resources. Unfortunately,
most oil-exporting states exhibited little interest in preventing marine
pollution ***. Inspections to verify compliance with equipment standards
could occur in developed oil-importing states, which had shown far more
interest in enforcement. The shift from the 100 ppm and 60 l/m limits
to total discharge limits improved dramatically the practical ability to
detect violations. The shift from total discharge limits to equipment
standards improved the regime further by increasing incentives for
monitoring among those who already had the practical ability to monitor.

Equipment standards dramatically eased the problem of obtaining
evidence needed to sanction a violator. The standards eliminated any
reliance on self-incrimination by the perpetrator of a violation. Detecting

---

[46] *MARPOL 73/78*, Annex I, Regulations 4 and 5.
[47] Personal interview with John Foxwell, Shell International Marine, London, 27 June
1991.

an equipment violation and identifying its perpetrator also were not time-sensitive. *** Authorities also faced several difficulties in transforming detection of a discharge at sea into a case worthy of prosecution. In what can be called "passive voice" violations, often a tanker could not be identified as responsible for a detected slick: authorities could only say a violation "had been committed." Even if a responsible tanker could be identified, determining whether the 100 ppm or 60 l/m criterion had been exceeded generally was difficult. The total discharge standard could have eliminated this problem, but oil-exporting states never established inspection programs. These flaws in the design of the discharge standards compliance system were not necessarily inherent or insurmountable. For example, some analysts proposed placing observers on all tankers to verify compliance with discharge standards.[48] *** However, such programs would have involved huge expenditures of resources to produce only a low probability of successful deterrence.

* * *

The entry into force of total discharge standards in 1978 allowed inspectors in oil-loading ports to assume that any incoming tanker with all tanks free of slops had violated the very low limit placed on total discharges. However, even those oil-exporting states that were party to MARPOL had strong disincentives to inspect ships in their ports: ports that were conducting inspections were less attractive loading sites than neighboring ports that were not conducting inspections. Not surprisingly, most governments did not alter their enforcement strategies in response to the greater potential for enforcement provided by the promulgation of total discharge standards. In contrast, considerable evidence confirms that the equipment regime significantly changed the ways in which nations and classification societies conducted tanker inspections. Many of the states that originally had opposed the 1973 and 1978 U.S. proposals for equipment regulations subsequently conducted the in-port inspections needed to detect violations. In 1982, the maritime authorities of fourteen European states signed a Memorandum of Understanding on Port State Control, committing themselves annually to inspect 25 percent of ships entering their ports for violations of maritime treaties, including MARPOL.[49] *** Even though several member states had voted against

---

[48] Cummins et al, "Oil Tanker Pollution Control," p. 171.
[49] "Memorandum of Understanding on Port State Control," reprinted in *ILM*, vol. 21, 1982, p. 1.

SBT, all fourteen have included checks of IOPP certificates in the thousands of inspections they conduct each year. * * * While * * * countries undoubtedly vary widely in how frequently and carefully they conduct inspections, all have made inspections for MARPOL-required equipment a standard element of their inspection programs.

The effectiveness of these governmental inspections depends at least in part on the initial issue of accurate IOPP certificates by flag states or classification societies designated by them. Reports to IMO for 1984 to 1990 show that missing and inaccurate pollution certificates declined steadily from 9 percent to 1 percent; the memorandum of understanding secretariat reports similar declines – from 11 percent to 3 percent.[50] These trends suggest that after an initial period of learning how to issue and inspect certificates, classification societies and governments both now issue thorough and accurate certifications. Like port state governments, flag states and classification societies appear to have altered their behavior to become active participants in the equipment subregime's compliance information system. * * *

The greater transparency of violations of equipment requirements served perhaps most importantly to reassure other tanker owners that their own compliance would not place them at a competitive disadvantage in the marketplace. An environmentally concerned tanker operator inclined to comply with the discharge standards could not escape the knowledge that others probably would not comply. The economic incentives to discharge oil at sea, the absence of transparency about who was and who was not complying, and the attendant inability of enforcement efforts to effectively deter discharges precluded any assumption other than that many competitors would violate the discharge standards to reduce their costs. The greater transparency of equipment requirements assured a tanker owner installing SBT and COW that all other owners also were doing so. * * *

The equipment standards provided the foundation for a compliance information system far more transparent than was possible under the discharge subregime. In response, even governments that had opposed the adoption of the requirements conducted inspections for compliance. The subregime's compliance information system channeled the behavior of both governments and classification societies into monitoring activities that supported the regime. It did so by ensuring that those actors

[50] Secretariat of the Memorandum of Understanding on Port State Control, *Annual Report* (The Hague: The Netherlands Government Printing Office, various years).

with incentives to monitor compliance also had the practical ability and legal authority to do so. * * *

Facilitating Potent but Low-Cost Sanctions

Greater transparency translated into higher levels of compliance with equipment standards only because the compliance system also induced likely and potent sanctions. The noncompliance response system of the discharge subregime failed to do the same. * * *

Detected discharge violations frequently remained unprosecuted because the subregime relied on customary international law with its deference to enforcement by flag states. Both OILPOL and MARPOL required a government that detected a discharge violation at sea to forward all evidence to the flag state for prosecution. * * * Flag states often lack the ability to prosecute, since tankers flying their flag may rarely enter their ports. They also have few incentives to prosecute because vigorous enforcement on their part would induce owners to take their registrations, and the large associated fees, to a less scrupulous state.[51] * * * In short, the flag states with the authority to prosecute lacked incentives to do so, and the coastal states with the incentives to prosecute lacked the authority to do so.

Under the discharge standards, even states sincerely seeking to prosecute and convict a violator faced major obstacles to success. As already noted, evidence of a violation often failed to produce a violator, and otherwise convincing evidence often failed to meet the legal standards of proof needed for conviction. Evidentiary hurdles should have decreased with the prohibition of discharges that produced visible traces. However, even with aerial photographs of discharges, tankers frequently avoid conviction.[52] Between 1983 and 1990, port and coastal states discarded for lack of evidence an average of 36 percent of cases occurring in territorial seas and successfully convicted and fined less than 33 percent of all detected violators.[53] An additional 20 percent of high-seas cases referred

---

[51] Paul Stephen Dempsey, "Compliance and Enforcement in International Law – Oil Pollution of the Marine Environment by Ocean Vessels," *Northwestern Journal of International Law and Business* 6 (Summer 1984), pp. 459–561 and p. 576 in particular.

[52] See ibid., p. 526; and personal interview with Ronald Carly, Ministry of Transportation, Brussels, 10 June 1991.

[53] Peet, *Operational Discharges from Ships*, pp. 17–18, Tables 11 and 12; and Marie-Jose Stoop, *Olieverontreiniging door schepen op de noordzee over de periode 1982–1987: opsporing en vervolging* (Oil pollution by ships on the North Sea 1982–1987: Investigations and prosecution) (Amsterdam: Werkgroep Noordzee, July 1989).

to flag states were not prosecuted for the same reason, and less than 15 percent of all referrals resulted in fines being imposed.[54] *** Many experts had hoped that the clearer evidence from inspections for total discharge violations would overcome these problems, but *** there is no record "of a single case where the one fifteen-thousandth rule was used for prosecution."[55]

When conviction was successful, governments rarely imposed penalties adequate to deter future discharge violations ***.[56] Most states' courts are reluctant to impose fines disproportionate to the offense to compensate for low detection and conviction rates. The principle that "the punishment should fit the crime" places an upper bound on fines that may be too low to successfully deter violation, if detection and prosecution is difficult. Since 1975, the average fine imposed by states never has exceeded $7,000 and *** has decreased over time.[57] Even when a large penalty is assessed, the delays between initial violation and final sentencing and the reluctance of most states to detain tankers for minor discharge violations often mean that the responsible tanker and crew have long since left the state's jurisdiction, making fine collection difficult. ***

In place of the discharge subregime's legal system of prosecution, conviction, and fines, the equipment subregime relied on quite different responses to noncompliance. The most immediate sanctions involved the ability of classification societies, insurers, and flag state governments to withhold the classification, insurance, and pollution prevention certificates that a tanker needed to conduct international trade. As John Foxwell put it, tankers "cannot get insurance without certification, and can't get certification without compliance."[58] These sanctions amounted to preventing any illegally equipped tanker from doing business. ***

Besides these market-based sanctions, the equipment subregime obligated port states either to detain tankers with false pollution prevention certificates or inadequate equipment or to bar them from port.[59] As administrative sanctions, these responses skirted both flag state and port state legal systems – and the associated sensitivities regarding legal

---

[54] Ronald Bruce Mitchell, "From Paper to Practice: Improving Environmental Treaty Compliance," Ph.D. diss., Harvard University, Cambridge, Mass., 1992, Table 5–1.

[55] Personal interview with E. J. M. Ball.

[56] *MARPOL* 73/78, Article 4(4).

[57] Mitchell, "From Paper to Practice," Table 4–5.

[58] Personal interview with John Foxwell, Shell International Marine, London, 27 June 1991.

[59] *MARPOL* 73/78, Articles 5(2) and 5(3).

sovereignty. Paradoxically, this strategy made port states more likely to use detention and flag states more willing to accept it. Detention also had the virtue that even low usage by a few major oil-importing states forced tanker owners to choose between risking detention and the more costly option of not trading to those lucrative markets. Authorizing developed states to detain violating tankers effectively moved the right to sanction to countries that had far greater domestic political pressures to use it.

Coupling the equipment requirements themselves with these administrative sanctions completely eliminated the legal and evidentiary problems that make even clear violations of discharge standards difficult to prosecute successfully. Detention imposed opportunity costs on a tanker operator of several thousand dollars per day, and forced retrofitting could cost millions of dollars – far exceeding the fines for discharge violations.[60] Detention had the positive quality that it was not so costly as to be considered a disproportionate response to the crime but was costly enough to deter other violations. In short, detention was simultaneously more likely and more costly.

* * *

Although few states detained ships, available evidence supports the conclusion that the subregime altered enforcement behavior. Not one of the states that detained ships began to do so until after MARPOL took effect in 1983.[61] Even the United States waited until that year – ten years after the detention provision had been accepted. Consider the counterfactual: it is unlikely that the United States would have detained tankers for breaching U.S.-only requirements for SBT, even though it had the practical ability to do so. Without MARPOL, such detentions would have constituted a major infringement of flag state sovereignty. If the use of the more costly detention sanction had reflected an exogenous increase in the interests of states in environmental enforcement, fines for discharge violations should have increased at the same time. Yet, as states began to use detention, fines did not increase dramatically.[62] * * *

The equipment subregime operated not by convincing reluctant actors to enforce rules with which they disagreed but by removing the legal

---

[60] Personal interviews with John Foxwell; and with Richard Schiferli, Memorandum of Understanding Secretariat, Rijswijk, The Netherlands, 17 July 1991.

[61] Personal interview with Daniel Sheehan.

[62] See Peet, *Operational Discharges from Ships*, annex 15; and Dempsey, "Compliance and Enforcement in International Law."

barriers that inhibited effective enforcement by those states and nonstate actors willing to enforce them. Classification societies had interests in ensuring that the tankers they classified were able to trade without fear of detention. The incorporation of equipment requirements into their classification criteria provided the foundation for insurers to penalize noncompliant tankers. The willingness of a few environmentally concerned oil-importing states to inhibit tankers that lacked the required equipment from trading freely posed an extremely potent threat to a tanker owner. However, the ability and willingness of these states to threaten this sanction depended on removing international legal barriers to its use. Once these barriers were removed, imposing sanctions involved few costs to those imposing them, whether classification societies, insurers, or port state authorities. It thereby made detention more likely, even though it created no new incentives for states to impose sanctions. In a case of "nothing succeeds like success," the various threats of the equipment subregime's noncompliance system led to initial compliance by almost all tankers, making it rare that sanctions ever needed to be imposed.

Building on Existing Institutions

The oil pollution control regime induced implementation of those provisions that involved few direct costs to governments. Monitoring and enforcement proved especially likely when their costs were pushed "off-budget" by deputizing private, nonstate actors to issue certificates and conduct inspections. ***

MARPOL's equipment subregime fostered monitoring by allowing governments to delegate responsibility for surveys to classification societies. *** MARPOL allowed [developing] states to fulfill their treaty commitments by assigning classification and inspection responsibilities to actors who often had greater access to and more resources with which to conduct such inspections. Classification societies also had strong incentives to conduct accurate surveys as a means of protecting their business reputations and avoiding problems with insurance companies. The strategy thus simultaneously removed these tasks and the resources they required from the hands of governments and placed them in the hands of actors who could more easily accomplish them. *** Adding pollution control to classification societies' long inspection checklists required only marginal changes to existing procedures.

The many inspection programs operated by developed port states parallel this pattern. [The] maritime authorities of the European memorandum of understanding states, the United States, and other states interested in enforcing the equipment requirements could make simple, low-cost alterations to port state inspections already being conducted for safety, customs, and other purposes. * * * In contrast, where states have had to incur significant new costs to implement treaty provisions, they have proved unlikely to do so. * * * Most developed states have not established large, ongoing surveillance programs. * * *

* * *

Coercing Compliance Rather than Deterring Violation

The compliance systems of the two subregimes differ most strikingly in the fundamental model underlying their regulatory strategies. The equipment standards subregime relied on a "coerced compliance" strategy, which sought to monitor behavior to prevent violations from occurring in the first place. The discharge standards subregime was deterrence-oriented, attempting to detect, prosecute, and sanction violations after they occurred to deter future violations.[63] This basic difference in orientation made the compliance task facing the equipment standards subregime more manageable than that facing the discharge standards subregime. The underlying strategy choice had important consequences for the level of compliance achieved: inhibiting the ability to violate treaty provisions proved far more effective than increasing the disincentives for violating them.

MARPOL's equipment standards created a remarkably effective system for detecting and sanctioning violations. * * * However, the equipment subregime's strength really came from the fact that it rarely had to use the more potent sanctions it made possible. * * * The subregime relied on surveying behavior and preventing violations rather than detecting and investigating them afterwards.[64] [The] equipment rules allowed identification

---

[63] Neither strategy was incentive-based, as was the funding of compliance under the Montreal Protocol and Framework Convention on Climate Change. For development of the distinction between these three strategies, see Albert J. Reiss, Jr., "Consequences of Compliance and Deterrence Models of Law Enforcement for the Exercise of Police Discretion," *Law and Contemporary Problems* 47 (Fall 1984), pp. 83–122; and Keith Hawkins, *Environment and Enforcement: Regulation and the Social Definition of Pollution* (Oxford: Clarendon Press, 1984).

[64] Reiss, "Consequences of Compliance and Deterrence Models of Law Enforcement for the Exercise of Police Discretion."

of potential violators and made it harder to actually commit a violation. Tanker captains faced many regular autonomous decisions about whether to violate discharge standards. In contrast, tanker owners only had to decide once between violating or complying with equipment standards, and their decision required cooperation from other actors and involved major economic consequences. *** Classification societies, insurance companies, and flag state inspectors could withhold the papers necessary to conduct business in international oil markets, thereby frustrating any tanker owner's attempt to reap the benefits of sidestepping these standards.

Experience with the discharge standards had shown that many states would not enforce pollution standards ***. Given the costs of SBT, if deterrence had been the major source of compliance, one would expect some tankers initially to have violated the equipment standards in an attempt to identify which and how many states actually would enforce the rules. Yet, compliance levels did not follow a pattern of initial noncompliance followed by stiff sanctions and subsequent compliance. The compliance system of the equipment subregime succeeded by effectively restricting the opportunities to violate it rather than making the choice of violation less attractive. The very low noncompliance levels suggest that in most cases an owner simply decided it would be impossible to convince a tanker builder, a classification society, and an insurer to allow the purchase of a tanker without COW and SBT. *** [Obstacles] to committing a violation played a major role in preventing such violations. New tankers have been built initially to MARPOL standards, not retrofitted later in response to deterrence threats. ***

The equipment subregime may have been as successful as it was precisely because it produced a redundant regulatory system. It established compliance information and noncompliance response systems that prevented most violations but could successfully deter any actors who might otherwise have considered violating it. *** The initial discharge standards subregime faced problems at almost every step of the process: detecting violations, identifying violators, prosecuting violators, and imposing potent sanctions. The shift to total discharge standards eliminated or mitigated some of these problems, but the problems remaining left overall deterrent levels essentially unchanged. A tanker captain evaluating the expected costs of violating OILPOL's or MARPOL's discharge standards could only conclude that the magnitude and likelihood of a penalty were quite small. Successful deterrence strategies must ensure that the whole legal chain operates smoothly, since the breakdown of any link can significantly impair its effectiveness.

CONCLUSIONS

Nations can design regime rules to improve compliance. This article has demonstrated that, even within a single issue-area, reference to design features of compliance systems surrounding particular provisions is necessary to explain observed variance in compliance. In the regime regulating intentional oil pollution, the same governments and corporations with the same interests during the same time period complied far more frequently with rules requiring installation of expensive equipment than they did with rules limiting total discharges of oil. Where theories of hegemonic power and economic interests fail to explain this variance, differences in the subregime's compliance systems readily explain why the former subregime led powerful actors to comply with it while the latter did not.

The equipment standards elicited significantly higher compliance because they selected a point for regulatory intervention that allowed for greater transparency, increased the likelihood of forceful responses to detected violations, built on existing institutions, and coerced compliance by preventing actors from violating them rather than merely deterring actors from doing so. *** [Policymakers] can improve compliance by regulating those sectors more vulnerable to pressures for compliance and by facilitating the efforts of those governments and nonstate actors more likely to implement and enforce such regulations. This matching of regulatory burdens to expected behavior places the careful choice of the regime's primary rules at the center of any effective compliance system.

Once such primary rules have been established, careful crafting of the compliance information system and the noncompliance response system can further increase the likelihood of compliance. Oil pollution regulations succeeded by facilitating the goals of, placing responsibilities on, and removing the legal and practical barriers limiting those governments and private actors predisposed to monitor and enforce agreements, not by imposing obligations on recalcitrant actors. Inducing compliance required an integrated system of rules and processes that placed actors within a strategic triangle of compliance so that they had the political and economic incentives, practical ability, and legal authority to perform the tasks necessary to implement the treaty.[65] When such efforts succeeded, governments and private actors acted differently than they would have in the absence of the regime. *** [Negotiators] can and should design and

---

[65] I am indebted to Robert O. Keohane for the notion of a strategic triangle of compliance.

redesign treaties to maximize compliance within the constraints that power and interests impose.

Eliciting compliance is only one of the criteria on which we would want to judge a regime's rules. Indeed, the value of compliance itself rests on the assumption that more compliance makes the treaty itself more effective. In the oil pollution case, compliance with the equipment rules involved at least as great a reduction in intentional discharges as did compliance with the discharge standards. Thus, we can safely infer that the higher compliance levels under the former rules also led to increased treaty effectiveness, a fact confirmed by a consensus among most experts that intentional oil discharges have declined since MARPOL took effect.[66] [Compliance levels are an important evaluative criteria in regime design.] The cheaper, more flexible, and more efficient discharge standards simply failed to induce the level of compliance needed to achieve a socially desired outcome; yet the costs of the equipment standards may have exceeded the benefits of that outcome. In cases in which more efficient solutions elicit compliance sufficient to achieve a policy goal, they are clearly preferable. If expected compliance with such solutions appears low, effective regime design requires evaluating whether the benefits of higher compliance outweigh the expense and inefficiency of alternative solutions.

Can we apply the findings developed from studying these two oil pollution cases to other issue-areas? Initial selection of a difficult collaborative problem with characteristics common to many international collaboration problems provides some confidence that we can do so. Other treaties provide anecdotal support for some of the findings reported herein. *** [Confirming the conclusions arrived at here requires considerably more research.] The solutions adopted in the oil pollution regime also undoubtedly cannot be applied to all regimes or even to all environmental regimes. Wildlife and habitat protection, for example, can rarely be achieved through technological solutions or quantitative requirements that can be easily monitored. *** The strategies available to international regulators will depend at least in part on features unique to the problem being addressed. Analysts have already shown how regimes influence behavior in realms involving security.[67] How the impacts of similar

---

[66] See Ronald B. Mitchell, "Intentional Oil Pollution of the Oceans," in Haas, Keohane, and Levy, *Institutions for the Earth*, pp. 183–248.

[67] See Robert Jervis, "Security Regimes," in Krasner, *International Regimes*, pp. 173–94; and Duffield, "International Regimes and Alliance Behavior."

compliance systems vary across security, economic, human rights, or environmental regimes remains one of many important future questions.

Whether the nations of the world can collaborate to resolve the many international problems, both environmental and otherwise, that face them will depend not on merely negotiating agreements requiring new behaviors but on ensuring that those agreements succeed in inducing governments, industry, and individuals to adopt those new behaviors. *** [Careful] crafting and recrafting of international treaties provides one valuable means of managing the various problems facing the nations of the world.

26

The Regime Complex for Plant Genetic Resources

Kal Raustiala and David G. Victor

International institutions have proliferated rapidly in the postwar period. As new problems have risen on the international agenda, the demand for international regimes has followed.[1] At the same time, international norms have become more demanding and intrusive.[2] *** Governance systems dominated by elites have given way to more participatory modes; the policy process has become more complex as a growing array of [actors] *** become engaged in decision making.[3] ***

These trends – in particular the rising density of international institutions – make it increasingly difficult to isolate and "decompose" individual international institutions for study.[4] Yet efforts to build and test theories about the origins, operation, and influence of international regimes have typically been conducted as though such decomposition was feasible. Most empirical studies focus on the development of a single regime, usually centered on a core international agreement and

---

[1] See Keohane 1983; Krasner 1983; and Hasenclever et al. 1997.
[2] Lawrence et al. 1996.
[3] See Howse 2002; Slaughter 1997; Skolnikoff 1993; Keck and Sikkink 1998; and Haas 1992.
[4] Keohane and Nye 2001.

We are grateful for comments on early drafts presented at Stanford Law School, New York University Law School, Duke Law School, Harvard Law School, and the American Society for International Law. Thanks especially to Larry Helfer, Tom Heller, Robert Keohane, Benedict Kingsbury, Peter Lallas, Lisa Martin, Ron Mitchell, Sabrina Safrin, Gene Skolnikoff, Richard Stewart, Chris Stone, Buzz Thompson, Jonathan Wiener, Katrina Wyman, Oran Young, and two anonymous reviewers for their feedback. Kal Raustiala thanks the Program on Law and Public Affairs at Princeton for support. We also thank our research assistants, Lindsay Carlson, Lesley Coben and Joshua House.

administered by a discrete organization. * Such studies occasionally note the complicated links among international institutions, but [do not focus] systematically on explaining institutional "interplay."[5] A few studies have explored institutional interactions in hierarchical or nested regimes in which certain rules have explicit precedence over others, but the theoretical implications are limited because international agreements are rarely hierarchical.[6] The prevailing scholarship on regimes has also taken a functional approach to analyzing cooperation and has not given close attention to how the legal and intellectual framing of issues affects the boundaries of regimes.[7] Lack of systematic attention to boundaries and to the interactions among institutions leaves a large hole in the existing body of theory. Yet the rising density of the international system makes it likely that interactions among regimes will be increasingly common.

In this article we address this gap in theory by advancing several arguments about regime interactions under conditions of rising institutional density. We develop and explore these arguments through the lens of an understudied issue in international relations: the control of plant genetic resources (PGR). The PGR case is important because it lies at the nexus of critical areas of world politics – intellectual property (IP), environmental protection, agriculture, and trade.

For most of history, PGR – such as genetic codes, seed varieties, and plant extracts – were treated as the "common heritage of all mankind." They were understood to be freely available to all and owned by none.[8] During the twentieth century, those rules changed radically; today, international and domestic rules declare PGR to be sovereign property and subject to private ownership through IP rights such as patents. We explain that transformation by examining the rules that govern PGR in their natural state – "raw" genetic resources – as well as the "worked" resources that humans improve through breeding and other [techniques.] Raw PGR are those found in the wild, such as a flower in the rain forest that contains a yet-undiscovered gene that could cure cancer. Worked genetic resources, by contrast, are the products derived from that flower – such as the marketed cancer-fighting drug. * Drawing on the work of Harold Demsetz, we show how new technologies allowed firms

---

[5] The few exceptions, using the term "interplay," include Young 2002; and Stokke 2001. See also Leebron 2002 for discussion of "conglomerate" regimes; and Weiss 1993 for a warning about "treaty congestion."

[6] Aggarwal 1985. * * *

[7] Exceptions include Young 2002; Wendt 1999; and Sebenius 1983.

[8] Kloppenburg 1988.

to create greater value in novel worked products, which in turn spurred them to demand special new forms of IP for worked PGR.[9] Raw PGR also rose in perceived value – both as inputs to the innovation of new worked products and as valuable environmental goods in their own right.

While new technologies and ideas created pressures for enclosure, the composition and configuration of international institutions created a highly uneven process of change. Rather than a single, discrete regime governing PGR, the relevant rules are found in at least five clusters of international legal agreements – what we call *elemental regimes* – as well as in national rules within key states, especially the United States and the European Union (EU). These elemental regimes overlap in scope, subject, and time; events in one affect those in others. We term the collective of these elements a *regime complex*: an array of partially overlapping and nonhierarchical institutions governing a particular issue-area. Regime complexes are marked by the existence of several legal agreements that are created and maintained in distinct fora with participation of different sets of actors. The rules in these elemental regimes functionally overlap, yet there is no agreed upon hierarchy for resolving conflicts between rules. Disaggregated decision making in the international legal system means that agreements reached in one forum do not automatically extend to, or clearly trump, agreements developed in other forums. We contend that regime complexes evolve in ways that are distinct from decomposable single regimes.

In this article we do not attempt a full derivation of a theory of regime complexes. Rather, our aim is to demonstrate, through our discussion of the PGR case, that there is utility in analyzing regime interactions systematically and guided by the concept of regime complexes. We explore four conjectures.

First, we expect that regime complexes will demonstrate path dependence: extant arrangements in the various elemental regimes will constrain and channel the process of creating new rules. The existing literature on regimes implicitly presumes that regimes are negotiated on a largely clean institutional slate. *** In regime complexes, by contrast, the array of rules already in force channel and constrain the content of new elemental regimes.

Second, we expect that the existence of distinct negotiating fora will spur [forum shopping.] We explore not only the factors that we expect will affect the degree of forum shopping – such as barriers to entry,

---

[9] See Demsetz 1967; Libecap 1989 and 2003; and Merrill 2002.

membership, and linkages among issues – but also the practical impact that forum shopping has on the evolution of regime complexes.

Third, we expect that a dense array of international institutions will lead to legal inconsistencies. Scholars have noted the move to law in world politics.[10] One implication is that much diplomatic effort will be focused on [assuring] consistency – treating like situations alike – because consistency is a core element of the legal paradigm. In standard theories of regimes, regime development is driven by political contestation over core rules. In regime complexes, we argue, that evolution is mediated by a process focused on inconsistencies at the "joints" between elemental regimes. *** There is no single, omnibus negotiation – rather, there are multiple negotiations on different timetables and dominated by different actors. The move to cooperation on issues that were previously the sole domain of domestic policy only exacerbates this harmonization problem, because it is no longer foreign ministries that dominate international diplomacy: instead, a raft of domestic agencies, often with distinct agendas, increasingly play active roles.[11]

Fourth, we explore how states contend with inconsistencies through the process of implementation and interpretation. The literature on domestic policy implementation has demonstrated that when the legislative agenda is complex and contested, lawmakers often adopt broad, aspirational rules.[12] *** Earlier studies of treaty implementation echo these findings, showing that diplomats often negotiate broad *ex ante* rules and then defer the task of working out detailed implications to the process of implementation.[13] We expect regime complexes to be particularly prone to such behavior. Where interests are varied and complex it is difficult to specify precise rules *ex ante,* and the transaction costs for making formal changes to rules that span multiple regimes is high. *** Consequently, states often work out solutions "on the ground" and, in turn, align formal changes in the rules with the most successful implemented remedies.

We begin by summarizing the PGR case and theorizing about the dramatic change in property right norms during the past century. We introduce each element of the regime complex and show how the interactions between elemental regimes have become more numerous as the international rules have become more expansive, intrusive, and demanding.

[10] Goldstein et al. 2001.
[11] Slaughter 1997.
[12] See Ingram 1977; Bardach and Kagan 1982; and Stewart 1975.
[13] See Victor, Raustiala, and Skolnikoff 1998; Weiss and Jacobson 1998; and Chayes and Chayes 1995.

We then explore the significance of the concept of a regime complex for the theories of international institutions ***.

EXPLAINING NORM CHANGE: THE RISE OF PROPERTY RIGHTS IN PLANT GENETIC RESOURCES

PGR have been a central part of human civilization since its inception, though genes were not well understood until recently. *** Whether in the wild or in seed banks, for centuries PGR were viewed as a resource that was shared in common and accessible to all – a system that did not assign private ownership of these resources and later became labeled the "common heritage of mankind." * We call this basic structure of property rights the "common heritage" system. While a particular specimen of a plant could be owned, genetic resources per se were not owned by individuals or states. Common heritage was coupled to open access, which meant that states did not generally restrict others from obtaining small samples of PGR, such as seeds ***.

In the twentieth century, this structure of property rights changed markedly. By the 1990s, governments viewed raw PGR as a sovereign resource rather than as common heritage; increasingly governments also afforded individuals a wider range of varied IP rights for worked PGR ***. [Not] all international agreements embraced this approach, and for some time there was considerable conflict among the various regime rules. (In some areas, the conflicts persist.) Ultimately, however, a broad consensus emerged ***. We call this new system the "property rights" approach. Some states kept those property rights for the state itself, often with the state asserting not just control over these rights but direct ownership. Many other states, however, permitted the creation of individual property rights and increasingly this is the norm.

To describe and explain this fundamental normative shift toward enclosure we look to the theory of property rights famously developed by Demsetz and elaborated by Libecap and others.[14] Demsetz suggested that the development of property rights is primarily a function of changes in value: "the emergence of new property rights," he argued, "takes place in response to the desires of the interacting persons for adjustment to new benefit-cost possibilities."[15] When the private value of a good rises, potential owners will agitate governments to change property rules

---

[14] See Demsetz 1967; and Libecap 1989.
[15] Demsetz 1967, 350.

to allow capture of the added value. An increase in the value of the resource because of an exogenous circumstance, such as a technological development, *** may create a sufficient incentive for the development of property rights ***.

* * *

One dimension of this *** debate concerned the rules for ownership of PGR – common heritage versus some form of property right. The other dimension was the mechanism for allocating benefits from raw and worked PGR. Even as states, in a Demsetzian dynamic, converged on a property rights approach there remained strong disagreements over the allocation of benefits. Developing countries desired state-controlled mechanisms that would force PGR innovators to share the benefits with those states that provided the raw PGR; industrialized states preferred a more free-market approach.

The transformation of property and allocative rules over PGR did not occur smoothly or according to a single plan ***. Nor did this transformation occur through a single, omnibus negotiation aimed at the creation of a new international regime. Rather, as we describe, there were six distinct strands of activity, each of which addressed some important, but partial, aspect of the PGR issue. Five of these strands are what we call an elemental regime – an international institution, based on an explicit agreement, that reflects agreed principles and norms and codifies specific rules and decision-making procedures. Three of these elemental regimes are focused on agriculture, and two extend far beyond agriculture to broader issues:

- The 1961 International Convention for the Protection of New Varieties of Plants (UPOV), as amended in 1978 and 1991, governs property rights over intentionally bred plant varieties. These treaties require members to recognize "plant breeders' rights," a form of IP protection widely implemented in industrialized countries.
- The United Nations (UN) Food and Agriculture Organization (FAO) is the locus for negotiation of two key accords: the 1983 International Undertaking on Plant Genetic Resources and the 2002 International Treaty on Plant Genetic Resources. ***
- The Consultative Group on International Agriculture Research (CGIAR) is an international network of crop research centers. Efforts to breed improved crops have been aided enormously by the tremendous wealth of samples in CGIAR's "gene banks."

- The World Trade Organization (WTO)'s Agreement on Trade-Related Aspects of Intellectual Property Rights (TRIPs) sets minimum international standards for the protection of IP rights.
- The 1992 UN Convention on Biological Diversity (CBD), which originated in efforts to protect global biodiversity as a natural resource, simultaneously promotes the sharing of the economic benefits that arise from the use of genetic resources.

In addition to these five international institutions, the PGR regime complex has been influenced by activities at the domestic level, notably in the United States, and, to a lesser degree, in the EU. The United States has been a key driver of change in the IP field. Innovations that began in the United States, such as the patenting of life-forms, have subsequently been enshrined, partly as a result of U.S. insistence, in agreements such as TRIPs. U.S. firms are also the dominant innovators in both the pharmaceutical and agricultural industries.

Figure 26.1 illustrates these two dimensions of rules – ownership and allocative mechanisms – and summarizes the complicated story that we present below about the transformation from the common heritage system to sovereign and private property rights.

The Common Heritage System

For most of human history, the rule of common heritage governed PGR. *** [Under this system] there were no property rights in PGR, nor did states bar access to genetic resources per se. As a result there was much international diffusion of PGR, particularly as long-distance trade expanded and imperial nations established central collections, such as Kew Gardens outside London, stocked with plants from around the globe.[16] To be sure, nations tried but often failed to maintain control over certain genetic resources; for example, China went to great lengths to preserve the silkworm monopoly, but ultimately lost it to two enterprising Nestorian monks.[17] Silkworms, rubber trees, and a few other special resources of obvious high value were the exception, however – otherwise, genetic resources were free for anyone who bothered to take them.

[16] Kloppenburg 1988.
[17] Stone 1994.

**Ownership of Plant Genetic Resources and
Mechanism for Allocating Benefits**

		Common heritage	Property rights	
			Sovereign (state-controlled)	Private and community
Mechanism for allocating benefits from PGR	Market-based	Traditional 19th-century system		Late 20th-century national patents: U.S. EU TRIPs UPOV treaties
	Regulated	FAO 1983 Undertaking FAO 2001 Treaty (R35, W35) CGIAR gene banks	FAO 1989 and 1991 revisions to Undertaking CBD (1992) FAO 2001 Treaty (other raw) CGIAR gene banks (immediately post-1992, before FAO 2001 Treaty)	FAO 2001 Treaty (other worked)

Note: The UN Food and Agriculture (FAO) Treaty distinguishes the rules that apply to both raw ("R") and worked ("W") plant genetic resources (PGR) for a core group of 35 staple food crops, denoted "R35" and "W35." The Consultative Group on International Agriculture Research (CGIAR) gene banks operated on the principle of open access (with regulated benefits – in the sense that the system was organized and maintained for public purposes, not private, market-based innovations), but the creation of the Convention on Biological Diversity (CBD) in 1992 posed a challenge to that system by claiming sovereign ownership of raw PGR. The FAO 2001 Treaty eliminated that challenge for the most important food crops. The same rules apply to 29 crops used for animal feed.

TRIPs: Trade-Related Aspects of Intellectual Property Rights.

UPOV: International Convention for the Protection of New Varieties of Plants.

FIGURE 26.1. *Two dimensions of debate.*

Under the common heritage system there was little difference in treatment between what we term "raw" and "worked" PGR. In agriculture, the dividing line between raw and worked was (and often remains) indistinct because worked materials, as well as new raw materials collected in the field, are the source of new worked materials.[18]

The first moves toward propertizing PGR addressed worked resources. *** By the 1920s, a limited, industrial business of breeding emerged, and with it political pressure for protection arose. The most prominent innovative activity involved hybrid plants, which had their own built-in mechanism for protecting IP – hybrids lose their vigor after one generation, and thus farmers must purchase new seed every season.[19] But many other innovations were more difficult to protect, such as cuttings from fruit trees that propagate asexually. Governments responded by tailoring special rules to plant innovators. In 1930, the United States passed the Plant Patent Act, allowing innovators to claim patents for plants that reproduce asexually.[20] Most countries, however, stopped short of granting patents; if they granted IP protection at all they did so through a limited mechanism known today as "plant breeders' rights." These property rights barred plant breeders from [the] outright copying of innovations, but the rights did not prevent a breeder from using a competitor's improved variety as an input to their own new variety. This was an important step toward property rights in PGR. ***

*** [The] 1961 UPOV agreement enshrined the concept of plant breeders' rights into international law.[21] Plant breeders were concentrated in the industrialized states that had the largest influence over UPOV's content, and the resulting UPOV agreement largely reflected their interests. Updated with new agreements in 1978 and 1991, fifty states eventually became parties to at least one of the UPOV agreements. * While UPOV introduced property rights for worked PGR, raw PGR was still treated as common heritage. Plant breeders and seed companies, as well as the major botanical institutions, continued to gather PGR from around the world in the belief that [raw genetic information could not be owned.]

---

[18] Indeed, one of the major continuing areas of contestation has been the treatment of traditional crop varieties that have been improved incrementally and informally by generations of farmers. This is the so-called "farmers' rights" issue; we discuss it briefly below.

[19] Griliches 1957.

[20] Rories 2001.

[21] Barton 1982. The United States also passed the Plant Variety Protection Act in 1970, which extended the 1930 Act to sexually reproducing plants.

The Demise of the Common Heritage System

While change was already afoot by the early 1960s, the major shock to the common heritage system was the invention of recombinant DNA technology in the 1970s.[22] By allowing innovators to work directly at the genetic level, the scope for innovation in plant resources increased dramatically. This technological change stimulated interest in creating stronger protection for worked PGR and ultimately in creating property rights for raw PGR as well. In Demsetzian fashion, actors demanded property rights in response to the possibility of increasing the value of plant genetic resources and the desire to appropriate that value for themselves. Most of the early changes in property rights occurred in the United States, but this domestic activity created pressure for changes in international rules.

The biotechnology revolution that began in the 1970s led to the creation of many new firms engaged in genetic engineering. These firms' business models required secure property rights to reap the benefits of their costly investments in research and development. A critical breakpoint in this story was the U.S. Supreme Court's 1980 decision, in the landmark case of *Diamond v. Chakrabarty*, extending patent protection to living modified organisms – in that particular case, genetically engineered bacteria.[23] Before *Chakrabarty*, the patentability of living innovations outside the narrow confines of the 1930 Plant Patent Act was unclear. After *Chakrabarty*, and subsequent cases that reaffirmed and extended it, U.S. firms could receive complete utility patent protection for a panoply of genomic techniques. That same year (1980), Congress passed the Bayh–Dole Act, intended to encourage innovation by allowing universities and private firms to claim property rights on government-funded research. *** In short, these two changes – one judicial and one legislative – transformed the U.S. domestic playing field with regard to property rights in genetic resources. Since 1980, the conventional wisdom in the United States has been that strong property rights – patents, in particular – are essential to the modern biotechnology-based innovation system. U.S. firms and the U.S. government sought to extend this new system globally.[24]

---

[22] Evenson 2002,

[23] *Diamond v. Chakrabarty* (1980). Some doctrinal uncertainties remained that are not germane to our argument; see *Ex Parte Hibberd* (1985), and *JEM Ag Supply v. Pioneer Hi-Bred* (2001).

[24] Ryan 1998.

The increasing protection of worked PGR under the domestic laws of industrialized nations as well as the UPOV agreement led developing countries to organize a counteroffensive: the 1983 FAO Undertaking on Plant Genetic Resources. The FAO Undertaking, which is not legally binding, was placed on the FAO agenda by a coalition of developing countries, mainly from Latin America, and a small number of sympathetic industrialized countries. Often rich in biodiversity, developing countries have been the source of many commercially valuable genetic samples. Yet the open access regime gave them little compensation, even as arrangements such as UPOV forced them to pay for innovations built (in part) on their own genetic heritage. These concerns resonated with the then-recent effort to establish a New International Economic Order, aimed at redistributing global wealth through new international institutions and reining in the powers of multinational corporations.[25]

The FAO Undertaking attempted to counter the emergence of property rights in worked PGR – such as in the UPOV agreements – by defining all genetic resources (raw *and* worked) as "common heritage." In its most controversial wording, the Undertaking propounded the "universally accepted principle that plant genetic resources are a heritage of mankind and consequently should be available without restriction;" PGR should be available "free of charge ... or on the most favorable terms." *** [The industrialized countries refused to accept the Undertaking's demand for open access to worked PGR.] Eight industrialized countries issued formal reservations to the Undertaking. In 1989, FAO adopted an Annex to the Undertaking to provide a general "agreed interpretation" that papered over this conflict and allowed most of these hesitant countries to join.[26] ***

Biodiversity and Bioprospecting

The uneven but accelerating dissolution of the common heritage system in the 1980s dovetailed with a new change afoot in an unlikely source: international environmental cooperation. Protection of special habitats (such as wetlands) and animals (such as whales) were politically expedient choices for the first efforts at global environmental cooperation in the 1960s and 1970s. By the 1980s, however, conventional wisdom was that a broader approach was needed. This conceptual shift was rooted in ideas

---

[25] Gilpin 1987, 298–301.
[26] FAO Annex 1 1989.

from conservation biologists that stressed the need to protect entire ecosystems and was consummated in the CBD ***.[27]

[In the late 1980s, when the CBD was taking shape,] developing countries began to see property rights in PGR as a mechanism for securing sovereignty and wealth, rather than solely as a device that "biopirates" from the North had rigged against them. *** The conceptual touchstone for this new political coalition in favor of property rules was the notion of "bioprospecting." Firms could prospect for valuable genetic resources just as miners had prospected for gold in centuries past. A famous 1991 deal, in which a U.S.-based pharmaceutical giant (Merck) contracted with a Costa Rican conservation institute (INbio) for bioprospecting rights in the Costa Rican rain forest, signaled to many the dawn of a new era of bioprospecting.[28] This conceptual innovation aligned the interests of environmentalists, biotechnology firms, and developing countries that were seeking to extract greater value from their biodiversity riches.[29] [Subsequent economic analyses – as well as a dearth of realized profits – suggest that the value of rain forest genetic resources was considerably overestimated, but in the 1990s the hopes for transformation were a more powerful elixir than the econometrics.[30]]

*** [The] realization by developing countries that they could benefit from asserting sovereign ownership over raw PGR was reflected much more rapidly in the FAO's Commission on Plant Genetic Resources. Unlike the omnibus CBD, the FAO commission was focused solely on the issue of PGR and thus could change course more nimbly ***. [In 1991, the FAO adopted a new Annex stating that] "the concept of mankind's heritage, as applied in the [1983 Undertaking], is subject to the sovereignty of states over their plant genetic resources." It also flatly asserted that "nations have sovereign rights over their plant genetic resources" – a complete reversal of the 1983 Undertaking that sought to establish that no nation owned PGR. [This almost exactly mirrored language in the draft texts, then circulating, of the CBD.[31]] The draft CBD text also made clear that states controlled access to PGR and that the open access norm of the past was

---

[27] On the intellectual shift toward the "ecosystem" concept see Golley 1993; on the history of wildlife protection, which until the late 1980s focussed on specific activities, regions and ecosystems, see Lyster 1985.

[28] See Tilford 1998 and Blum 1993.

[29] Reid 1993.

[30] See Peters et al. 1989; and Godoy et al. 1993.]

[31] The only difference being that the CBD language referred to all biological resources, not just genetic resources.

gone. Through these simultaneous assertions of sovereign rights in the CBD and the FAO, a new approach to PGR coalesced.

The Legalization of Property Rights

The early 1990s represented a watershed in the development of the PGR regime complex – the final break from the primacy of common heritage. *** Yet the CBD was a broad agreement that had been crafted through a process dominated by relatively weak environment ministries; likewise, the FAO was dominated by agriculture ministries who also had limited influence. Although abundant in symbolism, the CBD and FAO had only minimal impact on the rules and practices that actually affected the flow of genetic resources.

At the same time that the new FAO Annex and CBD were finalized, nearly all the same states – represented by their more powerful trade ministers – were also in the final stages of negotiating a new round of international trade rules. These negotiations included a novel set of rules on IP, which were placed on the trade agenda because firms in entertainment, Pharmaceuticals, and other "knowledge industries" insisted on stronger international protection of IP. *** Backed by the power of the United States, these rules were codified into TRIPs. TRIPs sets minimum standards for IP protection; in practice these standards were closely modeled on U.S. or EU law.[32] Moreover, TRIPs was folded into the new WTO structure, which included a powerful, retooled system for enforcing dispute settlement. The large number of developing countries that joined the WTO seeking greater access to markets found that their membership also required a transformation in their domestic rules for IP. *

TRIPs contains specific language on genetic resources, which mandates that countries must grant patents for microorganisms and, in Article 27.3b, expressly requires either patents or a *"sui generis"* system for worked PGR.[33] The UPOV system of plant breeder rights was the concept that some TRIPs drafters had in mind for a *sui generis* system, but not all states wanted to endorse UPOV, forcing the drafters to leave this provision vague. These states instead sought clarity from the bottom up – each state would interpret and implement Article 27.3b as it saw fit, and a later systematic review would take stock of the experience. ***

---

[32] See Maskus 2000; Ryan 1998; and Sell 1995.
[33] A *"sui generis"* system simply means a unique system tailored, in this case, to the needs of PGR.

Thus from the mid-1980s, the number of international institutions within the regime complex grew, and the boundaries between the elemental regimes blurred. This expansion was driven by the large number of new issues that touched on PGR – such as protection of biological diversity and the expanding agenda of international trade policy – as well as the desire by key stakeholders to codify the emerging consensus in favor of property rights. * * *

The seismic change in property rules rippled through the rest of the regime complex, affecting how key stakeholders saw their interests served in many other rules. The main front line was now the allocation of benefits from PGR – the second dimension in Figure 26.1. Should the market be left to itself to allocate the benefits of PGR, or should governments regulate the allocation of benefits? Distributional issues often confound efforts to secure property rights. As Libecap argues, "all things equal, skewed rights arrangements lead to pressure for redistribution through further negotiations."[34] The history of PGR exemplifies this pattern. Wary of market mechanisms, developing countries sought to create special mechanisms that would force innovators to share the benefit stream with the states that provided the raw PGR. Property rights alone, these countries argued, would not be enough to force biopirates to disgorge a fair share of profits.

These efforts to elaborate an international benefit-sharing scheme arose mainly in the CBD * * *. The widest in scope of all the elemental regimes, the CBD was a convenient forum for actors who wanted to expand the debate. At the same time, powerful states that wanted to insulate the normative structure of other (in their view, more important) elemental regimes – notably the WTO – often found it convenient to allow the CBD to become a holding pen for these new concerns * * *. The CBD addressed the benefit-allocation issue through several controversial provisions. Most notably, it obligated each party to enact measures aimed at "sharing in a fair and equitable way ... the benefits arising from the commercial and other utilization of genetic resources with the [state] providing such resources."[35] This redistributive language was strongly opposed by the United States, and contributed to the U.S. decision not to ratify the CBD.

* * *

---

[34] Libecap 2003.
[35] Article 16. Similar language appears in Article 8(J) of the CBD. On the use of CBD as a holding pen and the incentives to shift between regimes see Helfer 2004.

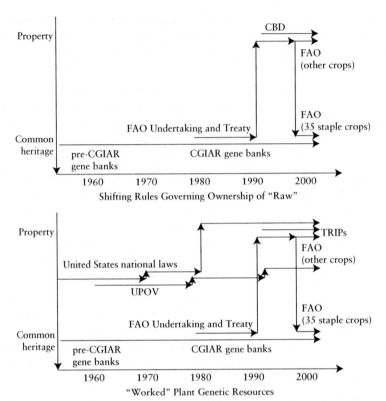

Shifting Rules Governing Ownership of "Raw"

"Worked" Plant Genetic Resources

Note: Institutions shown only on panels for which they have relevant rules. The International Convention for the Protection of New Varieties of Plants (UPOV), for example, relates only to worked plant genetic resources (PGR). Consultative Group on International Agricultural Research (CGIAR) gene banks are shown as "raw," although perhaps two-fifths of their collections have been worked in some way. The Convention on Biological Diversity (CBD) is not shown on panel B, although the CBD does include a clause that pertains to worked PGR.

Lines shift at major events that alter the rules within a given institution.

Major events for raw PGR: The annex to the International Undertaking (1991); the UN Food and Agriculture (FAO) treaty that distinguishes rules for 35 staple crops from those for nonstaples (2001).

Major events for worked PGR: The U.S. Plant Variety Protection Act (1970) and the *Diamond* case in the United States (1980); revisions to UPOV (1978, 1991); the annex to the International Undertaking (1991).

TRIPs: Trade-Related Aspects of Intellectual Property Rights.

FIGURE 26.2. *Changes in property norms for raw and worked PGR.*

In sum, by the end of the 1990s the international rules governing PGR were radically different from those that existed seventy-five years earlier. Figure 26.2 summarizes this shift – for raw PGR (top panel) as well as "worked" PGR (bottom panel).

*** [The realignment of the late 1990s did not erase existing political controversies.] Thus international norms were cast broadly to allow some diversity in local circumstances. *** In some cases, such as the core crop plants addressed by the 2002 FAO treaty (discussed below), the costs of administering property rights turned out to be so high that states collectively reverted to the common heritage concept – an outcome consistent with sophisticated versions of the Demsetzian thesis.[36] As property theorists have noted, a resource will operate without property rights as long as the cost of implementing and enforcing property rights is "higher than the value of the increase in the efficiency of utilization of the resource gained by the introduction of a property regime."[37] This was the case for many common food crops because of the extreme difficulty of demarcating and enforcing property rights – and the relatively small gains from doing so in this area – and consequently the system revived the common heritage approach in this circumscribed domain.[38] On the whole, however, the demands for property rights in PGR were largely met by the mid-1990s. Enclosure had triumphed over common heritage and open access.

REGIME COMPLEXES AND THE STUDY OF REGIMES

Many studies of international cooperation have noted the tremendous rise in the number of international treaties and organizations, particularly since 1945.[39] Yet few studies have given systematic attention to the implications of this increase in institutional density.[40] *** This rise in density occurs against a backdrop of increasing legalization in world politics. The international legal system is, however, nonhierarchical: generally,

---

[36] See Libecap 1989; Merrill, 2002; and Levmore 2002.

[37] Benkler 2002, 402.

[38] See the list in the 2002 FAO Treaty on Plant Genetic Resources. As Libecap notes, the physical nature of an asset affects the cost of calculating and assigning value, in turn affecting the costs of marking and enforcing property rights. Libecap 2003, 150.

[39] Shanks et al. 1996. In-depth studies of particular areas of international cooperation – such as trade, arms control, or human rights – all point to the same general pattern of rising numbers of institutions.

[40] Partial exceptions include Young 2002; Stokke 2001; and Leebron 2002.

no one regime is supreme over others as a legal matter. Moreover, the international legal system is disaggregated. Regimes and rules are developed in one forum that frequently implicate or even challenge regimes and rules developed in other forums.

As the PGR case illustrates, one result of rising density in this context is the development of overlapping but discrete regimes, often with conflicting rules during periods of transition to new interests and rules. * * *

In the remainder of this article we use the PGR case to illustrate and probe the conjectures about regime complexes described in the introduction. Our argument is not that existing regime theory is fatally flawed, but rather that it is oriented around a model of regime development that fails to reflect the growing concentration and interconnection of institutions in the international system.

No Clean Slate

Existing scholarship on international regimes has generally, if implicitly, assumed that the process of regime formation begins with an institutional clean slate. In most empirical studies of regime formation negotiators arrive at the task of creating a regime without any explicit international rules in place; previous arrangements – if they exist at all – are readily discarded or adjusted. In these accounts, states with different interests vie to shape the outcomes, and institutions are crafted to serve the political agreement. * * *

In a regime complex, by contrast, negotiations over most substantive rules commence with an elaborate and dispersed institutional framework already in place. The institutional slate is not clean. Ideas, interests, and expectations frequently are already aligned around some set of existing rules and concepts * * *. Consequently, power, interests, and ideas do not directly map onto the norms that become enshrined in the agreements at the core of the regime; the content and evolution of rules does not trace neatly back to changes in the underlying driving forces. We expected that the lack of a clean slate would affect the development of the rules in the elemental regimes in a path-dependent manner – and, consequently, the evolution of regime complex as a whole. Despite the history of PGR being one of dramatic change – a normative shift, over many years, from common heritage to propertization – in many respects this expectation was borne out. We found path dependence at the meso scale, in that particular rules affected and constrained the architecture of subsequent rules. Yet at the macro scale the regime complex exhibited marked change.

One example of how previous expectations and institutional accretion affect outcomes in a regime complex is the creation of strong property rights for worked PGR. When negotiators in TRIPs began crafting rules for PGR in the late 1980s, there were several sets of rules already firmly in place. For decades, the community of plant breeders had built up the concept of plant breeders' rights and enshrined it in both international and domestic law. Some who opposed even this weak form of IP, predominantly concentrated in the developing world, had already established a marker in the 1983 FAO Undertaking. ***

With conflicting interests as well as divergent rules already on the books, it was impossible to gain consensus on a single approach to property rights. Yet the TRIPs negotiation, part of the omnibus Uruguay Round, could not be halted, so the negotiators adopted a broad umbrella approach. *** This approach contrasts sharply with more familiar cases of regime formation such as that of the Montreal Protocol on ozone depletion, where negotiators had diverging interests but the negotiation process was unconstrained by existing rules on ozone depleting chemicals.[41] Faced with a clean institutional slate, the Montreal Protocol negotiators could strike a political compromise that directly reflected the power, interests, and knowledge within that issue-area, codified in precise rules with unambiguous timetables. The negotiators in the ozone regime were worried about how their decisions might affect other issue-areas – notably, they feared that provisions to apply trade sanctions against countries that refused to implement the Protocol's rules would run afoul of the GATT. The negotiators solved the problem by crafting trade restrictions narrowly and trying to navigate around any possible interactions with other regimes. * The negotiators of PGR provisions in TRIPs – which overlapped with rules being adopted in the FAO as well as in the CBD and the international gene bank system – faced a quite different situation. A multiplicity of overlapping rules and norms made it impossible to create a legal system that was isolated from the other elemental regimes.

The lack of a clean slate has at least two implications for the evolution of rules in a regime complex. First, when wary of conflicts between rules, the architects of new rules will attempt to avoid conflicts by demarcating clear boundaries. They will negotiate devices such as "savings clauses" and other mechanisms for disentangling one regime from another ***. Disentangling and demarcation appear to be viewed as a first best solution ***. (In a few cases, however, we observe explicit efforts to create

[41] See Benedick 1991; and Parson 2003.

conflicts to force change in another regime – what we term "strategic inconsistency" – which we also discuss further below.)

Second, the sheer complexity of the interactions at high institutional density suggests that it will often prove difficult to demarcate boundaries clearly. In this context, the PGR case suggests that rules may evolve by a special pattern. When PGR-related matters have been linked to a much larger array of issues, the negotiating processes usually arrived at some agreement even when views were diverse and conflicting. *** Analysts often assume that broader negotiations allow for "negotiation arithmetic" that explores tradeoffs and seeks Pareto-superior deals.[42] However, in the PGR regime complex the benefits or detriments of issue linkage were not critical ***. The "agreements" that resulted were usually broad to paper over differences, deferring resolution until later. The TRIPs rules on PGR exemplify this.

A quite different pattern appeared in elemental regimes that were specialized for PGR purposes – such as the FAO Undertaking. Unsurprisingly, serious negotiations yielded rapid agreement when key stakeholders shared core interests. For example, in the late 1980s the FAO was the first elemental regime to shift from the principle of common heritage to rules that allowed states to assert sovereign ownership of raw PGR. Indeed, the FAO employed exactly the language that was under negotiation in the CBD before it had been adopted in the CBD. The substantive narrowness of the FAO process made this rapid shift possible. ***

This pattern of evolution may help to explain why some interactions between elemental regimes are supportive and others yield rules that clash. The narrow, specialized elemental regimes that were under less political pressure to reach agreement tended to codify rules that reflected an emerging consensus. But agreements reached under pressure of a credible political deadline – such as the CBD and WTO – tended to yield more conflict. The CBD, for example, contained language on the scope of IP rights and requirements that governments adopt schemes to share the benefits of worked PGR – language that the U.S. government and many firms saw as aimed at undermining TRIPs.[43] The PGR case suggests a propensity for negotiators in highly complex areas to adopt broad and general agreements, if only because some of the complexity and conflict may resolve itself autonomously – in the sense that exogenous events or new political shifts may in time render the underlying conflict moot.

[42] See Sebenius 1983; and Tollison and Willett 1979.
[43] Raustiala 1997.

Thus the 1989 Annex to the FAO Undertaking was a general effort to paper over different interpretations of the concept of "common heritage," which just two years later was made obsolete by new interests that favored sovereign property rights.

Forum Shopping

The defining characteristic of a regime complex is the existence of multiple, overlapping elemental regimes. Given the availability of multiple fora for developing or elaborating international rules, we expected actors would attempt to select the forum that best suited their interests. The PGR case is consistent with this expectation.

The FAO, for example, served as the forum for the 1983 Undertaking that declared both raw and worked PGR to be the common heritage of all mankind. As part of the UN system and open to all states, the FAO was dominated by developing countries and thus became a favorable forum for asserting demands for wealth redistribution. By contrast, the United States and (to a lesser extent) the EU sought a different forum – the trade negotiations leading to the WTO – to push for new IP rules. The omnibus nature of WTO commitments and the exclusive membership criteria created high barriers to entry and made it easier for the United States to link IP issues *** to broader market access. ***

Created under the auspices of the UN Environment Programme, the negotiations that lead to the CBD originally centered on conservation ***. The UN Environment Programme (like FAO) was an open forum with low barriers to entry. Thus developing countries found it relatively easy to graft their IP agenda onto the CBD negotiations. What they were unable to achieve in other fora – notably TRIPs – developing countries tried to gain through linkages to biodiversity. The result was two diverging and distinct sets of rules, with the CBD rules on IP – mostly related to benefit-sharing – partly undercutting those in TRIPs. This divergence in substantive rules occurred despite the fact that the CBD and the WTO have broadly the same membership. The two institutions offered two distinct fora, with different bureaucratic representation, leading to different expressions of state interests and issue linkages. ***

Legal Consistency

Noting the general trend toward legalization in world politics, we expected that regime complexes would evolve in ways that reflect the increased role of legal arguments and legal concepts in international cooperation.[44] One of the signal attributes of this shift to law is pressure for legal consistency. We expected that it might be extremely difficult to maintain legal consistency within a regime complex because of the complexity of issues and interests in the far-flung elemental regimes [and because the international legal system has no formal hierarchy of treaty rules.] * * *

We found that the drive for consistency – a hallmark of legalization – has had a strong impact on the evolution of the PGR regime complex. The extremely large number of issues and complex interactions made it difficult for negotiators to ensure legal consistency; areas of persistent inconsistency became focal points for efforts at reconciliation and further bargaining. States responded to legal inconsistency in two linked ways. They first attempted to implement or interpret international norms such that inconsistencies evaporated. If those efforts failed then the inconsistencies set the agenda for subsequent negotiations. We find that these inconsistencies rarely persist within each elemental regime; rather, they arise at the "joints" between the elemental regimes.

This mode of development – driven by concern about achieving legal consistency – is illustrated in several conflicts surrounding PGR. * * *

For example, when states in the late 1990s took up the task of negotiating the first protocol to the CBD – the Biosafety Protocol, intended to regulate trade in bio-engineered goods – they did so against the backdrop of provisions in the WTO that prohibited discriminatory barriers to trade.[45] The result was a massive bargaining effort focused on a "savings clause:" a legal provision inserted into the Biosafety Protocol that purported to immunize the WTO provisions from any inconsistency with the Biosafety Protocol. Similarly, the negotiation of the new Treaty on Plant Genetic Resources in the FAO was conducted against the backdrop of TRIPs and its strict IP rules. The result was a debate over whether to include a savings clause with the same aim: to protect the TRIPs provisions in the event of any inconsistency between the treaties. (Whether these savings clauses actually help to demarcate boundaries and establish priorities in the application of conflicting laws remains a proposition that lawyers debate).[46]

---

[44] Goldstein et al. 2001.

[45] Notably the Agreement on Technical Barriers to Trade and the Agreement on the Application of Sanitary and Phytosanitary Measures – both part of the Uruguay Round negotiations.

[46] Safrin 2002.

While efforts at achieving consistency drive much of the action within a regime complex, [states] may also attempt to create what we term *strategic inconsistency*. Cognizant that the growing legalization of world politics means that legal conflicts focus efforts at solutions, states at times attempt to force change by explicitly crafting rules in one elemental regime that are incompatible with those in another. For example, developing countries led the establishment of the original FAO Undertaking in a radical attempt to refocus the agenda toward a broad and controversial common heritage principle for all PGR. The CBD's rules on IP rights are another example – the CBD purposefully included language that [appeared to contravene the content of TRIPs.] For diplomats operating in a legalized setting, the existence of a glaring inconsistency across regimes sets the agenda for future efforts, which in the legal paradigm typically focus on ways to restore rule alignment.

Regime Development Through Implementation

In the traditional model of regime development, parties that seek a change in regime rules press their cause through formal negotiations leading to new rules; the implementation process follows thereafter in a "top down" fashion. Rules beget changes in behavior and compliance. The actual practice of regime implementation, however, is not linear or neat. Earlier studies have shown that when international rules are demanding and intrusive, they are more likely to conflict with other national commitments – making it difficult to plan and anticipate the process of implementation.[47] * * *

We hypothesize that the existence of a regime complex resolves this tension in favor of a "bottom up" style of evolution. Negotiators adopt broad rules because it is extremely difficult to work out the fine detail for all contingencies *ex ante*. Where that is not possible, they adopt specific rules that often yield conflicts in other elemental regimes. This approach, amply evident in the PGR case, in effect relies on the implementation process for experimentation with different solutions to the ambiguities and inconsistencies that arise from divergent rules and interests. The parties used their implementation experiences as guides for subsequent changes in the formal rules. This process certainly occurs in the domestic context.[48] In that setting, however, courts often exist to elaborate and fill

---

[47] See Victor, Raustiala, and Skolnikoff 1998; and Evans, Jacobson, and Putnam 1993.
[48] See Ingram 1977; Bardach and Kagan 1982; and Stewart 1975.

gaps in statutes; internationally, aside from a handful of distinctive regimes, courts do not exist to play that role. This implies that the feedback loop from implementation to formal rules is even more significant in the international than in the domestic context. Three episodes in the history of the PGR regime complex reveal this bottom-up process of rule development through implementation and interpretation.

First, the evolution of access rules for the international gene banks shows how incompatible interests led states to adopt broad rules with the hope that conflicts could be resolved *ex post* as implementation progressed. The CGIAR system was built on the principle of common heritage. The system's gene banks were open to all, a core principle challenged when developing countries shifted preferences in the late 1980s toward sovereign rights over raw PGR. ***

[The solution was codified in the 2002 Treaty on Plant Genetic Resources.] The treaty's principal purpose was to resolve some of the inconsistencies that had arisen in the regime complex. It created a special "multilateral system" for core crop resources, including the collections of raw PGR in the gene banks. In a sea of sovereign and private property, it carves out a special collective property right for a limited number of staple food and feed crops:

> In essence, the multilateral system is a communal seed treasury composed of 35 food and 29 feed crops . . . in exchange for access to this common seed pool, those who commercialize products that incorporate plant genetic resources received from the multilateral system must pay a percentage of their profits into a fund to be administered by the Treaty's Governing Body. That fund will be used to promote conservation and sustainable use of plant genetic resources, particularly by farmers and indigenous communities, whose rights and contributions to genetic diversity the [2002 Treaty] expressly recognizes.[49]

For these key crops, the economic gains from property rights were outweighed by the costs of creating and policing those rights, and thus actors sought a reversal of propertization. This solution was the culmination of a process that, we suggest, is a generic feature of regime complexes. The parties started with broad and conflicting rules. They tried to work out the problems, attempting first those solutions that were easiest to implement – actions "on the ground" that sought to interpret and adjust legal commitments in favorable ways. As those failed they sought remedies that required progressively greater legal coordination – creating a new legal agreement as the last resort.

---

[49] Helfer 2002.

A second example of evolution through implementation is the ongoing attempt at reconciliation of the various weak forms of IP for improved plant varieties, * * * with the strong patents that many countries now grant. TRIPs accepts all of these systems because it was impossible to gain agreement on a precise rule *ex ante* * * *. The TRIPs architects hoped that the implementation process would reveal which systems were most compatible with the diverse interests involved, and they built in a planned review of those experiences as a result. This review is proceeding slowly * * * which underscores an earlier point about the dynamics of a regime complex: the codification of international norms is driven by credible deadlines, but the implementation process often drags on because politically the easiest solution in the face of conflict is to keep the rules broad and then defer the details until later.

The third example, still ongoing, involves two recent concepts in IP: "farmers' rights" and "traditional knowledge." [Modern IP law is] largely organized to protect discrete innovations that occur at a moment in time by identifiable persons; they are generally unable to protect innovations that reflect the slow accumulation of novel concepts by many (unknown) members of a community.[50] Farmers' rights are "rights arising from the past, present and future contribution of farmers in conserving, improving, and making available plant genetic resources."[51] * * * From the 1970s, the farmers' rights movement called into question the dividing line between raw and worked resources, asserting that much of what is taken to be raw is in fact worked. * * * The farmer's rights movement has gained momentum as a broader group of indigenous communities – not just farmers – have realized that they could be victims of the same dividing line between "raw" and "worked" knowledge. As this broader coalition organized, it adopted a more general term: "traditional knowledge."

* * * Thus far efforts to protect traditional knowledge and to mandate the sharing of benefits that arise from its commercial use have not yielded much practical change * * *. Now the World Intellectual Property Organization, which has been a peripheral actor in the PGR story, has convened a new working group to generate rules that recognize and reward traditional knowledge. This development may herald the arrival of a new element in the PGR regime complex. We expect that advocates for traditional knowledge will seek, through new WIPO rules, strategic inconsistency in the rules governing the allocation of benefits from PGR,

[50] Boyle 1997.
[51] FAO 1995.

which in turn will force efforts to resolve the conflict through the various mechanisms and processes we have illustrated.

CONCLUSION

Genetic resources, while seemingly esoteric, are increasingly an arena of global conflict in world politics. The struggle over the control of plant genetic resources is at the core of this battle. During the past century, the international rules for PGR protection shifted quite dramatically from a common heritage, open access system to a system of sovereign resource rights and private intellectual property rights. We have argued that this transition was driven by the perception – and the reality – of the rising value of PGR, in particular as new techniques of genetic manipulation permitted innovators to add substantial value to plants. Propertization, initially resisted by the plant-rich developing world, decisively triumphed over common heritage.

This transition to an international property rights system did not occur smoothly. Rule evolution in the PGR case involved several distinct but overlapping international regimes interacting with each other as well as the domestic practices of key states. Whereas existing studies of international regimes have generally focused on regimes as single, self-contained entities, often built around a single treaty, the hallmark of the PGR story is the lack of any central, hierarchical international institution. The principles, norms, rules, and decision-making procedures that govern PGR have arisen and evolved in ways that are distinct from the existing body of theory about international regimes [– a regime complex rather than a regime.] The horizontal, overlapping structure and the presence of divergent rules and norms are the defining characteristics of a regime complex.

The regime complex for plant genetic resources is unlikely to be the first or the last such institution in world politics. Indeed, there are good reasons to believe that regime complexes will become much more common in coming decades as international institutions proliferate and inevitably bump against one another. *** Indeed, regime complexes may already be abundant – looking through this new conceptual lens, regime complexes may appear where previously analysts saw only individual decomposable regimes. ***

*** In a regime complex rules evolve against a thick backdrop of existing rules: there is no clean institutional slate on which actors pursue interests or wield power. This backdrop defines the regime complex but also generates its distinctive dynamics. In an international system characterized by increasing legalization, the lack of legal consistency that flows from differing and overlapping rules pushes states to seek resolutions and to negotiate broad rules. At times, states also create strategic inconsistency as they seek to jolt rules in one or another direction.

Our work on regime complexes suggests not only some extensions for the theories of regimes but also advances the study of legalization in world politics. A hallmark of the regime complex is a shift in the locus of action – away from elemental regimes and toward legal inconsistencies that tend to arise at the joints between regimes, and away from formal negotiations and toward the more complicated processes of implementation and interpretation. As the scope of the regime complex grows and rules become more demanding and intrusive, the style of rule change shifts ever more to this more messy and complicated "bottom-up" system and away from the top-down mechanisms that are implicitly assumed in [mainstream regime scholarship.] *** More research that uses regime complexes as the unit of analysis will reflect a growing empirical reality. This type of research will also extend one of the most productive research programs in international relations – the study of international regimes – by integrating insights from studies on law and legalization, policy implementation and the role of institutions.

References

While citations within articles have been maintained, complete references have been omitted from the book. However, a complete set of references for each of the chapters in the book may be found at http//:www. cambridge.org/9780521861861.

Index

Note: Page numbers printed in *italics* followed by a lower-case *f* or *t* refer respectively to figures and tables.